Working with
School-Age Children

Working with School-Age Children

Marlene A. Bumgarner

Gavilan College

Boston   Columbus   Indianapolis   New York   San Francisco   Upper Saddle River
Amsterdam   Cape Town   Dubai   London   Madrid   Milan   Munich   Paris   Montreal   Toronto
Delhi   Mexico City   Sao Paulo   Sydney   Hong Kong   Seoul   Singapore   Taipei   Tokyo

Vice President and Editor in Chief: Jeffery W. Johnston
Senior Acquisitions Editor: Julie Peters
Editorial Assistant: Tiffany Bitzel
Vice President, Director of Marketing: Margaret Waples
Marketing Manager: Erica DeLuca
Senior Managing Editor: Pamela D. Bennett
Project Manager: Kerry J. Rubadue
Senior Operations Supervisor: Matthew Ottenweller
Senior Art Director: Diane Lorenzo

Text Designer: Aptara®, Inc.
Cover Designer: Candace Rowley
Photo Coordinator: Lori Whitley
Permissions Administrator: Rebecca Savage
Cover Art: Getty Images
Full-Service Project Management: Jogender Taneja, Aptara®, Inc.
Composition: Aptara®, Inc.
Printer/Binder: Edwards Brothers Malloy
Cover Printer: Edwards Brothers Malloy
Text Font: Galliard

Credits and acknowledgments borrowed from other sources and reproduced, with permission, in this textbook appear on appropriate page within text.

Photo Credits: Marlene A. Bumgarner, pp. 3, 9, 35, 40, 42, 61, 62, 90, 106, 115, 119, 122, 162, 184, 201, 205, 210, 212, 214, 253, 278, 282, 284, 285, 323, 412, 428; John Loyd, pp. 10, 68, 195, 260, 289, 304, 354, 357, 405; Jennifer Dahnke/Collaborative Communications Group, p. 77; Anthony Magnacca/Merrill, pp. 92, 437; Shutterstock, p. 101; Maria D. Rico, pp. 135, 143; Laima Druskis/PH College, p. 153; Thinkstock, p. 159; Punchstock–Royalty Free, p. 176; Norman Haughey, p. 248; Katelyn Metzger/Merrill, p. 315; Courtesy of City Vision, p. 391; Getty Images–iStock Exclusive RF, p. 395; Creatas Images/Thinkstock, p. 410; Laura Bolesta/Merrill, p. 439; Valerie Schultz/Merrill, p. 441.

Every effort has been made to provide accurate and current Internet information in this book. However, the Internet and information posted on it are constantly changing, so it is inevitable that some of the Internet addresses listed in this textbook will change.

Library of Congress Cataloging-in-Publication Data
Bumgarner, Marlene Anne
  Working with school-age children/Marlene A. Bumgarner.
    p. cm.
  ISBN-13: 978-0-13-208085-9
  ISBN-10: 0-13-208085-0
  1. Afterschool programs—United States.   2. School-age child care—United States.   3. Child development—United States.   I. Title.
  LC34.4.B86 2011
  371.8--dc22   2010022323

10 9 8 7 6

ISBN 13: 978-0-13-208085-9
ISBN 10:   0-13-208085-0

Preface

This book was written primarily for people who work with school-age children outside the regular classroom or plan to do so in the future. It provides a foundation of child development theory and age-appropriate day-to-day practice in out-of-school or afterschool programs. Both of these aspects are necessary to create and maintain high-quality programming for children of any age. (Note: The term *out-of-school* has wide usage in certain regions of North America, while *afterschool program* and *school-age care* are more commonly used in other areas. Therefore, all three terms appear in this text.)

THE PURPOSE OF THIS BOOK

As a parent of four children, I was for many years a regular consumer of school-age programs. In my role as a college instructor and board member of organizations such as the YMCA, American Red Cross, and Girl Scouts of America, I frequently found myself funding, supervising, and working directly in programs for school-age children.

As the need for afterschool programs gradually, then rapidly, grew in my community and in the nation, I became drawn into the world of lawmaking, fundraising, and advocating for the needs of school-age children. My own children's views of the programs in which they spent so many afterschool hours, combined with my growing awareness of the multiple factors that contribute to quality, led me on a 20-year quest to improve school-age programs.

During these two decades, I have had many opportunities to lead workshops and trainings and to serve on local and statewide task forces, professional organizations, and grant-writing and grant-evaluating committees. I have supervised student interns, served as a National Afterschool Association accreditation endorser, and provided technical assistance for quality-improvement projects. Many afterschool programs have invited me to visit, and I have seen some of the best in the country.

Both personally and professionally, I continue to be committed to improving the quality of out-of-school time. In addition to documenting what I have learned and encouraging new and experienced staff in school-age settings to create wonderful programs for children, I have provided information on continuous quality improvement. I believe that an external accreditation system is important to the development of high quality school-age programming, and urge program directors to participate in that process.

AUDIENCE FOR THIS BOOK

This book was written primarily as a stand-alone text for college and university courses designed for people who work, or will work, with school-age children outside the regular classroom. However, it can be used by others in a wide variety of ways:

- ❀ For in-service afterschool staff in child and youth work, recreation, or leisure studies.
- ❀ For board members, administrators, funders, and parents as an introduction to the role that communities play in providing out-of-school services to children and families. It also can serve as an introduction to the characteristics of high-quality, sustainable programs that have been shown to improve academic success, reduce crime between the key hours of 2:00 and 6:00 p.m., and promote responsible citizenship.
- ❀ For people who already work in afterschool programs as directors, teachers, group leaders, recreational directors, aides, line staff, or activity planners, as a useful source of information, ideas, and guidance. This book can also serve as a reference for camp counselors; 4H, Junior Achievement, Trailblazer, and Scout leaders; athletic coaches; and countless other volunteers who work with school-age children in a variety of settings.

CHAPTER FEATURES

Throughout the text, I have drawn heavily from the experiences of real people, revealing a diversity of experience and needs and seeking to define the role of professional child and youth workers in the lives of children and families. To ground the valuable work done by these people in a context, a historical overview is provided as well as an overview of school-age care in other parts of the world.

The necessary attributes and skills of people who work with school-age children are described, as are the issues faced by children in today's world and some strategies for helping children deal with the fear and anxiety that often result. The organization of the chapters is guided by key elements in quality school-age care identified through research; the importance of human relationships, environment, guidance strategies, and continuous quality improvement provide a foundation for later chapters on behavior and guidance, curriculum development, and child-centered activity planning.

In response to a growing awareness of the need for programs for older children, a separate chapter addresses the ideal characteristics of those programs. Another chapter suggests ways in which staff in school-age settings can develop partnerships with parents and community agencies to develop cohesive and responsive programs that offer a wide range of activities and services to families and are sustainable without continual external funding. The final chapter provides an overview of the administration function within school-age programs.

"Perspective" boxes are featured within each chapter to highlight one or more of the concepts contained within that chapter. The essay within each box has been written by a practitioner or researcher familiar with school-age programming and reflects the point of view of the writer.

"Consider This" boxes are featured within each chapter to expand students' knowledge and practical application of concepts. Each box asks students to pause and reflect upon their experiences with children and offers ways to implement ideas or handle difficult situations in the afterschool setting. Questions require the student to connect the theories and strategies within the chapter to real life.

This book is a work in progress. If there is an area that you believe needs to be expanded or added to in future editions, please let me know.

ACKNOWLEDGMENTS

In the preparation of this manuscript, I have had the help of many wonderful people. I am indebted to the professionals in the field who read part or all of the manuscript for this book and provided thoughtful and constructive comments and criticism. They include Jamie Cardenas Smith and Mindy Bostick, A Children's Garden; Mary Hoshiko, Santa Clara County Metropolitan YMCA; and Dr. Barbara Malaspina, Santa Clara Unified School District (retired).

I would like to thank the following individuals who reviewed the manuscript and offered their expertise: Toni Cacace-Beshears, Tidewater Community College; Marilee J. Cosgrove, Irvine Valley College; Lisa Fuller, Cerro Coso Community College; Kathryn B. Hollar, Catawba Valley Community College; Mary Hoshiko, Gavilan College; Norman Lorenz, Sacramento City College; Michelle B. Morris, Wor-Wic Community College; Dawn S. Munson, Elgin Community College; Karen L. Peterson, Washington State University, Vancouver; Helen Napier Thomas, Guilford Technical Community College; and Marlene Welch, Carroll Community College.

Thanks also to my editor, Julie Peters, who guided me through the writing of this book with grace and patience; to Tiffany Bitzel, who read all the chapters and provided feedback; to my research assistant, Carolyn Bowers, without whose unwavering dedication this project would never have been completed; and to my partner, Dennie VanTassel, who proofread every chapter, tested all the Web sites, and contributed a male perspective when it was needed.

A special thanks goes to the Gavilan College students who have read portions of the text at various stages of completion and suggested additional topics or better ways of presenting the material. Several students allowed me to use curriculum planning ideas or other material they had developed. Their names are cited at the appropriate places in the text.

Finally, I want to express my gratitude to the four young people who inspired me to write this book in the first place, who provided many of the stories and topics, and who lived through all the years of researching, writing, and refining the material. They are experts indeed in the strengths and challenges in out-of-school care—my children, Doña, John, Jamie, and Deborah.

Brief Contents

Chapter 1   Where Are Our Children After School?   1

Chapter 2   A View of the Field: School-Age Care and Youth Development   24

Chapter 3   Developing and Ensuring Program Quality   56

Chapter 4   What Does It Take to Work with School-Age Children?   76

Chapter 5   Theories of Child Development   96

Chapter 6   The Adult's Role in Socialization and Development   128

Chapter 7   Issues Facing Today's Children   151

Chapter 8   Understanding and Guiding Children's Behavior   175

Chapter 9   Environments of School-Age Children   199

Chapter 10   Cooperative Program Planning   235

Chapter 11   A Health and Fitness Curriculum: Fighting Back Against Childhood Obesity   271

Chapter 12   Engaging Children in Indoor Activities   302

Chapter 13   Engaging Children in Outdoor Activities   343

Chapter 14   Working with Older School-Age Children and Teens   370

Chapter 15   Developing Partnerships with Families, Schools, and the Community   401

Chapter 16   Administrative Issues: Licensing, Policies, and Personnel   426

Appendix   National Afterschool Association Code of Ethics January 2009   446

Index   457

Contents

Chapter 1   Where Are Our Children After School?   1

Afterschool in Earlier Times   3
Afterschool Care Today   4
Meeting the Unique Scheduling Needs of School-Age Children   5
Meeting the Needs of Children and Families   5
What Do Children Want in Before- and Afterschool Programs?   7
What We Can Learn From Parents   12
What We Can Learn From Classroom Teachers   13
What We Can Learn From Research   14
A Brief History of Afterschool Programming   15
   Settlement Houses   16
   4-H Programs   17
   Boys and Girls Clubs   17
   Young Men's and Women's Christian Associations   18
   Youth Scouting Movement   18
   The Importance of Historical Influences   18
Today's Family's Need for School-Age Care   19
Summary   20
Terms to Learn   20
Review Questions   21
Challenge Exercises   21
Internet Resources   21
References   22

Chapter 2   A View of the Field: School-Age Care and Youth Development   24

Varieties of Care Options for School-Age Children   25
   Self-Care   25
   In-Home Care   27
      Relative Care   27
      Non-Relative Care   29
   Out-of-Home Care   30

Licensed Family Child Care Homes   30

Publicly Funded School-Age Programs   32

Privately Funded Programs   36

Nonprofit Programs   36

Grassroots Solutions   37

Informal Care   38

Nontraditional Hours and Services   39

Drop-in Programs   41

Athletic and Recreation Programs   41

Enrichment Programs (Music/Art /Community Service) and Youth
Groups   41

Programs at Public Libraries   42

School-Age Care in Other Countries   43

Europe, Canada, and Australia   45

Africa, Asia, India, the Middle East, and Latin America   47

Elements of an Effective Before- and Afterschool Program   50

Summary   52

Terms to Learn   52

Review Questions   52

Challenge Exercises   52

Internet Resources   53

References   53

Chapter 3   Developing and Ensuring Program Quality   56

Continuous Program Improvement and Accreditation   56

The Challenge of Rapid Growth   57

The Quality Pyramid   59

Program Organization, Procedures, Policies   60

Human Relationships   60

Safety, Health, and Nutrition   61

Environment (Indoor and Outdoor)   62

Activities   63

The Role of the Quality Pyramid in School-Age Programming   63

Other Models of Quality   64

*The Role of Assessment and Accreditation in Program Quality
Improvement   66*

Assessment   66

Accreditation   67

The Goals of Accreditation   67

The Process of Accreditation   68

The Development of a National Improvement and Accreditation
System   70

Accreditation Today 71
   Council on Accreditation Afterschool Standards 71
   Achieving Accreditation 71
Developing and Ensuring Program Quality 73
Summary 73
Terms to Learn 74
Review Questions 74
Challenge Exercises 74
Online Resources 74
References 74

Chapter 4   **What Does It Take to Work with School-Age Children? 76**
People Who Work With School-Age Children 77
   Afterschool Program Leader 78
   Afterschool Inclusion Aide 78
   Classroom Aide 79
   Community Volunteer 79
   Service Club Leader 80
   Family Child Care Provider 81
   School-Age Program Site Supervisor 81
The Common Need: A Knowledge of Child Development 82
Educational Options for People Who Want to Work With Children 82
   College and University Certificates and Degrees 82
   Credentials and State-Issued Certificates 85
   Professional Development 85
Are You a Good Fit as a Leader in a School-Age Setting? 86
   Personality, Temperaments, and Dispositions 86
   Truly Enjoy Interacting With School-Agers 86
   Serve as Positive Role Models 87
   Basic Understanding of the Developmental Needs of School-Agers and How to Meet Them 87
   Energy 89
   Flexibility 89
   Sense of Humor 90
   Effective and Positive Style of Guidance and Discipline 90
   Ability to Work Well With Other Adults 91
   Competencies: Skills and Knowledge 91
Summary 93
Terms to Learn 94
Review Questions 94
Challenge Exercises 94
Internet Resources 94
References 95

Chapter 5 Theories of Child Development 96

Why Do We Have Theories of Development? 96
Characteristics of Theories 97
Domains of Development 97
Physical Growth and Development 98
Arnold Gesell (1880–1961): Maturation Theory 98
Gesell's Growth Gradients 98
Using the Maturational Theory 98
Social–Emotional Development 100
Erik H. Erikson (1902–1994): Psychosocial Theory 100
Erikson's Life Crises 100
Stage One: Basic Trust vs. Mistrust (Hope) 101
Stage Two: Autonomy vs. Shame and Doubt (Will) 102
Stage Three: Initiative vs. Guilt (Purpose) 102
Stage Four: Industry vs. Inferiority (Competence) 102
Stage Five: Search for Identity vs. Role Confusion (Fidelity) 103
Stage Six: Intimacy vs. Isolation (Love) 105
Robert Havighurst (1900–1991): Developmental Tasks 106
Using Social–Emotional Theories 108
Cognitive Development 108
Jean Piaget (1896–1980): Constructivist 108
Piagetian Stages of Cognitive Development 108
Sensorimotor 109
Preoperational 109
Concrete Operational 110
Formal Operational 110
Lev Vygotsky (1896–1934): Sociocultural Theory of Cognition 111
Howard Gardner (1943–): Theory of Multiple Intelligences 112
Using Theories of Cognitive Development 113
Learning Theory 115
B. F. Skinner (1904–1990): Operant Conditioning 115
Albert Bandura (1925–): Social Learning Theory 116
Using Learning Theories 116
Moral Development 117
Lawrence Kohlberg (1927–1987): Moral Reasoning 117
Carol Gilligan (1936–): The Ethics of Caring 118
Nell Noddings (1929–): Caring and Relationship 119
William Damon (1944–): Moral Development Through the Life Span 120
Using Theories of Moral Development 120
Ecological Systems Theory 121
Urie Bronfenbrenner (1917–2005) 121
The Microsystem 122
The Mesosystem 122

The Exosystem 123
The Macrosystem 123
Using the Ecological System Theory 123
Summary 124
Terms to Learn 124
Review Questions 125
Challenge Exercises 126
Internet Resources 126
References 126

Chapter 6   The Adult's Role in Socialization and Development 128

The Process of Socialization 128
Agents of Socialization 129
Types of Socialization 129
The Role of Culture 130
Adults and the Development of the Personality 134
The Role of Others 134
Adults as Teachers 136
Life Skills and Job Skills 137
Social Skills and Strategies 138
Support for Academic Achievement 139
The Impact of Poverty 140
Problem Solving and Competence 140
Literacy and a Love of Learning 141
Lifelong Habits of Health and Fitness 143
Self-esteem 144
Competence 145
Power 145
Acceptance 145
Moral Virtue 146
Moral Reasoning and Values Clarification 147
Summary 148
Terms to Learn 148
Review Questions 148
Challenge Exercises 148
Internet Resources 149
References 149

Chapter 7   Issues Facing Today's Children 151

Parents' and Children's Fears and Concerns 151
Concerns of Parents 152
Concerns of Children 153

Children's Need to Feel Safe 154
    Abraham Maslow's Hierarchy of Needs 154
What Is Normal? 156
Generational Fears 158
Some Strategies That Can Help 159
Family, School, and Community Issues 162
    Societal Issues 164
    Gender-Related Issues 165
        Learning Gender Roles 165
        Gender and School Success 166
        Implications for Programs 168
    The Disappearance of Play 169
    Children's Use of Tobacco, Alcohol, and Drugs 170
Summary 171
Terms to Learn 171
Review Questions 172
Challenge Exercises 172
Internet Resources 172
References 173

Chapter 8   Understanding and Guiding Children's Behavior 175

Conditions Affecting Children's Behavior 175
    The Guidance System 175
        The Children 176
        The Importance of Friendships 178
        The Environment 181
        The Adults 183
Guiding Children's Behavior 185
    The Theories Behind Child Guidance Techniques 185
        Effective Child Guidance Techniques 186
        Setting and Enforcing Limits 192
    Involving Parents 194
Summary 196
Terms to Learn 197
Review Questions 197
Challenge Exercises 197
Internet Resources 197
References 198

Chapter 9   Environments of School-Age Children 199

Physical Settings Used for School-Age Programs 199
    Private Homes 200
    School-Site Centers 201

Places of Worship   201
Other Community Facilities   202
Permanent or Relocatable Buildings   202
The Three Dimensions of Environments for Children   202
The Physical Dimension   203
The Temporal Dimension   204
The Interpersonal Dimension   204
A Nurturing Environment   205
The Challenge of Shared Space   212
An Attractive Environment   215
Furnishings (Including Equipment and Materials)   215
Light and Color   217
Sound   218
Provision for Privacy   218
An Interesting Environment   219
Variety of Materials   219
Room Arrangement and Interest Areas   221
A Safe Environment   221
Setting the Standards for Supervision and Practice   224
Teaching Children to Use Specialized Equipment   225
Reducing Hazards in the Afterschool Environment   226
Selecting Hazard-Free Art Materials   226
Developing a Safety Checklist   227
Responding to Accidents and Injuries   227
Ensuring That Your Environment Is Accessible to All Children   229
Evaluating Your Environment   230
Summary   231
Terms to Learn   231
Review Questions   231
Challenge Exercises   232
Internet Resources   232
References   232

Chapter 10   Cooperative Program Planning   235
The "Curriculum" of School-Age Programs   235
An Emergent Curriculum   236
Finding a Balance Between Academic Enrichment and Recreation   238
Developing Curriculum Plans   239
Planning Activity Areas   239
Clubs   241
Brainstorming Curriculum Ideas   241
The Benefits of Advance Planning   242
Scheduling Key Areas   243

Obtaining Materials, Equipment, and Supplies   244
Scheduling Staff   244
Encouraging Children to Contribute Their Ideas   245
Learning Important Skills   245
Enjoying the Anticipation of the Event or Activity   246
Achieving the Stated Goals of the Program   247
Planning the Year   247
Identifying Goals, Objectives, and Leadership Strategies   249
Ensuring a Balanced, Integrated Curriculum   250
Planning the Season   252
Planning the Month   252
Monthly Staff Planning Calendar   252
Monthly Family Calendar   255
Planning a Week   255
Planning a Day   256
Planning an Activity   259
Planning Long-Term Activities   259
Thinking Broadly About Your Program   262
Evaluating Curriculum   263
Summary   267
Terms to Learn   268
Review Questions   268
Challenge Exercises   268
Internet Resources   269
References   269

Chapter 11   A Health and Fitness Curriculum: Fighting Back Against Childhood Obesity   271

An Epidemic of Obesity   272
The Dangers of Obesity in Children   273
Understanding the Causes of Childhood Obesity   274
Food and Fitness   274
Government Policies   274
Trends in Activity Levels and Eating Habits of School-Age Children   276
Developing Habits of Lifelong Health and Fitness   277
Your Role in Modeling Health and Fitness   277
Increasing Physical Activity   279
Factors Affecting Physical Growth   280
Good Nutrition   280
Emotional Well-being   280
Culture   280
Teaching and Modeling Healthy Food Choices   281
A Nutritious Snack Curriculum   281

USDA Food and Nutrition Service Guidelines for Afterschool Program Snacks   282

Preparing Snacks With Children   284

Incorporating Aerobic Activity Into Your Program   285

Encourage Children to Walk or Bike to School   285

Dance, Yoga, and Music   289

Dance   289

Yoga   290

Music   290

Other Creative Ways to Get Children Moving   292

All Children Exercise Simultaneously   294

Virtual Trail Walking   294

Fit for Learning, Fit for Life   295

Electronic Interactive Exergames   296

Fit Kid Activities   297

Summary   298

Terms to Learn   298

Review Questions   298

Challenge Exercises   298

Internet Resources   298

References   299

Chapter 12   Engaging Children in Indoor Activities   302

The Importance of Choice and Play: Naps, Snacks, Raps, and Laps   302

Structured vs. Unstructured Play   303

The Importance of Play   303

Strategies for Involving Children in Activities   304

Balancing Academic Enrichment and Applied Knowledge   304

Using the Project Approach to Teach Life Skills   307

Afterschool Programs and Academic Standards   308

The Use of Seven Key Learning Areas to Balance Curriculum   310

Activities That Support Literacy Learning   311

Creating and Using Curriculum Webs   311

Benefits of Creating and Using Curriculum Webs   312

Connecting Geography to a Pen-Pal Activity   312

Learning to Write a Personal Letter   313

Technology Tie-in: Teaching Children to Use E-mail   316

Some Benefits of Writing Letters and Pen Pals   316

Simple Science Projects   316

Benefits of Simple Science Projects   319

Math Problem Solving   319

Cooking in the Classroom   319

Teaching Food-Preparation Skills   321

Other Activities That Strengthen Math Problem-Solving Skills 324
  Benefits of Math Problem Solving 325
Creative Arts 325
  Learning to Use a Sewing Machine 325
  Benefits of Learning to Use a Sewing Machine 326
  Making Puppets 326
  Benefits of Making Puppets 327
  Making Jewelry 327
  Benefits of Making Jewelry 327
  Tie-Dyeing 327
  Benefits of Tie-Dyeing 328
Dramatic Activities: Fantasy Play, Staged Plays, Prop Boxes, and Puppets 328
  Fantasy Play 328
  Benefits of Fantasy Play 329
  Staging a Play 329
  Benefits of Staging a Play 330
  Prop Boxes 330
  Benefits of Prop Boxes 331
  Puppet Play 332
  Benefits of Puppet Play 333
Fitness and Nutrition: Organized Active Games 333
  Indoor Hide-and-Seek 333
  Follow-up Activities 334
  Leapfrog 334
  Duck, Duck, Goose 334
  Follow-up Activities 335
  Freeze Dance (Statues) 335
  Benefits of Active Indoor Games 336
Technology 336
  Integrating Technology Into Afterschool Programs 336
  Industrial Technology 336
  Computer Technology 337
  Large Constructions 337
  Benefits of Large Constructions 338
  Photography 338
  Benefits of Photography 339
Summary 339
Terms to Learn 339
Review Questions 339
Challenge Exercises 340
Children's Books 340
Internet Resources 340
References 341

Chapter 13 Engaging Children in Outdoor Activities 343

Creating an Outdoor Environment for Children 343
Benefits of Outdoor Play and Activities 344
Most American Children Live Indoors 346
Modifying Outdoor Environments and Maintaining Safety 347
Facilitating Unstructured Outdoor Play 347
Increasing Opportunities for Engagement 348
Encouraging Different Types of Play 349
Thinking Creatively About Outdoor Activities 350
Benefits of Unstructured Outdoor Play 350
Nature and Ecological Activities 350
Field Trips to Outdoor Places 351
Follow-up Activities 351
Benefits of a Field Trip to the Woods 351
Planting a Garden 351
Follow-up Activities 355
Benefits of Planting a Garden 355
Greening the Planet 356
Benefits of Greening the Planet 356
Outdoor Games and Sports 357
Parachute Games 357
Bounce the Beach Ball 357
Slithering Snakes 358
Parachute Cave 358
Benefits of Parachute Games 358
Hiking, Cycling, and Skating 358
Benefits of Hiking, Cycling and Skating 359
Team Sports 359
Benefits of Team Sports 360
Organized Outdoor Games 360
Volley-Up 361
Stop and Go 361
Scramble 362
Tag and Freeze Tag 362
Benefits of Outdoor Games 362
Other Outdoor Pursuits 363
Water Fun 363
Benefits of Water Fun 364
Working With Wood 364
Benefits of Working with Wood 365
Building and Flying Kites 365
Benefits of Making and Flying Kites 365

Raising Animals 366
    Benefits of Raising Animals 367
Summary 367
Terms to Learn 367
Review Questions 367
Challenge Exercises 367
Children's Books 368
Internet Resources 368
References 368

Chapter 14   **Working with Older School-Age Children and Teens** 370

Older School-Agers and Teens: Intermediate Grades, Middle School, Junior High, and High School 370
Definition of Terms 370
Safety of Older School-Age Children 371
Developmental Characteristics of Older Children and Teens 372
Some Differences in Programs for Older Children and Teens 374
Create Separate Programs for Older School-Agers, Middle School Youngsters, and Teens 374
    Dimensions of Programs for Older School-Age Children 377
    Implications for School-Age Staff 378
Make the Program Look Different 379
Change the Role of the Staff 381
Give Older Children a Room of Their Own 384
Characteristics of Successful Programs 385
Offer Extended Day Programs 385
Involve Youngsters in Planning and Leading Activities 386
Ensure Flexibility for Individual Needs 386
Provide a Wide Variety of Activities 387
    Request Donations of Musical Instruments 387
    Invite a Local Scientist or Mathematician 387
    Invite the Local Community Theater 388
    Design an Environment That Invites Older Youngsters 388
    Make Homework an Integral Part of the Program 388
Challenge Their Skills, Encourage New Abilities, and Supervise Safe Risks 389
Create and Nurture Links with Community Agencies 390
Programs for Teens 392
    A Model Program: LEAP 394
    Nighttime Programming Challenges and Solutions 394
Create Safe and Friendly Havens for Adolescents 395
The Role of the Adult in Programs for Teens 396
Summary 397
Terms to Learn 397

Review Questions   397
Challenge Exercises   397
Internet Resources   398
References   398

Chapter 15   Developing Partnerships with Families, Schools, and the Community   401

Building Relationships With Families   402
  The Role of Adults in the Family–School Partnership   403
  Setting the Tone at the First Contact   404
  Admission and Enrollment Policies   405
    Enrollment Packets   406
    Parent Handbooks   406
  Schedule Open Houses, Back-to-School Nights, and Parent Conferences   406
    Open Houses   408
    Back-to-School Night   408
    Parent Conferences   409
  Family Fun Nights and Parent Information Meetings   409
  Parenting Education and Support   411
  Including Fathers and Other Males in Family Activities   411
  Day-to-Day Communication   412
    Your Public Front Door   413
    Bulletin Board   413
    Newsletters   414
    Personal Conversation   414
    Telephone Contact   414
    Notes   414
    Photos   416
    Results of Effective Parent Partnerships   416
  Resolving Parent–Staff Differences   416
Developing Partnerships With Schools   417
  Advantages   417
  Concerns   418
Developing Community Partnerships   419
  Forming Partnerships With Businesses, Community-Based Organizations, and Public Agencies   419
  Partnerships That Strengthen Students' Academic Performance   420
  Workforce Development Through Community Partnerships   421
  Building the Capacity and Sustainability of Out-of-School Programs   422
Summary   423
Terms to Learn   423
Review Questions   423

Challenge Exercises   423
References   424

Chapter 16   Administrative Issues: Licensing, Policies, and Personnel   426

Licensing Issues   426
   Licensing and Regulations   427
      The Challenge of Varied Licensing Regulations   427
      Understanding the Licensing Provisions That Apply to Your Program   428
   Liability: Who Is Responsible?   429
      Types of Ownership and Liability   430
Policy Issues   431
   Contracts With Parents   431
      Mission Statements   431
      Developing Admission Agreements   432
      Parent Handbooks   433
   Staff Policies and Procedures Manual   433
   Determining an Operating Schedule   434
   Funding and Finances   436
   Transportation and Parking   436
   Getting Along With Your Neighbors   437
Personnel Issues   438
   Staffing Considerations   439
      Blurring of Roles and Shared Decision Making   439
      Hiring and Retaining Effective High-Quality Staff   441
Summary   444
Terms to Learn   444
Review Questions   444
Challenge Exercises   444
Internet Resources   445
References   445

Appendix   National AfterSchool Association Code of Ethics
January 2009   446

Index   457

Chapter

1

Where Are Our Children After School?

Do you ever think about where children go after school? Unless we have little brothers or sisters, or children of our own, few of us spend much time thinking about children. Locked away in safe school buildings most of the day, they appear on the city sidewalks for an hour in the morning (you might notice the heavy automobile traffic jam if you have to drive in the vicinity of a school) and again in the afternoon. However, there are approximately 36 million children between the ages of 5 and 13 in the United States, and they all head away from school sometime between two o'clock and four o'clock each afternoon. Where do they go? Here are the stories of several children to illustrate the varieties of ways in which they spend their time.

STUART and JESSE. Twelve-year-old Stuart arrives home from middle school each day on a city bus, having stopped partway along the route to retrieve his 8-year-old brother, Jesse, from the Extended Care room at his elementary school. Together they board another bus and get off a few blocks from their apartment, where they stay until their father arrives home a few hours later. Although Stuart and Jesse may talk on their cell phones, they are restricted from using the house telephone, visiting friends, or having friends visit them during this time. In the event of an emergency, Stuart can refer to a list of telephone numbers, including those of the local Red Cross and a neighbor who cares for younger children in her home. The neighbor also compiled a list of safe Web sites and e-mail addresses that he can use to get help with homework, although he rarely uses them. The afternoons are long, especially in the winters, when the darkness arrives long before their father. On Wednesdays, Jesse attends a Cub Scout meeting at his school, and Stuart goes to a drop-in tutoring program at the public library until Jesse's meeting ends. The Cub Scout leader has seen the boys' father only once, at the parent-orientation meeting in the fall. She sends notes and permission slips home with Stuart when he comes to pick up his brother, however, and permission slips are usually signed and returned promptly, so Jesse is able to participate fully.

DIANNE and KWAME. After school on Tuesdays, Dianne and Kwame, both aged 7, cross the street in front of their school and enter the public library. Selecting seats against the back wall, they take out paper and books and begin their homework. Their mothers, both teachers, will pick them up in an hour or so. Since there are so many unaccompanied children in the library each afternoon, the staff has been increased during these hours, and librarians alternate between helping children find books or magazines and running special programs to keep them from disturbing the other library patrons. Twice a week the librarians stage a puppet show for the younger children, and sometimes the girls help out. High school students sometimes come to the library and help the younger children with homework. One of the boys helping Dianne with her math homework told Dianne that he does this for community service credit at school.

JAMAL. Ten-year-old Jamal could go directly home after school if he wished; his parents have arranged for a neighbor to keep an eye on him until they come home from work. But Jamal feels that he is too old to be watched by a "babysitter" and prefers to play basketball at the YMCA for an hour and then stop at the video arcade around the corner from his house until dinner time. On Tuesdays he has piano lessons, which take nearly an hour, including walking to the teacher's house, and on Thursdays his school has an after-school basketball league. By moving from one activity to another throughout the week, Jamal never has to do more than check in with the neighbor, and he rarely enters his own lonely house.

TERESA, ESPIE, and JAMES. Teresa and Espie are 9-year-old twins. Their 13-year-old brother is supposed to be watching them after school, but James is more interested in being with his friends and usually shoos the girls away. The row houses along their street are filled with unemployed and discouraged people, the alleys and culverts with homeless teenagers. Teresa and Espie used to be afraid to walk home alone, and even more afraid to stay in their house when James brought his rough-talking friends over. Their mother works hard, and they don't want to make her life harder by tattling on James. A gang-prevention agency opened a drop-in recreation center for children in their neighborhood, and one afternoon the girls entered the doors, curious. Now they go there often after school. They especially like the crafts and playing volleyball. There are tutors there who have a list of homework assignments their teachers have assigned, and they even offered to help them with their big social studies project, so now that it is getting dark earlier, they stay at the center until their mother can pick them up on her way home from work.

These four scenarios illustrate some of the ways families try to ensure the supervision of school-age children during the gaps between their school hours and the availability of their parents to care for them. Some are formal; others are less so. Generally, **formal child care** falls into one of three categories: (1) in-home care, (2) out-of-home care, and (3) relative care. **Informal child care** includes the use of community services such as the public library or drop-in centers, music or art lessons, and organized sports. More information about the types of child care and the advantages and disadvantages of each will be presented in later chapters.

AFTERSCHOOL IN EARLIER TIMES

The need for before- and afterschool supervision of children is not new, and there really never has been a time when all children had a parent at home to care for them (Coontz, 2000). Mothers have worked in the fields, in hospitals and class-rooms, in factories, and in the service sector for many generations. In earlier gen-erations, and even today in some communities, children have been cared for by grandparents, aunts or uncles, or siblings, as well as by nannies, governesses, and tutors, depending on the income and social class of the family. Or they may have simply stayed home alone. During the wave of immigration from Europe in the late 19th century, settlement houses, developed to meet the financial, social, and educational needs of immigrants, offered activities after school that included cooking, sewing, woodworking, English lessons, and tutoring in school subjects. Many children spent the long hours after school in such centers, keeping safe and learning how to become American citizens (Koerin, 2003).

During World Wars I and II, women were called to serve in factories to re-place the men who had gone overseas, and afterschool programs were hastily opened to care for their children while they worked. For a decade or so following World War II, the expanding U.S. economy allowed some middle-income moth-ers to remain at home until their children were grown, but by 1980 nearly two-thirds of all young wives were working (Coontz, 2000).

Nearly a million American children participate in afterschool enrichment programs.

At the same time that many families were enjoying a postwar prosperity, others were facing new challenges. Mothers continued to enter the workforce in larger numbers than before, and new waves of immigration brought displaced families into communities and schools where it seemed everyone was chasing the "American Dream" of home ownership, a car in the driveway, and matching furniture inside. In that one-car economy, transplanted wives were often trapped in the suburbs with their children, and many single mothers, unable to find child care, were forced to go on governmental assistance to stay home with their youngsters.

The 1960s and 1970s saw increased stress, unstable relationships, rising divorce rates, and the emergence of thousands of single-parent households. The resulting increase in primarily female-headed households led to a drop in the average income of families with children (Coontz, 2000), and even families with two parents at home often found their standard of living in jeopardy as the years went by. A single generation of mothers staying at home to care for children had led many people to believe that this was how it should be, and for a number of years the American voters were unwilling to underwrite a system of caring for school-age children to solve the problem. Most afterschool programs at that time were those operated by community organizations, such as the YMCA, Boys and Girls Clubs, and the Boy Scouts of America (Gayl, 2004).

❀   *Consider This:*   ❀

Talk with other members of your class about afterschool arrangements when they were in elementary school. Did any of you go home to an empty house? Did someone care for you other than your mother and father? How old were you when your family allowed you to be alone on a regular basis? Did you find yourself in any unsafe situations while you were home alone?

AFTERSCHOOL CARE TODAY

Fortunately, attitudes have changed, and this social issue, long regarded as a private family matter, is now the subject of public discussion, government policy, and community endeavor. Today, nearly a million school-age children participate in afterschool enrichment programs and other youth-development and support programs under the umbrella of the federal 21st Century Community Learning Center Program (National Institute on Out-of-School Time, 2007), and many others attend programs funded by state and local measures as well as with private funds. However, 15 million children still regularly return to empty homes after school, and only about 8.4 million are in afterschool programs (Afterschool Alliance, 2009). Most school-age children experience a patchwork of multiple arrangements during a typical week (Capizzano, Tout, & Adams, 2000; Chung, 2005). However, seeing a relationship between unsupervised children and growing juvenile crime rates, many communities have since addressed the need for a comprehensive system of afterschool care and recreation programs, and a variety of creative solutions are emerging.

DEBORAH. At the end of each school day, 8-year-old Deborah walks only a few yards to her afterschool program. An agency that operates school-age care centers with federal money has placed a portable building in a corner of the school playground, and Deborah attends three afternoons a week, while her mother, a hair stylist, completes her afternoon appointments.

There she can do her homework at a table with her friends, play board games or use the computer, help make a snack or sew, or participate in construction or recreational activities outside as weather allows. An only child, Deborah enjoys this wind-down time until one of her parents comes to get her in the evening. She has been in group care since infancy and seems to be content there.

MEETING THE UNIQUE SCHEDULING NEEDS OF SCHOOL-AGE CHILDREN

Unfortunately, as the number of working mothers and single-parent families (now including many male-headed households) has grown, so have the challenges surrounding the supervision and care of their school-age children. As Jodi Grant states in Perspective 1.1 on next page, advocacy is necessary to ensure that the needs for seamless afterschool services are met. Many afterschool programs close during winter and spring breaks and even during summer vacation. Some do not provide services on teacher professional-development days or school holidays, which may not be holidays for the parents. Some schools close early one or two days a week for teachers to attend meetings or prepare lessons. Parents must find alternative care during these days, which may amount to as many as a quarter of their workdays, or be forced to leave children at home alone.

Year-round schools offer a different kind of challenge, requiring full-child care for a segment of the community's children for several weeks at a time. Imagine the child-care nightmare of a family whose 8-year-old attends one school from 8:00 a.m. to 2:00 p.m., whose 10-year-old attends a year-round mathematics magnet on the other end of town (3 months on-track, 6 weeks off), 8:30 a.m. to 3:15 p.m., and whose 12-year-old can walk to junior high but doesn't start class until 9:00 a.m. or return home until nearly 4:00 p.m.

MEETING THE NEEDS OF CHILDREN AND FAMILIES

GREGORIO. Eleven-year-old Gregorio has a 25-minute bus ride from his special day class to a developmental center on the other side of town. Gregorio has Down syndrome. His extended day program teaches community-living skills and offers recreation in community settings. Gregorio's mom is a bookkeeper at an auto parts store, so she has some flexibility in her work hours, but the distance to his afterschool program makes it difficult to participate or even visit often. She would rather have him in the afterschool program at his own school, which is closer to where she works, but the staff at

PERSPECTIVE 1.1

Looking Ahead: Opportunities in a Disappointing Budget

Reflections on the President's 2010 Budget

by Jodi Grant, May 14, 2009

After a tough winter, we all hoped for a bright spring. When we learned that the President's FY 2010 budget did not propose an increase in afterschool funding, we were more than a little disappointed. Given President Obama's campaign promise to double afterschool investments, and the Department of Education's enthusiasm for afterschool, summer and expanded learning, we had anticipated—even expected—to see an increase.

That's not to say all is lost. As advocates—and community organizers—like to say, advocacy is never over. We can, and should, take pride in the strides we have made: winning an increase in funding in FY09 even though President Bush called for a cut; having several congressional offices working to advance new afterschool bills to support older youth and rural communities; hearing Education Secretary Arne Duncan applaud our field at the Afterschool for All Challenge late last month.

And, as is true with the American Recovery & Reinvestment Act, there are numerous opportunities in the President's budget to provide additional resources to afterschool programs. The budget includes an increase of more than $1 billion for Title I, $100 million for innovations in education, and $50 million for a social innovation fund; all of these are potential funding sources for afterschool programs. We will pursue each vigorously, to ensure that every possible dollar goes to help the millions of children who urgently need afterschool programs.

I want to thank everyone who reached out to the White House to voice their disappointment in the President's budget. Our message was heard. Afterschool Alliance leaders will be meeting with White House officials next week to discuss how we can help the President keep his promise to increase afterschool funding.

We are truly stronger than we've ever been. Even in hard times, we are finding ways to keep kids safe, inspire them to learn and help working families. Our good work, and our powerful and steady advocacy, continues to make a difference.

As spring becomes summer and then fall, we look forward to *Lights On Afterschool* and other events that will give us the chance to call for the afterschool investments the nation needs. We also will continue working hard to ensure that the lessons of afterschool influence changes in our nation's education system. We will ask Congress to step up, once again, and help get us on the path to 'afterschool for all' by increasing funding for 21st CCLC in the 2010 budget. We will continue seeking opportunities in the American Recovery and Reinvestment Act, and pressing for positive changes in the reauthorization of No Child Left Behind.

We do it because we know our kids need afterschool supports to succeed. With more than 14 million children unsupervised after the school bell rings, we can and will continue the fight to bring much needed afterschool supports to all our children and youth. And together, we will prevail.

Jodi Grant is executive director at the Afterschool Alliance.

Source: This article appeared in the May 2009 issue of the *Afterschool Advocate*, published by the Afterschool Alliance. Used with permission.

that center was hesitant to include a child with his particular special needs, which include a hearing deficit and the need to wear a heart monitor. "I suppose I could fight it under the ADA," she says, referring to the Americans With Disabilities Act, "but I just don't have the energy. Besides, he can go to the developmental center until he turns 21."

Parents of children with special needs face many challenges. Like all parents, they want a safe, welcoming environment for their children while they work to support their family. However, programs that are suitable for children with physical or cognitive limitations may not be located near transportation hubs or convenient to schools. They may have long waiting lists or be limited in their capacity to serve children by a shortage of trained staff.

Although the Americans With Disabilities Act prohibits programs from discriminating against children based on disability, it may still be difficult to find an appropriate placement. Many programs do not have staff members trained to meet the unique requirements of a specific child. Some children have extensive medical challenges that make group care difficult or impossible. It can be a daunting task to find programs for children over 10 or 11 that engage them sufficiently to make them enjoy participating. As well, some older youth resist attending programs that are labeled (or even look like) "child care." Gregorio's mother is fortunate to have found a program that her son enjoys and where the staff and administration work hard to teach the children workplace and self-care skills.

Children who do not speak English, or are learning it as a second language, also face many challenges. In many parts of the country, second-language learners such as José Luis Ríos (see Perspective 1.2 on next page) have a difficult time finding safe adults away from home who speak their language. This can be even more difficult in urban communities where dozens or even hundreds of dialects or languages coexist. Cultural differences between parents and staff of after-school programs, coupled with the increasing numbers of biracial and or bicultural children, make for interesting challenges, both linguistically and socially. Communication styles are likely to be different, as are some values and assumptions about roles and behaviors.

Fortunately, most of the problems have been identified, and many people are committed to solving them. However, to develop and implement a high-quality and effective system of programs for children during their out-of-school time, it is important to understand all the factors that contribute to the success of a program. One way to begin this process is to meet the children themselves and talk to them, getting to know what matters to them and what kinds of experiences they want to have when they aren't in school. Below are examples of what you might hear if you were to do that.

WHAT DO CHILDREN WANT IN BEFORE- AND AFTERSCHOOL PROGRAMS?

Jesse says, "My teacher has an iguana named Irma that we keep in our classroom. Irma is really cool and likes to sit on our shoulders while we work. If we finish our assignments, sometimes we get to clean out Irma's house or give her food or water. It is important to make sure that on cold days the light is close to the place she likes to sleep, and sometimes we put a blanket over the terrarium to keep in the heat. I really like taking care of Irma. She's cool. My mom and I live in an apartment, and my mom works lots of hours, so we can't have a cat or a dog. Sometimes I get to visit my grandparents, who have horses. But I can see

PERSPECTIVE 1.2

Working in La Fresa

José Luis Ríos

Nine-year-old José Luis Ríos lives with his large extended family in a small house in Las Lomas, California. All of his relatives work in the fields, including his brothers and sisters. José Luis is often taken out of school to work alongside his family. The owner of the land where the Ríos family works has been charged by the investigators of the Labor Department for violating some 60 provisions of the federal Migrant and Seasonal Agricultural Worker Protection Act.

My name is José Luis Ríos, and I am in third grade. We live with our parents and aunt and uncle and cousins in Las Lomas. My grandparents live in Michoacan, Mexico. If they were here right now, I'd ask them to come and visit because I don't know them. My parents told me they used to work in the fields picking strawberries, garbanzos, lentils, and corn. All my relatives that I can think of work in the fields.

My parents work in *la fresa* (the strawberries) and *la mora* (the raspberries), and my mom sometimes packs mushrooms. During the week, they leave in the morning around six o'clock, I go and help them, mostly on weekends. I help pick the strawberries and put them in boxes. Last year my father took me to the fields a lot during the week, too, instead of bringing me to school. I would find out I was going because he would say, "Let's go pick strawberries now." I like going to the fields with my father because it is pretty out there.

The longest day in the field was when we picked a lot of strawberries. I felt bad and it was getting dark. We were out there so long. I said to my parents, "Let's go home," and finally they said, "We're going." It was hard to work so long. My body gets tired, and when it is muddy, my feet get covered with mud and it is hard to walk. Also, when it is muddy, my uncle has to park the truck far away, and I get tired and cold when I have to walk back to the truck. . . .

Sometimes when I'm there, my aunt and uncle that live with us are in the fields working.

My cousins are there, too. I play with my cousin Andreas. He is seven. I like to play with him because he is a *buena gente* (good person). We play tag in the fields. My brothers work in the fields but not usually my sisters. They go to school. Rogelio, my little brothers who's two, comes to the fields, but he just plays. He doesn't make any trouble.

When I work in the fields, I don't get paid. I don't want them to pay me because it's not good. They pay my parents for what I pick. I like that my parents get paid because then they buy me toy cars and trucks or maybe a bicycle. My brothers get paid. Ignacio is eighteen, and he works during the week. He doesn't go to school now, but he used to go to high school. Manuel is the oldest, and he works in the fields in Salinas. I want to work in the fields like my brothers when I'm older, because I can eat a lot of strawberries and out there you can watch the birds.

But sometimes it is hard and I'm tired in school on Mondays because I worked on the weekend. I also get a lot of bad headaches, so sometimes I have to leave school early or go and rest in the nurse's office. When my father took me to the fields last year during the week, it was hard to study when I got home because I was tired. It is hard to work and go to school at the same time.

I like coming to school better than working in the fields. I go to school on the bus at seventhirty. I like going to school to learn because then you know things. If you don't know anything and you go somewhere and somebody asks you to write something, you won't be able to. And when you're older you won't know anything. The people who haven't gone to school, they work in the fields.

I'm trying to learn English at school, but I like to speak Spanish because I'm understood better. I have more friends that speak Spanish than English. My parents tell me to study English, but I like studying the Native Americans best because they wrote, they did drawings, and they hunted buffalos. I like the Mayans. They made houses so the water couldn't get in when it rained. In school I like to write, too. I write about the birds because they are pretty and they fly. And I like to write about sheep and animals and also the Ninja Turtles.

When I get home from school, I have cookies. I eat most of my meals at school. My older brothers and sisters are there when I get home. They take care of me because my parents are working in the fields. My big sisters Carmela and Amelia help me with my homework and make cookies and coffee. Sometimes we take the strawberries from the fields home to eat. We make *fresa molida*—it's kind of a milkshake. Sometimes I take care of my little brothers and sister. I give them coffee and cookies. I have to watch out when I take care of them because cars come up our driveway and they could hit them. That's what happened to my little cousin. And sometimes we play right by the driveway. I play marbles with my brother Carlos and my cousin Jorge. I like to play hide-and-seek with my little sister Maria. My favorite place to hide is in the car.

Source: From *Voices from the Fields* by S. Beth Atkin. Copyright 1993 by S. Beth Atkin (text and photographs). By permission of LITTLE BROWN & COMPANY.

Irma every school day, and I like that. If I were in an afterschool center, I'd like to have a pet that I could take care of there, who knew me and trusted me like Irma does."

And what about the other children we met earlier? What would they like to have in an out-of-school setting? Stuart, for instance, has a science fair project to build this year. He has a computer at home, and his father has been helping him with ideas. But he has a friend, Aaron, who wanted to work with him, maybe to build a suspension bridge or an arch. Stuart can't have friends over after school, and Aaron's not allowed to go out after dinner or on Saturdays, so it's difficult for them to work together. Both Aaron and Stuart would like a place where they could work on their project together after school, with computers and books about engineering, as well as a workbench and tools.

Dianne and Kwame like going to the library, and they really enjoy working with the preschool children and the puppet shows, but they know the librarians don't like it when children are left there alone. They wish that there was a special room at the library that was set up for kids to study and talk, where it was actually

Some afterschool programs have pets that children care for.

Most children prefer the company of their peers to going home alone.

okay for them to be and where no one got upset because they were there without their parents.

Jamal has already learned his way around the neighborhood, and most of the time he's pretty happy with his informal afterschool arrangements. However, when pressed, he admits that he hardly ever starts doing his homework until after his parents come home, and then sometimes he gets involved playing games with his dad or watching TV, and things don't get done that should. When the weather turns cold he wishes there was somewhere warm where he could go right after school besides the neighbor's home or his empty house.

Gregorio likes his afterschool center, and he likes the ride on the bus. He watches people, he'll tell you, and there are lots of trucks on the road. He likes trucks. However, he also misses being with Carlos, his best friend from school. Carlos can't go to the same afterschool program where Gregorio goes, and Gregorio can't go to the afterschool program at his regular school, where Carlos goes every day. He'd like it better if they could both be in the same program after school.

You can tell from the way Teresa and Espie regularly attend the drop-in center that they are happy it opened. But sit with them for a while and talk, and they will tell you that their favorite teacher, Ada, doesn't work there anymore. She left to work at a Head Start program where she can make more money. She explained it to the girls when she said good-bye, and they understand, but are sad she left.

Eight-year-old Deborah is still quite happy at her child care center. However, one of her friends, Karolina, is not so happy. At 12 years old, Karolina is the only sixth grader in the afterschool care program, and there are only four fifth graders. She complains that there's nothing to do there and that all the toys are for "babies." She works on her homework most of the time, helping younger children like Deborah with their math or teaching them how to play card games. Karolina would like to go home alone after school, but since her mother won't let her, she wishes that there were more older kids and something more interesting to do.

❀   *Consider This:*   ❀

How did you spend your free time when you were in elementary school? Did you have hobbies? Participate in sports? Go to music lessons? Ride your bike? In what ways do you think this differs from spending 2 to 4 hours of time every day in a group setting?

Ask a group of children in an afterschool program how they would like to spend their time if they were able to make the choice.

What should a school-age program look like? School-age children have lots of ideas and often very strong opinions about what they want to do when they're not in school. As a way of getting at this information, I asked a group of fifth and sixth graders to make a list of things they would like to be able to do in the "dream" afterschool program. This is what they wrote:

When I go to my center I want to . . .
- ❀ be left alone.
- ❀ go home as soon as I can.
- ❀ not have to do my homework.
- ❀ do whatever I want.
- ❀ be with my friends.
- ❀ call my mom.
- ❀ visit places.
- ❀ eat lots of junk food.
- ❀ watch TV.
- ❀ be on a soccer team.
- ❀ read my book all afternoon.
- ❀ play basketball.
- ❀ do lots of art projects.
- ❀ have men teachers.
- ❀ play video games.
- ❀ chew gum and eat candy.
- ❀ have lots of time with the teacher.
- ❀ go down the hall to the bathroom without a buddy.
- ❀ learn how to play the drums.
- ❀ work on my trading card collection.
- ❀ build things.
- ❀ have a break from homework and school.
- ❀ play pool.

It might not be reasonable to offer all these things in an afterschool program (especially the junk food!), but it would be very smart to keep them in mind as you plan your program.

WHAT WE CAN LEARN FROM PARENTS

It is also helpful to hear what parents have to say about their children's likes and dislikes and how they view their out-of-school activities. After all, they know their children best, and they see them in a variety of environments. But parents also have their own issues, hopes, and fears. Some parents read books and talk to teachers and to one another, trying to reassure themselves that their children are developing and growing like other children do or helping one another cope with behavioral changes or personality traits.

One father picking up his 7-year-old daughter from a Brownie meeting remarked to the leader, "Melissa and I are not getting along very well this week. She seems to be whining about something all the time. Everything is *boring*, or *dumb*, or *gross*." Smiling knowingly, the young woman, the mother of Melissa's best friend, agreed. "Yes, Melissa does like to dramatize events. But so does Lacey. I think it's just part of being 7 years old. However," she went on, "Melissa gets just as intensely interested in something she wants to do as she gets intensely bored with something we've suggested that she doesn't like. Take, for example, those friendship bracelets we made last week. She didn't want to stop working on them even when you came to pick her up, remember?" Melissa's father likes having a professional spending time with his daughter, and he appreciates knowing that she understands child development enough to explain it to him.

Another parent, juggling a toddler and an infant as her 9-year old opened the car door, praised her oldest child's cooperative spirit. "I don't know what I would do without Gurnoor. Since Jassim was born, I never seem to have enough hands. But Gurnoor helps me get in and out of the house and entertains his little sister while I feed and change Jassim. He's suddenly become so helpful!" School-age children are moving away from the dependence on adults that has characterized their early childhood. According to Erik Erikson (1959), between the ages of 6 and 12, youngsters are in a stage of development he labeled "Industry vs. Inferiority." As Gurnoor's mother had noticed, they are growing up and like to demonstrate that they can be responsible and take on adult tasks. Good after-school programs offer children opportunities to learn new skills, such as cooking, gardening, computer graphics, conflict resolution, and theater arts, and develop apprentice-like relationships with caring adults as they learn how to "do" things in an increasingly mature manner.

A 2007 survey of directors of school-age programs conducted by Child Care Exchange found that, on the whole, parents agree with Erikson's observations. However, Figure 1.1 illustrates two responses that reflect contemporary culture: (1) parents want their children to be safe, and (2) they want them to do their homework while they are at their afterschool program. Other expectations parents had for their children were "having fun, learning, academics, and developing social skills" (Neugebaeur, 2007). Parents want to know that their children have opportunities to grow and learn in a safe environment outside of the classroom.

A cluster of parents watching their 7- and 8-year-olds playing with superhero characters at a park remarked on the complicated script the children had worked out. Each child had at least two different characters to move around, yet none seemed to have trouble remembering each of the other characters' names and extensive attributes or the story line that had emerged during the last hour.

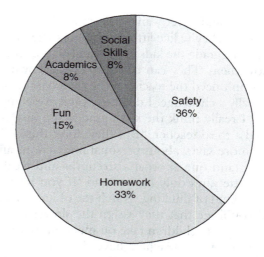

FIGURE 1.1 Parent Expectations for School-Age Care.

Source: Lawrence National Center on Children in Poverty Report. Cited in Neugebauer (2007), *Exchange*. Used with permission of Exchange Press, Inc.

"You should hear all the rules they've made about this game," one of the parents marveled. "If they jump from the picnic table it means they've transported to another galaxy, but if they're *under* the table they have their shields on. Only certain characters can be invisible, and if they get hit by a missile of some kind, they lose their powers. I'd need a rule book to keep it all straight." "I know," agreed another. "But it gets even better as they get older. My 10-year-old daughter keeps reminding me of the moves whenever we play chess, and she's only been playing for a year. I have trouble remembering all the rules in *Jeopardy!*"

School-age children are also growing intellectually. They are developing logical thought and new social skills that allow them to think about people, places, and events that are far away from their daily lives, perhaps even imaginary, and they enjoy being involved in complex games, problem solving, and long-term projects. These parents are pleased that their children are having opportunities to play with one another and develop their social skills. They also appreciate that they can stretch their minds, not only by pretending to be space explorers but also by playing challenging games such as sudoku, chess, Clue, or Connect Five, with older children and adults.

Talking to parents can help you to understand what parents need and want in an afterschool program. Conversations with parents can also help you to understand the sometimes confusing temperaments and developmental changes of children, as well as changing family dynamics.

WHAT WE CAN LEARN FROM CLASSROOM TEACHERS

"I really enjoy teaching first grade," remarked a first-year teacher during a staff meeting at a small neighborhood school. "The children want so much to please you and are loving and kind to one another. I did my student teaching in fourth grade, and found the kids really hard to handle at first."

"I would never want to teach 5- and 6-year-olds," disagreed the fourth-grade teacher. "They're like little ducklings; some of them follow you around all the time. By fourth grade the kids understand all the school rules and make sure their friends follow them. They can take care of their own emotional needs in the peer group and don't need the teacher to be their nanny. But get much older than 9, and they are really a challenge. I definitely prefer teaching fourth and fifth graders."

"I really think the sixth graders are just as sweet as the first graders," interjected a third teacher. "But they don't think it's cool to let you know it. They're a lot more savvy about personal interactions and how friendships work, but they understand one another's strengths and weaknesses and often allow for them. The little guys only understand 'If you let me play with your toy, I'll be your friend' kind of thinking. Watch the older children working in groups on a project, and you'll see that they assign the slower kids things they can handle, while the more capable children take on much more responsibility."

What these teachers have discovered, and afterschool professionals know also, is that school-age children are very different from preschool-aged children. Each birthday brings with it new and exciting skills and challenges. Just as their parents expect more of older children, afterschool programs must offer more stimulating activities and experiences appropriate for youngsters as they become capable of more abstract thought and complex moral reasoning. Long-term construction projects, play production, writing a newsletter, planting a garden—these kinds of activities offer older children real challenges in the developmental domains of intellectual and language development. School-age children can also become concerned about the right and wrong of one another's behavior, and adult staff can use intervention techniques to provide opportunities for peer relationship building and facilitate moral development that can have positive and wide-ranging effects, even outside the program (Metz, Goldsmith, & Arbreton, 2008).

WHAT WE CAN LEARN FROM RESEARCH

Classroom teachers, more than any other group of people, see children in age-related **cohorts**, which allows them to see behavioral similarities among children of approximately the same age. Just as 2-year-olds have certain common traits, so do 6-year-olds, 9-year-olds, and 10-year-olds. Researchers have identified developmentally related **cohort effects**, such as characteristic behaviors at different ages, and it is useful to know what they are, always keeping in mind that each child is unique and growing on his or her own timetable. **Temperaments** and **life experiences** also differ, influencing individual children's responses to similar situations. Children are influenced by their families and the society in which they live as well as by their internal developmental calendar (Bronfenbrenner, 1979; Chess & Thomas, 1996).

Child psychologists have observed that developmental changes in children tend to be orderly, directional, and stable (Lightfoot, Cole, & Cole, 2009). **Orderly** means that changes tend to occur in a sequence or series and can usually be predicted, because in many cases they are similar for all children. For example, most children learn to crawl before they walk and walk before they run. **Directional** refers to the fact that these changes build on one another; they show some kind of progression or accumulation of the parts of development. It's much like learning the moves in a video game—it's easier for the player if each level builds on the skills that were required in the earlier levels. And **stable** means that these changes stick around for a while once they appear. In general, once a child, for example, conquers his fear of the dark, he remains less frightened than before. Once a child learns to ride a bicycle, she continues to know how to do so (Erikson, 1950/1963; Piaget & Inhelder, 1969/2000). However, development is not always smooth, or continuous; sometimes a new skill or attribute seems to occur all at once. Researchers call this occurrence **discontinuous development** (Piaget, 1971).

In addition, child-development professionals tend to divide their analysis of development into separate areas, called **domains of development**. For example, *physical growth* and *motor development* are considered separately from *social* and *emotional development*, as are *cognitive* and *language development* and *ethics* or *moral development*. Researchers observing children as they grow up in families around the world can provide child and youth professionals with information that is helpful when they work with children of various cultures and abilities, spending as they do large portions of their growing-up time in environments away from home. Learning about typical development can help you to apply the results of research to your selection of activities, guidance techniques, and policies in a variety of situations.

Researchers such as Erikson, Piaget, Bronfenbrenner, and Vygotsky have developed theories to explain what they have observed about children at different stages of growth and development. Most theorists focus their study of development on one or two domains, so it is important to consider the viewpoints of several different people to build a complete picture of the developing child. Curriculum and guidance decisions can be informed by these theories, which are discussed in more detail in Chapter 5. Meanwhile, it is important to understand the supervision needs of children after school and how their communities are trying to meet those needs.

A BRIEF HISTORY OF AFTERSCHOOL PROGRAMMING

It is easy to think of the field of school-age care as being quite new. However, **child and youth development**, sometimes referred to as **youth work**, which overlaps the provision of care, enrichment, and recreation for school-age children, has a very long history. The youth-development field is quite broad, with recreation, affiliation, academic enrichment, and crime prevention among the stated goals of the various groups that run programs for children and teens (Boys and Girls Clubs of America, 2009; Girl Scouts of America, 2000). All developmental domains are interrelated and inseparable (e.g., social–emotional, cognitive, and physical). Likewise, the terms *school-age care, youth development,* and *child and youth work* are used somewhat interchangeably in the pages to follow.

The term **school-age care** first appeared in 1977, when the School Age Child Care Project began at the Center for Women at Wellesley College in Boston. Michelle Seligson, director of the project, founded the National Institute on Out-of-School Time (NIOST) and drew national attention to the need for high-quality school-age care and enrichment for children ages 5–12. Soon, school-age care became a recognized program type. In 1980, Rich Scofield began publishing "School Age Notes: The Newsletter for School Age Care Professionals," and a new profession was born.

In 1986, the National School-Age Child Care Alliance (NSACCA), now the National Association for AfterSchool (NAA), was founded "to promote national standards of quality after school child care," and this organization introduced the terms **out-of-school time** and **afterschool**.

The need for increased programming specifically focused on the hours before and after school was the focus of intense discussion and legislation in the 1990s. As a result, thousands of new school-site programs were added to the approximately 17,000 local youth-serving organizations and approximately 25 national youth-serving organizations that served more than 30 million young people in the United States at that time (Borden & Perkins, 2006). New research shows strong support for the value of *high-quality* youth-development programs, and later chapters will discuss quality in more detail. However, the grassroots organizers who had quietly provided programs for children in the previous century had already laid the foundation for these new efforts, and they had known their work was important long before research findings validated them:

> Many classes have been formed. The first idea was to make a little centre of social life and brightness, then, finding those who wish to work and study, to show that social life can be carried on in these higher ways. There is a club of working girls, enjoying George Eliot's Romola, with beautiful Florentine photographs. There are also clubs of boys, large and small, to whom books are lent. One afternoon is devoted to school girls, and one evening to working girls. . . . A drawing class has done some excellent work in charcoal. . . . In the morning a small kindergarten goes on in the beautiful reception room.
>
> *(Addams, 1890)*

Settlement Houses

The description above is of a Chicago **settlement house** run by Jane Addams and Ellen Starr, the best-known example of the settlement movement of the late 19th and early 20th century. According to one historian, this movement was fueled by "a rapidly growing immigrant population, large-scale industrialization, and the problems of urban slums" (Koerin, 2003). Settlement leaders, often volunteers, developed a range of services that were at first targeted at immigrants. These included classes in English and citizenship, child care, homemaking and woodworking for the parents, and nurseries, kindergartens, and afterschool programs for their children.

Settlement programs were designed to meet the unique needs of the neighborhoods in which they were established and accordingly were often quite different in scope and personality from one another. In addition to programs for young children, teen programs in the early settlement houses included truancy and delinquency prevention and vocational training. In time, settlement programs were opened to a wider audience. One of the first playgrounds in the United States began as a large sand pile that was placed in the yard of the Boston Children's Mission on Parmenter Street after a local doctor observed supervised similar play areas in Berlin. These "sand gardens" were thought to promote the good health of children, and by 1899, 21 such playgrounds were open throughout Boston. Many settlement houses eventually became community centers, and some still exist today (Blank, 1998; Ruiz & Korrol, 2006). For example, the Houchen Settlement House in El Paso, Texas, was founded in 1893 and from 1930 to 1950 provided services to as many as 15,000 to 20,000 people a year. Today, under the auspices of a Methodist church, Houchen continues to provide child care, afterschool tutoring, and youth sports (Koerin, 2003). The United Neighborhood Houses of New York City currently runs 28 afterschool programs at settlement houses, including programs in Manhattan, Queens, and the Bronx.

4-H Programs

In the late 1890s, 4-H programs began throughout the country in response to the need to provide young people with a modern agricultural education. The events of the earliest years are not recorded, but in 1901, A. B. Graham, a school principal in Ohio, began to promote vocational agriculture in rural schools in out-of-school "clubs." In 1902, Graham formed a club of boys and girls with officers, projects, meetings, and record requirements. He sought the assistance of the Ohio Agricultural Experiment Station and Ohio State University. At the same time, the club concept was adopted in Iowa, perhaps through some unknown personal connection. In about 1908, the first emblem used nationally was designed. The four-leaf clover design originally stood for "head, heart, hands, and hustle" but eventually was changed to symbolize "head, heart, hands, and health."

In 1912, O. H. Benson began to establish federal–state–county programs through cooperative agreements, which tied the three entities of Agricultural Extension together. Twenty-eight such early cooperative agreements between the Office of Farmer Cooperative Demonstration Work and the land-grant colleges promoted youth club work. In 1987, 4-H entered the field of school-age care when several universities, under the auspices of their colleges of agriculture, provided grant funds for community trainers to work with child care providers. As surveys identified a growing need, new programs were opened and 4-H youth-development staff developed a curriculum for child care staff to use with 6- to 12-year-olds in afterschool programs, child care centers, and family child care homes. Partnerships with local schools, neighborhood centers, and community organizations led to 4-H afterschool programs in a wide variety of settings, including enrichment opportunities for youth in lower income neighborhoods (Gleason, 2004; Wisconsin 4-H Youth Development, 2002).

Boys and Girls Clubs

Boys and Girls Clubs of America had their beginnings in Hartford, Connecticut, in 1860. Some of the earliest Boys Clubs met in settlement houses, and club activities in the early days included snooker, trampoline, judo, table tennis, cross-country running, wrestling, and football. Fundraising took much of the time of both the organizers and the boys who came to the clubs every afternoon. In 1990, the name was changed to reflect the participation in programs by girls as well as boys (Boys and Girls Clubs of America, 2009).

Young Men's and Women's Christian Associations

The Young Men's Christian Association (YMCA) started in London in 1844 with a small group of men opening hostels where men could stay who were new to the city. The Young Women's Christian Association (YWCA) began constructing similar hostels for women in 1855 during the industrial revolution in Great Britain. Young women, drawn by plentiful jobs in the city, left their rural homes and appreciated the safe housing and social network these programs provided. Both organizations soon went worldwide, and by 1875 there were chapters of both in many major cities in the United States and Canada. From its earliest years, the YWCA provided supportive services for working women, and that often included child care. In urban areas, the YWCA ran self-supporting boarding houses and in those locations offered sewing schools, libraries, prayer meetings, and Bible study as well as activities for children in the afternoons while their mothers worked. During the 1880s, the YMCA began constructing buildings in large numbers, and those facilities housed the variety of services that were available to men and boys (eventually also women and girls): swimming pools, gymnasiums, bowling alleys, basketball and volleyball courts, help with reading and studying, and Bible study. Today the YMCA serves youth and teens, families, adults, and communities throughout the United States. Their mission statement is "We build strong kids, strong families, strong communities," and one of the ways the organization addresses this mission is by providing high-quality school-age child care programs in thousands of communities.

Youth Scouting Movement

Boy Scouts began in England in 1908, created by General (later Lord) Robert Baden Powell. The story goes that when he learned boys were using his text on military scouting as a guide to outdoor activities, he came up with a program that used many of the same ideas but in a peaceful context. Juliette Low, an American, met Lord Baden Powell while she was living in England. Baden Powell's sister Agnes established Girl Guides in 1910, and Juliette Low took the idea back to her native Georgia, where the first troop meeting was held in Savannah on March 12, 1912. Early activities placed a heavy emphasis on the "arts of housewifery," but in 1916 were broadened to include ecology, physical fitness, and even aviation (Girl Scouts of America, 2000). Most Girl Scout troops met in the afternoons after school, but Boy Scouts usually met in the evenings when their male leaders had finished work for the day.

The Importance of Historical Influences

Present-day school-age staff can learn from these early youth-serving organizations. Their leaders have worked with children in urban and rural environments during the Industrial Revolution, through numerous waves of immigration, the Great Depression, and several major wars. More recently they have faced the challenge of a changing demography and cultural and societal changes that have resulted in even more school-age children without adequate supervision in the early mornings and late afternoons. The line staff, volunteers, and administrators of these programs have learned many lessons from history, and school-age professionals who work in programs influenced by these established ideas have a wonderful opportunity to benefit from that knowledge.

TODAY'S FAMILY'S NEED FOR SCHOOL-AGE CARE

In the past century, families have changed, society has changed, and children have changed. One of these changes is families' confidence about the safety of their children after school. Many parents report that they do not feel their children are safe walking home from school, to a friend's house, or to music lessons or soccer practice, even in places where a generation ago children played happily together after school each day (Berkeley Parents Network, 2005). These fears are not unfounded, and there is even a name for this concern: **parental afterschool stress** (Barnett & Greis, 2006).

Families today tend to be **nuclear** (single generational) more often than **extended** (several generations in one household), and parents are more likely to live far away from other relatives than once was the norm. Nuclear family groupings vary from father, mother, and child to single parents raising children alone, and variations on the **blended** or **reconstituted** family that may include unmarried couples and same-sex parents, children being raised by their grandparents, or families that are built through a combination of biology and adoption. (Such families typically include children from previous marriages of one or both parents.)

Family structures vary, but the one attribute these diverse families are likely to have in common is that most of the time they function in relative isolation, and they cannot always keep their children safe without help from others.

Families are also busier than they were in earlier generations, and so are their children, a trend that led to what developmentalists call the **hurried child syndrome**, in which children are pressured to grow up too quickly (Elkind, 1981; Grose, 2005; Gross, 2004). One of the antidotes for this syndrome, according to Michael Grose, a leading parent educator, is to change children's schedules to afford them "plenty of free time when they can just hang around and basically do nothing" (2005, p. 2). But without adult supervision, unscheduled time in a safe environment is at a premium for many modern children.

Many communities have moved to mixed-use zoning, which integrates services and residential buildings. Wandering around the neighborhood was never an ideal play activity, but rural, suburban, and urban neighborhoods were home base for many children, as they had been for their parents and grandparents. Today's neighborhoods have a different feel to them; they may include strip malls, convenience stores, video arcades, and families who move in and out of houses and apartments in less than a generation (sometimes in less than a few years). The isolation and disengagement that result from living among strangers seems to go hand in hand with statistics that tell us there is now much more violence committed by children and teens, more suicide, more depression, more eating disorders, and more drug and alcohol abuse, especially in the hours between school letting out for the day and parents arriving home from work. America's law enforcement leaders call the hours between the end of school and the time parents' return home "prime time for juvenile crime" (Newman, Fox, Flynn, & Christeson, 2000).

In the hours after the school bell rings, violent juvenile crime soars and the prime time for juvenile crime begins. The peak hours for such crime are from 3:00 to 6:00 p.m. These are also the hours when children are most likely to become victims of crime, be in an automobile accident, smoke, drink alcohol, or use drugs. A recent poll shows that the number one concern of working parents is the safety of their children during the afterschool hours. Afterschool programs that connect children to caring adults and provide constructive activities during these hours are among the most powerful tools for preventing crime.
(National Institute on Out-of-School Time, 2007, p. 3)

What this means in many communities is that children and youths are no longer safe unsupervised for long periods of time *even in their homes*. The referenced youth alcohol, drug, and crime involvement tells us that, street smart or media savvy as they may appear to be, young people continue to need the guidance of caring adults, support of their communities, and interesting things to do in their out-of-school hours (Search Institute, 2006). The good news is that all of these things are available to children and youth in most communities, in a variety of forms. Many recreational and care programs exist outside the community child care system, which tends to emphasize infant, toddler, and preschool care, and the environments in school-age programs look and feel different than those designed for younger children. To understand the framework within which various school-age programs function, it is important to be aware of the whole range of childrearing and supervision options available during out-of-school time.

SUMMARY

Children whose parents cannot care for them every day after school face different challenges. Parents can find a variety of solutions. Some families allow their children to go home alone after school, whereas others make informal supervision arrangements with neighbors or organizations. Still others make use of afterschool programs in their communities that offer enrichment experiences or recreational activities. Theorists study various domains of child development, and their research can inform afterschool staff as they plan environments and curriculum for school-age children. People who work with school-age children can also learn a great deal by reading the findings of researchers and by talking with children, their parents, and their teachers. Modern afterschool programs often build on the experiences of child and youth workers in programs such as YMCA and YWCA, Boys and Girls Clubs, and Scouting, which have long histories of serving youth and families, as well as the work of settlement house pioneers.

TERMS TO LEARN

afterschool
blended/reconstituted family
child and youth development
cohorts/cohort effects
directional
discontinuous development
domains of development
extended families

formal child care
hurried child syndrome
informal child care
life experiences
nuclear families
orderly
out-of-school time
parental afterschool stress

school-age care   temperaments
settlement houses   youth work
stable

REVIEW QUESTIONS

1. Make a list of each of the children described in this chapter. Which of them would be considered to be under the care and supervision of an adult? Who is not? Do you feel that these children are adequately protected from harm?

2. Think about each of the children described in this chapter. Do any of them seem like any children you know? Why or why not?

3. What is meant by the term *out of school*? How does that differ from *after school*? *School-age care*? Explain how these various terms evolved.

4. What is "prime time for juvenile crime"? Explain and discuss.

CHALLENGE EXERCISES

1. Research programs for school-age children in your community. Look in the telephone directory, in the newspaper classified ads, and on the Internet. How many are there? Do you think the provisions are adequate?

2. Interview members of a family in which both parents (or a single parent) work outside the home. Talk to the parent(s) separately from the children; ask what their children prefer to do before and/or after school. Ask the child or children the same question. Compare the answers.

3. Create a composite child, aged 5 to 12. Give the child a gender, an age, and a name. Describe him/her physically, behaviorally, and socially. What kind of scenario can you create for this child's before- and afterschool situation? Is it realistic? Why or why not?

4. Who do you think should be responsible for the before- and afterschool care of children? Parents? Schools? Local, state, or federal government? How about summer and holiday care? Who should pay for it? How should the funds be raised? Where should this care be located?

INTERNET RESOURCES

Afterschool Alliance:
   http://www.afterschoolalliance.org
Americans With Disabilities Act of 1990:
   http://www.ada.gov/pubs/ada.htm
Boys and Girls Clubs of America:
   http://www.bgca.org
4-H afterschool programs:
   http://4-h.org/b/Pages/Afterschool/about.html
Girl Scouts of America:
   http://www.girlscouts.org
YMCA:
   http://www.ymca.net/
YWCA:
   http://www.ywca.net

REFERENCES

Addams, J. (1890). The Chicago Toynbee Hall. In J. Dow (Ed.), *Unity: Hull-House scrapbook I*. Chicago: University of Illinois.

Afterschool Alliance. (2009). *America after 3PM: Key findings*. Washington, DC: JCPenney Afterschool.

Armstrong, T. (2004). The hurried child syndrome: What you can do about it. The National Parenting Center. Retrieved April 13, 2010 from http://www.tnpc.com/

Atkin, S. B. (1993). *Voices from the fields: Children of migrant farmworkers tell their stories*. Boston: Little, Brown and Company.

Barnett, R. C., & Greis, K. C. (2006). Parental after-school stress and psychological well-being. *Journal of Marriage and the Family, 68*, 101–108.

Berkeley Parents Network. (2005, November 14). *When is it safe for kids to walk alone?* Retrieved July 14, 2008, from http://parents.berkeley.edu

Blank, B. T. (1998). Settlement houses: Old idea in new form builds communities. *New Social Worker, 5*(3), 6.

Borden, L. M., & Perkins, D. F. (2006). Community youth development professionals: Providing the necessary supports in the United States. *Child & Youth Care Forum, 35*(2), 7.

Boys and Girls Clubs of America. (2009). Who we are: The history of Boys and Girls Clubs of America. Retrieved March 26, 2009, from http://www.bgca.org/whoweare/history.asp

Bronfenbrenner, U. (1979). *The ecology of human development: Experiments by nature and design*. Cambridge, MA: Harvard University Press.

Capizzano, J., Tout, K., & Adams, G. (2000). *Child care patterns of school-age children with employed mothers*. Washington, DC: The Urban Institute.

Chess, S., & Thomas, A. (1996). *Temperament: Theory and practice (basic principles into practice series)* (Vol. 12). New York: Brunner/Mazel.

Chung, A. M. (2005). *Afterschool programs: Keeping children safe and smart*. Washington, DC: Partnership for Family Involvement in Education.

Coontz, S. (2000). *The way we never were: American families and the nostalgia trap*. New York: Basic Books.

Elkind, D. (1981). *The hurried child: Growing up too fast too soon*. Reading, MA: Addison-Wesley.

Erikson, E. H. (1959). *Identity and the life cycle in psychological issues*. New York: International Universities Press.

Erikson, E. H. (1963). *Childhood and society* (2nd ed.). New York: Norton. (Original work published in 1950)

Gayl, C. L. (2004). *Afterschool programs: Expanding access and ensuring quality*. Washington, DC: Progressive Policy Institute.

Girl Scouts of America. (2000). *History of Girl Scouts*. Retrieved March 26, 2009, from http://www.main.org/gsusa/histry.htm

Gleason, W. (2004). *The early history of Wisconsin 4-H*. Madison: Division of Cooperative Extension of the University of Wisconsin-Extension.

Grose, M. (2005, June). *Let's not hurry children through childhood*. Retrieved April 13, 2010, from http://ezinearticles.com/?expert_bio=Michael_Grose

Koerin, B. (2003). The settlement house tradition: Current trends and future concerns. *Journal of Sociology and Social Welfare, XXX*(2), 53–68.

Lightfoot, C., Cole, M. C. S., & Cole, S. (2009). *The development of children*. New York: Worth.

Metz, R. A., Goldsmith, J., & Arbreton, A. J. A. (2008). *Putting it all together: Guiding principles for quality after-school programs serving preteens*. Philadelphia: Private/Public Ventures.

National Institute on Out-of-School Time. (2007). *Making the case: A fact sheet on children and youth in out-of-school time*. Boston: Wellesley Centers for Women at Wellesley College.

Neugebaeur, R. (2007, September/October). School-age child care trend report: Views from the field. *Exchange*, 4.

Newman, S. A., Fox, J. A., Flynn, E. A., & Christeson, W. (2000). *America's afterschool choice: The prime time for juvenile crime, or youth enrichment and achievement.* Washington, DC: Fight Crime: Invest in Kids.

Piaget, J. (1971). *Genetic epistemology* (4th ed.). New York: W. W. Norton & Company.

Piaget, J., & Inhelder, B. (2000). *The psychology of the child.* New York: Basic Books. (Original work published in 1969)

Ruiz, V., & Korrol, V. S. (2006). *Latinas in the United States: A historical encyclopedia*: Bloomington Indiana University Press.

Search Institute. (2006). *Pass it on! Ready-to-use handouts for asset-builders* (2nd ed.). Washington, DC: Author.

Wisconsin 4-H Youth Development. (2002). 4-H youth development history. Retrieved April 13, 2010, from http://4h.uwex.edu/about/historydates.cfm

Chapter
2

A View of the Field: School-Age Care and Youth Development

More than 28 million school-age children have both parents or their only parent in the workforce, and experts estimate that more than 15 million children go home alone on any given afternoon (Afterschool Alliance, 2009). For most of human history, in nearly all cultures, extended families have helped one another to raise the society's children and keep them safe until they were old enough to do so themselves. Childhood in developed nations has been until recently characterized by a certain amount of freedom and unscheduled time. For a variety of reasons, however, in the United States and other industrialized nations of the world this is no longer the case.

Dr. Christine Todd, child development specialist at the University of Illinois, studied the variety of experiences school-age children may have while their parents work. Table 2.1 presents that conceptual framework. Using Todd's analysis, children in solitary self-care fall at the lowest end of the supervision continuum, **no supervision**, and probably suffer the greatest vulnerability to the risks described in Chapter 1. This would be where brothers Stuart and Jesse (also introduced in Chapter 1) would appear on the chart.

Some communities have initiated telephone help lines, family education programs, or "check-in" programs, where qualified staff run drop-in or call-in centers to assist children in self-care to deal with loneliness, fear, or specific problems such as homework, preparing meals, or first aid for simple injuries. Once they begin participating in this type of a program, or if Jamal from Chapter 1 checks in with the neighbor as his mother desires, these children are now considered to have **distal supervision**, or supervision from a distance. Commercial check-in programs present a niche opportunity in communities where they are not yet an option.

Families who schedule their children into after-school sports programs, as Jimmy and Jorge's parents did, or recreation programs, music lessons, Scouts, or

TABLE 2.1 A Continuum of School-Age Child Care Options.

HIGH	Degree of Adult Supervision		LOW
Adult Supervision with Full Accountability	**Adult Supervision with *Some* Accountability**	**Distal Supervision**	**No Supervision**
Relative care; nanny care	Short-term recreation programs	Self-care with parental monitoring	Self-care with no parental monitoring
Licensed family child care	Enrichment activities (e.g., music/art lessons)	Sibling care	Telephone help lines
Formal before- and after-school care programs	Youth groups (4-H, Scouts, sports)	Check-in programs (neighbors or community based)	

Source: Adapted from, Todd, C., Albrecht, K. & Coleman, M. (1990). School-Age Child Care: A Continuum of Options. *Journal of Home Economics,* Spring, 46–52. Used with permission from the American Association of Family & Consumer Sciences.

other youth groups, are providing **adult supervision with some accountability**. The most preferable situation, of course, is **adult supervision with full accountability**, and that would include in-home care and out-of-home care in a school-site or center-based program or licensed family child care home.

VARIETIES OF CARE OPTIONS FOR SCHOOL-AGE CHILDREN

Expanding on the four degrees of supervision identified by Todd and her colleagues, the varying arrangements parents make for children can be thought of as falling into three major types: self-care, in-home care, and out-of-home care. Each has its advantages and its disadvantages, and all types of care can function in the community to support the needs of school-age children and their families. The following sections describe these care options in more detail, and Figure 2.1 shows their percentage of use.

Self-Care

Over a third of all school-age children in the United States go home to empty houses each afternoon (Vandivere, Tout, Zaslow, Calkins, & Capizzano, 2003). One common element for these youngsters, traditionally called **latchkey children** because of the key they carry to open their door latch, is the loneliness they experience, the boredom, and the pressure to be self-sufficient. Although the popular *Home Alone* films romanticized the notion of self-care, in reality many children find it a rather unpleasant experience. Children who enter empty houses, heat snacks in the microwave, and spend their afternoons in solitary confinement do not always praise this option, and many child-development professionals discourage it (Alexander, 1986; Kaplan, 2006). Unstructured hours spent with little or no adult supervision can result in physical injury to children, as well as emotional and psychological harm.

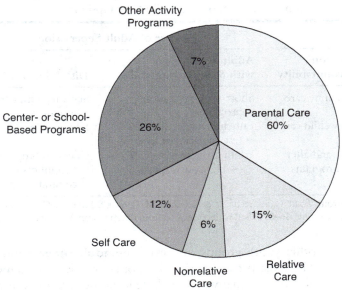

Note: Because some children are in more than one arrangement, percentages do not add up to 100.

FIGURE 2.1   Children in Various School-Age Care Arrangements.
Source: Lawrence National Center on Children in Poverty Report. Cited in Neugebauer (2007), *Exchange.* Used with permission of Exchange Press, Inc.

❀   *Consider This:*   ❀

What activities would you provide for a child who needed to be alone at home for several hours each evening? If you were the parent of a 10-year-old child and no after-school program were available, what kinds of steps would you take to ensure his or her safety?

To be fair, most parents do not usually *choose* self-care but rather settle for it when working arrangements keep them from their children before or after school, and no feasible or economic alternative is available. The parents of 15.3 million children say their children would participate if an after-school program were available (Afterschool Alliance, 2006).

There are conflicting opinions on the effects of latchkey arrangements, but four types of adjustment risks are associated with extended hours of self-care. Children who are home alone may *feel badly, act badly, develop badly,* or *be treated badly.*

In other words, children who spend extended time alone may begin to feel rejected and alienated from peers and family or possibly experience high levels of fear. Left to their own devices, and frequently bored, such children may begin to engage in antisocial or delinquent behavior. In addition, children with no feedback or regular interaction with peers or adults may develop emotional or health problems or begin to fall behind in their schoolwork. Finally, children without supervision may become victims of crime or abuse and are at a higher risk for accidents than are children in care (Capizzano, Tout, & Adams, 2000; Fight Crime: Invest in Kids, 2007; Kaplan, 2006; Vandivere et al., 2003).

One way some communities have approached the large number of children in self-care arrangements is with education programs designed to make parents aware of the risks and help children become more able to care for themselves. Often these programs use as a text one of the many commercial books designed to help children in self-care handle routine events or emergencies that might occur while they are alone. Other communities fund check-in programs where children sign out with the program supervisor before going to any activity and sign back in when they return (Arlington Public Schools, 2008; Upper Dublin Parks & Recreation, n.d.). Figure 2.2 shows a flyer advertising one such program to local parents. School-sponsored check-in programs, usually designed for children 10–14 years old, also require children to sign in and out when leaving for an activity. Check-in students have a place to study, relax, or participate in organized activities and may be able to participate in their school's regularly scheduled intramural sports and clubs.

In-Home Care

While support systems for latchkey children such as check-in programs, educational workshops, and self-help books can help to increase children's safety and welfare, it is important to understand and continue to educate children, parents, and the entire community that the best place for children before and after school is not alone but in the care of a responsible adult. This care may take place in the child's own home or elsewhere in the community.

Relative Care   Even today, some children have one or more parent at home to welcome them after school and to supervise their activities. Increasingly, both fathers and mothers seize opportunities to run small businesses from their homes or take work home so they can be with their children after school, or they work different shifts from one another to maximize the time an adult is available. Many parents, however, depend on a patchwork of out-of-school activities to fill in the gaps.

A single father in a rural Minnesota community, an electrician, can adjust his workdays as long as he achieves the total hours needed to earn an acceptable income and satisfy his supervising contractor. For several years, Niels arose at 4:00 a.m. each day and carried his two sleeping children to his mother's nearby home so that he could be with them after school and drive them to athletic activities and music lessons. He bragged that he had never missed a first day of school or a parent's night, and the only outside care his children received were summer recreation programs to give his mother a break from her high-spirited grandchildren. A regular family presence is an important component of Niels' relationship with his children, who are very close to him and appreciate the interesting life and varied activities he and his mother have been able to afford them.

Traditionally, grandparents, older youths, and adult siblings helped young parents care for their children. Increasingly, grandparents are also working away from home, juggling their lives around train schedules or long commutes, and they are retiring later than historically has been the case. Even parents' younger siblings—the aunts and uncles of school-age children—are likely to live far away from their families and work or commute longer hours than in earlier generations.

Community Parks & Recreation for a Lifetime

After-School Hangout at the EPI-Center (Oreland)

Monday, January 26 to Friday, April 3 - Winter

Monday, April 13 to Thursday, June 18 - Spring

(site is closed on 2/13, 2/16, 3/11, 5/25)

Weekdays 3p-6p

After-School Hangout is for children who are currently enrolled in Grade 6. Grade 7 and 8 will be placed on a waitlist.

AFTER-SCHOOL HANGOUT INCLUDES…
organized games and activities, homework time and arts/crafts time. UDP&R will also provide a snack or participants can provide his/her own (please list any allergies on registration form).

1/2/09

AFTER-SCHOOL HANGOUT REGISTRATION begins:
FRIDAY, JANUARY 2 at 9a

Online Registration available at www.upperdublin.net

"Pay as You Play" Fee Schedule
You have the flexibility to register and pay for the days of the week your child will be attending throughout the session.

1. Submit all registrations at the UDP&R office or online at www.upperdublin.net.

2. If registering at the UDP&R office, please find a REGISTRATION FORM available Friday, January 2 at 9a, outside of the UDP&R office. Complete, SIGN and submit with FULL payment (cash, Visa, MasterCard, Discover or check made payable to Upper Dublin Township). Parent/Guardian MUST sign form for registration to be processed. Forms will be available 24 hours a day in the bins outside of the UDP&R office.

3. Registration is limited to 10 minimum/20 participants maximum.

4. RESIDENT/NON-RESIDENT FEES: Our doors are open to children who live outside of Upper Dublin with the payment of a non-resident fee. Non-resident fees apply to any child who does not reside in Upper Dublin Township year-round. **Proof of residency will be required** before your registration is accepted or fully processed. Please bring a driver's license with you to walk-in registration. If there is any question regarding a mail-in, online or drop-off registration, you will be contacted by a CSR.

5. Parents have the option to choose what days of the week they want to sign their child up. Note that if you sign up for all 5 days during the session you will receive a 10% discount.

SUPERVISION
The After-School Hangout is managed by a qualified staff specifically one full-time UDP&R staff member and at least two After-School Aides (high school aged & older). Our Staff to a child ratio is no greater than 1:7.

There's *always* something going on at UDP&R! Keep an eye out for special events, activities and off-site trips that will be announced

 Your child wants a fun place to go after-school, to be with friends, to play games and sports, to create arts and crafts and to learn new things! You want to provide all of these opportunities *plus* be safe and secure. UDP&R can offer both…

WHY CHOOSE UDP&R? IT'S SIMPLE…

For decades, UDP&R has offered quality programs for the children in the community. Some of these programs include a variety of summer camps, 'Tween Carnival, Movies in the Park and many more! We have children and grandchildren of past participants involved in our programs . . . now *that* says something! Each day is different with a variety of carefully planned activities - including arts and crafts, organized games and homework time. A snack and drink will also be provided (please indicate any allergies on registration form). The After-School Hangout is managed by a qualified staff, specifically one UDP&R **full-time staff** member and two or more **After-School Aides** (high school age & older). Our staff to child ratio is no greater than 1:7

CHECK-IN / CHECK-OUT SAFETY

So that we know they are on site, children check-in daily at the Upper Level of the EPI-Center. The After-School Hangout will start at 3p. Children will have the option of riding the bus, walking or riding a bicycle to the EPI-Center (approximately 0.5 mile from SRMS). Please indicate on the registration form what type of transportation the participant will be using. *If traveling by bus please contact the Upper Dublin School District Transportation Office to arrange a spot on the bus.* Children who ride bikes are required to wear helmets. In case the child misses the school bus, please inform the staff.

Children will check-out and be dismissed no later than 6p. Notes signed by the parent/guardian and given to the staff are required should your child be traveling home at other than the usual time or by other means. *Always seek out a staff member to sign your child out if your child is to leave at odd times.*

FIGURE 2.2 Some Afterschool Programs Have Check-in, Check-out Policies.

Source: After-School Hangout at the EPI-Center, by Upper Dublin Parks & Recreation. (n.d.). Port Washington, PA: Township of Upper Dublin. Used with permission.

However, when patterns of employment do allow families to help, and when families live close enough to one another to make it possible, they often participate in shared parenting. Grandparents or aunts and uncles take children to the dentist after school, drive them to practice or music lessons, and help them with their homework. Often some care takes place in the child's own home; at other times, children walk or take public transportation to the relative's home after school. In either case, relative care provides an important support system for working parents and can help to keep families functioning during the years when children need more supervision than their parents can provide.

Non-Relative Care   When relative care is not a possibility, one solution is to hire a nanny. The live-in nanny, once the private domain of British upper-class children, is increasing in popularity in the United States. Nanny training programs in private institutions and public colleges prepare professional child care workers to interact with parents and children of all ages within a home setting. The Urban Institute reports that 4% of children aged 6 to 12 were cared for by nannies in 1997 (Capizzano et al., 2000). Most nannies are hired by families at the birth of a child, but some become such a part of the family's life that they are asked to stay on even when the children start school. Some nannies have the luxury of a private room and a bath; others live elsewhere, arriving each morning before breakfast to help ready children for the day and leaving in the evening when parents return. Perspective 2.1 describes the personal experience of a nanny in California.

While hired most often by parents of very young children, well-chosen nannies can become devoted companions to older children and provide the peace of mind necessary for parents to meet their professional responsibilities away from home. When trained in child development, health, and safety, the nanny can become a respected member of a parenting team and assist in family decisions surrounding homework, chores, bedtimes, and allowances. Parents who can afford it realize that the continuity of having this trusted adult waiting at the schoolyard gate can make all the difference in their child's feelings of safety and security—and the parents' stress levels.

Christopher Robin Milne, of *Winnie the Pooh* fame, had this to say about the importance of his nanny:

> She had me when I was very young. I was all hers and remained all hers until the age of nine. Other people hovered around the edges, but they meant little. . . . Was she a brilliant teacher? Not specially. She was just a very good and very loving person; and when that has been said, no more need be added. (Milne, 1974)

There is a great variation in nanny training. Some nannies have academic backgrounds and significant experience; many do not. However, as the demand for in-home caregivers has grown in recent years, parents are increasingly demanding evidence of child-development education and professional affiliation. The International Nanny Association (2008) reported in their 2006 Salary and Benefits survey that 45% of nannies had 1 to 3 years of college education, and 18% had more than 10 years' experience working with children. The rewards are significant—a third of the nannies who responded to this survey of 1,119 individuals reported earnings of from $600 to $1,000 per week.

Being a Nanny

Bonnie Crowe, Gilroy, California

Being a nanny has been a rewarding and educational experience for me. I had already taken a few child-development classes toward an associate's degree, so being able to work within a family helped to reinforce what I had learned. After I had done occasional child care for the family for a year, the children's mom needed to go back to work. She and her husband invited me to be a live-in nanny so that the children didn't have to be in a child care center 8 or more hours a day. My day usually starts after breakfast with crafts or doing outside activities (usually structured) if the weather permits. Then we have lunch, and I put the smaller children to bed. When the older child comes home from kindergarten, I can be with him one-on-one, to do activities that we cannot do with little ones around. When the younger children get up, it is playtime, usually doing whatever the kids want. Toward the end of the day, we listen to music or read books so we can calm down and get ready for dinner, by which time the parents are home. I have my own room and bath, and sometimes eat with the family, but they don't expect me to do that every day. I attend evening classes at the community college and have some free time on Saturdays and Sundays. The thing I like the most about being a nanny is being able to share so many precious moments with the children while they are growing up that a person can't normally see when working in a child care center or just seeing the children for an evening at a time. The hard thing about being a nanny, though, is you have to eventually say good-bye to the children, and they really come to love you and you them.

Source: Used with permission of Bonnie Crowe.

Out-of-Home Care

All the variations of care discussed so far offer children a regular adult presence and more or less healthy opportunities for normal social development within a home environment. However, an in-home caregiver can be very expensive, out of reach of most families, and some families are without friends or family who are available to help care for their children. Even families who have a network of care in place may prefer a more consistent solution.

There are many different types of out-of-home care. Some are small programs that focus on a specific set of activities, such as sports, drama, or tutoring. Others are larger with a wider range of activities or may emphasize academic enrichment. Some programs are located on school sites; others in churches, storefronts, or purpose-built facilities. In the sections to follow, several types of school-age programs will be described, ranging from licensed child care in a private home to a variety of options for supervision, recreation, and enrichment provided by public and private organizations. Table 2.2 summarizes various aspects of formal center- or school-based programs.

Licensed Family Child Care Homes   Licensed family child care consistently accounts for the supervision of more than a quarter of American school-aged children in out-of-home care (National Institute on Out-of-School Time, 2007). In most parts of the country, home-based family child care providers are licensed and certified separately from preschool and afterschool professionals. They may also be required to complete fewer numbers of postsecondary education courses (sometimes none) than those who work in center-based programs. Some parents think

TABLE 2.2 Variations in Center- or School-Based Program Types.

Program Type	Characteristics	Employment Requirements/Compensation
Licensed family child care	Mixed-age groupings Family-like setting Small group size	Varies by state; usually fewer college units than center-based care; first aid/CPR certification; owner operated; few employees
Publicly funded	School sites Community/recreation centers Storefronts Often several hundred children housed in a multipurpose room or classrooms Funded by tax revenues; subject to state or federal guidelines	Varies by funding; typically 1–2 years of college child development or education courses; some programs require an elementary teaching credential; others require no specific course work, only college units Government-funded programs offer higher salaries than privately funded programs; first aid/CPR certification
Privately funded	Housed in portable classrooms, houses, purpose-built facilities, churches, shopping malls, some on-school sites; historically less likely than publicly funded programs to be academically oriented; more recreational, crafts, socio-emotional emphasis Operate at a profit, so subject to parent pressures	Varies by state; usually 1–2 years of college child development or education courses; usually lower salaries than publicly funded; first aid/CPR certification
Nonprofit	May be privately or publicly funded; sometimes have a specific focus, such as reduction of obesity, environmental awareness, or target a specific clientele, such as children with disabilities or with incarcerated parents; usually administered by church groups, community-based organizations, or private schools	Varies by agency; usually 1–2 years of college child-development or education courses; privately funded programs have lower salaries; often seek volunteers; first aid/CPR certification
Grassroots solutions	Staffed by creative, politically savvy people, often motivated by a cause; usually quite dedicated to their work on behalf of children and families; can be excellent working environments, although salaries are usually low	May operate on bare-bones budgets, depend on volunteers and staff who can survive on low salaries or who share a passion for a cause; working hours may be long due to inadequate staffing

of home-based child care as more suitable to the needs of infants and toddlers than of school-aged children. However, if the practitioners provide a lively and developmentally appropriate environment and curriculum, licensed family homes can be excellent arrangements for all ages. Ideally, the caregiver would live in the same neighborhood as the elementary school the children attend, so that they can participate in school-sponsored activities and play with children who live nearby.

There are some excellent pedagogical arguments for the mixed age grouping of children typically found in a family child care setting. The day-to-day interactions in a nurturing homelike environment can help youngsters develop in positive ways and to learn how to avoid, or at least how to cope with, behavior problems and conflict. Knowledgeable family child care providers can address the needs of *all* the children in their care.

For example, sensitive caregivers do the following:

- ⚘ Listen to older children's requests for private spaces away from toddlers
- ⚘ Respond to their need to talk about the events of the day
- ⚘ Provide them with challenging games and a chance to socialize as well as study and work on homework

Younger children may require closer supervision and more one-on-one attention from the caregiver, but when those children are asleep or quietly occupied, caregivers can turn their attention to the older children, using that time to help them plan future activities, assist with problem solving, or simply listen. When developmental issues are taken into consideration, most school-age children thrive in family-like settings that emerge in family child care homes.

⚘　　*Consider This:*　　⚘

What are the advantages of working at home as a family child care provider? Have you ever considered doing this yourself? How do you suppose family members adjust to having other people's children in their house all day?

Some school districts prohibit transportation of children to sites other than their own homes, and licensing regulations frequently stipulate "line of sight" supervision, which means that the children must be in view at all times. This provision precludes school-age children from going home first, and then checking in with a caregiver, and perhaps returning home or to a friend's house later. Active efforts from child care associations and parents have successfully changed some of these restrictions, and innovative programming can result in programs that meet children's needs and satisfy lawmakers' concerns, but all out-of-home programs must work within federal, state, and local guidelines.

Publicly Funded School-Age Programs　State and federal governments fund many school-age programs. The most common examples of **publicly funded** programs are stand-alone academic instruction/tutoring programs. Such programs focus almost exclusively on improving student performance in core academic subject areas such as math, reading, and science. Examples include Supplemental Education Services (SES) in schools that did not make sufficient progress under the provisions of the No Child Left Behind Act (NCLB), stand-alone programs that focus on improving academic skills in children who are at risk of school failure, and programs that provide additional academic exposure for students who are doing well in school (Parsad & Lewis, 2009).

One example of how government support for afterschool programming can fluctuate is in California. Historically, that state funded school-age care under the auspices of the School-age Community Child Care Act of 1985, which distributed $15 million in grant funds to 190 programs in its first year of operation. Recently, however, state funds have diminished, and the major publicly funded programs in California are administered by the California State Department of Education, Child Development Division. The two largest programs are the state-funded After School Education and Safety (ASES) program and the federal 21st Century

Community Learning Centers. ASES was created in 2002 after voters approved Proposition 49, which provided funds to school districts or local government entities to offer programs focusing on literacy, academic enrichment, computer training, homework assistance, fine arts, youth development, and physical fitness. In 2008–2009, the ASES budget included $490 million to serve more than 300,000 students (Afterschool Alliance, 2009).

The U.S. Department of Education's 21st Century Community Learning Centers are similar to California ASES programs, although the target audience is different. This federal program serves students from kindergarten through high school, with 50% of the money going to high school programs. As with the ASES program, each 21st Century program site must provide both an educational component and an educational enrichment element. These centers particularly target students who attend high-poverty and low-performing schools. The curriculum and staff help students meet state and local standards in core academic subjects, such as reading and math; offer a broad array of enrichment activities that can complement their regular academic programs; and provide literacy and other educational services to the families of participating children. The ratio of 1 adult to 20 children is not ideal, but it keeps the programs more cost effective.

Most publicly funded before- and afterschool education services are housed on public school sites. Others can be found in community centers, church buildings, and storefronts. The number of public programs has grown tremendously in recent years, driven by research that links participation in such programs to significantly lower involvements in risky behaviors (Miller, 2003). There is also a growing conviction that afterschool programs can improve student achievement (California School-Age Consortium, 2008; National Childcare Accreditation Council, 2008; National Institute on Out-of-School Time, 2007; Viadero, 2007).

An example of a successful 21st Century Learning Center is located at the Boys and Girls Club of Greater Gardiner, Maine. The club started in 1993 with a small program for six children at the River View Community School. Today, with the help of 21st Century funding, the club offers 250 middle and high school youngsters a safe environment from 6:30 a.m. until 5:30 p.m. daily. Besides the teen program, the club offers care for elementary children and sporting activities. Gardiner's mission is "to enable all young people especially those who need us most, to reach their full potential as productive, caring responsible citizens" (see http://www.club4me.org for more). The club operates on a $1 million budget and also receives money from the city to pay a portion of its operational costs. Amy Princiotta, a student at Gardiner, describes her experiences in Perspective 2.2.

In an ideal situation, publicly funded before- and afterschool centers are located at each school in a district. One advantage of this is transportation. However, even if only certain schools are designated as afterschool sites, shuttle service between schools can usually be arranged by the district transportation office. A second advantage of locating programs on school campuses is increasing the utilization and safety of publicly owned facilities. Many school districts are being challenged for their **underutilization** of school buildings, which are at risk for **vandalism** during the unused hours of the day. One of the strongest arguments for school-site care is that the community-education model of facility usage creates a natural buy-in, or "protection" role, for community members who use the facility outside school hours (Grace, 2001; Zigler & Ennis, 1988). Since most identified

PERSPECTIVE 2.2

21st Century Learning Centers

My name is Amy Princiotta and I am a ninth-grade student at Gardiner Area High School. I was recently named the 21st Century Community Learning Center Youth of the Year for the State of Maine. I received this honor because I won an essay contest about afterschool programming.

As the Youth of the Year, I spoke at the Lights On Afterschool event last October at the Capitol in Augusta and [at] a Nellie Mae luncheon this summer in Portland. Although speaking at these events was a little nerve-wrecking [sic], it was (and always is) my great pleasure to share my afterschool experience with others, especially those who don't realize how valuable afterschool programming truly is.

I feel that it is very important for every student to have a safe place to go after school. My place is the Boys and Girls Club of Greater Gardiner. I go there every day after school for many different reasons. I like the activities they offer, I like that I have a place to hang out with my friends, and I especially like the Community Learning Center (CLC) program. Before I came to the CLC, I had a really bad math phobia, which made me stressed out about school. At school, I felt rushed and pressured to finish my math work, but my CLC tutor, Mrs. Graves-Leclair, always made time to help me. She let me know that she cared about me and not just my grades. The CLC has also helped me improve my grades and make sure that my homework was done correctly and on time.

The Boys and Girls Club of Greater Gardiner provides fun club activities and opportunities to go on trips. I am currently the vice president of our club's Torch Club community service team. This year, my team and I walked for MS [Multiple Sclerosis], made more than 50 quilts for a local nursing home, collected more than 100 brand new toys for the Salvation Army at Christmastime, and raised over $600 for a new porcupine exhibit at the Maine Wildlife Park. As a reward we were allowed to name the porcupines and spend the night at The Wildlife Park. I also participate in the Club's horseback riding lessons, the swim classes at the YMCA, and now I am taking part in the Club's CIT [Counselor in Training] program, which will prepare me to someday be a staff member at the Boys and Girls Club.

When I grow up I'd like to do a bunch of things like teaching, having my own day care, or any kind of job involving children. I'd also like to help others through community service. Someday I hope go to college and become a good role model to others, just like Mrs. Graves-Leclair and the other staff at the Boys and Girls Club are to me.

The staff at the 21st Century Community Learning Center and the Boys and Girls Club have taught me to never give up, to always work hard, and to always be the best I can be. They've made me feel confident and they let me know that they appreciate me. I think that's the best thing anybody can do for a teenager. I hope that what I've learned here will help me throughout my life. I also hope that by writing about my experience and speaking to adults who can make a difference, I can help more people realize how important afterschool programs are to kids like me and encourage them to be advocates for programs that provide a safe place for kids to go after the bell rings.

Source: www.afterschoolalliance.com. Used with permission of Afterschool Alliance.

vandals are between the ages of 7 and 18 (Fight Crime: Invest in Kids, 2007), it also seems reasonable that providing programs for children in that age range will help to reduce the total amount of vandalism in the community.

As federal block grant money and state-initiated funding became available for the creation and implementation of school-age care programs, a common way funds were allocated was through a competitive bid process. Child- and youth-serving

Many established agencies have entered the field of
out-of-school care.

organizations that have competed for public funds include community park and
recreation centers, nonprofit child care centers, and established youth-serving organizations such as the YWCA/YMCA, Campfire, and Boys and Girls Clubs. Private
corporations previously offering care for younger children also competed for funds.
Like Gardiner's Boys and Girls Club, many programs count on funding from several
sources—public and private—to piece together an adequate operating budget.

Federal provision for school-age care primarily takes the form of funding for
planning, development, establishment, expansion, and improvement of programs,
and the government has increased that funding in recent years. A total of $3 mil-
lion was distributed to states and territories between 1986 and 1989 under the
Human Services Reauthorization Act, with the stipulation that the funds be used
only for school-age child care services (National Research Council, 1990). Those
numbers were dwarfed by the No Child Left Behind (NCLB) legislation, which
appropriated $981 million in fiscal years 2006 and 2007 for care and enrichment.
Even so, at an average cost of $1,000 per student, less than 1 million children
and/or youth were able to benefit from the 21st Century Community Learning
Centers funded with that money (Afterschool Alliance, 2006). The Child Care
and Development Fund (CCDF) represents an additional public investment that
amounted to $5 billion federal dollars and an estimated $2.2 billion in state funds
in fiscal year 2006 (National Institute on Out-of-School Time, 2007).

Privately Funded Programs   Many individual entrepreneurs and large corporations open school-age centers that they run as commercial businesses. Others have added school-age programming to existing sites built for preschoolers and younger children. Programs may be open before and after school and all day on holidays, release days, and vacations. **Privately funded** programs may be located in classrooms or portable buildings on school sites, in large buildings built specifically for the purpose, in converted houses, churches, or storefronts, and in shopping malls. Because they are profit driven, these commercial school-age programs may offer a greater variety of hours, activities, materials, and equipment than those funded with public money. Since local needs and parent opinions are important to being successful, programs tend to be reflective of regional priorities.

In for-profit programs, cash flow can be a problem, and staff salaries are often below those in the public sector. When money is short, it may be necessary to limit supplies and materials and keep staff–child ratios to the higher numbers allowed by health and safety regulations. While many for-profit school-age programs are excellent, there is a danger of becoming warehouses for bored children. Privately funded for-profit centers need enthusiastic, dedicated program managers to create developmentally appropriate programs that will nurture, rather than merely house, children while their parents work and a clearly delineated career ladder to attract and keep professional staff. This may be a role that you can take; it is certainly an important one.

Nonprofit Programs   Some programs are operated by nonprofit corporations, which mean they are legal entities formed for the purpose of providing care under a legal provision where no individual (e.g., stockholder, trustee) will share in profits or losses of the organization. Nonprofits are usually granted tax-free status, and donations to the organization may be tax deductible as well. Most nonprofit school-age programs are supervised by a board of directors, which hires the program director and the staff. A constant challenge in nonprofit programs funded by government agencies is costs that increase annually while reimbursement rates stay level, sometimes for 5 to 10 years.

Nonprofit programs may look just like for-profit programs, but sometimes they have a specific target clientele, such as children with disabilities, or a specific programmatic focus, such as raising environmental awareness or developing healthy eating habits. Examples of nonprofit programs with a targeted mission include five Salvation Army programs in the greater Columbus, Ohio, area, the Monkey Tail Gang After-School Club in Philadelphia, and Heart House in Austin.

The Salvation Army programs target low-income and one-parent families and provide activities intended to help children improve school grades, attendance, and social behaviors. These programs collaborate with Boys and Girls Clubs and the United Way to keep the children's fees low. They also may rely on volunteers to keep their costs down.

The Schuylkill Center for Environmental Education provides a variety of indoor and outdoor environmental activities for the Monkey Tail Gang on school days. Supported by a team of professional program leaders, an environmental educator teaches ecological principles and engages children in inquiry and problem solving around local and global environmental issues.

Heart House, funded by the KDK-Harman Foundation, is a free program that provides a safe environment and strong academic support to low-income children in the Austin area while also encouraging them to become good citizens. Web sites for these three nonprofit programs are listed at the end of the chapter.

Grassroots Solutions   What if there are no afterschool programs in a community? Sometimes pressure from parents demanding care for their school-age children can result in rather dramatic successes. Employees of the American Home Economics Association (AHEA) solved a problem for working parents by organizing an afterschool program in rural Arkansas after they were approached for help. One parent, after requesting information from the county department of human services regarding afterschool care for her child, was dismayed to discover that, not only were there no centers offering care for school-age children in this rural town, but there was no resource and referral system to locate family child care providers or even babysitters.

Following discussions with other parents, the AHEA was contacted. Under the umbrella of Project Home Safe, sponsored by the Whirlpool Foundation and designed to provide training, technical assistance, materials, and other resources to promote solutions to the school-age child care problem, the AHEA conducted a 3-day workshop and followed up with guidance to launch an afterschool program. The formulation of a community coalition, fundraising plan, facilities location committee, and publicity package was the responsibility of the interested parents, who gave far more than the required 40 hours of community service each necessary to qualify for Project Home Safe assistance. The result was the opening of a summer program for 42 children, followed by an afterschool program the following fall (Warnock, 1992). This kind of community organizing is known as **grassroots** organizing.

A similar program emerged in Orange County, Florida, in 1996. To meet the needs of the community, the Union Park Action for Safe Families collaborative growth initiative was created, and funding was secured from the Orange County Citizens' Commission for Children. The collaborative partners consisted of four member agencies spearheaded by the University of Florida's Orange County Cooperative Extension Service and an advisory group consisting of parents, school and community leaders, and member agencies (Ferrer & Chambers, 1999).

Parents in Native American communities have also worked with funding agencies to integrate solutions to child care challenges. In Leelanau County, Michigan, the Benodjehn Child Care Center provides Head Start (preschool) and school-age care for approximately 100 Ottawa and Chippewa families. The Grand Traverse Band established the combination facility in 1989 and kept it open 21 hours a day so that parents could work at the community's major revenue source, the casino/hotel (Krohn, Charter, Beniak, Anderson, & Sordelet, 1993). Over time, the Benodjehn Center expanded to offer education, medical and dental services for the whole family, meals, nutritional information, and transportation (Napoli, 2002).

In Oklahoma, the Osage Nation combined several different funding streams to build and support the Youth Enhancement Facility (YEF), which offers programs for elementary, middle, and high school youth. Sources of support included an Oklahoma juvenile justice grant, a state health and fitness program, state childhood obesity-prevention funds, and a grant provided by the Native American Housing Assistance and Self-Determination Act. The YEF afterschool program has shown several positive results, including a reduction of parent stress, an increase in children's physical activity and healthy eating, and an increase in homework completion (U.S. Department of Health and Human Services, 2004).

Grassroots development of school-age care provision takes place in urban areas, as well. Kristin Rowe-Finkbeiner and Joan Blades, co-founders of the online organization MomsRising.org, share a common concern about the need to build a more family-friendly America. This grassroots effort, supported by a media base in Washington, DC, aims to mobilize mothers across America as a cohesive force for change. They are developing a corps of activists who lobby legislators and community organizers for before- and afterschool facilities as well as family child care, preschool, and other measures that can make family life and the workplace more compatible (Corday & Casey, 2006).

All of these examples underscore the challenges in providing high-quality afterschool programming for children. Locating and maintaining a funding stream, hiring and training a qualified staff, and meeting the diverse needs of families are major challenges. The National Institute for Out-of-School Care at Wellesley College is a good source of additional models and expertise for parents and organizations wishing to develop their own community-based programs. The Afterschool Alliance can also provide statistics, examples, and contact information for people working in their communities to develop programs for school-age children (Afterschool Alliance, 2007; Seligson, 2001; Seligson & Stahl, 2003).

Informal Care

In close-knit neighborhoods, parents who are available to their children for some or all of the afternoon hours may share the responsibility with other parents nearby, facilitating the increased freedom of movement desired by older school-age children. This arrangement replicates the pattern of rural and suburban child-drearing depicted in television reruns, where groups of children flow from one backyard, tree house, or empty lot to another, passing by one another's kitchens for snacks on the way. Some at-home parents, voluntarily or not, absorb the occasional care of several children in the neighborhood, as the balance changes from one or two children whose parents cannot be home in the afternoon to one or two children whose parents *can*. An example of that is one of my own neighbors.

Miss Joan, who teaches piano in her home, remembers a time when all parents drove their children to lessons and picked them up promptly when the lesson was over. For many years now, because their parents are not at home, most children walk directly to her house after school, even if their appointment is not until much later. Responding to the ever-present groups of children sitting on her front lawn or in her kitchen, Joan began setting out bowls of nuts and raisins on her dining room table and allowing children to come in (quietly) and study or read together while they awaited their turn at the piano. Sometimes they would return to the table following their lesson to await a parent's arrival after work. Joan has become, in effect, a part of the child care solution for many parents who would, she realizes, be forced to cease their children's lessons altogether if she were not responsive to their needs. She works closely with parents to schedule appointments at the most convenient times, and she follows up on children who do not arrive for appointments to be sure they are not stranded between school and home. One might argue that child care is "not her job," but Joan believes her flexibility is a boon to the community, and the parents of her students would definitely agree with her.

Nontraditional Hours and Services   Parents do not always work during traditional daytime hours. About 20% of American workers have night and swing shift responsibilities, but most child care centers operate between 7:00 a.m. and 6:00 p.m. According to a report issued by the Department of Labor, this situation affects about 7.2 million working mothers with 11.7 million children under the age of 15 (Mathematica Policy Research, 1996). Single mothers are more likely than married mothers to work at nonstandard times. (They also work longer hours.) According to National Data Source, about one-fourth of single mothers with children work nonstandard hours, and more than one-third worked weekends (Presser, 2003). Children 6 to 9 years old whose parents work nontraditional hours are less likely to be in self-care arrangements, and although fewer have a school-age program as their primary caregiver, they are likely to need supervised care for more hours a day than children whose parents work traditional hours (Capizzano et al., 2000).

Providing evening or nighttime care of school-age children presents significant challenges, but some programs attempt to address them. In Florida, for example, there is a heavy service industry, and parents are often employed in hotels, hospitals, or restaurants that are open 24 hours a day. Many family child care homes offer evening care in the Tampa Bay area, and at least one afterschool center does also. The Second Street Learning Center at Opportunity House in Reading, Pennsylvania, provides around-the-clock care to serve second- and third-shift parents and in 2006 was serving 300 children (Negley, 2007). Several 24-hour child care centers opened in Sioux Falls, South Dakota, after an increase in requests came into the city's 211 HelpLine from call center operators, hospital staff, and meatpacking plant workers needing consistent care for their children (Gruchow, 2007). Residents of the District of Columbia are eligible to receive nontraditional child care subsidy payments through the Department of Human Services, Income Maintenance Administration, Child Care Services Division. Nontraditional child care is a service offered to parents whose work schedule is outside of the standard hours of 7 a.m. to 6 p.m., Monday through Friday. Parents can receive child care services on the weekend, nights, and evenings. Eligibility is based on the customer's employment and/or training schedule (see http://dhs.dc.gov for more information). Minnesota had such a demand for programs that were open at nontraditional hours that they developed a full set of licensing standards for overnight care centers (Bales, 1998).

Other programs have emerged to meet the needs of parents outside traditional hours. For example, KidsPark, originally opened in California as a center-based hourly care service that was open days, evenings, and weekends, has developed into a franchise with seven locations in California and others in Kansas, Texas, Arizona, Florida, Tennessee, and Pennsylvania. The staff at KidsPark cares for children from 2 to 11 years of age while parents work, run errands, or go out to dinner and a movie. "The family-support structure that we used to have is no longer there,"

KidsPark has provided hourly childcare to families in the San Jose, California area since 1988.

explained Debbie Milner, KidsPark founder and chief executive officer. "We have replaced grandparents in the family infrastructure." Milner opened her first center in San Jose in 1988 when, as the mother of a young child, she needed more flexibility in her own schedule. KidsPark, offering an average teacher–child ratio of 1 to 8 (Johnson, 2006), provides meals, a play structure, toys, crafts, and activities. A recent innovation is an additional space specifically for school-age children, who are known as the Blue Crew. Here children can participate in more detailed art, age-appropriate games, and nonviolent video games. They can also do their homework and get help from the staff at no extra charge. During school breaks, theme-based Blue Crew Camps offer a changing menu of activities and games.

In Dade County, Florida, a company called KidMover offers transportation services for school-age children (http://www.kidmover.com/registerforschoolyear. asp). This van service transports children between school and dental appointments, soccer practice, or other scheduled activities and returns them to a child care program or home when they are finished. Parents who contract with the service by the month or year can contact the dispatcher as little as 2 hours before the scheduled activity, providing a welcome flexibility for families.

The emergence of such niche companies as these reflect a need on the part of families to get help caring for their children around the clock and during the night, and under some rather challenging circumstances. It also raises some important questions. As the service sector becomes the core of U.S. industry, parents are increasingly away from home at times when their school-age children need supervision. How can they be sure that their arrangements are safe? Most licensing agencies do not regulate short-term care or transportation services in the same way they do other school-age settings. It would be wise for advocacy organizations such as the National AfterSchool Association and the Afterschool Alliance to take a

FIGURE 2.3   Communities Can Protect Their Youth with Drop-in Programs.

In 1993, the Morgan Hill, California, gang-prevention task force began opening a middle school gymnasium on Friday nights for pick-up basketball games. Known originally as Friday Night Jams, the program later added activities for younger children. Its immediate popularity encouraged neighboring Gilroy to start a similar program. The Gilroy site included a video room, a game room with a pool table, tutors and counselors, and an open kitchen with sodas and snacks available at modest prices. The Gilroy Community Youth Center now resides in a converted public utility building and serves children from 6 to 17 years of age. It is administered by the Mexican American Community Services Agency, and in 2005 it received a $100,000 grant to build a new facility (Gruner, 1994; Munson, 2005). A few concerned parents, working with business leaders and local agencies, have made a huge difference to children in their communities.

lead in developing needs assessments, guidelines for programming, and training of staff for these settings involving an extremely extended day. You can attend meetings of these organizations in your area and local child care planning groups and learn how you can help.

Drop-in Programs   Although they have now entered the field of school-age care with formal working-hours programs, the YMCA/YWCA and Girls and Boys Clubs continue to offer valuable **drop-in programs** for the youth of urban areas as they have done for generations, and they have added many programs in suburban areas, as well. In addition, community-based anti-drug and gang-prevention programs fund recreational and social activities based on the successful drop-in model. A homework club started by a single mother in Charleton, South Carolina, was recognized by the Save the Children Out-of-School Time Rural Initiative project and received external funding to expand and continue her work (Chung, 2005). Programs like these and the ones described in Figure 2.3 offer youngsters an alternative to gangs, violence, and other negative behaviors that too often result from endless weeks and months of loneliness and boredom.

Athletic and Recreation Programs   Other programs that offer adult supervision but are not commonly thought of as "care" include community-sponsored or afterschool sports teams, such as swimming, gymnastics, basketball, baseball, soccer, football, or recreation programs that meet once or twice a week to play games or make arts and crafts. In addition, in some communities, public gyms offer the use of a trampoline, basketball courts, or swimming pool on a drop-in basis. The most formal of these arrangements is the competition athletic team, since coaches are likely to require two or more practices a week and may contact parents if their children do not show up regularly or if a child seems troubled or behaves in an unusual way. The less structured programs do not usually involve regular communication with parents, who may not know if their child fails to arrive or leaves early. However, the activities in and of themselves are beneficial to school-age children, and the interaction with adult staff is a valuable part of the community care network.

Enrichment Programs (Music/Art/Community Service) and Youth Groups
These programs include art or music lessons, choir practice, Trailblazers,

In many communities, organized sports programs provide children with challenging activities during out-of-school time.

Scouts/Guides, Campfire, 4-H, and Junior Achievement. Traditionally, Scout meetings and choir practices met at night. As a result of increasing pressures on families in which both parents work, and in which the little time they have to spend with their children is too precious to share with others, these activities now often take place immediately after school.

Some afterschool programs contact sponsoring organizations to initiate a group to meet at their site; others make transportation arrangements so that their children can participate. Some children walk to meetings, especially if they meet in a room at their school or at an easily accessible location such as the public library. Scouting, YMCA, Campfire, and other groups can be chartered to meet at homeless shelters, youth centers, and in group care facilities.

In most cases, the leaders of community-enrichment programs begin with little or no training, although sometimes they are retired members of the teaching or social work fields. This can be a fulfilling kind of work, as it helps children to feel connected to their communities and the adults who live in them. If you are preparing to work with youngsters in any capacity, consider volunteering; such work can provide valuable experience in group dynamics, developmental characteristics, and curriculum planning.

Programs at Public Libraries　In some communities, public libraries address the interests and needs of children after school. For example, historical associations, Explorer Scouts, or business leaders may develop programs on local history, fingerprinting, or getting a summer job. Children's librarians are increasingly designing programs that address the homework, research, and supervision needs of elementary and middle school children in their service areas. A national study revealed that most of the 110 large public libraries surveyed in 1990 experienced unattended children whose families used the library as child care after school (Dowd, 1991). Only a minority of libraries reported "significant" problems or concerns regarding medical emergencies or accidents, the need for increased security measures, reallocation of staff to cover afterschool hours, or legal liability. In fact, many of the libraries polled by the study had already increased the number of drop-in activity programs, story hours, and clubs. Google "library afterschool programs" today and you will find dozens of links to libraries around the country that have developed programs for school-age children. Many libraries now hire separate staff members to run afterschool activity programs, leaving librarians free to help youngsters with homework projects and locating reference materials.

The public library association in New London, Connecticut, is one of many that have developed programs for children after school. The children's librarian supplements the program, which is staffed by the local YWCA, with films and reading materials. In Georgia, the DeKalb County Public Library began Homework Libraries, which included typewriters, computers, read-along books, and learning games, after many requests from parents to provide afterschool programs (DeKalb Public Library, 1990; Dowd, 1991). The program grew so much that a youth program coordinator, Steve Roman, was hired. In 2008, Roman initiated a Teen Advisory Group to "help advise and discuss which items, resources, and programs the DeKalb Public Library needs for its teen patrons" (personal communication, 2008). Their plans now include book discussions, strategy sessions, and food. Similar programs can be found in libraries all over the country.

A particularly notable early program was the Seattle Public Library's After School Happenings (SPLASH), held at several branches of the library in the mid-1990s. The activities, which included making dollhouse furniture, gardening, stories, sing-alongs, and homework, were tailored to meet the needs of each individual neighborhood served by branch libraries. Three of the 10 goals of SPLASH were "to promote reading as a life-long pursuit, establish services for new Asian immigrants, and to provide activities which will help develop self-esteem, self-worth, and creativity" (Seattle Public Library, 1998). Sadly, funding for SPLASH ended, but the Seattle libraries continue to work with community organizations to provide regular activities for children and teens and have homework helpers available most evenings. I visited the downtown library in 2008 and discovered welcoming niches designed specifically for school-age children and teens. A Seattle Public Library poster from 1998 advertising summer activities is shown in Figure 2.4. It would be wonderful if this and other programs could offer the broader activity programs of the original SPLASH.

School-Age Care in Other Countries

Most Western nations are still developing clear public policies around the needs of school-age children. In developing countries, older children may be expected to help with the care of younger siblings, food preparation, agricultural tasks, or

FIGURE 2.4 Summer Activities for Children and Youth at the Seattle Public Library.
Source: Used with permission of Letterpress Studio, Seattle, WA.

participation in some cottage industry with other members of the family. Afterschool arrangements vary, as does the provision of educational opportunities for children.

Europe, Canada, and Australia   Child care as a social policy is a high priority in the European Union. However, as demand increases for more and higher quality programs, it has become clear that there are gaps in availability of services and serious problems attracting professionals to work in the field. One recent study carried out across the 25 EU member states found wide disparities in availability, approach, and quality of programs. The report also reviewed the current EU policy context for addressing child care for school-age children and identified good-practice employment initiatives. The conclusion of the researchers was that "improving the quality of the training and qualifications of workers is a key starting point to enhancing employment possibilities and ensuring overall quality in the sector" (Larsen-Elniff, Dreyling, & Williams, 2006).

Denmark and Sweden have both developed comprehensive systems of school-age care, serving children and youth from age 7, when they enter school, to age 21. Child care is considered a public responsibility and is financed by the state, local municipalities, and parent fees. In fact, municipalities in Sweden are obliged to provide programs for children up to and including the age of 12 whose parents are working or studying. Their charge is to "help provide an environment that stimulates children's development and learning, and enable parents to combine parenthood with work or studies" (Swedish National Agency for Education, 2008).

Parents sending their children to child care centers, family child care homes, or leisure centers receive partial state subsidies, and most programs are run by graduates of special training colleges. The municipality is supposed to take parents' wishes about what type of care they want into account as far as is reasonable. Care of children aged 10–12 can also be run as open leisure-time activities, which means that the children are not registered and their families decide when and how often the children will participate.

Many nations face school-age care challenges. Most Western European schools have traditionally scheduled long lunch breaks, when historically children would return home for the main meal of the day. In France there is still no school on Wednesdays. Some countries with an agricultural history continue to close school for 3 to 3½ months in the summer; in France and Greece the break is 4 months. Clearly, none of these schedules was designed with two working parents in mind, and they are increasingly undergoing change (ESL Teachers Board, 2008; Hein & Cassirer, 2009; Moss, 1991).

❀   *Consider This:*   ❀

How do you think school-age programs would look if they were all paid for with government money? Would they offer more or less variety in programming? Higher or lower quality? Do you think the curriculum would emphasize social development, physical fitness, or academic enrichment? How about teacher qualifications and pay?

Sometimes it takes parent action to ensure that programs understand families' needs. For example, a group of parents in the Netherlands, faced with school hours and timetables that differed for each level of schooling, petitioned the city to have the same hours for children at all ages, the same holidays for all schools, and no unscheduled school closures (previously a common event). The result was more consistent scheduling within age ranges and permission for the parents to organize child care on the school sites during the lunch hour and over holidays (Meijvogel, 1991). In France, after a surge of requests from parents, Leisure Centers (Centres de Loisirs Sans Hebergement) are now open all day on Wednesdays and school holidays (Eurostat, 2003).

Denmark saw a phenomenal increase in all types of government-sponsored child care between 1972 and 1986 (41,500 children served). Today, 98% of children aged 6–9 are enrolled in out-of-school programs provided primarily through government funding (Organisation for Economic Co-operation and Development, 2006). Supervision is provided for children from a few months of age to 14 years, primarily in mixed-age groupings, often using primary school facilities. School-based care is funded by the education sector, while center-based care is social-welfare funded. Twenty percent of the children aged 7–10 attend youth centers known as *fritidshjem*, or "leisure homes" (Adema, 2002; Jensen, 1991).

Some large French schools employ graduate students from related university courses to lead play sessions after school. This is not such a new idea; in the early part of the twentieth century, afterschool recreation programs were common in industrial cities in Europe, and they were often staffed by teachers and older students (R. Skirrow, personal communication, 2008; Trevelyan, 1919). What is new, however, is that professional child care workers in France are now integrated into the total economy and enjoy the same benefits as other French workers, such as social security, illness and vacation pay, and retirement benefits. Taking advantage of their well-educated and professional staff, these school districts are able to offer a wide range of afterschool activities, including scouts, art, needlecraft, drama, ballet, chess, technology, and sports. A late bus transports children home after the activities end.

In the United Kingdom, Ireland, Canada, and Australia, an extensive network of school-age programs exist, supervised by government agencies and children's advocacy groups. Leaders have made efforts to expand the availability of out-of-school care into all communities and to develop a comprehensive program of program assessment and improvement (Gammage, 2003). In the UK, the Aiming Higher Framework 0–19 offers school districts and other organizations a set of comprehensive quality guidelines across program types as well as training, support, accreditation and self-certification, and audits to ensure standards and quality. The National Quality Improvement Network, funded by the Department for Children, Schools and Families, supports continuous quality improvement in programs for all age groups. PlayCare Clubs were set up across Northern Ireland starting in 1996, funded through the European Union Special Programme for Peace and Reconciliation. Currently, all out-of-school hours programs for children up to the age of 12 in Northern Ireland are registered by Early Years teams within the local Health and Social Services Trusts (Child Care Directorate, 2005).

In Ireland, center-based school-age child care is a relatively new concept, but many unconnected individuals and organizations are attempting to close the gaps between school hours and parents' availability. A miscellany of names are given to these services: Afterschool Care, Out of School Care, After School Clubs, Summer Schemes, and Homework Clubs being among them (Child Care Directorate, 2005).

The Canadian government made a commitment to develop a National Children's Agenda but reviews of the progress of that agenda have shown a tendency to focus on early child development at the expense of school-age programs. Even the National Child Benefit, which invests heavily in assistance to low-income families, has primarily targeted younger at-risk children (Mahon & Beaufais, 2001). Private corporations such as the Royal Bank of Canada, CIBC, and Sears Canada have provided the critical financial support for high-quality school-age programs to survive in many communities.

"Getting family-friendly policies right will help reduce poverty, promote child development, enhance equity between men and women and stem the fall in birth-rates." This is the message of Willem Adema, author of *Babies and Bosses, Reconciling Work and Family Life*, a four-volume report published by the Organisation for Economic Co-operation and Development that compares the approaches taken by 30 different countries to help parents balance their work and family commitments. These four volumes contain a wide variety of funding, staffing, education, and mission statements and can serve as a valuable resource for any organization working to improve afterschool arrangements for children (Adema, 2002).

The commonwealth government in Australia provided a detailed handbook in 2000 outlining requirements for what it terms "Outside School Hours Care." Considerable technical and financial support is available to facilitate new school-age programs and also to support the child care needs of parents. The focus of the development model provides incentives to both community-based organizations and private child care providers. Most school-age programs in Australia are supported through fee-for-service. However, if families satisfy certain income and residency criteria, a child care benefit may be paid to parents or directly to the service provider.

Africa, Asia, India, the Middle East, and Latin America   In countries where children contribute to the family labor pool as soon as they are able, compulsory education laws are difficult to enforce. Such is the case in parts of Kenya and Liberia, where social agency personnel have struggled for decades to provide child care centers for the children of low-income families (Hildebrand, 1997). School-age programs are nearly nonexistent there. Even South Africa, a richer nation with a more highly educated population, faces huge obstacles in afterschool programming. In 2008, the National AfterSchool Association was invited to participate in an Afterschool Summit held in Capetown. Judy Nee, NAA president and CEO, participated by teleconference in the summit, which brought together South African government officials, the U.S. embassy there, and experts and practitioners in the greater Cape Town area in an effort to build a community of practice and professionals in their country (National AfterSchool Association, 2008).

❀   *Consider This:*   ❀

What can we learn from the successes and challenges faced by child and youth professionals in other countries? How can we apply this information to our own situation?

Japanese schools are open from 8:00 a.m. until 5:00 p.m. in many areas, and youngsters are encouraged to play actively after the noon meal and then sleep for 1 to 2 hours. When school-hours stretch to fill the adult workday, separate programs for before- and afterschool care are not necessary. However, in some districts, afterschool clubs (*kurabu katsudō*) provide an important respite from high-stress academic classrooms. *Buraban* (school band) is reported to be the most popular activity for girls. However, some elementary schools offer recreational programs, and increasing numbers of parents are enrolling their children in them. For example, at Shinanodai Elementary, there are six afterschool clubs for fifth and sixth graders, with themes ranging from story making or music to sports. Basketball and baseball clubs are also available at some elementary and middle schools (Ministry of Foreign Affairs of Japan, 2009). Sports, recreational reading, and watching television are also well-liked leisure activities, but schoolwork remains the focus of the daily lives of most Japanese children. Looming secondary and college entrance examinations greatly influence their free time and study habits. In both Japan and Korea, afterschool programs are more likely to be of the "cram school" variety, the focus of which is to help children attain entrance into a good high school and help high school students make it into a good college. Cram schools are usually privately owned and have a very narrow, academic focus (Jiyeon, 2008).

In Vietnam, there is a big difference between urban and rural areas. Very few rural children stay in school beyond fifth or sixth grade, especially girls, who are encouraged to work around the house and/or on the farm, and most children return home immediately after school, whether someone is there or not. In Ho Chi Minh City, charity groups provide accommodation, education, recreational activities, and opportunities for street children and orphaned children, but in many areas, relatives take care of their own school-age children based on kinship (Ruiz-Casares & Heymann, 2009; WLS International, 2010).

In Sri Lanka, just off the southern coast of India, the situation was similar until the tsunami in 2004. After that disaster, UNICEF and local nongovernmental organizations organized afterschool programs for children who had been affected. These programs helped children confront and overcome the trauma and stress they had faced and also continue to serve a longer-term peace-building purpose, since children of many different ethnic groups are served by the programs (Mitchell, 2005).

In many cities of the world, including those in India, the Middle East, and Latin America, millions of children live on the streets, eating from garbage cans and sleeping in railway stations (Street Kids International, 2006). According to the United Nations, about 40% of those children are homeless, and the other 60% work on the streets to support their families (Fernandes & Vaughn, 2008).

Trying to address this problem in India, the YMCA opened several night shelters in Visakapatnam and other urban centers that offer informal education and training in carpentry, car and cycle repairs, bookbinding, welding, tailoring, and office work. Since street children have in a sense lost their childhood, the program staff also encourages children to play volleyball, kabaddi, and chess and go on trips to the beach, zoo, and park (Kumar, 1995; YMCA International, 2009).

In modern India, the number of working women in all the major cities is increasing tremendously. Many of these mothers face the "insecurity of leaving the child behind at home in the care of unwilling relatives or untrained, unreliable domestic help who have little idea of cleanliness, hygiene or the knowledge of how to deal with an emergency" (M. Dasgupta, executive director of Dolna Day Trust, personal communication, 2004). **Crèches**, or child care centers for very young children, have been common in India for many years. In recognition of the problems faced by this new generation of working parents, some crèches in Kolkata were expanded to include children up to 16 years old. In addition to keeping the school-age children safe, these crèches offer painting, drawing, singing, instrumental music, dancing, and even computer studies.

A creative approach to addressing the need for affordable child care in both industrialized and developing countries is to help parents access non-family care through workplace programs. Partnerships between employers, trade unions, national and local governments, and various types of child care programs have emerged in unlikely workplace settings (Hein & Cassirer, 2009). One example of this is Mumbai Mobile Crèches, which operate in Delhi, Bombay, and Pune to care on-site for the children of migrant construction workers. In many cases, older siblings, lacking access to school or health centers, were being required to care for younger siblings at the construction site. Consequently, crèche staff accept children up to age 12 and employ non-formal education methods to gradually introduce the older children to the skills they will need as well as assistance to enter the formal educational system (Mahadevan, 2009).

> Over the last three decades, MMC [Mumbai Mobile Crèches] has developed and pioneered a model that supports the development of the very young child, frees older children from the burden of looking after younger siblings, helps children applying to school and ensures they stay in school. Such an approach—which has the needs of young children at its core—creates the foundations for healthy development and overall growth of our society. (Mahadevan, 2009)

Throughout the world, child and youth professionals share a common belief: Leaving school-age children unattended is not healthful or wise. Most governments also know this, and funding streams designed to protect and educate children during the hours their parents work are in evidence in most nations. However, children who have grown accustomed to taking care of themselves may not appreciate these efforts.

Louis Aptekar, an anthropologist who lived and worked among the street children in Colombia in order to study them, described the need for both **macroprograms**, which are on a larger scale and are concerned with changing people's attitudes about childhood and street children in particular, and **microprograms**, which serve the needs of the children themselves. Yet even as he proposed solutions for the community, Aptekar expressed a respect for the culture of the **gamines**, or street children, who functioned independently of family and society yet exhibited many healthy characteristics of a working social group.

However, these children had assumed many of the rights of adults, he warned, and would not easily or happily respond to efforts to return them to childhood (Aptekar, 1988). He was correct: Clearly, there is a great deal of variation in the lives of the world's children. And there is much work to be done developing appropriate out-of-school programs to serve them (Aptekar, 2003).

❀   *Consider This:*   ❀

A macroprogram in the United States might educate parents about the risks of leaving school-age children unsupervised for long periods of time. A micropro-gram could provide funding for recreational activities and homework help at a community center housed in an apartment complex.

ELEMENTS OF EFFECTIVE BEFORE- AND AFTERSCHOOL PROGRAMS

While we still have much to learn about the best ways to provide supervision and guidance for children during the out-of-school hours, there are some common threads to be found in the examples presented above. The most effective arrangements accommodate the working schedules of parents and school calendars of children. For children who attend structured school settings, effective programs allow children to feel that "school is out" and that this is their "free" time rather than simply more of what they have been doing all day. For children in some situations, this "out of school" time is the closest they will get to a formal education. What is most important is that all excellent programs allow children to grow in responsibility and freedom as they develop in reliability and trustworthiness.

In afterschool programs, there are often competing needs: Parents express their need for a safe and pleasant environment, for adequate care, and for the opportunity for their children to do their homework (see Figure 2.5). Children tend to vote for recreational games, plenty of time to talk to their friends, free choice of a variety of activities, and usually no homework (one staff member calls this Food, Friends, and Fun). Professional afterschool staff want to extend and enrich children's learning and encourage positive socialization (M. Bostick, owner of A Children's Garden

FIGURE 2.5   Guidelines for Developing Effective School-Age Programs.

- The program addresses a community need.
- Hours and days of operation accommodate the working schedules of parents and school calendars of children.
- If private, the program works with public agencies to secure adequate funding.
- If public, the program works with private agencies to raise standards and develop a professional workforce.
- The program offers fair compensation to staff members.
- The staff meets children's social and emotional needs and helps them with academic skills.

child care center, private communication). They also want to provide a private space and time for each child who needs it and for opportunities to exchange confidences with and receive reassurances from other children and nurturing adults.

Michelle Seligson (2001), founder of the Wellesley School-Age Child Care Project, identified several characteristics that should be present in programs for them to meet children's needs and keep them interested. She describes the optimum environment as an atmosphere of informal learning that allows children to do the following:

* ❀ Make choices
* ❀ Expand their cultural horizons
* ❀ Achieve a gradual sense of independence as they grow
* ❀ Participate in peer culture

In the United Kingdom, "out of school" clubs form part of the government's extended-schools agenda, along with breakfast clubs and holiday clubs. Extended schools are designed to help balance work and family commitments, while providing children with study support and offering them a broader range of experiences and interests than they could otherwise obtain in the normal school day. Under the UK government's "extended services" initiative, all schools had until 2010 to provide access to child care, either on their own premises or nearby, from 8:00 a.m. to 6:00 p.m. The British national afterschool organization guidelines generally promote the creation of afterschool clubs that are warm and welcoming and where all children and staff are valued and respected. Leaders learn to recognize and value children as individuals, build close relationships with them, and include them in the running of the club. Club rules are designed to promote safety, enjoyment, comfort, and positive behavior (Out of School Alliance, 2009).

In a report to supporters of the Dolna Créche program, in India, the executive director wrote the following:

> All over the world today, life has become a whirlwind of activities and in the general hustle and bustle no one has any time to "stand and stare." Parents are losing the enjoyment of watching their children grow-up and children are losing out on the comfort, solace, understanding and guidance that they need, from their grandparents and parents, especially in their formative years. A direct result is the increase in the number of children straying from acceptable norms in society and adopting wayward habits and culture. It is because of these reasons that value-oriented education is assuming a special place in modern-day society. Institutions like Dolna have come forward to give the children those inputs that will instill a clear sense of values in them, teach them that they have positive responsibilities towards their families, their culture and their heritage. The children must appreciate Indian culture and the values that are its heritage. At the same time, they should also learn to glean the best of what the modern western world has to offer.
>
> *(From "Dolna's Services Today" by M. Dasgupta, Founder, Dolna Day School & Creche.*
> *Used with permission.)*

We are a world of diverse cultures, yet the goals for our children are not so different from one another. To attain these important goals, it is clear that a continuum of care needs to exist within each community and that private and public agencies must work together with parents and youngsters to assure that these arrangements suit them. The field of school-age child and youth work offers a broad range of employment and volunteer options. It is terribly important for the future of our children that the adults doing this work do so with a clear understanding of their role, their significance, and their responsibilities. Chapter 4 will address those topics.

SUMMARY

Communities in all industrialized nations are facing the need to provide care and supervision of school-age children before and after school and during holidays. The varieties of ways in which children's needs are being met in their own homes include flexible parental working hours and assistance from relatives, neighbors, community volunteers, and nannies or au pairs. Many children are left at home to fend for themselves, sometimes with telephone numbers they can call in case of loneliness or emergencies. Some communities offer telephone help lines or drop-in activity programs for these children. Out-of-home care can include licensed family child care homes, center-based programs on and off school sites, and a variety of activity, sports, and enrichment programs. Professional school-age care organizations have developed guidelines for supervision and care programs, which can serve to guide community agencies, program planners, and parents in the development of new programs and evaluation of existing ones.

TERMS TO LEARN

adult supervision with full accountability
adult supervision with some accountability
crèche
distal supervision
drop-in programs
gamine
grassroots
latchkey children

macroprogram
microprogram
no supervision
privately funded
publicly funded
underutilization
vandalism

REVIEW QUESTIONS

1. Referring to the scenarios given, identify some of the times during a typical school day and a school year when children are most likely to benefit from having access to an afterschool program.

2. How can communities meet the needs of families who need programs for their children only part of the time?

3. What kinds of activities are likely to take place in a program that operates for an hour or two before the school day? How would they differ from the activities usually found in afterschool programs?

4. What are the advantages and disadvantages of family child care for school-age children?

5. Why is public funding necessary for adequate provision of programs for school-age children?

CHALLENGE EXERCISES

1. Interview a parent, a school-aged child, and a community member about the out-of-school programs in your community. Ask them what they think *should* be available, and compare it to what *is* available.

2. Visit a before- or afterschool program while it is in progress. If possible, interview the leader and identify the goals of the program. List all the different ways children are occupying their time. Note where the adults are and what they are doing. Describe what you observe. Does this program appear to meet the guidelines given in this chapter?

3. How do you feel about coaches, music teachers, and librarians being referred to as "caregivers"? Ask one of these people what he or she thinks about being thought of in this fashion.

4. What do you think are the responsibilities of programs that offer out-of-school programs? List four services you think they should provide.

5. Do you know your county or state's procedure for obtaining a license to care for school-age children in one's own home? Locate this information on the Internet and bring it to class to discuss the steps with others.

INTERNET RESOURCES

Modern settlement houses in New York City:
http://www.nynp.biz/index.php/points-of-view/433-settlement-houses-and-public-housing-a-contemporary-solution

Salvation Army afterschool programs:
http://www.salvationarmycolumbus.org/programs/after_school.html

The Monkey Tail Gang Environmental Education After School Program:
http://www.schuylkillcenter.org/programs/afterschool/

Heart House Free Afterschool Program:
http://www.hearthouse.org/

Mumbai Mobile Créches, India:
http://www.mumbaimobilecreches.org

REFERENCES

Adema, W. (2002). *Babies and bosses: Reconciling work and family life, Vol. 1, Australia, Denmark and the Netherlands.* Retrieved April 11, 2009, from http://www.childcareinachangingworld.nl/sd-adema1.html.

Afterschool Alliance. (2006). *21st century community learning centers: A foundation for progress.* Washington, DC, publisher and author: Afterschool Alliance.

Afterschool Alliance. (2007, September). Afterschool partnerships with higher education. *Afterschool Alert: Issue Brief, 2.*

Afterschool Alliance. (2009). *America after 3PM: Key findings.* Washington, DC: JCPenney Afterschool.

Alexander, N. P. (1986). School-age child care: Concerns and challenges. *Young Children, 42*(1), 3–10.

Aptekar, L. (1988). *Street children of Cali.* Durham, NC: Duke University Press.

Aptekar, L. (2003). Cultural problems for Western counselors working with Ethiopian refugees. In F. Bernak, R. Chung, & P. Pedersen (Eds.), *Counseling refugees: A psychosocial approach to innovative multicultural innovations.* Westport, CT: Greenwood Press.

Arlington Public Schools. (2008). *Programs and services: Check-in program.* Retrieved February 22, 2009, from www.apsva.us.

Bales, D. (1998). Cooperative extension service, University of George, Athens.

California School-Age Consortium. (2008). *After school: Policy brief.* San Francisco: After School Corps: CalSAC's After School Workforce Development Project.

Capizzano, J., Tout, K., & Adams, G. (2000). *Child care patterns of school-age children with employed mothers.* Washington, DC: published by The Urban Institute.

Child Care Directorate. (2005). *Developing school age childcare.* Dublin: Department of Justice, Equality, and Law Reform.

Chung, A. M. (2005). *After-school programs: Keeping children safe and smart.* Partnership for Family Involvement in Education, Washington, DC.

Corday, K., & Casey, J. (2006, November). MomsRising: Online grassroots organizing around family issues. *Sloan Work & Family Research Network,* Corday Boston College, Boston, MA 8(11).

Dasgupta, M. (2009). *Dolna's services today* [Newsletter]. Dolna Day Trust.

DeKalb Public Library. (1990). "Dear Parent" form letter and brochures.

Dowd, F. S. (1991). *Latchkey children in the library and community: Issues, strategies, and programs.* Phoenix, Arizona. Published by Oryx Press.

ESL Teachers Board. (2008). Online message board for teachers of ESL. Retrieved April 11, 2009, from http://www.eslteachersboard.com/

Eurostat. (2003). *Development of a methodology for the collection of harmonized statistics on childcare.* Geneva: Author.

Fernandes, G. T., & Vaughn, M. (2008). Brazilian street children. *International Social Work, 51*(5), 669–681.

Ferrer, M., & Chambers, J. (1999). Union Park action for safe families. *Journal of Extension, 37*(4). Retrieved April 15, 2010, from http://www.joe.org/joe/1999august/iw3.php

Fight Crime: Invest in Kids. (2007). *After-school programs prevent crime.* Oakland, CA: Author.

Gammage, P. (2003). *Outside school hours care: Does it matter?* [Keynote address]. Paper presented at the School Age Care Symposium. South Australian Department of Education and Children's Services, May 4, 2003.

Grace, M. (2001, August 8). Gresser: Put buildings to use after school. *New York Daily News,* p. 2.

Gruchow, M. (2007, May 18). Need for day care expands into night. *Army Times.* Retrieved April 15, 2010 from http://www.marinecorpstimes.com/careers/second_careers/military_niche_childcare_070518/

Gruner, A. (1994, August 12). Kids find themselves in a jam. *Dispatch,* p. 1 and 8.

Hein, C., & Cassirer, N. (2009). *Workplace solutions for childcare.* Geneva: International Labour Organisation.

Hildebrand, V. (1997). *Introduction to early childhood education* (6th ed.). Columbus, OH: Merrill.

International Nanny Association. (2008). *International Nanny Association (INA) 2006 survey: Results and observations.* Houston, TX: Author.

Jensen, J. J. (1991). School-age child care in the Danish social context today. *Women's Studies International Forum, 14*(6), 607–612.

Jiyeon, L. (2008, May 6). S. Korean cram school gulag is all books, dreams. *Reuters Life.* Retrieved April 15, 2010, from http://www.reuters.com/article/idUSSEO4837020080506

Johnson, K. (2006, November 17). Growing chain of child-care centers to add four area locations. *Sacramento Business Journal,* p. 3.

Kaplan, S. (2006). *Children's views of self-care: Concepts of autonomy and risk.* Unpublished paper presented at the annual meeting of the American Sociological Association, August 10, 2006.

Krohn, S., Charter, M., Beniak, T., Anderson, J., & Sordelet, G. (1993). Tribal child care innovations. *Children Today, 22,* 3.

Kumar, M. (1995). *Street life.* Visakapatnam, India: YCARE International.

Larsen-Elniff, A., Dreyling, M., & Williams, J. (2006). *Employment developments in childcare services for school-age children.* Brussels, Belgium: European Foundation for the Improvement of Living and Working Conditions.

Mahadevan, D. (2009). *Mumbai mobile creches: Laying the foundations for childhood on construction sites.* Colaba, Mumbai: Mobile Creches.

Mahon, R., & Beaufais, C. (2001). *School-aged children across Canada: A patchwork of public policies.* Ottawa, ON: Canadian Policy Research Networks.

Mathematica Policy Research. (1996). *Sustaining employment among low-income parents: The problem of inflexible jobs, child care, and family support, a research review.* Princeton, NJ: Author.

Meijvogel, R. (1991). School-age child care in the Netherlands: The shift from equality aims to the interest of the child. *Women's Studies International Forum, 14*(6), 557–560.

Miller, B. M. (2003). The promise of after-school programs. *Educational Leadership, 58*(7) 6–12.

Milne, C. (1994). *Enchanted places.* London: Mandarin Paperbacks. (Original work published in 1974)

Ministry of Foreign Affairs of Japan. (2009). *KidsWeb Japan.* Retrieved April 11, 2009, from http://web-japan.org/kidsweb/

Mitchell, L. (2005, December). *Tsunami: One year update.* Washington, DC: UNICEF.

Moss, P. (1991). School-age child care in the European community. *Women's Studies International Forum, 14*(6), 539–549.

Munson, C. (2005, December 12). $100,000 for youth center. *Dispatch,* 1.

Napoli, M. (2002). Native wellness for the new millennium: The impact of gaming. *Journal of Sociology and Social Welfare, 29*(1), 17+.

National AfterSchool Association. (2008). *The future of NAA's role in program accreditation.* Boston: Author.

National Childcare Accreditation Council. (2008). *Quality child care for school age children: A NCAC factsheet for families.* Surry Hills, New South Wales: Australian Government.

National Institute on Out-of-School Time. (2007). *Making the case: A fact sheet on children and youth in out-of-school time.* Boston: Wellesley Centers for Women at Wellesley College.

National Research Council. (1990). *Who cares for America's children: Child care policy for the 1990s.* Washington, DC: National Academy Press.

Negley, E. (2007, July 2). Day care, night care. *Reading Eagle,* p. 3.

Organisation for Economic Co-operation and Development. (2006). *Starting strong II: Early childhood education and care.* Paris: Author.

Out of School Alliance. (2009). *The one-stop shop for out of school clubs.* Cambridge, UK: Author.

Parsad, B., & Lewis, L. (2009). *After-school programs in public elementary schools: First look.* Washington, DC: U.S. Department of Education.

Presser, H.B. (2003). *Working in a 24/7 economy: Challenges for American families.* New York: Russell Sage Foundation.

Ruiz-Casares, M., & Heymann, J. (2009) Children home alone unsupervised: Modeling parental decisions and associated factors in Botswana, Mexico, and Vietnam. *Child Abuse & Neglect, 33*(5), 312–323.

Seligson, M. (2001). School-age child care today. *Young Children,* (56), 4.

Seligson, M., & Stahl, P. (2003). *Bringing yourself to work.* New York: Teachers College Press.

Street Kids International. (2006). *Annual report, 2006–2007.* Toronto: Author.

Swedish National Agency for Education. (2008). *Quality in leisure time centres: Guidelines and comments.* Retrieved April 15, 2010, from http://www.skolverket.se/sb/d/190

Trevelyan, J. P. (1919). *Evening play centres for children.* London: Methuen.

U.S. Department of Health and Human Services. (2004). *Innovative strategies for providing school-age care.* Washington, DC: Administration for Children and Families.

Upper Dublin Parks & Recreation. (n.d.). *After-school hangout at the EPI-center.* Port Washington, PA: Township of Upper Dublin.

Vandivere, S., Tout, K., Zaslow, M., Calkins, J., & Capizzano, J. (2003). *Unsupervised time: Family and child factors associated with self-care.* Washington, DC: Urban Institute.

Viadero, D. (2007). High-quality after-school programs tied to test-score gains. *Education Week, 27*(13), 1–13.

Warnock, M. (1992). After-school child care: Dilemma in a rural community. *Children Today, 21*(1), 16–30.

WLS International (2010). *Volunteer projects in Ho Chi Minh City, Vietnam.* Retrieved April 15, 2010, from http://www.gapyearinasia.com/vietnam-projects.html

YMCA International. (2009). *World alliance of YMCAs.* Retrieved November 25, 2009, from http://www.ymca.int/

Zigler, E. F., & Ennis, P. (1988). Child care: A new role for tomorrow's schools. *Principal, 68*(1), 10–13.

Zigler, E. F., & Lang, M. E. (1991). *Child care choices: Balancing the needs of children, families, and society.* New York: The Free Press.

Chapter

3

Developing and Ensuring Program Quality

Between 1981, when I was seeking someone to help me care for my two oldest children, and 1989, when my youngest child entered kindergarten, our small community sprouted six afterschool programs and two large corporate child care centers. In addition, two established preschools had added portable buildings to serve school-aged children before and after school. Our community was mirroring a national trend. In the 1980s, social services agencies throughout the country, including those serving young children and youth, received millions of dollars to address such problems as drug abuse, teen pregnancy, and school dropout rates. By 1991, more than 50,000 afterschool programs across the United States served an estimated 1.7 million children and their families (Seppanen, Love, deVries, Bernstein, & Seligson, 1993).

A broad national examination of U.S. out-of-school programs reported "significantly improved" opportunities for working parents to find a safe environment for their school-age children during non-school hours (Seppanen et al., 1993). The trend continued with increased interest from school districts and other educational agencies, and still more public money. By 2003, 11% of the nation's K–12 children (6.5 million) were in afterschool programs, and the parents of 9.7 million children of working families who were not participating indicated that they would like their children to do so if such a program were available (America After 3 PM, 2004).

CONTINUOUS PROGRAM IMPROVEMENT AND ACCREDITATION

American families desperately needed this increase in afterschool programming, but such rapid growth brought challenges. New and expanded programs were faced with identifying and meeting community needs, finding and keeping a well-trained workforce, and maintaining a quality program while meeting the demand for increased services. Simply increasing the quantity of programs and spaces was not going to be enough. Researchers specified high-quality programs when they reported social, behavioral, and academic improvements for children in out-of-school programs. But what, exactly, is **quality**? That was the question confronting the rapidly growing field, as well as the agencies, funders, and researchers called upon to evaluate the effects of various types of programs for children (Seligson & Stahl, 2003).

The Challenge of Rapid Growth

As the number of school-age programs increased, opportunities for professional networking also increased. Professional organizations were formed in many states, creating loosely affiliated networks at first, then more formal professional associations often affiliated with the National School Age Care Alliance (NSACA), now the National AfterSchool Association (NAA). Given opportunities to meet at regional, state, and national conferences, the administrators and staff addressing a variety of goals and objectives "conferred, discussed, and argued about purpose, philosophy, and their role in children's lives" (Halpern, 2006).

In the 1990s, the conversation moved into the legislature and the public press. As the value of before- and afterschool programs became more widely recognized and promoted, they became the focus of research and analysis and of increased public scrutiny. An important outcome of all this interest was a series of research studies in which children attending formal school-age programs were compared with children in other afterschool activities, or in self-care (Rosenthal & Vandell, 1996). The earliest comparisons looked at social relationships and emotional well-being. Research after 2000 focused on the effectiveness of afterschool programs at boosting academic achievement (Halpern, 2006).

The findings were not always clear. One report concluded that children participating in high-quality school-age programs were "more likely to show improvements in social behavior, ability to handle conflicts, leadership skills, range of interests, academic performance, and school success" (California Department of Education, 1996). The report also stated that participating children were less likely to be retained in the same grade, placed in special education programs, or exhibit behavior problems or vandalism in and around schools.

Other studies showed that afterschool programs could link the values, attitudes, and norms of students' cultural communities with those of the school culture (Cooper, Denner, & Lopez, 1999), lower children's involvement in risky behaviors (Miller, 1995), or give them a boost in test scores (Viadero, 2007). One study observed staff–child interactions and rated programs in terms of flexibility and age appropriateness (Rosenthal & Vandell, 1996). An evaluation of the Boys & Girls Club's Project Learn showed an increase in grade average, school attendance, and study skills (Schinke, Cole, & Moulin, 1998). But even after all this research, none of the studies defined "quality" very clearly, nor suggested how to measure it.

In my work supervising student teachers, I see many afterschool programs. No two are alike, and they function at very different levels of effectiveness, depending on stability of staff, support from the community, funding sources, and educational requirements of the agency. The most helpful explanation I have found in making sense of these fundamentally different characteristics of programs was a description of the "generations" model of school-age programs developed by Laurie Ollhoff when she was teaching in Concordia University's graduate program in school-age care. Figure 3.1 presents this model. Her message is that as a profession, we have gone through several phases in our understanding of what is needed to provide optimum experiences for children in their out-of-school time. Similarly, many programs also go through those phases, especially if they were originally developed, supervised, and staffed by people new to the concept of school-age care. After more than two decades of research and implementation, we are all hopefully moving into Generation 3.

Since the days of settlement houses and the early kindergarten movement, **child and youth workers** have recognized that in order to effectively meet the broad needs of children, families, and society, programs must be designed thoughtfully, based on knowledge of the communities and families they serve (Youcha, 2005). In addition, programs for school-age children should be administered and implemented by people with a solid understanding of children's development and characteristics, as well as the "generations" concept of program

FIGURE 3.1   Three Generations of School-Age Care.

School-age care is a young profession. Young professions require periodic reevaluation of their role and purpose for existing. The generational model is a tool for understanding the way school-age care is perceived. The different ways people understand school-age care are identified by each generation. Each generation has distinct characteristics. Movement within the generations takes commitment, self- and program reflection, and the desire to learn. Meeting the best needs of children can be a challenge and sometimes can stagnate or stifle us in everyday activities.

GENERATION ONE: The goal of school-age care is to provide a safe place for children to wait for their parents to pick them up. School-age care is a holding place. The ideal site provides a polite, quiet atmosphere with obedient children. Safety is considered the key reason to have children in school-age care. The adult's job is to supervise children so that no one gets hurt. Adults do not usually get involved in the children's activities. Adults are police officers.

GENERATION TWO: The goal of school-age care is to provide a fun and exciting curriculum—so that kids will want to continue in the program. The ideal site is a fun site with lots of learning activities. The primary value is to give kids the choice of activities. The adult's job is to create environments that foster creative choice. Adults lead activities and find new ideas to entertain children. Adults are activity directors.

GENERATION THREE: The goal of school-age care is to create a network of families, schools, and community to guide and mentor the optimum development of life skills. The ideal site is where children learn peaceful living skills. Children and their social and emotional growth are the primary values. The adult's job is to teach social skills—which is usually done through the process of games and spontaneous play. Adults are facilitators of positive development.

To which generation of thinking do you or your program belong? I challenge all of you involved in school-age care to become reflective thinkers and move towards third generation thinking.

Source: School-Age Care Planner: A Guide to Planning for Children and Youth During Out-of-School Time, by L. Ollhoff, 2002, Sparrow Media Group: Eden Prairie, MN. Used with permission.

development. School-age children can "vote with their feet," meaning that if they are not engaged in program activities and don't look forward to attending, they will convince their parents to find another option, simply opt out of active participation, or, worse, become behavior problems. The emerging vision of high-quality programs grew out of this historical perspective and continues through the discourse and collaboration of child and youth workers throughout the nation.

The Quality Pyramid

Once the staff of a school-age program is ready to think about improving quality, it is helpful to have some way of envisioning the goal. Figure 3.2 shows a model that has been used by many school-age programs and found to be helpful. Each major component is shown in proportional relationship to the others, indicating the importance of each element by its size and placement on the pyramid.

The base of the pyramid is constructed of the program organization, procedures, and policies. Moving up the pyramid are the building blocks of safety, health and nutrition, and the outdoor and indoor environments in which the activities, the day-to-day curriculum, take place. Figure 3.3 defines the terms in each section of the pyramid, and the following sections describe each of these components in more detail.

FIGURE 3.2 The Quality Pyramid. Standards for Quality School-Age Care.

Source: From *The NAA Standards for Quality School-Age Care,* by the National AfterSchool Association, 1998, Boston: National AfterSchool Association. Copyright © 1998 by the National AfterSchool Association. Adapted with permission.

FIGURE 3.3   Guiding Principles for Afterschool Programs.

Guidelines for Quality Programs

1. **Program Organization, Procedures, Policies:** This consists of the mission statement, goals and objectives, and staffing plan. The policies and procedures manual provides a blueprint for day-to-day operation and clear direction for the program leaders and line staff.

2. **Human Relationships:** Without well-trained staff, and an interpersonal environment in which adults and children communicate effectively and nurture one another's needs, the mission of the program will fail.

3. **Safety, Health, and Nutrition:** The physical environment should be safe, clean, and designed with the goals of the program in mind, and the curriculum should teach good health and nutrition both by model and instruction.

4. **Indoor and Outdoor Environment:** Work within the limitations of your physical environment to ensure that children have many opportunities for active play. Be creative in playground design and furniture arrangement so that children can participate in a wide variety of activities as well as find private spaces for solitude.

5. **Activities:** Plan most of your activities to promote the goals and objectives of the program, but provide others to balance the curriculum. Check in frequently with children to get ideas for new activities and guidance for which ones to retire.

Source: Wisconsin Afterschool Network (WAN). Used by permission.

Program Organization, Procedures, Policies   This section contains the elements making up the base of the quality pyramid. High-quality programs identify clear goals and objectives at the outset and develop the remainder of the program to achieve those goals. The value of having a focused and intentional strategy is that your program can measure everything, from curriculum plans to parent information nights to attendance policies, against the original intent of the program to be sure that they make sense (Metz, Goldsmith, & Arbreton, 2008). This section of the pyramid encompasses many aspects of program administration. Group sizes and ratios of adults to children are important, as are provisions for older children to move in and out of the direct line of supervision of adults. Do staff members support and encourage family and community involvement in the program?

Evaluators measure this component by observing how teaching staff orient family members to the program goals and activities, how frequently and effectively they communicate with parents and community members, and how much the administrators and teachers encourage children and families to provide input and be involved in program activities. This criterion also addresses staff qualifications for working with children at several levels of responsibility, their training on the job, and their compensation. Chapters 10, 15, and 16 address the issues in this section of the pyramid in more depth.

Human Relationships   It could be argued that the most important component of school-age programming is the quality of the human relationships they produce (M. Bostick, personal communitcation, 2009; Seligson & Stahl,

Skillful teachers promote positive interactions with children.

2003). People who spend hours together each day affect one another's lives. An examination of the elements of adult–child, child–child and adult–adult interaction can identify which attitudes, behaviors, and assumptions contribute to positive experiences for adults and children. Children learn **prosocial behavior** from significant adults, and observing teamwork and respectful communication among teachers, parents, and administrators can help them feel safe and contributes to their sense of belonging. Children's relationships with one another are also important. Do children value one another's unique characteristics, or do they form cliques that freeze out individuals who do not share their views? Do child and youth workers really listen to children and respect their feelings about things they care about? Children who experience healthy relationships are less likely to exhibit aggressive behavior, and children who learn how to maintain healthy relationships may be less likely to experience aggressive behavior from others.

In effective programs, administrators develop and facilitate two-way communication with staff, children and youth, families, school personnel, and the community. Skillful teachers, counselors, and coaches—anyone who works directly with children—should promote positive interaction, demonstrate mutual respect, and model healthy relationships. In other words, staff, children, and families relate to one another in positive and helpful ways. Chapters 4, 5, and 6 address the characteristics of people who work successfully with school-age children and identify many of the ways to ensure that these guidelines are being met in your program.

Safety, Health, and Nutrition   This component is often the first one mentioned by parents when they describe what they seek in an afterschool program for their children. Most states address health and safety basics through licensing **standards**. However, there is more to consider than minimum requirements. The physical environment should be safe, clean, and appropriate for the goals of the program. The physical health of children is a high priority and should be considered when planning snacks and activities. Especially with an obesity epidemic in our midst, we need to serve and teach the preparation of healthy foods, support children's need to eat varying amounts at different times, post children's allergies and respect them, and include children in building menus. Be sure that children's prescription medications are recorded accurately, administered correctly and on time, and securely locked away.

Model positive behavior in your own food choices and efforts to maintain good health and fitness. Plan high-interest activities that motivate children to "get off the couch" and move their bodies in games and dance—and move your own body right along with them. The emotional health of children and staff is also an important consideration. Programs should encourage children to interact positively with one another, make responsible choices, and respect cultural identity and individual preferences. Familiarize yourself with the School-Age Code of Ethical Conduct (see Appendix) and use it to guide both the staff and the children in their interactions with one another, schools, families, and the community. Health and fitness are addressed in more detail in Chapter 11.

Environment (Indoor and Outdoor)   Both the indoor and outdoor space utilized by the program should be appropriate for the ages of the children or youth participating in the program. The indoor space should be sufficient to allow free movement of children, support a wide range of activities, and allow independent

Youngsters should have the option to sit in large or small groups or alone.

exploration of a variety of interests. Place furnishings in such a way that young-sters have the option to sit in large or small groups or alone. Ensure that the outdoor environment is free from hazards and protected from foot or vehicle traffic by fences or other means. Encourage physical activity. Chapter 9 provides specific suggestions for the design and utilization of indoor and outdoor environments.

Activities   The curriculum in afterschool programs is most effective when it does not merely duplicate what youngsters experienced in their regular daily classroom (Bodily & Beckett, 2005; Northwest Regional Laboratory, 1999). Ideally, activities are child initiated or at least self-selected and include opportu-nities for active physical play, creative arts, quiet activities, and socializing, as well as various forms of academic enrichment. For example, following a snack and "vege out" time after school, organize sides to play elbow tag, hagoo, soccer, or traditional playground games such as Capture the Flag and Steal the Bacon (game instructions can be found in Chapter 13). Once inside, children may engage in homework, math or reading skill practice, or one-on-one reading with a staff member. After that, a variety of arts, crafts, carpentry, or board games should be made available, or youngsters may just want to sit alone or in groups and chat.

Within the goals of the program, children should have the opportunity to participate in short- and long-term projects, exercise small and large muscles, develop independence, learn conflict-resolution skills, and have fun. Whether the curriculum is primarily academic or recreational, addresses a community issue such as alcohol and drug prevention, or is administered by a faith-based organi-zation, activities should always be developmentally appropriate and engaging. Chapter 10 introduces the concept of collaborative program planning in school-age programs. Chapters 11, 12, and 13 provide many examples of enriching and interesting activities.

The Role of the Quality Pyramid in School-Age Programming

The NAA Quality Pyramid was originally developed as part of an early quality-improvement movement, during which a team of researchers determined that quality improvement must emerge from inside the field rather than be exter-nally imposed by funders or government agencies. The idea of the pyramid comes originally from Abraham Maslow's Hierarchy of Needs, his model of human development (Maslow, 1970), which suggests that as we grow and learn there are certain basic needs that must be met. In 2005, a slightly differ-ent Pyramid of Program Quality appeared in an assessment tool for use in pro-grams for older youth. Staff members familiar with a quality pyramid concept and who use it in their planning are more likely to emphasize **human rela-tionships**, **engagement**, and **interaction** since those elements make up part of the broad base of the pyramid, and less likely to depend on **activities**, repre-sented by a small triangle at the top, to carry their program. I suggest that you post a copy of the NAA Quality Pyramid in your staff work room and refer to it often.

Other Models of Quality

In 2003, the Forum for Youth Investment reviewed 13 statements of standards and guidelines for child and youth program quality. Most were developed by organizations or accrediting groups that focused on only one area of the youth development field, such as school-age care, youth leadership, or summer camps (Granger, Durlak, Yohalem, & Reisner, 2007). The authors of the report found that, even though differences in program purpose and content existed in the standards, there was a clear emphasis on interactions among program staff and participants (Forum for Youth Investment, 2003). In 2007, the Forum expanded its research and published reviews of nine other instruments designed to measure the quality of programs for children and youth (Yohalem & Wilson-Ahlstrom, 2007). From having no guidelines to measure quality, the school-age field now had 24.

Because each program differs in its desired outcome and funding sources, it is important to select an assessment tool that matches your program mission and goals. It is also important to include the stakeholders who will be using the evaluative data to make programmatic changes in the decision about which instrument(s) to use.

Table 3.1 compares eight tools that can be used by program staff for evaluating and improving program quality. Instruments designed specifically for research were not included.

TABLE 3.1 Tools for Program Quality Improvement.

Name	Overview	Primary Purpose	Target Grades	Content	For More Information
Assessment of Afterschool Program Practices Tool (APT)	Helps programs examine aspects of program quality to support learning and development; two questionnaires, one to gather information, the other used during observation.	Program improvement Monitoring Accreditation	K–8	Program climate Relationships Approaches and programming partnerships Youth participation	www.doe.mass.edu/21cclc/ta/
Out-of-School Time Program Evaluation	Designed to help staff assess the feelings of students, parents, program staff, and teachers through stakeholder surveys and focus group questions.	Program improvement	4th and above	Student, teacher, parent and staff surveys Student, parent and staff focus group Focus group protocol and questions Partnership survey Comprehensive instruction manual	www.nwrel.org http://www.nwrel.org/ecc/21century/publications/ost_tools.pdf
Program Observation Tool (POT)	Measures 36 "keys of quality" organized into six categories; designed to help programs assess progress against the Standards for Quality School-Age Care.	Program improvement Monitoring Accreditation	K–8	Human relationships Indoor environment Outdoor environment Activities Safety, health, and nutrition Administration	http://naaweb.yourmembership.com/?page=NAA Accreditation

TABLE 3.1 (*Continued*)

Name	Overview	Primary Purpose	Target Grades	Content	For More Information
Program Quality Self-Assessment (QSA)	Intended to help program leaders and staff, in collaboration with other stakeholders, to better understand the indicators of a high-quality program and reflect on all aspects of their program's operation. Requires a combination of observation, interview, and document review.	Program improvement	K–12	Environment and climate Administration and organization relationships Staffing and professional development Programming and activities Linkages between day and afterschool youth participation and engagement Parent, family, and community partnerships program Sustainability and growth Measuring outcomes and evaluation	www.nysan.org
Quality Assurance System (QAS)	Developed to help programs conduct quality assessment and continuous improvement planning. Requires a combination of observation, interview, and document review.	Program improvement	K–12	Program planning and improvement Leadership Facility and program space Health and safety staffing Family/community Connections Social Climate	http://qas.foundationsinc.org/start.asp?st=1
School-Age Care Environment Rating Scale (SACERS)	Focuses on social interactions within the setting as well as space, schedule, and materials. Can be used by program staff as well as trained external observers.	Program improvement Monitoring Accreditation Research/evaluation	K–8	Space and furnishings Health and safety Activities Interactions Program structure Staff development Special needs	www.fpg.unc.edu/~ecers/
Youth Camp Outcomes Questionnaires	Purpose is to help administrators evaluate camp program goals and document changes in campers to share with parents, funders, staff, etc.	Program improvement	6–17	Friendship skills Independence Teamwork Family citizenship Perceived competence Interest in exploration Responsibility	www.acacamps.org

(*continued*)

TABLE 3.1 Tools for Program Quality Improvement. (*Continued*)

Name	Overview	Primary Purpose	Target Grades	Content	For More Information
Youth Program Quality Assessment (YPQA)	Purpose: Encourage individuals, programs and systems to focus on quality of experiences young people have in programs and the corresponding training needs of staff.	Program improvement Monitoring Accreditation Research/ evaluation	4–12	Social processes: Interactions between and among youth and adults Youth engagement Program resources Organization	http://www. highscope. org/ Content.asp? ContentId= 117

Sources: Adapted From American Camping Association, 2007; National Institute on Out-of-School Time, 2007; Northwest Regional Educational Laboratory, 2003; Yohalem & Wilson-Ahlstrom, 2007.

The Role of Assessment and Accreditation in Program Quality Improvement

Assessment and **accreditation** are used for ensuring and improving program quality. Unlike standardized tests commonly used by school districts and universities, these tools evaluate the program, not the children, and provide guidelines to help you develop strategies for continuously improving the program.

Assessment

Program quality assessment, as we have been discussing it, is a process that allows staff and parents to look at the program objectively. For a single-program site, this examination can be as simple as a one-evening information-gathering session with the staff and parents, followed by a potluck meal—or it can be a rigorous, year-long process that includes children, parents, staff, and community members and culminates in a written report. Thinking about the program in a methodical fashion, considering the various aspects of each day or week or the whole year, and asking **stakeholders** in the program how they feel about each of these aspects can be extremely helpful. This self-assessment is an important tool in determining areas of strength and areas needing strengthening, and it is an important first step to building program quality.

However, a limitation of **self-study**, even with the plethora of evaluative instruments to choose from, is that it can be difficult to get a clear picture of how your program compares to other programs with similar goals. Self-study and reflection are an excellent first step, but they can take your program only so far. Once you have gathered information from the various groups, measured your program against an external set of standards, and made some improvements, the conversations that follow may eventually lead you to desiring an evaluation by professionals outside the organization. Accreditation is such an external evaluative process.

Accreditation

As the awareness of the positive effects of high-quality school-age programs grew, so did the interest in developing a national accreditation system. Other countries were moving in this direction at the same time, and in collaborative workshops at several national conferences, common elements began to emerge. In the United States, the Army worked with the Council for Early Childhood Professional Recognition to publish an assessment system and set of competency standards, resulting in the ASQ: Assessing School-Age Quality (O'Connor, Harms, Cryer, & Wheeler, 1991). Teachers College Press added the *School-Age Care Environment Rating Scale* to their selection of environmental checklists (Harms, 1996). Drawing on 10 years of research and discussion with each of these groups, the National School-Age Care Alliance (NSACA) published *Standards for Quality School-Age Care* (1997) and initiated a national accreditation process specifically for school-age programs.

A powerful part of any accreditation process is the development of a local team of people who care about the program. This team participates in a rigorous self-study, develops a plan for improvement that becomes part of the accreditation application, and then meets with the accreditation endorsers. Accreditation can be a powerful tool, because it provides a structure that encourages professionals and families to work closely together. By carefully examining each component of your program, and comparing it to the same set of external guidelines that the endorsers will be using, you can develop the momentum needed to identify areas needing improvement and make the necessary changes to allow your program to grow toward excellence.

❀   *Consider This:*   ❀

Who would you select to be team members in an accreditation of your program? It is common to include a group leader, a parent, a classroom teacher and/or principal from the neighboring school, and a child. Who else would you include?

It is important to train all participants in the self-study process at the beginning of the evaluation period. Rosa Andrews, a former National AfterSchool Association accreditation endorser and a National AfterSchool Association board member, describes well-implemented training as being "extremely motivating." "The training . . . prepares staff to evaluate their programs and make needed quality improvements . . . . I think any time program staff have the opportunity to network together and gain explanations and information in their field the outcome is positive" (personal communication, July 2008).

The Goals of Accreditation   The accreditation process ideally serves three functions. First, it encourages the school-age community to make a public statement about what is expected of a program by the selection of specific standards and to certify that a program is meeting those standards. In other educational endeavors, this kind of certification protects children and families from institutions that make unsupported claims about their enterprise. It protects staff and

Preparing a site for an accreditation visit can raise staff morale and create a sense of excitement.

administration by letting them know whether their program is operating within the framework agreed upon by their peers.

Second, accreditation certifies to state or federal agencies and other organizations that a program meets more than minimum standards for quality. Although accreditation is a nongovernmental process, it can be used by government agencies as a criterion for certain financial support in the form of grants, loans, subsidies, etc.

The third (and perhaps the most important) function of accreditation is to encourage the administrators and staff to formally review the programs on a regular basis and to provide tools for improvement. The accreditation process is based on the assumption that if an institution looks at itself often enough and carefully enough, it will identify its flaws and limitations and address them.

The Process of Accreditation   Following an awareness of quality standards and a period, sometimes several years, of internal evaluation and assessment using one of the tools shown in Table 3.1, it is a natural next step to consider applying for accreditation. Most publicly funded educational programs are required to undergo an accreditation process periodically, and many privately funded programs choose to pursue it as well. During accreditation, programs measure themselves against a set of commonly agreed-upon standards and then invite a team of external examiners to visit their site and do the same. The two sets of findings are compared. If accreditation status is awarded, that means that the program does, indeed, meet the standards. If the visiting team members, known as **validators** or **endorsers**, do not agree with the findings of the self-study, accreditation will be **deferred** until agreed-upon improvements or changes in the program can be made. The award of accreditation status assures parents and community members that a school or child care program has thought through a broad range of issues and offers a coherent and appropriate program to their children. Perspective 3.1 explores the role of accreditation in program quality.

PERSPECTIVE 3.1

*Where Are We Headed
With Center Accreditation?*

Roger Neugebauer

With a new administration in Washington, DC, poised to expand federal support for early childhood and school-age services, it is important that our profession take a close look at how we can assure parents that we are providing the high-quality services they need and deserve.

What accreditation options do centers have? For a decade after its launch in 1985, NAEYC accreditation was practically the only show in town. However, in recent years, a variety of organizations have launched new accreditation systems. Of course, all accreditation systems are not equal—they vary considerably in terms of standards assessed, procedures for assessment, numbers accredited, types of programs served, and cost. Many of the newer accreditation systems are targeted at specific niches in the field.

Around the turn of this century, a new approach for monitoring quality came into vogue—quality rating and improvement systems. According to the National Child Care Information Center, today 17 states have statewide quality rating systems in place. Usually these systems benchmark all licensed programs against specified levels of quality. Center accreditation is typically incorporated into these systems as a means of achieving the highest levels of quality.

With growing numbers of states enacting quality rating systems, where does this leave center accreditation systems? Do they fit hand in glove, with the lower levels of quality rating systems (QRS) providing stepping stones on the way to the ultimate goal of accreditation, or will QRS gradually replace accreditation as the marker of quality? Here is what some of our trend watchers observed:

While it is too early to tell if quality rating systems will replace or support accreditation systems, there are two areas where quality rating systems appear to offer significant advantages. . .

❋ They are visible. One of the major criticisms of all accreditation systems is that they are not household names to parents. In surveys published in *Exchange* magazine surveys, center directors frequently cite the positive impact on staff motivation from participation in the self-study portion of accreditation. Yet they nearly unanimously observe that being accredited has not attracted any parents to their center. On the other hand, since quality rating systems rate all centers in a state, parents soon seize upon this as a quick way to judge center quality (whether they consider this a key factor in their final selection is not so clear).

❋ They incent programs to improve. In many states, being accredited by certain of the accreditation systems enables programs to receive a higher rate of reimbursement. In most states with quality rating systems, centers receive increasing levels of reimbursement through all the steps in the process, thus offering some incentive to centers who may not be able to achieve accreditation.

AN UPBEAT PROGNOSIS

It is the American way to "let a thousand flowers bloom." Instead of decreeing one right way of doing business, we let the market work things out. Beta and VHS technology competed for years before VHS eventually became the *de facto* standard.

Having dozens of quality rating and accreditation systems in play at the same time is certainly confusing. And it splinters quality-enhancement efforts in a number of directions. But if we view this as a grand experiment, we are testing out a range of avenues for broadcasting quality. In time, cumbersome, ineffective systems will fall away and we will start reaching consensus on which systems are most useful. As statewide quality rating systems are refined and coordinated, they will be seen as the way to provide a convenient, across-the-board rating of programs. But for monitoring quality at the highest level, program accreditation systems will continue to provide the truest, in-depth assurance of quality for parents, regulators, and funders.

Source: Neugebauer, R. (2009). *Exchange EveryDay Magazine;* Upbeat about Center Accreditation, 4/23/2009. Used with permission.

Programs with areas that need improvement can use information provided by the self-study and accreditation process to guide them in setting their goals. After participating as an endorser and quality-improvement consultant in the accreditation process, Rosa Andrews, National AfterSchool Association board member, concluded that "motivation is very definitely created through this process. The excitement that this kind of quality is possible is contagious . . . the process empowers the staff to ask for what they need to improve their programs" (personal communication, July 2009).

While state-mandated licensing, required in most areas, is a necessary and helpful tool for assuring a reasonable level of program safety and effectiveness, it requires programs to meet only a *minimum* set of standards. Even self-study using an assessment tool is limited by the ability of your program to honestly critique itself. The accreditation process encourages programs to see themselves through the eyes of others and encourages continued growth toward higher quality. The receipt of accredited status shows that a program is performing with a high degree of excellence and meeting professional standards.

Accreditation criteria are developed by professionals who have visited many programs and reviewed by researchers and program staff to analyze the components that result in program quality. For many years, two nationally recognized accreditation options were available to out-of-school programs: (1) the Early Childhood Program Accreditation process, administered by the National Association for the Education of Young Children (NAEYC), and (2) the National Improvement and Accreditation System, until 2008 administered by the National AfterSchool Association (NAA). Beginning in 2008, the Council on Accreditation began overseeing accreditation of afterschool programs. NAEYC and NAA no longer provide accreditation services for school-age programs, although existing accreditation awards are valid for the life of the certification awarded.

The Development of a National Improvement and Accreditation System
Creating a national accreditation program took many years. First came an awareness that before- and afterschool care programs needed their own system of assessment, one that was specifically designed for school-age programs. The National School-Age Care Alliance (NSACA) distributed a set of pilot standards based partly on the ASQ (O'Connor et al., 1991), which was in use by the U.S. Army school-age programs. A pilot project, conducted with 74 programs, collected information on how the system and standards could be revised and strengthened to better fit the diversity of programs around the country. A second pilot was conducted with the revised standards, which were then approved and published as *The Standards for Quality School-Age Care* (National AfterSchool Association, 1998).

These standards formed the core of a nationwide school-age Program Improvement and Accreditation project. Over the next 9 years, over 100 accreditation endorsers were trained and visited school-age programs throughout the United States. The list of newly accredited programs on the NAA Web site grew every year. In fact, the demand for accreditation grew more quickly than the small NAA staff in Boston could accommodate, and in 2007 the decision was made to transfer the accreditation function from NAA to the much larger Council on Accreditation (COA). The Council surveyed the field to understand the nature and size of the challenge and developed an accreditation process that was "based on generally accepted standards of best practice, outcomes-oriented, responsive to the unique needs and diversity of afterschool programs, financially affordable, and effective in advancing quality" (Council on Accreditation, 2008). It is likely that the COA process and the standards on which it is based will be revised periodically to reflect changes in the field.

Accreditation Today

The Council on Accreditation worked with the National AfterSchool Association (NAA) to develop a transition set of standards that reflected generally accepted elements of best practice and paralleled other accreditation tools used by the COA. These standards are outcomes-based, which means they are measured by observing results. Seeking and preparing for accreditation is considered a program-improvement process, which leads to a gradual increase in the effectiveness of the program to address the unique needs and diversity of families in its community. A program that began the process as a generation-one environment for children will mature into a generation two and eventually emerge as generation three (Ollhoff & Ollhoff, 1999).

Council on Accreditation After School Standards   COA's After School Standards are organized into three sections: (1) After School Program Administration, (2) After School Human Resources, and (3) After School Programming and Services.

- ❀ **Administration:** The administration standards review practices related to continuous quality improvement, financial management, risk prevention and management, and ethical practice.
- ❀ **Human Resources:** The human resources standards address recruitment and selection of staff, training and professional development, support, and supervision.
- ❀ **Programming and Services:** The programming and services standards identify recommended practices for working with children and youth in out-of-school time.

Achieving Accreditation   Each of the three sections of the accreditation document is divided into subsections, listing *practice* standards, *concept* standards, and *purpose* standards. All three types of standards may be accompanied by interpretations that elaborate on the meaning of the standard. Figure 3.4 shows the steps to accreditation. With the use of specific tools provided by the accrediting agency, the program seeking accreditation documents each standard using written material (policies and procedures manuals, parent newsletters, snack menus, etc.) and staff or student files. During the site visit, endorsers observe interactions between staff, children, and parents and compare them to the standard and the documentation to determine if the standard has been met.

Accreditation can take a long time to achieve, and it is helpful to have some markers along the way. Under the Council on Accreditation, the **continuous**

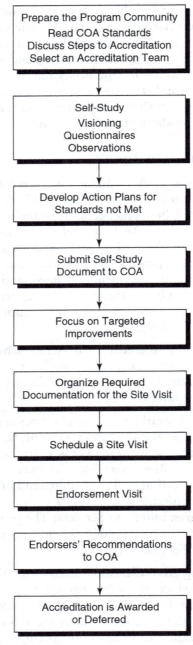

FIGURE 3.4   Steps to COA Program Accreditation.

Source: Used with permission of the Council on Accreditation, Inc.

program improvement process consists of three phases: *registration, certification,* and *accreditation.*

Registration is a 3-year progressive process that allows small and new programs to demonstrate their commitment to quality by familiarizing themselves with the COA standards and building their capacity for positive outcomes.

Certification requires a self-study to be reviewed by an endorser, but not a site visit, and lasts for 3 years. This step "provides programs with a process to expand their capacity and quality prior to applying for accreditation" (Council on Accreditation, 2008).

Following the full self-study, action plan, site visit, and award process, accreditation status is awarded for 4 years, and during that time the administration and staff commit to completing a self-review annually to ensure that the program stays on track. Together these three steps result in one cycle of continuous program improvement.

Participating in accreditation is a bold step toward assuring quality in school-age programs. As described at the beginning of this chapter, programs typically go through several stages of development and consolidation as they learn how to meet the needs of children in their community, and it is not useful to rush into accreditation before you are ready (Ollhoff & Ollhoff, 1999). However, once a program achieves accreditation status, you can be proud that you are providing a wonderful place for children to grow and develop in the hours they are out of school and away from home. For more information about the COA accreditation process, or to receive accreditation materials, contact:

Council on Accreditation
120 Wall Street, 11th floor
New York, NY 10005
voice: 212-797-3000
fax: 212-797-1428
http://www.coaafterschool.org

Developing and Ensuring Program Quality

This chapter has identified the components of a high-quality school-age program, emphasizing program organization, procedures and policies, and human relationships as the base of a quality triangle, followed by safety, health and nutrition, indoor and outdoor environments, and activities. The following chapters will address each of these components in more detail.

SUMMARY

In response to a pressing need for safe environments for school-age children, many agencies and organizations have established afterschool recreation and enrichment programs. In our enthusiasm for increasing the *quantity* of school-age programs, however, we must not forget the importance of *quality* in those programs. By using a program assessment or accreditation process, program managers, staff, parents, and children can examine and improve components of their programs. Many tools for evaluation and assessment have been developed. The NAA quality-assurance process was developed specifically as an accreditation system for school-age programs. In 2008, the afterschool program-accreditation process was assumed by the Council on Accreditation.

TERMS TO LEARN

accreditation
activities
assessment
child and youth workers
continuous program improvement
endorser
engagement
deferred

human relationships
interaction
prosocial behavior
quality
self-study
stakeholders
standards
validator

REVIEW QUESTIONS

1. What outcomes have been associated with high-quality school-age programs?

2. Distinguish between *assessment* and *accreditation*.

3. Why is it important to continually review the components of a school-age program?

4. What distinguishes a self-study from the process of accreditation?

5. Describe the three functions of the accreditation process.

CHALLENGE EXERCISES

1. Inquire in your community to see if any of the school-age programs have completed a self-study assessment process. Meet with the director to discuss the process and its outcomes. Summarize and share with the class.
2. Describe the characteristics of a program that demonstrates a high quality of human relationships. Compare your description to your observation notes from site visits made to school-age programs in your community. Discuss.

ONLINE RESOURCES

Boys and Girls Club Project Learn:
http://www.nydic.org/nydic/programming/newideas/documents/ PROJECTLEARN.pdf

Council on Accreditation:
http://www.coaafterschool.org/

National AfterSchool Association accredited sites:
http://naaweb.yourmembership.com/

National Association for the Education of Young Children accreditation:
http://www.naeyc.org/academy/

REFERENCES

America After 3 PM. (2004). *Working families and afterschool.* Washington, DC: Afterschool Alliance.

American Camping Association. (2007). *Enhancing the importance of the camp experience.* Martinsville, IN: Author.

Bodilly, S., & Beckett, M. K. (2005). *Making out of school time matter: Evidence for an action agenda*. Santa Monica, CA: Rand Education and Rand Labor and Population.

California Department of Education. (1996). *School-age care in California*. Sacramento: Child Development Division.

Cooper, C. R., Denner, J., & Lopez, E. M. (1999). Cultural brokers: Helping Latino children on pathways toward success. *Future of Children, 9*, 81–95.

Council on Accreditation. (2008, May 7). *Afterschool program initiative*. New York: Author.

Forum for Youth Investment. (2003). *Quality counts: Forum focus*. Washington, DC: Impact Strategies.

Granger, R. C., Durlak, J., Yohalem, N., & Reisner, E. (2007). *Improving after-school quality* (Working paper). New York: William T. Grant Foundation.

Halpern, R. (2006). *Confronting the big lie: The need to reframe expectations of afterschool programs*. New York: Erikson Institute for Graduate Study in Child Development.

Maslow, A. (1970). *Motivation and personality* (2nd ed.). New York: Harper & Row.

Metz, R. A., Goldsmith, J., & Arbreton, A. J. A. (2008). *Putting it all together: Guiding principles for quality after-school programs serving preteens*. Philadelphia: Private/Public Ventures.

Miller, B. M. (1995). *Out-of-school time: Effects on learning in the primary grades*. Wellesley, MA: Center for Research on Women, National Institute on Out-of-School Time.

National AfterSchool Association. (1998). *NAA standards for quality school-age care*. Boston: Author.

National Institute on Out-of-School Time. (2007). The afterschool program assessment system (APAS). Boston: Wellesley Center for Women, Wellesley College.

Northwest Regional Educational Laboratory. (2003). *Out-of-School Time Program evaluation*. Portland, OR: NREL.

Northwest Regional Educational Laboratory. (1999). *After school programs: Good for kids, good for communities*. Portland, OR: NREL.

O'Connor, S., Harms, T., Cryer, D., & Wheeler, K. (1991). *Advancing School-Age Child Care Quality (ASQ) program observation instrument and questions for the director*. Wellesley, MA: National Institute on Out-Of-School Time-Age Care.

Ollhoff, L. (2002). *School-age planner: A guide to planning for children and youth during out-of-school time*. Eden Prairie, MN: Sparrow Media Group.

Ollhoff, L., & Ollhoff, J. (1999). *The generations of school-age child care*. Paper presented at the National School Age Care Conference, April 1999, San Antonio, TX.

Rosenthal, R., & Vandell, D. L. (1996). Quality of care at school-aged child-care programs: Regulatable features, observed experiences, child perspectives, and parent perspectives. *Child Development, 67*(5), 11.

Schinke, S. P., Cole, K. C., & Moulin, S. R. (1998). *Thirty-month data and process findings: Evaluation of educational enhancement program of Boys & Girls Clubs of America*. New York: Columbia University School of Social Work.

Seligson, M., & Stahl, P. (2003). *Bringing yourself to work*. New York: Teachers College Press.

Seppanen, P., Love, J., deVries, D., Bernstein, L., Seligson, M., Marx, F., & Kisker, E. A. (1993). *National study of before- and after-school programs (Final report)*. Portsmouth, NH: RMC Research Corporation.

Viadero, D. (2007). High-quality after-school programs tied to test-score gains. *Education Week, 27*(13), 1–13.

Yohalem, N., & Wilson-Ahlstrom, A. (2007). *Measuring youth program quality: A guide to assessment tools*. Washington, DC: The Forum for Youth Investment.

Youcha, G. (2005). *Minding the children: Child care in America from colonial times to the present*. Cambridge, MA: DeCapo Press.

Chapter

4

What Does It Take to Work with School-Age Children?

It takes a whole village to raise a child.
—AFRICAN PROVERB

In the course of a single day, most school-age children come in contact with many different adults. After leaving home in the morning, they may pass neighbors and businesspeople on their way to a bus or train; they may be driven to school in a neighborhood car pool or slip into a friend's house or apartment before walking to school together.

Once at school, in addition to teachers, children encounter many other people who take important roles in their lives—custodians, librarians, attendance clerks, the school secretary, librarian and/or the nurse, perhaps the principal, yard duty supervisors, cafeteria staff, buildings and groundskeepers, and classroom aides or volunteers. After school, if they do not attend a formal program, youngsters may stop for a snack at the convenience store, look at magazines at the supermarket, or play video games before heading home, exchanging conversation with some of the adults they encounter.

Each of these people plays an important role in the socialization of the children they meet and helps them learn to develop relationships with adults. Some have greater influence than others, but everyone is important. Children greatly benefit from these interactions with adults in a variety of settings. I spent many afterschool moments talking to the ice-cream man, or to Mrs. Mayer, who ran a 1950s version of a neighborhood convenience store. Some of my friends took music lessons after school and told their piano or saxophone teachers about the events of their day. My youngest daughter shared confidences with an approachable soccer coach who transported her from her afterschool program to practice twice a week. Research suggests that every youngster needs to receive emotional support from at least three non-parent adults. Communities that provide young people with sustained adult relationships report that their youngsters exhibit

"We need to make sure that no boy or girl in America is growing up without having in his or her life the presence of responsible, caring adults. Where else does a child learn how to behave? Where else does a child learn the experiences of the past, the totems and traditions of the past? Where else does a child look for the proper examples except from responsible, caring, loving adults in his or her life?"

—America's Promise founding chairman, General Colin L. Powell, at 2009 NAA/NAESP Conference, New Orleans, Louisiana

fewer negative behaviors and more positive social skills, responsible values, and positive identity than children in communities that do not provide that social asset (Search Institute, 2003).

So how do afterschool staff members fit into this picture? Before- and after-school programs complement the structured school day that most children experience, and are an ideal setting in which to provide these positive adult relationships. Often, due to their varied roles, adults outside of school have more time and opportunity to respond to children's emotional needs than do classroom teachers.

PEOPLE WHO WORK WITH SCHOOL-AGE CHILDREN

People who work with school-age children come to their positions with many different backgrounds and experience. There are a variety of pathways that lead one to become a skilled professional, someone who can provide children with a nurturing adult relationship. While many people complete a specific college course of study specifically designed for child and youth workers, some do not. The following sections will provide you with several examples of career paths and will highlight some of the ways in which a variety of child and youth workers have prepared themselves for the position they have today.

Afterschool Program Leader

Maria works at an afterschool program on an elementary school campus, where she leads enrichment and recreational activities and helps children with their homework and school projects. After high school, Maria attended a community college, planning to transfer to the nearby state university. Meanwhile, she satisfied a service learning requirement by tutoring elementary school children after school. She enjoyed working with children so much that, before transferring, she completed a 2-year certificate in school-age child care and applied for a position working in the same school where she had been tutoring. She was required to show proof of 2 years of college and 1 year working with children and had to submit to a health screening and a background check.

Now that she is settled into her job, Maria has returned to the community college at night to complete the remainder of the courses needed for transfer. Her goal after completing a bachelor's degree is to run an afterschool program. The director of the program where she works hopes to retire in a few years, and Maria plans to apply for his position when it becomes available.

Afterschool Inclusion Aide

After obtaining the required certification through a year-long course at a regional training center, Lucy spent 10 years working part-time in a Montessori preschool. She enjoyed being with the children and truly believed in the Montessori educational philosophy. When her own two children entered elementary school, she began thinking of working full-time. Just then, the director of the Montessori school expanded into elementary education and enrolled 15 children between 6 and 10 years of age. Lucy applied to teach in the new program. During her interview, the director said that she had noticed several courses in psychology and special education on Lucy's college transcripts. She offered Lucy a position as an inclusion aide.

Lucy's role is to assist children with developmental delays integrate into the school day. Most of her time is spent much like it was in the preschool program—setting out arts-and-crafts projects, supervising children as they select prepared materials from their customary locations around the classroom, and leading small groups in lessons, music, arts and crafts, and outdoor play. However, she primarily focuses specifically on two children in the program who need special assistance to develop small-muscle and eye/hand coordination and to manage their behavior. She does this using positive reinforcement strategies and techniques. Lucy monitors all of the children in her care during class activities, outdoor playtime, and lunch, but her main focus is always on her two special charges. Her support allows them to participate more fully with other children (see the account of Jeremy Orr in Perspective 4.1, it addresses the importance of intentionality when interviewing for a position in an afterschool program). Lucy quickly learned that school-aged children, even children with developmental or physical challenges, are quite different from preschoolers. The years she spent working with preschoolers has provided a good foundation for her new role, but every week she learns something new.

PERSPECTIVE 4.1

The Americans With Disabilities Act 10th Anniversary

Faces of the ADA: Jeremy Orr

For several months, 9-year-old Jeremy Orr had been attending an afterschool program at a KinderCare center in California, when suddenly his parents were told that, in 30 days, he would no longer be able to attend the program because his disabilities prevented him from participating in activities in the same manner as the other children in his program. Like any other kid, Jeremy enjoys his friends, computer games, Halloween costume parties, and field trips. Because he has multiple disabilities, including developmental disabilities, low vision, and a mild seizure disorder, he needs some extra help. When KinderCare refused to let Jeremy attend their program even with an aide paid for with state funds, Jeremy's parents filed an ADA lawsuit. The Department of Justice filed an amicus brief supporting Jeremy. The case was settled, and KinderCare changed its policy. Jeremy remained in the afterschool program, with his aide, with the friends he had made. His mother, Sherry Johnson, summarized: "The benefit Jeremy received at KinderCare was that he was treated like other children. He was included in the holiday parties and field trips like the annual Halloween costume party—he was a Power Ranger and Batman. Jeremy attended the field trips and participated in other children's parties at the center and even got invited to a few parties outside of the center.

"As a parent, the biggest benefit I received was in the day-to-day observation of his inclusion and acceptance by other children during the time he attended the center. Whether it was the time he came to the table to join some younger children in a coloring project and one girl remarked, 'Where is his walking chair?' or whether it was sitting behind the boys playing computer games and their suggestion that it was his turn to play, Jeremy was their friend and part of their day-to-day activities.

"During Jeremy's graduation from KinderCare, I proudly watched all the cool boys sit with Jeremy. I know Jeremy has made an impact on the children in his community because when we go to the store or public events or when he is attending public school, some child will yell out, 'Hey, Jeremy! How are you?' I usually don't know or recognize the child, but it's enough for me to know that they know Jeremy."

Source: Used with permission from the U.S. Department of Justice/Civil Rights Division.

Classroom Aide

When her daughter, Sita, entered kindergarten, Rashmi volunteered to work in her classroom on Fun Fridays. Sita's kindergarten teacher planned arts-and-crafts activities and a cooking project each week and depended on parent volunteers to help carry them out. After a year of working in the classroom, Rashmi began working as a classroom aide at a different elementary school. Now she helps children with their reading and math projects while the teachers take small groups of children for oral reading. Some years earlier, Rashmi had nearly completed a college degree in business administration, so she met the new federal standards for the position, and she passed the basic skills test easily.

Community Volunteer

Ever since moving away from home, Luke has been volunteering at a homeless shelter several evenings a week; his girlfriend, Chibi, helps out in the tutoring program offered for children whose families live at the shelter. Both young adults grew up in communities where gangs claimed many of their school friends, and they are trying to keep that from happening in the town where they hope to raise their own family. The youngsters who spend time here "aren't used to trusting adults," explains Luke. "At first they figure there's something in it for us, even though they don't know what it is. After a while, when they get to knowing us better, I think they get that we actually care about them."

❀　　*Consider This:*　　❀

What do a community volunteer and a classroom aide have in common? What skills do they need to work successfully with the youngsters in their programs?

Chibi agrees. "Yes," she says, "these kids appreciate having us here. You just have to understand that they can't really show it, because that's not cool." Luke and Chibi have not yet completed their formal education, and they haven't found their career path just yet. However, the experience they are gaining working with homeless youngsters can be directly transferred to many other kinds of work with children and youth, and is valuable **social capital**.

Service Club Leader

Marco is a YMCA staff member. For many years he volunteered as an activity leader, accompanying his own two sons to camp and Y-Guide meetings and attending many training workshops and classes. And, he is quick to add, those trainings included far more than how to collect dues, lead crafts activities, and plan field trips. The trainers also provided valuable insights into children's capability and skills at different ages and outlined safety precautions to take with children of different ages. While still a volunteer, Marco also completed two sessions of conflict-resolution training, which help him understand some of the nuances of interpersonal relationships between children and other children and between children and adults. Last year, Marco sold his tax accounting business and went to work at the YMCA afterschool program full-time. He works with children from 5 to 12 years of age, leading games and helping the youngsters plan long-term projects, such as plays, a vegetable garden, or community service projects.

Jorge, Marco's adult son, agrees that on-the-job training can be very helpful. "I've worked at the Boys and Girls Club for 2 years now, but at first I wasn't sure I wanted to work with kids after all." Jorge had taken psychology classes in college but still didn't know how to handle it when the kids argued with one another or were rude to their parents or the other adults in the program. He found it frustrating when youngsters didn't show up as they had promised—for instance, when other kids were counting on them to make up a team. Or they would forget they had volunteered to bring snacks for a field trip or special ingredients for something the group was planning to cook. The Boys and Girls Club holds monthly training sessions for volunteers, as well as frequent staff meetings, and they helped Jorge stay with it. Now, he reports, "I think I'm finally beginning to understand the kids and develop good relationships with them."

Family Child Care Provider

Gloria has cared for other people's children in her home since she was a new bride 14 years ago. At first she took only babies and toddlers and asked parents to find a new place for them when they entered preschool. But then her own two children were born, and when they entered preschool and kindergarten she encouraged parents to leave their older children in her care so her own children would have friends to play with after school.

Now her licensed family child care home has 12 children ages 2 to 11 years. "I took some child development classes when I first started doing child care, but they only talked about children under 5. This older kid thing about 'I won't be your friend if you don't let me play with your truck' really began to get to me. They always seemed to be fighting! So I went back to the community college last year when a friend told me they had special courses for people who work with school-age children. I've learned a lot now about developmental stages of children from 6 to 12, and I've even brought home some good ideas for activities."

School-Age Program Site Supervisor

When Scott's wife died, their three children were 5, 7, and 12. They attended two different schools, and there were no home-based family child care providers near their home who could arrange to pick them up from school and care for them. "I wished desperately then that there was someplace near the elementary school where the two youngest children could go," he remembers. "Instead, they walked home together and their sister took care of them when she got home from junior high. I hated it and lived in fear that something bad would happen before I got there."

Today, Scott, an elementary school principal, supervises a before- and after-school program on the grounds of the school where his youngest children once attended. "Our program receives funds from the district to lease a portable classroom, and a local resource and referral agency wrote a proposal to fund the day-to-day operation of the center. Some parents pay full cost and others a sliding fee. It's hard to believe that the school district didn't do this earlier, but now children in our neighborhood have a safe place to go to after school. We have a wonderful staff with a wide variety of ages, gender, culture, education, and experience, so the children have an interesting place to come after school, a home away from home where they can get help with homework and school projects, learn to play chess or sew or plant a garden, and make new friends. I'm very proud of what we have created here."

Scott holds a master's degree in supervision and administration and an elementary teaching credential. He thinks formal education is important for after-school staff. He looks for staff with at least 2 years of college and requires program leaders to have a bachelor's degree.

THE COMMON NEED: A KNOWLEDGE OF CHILD DEVELOPMENT

Whatever the reason they came into their situation, each of these adults and young people recognizes the importance of understanding the developmental characteristics of school-age children as well as how to organize and run a program. With that knowledge, you can put children's often-confusing behavior into context and develop activities and experiences that are **developmentally appropriate**, meaningful, and fun.

A common belief is that all you need to work with children is to "like kids." Nothing could be further from the truth. In fact, the people who are most sensitive to the needs of children and who enjoy spending time around them often voice the loudest frustration with the confusing behavior of school-agers. A 2-year-old child throwing a temper tantrum has the charming attribute of being cute, at least at nap time or when he snuggles in your lap for a story. A 9-year-old may not be quite so charming, especially when she is challenging the authority of the adult in charge or calling a 6-year-old disgusting names.

But where can you learn about the **age-specific development** of children? And how do you know what other information you will need? Because so many people enter this career pathway without a clear notion of where they will be working in the future, it is common to be confused about educational requirements and how to attain them. The varied names that are used to describe child and youth workers, and the programs in which they work, don't help either. While much can be learned on the job, many child and youth workers find it helpful to pursue a formal **course of study** at a community college or university. Others rely on targeted training provided by their employer, affiliates of the National AfterSchool Association, or other agency. While many employees come to the field after completing a degree in education or psychology, others begin their educational journey after they start working with children. Here are some possibilities for you to consider:

EDUCATIONAL OPTIONS FOR PEOPLE WHO WANT TO WORK WITH CHILDREN

College and University Certificates and Degrees

Some colleges and universities offer coursework specific to the needs of child and youth workers, including afterschool staff. Perhaps you are reading this textbook because you are taking such a course right now.

Many community colleges have developed **academic programs** specifically for staff at school-age centers and may offer various career certificates or associate's degrees in school-age care, child and youth work, or afterschool education. Figure 4.1 shows a typical course of study for a student wishing to pursue either a transfer degree or certificate in afterschool studies. Others offer related majors that can prepare you for work with school-age children in a wide variety of settings. Online resources to help you locate these institutions include the College Board, which has an excellent "Find a College" Web site; private online directories

PERSPECTIVE 4.2

*Getting Ready for the Job Interview:
A Director's Point of View*

*A Children's Garden Childcare and Learning
Center, Morgan Hill, California*

Jamie R. Smith, Resource Director

What kind of teacher do you believe yourself to be? The first impression a candidate gives a prospective employer communicates personal and professional style, mannerisms, temperament, and knowledge. It also provides an opportunity for the interviewer to determine if there is a match between the philosophy of the program and that of the applicant.

Working with children, youth, and their families is a very personal experience, and it is vital that the teaching philosophy of both the candidate and the program are in partnership. What is your teaching philosophy? Why is it as such, and how did you come to it? Quality school-age programs (accredited or not) should have a written mission statement that you can study and reflect upon before and after your interview. If you are not clear how this mission statement is implemented in the program, prepare some questions to ask. Employment interviews work in both directions; the employer will be interviewing you, but you should also be interviewing the employer.

It is important that you come in to the interview with evidence of who you are as an individual. Employees who feel comfortable in the program environment will enjoy their work and be better able to contribute than those who recognize an ill fit. What assets and qualities do you bring to the position? In which areas do you still want to develop? How do you keep yourself aware of new research, teaching strategies, and legislation? Employers appreciate candidates who are open, honest, and enthusiastic about sharing who they are (and who they are not), what they are still learning, and where their strengths lie.

Employers also want to know that the children will be cared for by people who understand the importance of physical and emotional safety at all times. What does physical and emotional safety look like to you? What is your role in developing a sense of community, an environment that minimizes physical conflicts and emotional putdowns? Programs need strong leaders who can create opportunities for social collaboration in afterschool settings that can have a positive compounding effect on the greater community.

Take a careful look at who you are as a person, and as a teacher. Reflect upon what it was like to be a child. When you were a child, who did you feel listened to you? How did the adults in your life speak to you? Did you feel empowered and respected by some adults? Were your ideas heard? If so, were you offered avenues to implement those ideas?

If your ideas went unheard, or you did not feel respected or empowered, can you remember how that felt? Did you persist in your efforts to be understood and listened to, or did you give up? As you ask yourself these questions, take time and reflect about those childhood experiences. It can be helpful (and sometimes emotionally painful) to put yourself back to that point in your life in order to assist you in honing your abilities in working with children.

As you continue to develop your philosophical outlook on teaching and working with school-age children, and prepare to apply for a position, consider these factors. Even after you have been working for a while, it is also important to reflect on these things. What you contribute today will probably have important effects beyond tomorrow, or next week, or even next month. Make every moment and interaction count, so that children know that they have a place in this world, and a voice, and that both are valued.

Source: Used with permission of A Children's Garden Childcare and Learning Center.

Child Development Program Requirements Course Checklist
2009-2010

_Afterschool Degree Track (Program Code AAS_C216)_
*denotes general courses for transfer program

General Courses (28 hours)

____	ENG 101	English Composition I	3
____	ENG 102	English Composition II	3
____		**MTH Elective** (100 or 116 or higher level math) (*MTH 110 for transfer)	3
____	SPH 107	Fundamentals of Public Speaking	3
____	PSY 200	General Psychology	3
____		**Humanities and Fine Arts Elective:** _Art Humanities, Religion, Theater Arts, Philosophy, Literature, Music, Foreign Language_	3
____		**Lab Science Elective:** (*BIO 101 recommended for transfer) _Astronomy, Biology, Chemistry, Physical Science, Physics_	4
____		**Computer Elective** (*CIS 146 recommended for transfer prerequisite)	3
____		**General Elective** (*BIO 102, History or Literature recommended for transfer)	<u>3</u>
		General Credit Hours	28

Major Courses (36 hours)

____	CHD 230	Introduction to Afterschool Programs	3
____	CHD 201	Child Growth and Development	3
____	CHD 202	Creative Experiences for Teaching Children	3
____	CHD 203	Children's Literature and Language Development	3
____	CHD 204	Methods and Materials for Teaching Children	3
____	CHD 231	Afterschool Programming	3
____	CHD 206	Children's Health and Safety	3
____	CHD 210	Educating Exceptional Young Children	3
____	CHD 214	Families and Communities	3
____	CHD 215	Supervised Practical Experience	3
____	RER 250	Introduction to Recreation	3
____	RER 257	Recreational Leadership	<u>3</u>
		Major Credit Hours	36
		Total Credit Hours	**64**

_Afterschool Certificate (Program Code STC_C216)_
(all certificate courses are part of the degree program, too)

____	ENG 101	English Composition I	3
____		**MTH Elective** (100 or 116 or higher level math) (*MTH 110 for transfer)	3
____	CHD 230	Introduction to Afterschool Programs	3
____	CHD 201	Child Growth and Development	3
____	CHD 202	Creative Experiences for Young Children	3
____	CHD 203	Children's Literature and Language Development	3
____	CHD 204	Methods and Materials for Teaching Children	3
____	CHD 206	Children's Health and Safety	3
____	RER 250	Introduction to Recreation	<u>3</u>
		Total Credit Hours	**27**

FIGURE 4.1   A typical course of study for an afterschool A.S. Degree.

Source: Jefferson State Community College Child Development Program Requirements Course Checklist 2009–2010, www.jeffstateonline.com/childdevelopment/PDFs/checklistAfterschool.pdf.

such as A2ZColleges.com; and state-specific Web sites that detail transfer agreements between community colleges and universities within the state (two examples are ASSIST in California and the Minnesota State Colleges and Universities transfer site, both listed in the Internet Resources section at the end of the chapter). For the widest range of majors to choose from, select "Education" at the beginning of your search, then follow the various career options to a major you like.

Credentials and State-Issued Certificates

Several states have developed **credentials** specifically for afterschool professionals. In Connecticut, the Credential in After School Education is a certification program that establishes educational and experiential competency standards for specialists in the care and education of children ages 5–15 outside of school hours. The Wisconsin School-Age Credential is administered by the Wisconsin After School Association in partnership with several Wisconsin colleges. Other credentials include the California Child Development Teacher Permit with a School-Age Emphasis and the Vermont Afterschool Program Director Credential. Other states are in the process of developing credential programs. The U.S. Department of Health and Human Services Administration for Children and Families maintains a registry of such credentials; for current information, consult their Web site (see Internet Resources at the end of the chapter).

Professional Development

There are many organizations and affiliates that offer workshops, short courses, and intensive training for the people who are already employed working with school-age children. A representative sample of them is introduced here, and others are listed at the end of the chapter.

The Partnership for After School Education (PASE) is a child-focused organization serving young people from underserved communities. PASE sponsors and publicizes trainings in the New York area on its Web site.

Foundations, Inc., conducts professional development workshops for afterschool staff, and they have recently expanded their activities from training providers to follow a written curriculum to developing staff skills more broadly in the contexts of their own program goals and objectives. Their Web site is listed in the Internet Resources section at the end of this chapter.

Most states have a professional organization for practitioners in school-age settings. If they are formally affiliated with the National AfterSchool Association, they will be listed on the NAA Web site, which is listed at the end of this chapter. State affiliates generally hold at least one conference a year, and regional affiliates may offer smaller workshops even more often. Joining NAA and your local affiliate will allow you to receive mailings and online reminders about professional development opportunities in your areas.

The American Camp Association offers conferences and professional development opportunities all over the country. Their Web site lists such workshops as the Professional Development Portfolio, Environmental Awareness, and Basic Camp Director course. They work closely with other organizations, such as the National Collaboration for Youth and the Forum for Youth Investment, to provide support and education for child and youth workers in a wide variety of work settings. By participating in **professional development**, adults in school-age programs are better able to create innovative, effective programs for young people.

ARE YOU A GOOD FIT AS A LEADER IN SCHOOL-AGE SETTINGS?

Many people who work successfully with children demonstrate certain identifiable characteristics. Reviewing them can guide you in your personal development and reassure you that your goal of working with school-age children is achievable. These characteristics can be divided into two major components: (1) personality, temperament, and disposition and (2) competencies, or skills and knowledge.

Personality, Temperaments, and Dispositions

A classic staff development publication advised program directors to hire "people who truly enjoy interacting with this age group, and who can serve as positive role models for children" (Bellm, 1990, p. 1). The author explained that while it was also important to understand the developmental needs of school-agers and how to meet their needs, activity leaders should bring energy, flexibility, and a sense of humor to the job. To be truly effective, they need to develop a positive style of guidance and discipline with children and show an ability to work well with other adults—both co-teachers and parents.

Bellm was primarily describing **personality characteristics**. The following sections address each of these valuable attributes.

Truly Enjoy Interacting With School-Agers   School-age children demand a high level of interaction with their adult companions. Younger youth workers may find interaction easier than older staff members, simply because the age differences between them and the children are smaller. However, many wonderful friendships have developed between 9-year-olds and their adult mentors. The trick seems to be the adult's self-confidence and ability to be comfortable with the young people.

If you have ever ridden with a busload of children traveling to summer camp or on a ski trip, sat in the same booth with them in a fast-food restaurant, or sung silly songs all the way home from the beach, and actually enjoyed yourself, then you are probably on the right career path. Ask yourself if you would ever spend time with 6-year-old children for *fun;* if not, how can you be sure you will enjoy doing it just because someone offers to pay you?

Observe a group of children visiting the local zoo, or museum, or other educational or recreational spot in your community. Now, observe the adults accompanying the children. Some of them probably look harried, tired, or out of sorts. Others are animated, engaging in conversations with the children about what they are seeing. For you to be successful working with school-age children, you must be like the second group of leaders more often than the first. Adults who lose patience with children's normal behavior, or whose energy level flags after a few hours, have more difficulty managing groups of children. Just like adults, children who sense you don't enjoy being around them won't enjoy being around you either. Adults may have learned to mask their emotions, or to simply avoid people who don't like them, but children—especially children who are required to remain in the same place with you for long periods of time—tend to be less tactful and may even go out of their way to irk you if they think it might make things more interesting.

A few things can help the inexperienced child and youth worker to enjoy working with school-age children. One is to try remembering your own childhood and replay feelings you had about experiences and people. Journal writing, group discussion, or role-playing are often helpful. Another important tool for enjoying children at any age is understanding what is normal for their developmental stage and what you can do to encourage movement to the next one.

Serve as Positive Role Models What often comes to mind when this characteristic is mentioned are impeccable morals and examples of good citizenship, such as not smoking, drinking, or swearing around the children. However, two of the most important examples youth workers can provide for youngsters are dispositions for cooperation and models of problem solving. **Dispositions** are personality traits such as integrity, persistence, creativity, and enthusiasm. Children who see adults working out their differences learn the same techniques for personal interaction. When they watch you repair a broken game, children learn economy and patience; as you share with them your plans for the future, they may begin to develop their own dreams. Other important behaviors to model include a propensity for lifelong learning, good eating habits, and regular participation in physical activities. Habits are also learned through modeling. When children see you recycle a bottle or turn off an unneeded light, the children learn that behavior. Likewise, when they see you throw a glass or plastic container into the trash instead of recycling it, they may well follow suit in the future.

Working with children is a way to build foundations for the future. Very young children require caregivers who provide consistent nurturing in order to develop trust; toddlers need adults who allow them to develop independence and autonomy. School-age children are trying out different personalities and demeanors as they search to find ones that fit them best (Erikson, 1993). The adults around them—at home, at school, on television, and in movies—provide the **models** for this experimentation. The more dynamic the models, the more likely the children are to emulate them long enough for the values they represent to become habits. It's a very big responsibility to be a role model, but very worthwhile.

Basic Understanding of the Developmental Needs of School-Agers and How to Meet Them Some years ago I visited an amusement park with my children. While waiting for them to return from a ride, I watched a group of school-age children interacting with their adult leaders. They were apparently on a class trip, about 25 fifth graders who obviously knew one another quite well and were in high spirits upon arriving near the long-awaited scary ride. Their teacher was cheerful and enthusiastic, but when she accompanied a group of girls to the restroom, she left the rest of her class in the charge of one of the other adults traveling with them. Immediately the tone of the group changed. "Everyone get in line," the woman said loudly, her large straw hat flapping as she waved her arms. "I want you to be ready to move as soon as your teacher gets back." The response was underwhelming: A few children came toward the woman, but most continued their talking, joking, and people-watching. One child quipped, "The lady in the big yellow hat lost her Curious George."

"Hurry up, or I'll leave you here while we go on the ride!" was the reply. Now the youngsters began to pay attention, and to grumble. "Who made her the boss?" was heard from within the ranks. "Who said that?" she demanded. "We're not moving until I hear an apology." No one answered. It was during this stalemate, which lasted another 5 minutes, that the teacher returned. "Who's ready to go on the ride?" she asked upon approaching the group. Waving hands signified that most of the children were interested and ready, but once again a few did not respond.

The teacher walked closer to two of the youngsters without hands up. "What would *you* like to do?" she asked. There were several ideas—buy a drink, go to the gift shop, wait somewhere in the shade. These were clearly children who did not want to go on the ride with the others. In short order, the teacher divided them into small clusters with an adult for each and left for the ride with the rest. "Last one in line has to load the suitcases," the teacher called as she broke into a trot. In contrast, the woman in the yellow hat could be heard calling, "Don't run . . . wait for me . . . you won't be able to go to the gift shop if you don't mind what I am saying!"

What was happening here? Clearly, the woman barking out commands was *not* comfortable working with 10-year-old children. She felt out of control and tried to impose order with commands and threats. Forcing an apology, or any other singling out of an individual child, can hinder relationships by reducing the children's level of trust and comfort. The children's teacher, on the other hand, felt comfortable enough with the children to suspend her authority over them and give them reasonable choices, even to play with them. That kind of confidence and enjoyment takes a while to develop, but understanding development and its influence on behavior is a big part of it.

When a 10-year-old child wisecracks, he is performing for his peers, not necessarily challenging authority. And even when mid-aged children *do* challenge authority, they do it in order to build themselves up, not necessarily to tear down the one they are challenging. The confident adult understands this and provides opportunities for children to grow into leadership rather than trying to squelch their budding confidence. School-age children, especially from ages 7 to 11, are trying to learn how to act like older people in authentic roles while struggling with the fear that they don't know what to do (psychologist Erik Erikson called this period a conflict between **industry vs. inferiority**). This is as true of children with disabilities and those who are learning English, as with all other children.

Erikson and the adult who understands children's need to master the world around them would encourage us to offer children lots of chances to make choices and decisions. The opportunity to do that, especially in situations where a wrong decision may be inconvenient or uncomfortable but not disastrous, provides valuable information for the growing child and enhances his confidence with future dilemmas (Erikson, 1993). In addition, confident children are usually much easier to get along with than children who feel they must always be challenging authority in order to stretch their wings.

Energy   Even adults who enjoy spending time with children may be short on energy if they are overworked, short on sleep, or in less than optimum health. Since energy is one of the most important ingredients in a working relationship with active children, child and youth workers should revitalize themselves when they can, taking a bike ride after work, for example, or listening to relaxing music and reading an enjoyable book. A well-balanced diet, regular exercise, and sufficient sleep go a long way toward creating energy. Each individual will need to develop a suitable schedule of work, study, and play that allows for sufficient vigor to make it through several intense hours of interaction with children each day. If all else fails, take vitamins!

Flexibility   Flexibility, however, does not come in a vitamin bottle. Flexibility means the ability to see more than one way to accomplish a task and the willingness to change the order of events or even abandon your plans if they don't seem to be working. The children in one afterschool program decided to stencil and paint murals on classroom windows during the pre-Christmas season. The adult in charge helped a planning group come to agreement about the choices of designs and colors of paints, who would draw the stencils, and who would paint the windows. Three creative fifth and sixth graders were assigned by their peers to sketch the large stencils on butcher paper; third and fourth graders were given the task of mixing paints and taking orders from the teachers. First and second graders would sponge-paint the lower portions of the windows, and third, fourth, fifth, and sixth graders would paint with brushes around the edges of the stencils and stand on step stools to sponge-paint the upper portions of the pictures.

Once the painting began, several children decided they were really not interested in doing this after all. One second grader became quite upset that she was not allowed to use a brush; she didn't want to use only a sponge. In the interest of fairness, the youth leader at first insisted that everyone should participate in the project and that the second-grader should use the sponge like everyone else her age. The children balked; she insisted, and they eventually complied. However, after thinking it over later that evening, he decided to try presenting the problem to the children who had set up the division of labor in the first place.

The next day, the leader presented the problem to the children as one both of fairness and of matching skills to tasks. The second-grade girl was thought of by her classmates as an artist, and they believed she deserved this exception. When they learned this, the older children didn't mind at all letting her use a brush. In fact, one of them suggested that she also be given a chance to draw a stencil. An unexpected outcome of the group meeting was that the children who were no longer interested in the project were freed from participating. There were plenty of hands still left to do the work, and the whole process went much more smoothly now that willing painters were painting.

Two important things happened here. In the first place, more children ended up satisfied with the results. A less flexible adult might have insisted on "equality" and "fairness" at the expense of harmony. In addition, by modeling flexibility (but not insisting upon it, which is a kind of inflexibility in itself) the adult leader taught the children a valuable skill: Some rules, even when arrived at thoughtfully, are arbitrary and can be changed.

Sense of Humor   This young man also showed an ability to put his own ego aside and accept the children's decision with a good sense of humor, even poking a little fun at himself for his initial desire to "play fair and hang tough." General Dwight D. Eisenhower (1968), 34th president of the United States and a respected military leader, said, "A sense of humor is part of the art of leadership, of getting along with people, of getting things done." Most of us would rather work with someone who sees humor in life than with a super-serious person who never cracks a smile. However, choosing the humor is another matter. School-age children hear lots of put-downs, snide remarks, and smart-aleck comebacks—especially from other youngsters. Avoid making these types of comments, even if they may seem funny at the time. They do not have a place in your program, because they make us laugh at someone else's expense. Good, nourishing humor enables us to laugh at ourselves for simply being human.

Effective and Positive Style of Guidance and Discipline   No gathering of school-age children will be entirely without problems. It would be naive to assume that if all the adults working with children are energetic, cheerful and flexible, and enjoy being with children, everyone will get along with everyone else all the time. Another important tool in the skills kit of a child and youth worker is a reasonable set of behavioral guidelines and how to implement them. (This topic will be covered in more detail later.) It is important to have a positive outlook on life in general, and on children in particular, if you want to be an effective child or youth worker. A positive attitude enhances your relationships with children and adults and creates a foundation for effective guidance strategies.

Children's relationship with adults help shape their values, morals, and self-perceptions.

Ability to Work Well With Other Adults   Do not overlook the fact that when you work with children you also work with adults. Parents, classroom teachers, and other adults in the afterschool program will each play a part in your daily work. Individuals have different values, different ideas, and different communication styles, and this is bound to show up in daily interactions. In addition, for the first time in history we have four different generations working side by side in many workplaces. It is quite possible that you will find representatives of all of them—veterans (also called traditionalists), baby boomers, Gen X, and Gen Y—working in your program (Hammill, 2005) (more about this in later chapters).

To work effectively with children, you must talk with their families about their collective and individual needs and possible contributions. You will also need to get along with the people who own your building or share their facilities with your program. Parents know what is happening in a child's personal life, and classroom teachers may hold the secret of children's grades, the key to the copy machine, and the availability (or not) of the very space used for your program. Day after day you will be working closely with other adults, trying to understand the behavior of growing children, trying to develop meaningful relationships, and trying to develop valuable skills to work with both children and adults. Each of the people with whom you come in contact have good and bad days; each will need from you the very best you have to offer.

Competencies: Skills and Knowledge

So much for personality characteristics. Now let us examine the skills and knowledge exhibited by people who work successfully with children.

Drawing on research, a guide for parents seeking quality programs stresses the need for children to experience caring, responsive relationships with adults. It advises them to select a program that demonstrates the following practices (National Childcare Accreditation Council, 2008):

❀ Adults in the program seek children's input in decision-making processes, and children's ideas and opinions are valued.

  • "Joe, what art project would you like to try today?"

❀ There is a strong focus on engaging children in meaningful and respectful conversations and interactions with peers and adults.

  • "Let's think about how to organize our garden project. Does anyone have an idea where we might obtain some inexpensive tools?"

❀ Support is provided for children to interact fairly and respectfully with others and to negotiate and resolve issues effectively.

  • "Kirin, I would like to help you and Sasha solve your disagreement. It doesn't appear that you can both use the world globe at the same time without fighting. Why don't the two of you walk to Mr. Carter's classroom and ask if you can borrow another globe from him, just while you finish your homework."

An important role of afterschool staff is to help children learn to resolve conflicts.

❀ Appropriate and effective behavior-guidance strategies give children opportunities to help regulate their own and others' behavior.

- "Bella, I know that you want to play chess today, too, but Kyla can't think with you looking over her shoulder. Please sit where you can still see the board but so that Kyla can have more space. I'll come and sit beside you, and we can try to figure out what strategy she should use next."

These practices incorporate a variety of effective **guidance strategies**. Guidance strategies are most effective when they reflect fairness and respect for children's intelligence, feelings, and ideas, and purpose. Figure 4.2 provides some examples.

A comprehensive set of school-age core competencies was developed by the Minnesota School-Age Care Alliance, in partnership with the Minnesota Professional Development Council and the Minnesota Department of Human Services, and can serve as a guide as you strive to prepare yourself to work with children

FIGURE 4.2   Effective Strategies for Guiding Behavior.

- Listen to children when they speak, and respond with interest and respect.
- Accept and value children's ideas and suggestions.
- Display a sense of humor.
- Respond with understanding to a child who is fearful, shy, upset, hurt, or angry.
- Teach children to be cooperative with one another.
- Promote problem-solving skills and a sense of independence.
- Set reasonable limits for behavior.
- Respond to inappropriate behavior in a fair and consistent way.
- Initiate conversations with the children other than giving instructions, announcements, and commands.

FIGURE 4.3   Minnesota Competencies for School-Age and Youth Care Practitioners.

- Understand how children and youth acquire language and develop physically, cognitively, emotionally, and socially.

- Establish an environment that provides learning experiences to meet each participant's needs, capabilities, and interests.

- Observe and assess what children and youth know and can do in order to provide curriculum and instruction that addresses their developmental and learning needs.

- Establish supportive relationships with children and youth and guide them as individuals and as part of a group.

- Work collaboratively with families and agencies/organizations to meet participants' needs and to encourage the community's involvement with programming for school-age children and youth.

- Establish and maintain an environment that ensures the health, safety, and nourishment of participating children and youth.

- Establish, implement, evaluate, and enhance operation of a school-age or youth care program.

- Serve children and families in a professional manner and participate in the community as a representative of school-age and youth care.

Source: Minnesota School Age Core Competencies (p. 2), by K. Kurz-Riemer, 2005, St. Paul: Minnesota Professional Development Council.

(Kurz-Riemer, 2005). The areas of competency correspond with traditional curricular areas in school-age and youth care programs. Each content area describes the knowledge and skills needed to work effectively with children in the targeted age group. The Minnesota competencies can be used to measure staff skills in a wide variety of settings and programs. A representative list of these competencies can be found in Figure 4.3.

So much for skill sets. But how about a "basic passion for working with children and youth"? Doesn't it matter that you "like kids"? Yes, of course it does. However, it is also important that you understand how it is that adults affect children's lives, what it is that makes school-age children unique in the human development continuum, and why it is important to develop the competencies identified as necessary to succeed in work with school-age children. If you are concerned that you don't know how to do all of these things, relax. Guidance strategies can be learned. You can also learn each of the competencies listed in this chapter. If you value children for their individual differences, respect their language, culture, and personality, and nurture their friendship, they will know that you care about them, and all else will follow.

SUMMARY

The lives of school-age children are affected by many adults, some of whom work with them for several hours a day in a variety of roles. School-age children interact with adults on the school playground, in organized athletic or recreational programs, and in drop-in youth centers. Others attend before- and afterschool care programs in family child care homes or child care centers. It is important for child and youth workers, if they are to be successful, to understand the basics of child growth and development and the unique characteristics of school-age children. It is also important that students considering a career working with school-age children evaluate their aptitude for this work and develop a set of dispositions and competencies that will allow them to succeed.

TERMS TO LEARN

academic programs
age-specific development
course of study
credentials
developmentally appropriate
dispositions

guidance strategies
industry vs. inferiority
models
personality characteristics
professional development
social capital

REVIEW QUESTIONS

1. Referring to the scenarios presented in this chapter, describe some similarities and differences in the responsibilities of adults in each of the following settings:

   a.   Classroom aide working inside a regular classroom or on a field trip

   b.   Group leader in an afterschool program at an elementary school

   c.   Recreational specialist at a drop-in youth center

   d.   A special-needs inclusion aide

2. In what ways do you think early childhood development courses prepare someone to work with school-age children? In what ways might that training be limited or inadequate?

3. What kind of problems and challenges might an athletic coach face with members of his team that are similar to those encountered by Scout leaders or summer camp counselors? What *different* kinds of problems might they face?

4. List four characteristics of child and youth workers that you think you have.

CHALLENGE EXERCISES

1. Identify two individuals in your community who work at least occasionally with school-age children. Prepare a set of questions to ask about how they came to be doing this work, what kind of training or education they have had, and what they like best or least about their work. Interview both people, and summarize your findings.
2. If you kept a journal or diary as a child, dig it out and review some of the passages. Note feelings, attitudes, and emotions. Summarize an event, identifying those characteristics. If you do not have a written source to draw on, try to recall a major event from your childhood—for instance, going away to camp, getting a new puppy, the birth of a sibling, or moving to a new home. Summarize the event as described above.
3. Research the educational requirements for professionals in school-age settings in your state. Do those requirements apply only to child care centers, or do they also include family child care homes, before- and afterschool homework programs, or recreational activities?
4. Find out what the afterschool options are for children in your community. How many different places can they go after school where they will be safe and supervised by adults? Who runs them? Visit one and report back to the class.

INTERNET RESOURCES

American Camp Association:
   http://www.acacamps.org/

Americans With Disabilities Act (Jeremy Orr's story):
http://www.ada.gov/fjerorr.htm

ASSIST (Articulation System Stimulating Interinstitutional Student Transfer):
http://www2.assist.org/exploring-majors/Welcome.do

Center for Afterschool Education:
http://www.caceafterschool.org/

College Board "Find a College":
http://www.collegeboard.com/csearch/majors_careers/profiles/majors/13.1210.html

Forum for Youth Investment:
http://www.forumforyouthinvestment.org

Foundations, Inc.:
http://www.foundationsinc.org/

Minnesota School-Age Core Competencies:
http://www.mnaeyc-mnsaca.org/

Minnesota State Colleges and Universities transfer site:
http://www.mnscu.edu/students/admissions/transfer.html

National AfterSchool Association:
www.naaweb.org

National Collaboration for Youth:
http://www.connectforkids.org/

New York State School Age Care Credential:
www.afterschoolworksny.org

Palm Beach County Core Competencies for afterschool practitioners:
http://www.primetimepbc.org/profdev_core.asp

Partnership for After School Education:
http://www.pasesetter.com/

U.S. Department of Health and Human Services Administration for Children and Families Credential Registry:
http://nccic.acf.hhs.gov/afterschool/results.php?category=15&state

Wisconsin After School Association:
http://waaweb.org

REFERENCES

Bellm, D. (1990). *Staff issues: Training, retention and recruiting.* San Francisco: California School Age Consortium.

Eisenhower, D. D. (1968). Some thoughts on the presidency. *Readers' Digest.* Retrieved April 10, 2010, from http://www.quotationspage.com/quotes/Dwight_D._Eisenhower

Erikson, E. H. (1993). *Childhood and society* (Reissue ed.). New York: Norton. (Original work published in 1963)

Hammill, G. (2005, Winter/Spring). Mixing and managing four generations of employees. *FDU.* Retrieved April 10, 2010, from http://www.fdu.edu/newspubs/magazine/05ws/generations.htm

Kurz-Riemer, K. (2005). *Minnesota school age core competencies.* St. Paul: Minnesota Professional Development Council.

National Childcare Accreditation Council. (2008). *Quality child care for school age children: A NCAC factsheet for families.* Surry Hills, New South Wales: Australian Government.

Search Institute. (2003). *Coming into their own: How developmental assets promote positive growth in middle childhood.* Washington, DC: Author.

Chapter
5

Theories of Child Development

Understanding child development theory can help child and youth practitioners understand children and design more effective and interesting programs. It's helpful, for example, to know that 10-year-olds are more likely to enjoy a rollerblading derby than 6-year-olds or that certain craft activities enjoyed by most kindergartners may be too simple for third graders. In the same way, understanding that there are distinct developmental stages of friendship can help you understand the dynamics of children's relationships and communicate more effectively with children who are having difficulty getting along with others. And with the media bringing visual images of world events into family homes, the application of cognitive development theory can help you respond to children's fears and concerns in a way that reflects their perceptions and ways of thinking about danger.

WHY DO WE HAVE THEORIES OF DEVELOPMENT?

The study of children is a scientific endeavor. In the nineteenth century, scientists such as Charles Darwin and G. Stanley Hall began studying child development, thinking it might support their views on the evolution of the human species. Hall used questionnaires and interviews to study large numbers of children, and published the first scientific study of child development in 1891 (White, 1992). Soon experts from other disciplines, such as medicine, psychology, biology, and education, were attracted to the inquiry. Each discipline has its own concepts, vocabulary, and theories, and the study of child development was no different. Eventually, the ways in which researchers described and explained the growth, development and behavior of children began to distinguish themselves from one another. Some theories explain the process as an unfolding, following a predetermined schedule of **developmental milestones**. Other theories emphasize the role of the environment and personal experiences in learning. Still others teach that all behavior can be molded, or shaped, by the use of natural and logical consequences or by rewards and punishments.

Characteristics of Theories

Children grow and develop in many different areas, called domains. Theories of development address each of those domains, including physical growth, psychological functioning, and personality; social, emotional, and gender identity; language development; learning; and memory. Some theories incorporate developmental stages into their descriptions, while others view development as a continuous process. To satisfy the scientific criteria of a theory, however, each must accomplish four things:

- ❀ *Guide the collection and interpretation of information.* A well-defined theory can help teachers, parents, and youth leaders observe children and document what they see and then study the collected data and analyze them within a framework of ideas and principles (Lightfoot, Cole, & Cole, 2009). Imagine a child taking home an unsatisfactory report card at the end of a grading period. Parents subscribing to a theory that emphasizes student effort as leading to academic success would direct the child to spend more time on homework in the ensuing term. However, if they used a theory that presents intelligence as being inherited and unchanging, or teaches that acquisition of knowledge is dependent upon physical maturation, they would not necessarily respond in that way.
- ❀ *Explain behavior.* To be useful, a theory of development will help you to explain and sometimes even predict behavior. A satisfactory theory of age-related behavior will allow a youth worker to develop activities for children of different ages, taking into consideration small and large motor skills, logical thinking (or its absence), and attention span.
- ❀ *Have broad applicability.* The most useful theories apply equally to children who are different from one another in culture, socioeconomic status, and gender. An example of a theory that would meet these criteria is one that explains learning as resulting from a combination of hereditary characteristics, experiences, and effort.
- ❀ *Can be tested.* One of the defining characteristics of scientific theory is that it remains **stable** over time (the explanation of behavior doesn't change each week or each month) and that its basic tenets can be tested. A theory that is tested repeatedly by teachers and parents is the notion that children can be encouraged to repeat desirable behavior by rewarding them each time the behavior occurs.

Domains of Development

As mentioned above, researchers tend to divide their analysis of child development into **domains**. Certain theories are most appropriate for understanding the way children develop in one or a combination of these domains:

1. Physical growth and motor development
2. Social and emotional development, including gender and cultural identity
3. Intellectual or cognitive development (memory, language, thinking, and problem solving)
4. Moral development

Although we know that children's development does not occur separately in four different areas, it is easier to understand the theories if we analyze them one at a time. Therefore, this chapter is also organized by domain, beginning with physical growth and development.

PHYSICAL GROWTH AND DEVELOPMENT

Children grow and develop at different rates, and some of the earliest developmentalists were interested in knowing the comparative influence of genetics and environment, known also as **nature vs. nurture**. One of the most influential of these theorists was Arnold Gesell.

Arnold Gesell (1880–1961): Maturation Theory

Best known for books about children's ages and stages bearing his name, Arnold Gesell held doctorates in both psychology and medicine and drew on those disciplines as he studied infant and child mental and behavioral development. He is credited with being the first school psychologist.

Gesell was especially interested in the developmental and behavioral characteristics of children at different age levels, and the wealth of data that he collected, as well as the ongoing interpretation of those data, has been his legacy to us. By encouraging parents to bring their children to the Yale Child Study Center, which he founded in 1911, for **well-baby clinics**, he was able to collect information using then-groundbreaking cinematography about growth and development of specific children for over three decades. Well-baby clinics concern themselves more with healthy infants than with ill ones, and during these visits, Gesell and his staff created tests, measuring procedures, and observation techniques that enabled them to describe children's status in a wide range of growth areas (Thomas, 2004). The research team gathered information about children who came to the clinic up to the age of 10. They also interviewed parents to learn about the children's behavior at home (Gesell, 1940). Colleagues and students continued his work at the Gesell Institute of Child Development, established after his retirement in 1950, and today the institute continues to provide resources for parents and teachers and research data to the field.

Gesell's Growth Gradients   Gesell proposed a development theory with three parts:

1. Development is primarily a result of genetic factors.
2. Each age produces characteristics and behaviors (stages) in a predictable fashion.
3. Alternating periods of equilibrium and disequilibrium result in "stable" and "chaotic" half-year periods in a child's family interaction.

Heavily influenced by contemporary thought, Gesell reluctantly acknowledged the role of environmental factors but as lesser influences, thus interpreting the data in terms of an unfolding organic calendar. His presentation of the material is therefore often called the **maturational theory**.

Using the Maturational Theory

Generations of parents and teachers have found Gesell's growth gradients or schedules helpful as they seek to understand child behavior. Parenting books published by the Gesell Institute remain popular after four decades. Table 5.1

TABLE 5.1 Gesell's Growth Gradients, Part I.

5 years	6 years	7 years	8 years	9 years
Control over large muscles is more advanced than control over fine ones. Likes to climb fences and go from one thing to another. Can skip. Attempts to roller skate, jump rope, and walk on stilts. Likes to march to music. Wants to hold adult's hands when unsure of self, as when descending stairs.	Very active; in almost constant motion. Activity is sometimes clumsy as he overdoes and falls in a tumble. Body is in active balance as he swings, plays active games with singing, or skips to music. Balls are bounced and tossed and sometimes even caught. Enjoys walking and balancing on fences. Has trouble choosing between two alternatives.	Shows more caution in many gross motor activities. Repeats activity persistently. There is a great desire for a bicycle, though is only ready to handle it within limits. Beginning to be interested in group sports. Girls may have a desire for dancing lessons. Fears stimulated by TV and reading.	Bodily movement is more rhythmical and graceful. Now aware of posture in self and others. Likes to play follow the leader. Learning to play soccer and baseball with a softball and enjoys the shifts of activity within the game. Goes out to meet the world but often overestimates own ability in meeting new challenges.	Works and plays hard. Apt to do one thing until exhausted, such as riding bicycle, running, hiking, skating, or playing ball. Interest in own strength and in lifting things. Boys like to wrestle and may be interested in boxing lessons. Great interest in team games and in learning to perform skillfully. Increasingly self-sufficient.

TABLE 5.1 Gesell's Growth Gradients, Part II.

10 years	11 years	12 years	13 years	14 years
Prefers to be active and loves the outdoors. Poised and congenial. Girls show signs of approaching adolescence during this year or the next. Even poor eaters are eating more than they used to. Both girls and boys seem positively to dislike washing, especially their faces. Love old clothes. Some fears from past may reappear. Great interest in "smutty" jokes.	Egocentric and energetic. Always on the go—eating, talking, moving about. Slow to respond and quick to criticize. Has trouble sitting still for long periods. Fiddles with things in hands; when standing, shifts from one leg to other. Needs lots of physical activity, yet also fatigues easily. Increased need for sleep. Most girls are growing quickly. Does not like to be alone.	Energy levels beginning to calm down. More capable of organizing their energy. Enthusiastic about things they like, especially sports. Occasional periods of extreme fatigue and bad temper. Rapid growth in height for girls. Appetites vary, but most children are hungry by midmorning and again after school even with adequate meals. Clothes are starting to matter.	Withdrawn, physically as well as emotionally. May actually seem unfriendly. Needs privacy to brood and think about all the changes taking place. Appetite calming down. Likes to be involved in lots of things. Responsibility for chores increasing, as skills develop. Unexplainable tears occasionally happen, usually behind a closed door. Rapid growth in height for boys.	Boundless energy, optimistic enthusiasm, and goodwill. Enjoy their friends and extracurricular activities, usually far more than school. Intellectual confidence in most cases. Generally criticizes parents and family freely and often. More outgoing, more straightforward, less on the defensive than earlier. Trying to find their own way, decide what paths are best.

Sources: Selected and adapted from *Your Ten- to Fourteen-Year-Old*, by L. B. Ames, F. L. Ilg, and S. M. Baker, Copyright © 1988 by Dr. Louise Bates Ames, Sidney M. Baker, Gesell Institute of Human Development, Tordes Isselhart, Carol Haber (for the Estate of Joan Ames Chase) and the Estate of Frances L. Ilg. Used by permission of Dell Publishing, a division of Random House, Inc.; and *The Child From Five to Ten* (Revised ed.), by A. Gesell, F. L. Ilg, and L. B. Ames, 1977, New York: Harper & Row.

outlines some of the age-graded characteristics of school-age children observed by Gesell's research staff. The characteristics represent experiences common to children of Gesell's time; long-awaited updated growth gradients will be released by the Gesell Institute in 2010. However, other than some inaccuracies resulting from the recent inclusion of girls into competitive sports, and the introduction of bicycles with training wheels for younger children, they are remarkably accurate, even now. Remember, though, that every child develops on a unique schedule, and some developmental milestones may also appear earlier or later in different individuals and cultural groups.

SOCIAL–EMOTIONAL DEVELOPMENT

Children develop the knowledge to function effectively within their own culture through the two-part process that includes personality development and socialization. Learning to recognize emotions in themselves and others, understanding the social interactions taking place at home and in school or child care, and matching their behavior to the situation are three ways in which children demonstrate their development in this domain. Erik Erikson, Robert Havighurst, and Urie Bronfenbrenner have provided us with a rich vocabulary, concepts, and explanations of the dynamics of this process.

Erik H. Erikson (1902–1994): Psychosocial Theory

Erik Erikson proposed a stage theory of development, based loosely on the work of Sigmund Freud (1856–1939), who had been his teacher. Freud was a physician and neurologist who became interested in the role of early experiences in the development of personality. Freud's contributions of concepts such as the **id**, **ego**, and **superego**, **defense mechanisms**, and psychosexual stages from birth to puberty are still taught in general psychology classes, but Erikson's modified (and simplified) theory has more practical application in our work with children. Erikson, who studied the entire human life span, believed that at each stage of development we focus on resolving a conflict between two disparate attitudes. Four key differences set his theory apart from Freud's:

- ❀ Erikson observed healthy personalities rather than patients seeking help.
- ❀ His explanation of development recognized that individuals could revisit earlier stages and resolve any unfinished conflicts.
- ❀ He presented a series of identity crises he believed each person must face.
- ❀ His believed that development is influenced by interactions with other people, including parents and peers.

Erikson's Life Crises   Critics of Freud, both during his lifetime and later, pointed to his work with neurotic personalities as an inadequate foundation for a theory of *normal* personalities. Erikson studied healthy people instead. Like Gesell and Freud, Erikson originally believed that children and adults develop in predetermined ways, determined primarily by genetic code. However, his description of eight life-span stages of normal psychosocial development, and the emotional conflict associated with each, clearly illustrates his belief in the

Erikson built on Freud's psychosexual theory, showing how life events influence children's personalities.

importance of the environment. One way of thinking about this theory is that while individuals work through each "crisis" on a fairly predictable timetable, the circumstances of their lives determine how they interpret each event and its outcome. Each stage builds on the successful completion of earlier stages. Erikson believed that failure to resolve the conflicts of any stage may lead to problems in later life but that these conflicts can be resolved at that time if the individual's life experiences or maturity allows thoughtful analysis of the difficulties.

The first six stages, from birth through adolescence, are described below.

Stage One: Basic Trust vs. Mistrust (Hope), Birth to 18 Months   During the first year of life, children develop their attitudes toward the people and circumstances of their world. Erikson described the eight stages as if each involved two emotions on opposite ends of a seesaw. In the case of **trust vs. mistrust**, for example, a child who experiences inconsistent care or outright neglect is likely to decide that life is not too dependable. This is likely to result in a child who either ceases to interact much with adults (assuming, probably correctly, that they won't meet his or her needs) or learns that acting out is the only way to get any attention. On the other hand, if all the basic needs of this first year are met, and especially if they are met in a caring and loving manner, the child might decide the world is a nice place to live. Thus, children develop either a trusting or a mistrustful outlook on life based on their experiences with it and develop adaptive behaviors to match their conclusions.

Is the result permanent? A common question. Each crisis carries with it the likelihood of a permanent influence. However, there is plenty of evidence—for example, with children removed from abusive homes into caring adoptive families—that much can be done to temper these initially formed attitudes. Children who develop one way of behaving in neglectful or inconsistent surroundings may change their behavior when they discover that the environment of their afterschool program is predictable, caring, and fair.

TABLE 5.2 Comparison of Psychosocial Stages of Development According to Freud and Erikson.

							Years of Life									
	0	1	2	3	4	5	6	7	8	9	10	11	12	13	14	
Freud	Oral		Anal		Phallic			Latency						Genital		
Erikson	Trust vs. mistrust and doubt		Autonomy vs. shame		Initiative vs. guilt			Industry vs. inferiority						Identity vs. role confusion		

Sources: Childhood and Society, by E. H. Erikson, 1993, New York: Norton. (Original work published in 1963); *General Psychological Theory* (8th ed.), by S. Freud, 1974, New York: Collier Books. (Original work published in 1963)

Stage Two: Autonomy vs. Shame and Doubt (Will), 18 Months to 3 Years   **Autonomous** is a good adjective to describe mostly Western 2-year-olds. The stereotypical toddler generally has two favorite expressions: "No!" and "*I* do it!" According to Erikson, this initial try at autonomy can be threatened by overly harsh care giving, especially surrounding the issues of self-care, which typically begins during the second year of life in many American homes. Although the ages at which children enter and leave these stages is approximate, Stage Two is generally considered to occur chronologically at the same time as the stage Freud called the anal period (See Table 5.2).

The way Erikson explained the crisis faced by 2- and 3-year-olds is that they are caught in a double bind. Mastering putting on and taking off articles of clothing is an ongoing challenge, and bowel functions are not yet under their conscious control. Yet, when they attempt these tasks and fail, they are often made to feel ashamed. If children refuse to cooperate in toilet training efforts, they may feel powerful (Freud) or autonomous (Erikson), but either way their self-image suffers when they end up soiled and scolded. Gentle teaching, Erikson cautioned, produces the best results: a confident child, able to control bodily functions and beginning to take care of himself with pride. Cultures that emphasize interdependence over autonomy, such as Japan, may promote the use of close body contact, swift reactions to infant and toddler distress, and avoidance of parent–child separation as a way of fostering security through this stage of development (Eisenberg, 2006).

Stage Three: Initiative vs. Guilt (Purpose), 3 to 5 Years   Adults who work with preschoolers and kindergarteners will witness this crisis playing out. Children of 4 and 5 have learned to build, climb, talk, reason, imagine. *Initiative* is Erikson's term for the process of exploring these new skills. The other side of the conflict is *guilt*, invoked when a creation gets out of hand somehow, perhaps gets broken, spilled, or too loud. The challenge for adults working with Stage Three children is to guide them safely through the exciting stuff without letting it get out of control. Children begin to develop an awareness of appropriate and inappropriate behavior during this period, which is important, but too much criticism or punishment for innocent acts can thwart youthful experimentation.

Stage Four: Industry vs. Inferiority (Competence), 6 to 12 Years   Freud called this period *latency*—a time when he apparently didn't think much was happening. In contrast, Erikson noticed that children between 6 and 12 years of age are not just marking time. Rather, they are tiring with the business of play and want to learn how to do useful things. Stage Four children form attachments to teachers and to parents of their friends, and they play-act doing grown-up work like those people do. Successful development during this period enhances self-esteem and gives children an accurate sense of their ability to work at useful tasks. If things do not work out so well, children's sense of inferiority can cloud their school years and stay with them for a very long while afterward. When you work in school-age programs, you will primarily see children working their way through this stage of development.

Erikson believed that school-age children should have many opportunities to complete tasks that they consider interesting and that the "real world" of adults considers worthy. It is especially helpful for children to work beside adults on the same or similar tasks and for them to receive (gentle) guidance when they hit rough spots. Projects that involve cooking or making things with tools, for example, are very appealing to children 7–9 years of age. (If a way can be found to raise money from the creations, you'll also have the interest of the 10–12-year-olds!) Perspective 5.1 addresses the differences between 5–8 year old children and those between 9 and 12.

Feelings of inferiority may develop in children who rarely succeed at the tasks they set for themselves or those that are set by others. These negative perceptions of self may also occur if most of the things children have learned to do well are considered insignificant by important adults and classmates (Thomas, 2004). You may have children in your program with negative views of their abilities and worth. Your role is to encourage these children to participate in activities where they can succeed, at least occasionally, even with all their self-doubts.

❀ *Consider This:* ❀

What are some activities that children could engage in during afterschool programming that offer a variety of opportunities for success? (For example, planting zucchini squash in a spring vegetable plot.)

Stage Five: Search for Identity vs. Role Confusion (Fidelity), 12 to 18 Years If you have worked with children in sixth grade or above, you know that puberty brings with it a whole range of new and confusing changes, both in youngsters' bodies and in their personalities. Erikson coined the term **identity crisis** to explain what is happening during this period.

This is the time when a child's **persona** seems to change weekly; hairstyle, favorite type of music, and clothing take on entirely new, and very significant, meanings for the young adolescent. Sometimes we say that a youngster *identifies* with a particular character in a movie or book or with a group of people who characterize themselves by dressing or acting in a particular way. This is a reference to Erikson's term and often signals a youth's desire or need to try out several different roles before deciding on the one to be worn for the rest of his or her life.

How we dress, speak, and act has a direct influence on the people around us. How they respond to us tells us important things about ourselves. One of the crucial results of this period is that a young person succeeds in finding a role to

The Middle Years: Piddling, Plundering, and Posturing

Herb Kohl

Everyone interested in starting after-school programs needs to understand who the middle years' child is. This is the perspective of Herb Kohl, author of 36 Children, Growing with Your Children, *and* Growing Minds. *Kohl is a strong advocate of progressive and alternative education and is a keen observer of human nature. He speaks from his experience as a classroom teacher.*

Different children reach maturity in different ways and in different orders of growth. Some speak much more precociously than they walk, while others walk much more confidently than they speak.

In terms of who these kids are, the age spread is so enormous and the needs so diverse until it's best to look at the 5–8 year olds separately from the 9–12 year olds. The 5–8 year olds have their internal needs related to growing, strength, independence and exploration of the world. They're discovering the mastery of the world that surrounds them and the mastery of their local world causes tremendous anxiety for adults. They no longer have to look around for approval. This is a period when fundamental detachments occur and they deal with a real sense of individuation, much of which is culturally determined.

In certain class and cultural settings, kids are given a great deal more freedom. The more freedom that abounds, the earlier the individuation sets in. In many ways, the safety valves of middle class communities often stifle that kind of individuation. In working class communities, necessity often facilitates the independence much earlier.

Another developmental characteristic is the desire for them to have the same power as the adults by whom they are surrounded. You often see it in 5 year olds when they pretend to read. That is a power that most adults have over children. Playing house, making a store, driving a car are also ways of modeling the adult world. A real instinctive use of the body occurs as well and it is during this phase a fairly sophisticated coordination takes place, i.e. running, chasing, throwing or catching a ball.

With the 9–12 year olds, especially the 11 and 12 year olds, sensitivity to and towards peer affection becomes important. Friendship and sexuality become an obsession. The onset of a very self-conscious and acute, almost microscopic, awareness of the body and sexuality emerge. The casual and easy play that exists amongst the younger group becomes complicated by the peer and sexual dynamics. . . .

I'm not so certain that we really understand how far kid's minds can really grow. That's why the fullest humanistic education possible between the ages of 5–8 is essential. Exposing them to numbers learned through manipulation and to the real world will encourage their minds to flow freely from one subject to another: music to math and poetry to physics. They really don't deserve to be drilled or turned into people who hate the development of the mind.

Nine–twelve year olds are fully capable of sophisticated production of work and experimentation within literature and science. They also have the ability to articulate what they are doing. The age of in-depth inquiry is most apparent in the 10, 11 and 12 year olds. That kind of creative inquiry certainly needs to be encouraged. But I feel we're doing the opposite and that is closing down minds instead of opening them up. . . .

Compassion as well as budding political and moral consciousness also begin to play a significant role during the middle years. Unfortunately, institutions are driving people towards the discouragement of their compassions. Schools often destroy its development through teachers humiliating some and overpraising other students. Television and sports function in a similar manner . . .

This is also a time in which kids have to learn to sort out relationships. For one of the more sensitive issues at this point is the relationship between affection and sexuality. Two girls who love the same boy find it hard to like one another. Or two boys become enemies because they have a crush on the same girl. . . .

The fact that they are older means they're often left out of experiences and situations that do continue to nurture them and help them grow. The after-school environment is an important part of those experiences. That environment can often be an oasis in the midst of the desert that school sometimes becomes. Some of the more sensible ways of providing that care would be through activities like music, reading, theater; noncompetitive or judgmental group events should be encouraged as well. The fact must be stressed that we want them to have education as opposed to schooling and nurturing as opposed to care.

Maybe if we put ourselves on notice to the fact that our children are in the process of becoming the people they will ultimately be, we might move differently in terms of fulfilling the needs they really have and not the ones we imagine they have. There is no time when it is more important to demonstrate compassion and hope.

From Kohl, H. (1985). The Middle years: piddling, plundering and posturing. *Children's Advocate*. Used by permission.

play that results in feedback from society that matches his or her own perception of self. In other words, a role that *fits*.

Here is where what has gone before has a powerful influence on what happens next. Erikson said it this way:

> The sense of ego identity, then, is the accrued confidence that one's ability to maintain inner sameness and continuity is matched by the sameness and continuity of one's meaning for others. (Erikson, 1959, p. 89)

In Erikson's view, a child who considers herself to be competent, connected with society, and attractive to others will feel most comfortable playing a role that reflects those characteristics. If, on the other hand, the child has learned to believe that he is a "troublemaker," "lazy," "no good," etc., he will be more likely to take on a demeanor that consistently brings those messages from people around him and, sadly, reinforces the negative self-perception developed during an earlier stage. Understanding this process can help you to interrupt the cycle, avoiding over-reacting to this week or this month's hairstyle or fashion statement and, when possible, even providing some gentle feedback to youngsters that will help them behave or dress in a way that will result in desirable responses from the world around them. But be aware that older school-agers may consider this to be "selling out." A lively discussion can continue for months on this topic.

Stage Six: Intimacy vs. Isolation (Love), 20 to 34 Years   Even before we have resolved our identity crisis, most of us notice a sexual attraction to others. The ages attached to this stage are 20 to 34, but many youth workers see adolescents who are trying to work through Stages Five and Six simultaneously, so it is included here. Erikson believed that only after we have established a clear identity are we ready to make long-term commitments to others. That is when we become capable of forming intimate, reciprocal relationships and more or less willingly make the sacrifices and compromises that such relationships require. The other side of this crisis is that if we are not eventually able to negotiate an intimate relationship, perhaps due to our own unresolved issues or perhaps just due to circumstances, we may feel isolated from society. Not a good thing.

The final two stages, generativity vs. stagnation (care) and ego integrity vs. despair (wisdom), are outside the scope of school-age work and will not be discussed here. For more information about Erikson's theory and an interesting analysis of it, read Dr. George Boeree's review, listed in the Internet Resources at the end of this chapter.

Robert Havighurst (1900–1991): Developmental Tasks

Coined by the Progressive Education Association in the 1930s, the term **developmental task** is usually attributed to Robert J. Havighurst, who popularized it in the 1940s and 1950s. Developmental tasks are those challenges a child must meet in order to successfully move through infancy and childhood into adulthood:

> A developmental task is a task which arises at or about a certain period in the life of the individual, successful achievement of which leads to his happiness and to success with later tasks, while failure leads to unhappiness in the individual, disapproval by society, and difficulty with later tasks. (Havighurst, 1953, p. 2)

While Havighurst identified five stages of development in 10 categories of behavior, in its simplest form the developmental task theory integrates well with Erikson's eight life crises. For example, the attainment of certain tasks in infancy (such as *establishing oneself as a dependent being* or *learning to adjust to others' expectations*) can serve as signals that the goal of basic trust vs. basic mistrust is being achieved.

Examples of developmental tasks of 5-to-7-year-old children (initiative vs. guilt, industry vs. inferiority) could include *becoming independent from a primary identification with adults, learning to fit in with peer groups, developing fine muscle coordination,* and *learning more realistic ways of observing and controlling physical objects.* Table 5.3 shows some of the developmental tasks Havighurst believed important during the school years.

One advantage of afterschool programs is that, unlike regular classrooms, children at different stages of physical, cognitive, and social development can play and work together.

TABLE 5.3 Some Developmental Tasks of Childhood.

	Early Childhood (2–3 to 5–7)	Late Childhood (5–7 to Pubescence)	Early Adolescence (Pubescence to Puberty)
I. Achieving appropriate dependence–independence pattern	Adjusting to less attention; becoming independent physically	Freeing oneself from primary identification with adults	Beginning to establish independence from adults in all behavior areas
II. Achieving appropriate giving–receiving pattern of affection	Developing ability to give affection; learning to share affection	Learning to give as much love as one receives; forming friendships with peers	Accepting oneself as worthwhile person, worthy of love
III. Relating to changing social groups	Beginning to develop ability to interact with age-mates; adjusting to family expectations for child as member of the social unit	Clarifying adult world vs. child's world; establishing peer grouping and learning to belong	Behaving according to shifting peer code
IV. Developing a conscience	Developing ability to take directions, to be obedient in presence of authority; developing ability to be obedient in absence of authority	Learning more rules; developing true morality	
V. Learning one's psycho–socio–biological sex role	Learning to identify with adult male and female roles	Beginning to identify with same-sex social contemporaries	
VI. Accepting and adjusting to a changing body	Adjusting to expectations based on improving muscular abilities; developing sex modesty		Reorganizing self-concept in the face of significant bodily changes; accepting one's appearance
VII. Managing a changing body and learning new motor patterns	Developing large muscle control; learning to coordinate large and small muscles	Improving skill in use of small muscles	Controlling and using "new" body
VIII. Learning to understand and control the physical world	Meeting adult restrictions on exploration and manipulation of expanding environment	Learning more realistic ways of studying and controlling physical world	
IX. Developing an appropriate symbol system and conceptual abilities	Improving one's use of the symbol system; great elaboration of concept pattern	Learning to use language to exchange ideas or to influence; beginning to understand casual relationships; making finer conceptual distinctions; thinking reflectively	Using language to express and clarify more complex concepts; moving from the concrete to the abstract; applying general principles to the particular
X. Relating oneself to the cosmos	Developing a rudimentary notion of one's place in the cosmos	Developing a scientific approach	

Source: Adapted from R. M. Thomas, *Comparing Theories of Child Development, 6e.* (c) 2005 Wadsworth, a part of Cengage Learning, Inc. Reproduced by permission. www.cengage.com/permissions.

While the exact nature and timing of these developmental tasks are influenced by culture and life circumstances, an awareness of the tasks themselves can be very helpful to people working with children of different ages. The developmental task model can be used to help you (a) recognize the nature of children's tasks at each age level, (b) provide opportunities for them to practice the tasks, (c) be patient with their attempts, and (d) furnish information and training necessary to promote their success (Thomas, 2004).

Using Social–Emotional Theories

Understanding theories of development can help child and youth workers as they structure play and enrichment activities, schedule staff, and interact with children. You can expect to see children forming friendships and growing in self-confidence during these years. They are also learning to use language in more complex ways, although sometimes they may appreciate your help in negotiating interpersonal relationships with peers, teachers, and even parents. For example, as children begin to understand that rules, especially those associated with games and group activities, can be changed, you can help guide them through the process of developing their own rules for homework time, a cooking activity, or even board games.

COGNITIVE DEVELOPMENT

As children's brains grow in size and complexity, and as they absorb and learn to use information, development is taking place in the cognitive domain. In this arena, children learn how to think, solve problems, talk, remember information, and use symbols. Jean Piaget suggested that children think differently than adults and proposed a stage theory to explain how that thinking comes about. He was the first modern theorist to note that children play an active role in developing their own knowledge. As a result, his theory is often termed *constructivist*.

Jean Piaget (1896–1980): Constructivist

Piaget's work has heavily influenced psychology and education, and with good reason. His interpretation of children's intellectual growth stages provided a vocabulary and a framework for understanding much that goes on inside children's heads. He was generally known as a constructivist, believing that children construct their own understanding of the world as they reflect on their experiences. Each time we have a new experience, we generate a **mental model** containing rules or explanations that we use to make sense of what happened. Learning, in Piaget's view, is the process of adjusting mental models to accommodate new experiences.

For child and youth professionals, Piaget's most important contribution may be the observation that many children do not begin to overcome perceptions with logic until around the age of 7 and that most children are unable to work effectively with hypothetical situations until even later.

Piagetian Stages of Cognitive Development   Piaget identified four stages of cognitive development: **sensorimotor**, **preoperational**, **concrete operational**,

TABLE 5.4   Piaget's Stages of Cognitive Development.

Approximate Ages	Stage	Characteristics
Birth to 18 months	Sensorimotor	Babies depend on motor actions and senses to provide information. They begin to use simple symbols, such as pretend play and single words, toward the end of this stage.
18 months to 6 years	Preoperational	By age 2, children can use symbols to think and communicate. While they tend to centrate on one attribute of an object, by the end of this stage they can begin to take others' point of view, classify objects, and use simple logic.
6 to 12	Concrete operational	Children can now think logically, at least about concrete and familiar objects. They can also consider more than one characteristic of an object at once. By the end of this period children can conserve liquid, matter, and number and ponder simple "what if?" questions.
12+	Formal operational	Youngsters can now operate in a truly logical environment. They can think hypothetically, organize ideas, and solve problems systematically.

and **formal operational**. Each period is characterized by a different way of thinking and knowing, and every child passes through each stage in the same order (see Table 5.4). However, as we know from observation, cognitive development is not always **continuous**. Attainment of a stage can seem sudden, and it can also be incomplete. Although most children in school-age programs will be in concrete operations, not all will be, so it is helpful to understand the types of thinking that characterize earlier stages.

Sensorimotor   In the beginning of postnatal life, babies depend on their senses to provide all of their knowledge. Sometimes infants lose interest in objects and people when they are moved away from them. Things are experienced by sight, sound, or touch, so when a 4-month-old accidentally pushes a rolling toy under the couch and can no longer mouth it or see it, the object appears to no longer exist for her.

Somewhere around the end of the second year, children begin to think symbolically, which we know because they search for objects that have disappeared (recognition of object permanence) or imitate actions that they saw on the previous day, and they "pretend." This signals the beginning of preoperational thought.

Preoperational   Children in this stage do not think logically, and they are **egocentric**, which means not only that they believe the world turns around them, the literal meaning of the term, but also that it is pretty much impossible for them to consider another person's perspective, either physically (determining which is the right hand of a person facing them, for example) or emotionally. An egocentric child will frequently select a birthday present for a friend (or a parent) using the criterion "I'd like one." It is nearly pointless to ask a preoperational child "How do you think Billy feels when you hit him?" because the child cannot yet imagine being in another's mental or emotional state. He can only tell you how he feels, which is why a common response to this question is "angry" or, sometimes, "sorry."

Because young children are trying very hard to understand their world, the limitations on their thinking processes at this age can cause them to oversimplify categories, making them appear quite stereotypical. As children move from simple sorting of people and things into social categories (clothing styles, gender roles, race, age) and into more complex understanding of social roles and behaviors, these stereotypes are gradually modified. That is one of the positive results of experiencing the world outside the constraints of family and neighborhood that happens in school-age programs, and it suggests a role for child and youth workers to offer challenges to oversimplified categories of ideas whenever they occur.

Concrete Operational   By the time children are 6 or 7 years of age, most are operating at least part of the time in **concrete operational** thought. The significance of this step is that they can now think logically, at least about concrete and familiar things. While in earlier stages of cognitive development a child would **centrate** on one attribute of an object (such as its color, its shape, its purpose) and find it difficult to consider other attributes at the same time, now it is possible to think about more than one characteristic at once.

The most commonly published example of centration is the **conservation of liquid** task, in which a child is asked to decide whether a container of water that is tall and narrow holds the same amount as one that is short and wide. Even after being shown that they both hold the same amount of liquid, preoperational children will insist that the tall one holds more because it is thin (or sometimes that the short one holds more "because it is fat").

By comparison, a child who is a concrete operational thinker will think, "If the water can be poured from one to the other with no spilling and no space left over, they must both hold the same amount." The same kind of **precausal thinking** appears in dividing cookies of different sizes, cutting sandwiches into several pieces, and understanding that the number of objects remains the same when they are rearranged. These examples demonstrate conservation of matter and conservation of number. Understanding the limitations of preoperational thought can help group leaders mediate a disagreement between two children at different levels of development—for example, between a kindergartner and a second grader.

Formal Operational   Children who exhibit **formal operational thinking**, which appears from about age 10 to about age 15, are no longer constrained to thinking about what they have experienced directly. They can deal with physical impossibilities ("imagine that this car ran on milk . . .") in order to consider plausible possibilities. This allows the study of higher mathematics, physics, the solution of social and political problems, and the enjoyment of arguing for the sake of experiencing the logical argument process. This can make working with older children a real treat if you understand what is going on. However, for adults with poor self-esteem, or who do not understand the developmental tasks at hand (using language to express and clarify more complex concepts, moving from the concrete to the abstract, applying general principles to the particular), it can be quite challenging.

While developmental psychologists today question some of the specific details of Piaget's theory, there is no doubt that he has caused us to think about childhood in a different way than was done in the past. He created a new

TABLE 5.5 Assimilation and Accommodation in School-Age Children.

Concept	Assimilation: applying preexisting knowledge to a new situation.	Accommodation: changing an action or belief in response to the environment.
Naming objects	Calling a camel a horse. The child knows what a horse is but when first encountering a camel assimilates the shape and size of a camel into her schema for a horse.	After being corrected by someone, the child accommodates new information by noticing the different properties of a camel compared to a horse, perhaps calling a camel a horse with bumps. When she eventually learns and uses the name camel, she has accommodated this information.
Making assumptions	Saying that girls can't run as fast as boys. The child may have heard this somewhere or may just believe it because they've never seen girls run fast.	Following an Olympics Day at school, the same child remarks, "Well, *some* girls can't run as fast as *some* boys!" Now he recognizes that running skills are individual and not necessarily gender related.
Analyzing the difficulty of a task	Estimating that her math homework will take only 20 minutes because that is what it usually takes.	After completing three problems, reevaluating the task and estimating that this time it will take closer to an hour.

vocabulary and a new respect for children's thought. His description of how children acquire knowledge is a good example of this.

To explain the process, he used two terms, **assimilation** and **accommodation**. When faced with new information, a child either ignores it or assimilates it into his existing worldview. You might think of assimilation much like picking up a pine cone or other object and placing it on a shelf or in a drawer of your mind. If, however, the information is at odds with the existing understanding (or doesn't fit on the shelf or in the drawer), the child either (a) rejects it or (b) accommodates to it—in other words, changes his existing perception to adapt to the information (builds a new shelf or finds a larger drawer).

When a child learns to spell a list of words, each new word is assimilated, or added to each of the words that came before it. Imagine, however, that the child comes to a word that he thinks he already knows how to spell and use but discovers that he doesn't. A good example, one that often confuses even college students, relates to the homophones *accept* and *except*. If the child has been using these two words interchangeably, understanding the two different meanings but believing them to be spelled the same, he is liable to stop for a moment to ponder this new information when he learns it. Assuming he trusts the word list from which he is working, he will change his **schema** (another Piagetian word), or mental model, of either the word that is pronounced *ek-sept* or the word that is pronounced *ak-sept*). This is accommodation. We don't always accommodate new information quickly. Sometimes the process is painful. (Remember algebra?) See Table 5.5 for other examples.

Lev Vygotsky (1896–1934): Sociocultural Theory of Cognition

Lev Vygotsky was a young literature teacher who began studying developmental psychology following the Russian Revolution near the close of World War I. He taught and wrote that the social and cultural context in which the child grew up and learned was the critical factor to intellectual development. The major theme of his theoretical framework is that social interaction and cultural context play fundamental roles in the development of thinking and problem solving.

Although Vygotsky's work was not widely studied in the United States until recently, he has had a strong following in Europe since 1962, when his text *Thought and Language* was translated into English. Two concepts that emerged from his observations are especially useful for people working with school-age children: the zone of proximal development and scaffolding (Vygotsky, 1962, 1963, 1978).

The **zone of proximal development** captures the range of difficulty with which a child can learn a new task or concept. Within this zone, Vygotsky explained, the task or concept is difficult, but not too difficult. Often, the child needs a little help to understand the concept or master the task. This assistance, which usually comes from a helping adult, is called **scaffolding**. Educators use scaffolding all the time, by asking pointed questions such as "How do you think you could write that a different way?" or sounding out the beginning of a word but not the end, and suggesting two words that a third word might be found between on a dictionary page.

The important message that Vygotsky has to teach us is that there is a strong relationship between social experience and cognitive development, and the adults and more able peers in the child's relationship can help to connect new knowledge to prior knowledge and abilities and increase the youngster's motivation to learn. Current educational practices such as **reciprocal teaching** and **guided instruction** are effective strategies that implement Vygotsky's theory.

Howard Gardner (1943–): Theory of Multiple Intelligences

Gardner reframed the concept of intelligence itself. In 1983, the Harvard professor published *Frames of Mind*, outlining the notion that there are at least seven separate human capacities, or "intelligences." In 1999, Gardner added two more. According to Gardner, human beings have nine different kinds of intelligence that reflect different ways of interacting with the world. Although we each have all nine intelligences, no two individuals have them in the same configuration.

For Gardner (1999), intelligence is the following:

❀ The ability to create an effective product or offer a service that is valued in a culture
❀ A set of skills that make it possible for a person to solve problems in life
❀ The potential for finding or creating solutions for problems, which involves gathering new knowledge

Figure 5.1 illustrates each of these nine intelligences with symbols that depict activities and materials that encourage their exploration.

A compelling idea to educators, Gardner's theory presents a strong case for multisensory education at all ages and brings into question the single-strand

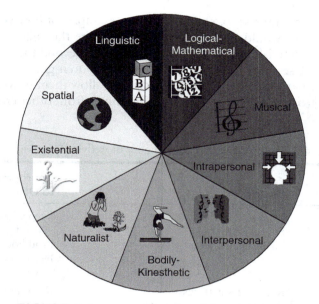

FIGURE 5.1 Howard Gardner's Theory of Multiple Intelligences.

Source: Based on Gardner, H. (1999). *Intelligence Reframed: Multiple Intelligences for the 21st Century.* New York, NY: Basic Books.

assessment that has been in place since the first intelligence tests were introduced to the public schools in the early 1950s. Gardner's view of intelligence explains not only how children learn best but also why different cultures might value different forms of intelligence differently.

Most people would agree that 21st-century airline pilots need to have strong logical–mathematical intelligence to fly modern jets. However, Gardner explains that if he were in an outrigger canoe in the middle of the Pacific Ocean without navigational instruments, he would hope to have a guide with well-developed *spatial* intelligence. That way the guide could find his way home by using constellations. Gardner uses this illustration in lectures to explain why one type of intelligence is more highly valued in some cultures than it is in others.

A list of Gardner's multiple intelligences is presented in Table 5.6, along with activities aligned with each intelligence. By guiding children toward a variety of activities, they can begin to understand—and you can, too—which of their intelligences is the best vehicle for learning. This information can be included in your activity planning, and it can also lead to children building an accurate self-concept.

Using Theories of Cognitive Development

You can use cognitive development theory to guide you as you work with children in a variety of ways. Creating an environment that provides opportunity for independent and collaborative discovery learning and paying attention to the developing interests of children are two examples of how you can do this. Vygotsky's theory would encourage you to challenge the children's abilities but not to present material or information that is too far beyond their current level of understanding. Use concrete experiences to help children grasp concepts needed for their homework or other school projects, and allow them to work in groups if they wish to, in order to get experience seeing things from other children's perspective.

TABLE 5.6 Using Multiple Intelligences Theory in Activity Planning.

Intelligence	Description	Appropriate Activities, Materials to Offer

Verbal/Linguistic	Likes to talk, listen
	Enjoys writing
	Likes rhymes, jokes
		Keep a journal, write a newspaper, do
		  word games
		Read books, magazines; write poetry, stories
		Debate hot topics; do crossword puzzles;
		  work with computers

Logical/
  Mathematical
	Recognizes patterns
	Works with abstract symbols
	Solves problems
		Keep stats for games; diagrams, charts,
		  graphs
		Checkers, chess, backgammon
		Measure things, do science experiments
		Run a math lab for younger children

Visual/Spatial	Likes color and design Describes scenes Likes to build things	Match nail polish color with fabric swatches Build castles/forts with cardboard cartons Make a wheat-paste topographic map, 3-D art
Bodily/Kinesthetic	Likes physical games Takes things apart and fixes them Good at sports Might play instrument	Relay races, sprints, hide-and-seek, sports Sandpaper numbers/letters for new readers Play-Doh, clay, making jewelry, weaving Dance/gymnastics sessions Rearrange the furniture
Musical/Rhythmic	Enjoys listening to music, playing instruments, possibly also dancing	"Name that Tune," Freeze Dance Simon (musical version of Concentration) Listen to music while doing homework Piano, rhythm instruments
Interpersonal	Works well with others Notices others' feeling High communicator	Group leader for planning session Jeopardy! host, Bingo caller, conflict manager Make phone calls to price food for party
Intrapersonal	Likes quiet corner Tends to play/work alone Thoughtful	Journal, earphones, lots of books Jigsaw puzzles, pen pal project Quiet spot for homework

Naturalistic	Can recognize, categorize, and use
	  features of the environment to
	  distinguish various living things
	  (plants, animals)
	Sensitivity to other features of the natural
	  world (clouds, rock configurations)
		Gardening, cooking, caring for animals,
		  rock climbing, cycling, surfing
		Journal of local wildflowers, temperature
		  changes, weather trends, cloud patterns
		Organize group hikes and neighborhood
		  walks

Existential	Sensitivity and capacity to tackle deep
	  questions about human existence, such
	  as the meaning of life, why we die, and
	  how we got here
		Debate, philosophy, religious studies
		Study great philosophers, work with a
		  spatial child to develop a wall chart or
		  graphic depicting their world views

Children with a strong interpersonal intelligence enjoy doing their homework with their friends, while intrapersonal children may prefer to study alone.

LEARNING THEORY

Learning theorists examine learning both as a product and as a process. Their point of view, in general, is that learning is not inherent but that it results from an accumulation of information and knowledge gained through experience. Learning theory can be used to explain development in all of the domains of development—physical, cognitive, social–emotional, and moral.

B. F. Skinner (1904–1990): Operant Conditioning

Harvard research psychologist B. F. Skinner was for 40 years the best known name in learning theory, also known as behaviorism. His behaviorist approach to the solution of educational, personal adjustment, and social problems resulted in four decades of controversy and notoriety. Teachers and parents, behavioral psychologists, and prison wardens have applied his principles of **operant conditioning** to increase desirable behaviors and decrease less desirable ones, sometimes with excellent results but often with disastrous ones.

At the base of his theory is the principle that a behavior will increase if it is followed by a **reinforcer** and decrease if followed by a **punishment**. Reinforcers can be the occurrence of a pleasurable event (eating an ice cream cone) or the removal of an unpleasant event (a ban on watching television), while punishment is always something that the child perceives as an unpleasant occurrence. The difficulty comes in identifying what is pleasant and what is unpleasant. The most common misconception among adults trying to use these principles is that children do not like to be scolded or singled out in a group. In actual practice, sometimes any attention is better than none, and so the child who is berated for his misbehavior in a particular setting may feel that he has been rewarded (simply by being noticed) and repeat the same behavior in order to receive the "reward" again.

Skinner provided a technique for undoing this problem once it is recognized. By eliminating the reinforcer (basically, ignoring the behavior), the likelihood that the behavior will occur again decreases (after a short period of increase as the child tries repeatedly for the expected reward). Once that decrease begins, the continued refusal on the part of the adult to reinforce it will eventually result in the **extinction** of the undesirable behavior.

Opponents of those who would use behaviorist techniques to modify children's behavior decry the techniques as manipulative and in violation of human rights. Supporters point out that parents and teachers have used these techniques all along; Skinner and others merely observed the process and gave it a vocabulary.

Albert Bandura (1925–): Social Learning Theory

Albert Bandura and his colleagues expanded learning theory to explain how children learn social behaviors. He proposed that most of a child's learning comes from actively copying, or **modeling**, the behavior of others. Reinforcement of behavior still occurs, but sometimes it can be vicarious reinforcement. In other words, if Zeke hears Kyle being rewarded for trying out a new play during football practice, he learns to do the same when he has the opportunity. Bandura (1977) developed three principles for explaining how children learn social behaviors:

1. The highest level of observational learning is achieved by first organizing and rehearsing the modeled behavior symbolically and then enacting it overtly. Coding modeled behavior into words, labels, or images results in better retention than simply observing.
2. Individuals are more likely to adopt a modeled behavior if it results in outcomes they value.
3. Individuals are more likely to adopt a modeled behavior if the model is similar to the observer and has admired status and the behavior has functional value.

Using Learning Theories

One of the more troublesome examples of social learning is television commercials. Commercials suggest that drinking a certain beverage or using a particular shampoo will make us popular and win the admiration of attractive people. Depending on the component processes involved (such as attention or motivation), we may model the behavior shown in the commercial and buy the product being advertised. Skinner felt that the process of learning from modeling occurred *only* in cases where the child was reinforced directly for the new behavior. Later social learning theorists pointed out that children think about what they see, hear, and feel and make decisions about the behaviors they adopt (Gordon & Brown, 2008). However one approaches the argument, understanding the concepts of learning theory can be helpful in understanding children's (and adults') behavior.

MORAL DEVELOPMENT

Moral development is the process through which children develop attitudes and behaviors toward other people in society, based on social and cultural norms, rules, and laws. The theories described above capture the mechanisms by which children learn knowledge, behavior, and skills. The theories that follow explain how children use that knowledge to learn moral reasoning and develop ethical behavior.

Lawrence Kohlberg (1927–1987): Moral Reasoning

A Harvard University professor of psychology and education, Kohlberg focused his doctoral work on the moral reasoning skills of North American boys from age 10 to 16. In this early work, Kohlberg identified a direct relationship between the passage through cognitive stages of thought and the potential for achieving identifiable stages of moral reasoning (Kohlberg, 1984, 1987). However, after recognizing that relationship, he acknowledged that intellectual development alone is not enough to determine moral judgment. A major portion of his theory is devoted to describing and explaining three additional factors (desire, social role taking, and justice structure) that interact with mental maturity to determine the way a child is likely to behave in any given situation.

Kohlberg arrived at his conclusions by presenting children with moral dilemmas. Probably the most famous dilemma is whether it would be acceptable to steal medicine for a loved one if it was impossible to purchase it and the loved one would die without the medicine (Kohlberg, 1969). By presenting children with these quandaries, many of which had no clear solution, he was able to identify the components of decision making and to identify how those components changed with experience and maturity.

Following his observations of 75 young American males struggling with these scenarios and dilemmas over a 10-year period, Kohlberg developed a hierarchy of three moral levels (**preconventional**, **conventional**, and **postconventional**). At the first level (pre-conventional), children base their decisions on a belief that an action is wrong only if it results in punishment. At the second level (conventional), the rules of society become the most important consideration. At the third level (postconventional), decisions are made according to universal principles of justice, even when those principles and public opinion or laws of the nation are in conflict.

While the contrived nature of the questions and the limitations on gender and culture have been acknowledged (Gordon & Brown, 2008), an understanding of Kohlberg's hierarchy can help us realize that children's moral decisions are indicators of a developmental stage process and of local influences and do not necessarily reflect on the inherent "moral fiber" of the child. It is not important exactly what the children decided—whether the husband should steal the drug—but how they come to their decision.

After completing his original set of interviews, Kohlberg came to believe that the levels and stages occurred in a regular sequence and were age related. He concluded that most children under age 9 thought about moral dilemmas in a preconventional way, but by the time they became young adolescents they began to reason in more conventional ways. By early adulthood a small number of people were using postconventional reasoning to sort out moral problems. Most people, according to Kohlberg, never use postconventional reasoning. He later studied children of both sexes from Mexico, Thailand, kibbutz communities in Israel, Malaysia, Turkey, Taiwan, and other areas. Following this research, Kohlberg concluded that the stages of moral development he identified are present in all cultures, but children move through the stages at different ages from one society to another.

Carol Gilligan (1936–): The Ethics of Caring

Harvard psychologist Carol Gilligan criticized Kohlberg's work as being male-value laden. Gilligan was a student and research assistant of Kohlberg's and while working with him came to believe that his theory was limited by its male-centered view. Girls and boys are socialized differently, she pointed out, and consequently develop different codes of morality. A woman's view of ethics "centers around the understanding of responsibility and relationships, just as the [male's] conception of morality as fairness ties moral development to the understanding of rights and rules" (Gilligan, 1993, p. 19).

She believed that differences in moral reasoning between males and females are based primarily on the fact that girls are generally raised by same-gender caregivers (mothers, grandmothers, and nannies, for example), while boys are generally raised by opposite-gendered adults. Gilligan asserted that this leads to differences in personality structure and therefore to different kinds of decision making in moral/ethical matters. Thus the male view of morality is based on **objectivity** (justice) and the female view on **connectivity** (caring). Gilligan suggested that women's responses on Kohlberg's scale were lower than men's not because they were less developed but because their moral thinking was more oriented toward interpersonal relationships.

When Gilligan's theory was first published it was seen by some as merely a feminist reaction to the male-centered personality psychology of Freud, Erikson, and Kohlberg. However, Gilligan's perspective is now an established point of view and one that can be helpful to you as you work with children and youth. In making moral decisions, she asserts, girls and women think more about the "caring" thing to do. Boys and men are more likely to consider the "justice" of the situation, defined by the rules or expectations surrounding the issue. Her earliest view that men and women differ in their moral reasoning has grown into the broader concept that men and women may use both justice and care dimensions in their moral reasoning. Table 5.7 illustrates the three basic stages of moral development postulated by Kohlberg and Gilligan.

TABLE 5.7 A Comparison of Kohlberg and Gilligan.

	Preconventional	Conventional	Postconventional
Lawrence Kohlberg	1. Avoid punishment 2. Gain reward	3. Gain approval and avoid disapproval 4. Duty guilt	5. Agreed-upon rights 6. Personal moral standards
Carol Gilligan	Individual survival	Self-sacrifice is goodness	Principle of nonviolence: Do not hurt others or self

Sources: In a Different Voice: Psychological Theory and Women's Development, by C. Gilligan, 1993, Cambridge, MA: Harvard University Press; and *The Psychology of Moral Development*, by L. Kohlberg, 1984, San Francisco: Harper & Row.

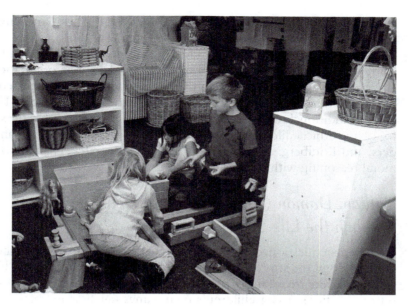

Children develop their moral reasoning by engaging in a reciprocal exchange of ideas with others.

⚘ *Consider This:* ⚘

One of the youngsters at the school where your program is located has posted pictures and information on the Internet that are hurtful to another child at the school. Two children in your program admit they know who did it but don't want to tell you or the principal, who has demanded that the offending party come forward and face disciplinary action. Using your knowledge of Kohlberg and Gilligan, how would you go about talking to the children in your program about this situation?

Nell Noddings (1929–): Caring and Relationship

Stanford researcher Nell Noddings carried Gilligan's ideas a step further with her work on the **cared-for** and the **one caring** (Noddings, 1984, 2002). Her argument for a morality based on natural caring, a femininist view rooted in **receptivity**, **relatedness**, and **responsiveness**, encouraged many schools to realign educational goals so that they more openly encouraged and rewarded sensitivity in moral matters.

In more recent years, Noddings has demonstrated the significance of caring and relationship, both as educational goals and as fundamental aspects of individual growth. Her argument begins with the position that care is basic in human life—that all people want to be cared for (Noddings, 2002). She then explained that **natural caring**, a desire for the feelings that result from the experience or memory of being cared for, and **ethical caring**, a state of being in relation to another person, characterized by receptivity, relatedness, and engrossment, are natural developments from that position (Flinders, 2001).

The work of Gilligan and Noddings has encouraged research by others. One study found that males are quite capable of displaying an orientation toward care and relationships and that, when they do, those boys and men score similarly to girls and women on Kohlberg's hierarchy of moral development (Lightfoot et al., 2009). Additional research revealed that there are more differences in approaches to solving ethical dilemmas between people of diverse cultures than between genders, and Kohlberg's hierarchy is unlikely to accurately characterize the levels of moral reasoning within those cultures.

William Damon (1944–): Moral Development Through the Life Span

Damon also questioned the appropriateness of Kohlberg's hypothetical dilemma methodology for studying young children, but mostly because he thought the questions were irrelevant to most children's experience. He developed a different set of questions, using children's own games (such as marbles) and questioned children's reasons for certain actions that were related to their interests (Damon, 1977, 2008).

Damon also studied the process of change in children's moral reasoning when they had opportunities to discuss ethical dilemmas with an adult or groups of other children (Damon, 1990). He presented various scenarios to the children and devised coding schemes to assess the way in which children presented their arguments and how they responded to the statements of others. He videotaped peer discussions for later analysis and then published the results. This research can help you understand the usefulness of talking with children about moral dilemmas and ethical decision making.

Damon's most useful discovery may have been that children grow and develop in their moral reasoning in a much more complex fashion than had previously been thought. Simple exposure to other people's ideas and opinions, even those of respected adults, are not, in and of themselves, sufficient to determine the kind of ethical decision making in which children will engage. This is great news, especially in light of the declining availability of high moral standards depicted by media, a major contender for children's free time. Damon (1982) concluded that one of the most effective change agents in children's thinking is **reciprocal interaction**. In other words, children exchange ideas with adults and one another in a two-way fashion, "extending, clarifying, or compromising with the other's statements" (p. 365).

Using Theories of Moral Development

Talking with children about real quandaries in their lives and the options available to them can be a very valuable exercise—both to increase your understanding of children's moral thinking and to help the children progress in it. The views of Kohlberg, Gilligan, Noddings, and Damon all have important implications for adults working with school-age children. They provide explanations for differing styles of communication, thinking, and decision making and remind us to be wary of any psychological model that is based on a single worldview.

ECOLOGICAL SYSTEMS THEORY

In its simplest form, the **ecological systems theory** defines four environmental systems, usually depicted as existing in concentric circles surrounding the child, who sits at the center. These four systems, identified with Latin prefixes that describe their position in the model, are the microsystem, mesosystem, exosystem, and macrosystem.

Urie Bronfenbrenner (1917–2005)

Urie Bronfenbrenner's model of childhood socialization, influenced by Vygotsky's sociocultural theory, incorporates all developmental domains and illustrates that human beings develop within the interrelationships of a social context. Even though we know that physical development influences social development, which is influenced in turn by cognitive development, most college instructors teach one domain at a time, using textbooks that also describe one domain at a time. The wonderful thing about Bronfenbrenner's approach to development is that it acknowledges and explains how children are simultaneously and repeatedly influenced by their family and home, school, community, and society. Figure 5.2 shows the four basic components of Bronfenbrenner's model, the microsystem, mesosystem, exosystem, and macrosystem. A fifth component, the chronosystem, refers to events in the child's life that happen over time, and is not pictured in the figure.

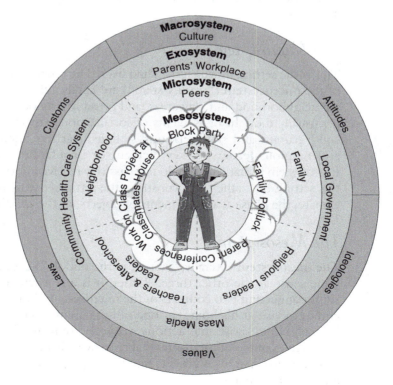

FIGURE 5.2   Bronfenbrenner's Ecological System Model.

Children's earliest socialization comes from their microsystem.

The Microsystem

This is the setting in which the child lives. The contexts usually depicted in models of the **microsystem** ("small system") are family, school or child care, the immediate neighborhood and play areas, and possibly religious settings. Most of the people usually thought of as agents of socialization exist in the microsystem with the child: parents and close relations, siblings, teachers, friends and close neighbors, and religious leaders. A key element of Bronfenbrenner's explanation of the microsystem is that children do not passively receive information and experiences in this setting but rather help construct the settings themselves—e.g., the emotional climate, the physical arrangements of objects, or the child's need for supervision.

The Mesosystem

The **mesosystem** (literally, "system in the middle") is not an actual setting in the same sense as the other three. Rather, it is a construction that reflects relationships connecting two contexts of the microsystem. For example, if a child's friend comes to visit at his home, or one of her parents communicates with her teacher by telephone, those interactions would be reflected in the mesosystem. A less concrete example of the contextual crossover that this system represents is that of a child whose parent is absent, representing rejection, finding it difficult to trust a teacher or other adult.

The Exosystem

The **exosystem** ("outer system") is made up of the wider community in which the child lives and which only indirectly affects development. Settings usually included in the exosystem are extended family, the parents' workplaces, the local economy, mass media, community health systems, legal services, social welfare services, and more distant friends and neighbors. However, since the child does not interact directly with the exosystem, these influences are felt only indirectly, such as when housing prices rise or fall or a parent is laid off from work.

The Macrosystem

The outer layer of Bronfenbrenner's model is the **macrosystem** ("large system"). In this layer reside the attitudes and ideologies, values, laws, and customs of the culture or subculture (or both) in which the child lives. These provide the broad ideological and organizational patterns that influence systems represented by the three inner circles. Macrosystems are not static and may fluctuate during the life of a child as a result of economic upheavals, war, or political or technological change.

Using the Ecological Systems Theory

Because it is a comprehensive model of environmental influences on children's development, the ecological systems theory provides professionals in school-age settings with a practical framework within which to understand children's behavior.

Here is an example of how this can work. During the last 50 years, our industrial-based society evolved first into a service economy and then into to a highly technology-based society and workforce. Most children interact regularly with members of four different generations of people in their microsystem: (1) grandparents or aunts and uncles, (2) parents, teachers, and classroom aides, (3) after school staff, coaches, and tutors, and (4) peers.

Grandparents, aunts, and uncles of school-agers are generally members of the baby boomer generation, born between 1946 and 1964. Most of today's parents and teachers, and some classroom aides, are members of Generation X, born between 1965 and 1980, and afterschool program staff, born between 1980 and 2000, are likely to be Generation Y. Growing up in an industrial-based society, baby boomers have learned to value involvement and commitment. Throughout their lives, they have placed a heavy focus on work and expect their children and grandchildren to do the same. Generation X members are more skeptical of the workplace, as many employers have mismanaged funds and laid off thousands of employees in recent years (Hammill, 2005).

Today's parents and teachers find their solace in fun and informality; they work shorter hours than their parents and worry less about deadlines and "getting ahead." As children begin to spend more time in out-of-school activities, they meet Generation Y: the recreation leaders, coaches, and tutors. Generation Y is realistic and confident; members of this technology-savvy generation stay connected through texting, social networking, and smart phones. Rather than obsessively saving their earnings, a characteristic of previous generations, today's young adults like to shop, driving from mall to mall to find the best deals or buying products online. Many afterschool staff members regularly check e-mail on their cell phones, view video clips on YouTube, monitor Facebook and MySpace for updates, download songs from iTunes, or refer to mapping sites to locate pizza or supplies. Children in afterschool programs see all of this and enjoy hearing about shopping trips, the latest tunes, and YouTube finds from their young leaders.

By using the framework of the ecological systems theory, it is easy to see that through interactions with members of each generation, children learn important lessons about values and behavior. By observing the connections that these individuals have across microsystems, youngsters evaluate the relevance and usefulness of the various messages, which may be in conflict with one another. Inevitably, as members of different generations move into leadership roles within the exosystem, the institutions themselves will change to reflect their values. Within each system, the varying beliefs, values, and behaviors of all the generations represented in today's society will influence the children growing up within it.

SUMMARY

Children grow and develop in a variety of areas—physical, socio-emotional, cognitive, and moral. Psychologists and educators have observed children and formulated theories about the way in which development progresses and some of the contributing factors. Arnold Gesell collected data over a 30-year period and developed guides for parents containing growth gradients and behaviors likely to occur at each age and stage. Psychoanalyst Freud studied his patients, developing a complex theory of personality development. One of his students, Erik Erikson, proposed a revisionist view based on a series of life crises influenced by environmental factors at work during each stage. Havighurst identified developmental tasks mastered at various stages of growth and development. Jean Piaget classified stages of logical thought, which provided a scaffold for Kohlberg's view of moral development. Lev Vygotsky showed how children's thinking and decision making is influenced by their culture and the adults in their lives. Howard Gardner expanded our understanding of children's thinking and the concept of intelligence. Skinner offered a behaviorist approach to the solution of educational, personal adjustment, and social problems. Albert Bandura expanded on that approach to explain how children learn social behaviors. Carol Gilligan proposed a feminist alternative to Kohlberg's theory, and Noddings and Damon identified factors that contribute to optimal growth in moral reasoning. Bronfenbrenner developed a multi-domain model of child development that illustrates the interrelationships between children and their family and home, school, community, and society. Each of these perspectives, or theories, provides frameworks, vocabulary, and explanations for behavior that can be helpful for people working with school-age children.

TERMS TO LEARN

accommodation	autonomous
assimilation	cared-for
autonomy vs. shame and doubt	centrate

concrete operational
connectivity
conservation of liquid
continuous
conventional
defense mechanism
developmental milestones
developmental task
domain
ecological systems theory
ego
egocentric
ethical caring
exosystem
extinction
formal operational thinking
guided instruction
id
identity crisis
identity vs. role confusion
industry vs. inferiority
initiative vs. guilt
intimacy vs. isolation
macrosystem
maturational theory
mental model
mesosystem

microsystem
modeling
natural caring
nature vs. nurture
objectivity
one caring
operant conditioning
persona
postconventional
precausal thinking
preconventional
preoperational
punishment
receptivity
reciprocal interaction
reciprocal teaching
reinforcer
relatedness
responsiveness
scaffolding
schema
sensorimotor
stable
superego
trust vs. mistrust
well-baby clinics
zone of proximal development

REVIEW QUESTIONS

1. What are the four domains of development studied by most theorists?

2. Match each of the following development areas with the correct theorist:

   physical growth and development   Gilligan
   psychosocial development   Erikson
   cognitive development   Gesell
   moral development   Piaget

3. Match the theorist below with the correct phrase:

   Erikson   developmental task
   Havighurst   life crises
   Vygotsky   growth gradients
   Kohlberg   stages of moral judgment
   Gesell   zone of proximal development

4. Explain how the moral development theory of Gilligan differs from that of Kohlberg. How might it affect children's decisions surrounding right and wrong?

5. In what ways does physical development influence social development? How might social development influence children's ability to make friends?

6. One theorist's ideas often influence another. Describe how Kohlberg's ideas about moral development relate to Erikson's life crises. How does cognitive development as described by Piaget relate to Havighurst's developmental tasks?

CHALLENGE EXERCISES

1. Interview three parents of school-aged children. Ask questions about their children's behavior, thinking, and ethical decision making. How closely do these children match the developmental stages presented by the theorists?
2. Interview three children about school, favorite activities, and friendships. What can you say about their moral development from their answers?
3. Design a project to build with a group of school-aged children. Work with them to plan the project, obtain the necessary materials, and construct it. Describe what you observe about their developmental differences as you work together.

INTERNET RESOURCES

Albert Bandura and the Bobo Doll Experiment:
   http://www.criminology.fsu.edu/crimtheory/bandura.htm
Urie Bronfenbrenner:
   http://www.news.cornell.edu/stories/sept05/bronfenbrenner.ssl.html
William Damon:
   http://ed.stanford.edu/suse/faculty/displayRecord.php?suid=wdamon
Erik Erikson:
   http://webspace.ship.edu/cgboer/erikson.html
Howard Gardner:
   http://www.infed.org/thinkers/gardner.htm
Gesell Institute:
   http://www.gesellinstitute.org/history.html
Carol Gilligan:
   http://its.law.nyu.edu/facultyprofiles/profile.cfm?personID=19946
Robert Havighurst:
   http://psychology.wikia.com/wiki/Robert_J._Havighurst
Lawrence Kohlberg:
   http://faculty.plts.edu/gpence/html/kohlberg.htm
Nell Noddings:
   http://www.cambridge.org/uk/catalogue/catalogue.asp?isbn=9780521807630
Jean Piaget:
   http://www.time.com/time/time100/scientist/profile/piaget.html
B. F. Skinner:
   http://www.sos.net/~donclark/hrd/history/skinner.html
Lev Vygotsky:
   http://tip.psychology.org/vygotsky.html

REFERENCES

Ames, L. B., Ilg, F. L., & Baker, S. M. (1989). *Your ten- to fourteen-year-old*. New York: Dell.
Bandura, A. (1977). *Social learning theory*. New York: General Learning Press.
Bumgarner, M. (1993). *Improving the understanding of learning styles in prospective early childhood education teachers through self-study and observation*. Unpublished manuscript.
Damon, W. (1977). *The social world of the child*. San Francisco: Jossey-Bass.
Damon, W. (1990). *The moral child*. New York: The Free Press.

Damon, W. (2008). *The path to purpose: Helping our children find the calling in life.* New York: The Free Press.

Eisenberg, N. (Ed.). (2006). *Handbook of child psychology: Social, emotional, and personality development* (Vol. 3, 6th ed.). Hoboken, NJ: Wiley & Sons.

Erikson, E. H. (1959). *Identity and the life cycle in psychological issues.* New York: International Universities Press.

Erikson, E. H. (1993). *Childhood and society.* New York: Norton. (Original work published in 1963)

Flinders, D. J. (2001). Nel Noddings. In J. A. Palmer (Ed.), *Fifty modern thinkers on education. From Piaget to the present.* London: Routledge.

Freud, S. (1963). *General psychological theory* (1974, 8th ed.). New York: Collier.

Gardner, H. (1999). *Intelligence reframed: Multiple intelligences for the 21st century.* New York: Basic Books.

Gesell, A. (1940). *First five years of life: A guide to the study of the preschool child.* New Haven, CT: Harper & Row.

Gesell, A., Ilg, F. L., & Ames, L. B. (1977). *The child from five to ten (Revised ed.).* New York: Harper & Row.

Gilligan, C. (1993). *In a different voice: Psychological theory and women's development.* Cambridge, MA: Harvard University Press.

Gordon, A., & Brown, K. (2008). *Beginnings and beyond* (7th ed.). Albany, NY: Thompson Delmar Learning.

Hammill, G. (2005, Winter/Spring). Mixing and managing four generations of employees. *FDU.* Retrieved April 10, 2010, from http://www.fdu.edu/newspubs/magazine/05ws/generations.htm

Havighurst, R. J. (1953). *Human development and education.* New York: Longmans, Green.

Huff, C. W. (2001). *Student handbook for Psychology 121.* Northfield, MN: St. Olaf College.

Kohlberg, L. (1969). Stage and sequence: The cognitive–developmental approach to socialization. In D. A. Coslin (Ed.), *Handbook of socialization theory and research* (pp. 347–480). Chicago: Rand McNally.

Kohlberg, L. (1984). *The psychology of moral development.* San Francisco: Harper & Row.

Kohlberg, L. (1987). *Child psychology and childhood education: A cognitive–developmental view.* New York: Longman.

Lightfoot, C., Cole, M. C. S., & Cole, S. (2009). *The development of children.* New York: Worth.

Noddings, N. (1984). *Caring, a feminine approach to ethics and moral education.* Berkeley: University of California Press.

Noddings, N. (2002). *Starting at home. Caring and social policy.* Berkeley: University of California Press.

Thomas, R. M. (2004). *Comparing theories of child development* (3rd ed.). Belmont, CA: Wadsworth.

Vygotsky, L. S. (Ed.). (1962). *Thought and language:* Cambridge, MA: Massachusetts Institute of Technology.

Vygotsky, L. S. (1963). Learning and mental development at school age. In B. Simon & J. Simon (Eds.), *Educational psychology in the USSR* (pp. 21–34). London: Routledge & Kegan Paul.

Vygotsky, L. S. (1978). *Mind in society: The development of higher psychological processes* (14th ed.). Cambridge, MA: Harvard University Press.

White, W. H. (1992). G. Stanley Hall: From philosophy to developmental psychology. *Developmental Psychology, 28,* 25–34.

Chapter

6

The Adult's Role in Socialization and Development

Dr. Marian Marion, a specialist on the subject of children's behavior, believes that the way children function in a group setting is heavily influenced by the interaction between the three components of what she calls the **guidance system**. Those components are the *adults,* the *children* themselves, and the *environment* (Marion, 2006). Anyone who plans to work with children should have an understanding of the ways in which these components interact. When you understand this dynamic you can more easily be an effective leader and mentor, and you will know how to create an environment in which positive interpersonal relations can develop. We have already discussed children and their development in Chapter 5. The next three chapters explore the role of adults in out-of-school settings. Chapter 9 will describe the features of an effective environment for afterschool care.

THE PROCESS OF SOCIALIZATION

The earliest lessons on how to live in the world are given to children by parents, grandparents, siblings, other family members, and caregivers. In a loving environment, children are taught that the world is a predictable and safe place, and they soon learn how to ask to have their needs met in acceptable ways (Erikson, 1993). Other children, especially those experiencing abuse or neglect, may learn to get their needs met by using less desirable methods (Levin, 2003). Even in those unfortunate settings, however, most children eventually learn to take turns and wait for things (lunch, a toy, going to the bathroom), how to do some things for themselves (eat, get dressed, go to the bathroom), and how to conduct themselves in public. Most of these skills are learned by imitation or instruction from family members, caregivers or teachers, and other children.

Agents of Socialization

Sociologists call the people who serve in this role **agents of socialization**. The term **socialization** means "the process by which we learn the ways of a given society or social group so that we can function within it" (Elkin, 1989, p. 2), and the agents are the facilitators of that process.

Educators Jim and Laurie Ollhoff (2007) believe that school-age professionals have a vital role to play in that process. "In the past," they wrote

> society was set up in a way that helped children learn social skills as they moved through life [but] today that is no longer true. Most mechanisms that helped facilitate social skills are gone. The extended family is gone. Time with adults is minimal and superficial. Instead of interaction, we have television. (p. 29)

All the more reason, then, for you to understand the importance of your influence on the children you work with. Sociologist Frederick Elkin (1989) described the traditional role of adults in the process of socialization:

> In the course of growing up, a child must acquire varied knowledge and skills, such as what utensils to use when eating specific foods; how to greet strangers; how to show or conceal emotion in different settings; when to speak and when to be silent. As children grow they move into a widening world of persons, activities, and feelings—all shaped by encounters with others who help define a socially organized world. (p. 2)

These "others" establish and communicate standards of right and wrong, and as a result children will begin to measure their actions against this moral compass and recognize when they do not meet their own expectations or the expectation of others.

As children enter school, the agents of socialization become the peer group, the media, and adults such as teachers, religious leaders, coaches, recreation workers, and afterschool staff. As an agent of socialization, you can help children learn to get along with one another, negotiate busy street crossings, behave in a variety of social settings, carry their side of a conversation, and play "fair." You will accomplish this both by what you *do* and by what you *say*.

Types of Socialization

Socialization is accomplished both *intentionally* and *unintentionally* by the agents of socialization. **Intentional socialization** might include "Don't put your feet on the furniture," or "Say please," or "Before you can play a new game, you need to put away the parts to the game you were playing with." **Unintentional socialization** takes place when children observe other people and absorb lessons from what they see and hear. An example of unintentional socialization would be eavesdropping on a phone conversation in which a child's older sister comforts a discouraged friend or calls in sick to work as she puts on her running shoes to go jogging. As you can see, children learn more than just **behaviors** through socialization—they also learn attitudes, appropriate **emotions**, and motivations, and they begin to **internalize** what they have learned, creating a kind of rule book for life. During this process, they form some lifelong assumptions about the world.

⚘   *Consider This:*   ⚘

What attitude might a child learn by watching an older sister comfort a discouraged friend? Watching her let another friend copy her math homework? Watching her work for several weeks on a science project and win first prize?

The Role of Culture

Culture plays an important role in this process. Each culture socializes its children to function within that culture, teaching and reinforcing behavior that reflects cultural values. Recent cognitive development theorists propose that when children interact with members of the same culture in certain situations many times, or talk about certain kinds of information with them many times, **cultural schemas** are created and stored in their brains (Nishida, 2005). Schemas are built from memories of past experiences that have been organized into related categories, and they guide children's behavior in familiar situations.

In a multicultural society, cultural schema development may lead to confusion for children as they receive one set of messages from family members, different ones from peers and teachers, and still others from the media. By being aware of this situation, adults who work in out-of-school settings can provide opportunities for children to discuss conflicts between the various parts of their lives and help them figure out what makes sense for them.

It's also important for children to see representations of role models of their own culture. Make a point of subscribing to several ethnically focused magazines such as *Right On, Hispanic, Face, Tribal Arts, Black Beat, ALO Hayati,* and *Ebony,* and develop a culturally rich selection of music, books, and posters. If you participate in hiring staff or recruiting volunteers, work toward cultural diversity, making a special point of reaching out to people from cultures and language groups represented by the children attending your program.

Attitudes, or the feelings one has about facts or conditions, can reveal a great deal about a child's cultural schema. "Nah, I can't do that. It's stupid," reflects an attitude. So does the omnipresent "Yeah, right. . ." Be watchful for comments like "He talks funny," or "Lisa is a pretty good runner, for a girl." Developers of the anti-bias curriculum at Pacific Oaks College have discovered that ignoring such slanderous words effectively validates them (Derman-Sparks, 2006; Derman-Sparks & ABC Task Force, 1989). To teach anti-bias attitudes, we need to notice biased statements and challenge them. For example, Marika, a tutor in an afterschool homework program, heard a fifth grader say, "But of course Tina scored higher than I did. Asians are better in math!" Marika immediately took the child aside and explained to her that Tina was good in math because she studied very hard. Tina's achievements did not come because of her Chinese ancestry. Leonard Pitts addresses the impact of attitudes on children in perspective 6.1.

Adults who work with children may hear statements reflective of a specific political or religious perspective. In the past, teachers hearing such statements would often assume that the children's words reflected the attitudes of their families. However, given the strong influence of the media in today's society, the greater mobility of families, and less dominant adult role models, that is less often

PERSPECTIVE 6.1

Talking About Racism

Leonard Pitts, Jr.
PARENTING Magazine

An African American father struggles with how to explain racism to his children.

My youngest daughter, Onjel, already knows that she is black. It was well over a year ago that I first heard her referring to "that white girl" or "that black girl." So I know that she has a sense of herself as someone different, someone apart. That bothers me. I wish she could have had a few more years just to be who she is. A few more years of freedom. Is that so much to ask? After all, she's only four years old.

I already know what will happen next, how she'll discover what black means. One day, too soon, she'll have a falling out with one of her playmates. And in the heat of the argument, the other child will brand my daughter with an ancient epithet that will make my pretty baby feel low and unclean and despicable. The other child will call my daughter a nigger.

And I know what will happen after that, too–I know it by heart. I'll take my anger to the child's parents. They'll profess astonishment, apologize, and tell me they haven't a clue where their little cherub picked up such foul language. Maybe I'll believe them. Probably I won't.

Then I'll lead my daughter back home. We'll find a quiet place to talk. She'll look up at me, waiting for Daddy to make sense of her pain. And my brain will become as empty as a politician's promise.

What do I say to my children about racism? I ought to have it down by now. Certainly I've had enough practice. Markise, who is now 20, was in grade school when he had his first brush with racism: A bully called him a nigger when my son refused to give up his place in line.

Monique, 17, was in second grade when another girl got angry because Monique wouldn't lend her a crayon. The other child said her father had always told her niggers were stingy.

Marlon, 12, doesn't even remember his first experience with prejudice because, he says, "it's happened so many times."

Bryan, who is 9, had his first encounter last year: A playmate's father said that because Bryan is black, the two children can't play together anymore.

At some point, it comes to every black child: Not just the knowledge that he or she is black, but the terrible understanding of what being black in America means. And then the child goes to the parent, who tries to explain it all but ends up relying on clichés.

What do I tell my children about racism? I tell them that they are good people. I tell them that anyone who seeks to judge them without knowing them is a fool. I tell them that there are many such fools in the world, but that they must dare and dream and aspire anyway. I tell them that the ignorance of others is always an obstacle but never an excuse.

As I said, clichés. Your child is hurting and looking to you to make it stop. But you can't. All you can give her is homilies. Few situations in the world have such an ability to make you feel so utterly useless, so completely impotent.

In a way, I'm almost thankful to have been raised in the racial isolation of inner-city Los Angeles. Yes, I grew up without the advantages my children enjoy, but I also never experienced the pain they have. Where I came from, everybody was black. I thought white people lived only on television, where they wore suits and dresses all day long and smiled in perpetual contentment because they had tigers in their tanks, Dodges in their garages, and Ty-D-Bol men in their toilets.

If my parents ever talked to me about racism, I don't remember it, More likely, it went unremarked, like air. You don't talk about air. Air just is. As racism just is. That is what makes it so hard for me to explain it to my own kids. Racism just is.

Racism is stupid, atavistic, a sure sign of an under-developed mind and a malnourished spirit. But for all that, it is. And likely always will be. The challenge is in teaching a child not to let it consume her. Because if you dwell on it, if you look for logic along its twisting, dimly lit passageways, you'll just make yourself crazy.

(continued)

And if you let it define you, you let it defeat you. So I tell my children that they must learn to distinguish between what other people think of them and what they know of themselves—and to always put their faith in the latter. I tell them to never play out a role scripted for them by somebody else.

Sometimes I think I harp too much on that point. Markise, a quiet, thoughtful young man, used to get so angry at his black friends when they were loud and rowdy. "They act just like white people expect them to!" he would seethe. Which is true enough. But, then, teenagers are supposed to be loud and rowdy. And white kids can act this way without fear that someone is going to project that behavior onto their entire race.

Is that fair? Of course not. But fair has got nothing to do with it. Never has.

There is something stubborn within all of us that refuses to yield to logic on this subject: Even though we should and do know better, we go right on hating and fearing that which is different from us simply because it is different.

"Can we all get along?" asked a shaky-voiced Rodney King at the height of the 1992 riots in Los Angeles. The question was too profound in its very simplicity for us to take seriously. It was too stark, too innocent, struck too close to the bone. It embarrassed us the way a child does when she asks the boss about his toupee at the dinner table. We resented King for not knowing better than to ask. So we made fun of his innocence and made a mockery of his question; better to hold it at a distance and avoid its ominous implications.

But was there anyone who, hearing King's question, didn't tremble a little in his own soul and fear that the truthful answer is no?

Sometimes I feel so bad for Markise. It seems like there's something more I could have told him that would make it easier for him when security guards follow him around department store. Or when police officers handcuff him at the curb, claiming, as they always do, that he looks "just like" the suspect in a recent robbery. Instead, I gave my son clichés, and now he gives me back potent frustration and a stunned bewilderment that things have to be this way, that people can hate and distrust him on sight without the minor inconvenience of getting to know him.

I know just how he feels. One day, on the way to taking my family to dinner, I stopped at an automatic teller machine. I was driving a minivan full of kids—including Onjel in her car seat. In the parking lot, the guy in the car next to mine looked at me and didn't see a family man. He saw a nigger and a thief.

So he called out to his female friend, who was at the machine. As I got in line behind her, she abruptly aborted the transaction and fled to the car.

I felt shamed. I felt furious. I felt tired. My frustration was older than I am. But I told myself the same thing I always do: Live with it. Racism just is. So how am I supposed to know what to say to Markise? How am I supposed to make it easier for him to accept moments like that when I don't even know what to say to myself?

From time to time, I read articles in which whites attempt to justify their fear of black people by claiming they are just being prudent—statistics, after all, suggest that blacks are criminally inclined out of proportion to their numbers. I always wonder why these people who have such faith in the statistics don't cite the rest of the equation, the part that shows that the primary victims of black criminals are, overwhelmingly, themselves black. Similarly, whites are most likely to be victimized by other whites.

Why doesn't it play that way on the evening news and in the arena of public perception? The answer is obvious, of course. Racism just is.

What do I tell my children about racism? I try to give them the tools that will make it possible for them to deal with it. Such as laughter: I laugh when I can't do anything else. Such as self-knowledge: When television hauls out the archival footage of the civil rights movement, I call the kids into the living room and make them watch. Afterwards, we talk. I take them to see *Glory* and Spike Lee's film *Malcolm X*. And we talk some more. When a local museum displays artifacts of black suffering in America, my family visits the exhibit. I explain to them the sacrifices their grandparents made for the freedoms we take for granted.

I try to give them some sense of perspective, too. Bigotry, I want them to understand, is a universal disease. I want my children to see it in context, to know that they are not hatred's only victims. I want them to remember the terrible feelings that racism engenders, to use that knowledge to understand why they must never make someone else a victim of that pain.

That's why I told them about Anne Frank, to broaden their perspective. And that's why, on a trip to Los Angeles, I took my two youngest sons to the Simon Wiesenthal Center Museum of Tolerance. My boys walked through the displays on hatred and civil rights, sat through the horrific films on genocide in the 20th century, toured the Holocaust exhibit. When we were finished, I asked them what they thought. They replied with some variant of "cool."

Sigh. That, of course, is the eternal conundrum with kids. You never know how much they're taking in and how much is just sliding between their ears without making an impact. You don't know if you've made a difference with your kids until they're not kids anymore. And then it's too late.

Still, I have reason to be hopeful. Markise is frustrated by the unfairness of life, but he's moving forward in the face of it. He's a college man studying for a career in law. I have high hopes for all of my kids.

I've spoken harshly of clichés, but that's frustration talking. It's just that I want to give my kids more than words—I want to make my children's pain go away. But I can't. All I can do is teach them how to use it.

"Let the pain motivate you to be better," I told Marlon just the other day. "You will need to be better than the best, my son." Why? Because growing up black is like growing up in a minefield: It takes courage, resolve, and no small amount of luck to make it safely to the other side. It calls on a person to be bigger, nobler, and grander of spirit than any of the low, mean forces that would bring him down.

But a parent can only tell children so much. Then they must go out there alone, away from your shelter, to live among those who would harm them, to make their own way. That's the hard part. That's when the frustration becomes acute. And you want to sweep your kids back in and tell them just one more thing—something that will keep them safe and well.

Instead, you let them go and you curse the impotence of homilies.

What do I tell my children about racism? Same as you. Not nearly enough.

Source: Used with permission from Leonard Pitts, Jr.

---

the case (Barbour, 2008). In fact, unless children initiate conversations with their parents about specific issues, they may not have any idea where they stand. Honesty, dishonesty, and respect (or lack of it) for other people can be learned in a wide variety of places—including programs for school-agers.

Emotions of shyness, sadness, anger, embarrassment, and pride are also feelings, often experienced so intensely that they seem physical. Most children experience a full range of emotions, whatever their age, language, or condition. Where the socialization process comes into play, however, is in determining which emotion is triggered by which situation and how that emotion is played out in behaviors. One child may feel grief at the death of a living creature; another may feel pride as he pulls off its wings. As with so many other things, these emotions and behaviors are learned by observing other people as they respond to various events in their lives. Adults play an important role in helping children to develop appropriate emotions for the society in which they live, by giving words to their own feelings, accepting the feelings of others, and helping children explore their feelings when they are confused.

Motivations are also learned. One child may study hard in school to please his parents, while his best friend does so in order to feel superiority over a sibling. A child may play with a blind classmate because she feels sorry for him, while another may do so simply because she enjoys his company. Some children tell the truth because they fear punishment, while others because they believe it is the moral thing to do. Motivations for social behavior are based on stages of development and on beliefs, sometimes mistaken ones, that children learn through interactions with the socializing influences in their environment (Dreikurs, 1990; Levin, 2003). We can help teach the "usefulness" or appropriateness of certain attention-getting aggressive behaviors, for example, by ignoring them and giving positive attention to children when they exhibit prosocial and cooperative behaviors. Keep in mind as you do so, however, that some behaviors (such as giggling, avoiding eye contact, or staring directly at you) may have different meanings in different cultures. An excellent resource for this kind of information is *Developing Cross-Cultural Competence: A Guide for Working With Young Children and Their Families* (Lynch & Hanson, 2004).

ADULTS AND THE DEVELOPMENT OF THE PERSONALITY

Related to socialization, or learning how to be a member of society, is the development of personality, or learning how to be an individual. Social behaviorist George Herbert Mead was one of the first researchers to offer an explanation for how children internalize society's rules and values. For Mead, the outcome of the socialization process that makes **self-regulation** possible at all is the development of the **self**. He described the self as having two parts: the **I** and the **me**.

Only humans can purposefully decide what it is that they wish to represent of themselves to others (Mead, 1934). As "me" I integrate the images of others into my self-concept ("You are an attractive woman; you are so clumsy"), but as "I," I regulate my behavior and present to others the view I wish them to see ("I am a capable person; I can do this"). Mead believed a cognitive process takes place, consciously or unconsciously, of modeling ourselves after what it is we think *others* wish us to be or after what it is *we* wish to be. He called this thought **internalized conversation**. You may know it as "self-talk." Children accomplish this process, wrote Mead, through two stages—**play**, during which children mimic what they understand adult roles to be (such as Mom going to the office and Dad teaching school or the mailman delivering letters) and **games**, which is more elaborate, requiring a set of rules and other people to play opposite parts. ("Pretend you're the space ship captain and I'm the engineer and I have this cool navigating tool that lets us change solar systems but you get hit by an enemy virus and I have to figure out how to pilot the ship.")

The Role of Others

Psychologists have studied this phenomenon for many years, and the role played by adults in the development of a child's personality is explained slightly differently by different theorists. Erik Erikson believed, as did Frederick Elkin, that children draw their models from many different people during childhood and adolescence, not just their parents, and incorporate bits and pieces of each of them into their developing personalities. As children's cognitive and social capabilities grow, they try new ways of interacting with other people. They watch how

Children need to see authentic images of their culture in order to develop a healthy self-image.

respected adults play certain roles, such as aggressor, peacekeeper, or comic, and they imitate those people's actions. This is also how he believed that children learn cultural identity and gender roles.

Some social learning theorists believe that children learn attitudes and behaviors through simple imitation (Blackmore, 1999; Tarde, 1969). Albert Bandura (1973) did not believe that children are passive observers but that they are actively trying to behave like trusted adults who have authority and whom they respect. However, Bandura did believe that visual images had a powerful influence on children and warned of the impact of media violence.

Bandura performed the classic Bobo Doll experiment to test his belief that children could acquire attitudes, emotional responses, and new styles of conduct through filmed and televised modeling. Children watched several video clips. Some children watched clips of adults hitting the Bobo Doll; others did not. Following the screening, the actions of the children were videotaped, and it was observed that children were more likely to behave aggressively toward the doll if the people in the video had behaved aggressively (Bandura, 1973).

Bronfenbrenner's (1979) ecological systems theory (Chapter 5) provides a model of socialization that can be useful when thinking about this phenomenon. The agents of socialization that primarily reside in the child's microsystem—his parents and grandparents, siblings, friends, close neighbors, and trusted adults—surround him and offer many opportunities for observation and analysis of behavior. Watch a youngster for a while during a family gathering and you will see many instances of unintentional imitation: mannerisms, style of dress, joke telling, even posture. Parents' and other adults' attitudes and behaviors may have been formed primarily within their own microsystem, but they are also subject to modification through interactions that take place in the exosystem and macrosystem. And those changes in attitude or behavior are then observed by children, who may imitate *them*.

Today, most theorists agree that children learn much of their behavior by imitating, or **modeling**, what they see or hear other people do and that they are more likely to model the behavior of someone they like and respect. This may lead to a boy becoming a gang member or an Eagle Scout. A girl might model the behavior of a female astronaut or her older sister who left high school at 16 to start a family. It is not necessarily the behavior that is valued by the child but the individual displaying that behavior.

Your role as an agent of socialization and therefore as a model for a developing personality is clearly significant, whether the children with whom you work are mimicking behaviors on purpose or inadvertently. In addition, children—Native American children, Chinese children, African-American children, Hispanic children . . . all children—*need* to see authentic images of members of their culture to develop a feeling of pride in their heritage and develop a healthy self-image and cultural schema. As adults working with children, you can use all of these theoretical frameworks to guide your practice and help you remember the value of modeling culturally relevant and morally sound behavior (see Table 6.1).

ADULTS AS TEACHERS

Traditionally in most cultures, teaching children to become productive, independent adults has been the task of families and school. However, recent observers of youth write that today's young people are failing to learn the basic skills they need to live and work productively (Blair, 1995; Glenn & Nelsen, 2000; Ollhoff & Ollhoff, 2007; Wallace, 1991). One explanation for this may be that in most families, especially those where both parents work outside the home or there is only one parent present, time is at a premium, and the members may spend less time together than they did in earlier generations. Whether family time is being stolen by long commutes to and from work, by the emotionally exhausting search for employment, by children's social and athletic activities, or by working a second job, most parents have less time available to spend teaching their children the skills of adulthood than their parents did.

TABLE 6.1   Guidelines for Modeling Culturally Relevant and Morally Sound Behavior.

Desired Behaviors	Leader Behavior
Responsibility, ethical decision making	Explain the rationale for your decisions; talk to children about your thought process.
Gender role awareness; appropriate professions for males and females; appropriate roles in relationships	Involve children in role-plays, using scenarios from literature or real life.
Self-efficacy	Set up a brainstorm session: Whose fault is it if you get a bad grade? The teacher's, your parents', or your fault? What factors contribute to doing well in school? How can you influence them?

Schools also face a time problem. As our society has changed from a manufacturing-based economy to an information-based one, teachers have been asked to add more and more material to their curriculum. Often this is done at the expense of traditional, practical pursuits, such as woodworking, cooking, sewing, or money management.

Life Skills and Job Skills

In this modern family, in which both parents probably work, or in which only one parent is trying to meet all the financial, emotional, and physical needs of the household, opportunities to teach domestic skills are often scarce. These are the skills everyone needs in day-to-day life, such as balancing checkbooks, buying groceries, cooking, cleaning, doing laundry, and mending clothes. Nor are there long stretches of family time available to spend building birdhouses or boats in the garage, hanging curtains, repairing bicycles or broken lamps, or even working together in the garden. Modern children believe that families used to do these things together—they've heard their parents and grandparents talk, and they've seen reruns of *The Brady Bunch* and *The Wonder Years*.

Some skill training has been transferred to schools, where vocational courses teach resume writing and how to find housing, but because of budgetary problems, or the crowding of the curriculum by "high tech" subjects, offerings of life skills classes may be limited. Also gone are lessons in manners and etiquette—the "social graces." Youngsters may argue these niceties have gone out of fashion, but the business pages of any major newspaper report the value of appropriate dress, polished manners, and grammatical speech in employment interviews.

Katharine, a counselor in a summer camp, teaches bed-making and other self-care skills to the children in her cabin. "I remember my mother teaching me how to make hospital corners," she explains, "but even if that skill hadn't been made unnecessary by fitted sheets, most of these children's parents are up at dawn and out the door before 7:00 a.m. I suspect they don't have time to make their own beds, let alone teach their children how." So Katharine does it instead. The issue here is not for children to make a bed so that a quarter bounces on it, as a Marine sergeant may require, but that they learn the value of orderliness and how to bring it into their lives. Katharine also stages formal luncheons where she teaches children how to select a meal from a menu of different types of food as well as how to use cloth napkins, numerous forks, or chopsticks. There are other ways to teach such things, and some might even argue that there is no longer a need for them at all, but Katharine reports that the children beam with pride when they demonstrate their knowledge of "fancy food stuff" to their families at the end of camp.

Raul Estrella grew up in a home with child parents. His mother was only 14 when he was born; his father barely 15. After struggling to keep their household together for several years, Raul's father abandoned his wife and three children when Raul was 7. Raul's mother began working long hours, leaving the two younger children with her mother for several days at a time. In the afterschool homework center where Raul went each afternoon, the tutor had a point system for special projects that children could complete when their homework was finished. Raul liked baseball cards, and he found he could earn them by sorting school papers, shelving books, and labeling file folders. By the time he left elementary school, Raul could type and file and knew how to use the lab computer. He returned to the homework center as a tutor while he was in middle school, and when he went to high school he worked in the school library. Raul's teachers see a college education in his future. Thanks to an adult who knew the importance of teaching a work ethic and practical skills, Raul got a lot more than just baseball cards from attending that afterschool program.

✿   *Consider This:*   ✿

What are some life skills that you learned outside your home? Who taught these skills to you? How old were you? What did it feel like to own these new skills?

Social Skills and Strategies

Social skills include getting along with others—on a city bus, in the supermarket, or at a baseball game. Learning how to enter a group, how to make someone else feel comfortable when he or she is the "new" or "different" one, working out disagreements, solving problems, and cooperating on a task—all these are social skills that must be learned and are heavily influenced by the actions and attitudes of the models/agents of socialization children have around them. You are "on" all the time when you are working with children. Negative attitudes among staff can be tremendously harmful and should be handled as soon as possible. That doesn't mean everyone has to agree all the time, but disagreements need to be resolved in productive ways. Adults encourage growth and independence in children when they teach the skills necessary for working with others.

Opportunities for children to learn the skills they need to live effectively in the society do not happen naturally in the course of a normal program day, so you may need to use imagination to create situations in which children can practice these skills. I saw one excellent example of this at an afterschool program. One of my students was working as a substitute group leader during the summer, and she had noticed that the children were extremely bored. It was hot, and the weeks stretched in front of them. Searching for something interesting to do, Julie brought in a book that her own children had enjoyed—*From the Mixed-up Files of Mrs. Basil E. Frankweiler* (Konigsburg, 1967/1973)—and began reading it to a small group of youngsters in the shade of a tree. The main characters in the story secretly leave home, travel by bus to the Metropolitan Museum of Art, take up temporary residence in the museum, and then become involved in solving a mystery.

As Julie talked to the children about the story, she realized that most of them had never ridden on public transit, nor did they know how to read a bus schedule or a map. The next day she brought in a map of their local community and they pored over it together, searching for familiar landmarks. Julie helped each child to find his or her home on a map, which they put on the wall with colorful pins marking all their locations. A few days later, continuing her daily reading of the book (to an increasing number of children), she brought in a map of the nearest medium-sized city and helped the children to plot a route from each of their homes to places they liked to visit, such as the hockey stadium, the mall, and the park. Finally, she obtained a bus schedule for each child, and together they planned routes to the city art museum, using the map and the schedules. As a culmination of the summer project, they traveled together to the museum and ate lunch together in a nearby park.

As Julie talked about her experience, she explained that she had been at the same time appalled at the children's lack of knowledge about how to get around and behave in public and then amazed at how much they had learned in one trip. As a young mother, she had stayed at home until her youngest child entered elementary school and traveled widely with her family. At first she expected that all children would know, as hers did, that you didn't run up and down the street while you were waiting for a crossing signal or trade seats constantly on public transportation. However, she discovered that for many of these children, this was their first outing other than family vacations. She had then accepted more willingly the role she played as a "parent," taught them what they needed to know, and rejoiced as they modified their behavior accordingly. In this circumstance, the adult learned as much from the interaction as the children did.

Many out-of-school settings offer opportunities for socialization. Coaches of athletic teams often travel to other cities for ball games; they have many opportunities to help children learn reasonable ways of behaving in motels, restaurants, rest stops, buses, airports, and airplanes. Scout leaders and youth group leaders take their charges to ski slopes, camps, fairgrounds, and other public places; in each case, they become agents of socialization. Sometimes child and youth workers find themselves feeling frustrated and even angry, believing that parents have been remiss by failing to teach their children to behave "properly." It is more effective, however, to consider that in today's world the role of socializing agent is of necessity being shared by the parents with others, and one of those **"others"** is you. Consider yourself to be part of the socializing team, and take your role seriously.

Support for Academic Achievement

Some out-of-school programs are primarily recreational and social in nature. Others integrate homework time and activities that encourage children to practice skills they are learning at school. Still others have academic support at the center of their mission, and group leaders provide a rich curriculum of choices and activities that include opportunities for literacy, language arts, math, science, social studies, health, safety, nutrition, art, music, drama, recreation, and physical activities (Kurz-Riemer, 2005). School-age children attending any of these programs can build on what they have learned during the regular school day, explore additional areas of interest, and develop relationships with caring adults, all of which are factors related to their success as adults (Miller, 1995).

The federal government provides funds directly to school districts to establish extended-learning programs after school, such as the 21st Century Learning Centers Program (Seligson, 2001). The goals of these programs include improving academic achievement, decreasing gaps in social development, and providing support systems designed to promote children's optimal development. State and local governments may also fund programs on school sites, or provide funding that private agencies and centers can apply for, in an effort to improve school achievement, raise scores on standards-based tests, and reduce the incidence of juvenile crime and victimization.

Child and youth workers employed in programs that emphasize supporting children's success in learning will need to design and implement activities that reinforce key learning concepts and develop systems for accountability regarding the program's involvement in children's learning (School's Out! Washington, 2005). In addition, it is important for staff to provide opportunities for English language learners to identify with and use their home language and to be knowledgeable about multiple intelligences and other learning style theories in deciding which activities to provide and how to structure them (Kurz-Riemer, 2005). While a certificated elementary or middle school teacher may be employed as the lead instructional staff member in academically oriented afterschool programs, college students are also valuable employees in such programs; because they are often closer in age to the children, the opportunities for mentoring and role-modeling are great.

The Impact of Poverty   A reality of today's society is the poverty of many children, often due to single-parent female-headed households (Bureau of the Census, 2004). Poverty may impede the development of children in many ways, related to the stresses that it generates within families. As a result of this stress, poor children have a higher incidence of disability and illness, diagnosed or undiagnosed, which may interfere with normal development. Unassisted poor children tend to do poorly in school and often drop out before high school graduation. Children from low-income families may be unable to participate in enrichment activities such as scouting, sports, or music lessons, and they cannot always take part in community-based programs intended to help them, due to low motivation or embarrassment. Poverty means that high-quality for-profit programs for school-age children may not be accessible to this group of children. It also means that the impact of such programs could be tremendous if sliding-scale fees are available. Child and youth workers in publicly funded drop-in recreational or tutoring programs may want to take these facts into consideration as they design their programs—if they are accessible, interesting, and enjoyable, they will be more effective at attracting the children who need them most.

Problem Solving and Competence   Closely related to a knowledge of social skills is knowledge of problem solving. Both the ability to know what to do in a social situation and what to do to solve a problem contribute to a child's feeling of **competence**, which in turn builds his or her **self-esteem**. Adults in the child's life have many opportunities to model problem solving and can also create situations in which children have opportunities to practice solving problems on their own.

Preschool teachers frequently ask children to set the table for snack; through repetitive trips for cups, crackers, napkins, and juice the youngsters learn about one-to-one correspondence and other elements of mathematics. Similarly, school-age children can be asked to develop a list of materials needed for a construction project or awarded the task of scheduling the computer so that everyone has an equal opportunity to use it. Many children do not have the belief in their own capabilities that comes from succeeding at these kinds of day-to-day tasks.

TABLE 6.2   Modeling Problem Solving and Competence.

- "No one brought the soccer net? Perhaps we could set up the traffic cones to designate the goal area."
- "Whoops, we're out of wheat paste for the papier-mâché! Let's see if we have some flour. I remember my teacher making paste from flour and water. Perhaps we can figure out how to do that, too."
- "The printer isn't working? Well, what are some of the things that can go wrong? Let's check the cables."
- "Annie can't reach the easel from her wheelchair. How can we set it up so she can paint, too?"

Because children are motivated to learn and perform from birth, they may begin to think of themselves as capable long before parents and siblings see them that way. Many toddlers, for example, want to help family members with household activities. "Me do it," they will declare as they follow their brother around with the vacuum cleaner or help Mom put groceries away. They want to sort clothes, do homework, put DVDs into the player.

Frequently, we discourage this frustrating behavior, telling children that they are too little to help or that they should get out of the way so they don't get hurt. If we do not replace the "annoying" helping behavior with "acceptable" helping behavior ("Here, Brandon, help me set the table please") we are likely to undermine children's sense of capability very early, and soon they will not only believe they are *not* capable, but they will also lose their interest in participating in family activities.

However, simply being asked to *do* a task is not enough. Children may need help to solve these problems, and it helps to see adults solving their own problems, too. Table 6.2 demonstrates several ways in which you can model problem solving and competence when working with children. Chances are that lots of learning, on both sides, will occur in your time together.

How many times in a day do you go through the problem-solving process? Do it out loud, let the children know what you are doing, and accept their suggestions as you brainstorm possible solutions. This is how they learn to do the same thing, and in the long run, whether your activity is playing soccer, making a Kwanzaa craft, adapting a project for a child with special needs, or producing a camp newsletter, it will run more smoothly as the children begin to feel more capable, more in charge of their own actions, more connected. The less children depend on adults to solve problems or give direction to their activities, the more independence and motivation they will begin to exhibit (Montessori, 1988).

Literacy and a Love of Learning

From age 5 to 8, children learn to study, to reason, to use the information coming in on all sides to develop concepts and ideas about the world. To do that well, they need to be well grounded in literacy skills—reading, writing, and listening. In a world where most adults receive the daily news on a computer screen, writing letters consists of e-mail or texting, bedtime stories have been replaced by videogames, and dinner-table conversation rarely happens, children get very few models, and even less practice, in developing these skills. Clearly, with at-home time limited by our fast-paced and busy society as well as the technological revolution, school has become the only real source of formal literacy education.

Yet despite research supporting a different approach, most schools are still curriculum centered rather than student centered. Such a pedagogical approach often leaves children with a sense of failure at a very early age, to the point that they may become discouraged about their ability to ever succeed in school. Discouraged or not, however, most of them will put in their time until they finish their state-mandated education and then are sprung on the society, unprepared to work and no longer interested in learning. The attitudes and motivations learned in schools that place an emphasis on achievement over development do not prepare children for lifelong learning, an absolute necessity in this technologically based society (Secretary's Commission on Achieving Necessary Skills, 2006). Even schools that have kept children's developmental needs at the center of their planning, try as they might, are often unable, due to class size or pressure for higher test scores, to devote much time to nurturing a love of learning. Here is where you come in.

Recreational and enrichment programs for school-age children can offer opportunities for them to try new things, to stretch their wings and choose their own activities. One of the most valuable endeavors for an afterschool program is to introduce youngsters to the joy of reading and independent learning. Traditionally, **literacy** is the term used to refers to one's ability to use language to read, write, listen, and speak. Today, the definition of *literacy* has been expanded to include facility in a variety of learning strategies that enable an individual to "achieve his or her goals, to develop his or her knowledge and potential, and to participate fully in the wider society" (UNESCO Education Sector, 2004).

Although attitudes toward literacy and learning begin early in life, the journey is ongoing and can be sparked by interesting experiences and enthusiastic companions. Learning to read and write, for example, are developmental activities, and youngsters can progress from where they are to the next stage at any age, even if the school curriculum has passed beyond (or has not yet reached) the skills they need to learn.

Youngsters need many opportunities to develop and practice emerging literacy skills through intelligent discussions with adults. Storytelling, reading and listening, games, and other activities and interactions can extend learning beyond the regular school day (Clark, 1989, 2002). Workers in child and youth settings who read interesting books, to themselves or to collected groups of children, and who share their own love of learning by seeking answers in libraries or online databases, provide models and motivations for children. These models and examples can have a tremendously positive influence on their future lives. Informal educational programs such as merit badge programs in Scouting, project work in 4-H, or mock business management in Junior Achievement or Future Business Leaders of America offer excellent opportunities for children; later chapters will suggest specific ways in which youngsters can be encouraged to overcome their fears and discouragement and to experience the enjoyment of learning.

School-age programs are also ideal environments for learning about individual and cultural differences as children develop solutions to problems within their microsociety. Their experiences working and playing together can serve as rehearsals for the very real problems our multicultural world will face in the decades to come.

Youngsters need many opportunities to develop and practice emerging literacy skills.

Lifelong Habits of Health and Fitness

The topics of fitness and health in childhood have received great attention in recent years. Pediatricians, concerned about the increasing incidence of **obesity** in school-aged children, have urged parents to improve family eating habits and increase children's opportunities for regular physical activity. One in five children in the United States between the ages of 6 and 17 is overweight (Centers for Disease Control and Prevention, 2006). In addition, researchers have determined that many American children have low aerobic endurance along with their high levels of body fact. Unfit and overweight children are more liable to show early signs of coronary heart disease, high cholesterol levels, and high blood pressure.

This is particularly troubling, because at the same time that childhood obesity is increasing, many youngsters, convinced that they are "fat" even when the mirror shows a different story, are taking unhealthy measures to keep their weight under control. Western society has long placed an enormous emphasis on physical appearance. This focus, combined with many youngsters' persistent belief that they must follow the example of actors and fashion models and hurry into adulthood, has made eating disorders such as **anorexia** and **bulimia** common during the middle school years. Seventy-six percent of reported anorexia nervosa cases in the United States were diagnosed between the ages of 11 and 20. While the skinny model image has been implicated in many cases of eating disorders, physicians now recognize that anorexia and bulimia are psychological conditions frequently resulting from low self-esteem and constant self-criticism. Youngsters with these conditions are often known to set impossible goals for themselves. When their goals are not achieved, they begin to control parts of their lives that they feel they can, such as food intake and weight.

Afterschool programs offer opportunities to address these issues. The good news is that most youngsters naturally want to be active, and after a long day of sitting in desks, nothing could feel better. The growing problem of obesity and lethargy in children can be partially blamed on extended hours of inactivity in school, often followed by an evening of television and video games. Breaking unhealthy eating and exercise patterns can be challenging, especially since children who have not been active lately may have low energy levels and little interest in doing anything about it. However, a positive attitude and good planning can encourage participation, and the more active children become during afterschool activities, the more active they are likely to be in the evenings and weekends at home with their families.

How do you fit into this picture? Once again, the adults in children's lives model behaviors, attitudes, and values that are internalized and eventually become part of their own personalities. Practice good eating habits, both while you are with the children and in your life away from the program as well. Make it a point to engage in a variety of physical activities, and tell the children about your experiences. In this way, you will find it natural and enjoyable to participate directly with children in physically challenging games and activities.

Capitalize on children's natural physical development. Provide materials, equipment, and opportunities for different kinds of physical activities—not just sports, but also dancing, dramatic performances, construction projects, and walking or cycling around the neighborhood. It is also important to provide activities in which children with a wide range of physical capabilities can be successful. Simple cooking projects and nutrition education can be an integral part of your afterschool program. Chapter 11 will discuss planning and implementing a health, nutrition, and fitness curriculum.

Self-esteem

The importance of positive self-esteem has received more than its share of attention in American childrearing culture. Depending on what you read, having self-esteem can lead one to happiness, success, and possibly a lucrative contract with your favorite basketball team. Lack of self-esteem, we are warned, is likely to result in alcoholism or drug abuse, school failure, teenage pregnancy, and unemployment. Nothing is quite that simple, and neither is the human quest for significance, purpose, or value. However, it is difficult to underestimate the value of believing oneself to be a valuable and competent member of society.

Contrary to the popular view that self-esteem can be "fed" to a child with regular doses of praise and compliments, a child's self-esteem actually develops from repeated self-evaluation. A classic and well-accepted definition of self-esteem is "a personal judgment of worthiness that is expressed in the attitudes the individual holds toward himself" (Coopersmith, 1981, pp. 4–5). Self-esteem is made up of two major components: **self-efficacy** and **self-respect**. Self-efficacy involves having the confidence that you can handle most things that you encounter and that you can effect change in your environment in order to improve the outlook for yourself or others. Self-respect, or self-worth, is more abstract. It gradually emerges as the realization that you are deserving of such feelings as happiness, success, love, and friendship and that you have the right to pursue them.

In measuring self-worth, children evaluate several different aspects of themselves. In evaluating self-esteem, they also often look to others for models and affirmation, and sometimes it is difficult to see how they draw their conclusions. Nancy E. Curry, Faculty Emeritus at the University of Pittsburgh, studied the development and values in young children and identified these four **dimensions of self-esteem**:

- ✸ Competence
- ✸ Power
- ✸ Acceptance
- ✸ Moral virtue

Competence   School-age children are striving for a balance between industry and inferiority (Erikson, 1993). They want to be able to make and do things and feel grown up, but their skill levels sometimes are insufficient to complete the tasks they begin. Robert Havighurst (1972) identified two developmental tasks of this period *as improving skill in the use of fine muscles* and *learning more realistic ways of observing and controlling physical objects.* You can see how reaching those developmental tasks can result in higher levels of that characteristic Erikson described as "industry."

Developing competence is a gradual process, and it is important that children realize the relationship of effort to ability. Praise small achievements, and encourage children to persist through confusion, frustration, even boredom. Share your own stories of achievement, including the times you thought you would fail, or did. Becoming competent may be its own reward, but receiving recognition for the effort it takes to get there can help children stay the course. However, false praise is just that—false—and most children see right through it. Too much praise for too little effort leads to false expectations in the future.

Power   Power in this context means taking control over one's own behavior rather than being a helpless victim of forces too strong to control (Curry, 1990). This is another way of saying self-efficacy. Children who see themselves as victims believe they are dependent on external forces (the teacher is boring) or their genetic makeup (our family isn't good at math). A sense of self-efficacy can provide a child with the courage to take academic or social risks, try out new skills, and seek new achievements. And, when they achieve success, self-efficacy also allows youngsters to take pride in it and recognize their own role in achieving it. To help children develop this characteristic, engage them in shared decision making about ordinary things. "I was thinking about moving the couch. Where do you think we should put it?" And talk to them about their small successes, reminding them that their skills and effort were the reason they achieved their goals. Encouragement is helpful, also. Reassure a child that "You can do this," if he becomes frustrated in the middle of a homework assignment or an art project. Even observing other children perform tasks can have a strong influence on self-efficacy. For example, a second grader who watches a group of third graders practicing the multiplication tables during afterschool time is more likely to approach the same task a year later with the attitude that he will be successful.

Acceptance   Listen to children when they share their doubts and fears about making and keeping friends, developing athletic skills, or learning how to read or solve algebraic equations. Knowing that they are being listened to and that their feelings are being acknowledged are powerful antidotes to the negative messages they may be hearing on the playground, in school, or at home. Children's social relations can be stormy and painful during the school years, and their self-doubts can be magnified when they have no one to reflect back to them. Your program may be the only place in their day where they feel safe and appreciated. Children need to learn how to deal with adversity and disappointment, but they also need to have someone who understands that they are doing so (Young-Eisendrath, 2009).

Moral Virtue   Create an environment of fairness in your program. For children in middle childhood, "fairness is the dominant moral standard" (Curry, 1990, p. 146). At age 24 my daughter still remembers the unfair treatment her best friend received at the hands of an elementary school teacher and came to realize that it began her friend's slide into discouragement and lack of motivation that took years to overcome. Many adults carry feelings of unworthiness and anger resulting from unjust treatment at the hands of adults in positions of authority. Set standards and expect youngsters to strive to meet them—equally. Watch for your own biases (we all have them), and guard against raising or lowering the bar based on your own perceptions of a child's capabilities. Research has shown that the more fairly adult leaders treat individual children and youth during after-school activities, the better the youngsters will treat one another. The adults serve as role models, setting a high level of expectation for how all members of the group should interact and get along (Grossman, Campbell, & Raley, 2006). Curry and her co-author, Carl Johnson, identified ways that adults can promote self-esteem and guide youngsters through the modeling and self-evaluation stages of development. Table 6.3 identifies some of those strategies.

In addition to setting up an environment for the development of self-esteem, it is important for youngsters to have many opportunities to *do* things and

TABLE 6.3   Using Curry's Four Dimensions of Self-esteem.

Competence	Praise small achievements.
	Encourage children to persist through confusion, frustration, even boredom.
	Share stories of achievement, including times you thought you would fail—or did.
Power/Self-efficacy	Engage children in shared decision-making about ordinary things.
	Talk to them about their small successes, reminding them that their skills and effort were the reason they achieved their goals.
	Encourage children who are struggling with a task.
	Allow children to observe other children performing tasks successfully.
Acceptance	Listen to children when they share their doubts and fears.
	Your program may be the only place in their day where they feel safe and appreciated.
Moral Virtue	Create an environment of fairness.
	Watch for your own biases.
	Guard against raising or lowering the bar based on your own perceptions of a child's capabilities.

Source: Based on Curry, N. E., & Johnson, C. N. (1990). *Beyond self-esteem: Developing a genuine sense of human value* (Research Monograph Volume 4). Washington, DC: The National Association for the Education of Young Children.

opportunities to *evaluate* the results of those activities. It is important not to offer empty praise to children—they are smart enough to know that is valueless. In fact, self-esteem-building exercises can backfire if they do not teach children to acknowledge and deal with their shortcomings as well as their strengths (Young-Eisendrath, 2009). People with high self-esteem are realistic about their strengths and weaknesses and are able to set goals and work toward them with optimism and humor. Adult feedback must be authentic and reflect the knowledge and understanding that every child is unique and his or her strengths and weaknesses integrate to create the whole child.

Michelle Borba (2003), a popular lecturer on the topic of self-esteem, considers the role of adults to be the providers of "building blocks," or life experiences that allow a child to gradually acquire the feelings listed above. Activities such as learning to read a bus schedule and travel to a nearby community, participating in an athletic event, or putting on a play for one's classmates and parents are all examples of these building blocks of self-esteem.

Moral Reasoning and Values Clarification

"SHAME," cried out the cover of *Newsweek* magazine in 2-inch-high letters. Subtitled "How do we bring back a sense of right and wrong?" the collection of articles inside described a society in which convicted embezzlers show no remorse, unmarried welfare recipients continue to bear children at public expense, and fathers openly avoid paying support for their families (Klein, 1995). Ten years later, Mueller (2005) wrote

> young people growing up in the postmodern culture have lost their sense of right and wrong as they grow up in the world without a clear sense of moral direction. They seek to find their way on their own, only to be molded and shaped by a postmodern media culture and circle of peers that is equally lost and confused. (p. 12)

One does not need to look very far in the newspaper or the evening news to find examples of moral decay among our corporate leaders, government officials, or highly paid athletes. How can we explain this to children and youth and convince them to live by a higher code of ethics?

The burden of teaching right and wrong has historically been placed with the family, but adults who work with school-age children become almost an extension of those families, partners with the parents in the socialization process. Positive role models can have a strong influence on children's **ethical decision making**, and an environment in which children talk about the confusing sets of values they see around them can add greatly to their moral development. It is also important to understand the way children of different ages perceive ethical dilemmas and how they arrive at their decisions.

Lawrence Kohlberg (1969) proposed a widely accepted theory of children's moral development. He outlined three levels of moral thinking, related to their understanding of rules, justice, and social order. Other theorists have developed explanations for the way in which children develop their moral compass (Damon, 1990, 1991; Gilligan, 1993; Piaget, 1932/1965). These theories are described in Chapter 5. Later chapters suggest ways you can provide school-age children with opportunities to develop moral values and self-control.

SUMMARY

Socialization, which can be intentional or unintentional, is the process by which children learn the rules and behaviors of their society so that they can function within it. Agents of socialization include parents, caregivers, teachers, peers, and the media. Outcomes of socialization include behaviors, attitudes, emotions, and motivations. Self-esteem requires knowing and accepting both your strengths and your weaknesses. When both parents work, the worker in the school-age setting becomes more influential in the socialization process. It is important that professionals in this realm understand socialization and provide models, activities, and opportunities for reflective communication with the children in their programs.

TERMS TO LEARN

acceptance	internalized conversation
agents of socialization	literacy
anorexia	modeling
attitudes	moral virtue
behaviors	motivations
bulimia	obesity
competence	others
cultural schemas	play
dimensions of self-esteem	power
emotions	self
ethical decision making	self-efficacy
games	self-esteem
guidance system	self-regulation
I/me	self-respect
intentional socialization	socialization
internalize	unintentional socialization

REVIEW QUESTIONS

1. How do "other people" function in the socialization process?

2. Give one example of intentional socialization and one of unintentional socialization.

3. List three agents of socialization.

4. List the four dimensions of self-esteem.

CHALLENGE EXERCISES

1. Name three people who have had an influence on your self-esteem.
2. Select a person you know to be a model for socialization. Describe the person, then try to imagine how a child might behave if he or she identified with that person.
3. Observe a group of strangers riding together in an elevator. Describe how they act. Do they talk with one another? Which way do they face? How do you suppose they all learned how to behave in this situation?
4. Imagine that you are about to embark upon a road trip with 20 children, aged 7 to 10. What preparation would you give the children for the trip? What kind of ground rules would you set for their behavior away from home?

INTERNET RESOURCES

The Bobo Doll Experiment:
http://www.criminology.fsu.edu/crimtheory/bandura.htm

Intentional and Unintentional Socialization:
http://www.education.com/reference/article/family-socialization

The Effects of Cultural Schema and Reading Activities on Reading Comprehension:
http://www.readingmatrix.com/conference/pp/proceedings/razi.pdf

REFERENCES

Bandura, A. (1973). *Aggression: A social learning analysis.* Englewood Cliffs, NJ: Prentice-Hall.

Barbour, C. B. N. (2008). *Families, schools, and communities* (4th ed.). Columbus, OH: Merrill.

Blackmore, S. (1999). *The meme machine.* Oxford, UK: Oxford University Press.

Blair, M. (1995, August 11). Class on manners alerts kids to changing times. *Dispatch,* p. D4.

Borba, M. (2003). *No more misbehavin': 38 difficult behaviors and how to stop them.* San Francisco: Jossey-Bass.

Bronfenbrenner, U. (1979) *The ecology of human development.* Cambridge, MA: Harvard University Press.

Bureau of the Census. (2004). *Income, poverty, and health insurance coverage in the United States: 2004* (Series P-70, No. 9). Washington, DC: U.S. Department of Commerce.

Centers for Disease Control and Prevention. (2006). *Prevalence of overweight among children and adolescents: United States, 2003–2004.* Retrieved April 19, 2010, from http://www.cdc.gov/nchs/pressroom/06facts/obesity03_04.htm

Clark, R. (1989). *The role of parents in ensuring educational success in school restructuring efforts.* Washington, DC: Council of Chief State School Officers.

Clark, R. (2002). Ten hypotheses about what predicts student achievement for African-American students and all other students: What the research shows. In W. Allen (Ed.), *African-American Education* (pp. 155–177). Oxford, UK: Elsevier Science.

Coopersmith, S. (1981). *The antecedents of self-esteem.* Palo Alto, CA: Consulting Psychology Press.

Curry, N. J. C. (1990). *Beyond self-esteem: Developing a genuine sense of human value.* Washington, DC: National Association for the Education of Young Children.

Damon, W. (1990). *The moral child.* New York: The Free Press.

Damon, W. (1991, Fall). Putting substance into self-esteem: A focus on academic and moral values. *Educational Horizons,* 12–18.

Derman-Sparks, L. (2006). *What if all the kids are White: Anti-bias, multicultural education with young children and families.* New York: Teachers College Press.

Derman-Sparks, L., & ABC Task Force. (1989). *Anti-bias curriculum: Tools for empowering young children.* Washington, DC: National Association for the Education of Young Children.

Dreikurs, R. S. V. (1990). *Children: The challenge.* New York: Plume.

Elkin, F. (1989). *The child & society: The process of socialization* (5th ed.) New York: Random House. (Original work published in 1960)

Erikson, E. H. (1993). *Childhood and society* (Reissue ed.). New York: Norton. (Original work published in 1950)

Gilligan, C. (1993). *In a different voice: Psychological theory and women's development.* Cambridge, MA: Harvard University Press.

Glenn, H. S., & Nelsen, J. (2000). *Raising self-reliant children in a self-indulgent world.* Roseville, CA: Prima.

Grossman, J., Campbell, M., & Raley, B. (2006). *Quality time after school: What instructors can do to enhance learning.* Philadelphia: Beacon Centers.

Havighurst, R. J. (1972). *Developmental Tasks and Education.* New York: Longman.

Klein, J. (1995, February 6). How do we bring back a sense of right and wrong? *Newsweek,* 12.

Kohlberg, L. (1981). *Essays on moral development, vol. I: The philosophy of moral development.* San Francisco: Harper & Row.

Konigsburg, E. L. (1973). *From the mixed-up files of Mrs. Basil E. Frankweiler.* New York: Dell. (Original work published in 1967)

Kurz-Riemer, K. (2005). *Minnesota School Age Core Competencies.* St. Paul: Minnesota Professional Development Council.

Levin, D. E. (2003). *Teaching young children in violent times: Building a peaceable classroom* (2nd ed.). Cambridge, MA: Educators for Social Responsibility.

Lynch, E. W., & Hanson, M. J. (2004). *Developing cross-cultural competence: A guide for working with children and their families* (3rd ed.). Baltimore: Paul H. Brookes.

Marion, M. (2006). *Guidance of young children* (7th ed.). Columbus, OH: Merrill.

Mead, G. H. (1934). *Mind, self and society.* Chicago: University of Chicago Press.

Miller, B. M. (1995). *Out-of-school time: Effects on learning in the primary grades.* Wellesley, MA: Center for Research on Women, National Institute on Out-of-School Time.

Montessori, M. (1988). *The Montessori method* (A. E. George, Trans.). New York: Schocken. (Original work published in 1912)

Mueller, W. (2005, June). Living and teaching right from wrong. *Youth Culture @ Today,* 12–13.

Nishida, H. (2005). Cultural schema theory. In W. B. Gudykunst (Ed.), *Theorizing about intercultural communication* (pp. 401–418). Thousand Oaks, CA: Sage.

Ollhoff, J., & Ollhoff, L. (2007). *Getting along: Teaching social skills to children and youth.* Farmington, MN: Sparrow Media Group.

Piaget, J. (1965). *The moral judgment of the child* (M. Gabain, Trans.). New York: The Free Press. (Original work published in 1932)

School's Out! Washington. (2005). Skills standards for school-age care professionals. Seattle, WA: Author.

Secretary's Commission on Achieving Necessary Skills. (2006, March 9). *What work requires of schools.* Retrieved July 28, 2008. http://wdr.doleta.gov/SCANS/whatwork/

Seligson, M. (2001). School-age child care today. *Young Children,* 56, 90–94.

Tarde, G. (1969). *On communication & social influence.* Chicago: University of Chicago Press.

UNESCO Education Sector. (2004). *The plurality of literacy and its implications for policies and programs* (Position paper). Paris: UNESCO.

Wallace, D. S. M. (1991, September). Are we preparing our kids for the real world? *Good Housekeeping,* 157–159.

Young-Eisendrath, P. (2009). *The self-esteem trap: Raising confident and compassionate kids in an age of self-importance.* New York: Little, Brown.

Chapter
7

Issues Facing Today's Children

Heffalumps and Woozles and Things that go Bump in the Night . . .
(MILNE, 1974)

The nature of childhood has changed significantly in the last several generations. The **social revolution** that began after World War II and continued each decade since has altered gender roles and individual and family responsibilities, and it has also resulted in the reapportionment of traditional childrearing responsibilities.

In the current economic climate, few families can afford to have one parent stay at home to make hot breakfasts, drive in a car pool, participate in the children's classrooms, and supervise them after school. In addition, the proportion of children growing up in single-parent households has more than doubled in recent decades (Snyder, McLaughlin, & Findeis, 2006). Female-headed families accounted for 7.5 million households in 2000, while in 2.2 million other homes, fathers raised their children without a mother present (Bureau of the Census, 2004).

In those families, unless there is significant participation from the other parent, it falls on the same person over and over to take time from work to care for ill children; transport them to the doctor, the dentist, and the orthodontist; and participate in classroom activities, including teacher conferences.

To effectively meet the social and emotional needs of children, therefore, professionals in school-age settings must work in partnership with time-strapped parents in the care of their children and design program environments to be nurturing and loving refuges from the sometimes rather overwhelming realities of daily life.

PARENTS' AND CHILDREN'S FEARS AND CONCERNS

To take on this role of partner, you will need to understand the specialized needs and concerns of today's children. Some of these are **developmental issues**, which reflect the different ways in which children interact with one another and with adults, how they use their bodies and minds, and how they view logical or moral dilemmas at different ages. In addition, each decade brings different **generational issues** that emerge according to the current social circumstances, economic realities, and media coverage as well as cultural and ethnic demographics.

As a way of understanding generational issues, it is helpful to compare typical school concerns in two different historical periods. In the 1940s, public school teachers reported the following kinds of rule infringement as top disciplinary problems: talking out of turn, running in the halls, chewing gum, making noise, and not putting paper in the waste basket (Evans, 1999). Today, teachers deal with bullying, robbery, personal theft, drug and alcohol abuse, teenage pregnancy, vandalism, and even murder (Noonan & Vavra, 2007). Children have learned that they may face horrifying situations and difficult decisions in their schools, their neighborhoods, and en route between them.

Concerns of Parents

In 2005, nearly 2,000 parents were surveyed about their concerns related to their children. Nearly 70% reported that their children were "too stressed," mostly about school, but also about divorce, separation issues, and family finances (Survey and Policy Research Institute, 2007). Depression also ranked high on the list of parental worries. In a later survey by the C. S. Mott Children's Hospital, adult Americans were asked to rate 17 different health concerns for children living in their communities. Topping the list were smoking and drug and alcohol abuse, teen pregnancy, and growing obesity numbers (C. S. Mott Children's Hospital, 2007).

A more recent study by the C. S. Mott Children's Hospital (2009) showed that parents across the United States are increasingly becoming concerned about their children's safety online. Eighty-one percent of parents reported their children ages 9–17 use the Internet and access Web sites without adult supervision. Forty-six percent reported that their children ages 9–17 who access the Internet by themselves have their own social networking profiles on sites like Facebook, MySpace and BlackPlanet. Of parents with youngsters online, nearly two-thirds are concerned about online sexual predators and about loss of privacy. About half of the parents worry about their children viewing pornographic material, especially the parents of boys, who also worry about their sons playing online games obsessively. A ranking of specific concerns with Internet safety showed that sexual predators concerned them the most, followed by loss of privacy, viewing pornographic material, playing online games, becoming a victim of online bullying, and online gambling (C. S. Mott Children's Hospital, 2009).

Health care and insurance are critical concerns for all American parents, but especially so for families of color. According to the Children's Defense Fund, African American and Latino children have less access to regular health care than white children and higher incidences of childhood illnesses. "Black children are 56 percent more likely than white children to have gone more than two years without seeing a doctor and almost three times as likely as white children to use the emergency room as their usual place of health care," wrote Marian Wright Edelman, president of the Children's Defense Fund (2009, para 3). In addition, "more than 30 percent of Black children and about 40 percent of Latino children report not receiving dental care" (para 4). The most common health problems

Violence is a harsh reality many children live with every day.

(obesity, high asthma rates, accidents, and substance abuse) can be directly related to poverty, and consistently poor health can lead to developmental delays that limit minority children's success in school. The Children's Defense Fund reported that nearly a million Black children under 18 were still living in extreme poverty in spite of the overall improvement in family income for Black families since 1999 (Children's Defense Fund, 2003). In 2007, Black and Hispanic children were more than twice as likely to live in poverty as non-Hispanic white and Asian children (Child Trends, 2009).

In addition, far too many families—of all ethnicities—live with the fear of violence in their homes, their communities, and their schools. An increase in parental concern about school violence specifically is evident in the results of Gallup's annual Crime Poll, conducted every October. In the 2006 study, nearly half of American parents reported that they "frequently" or "occasionally" worry about "having a school-aged child of yours physically harmed while attending school." That is one of parents' top crime fears along with having their home burglarized when they are not home (50% worry at least occasionally about this) and having their car stolen or broken into (Jones, 2006).

Children who grow up in neighborhoods where violence is common find it difficult to concentrate and to learn, and they may show signs of **depression** and **learned helplessness** because they see no way of escaping their personal nightmares. Parents report high levels of stress and absenteeism as a result of these problems.

Concerns of Children

In 2003, 200 children aged 10–14 were surveyed to evaluate how threatened they felt by terrorism and the possibility of nuclear war. Nearly a third of the participants ranked terrorism as the most important problem America faces today, with the threat of nuclear war only slightly below it (Garatti & Rudnitski, 2007). As American servicemen and -women continue to carry out military missions overseas, their families experience varying amounts of worry and fear. The Scripps Howard News Service identified over a thousand children who had lost a parent in Iraq and interviewed military families to understand the effects of their parents' military service on children. They learned that, in addition to the terrible grief and privation faced by families who have lost someone, all children whose mother or father had been deployed overseas lost sleep and peace of mind while their parent was in harm's way (Rosenberg, Gegax, Wingert, Briscoe, & Shenfeld, 2005).

In contrast, however, many children's statements about what concerns and frightens them appear to be the same today as what children have feared in the past. These issues relate as much to the developing mind and body as to the specific and chronological circumstances of life.

In 1968, a group of researchers asked children to rank their fears, using a list of 80 items. Three of the top ten were getting poor grades, being sent to the principal, and having their parents argue. In 1985, the same list was presented to children over 7 years of age. Only two new fears had joined the top ten: a burglar breaking into the house and falling from a high place. In both lists, however, more than a third of the children were afraid of "bombing attacks—being invaded" (Schachter & McCauley, 1988). Eighty percent of the children in a 1983 study listed being killed or a family member dying, and 70% worried about the house burning down, being followed by strange people and being kidnapped (Schachter & McCauley, 1988). Interestingly enough, in spite of periodic media coverage of school shootings in various parts of the country, only 12% of parents with children in kindergarten through Grade 12 polled by Gallup (August 13–16, 2007) said their child had recently expressed worry or concern about feeling unsafe at their school. The same poll indicated that 24% of parents feared for their children's safety at school (down, however, from 2006, when the poll took place only a week after 32-year-old Carl Charles Roberts IV shot 10 schoolgirls, ranging in age from 6 to 13 years old, at the one-room West Nickel Mines Amish School in Lancaster County, Pennsylvania).

Children's Need to Feel Safe

Events and fears that concern children may not be the same as those that keep adults awake at night, but they are often quite intense, troublesome, and definitely *real*, and they should never be ignored. There are some predictable things that all children fear at certain ages, but there are others that relate to the current circumstances of their family or culture. However, whatever these fears may be, if ignored they can have a serious impact on children's ability to grow, develop, and learn.

Abraham Maslow's Hierarchy of Needs   A psychologist who was interested in understanding this kind of dynamic was Abraham Maslow (1908–1970). He formulated a theory of human motivation that was based on a hierarchy of basic and growth needs. Maslow proposed that each of us has the strongest need for a solid foundation that consists of basic **survival needs** (food, water, clothing, shelter, air). This foundation is depicted in Figure 7.1 as the base of a triangle. Then, resting upon the basic **physiological needs**, are **safety and security needs**, which, when met, allow you to feel confident that your family and home will offer you

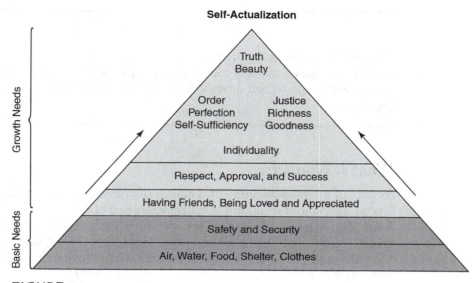

FIGURE 7.1   Maslow's Hierarchy of Needs.

Source: Based on *Motivation and Personality* (2nd ed., p. 74), by A. Maslow, 1970, New York: Harper & Row.

stability and protection. This is the area in **Maslow's Hierarchy of Needs** that flares up when children's parents lose their jobs or their home or when their neighborhoods are unsafe.

Until the first set of needs—air, water, food, clothing, and shelter—are satisfied, the second set has little meaning. If you're hungry or thirsty, for example, it's difficult to think about much else. Once the survival needs are met, the need to secure that survival (quite literally, "hold on to your food") becomes the most important consideration in the life of the child until that need is satisfied also. Only when children are warm, fed, and housed, with some confidence that they will be able to maintain that condition, can they begin to move up the hierarchy and think about having friends, being loved and appreciated (**social needs**), and trying to earn respect, approval, and success (**esteem needs**).

For children to be able to form friendships and develop a culturally sensitive morality, two developmental tasks of this period (Havighurst, 1953), they need to be relatively free from worrying about their physical safety and comfort and security. Only then will they be able to achieve more abstract, but appealing, goals such as a sense of belonging, respect from others, confidence, self-respect, and achievement. Maslow's research rested on the Western worldview of individualism, and he presented the highest level of the hierarchy as the need for self-actualization, or "being all that you can be." In his view, to become self-actualized (which to him meant "complete"), you need to have all the other needs met up to that point. A family may not share Maslow's worldview. Many cultures value interdependency over individualism. However, even if the goal is simply to help children become competent and confident adults, the theory has value for anyone who works with children. In summary: *In order to thrive, children need to be well nourished and safe and know they are loved.*

What kinds of things frightened you when you were a child? Do you remember any specific fears that kept you awake at night or made it difficult to do certain things, such as go to bed or walk down the hall to the bathroom in the middle of the night?

What Is Normal?

As part of a school assignment, child development students asked youngsters in several afterschool programs what they worried about at night. Answers ranged from "I'm scared I won't pass my spelling test on Friday" and "Who will take care of Fluffy (a rabbit in the third grade classroom) during summer vacation?" to "My dad might lose his job and we might have to move to Tennessee." or "What happens if our house catches on fire during the night?"

Common childhood fears are very similar even in different cultures, but they may differ considerably by age and by gender (Dong, Yang, & Ollendick, 1994; Ollendick, King, & Muris, 2003). In other words, as the children develop and grow, what frightens them and how they react to it changes.

Very young infants, for example, do not usually express fear when their parents or caregivers leave the room, while 8- or 9-month-old children (in the United States) develop **separation anxiety** as they develop an understanding of their own separateness and vulnerability to abandonment. We typically describe this separation anxiety as "normal." In more interdependent cultures, where young children are rarely, if ever, left alone in a room, separation anxiety may not occur until much later—at the start of school or even when the youngsters depart for college.

Developmental psychologists remind us that children become frightened of things only once they experience them or begin to understand the possibilities for hurt or sadness. Their understanding changes as they develop more complex thought. By the age of 5 or 6, children begin to understand and fear real-life dangers, such as fire, burglaries, or national disasters. Around age 8 or 9, fears about thunder, dogs, doctors, or the dark begin to give way to **social anxiety**, or worries about measuring up to their peers. Is my hair okay? How about my skin? I can't remember my spelling words! What if I forget my lines (or the music, or miss the ball . . .)? Twelve-year-olds worry about their hair, their clothes, their skin, but they also fear more abstract economic problems such as layoffs, homelessness, and hunger, and by this time they are very much more aware of the potential for chaos and inequity in the world. Adolescents may experience anxiety related to social acceptance and academic achievement.

Some fears, therefore, appear and disappear as part of a child's normal development. Fear of animals, loud noises, doctors, and the dark will be outgrown. As a child grows, one fear may disappear or replace another. For example, a child who couldn't sleep with the light off at age 5 may enjoy a ghost story at camp 6 years later. And some fears may extend only to one particular kind of stimulus.

FIGURE 7.2 Children's Fears and Anxieties Change as Children Grow and Develop.

- Babies experience stranger anxiety, clinging to parents when confronted by people they don't recognize.

- Toddlers exhibit separation anxiety, becoming emotionally distressed when one or both parents leave.

- Children ages 4 through 6 tend to fear things not based in reality, such monsters and ghosts. They also may experience separation anxiety when they enter preschool or kindergarten. Magical thinking makes them think they cause bad things to happen.

- Youngsters ages 7 through 12 fear circumstances that could actually happen to them, such as bodily injury and natural disasters. Concerns may be triggered by media coverage of events that take place far away.

- Adolescents experience anxiety related to personal appearance, social acceptance, and athletic or academic achievement. They also worry about human rights, government policies, and injustice in all places.

A child may want to pet a lion at the zoo but wouldn't dream of going near the neighbor's dog. Figure 7.2 lists the way in which normal fears change as children develop.

How important is it that you recognize and address children's fears and anxieties? Many adults are tormented by fears that stem from childhood experiences. An adult's fear of public speaking may be the result of embarrassment in front of peers many years before. If anxious feelings persist, they can take a toll on the child's sense of well-being. Even the anxiety associated with social avoidance (staying alone instead of with friends) can have long-term effects. For example, a child who fears being rejected may fail to engage with other children in ways that would help him learn important social skills, resulting eventually in social isolation and loneliness.

Children in school-age programs may also be at personal risk from violence, not only in their neighborhoods but in their own homes. Such children may develop behaviors such as biting, hitting, or destroying other children's property, or they may turn within themselves, cry easily, lose their appetites, or cling to a toy or a trusted person. The more violence they experience, the more serious these behavioral clues may become (Paul, 1995; Rossman, 2001).

It is important for workers in child and youth settings to recognize and identify the signs and symptoms of children's anxieties shown in Figure 7.3 so that these feelings do not become an obstacle to children's normal emotional development (King, Muris, & Ollendick, 2005).

After children begin formal operational thinking, around 11 or 12, **societal concerns** enter their awareness. Now worries about homeless people, AIDS victims, children starving in Third World countries, and personal fears of family bankruptcy, divorce, or burglary appear. The natural process of developing a conscience carries with it a gradually dawning awareness of unfairness, unevenness of wealth and opportunity, and eventually a more global view of humankind's inhumanity to humankind. This growing awareness is a positive sign in terms of a child's development, but the first symptom many children have of this new thinking ability is fear or anxiety.

FIGURE 7.3 Signs of Anxiety in Children.

Some signs that a child may be anxious about something may include the following:

- Becoming clingy, impulsive, or distracted
- Nervous movements, such as temporary twitches
- Problems getting to sleep and/or staying asleep longer than usual
- Sweaty hands
- Accelerated heart rate and breathing
- Nausea
- Headaches
- Stomach anxiety

These signs stay with us as adults.

Source: Based on "Anxiety in Young Children," by A. S. Berger, 1971, *Young Children, 27*, pp. 5–11.

Generational Fears

Like children of every generation, today's children reflect the traumatic events and conditions they encounter in the anxieties they feel. A year after the September 11th attacks on the World Trade towers in New York City resulted in 24-hour television coverage for a week, many children around the country were still anxious and afraid of a repeat attack. Reflecting on the increased incidence of post-traumatic stress disorder in these children, Shannon Smith and Cynthia Reynolds (2002) wrote, "The innocence that once existed amongst our children is now lost forever. No longer do they feel the safety and security that once existed in generations past" (p. 27). Thousands of children were uprooted and their lives changed forever by Hurricane Katrina when it hit New Orleans on August 29, 2005. However, children in every part of the country were also affected and will always remember the images of displaced and traumatized children during the aftermath of that event.

However, these **generational fears** have existed in the lives of every generation alive today, usually resulting from dramatic events that took place during their formative years. Traditionalists, those people born before 1945, still tell stories about post– Depression era food shortages, World War II, and the bombing of Pearl Harbor. Baby Boomers remember the days that President Kennedy, Martin Luther King, Jr., and Robert Kennedy were shot. Growing up in a home with great grandparents and grandparents, children may observe behaviors and attitudes that reflect those earlier experiences. Traditionalists still scrape half the butter off a piece of bread, 50 years after World War II food rationing ended; Baby Boomers still vote for gun-control legislation. It is these generational differences that shape us and contribute to our values, beliefs, and attitudes. However, it also contributes to what we lightly call the "generation gap"—that difficulty in understanding the fears, concerns, and attitudes of people who are significantly older or younger than we are.

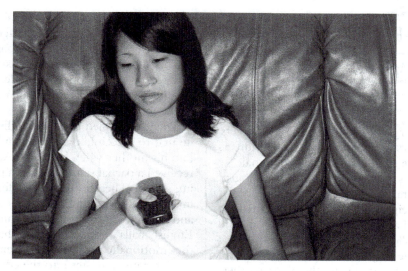

Media coverage of frightening events may be a source of stress or anxiety for some children.

Some Strategies That Can Help

So, whose job is it to fix all this? How do you, as a professional youth worker, respond to parents' worries and children's fears? Knowing what it is that frightens children is a big help. So is understanding the changes that are taking place in society and how some people are learning to handle their own and children's concerns. It is also helpful to know what you *cannot* expect to do, or should not attempt.

An afterschool program can be a good environment in which to address children's fears. Never try to minimize or denigrate children's feelings. That is likely to result in the frightened child keeping his feelings locked up inside, not only afraid of what originally frightened him but now also frightened of sharing the fear with others. When you model respect for children's fears, the other children in the program will learn sensitive ways to respond to their friends' private monsters. In Perspective 7.1 Marion Wright Edelman illustrates two examples of how afterschool programs can play a protective role in children's lives.

Sometimes play activities, such as "let's pretend," can help children master specific fears. Very young children who are afraid of the dark, or of animals, may benefit from playing "We're Going on a Bear Hunt" (Rosen & Oxenbury, 1997); older children can pretend to be marooned on a desert island or at summer camp and role-play scenarios with their friends. In the case of major disasters, children can be encouraged to act out the events they see on the news and try to get control over the outcome. Play activities that relate directly to hurricanes, for example, are building houses and knocking them down (and building them back up), playing with boats and water, and pretending to be rescue workers (Myers-Walls, 2005). In this way, children can work on the fear while maintaining a boundary between fantasy and reality. Other methods for working through fears in a group include painting the frightening situation, then talking about it, and performing puppet shows with one character acting out the frightened child and another a helpful friend.

PERSPECTIVE 7.1

Proof That After-School Programs Work

Marian Wright Edelman, Children's Defense Fund President

Jennifer Lowery sings in her church choir, acts in school plays, coaches swimming, volunteers at the Baltimore Aquarium and the National Zoo, and dreams of becoming a marine biologist. Diego Ivan Duran works part-time, mentors a small group of eighth graders, runs and advocacy group for Latino students at his school, and is aiming for college and then graduate school.

As remarkable as these Maryland students are, what's even more amazing are the obstacles they have overcome to accomplish so much. That's why CDF recently honored them for *beating the odds*. Jennifer and Diego have reminded me once again that avoiding school failure, alienation, too-early pregnancy, and resisting violence are possible when young people possess reserves of inner strength, have positive adult role models, and are engaged in productive activities when they're not in school. It is these extracurricular activities that have boosted their self-esteem and given Jennifer and Diego a feeling of connectedness to the community, despite the daunting circumstances in their personal lives.

Jennifer, 17, grew up in a home where her father battered her mother and regularly hurled verbal insults at his two children. When Jennifer was a sophomore, her father announced that he had put the house into foreclosure and allowed the car to be repossessed. Then he abandoned the family.

A shelter was home for the family until Mrs. Lowery—who had never worked outside the home—got a job managing a retail store. Making ends meet is still hard. Yet Jennifer, thanks to her mother, guidance counselor, and math teacher, has maintained her focus. "Involvement really keeps people out of trouble," notes Jennifer, after reciting her range of positive after-school activities that mean so much to her.

Diego struggled to learn English after he emigrated to the United States from Venezuela to join his mother when he was 9. At age 13, he received a partial scholarship at a private boarding school. Then his mother suffered a spinal injury, and Diego had to leave boarding school and go to work to support the family. His shaky English skills mistakenly landed him in a school for emotionally disturbed children.

Determined to get into the educational mainstream, Diego taught himself how to read and write English, and within a year he was attending his local public high school. Now 18 and a senior, Diego has devoted himself to helping others by forming a school-based tutoring and community service project.

"There are things you can learn from after-school activities that you can't learn from a book, like how to deal with people," says Diego, who credits his adviser Daniel Garcia and his mother for keeping him on the right track. "It prepares you for life."

These two are living proof that after-school programs are one of the essential keys to a bright future. They not only offer emotional support and positive friendships for young people but also provide a sense of community that is so often lacking today.

Source: Edelman, M.W. (1997). Proof that after-school programs work, *A Voice for Children*. Used by permission of the Children's Defense Fund.

Refer parents to books that address children's fears, and read them yourself. An excellent resource is *Taming Monsters, Slaying Dragons* (Feiner, 1988). A broad selection of children's normal developmental fears are described, along with some strategies for helping frightened children to overcome or manage their fears. A discussion of family systems and support networks contained in the book can also be also helpful for you as you work with children in the afterschool environment. Some of the scenarios are quite plausible, such as fearing loss of a home when a parent is unemployed or deployed overseas, or fearing a bully who lives in the child's neighborhood. Sometimes it is not possible to remove the situation causing the fear, and unresolved fear can be crippling and paralyzing. You can also help children resolve their fears by using some of the strategies in this chapter.

Some workers in child and youth settings help reduce children's vulnerability directly by volunteering in the community to develop neighborhood watch groups and other support services for parents and youth to help them cope with situations that threaten their safety, such as a walk-to-school program that provides help for children to get to and from school safely. In this way you can learn more about the specific situations children in your program are facing and increase the likelihood that solutions will be found.

Young school-aged children are still learning the difference between fantasy and reality. Their fears frequently reflect **magical thinking,** or believing that their thoughts can influence circumstances around them. Older children respond well if you appeal to their growing logical notions of cause and effect, historic and present time, and the ability to discriminate size, weight, and volume of objects, including fearsome ones. "It is harder to fear something if you are busy analyzing how it works" (Schachter & McCauley, 1988). Another valuable resource is *How to Talk to Your Kids About Really Important Things: Specific Questions and Answers and Useful Things to Say* (Shaefer & DiGeronimo, 1994). In this book, the authors address adoption, alcoholic parents, death of a loved one or pet, hospital stay, repeating a grade, sleep-away camp, HIV/AIDS, homosexuality, war, and others topics that may trouble youngsters in some way.

As a result of the media blitzes following the 9/11 terror attacks and Hurricane Katrina, several child development professionals developed guidelines for practitioners to use with their children. Figure 7.4 provides a summary of these ideas.

FIGURE 7.4 Guidelines for Helping Children Cope With Fear.

---

1. **Take some time to organize your own feelings and thoughts.** You need to be your most thoughtful, calm, and emotionally stable self when you talk to children. Be prepared for the inevitable difficult questions about why people kill, why war happens, why people die, and why people hate. Convey stability and calmness.

2. **Take your cues from the children themselves.** Don't initiate discussion about events the children don't otherwise know about. If they have heard about something that is upsetting them, respond at first to their questions, then see where the discussion leads.

3. **Find a way to make the tragedy or conflict understandable to the child.** Every child is different, and the explanation of national and world events should match the child's developmental understanding.

4. **Respect the growing ability of children and teenagers to understand issues, and be honest with them.** Many older children for the first time may become interested in larger issues of life in other countries, the military, war and peace, world religions, poverty, tolerance, and life and death.

5. **Focus on positive steps for prevention.** Seek professional help. Demonstrate security measures. Use children's anxiety to reinforce the importance of locks and keys, safety rules, etc.

6. **In every conversation, stay alert to signs of racism and stereotyping, and work for cross-cultural understanding and respect for others.** Be at your best as a human being.

Source: Based on material in *What Happened to the World? Helping Children Cope in Turbulent Times,* by J. Greenman, 2002, Watertown, MA: Bright Horizons Family Solutions; *When Your Child Is Afraid: Understanding the Normal Fears of Childhood From Birth Through Adolescence and Helping Overcome Them,* by R. Schachter, and C. S. McCauley, 1988, New York: Simon and Schuster; and "Helping Children Cope With Tragedy," by R. Scofield, 1995, *School-Age Notes, 15*(9), pp. 2–6.

FAMILY, SCHOOL, AND COMMUNITY ISSUES

Even their own family situation can be a source of concern for children. Parents of children who regularly attend a school-age program probably work outside their homes. Many of your children's parents are likely to be divorced or experiencing separation. At some time during their lives almost all parents are less attentive than they would like to be. At least 7 million American children have alcoholic parents, and 23.8% of children (17 million) live in a household where a parent or other adult is a binge or heavy drinker (National Center on Addiction and Substance Abuse at Columbia University, 2005). These are shocking numbers, and alcohol and drug abuse are family diseases with severe consequences for children.

Children in reconstituted, or blended, families face their own set of challenges. When previously married parents form a new family, the children must learn new rules, new structure, and new traditions. The authority structure changes, as do the respective roles of each of the parents. Some children find it very difficult to adapt to these changes.

In addition, there are more than 1 million homeless children living in the United States, and some of them may be in your program (National Center on Family Homelessness, 2008). Homeless children face disruption of friendships, schoolwork, and structure. They have lost pets, clothing, and possessions, and along with these precious things, many have also lost their self-esteem. Many children are either hungry or on the brink of hunger.

❀ *Consider This:* ❀

Think about a time in your life when you were separated from friends and family or your home and community. How did you feel during that time? In what ways did you cope with this situation?

Divorce, single parenthood, and remarriage all bring with them stresses on children.

When fears or concerns arise out of personally experienced circumstances, individual children may not find a large-group brainstorming session to be helpful or even desirable. Sometimes small groups of children experiencing similar problems can support one another as they deal with frightening changes in their lives or possibilities that have not yet materialized.

One such approach, Rainbows for All Children, is an international peer support program developed for use with children grieving over the loss of a parent through death, divorce, separation, or abandonment. The aim of the program is to help troubled children believe in their own goodness and the value of their own family, whatever its form. Child care professionals and teachers attend training sessions where they learn to provide emotional support for the children by listening with empathy and compassion, sharing feelings, involving them in planning and decision making, and helping forgiveness and acceptance happen. Rainbows is also effective in helping children deal with the sale of the family home, parental unemployment, siblings who go away to college, or pets who die. Operating much like a weekly "club" for anyone who wishes to participate, programs such as Rainbows for All Children can provide a helpful tool for adults working with normal children living through troubled times (Marta, 2003). Divorce is an issue that troubles many children, even long after the grieving and anger have begun to fade. The day-to-day mechanical issues of living in two homes (or traveling long distances to visit a relocated parent) can take a toll on a child's patience, and sometimes failure to figure out how to do this in an organized way can lead to lost homework assignments, missed appointments, late arrival at school, and other events that signal a downward spiral of discouragement and often failure.

Everyone who works with children should be trained to recognize signs of abuse and neglect and work with families at risk to seek help whenever possible. Invite a social worker or counselor from the child protective services in your community to present an in-service workshop to staff and interested parents. Beyond reasonable awareness, it is not within our power to prevent the hurt inflicted in the hearts of children by family disruption or violence. However, engaging children in projects and helping them to develop relationships with others can help them cope with their sadness and distress. Programs that provide a clear structure consisting of boundaries and expectations can provide a sense of security to children from chaotic home environments. Other helpful strategies focus on supporting the families themselves:

- ❀ *Know the parents, know the community.* Know the families you serve, and drive through the communities in which they live. This will put you in tune with the lives of the children you serve. When disruption and violence occur, you are then more likely to sense whether it is coming from the community, the home, the media, or a combination.
- ❀ *Offer parenting advice.* Model good practice with children and share with parents what you know about how children of different ages respond to scary things. Encourage parents to restrict children's viewing of violent videos and television shows, and discuss alternatives to violence-oriented action figures. Parenting workshops combined with potluck dinners can be good settings to present some of these ideas and also good settings in which to initiate friendly relationships with parents.

⚘ *Improve referral networks.* You can serve as a bridge to community support services: for instance, when you provide a telephone number, offer to make an appointment for a parent, or arrange for the social worker, psychologist, or other professional to meet the parent after work at your site. When children are frightened, it is often the case that their parents are also frightened. You can help the child by helping the parent.

If a program like Rainbows exists in your community, invite a representative to speak at a parent workshop. Program staff can also help children adjusting to family situations by being patient listeners, understanding the complications of life that lead to late pickups, lost possessions and homework, short tempers, and unexpected tears (not just of the child, but sometimes also of the parents). Divorce usually is accompanied by a change of residence, of parents changing their usual patterns of work and play, of a loss of old and trusted friends, and an expectation that children will make new friends as the parents' social lives bring new people into their lives. Homelessness and alcoholism increase when the economy is uncertain. Assurances that things will be better in 6 months, in a year, can sometimes help. Use realistic time frames that can help children to look forward to improvement. Things probably *won't* be much better in a week, or in a month. Help children to understand that change takes time, and meanwhile they can learn to cope with their fears and emotions.

If a formal program does not exist, you might try a strategy that was developed by an Australian psychologist whose own daughter sometimes couldn't sleep at night. Dr. Doris Brett (1988) developed a series of stories that mirror many of the real-life situations that make children anxious, such as nightmares, the birth of siblings, starting school for the first time, and coping with divorce or the death of someone close. Designed to calm the fears and build the confidence of her daughter, *Annie Stories: A Special Kind of Storytelling* allows children to explore the situations with an adult storyteller through the experiences of an imaginary boy or girl much like themselves. Storytelling is an art that takes some practice, but these stories make it easy to get started.

In addition to telling stories, reading books to children about potentially frightening events or creatures can help youngsters develop a stronger sense of control over their own safety. For instance, reading about natural disasters such as earthquakes, tornadoes, and hurricanes can show how rarely these events actually occur. Look for stories that illustrate the effectiveness of seat belts to help a child overcome his fear of auto accidents. Depending on the specific concerns, other effective tools are geographical atlases (to show how far away the military zone is) and books about reptiles, spiders, or dogs to build familiarity with animals that are often the object of fear.

Societal Issues

Sometimes the issues that trouble children are outside their own personal spheres. One 9-year-old became distressed about a homeless man she and her mother passed each day on their way to school. Watching him each morning, sitting on the side of the road near the edge of town, blowing on his chapped and cold hands, she worried that he would become ill or be hungry all day. The youngster shared her concern with a staff member at her afterschool center, and after some discussion they decided to learn more about the man. Eventually it came to light that this particular person had turned down an offer of shelter in town and preferred to stay where he was and had been sleeping in a grove of trees nearby for several weeks. He did accept the offer of a warm jacket and some bread and cheese that the children at the center provided, and the worried child felt comforted that something had been done.

As a result of this incident, however, the anxious young lady learned what provisions were being made in her community for homeless people and troubled adults like her new friend and how she and her classmates could assist in fund-raising or other activities. Finding an avenue of service provided her with a means to channel the concern that she felt for him and other needy people. More will be said about this in a later chapter, but this is a role that you can, and probably should, take on—to be a resource to children who have questions about their communities and to help connect them with other people in their community who are concerned about the same things they are. Parents may be at work during the hours when community agency telephones are answered, and this kind of research often needs to take place during that time.

As with the 9/11 attacks and the New Orleans hurricane, sufficient numbers of children in a program may experience anxiety or fear about the same event that it becomes a serious concern of the entire staff. This is common after any major cataclysmic event, such as a hurricane, earthquake, economic setback, or major news story. Dinner-table conversation and the evening news may have a strong influence on children's feelings about the event, especially when it relates to fears and concerns already present in their minds. So, too, can discussions that you lead with groups of children in your program.

Gender-Related Issues

The school years offer children many opportunities for growth and change. Their awareness of people and events broadens from those things that happen within their family and the neighborhood to events that have meaning to the wider community. By fourth or fifth grade, most American children are at least superficially conversant with current events and the existence of other nations, although their knowledge of world geography may be limited. Erik Erikson (1993) described this period as a time when children are learning how to conduct themselves in the world of adults. (Refer to Chapter 5 for a review of Erikson's stages of development.) Erikson believed that social institutions such as schools, the police force, banks, etc. can offer children glimpses of their own future, in the form of adults already in the working world. Erikson had found opportunities to develop autonomy, initiative, and industry in his own life by observing that "decency in human relations, skill in technical details, and the knowledge of facts" (p. 323) would permit him freedom of choice in his pursuits. In the same way, boys and girls draw conclusions about masculinity or femininity, individual worthiness, and how to behave from years of hearing, observing, and reacting to society's messages.

Learning Gender Roles Both girls and boys learn their gender identity through the **microcultural** influences of parents and family and the **macrocultural**

definitions from the wider society. Children monitor their own behavior to match their view of how society wants them to behave. Kindlon and Thompson (1999) believe that much of what boys see and hear is painful and causes them to modify their natural behavior in order to be accepted and to avoid negative responses from others. In the same way, some girls will conform more closely to gender stereotypes than others (Kindlon, 2006).

It is not easy to figure out how to be a boy or a girl today. And a related issue is that when it comes to deciding what they want to do when they grow up, children's choices may be limited not only by their gender role but also by how well they do in school, usually considered to be an indicator of future career success.

Gender and School Success   In 1960, young women made up barely 39% of the undergraduates in U.S. universities, and far less than that number completed an academic degree. In 2006, women were the majority of U.S. college students, and they also completed more bachelor's degrees than men (Goldin, Katz, & Kuziemko, 2006). In between, there had been an intense discussion among scholars and educators about the "plateau effect," the leveling off of previously successful girls' academic achievement in middle and secondary school (Love, 1993; Ornstein, 1994; Sadker & Sadker, 1982, 1994). A review of the early research showed that although boys and girls differed in their physical, emotional, and intellectual development, there was no biological reason for their disparate educational performance. What did differ, however, and still does, is that boys and girls may have different learning styles, and as educators we need to address them (Gallagher, 2001).

After the first wave of research encouraged teachers to select texts that showed girls in active, energetic roles; call on girls as often as they called on boys to answer questions; and offer opportunities for group projects and collaborative decision making (especially in math and science classes), some researchers began to be concerned that the efforts to level the playing field for girls had inadvertently created a toxic academic environment for boys. As early as 1999, Kindlon and Thompson observed:

> From kindergarten through sixth grade, a boy spends more than a thousand hours a year in school, and his experiences and the attitudes of the teachers and other adults he encounters there are profoundly shaping. Some boys are ahead of the others on the developmental curve, and some girls lag behind, but when we compare the average boy with the average girl, the average boy is developmentally disadvantaged in the early school environment. (p. 23)

Professions such as doctors and lawyers, typically male-dominated occupations, are now employing a majority of females. What does this do for the boys? The statistics are not good. According to the National Center for Educational Statistics:

- ❀ Boys are 30% more likely than girls to fail or drop out of school.
- ❀ When it comes to grades and homework, girls outperform boys in elementary, secondary, high school, college, and even graduate school.
- ❀ Boys are four to five times more likely than girls to be diagnosed with attention deficit hyperactivity disorder (ADHD).
- ❀ Women outnumber men in higher education, with 56 percent of bachelor's degrees and 55 percent of graduate degrees going to women.

According to the U.S. Department of Education:

❀ Boys make up two-thirds of the students in special education.
❀ Boys are five times more likely to be classified as hyperactive.

What has happened? Most educators agree that boys haven't changed; schools have. The elementary curriculum has become more language-based and demands more seat work sooner than in earlier generations. "At age five, many boys are not ready to learn to read," says teacher and author Jane Katch (2001). "When I began teaching in the '70s, children were not expected to read in kindergarten. Some first grade teachers actually preferred that children wait to learn the alphabet in first grade, where they could learn to do it 'the right way'!"(para 3).

Schools have cut down on recess and outdoor play in order to make time for meeting state academic requirements, which is a shame, because participation in physical activity may actually help some children learn more effectively (Gardner, 1999). Research tells us that that regular active physical play is essential for both boys and girls, but especially boys. Unfortunately, as the amount of time spent on academic curriculum has increased, the opportunities for play during the school day have decreased, with disastrous results. Some children, especially those with ADHD, need much more rough-and-tumble play than they get, especially since with greater amounts of activity, their behavioral symptoms often decrease (Panksepp, Burgdorf, Turner, & Gordon, 2003). And how much more do children actually learn during the extra hours of academic instruction? "Our demand for more and earlier skills, of exactly the type that boys are less able to master than girls," explains Katch (2001), "makes them feel like failures at an early age" (para 5).

Joseph Tobin (2000), professor of early childhood education at Arizona State University, calls the culture of schools "feminine," explaining that there are almost no male early childhood educators. Tobin and others believe that many teachers of young children find boys' interests in violence, gross things, and bodily functions to be boring or stupid.

> Boys' mothers and female teachers find some of their favorite thoughts, like "good guys making the world safe by killing bad guys," disturbing. Afraid that these thoughts indicate a worrisome propensity to violence, adults try to prohibit these thoughts and the toys that represent them, although boys see images all around them encouraging the fantasies and recommending the toys. (Katch, 2008)

In addition to requiring boys to sit inactive for long periods of time, and struggle with pencil-and-paper tasks that demand fine motor control that is beyond many of them in the early grades, the elementary education environment offers few subjects of interest to most boys. Tobin concludes that just as teachers were taught to ask themselves in the 1970s, "In what ways am I being sexist in my treatment of girls?" we should now be asking, "In what ways are we discouraging boys' interests in our classrooms?" (Tobin, 2000).

Being a boy in today's educational environment can be especially tough, and it is clear that we need to address this in programs for children.

One very important element in gender role development—and the resulting development of competence and self-esteem—is the availability of same-sex adults who can serve as sounding boards and role models. Tobin is correct. Since the

1950s, there have always been far more women than men teaching in the elementary grades, especially in grades K–3 (Snyder, Hoffman, & Geddes, 1996). Kindlon and Thompson (1999) are also concerned about this. They wrote that the primary school classroom "is largely a feminine environment, populated predominantly by women teachers and authority figures, that seems rigged against boys, against the higher activity level and lower level of impulse control that is normal for boys" (p. 23). Unfortunately, while it is clear that America's children would benefit from having more male teachers in elementary schools, that change is not likely to come quickly enough for the boys presently between 5 and 10 years of age and already in school.

Implications for Programs   Afterschool administrators who hire male staff in nearly equal ratios to females, however, can provide the balanced environment that is so necessary for the healthy development of children. Here is a wonderful argument for youth-serving organizations—including service clubs, recreational and enrichment programs, competitive sports, and even academically oriented school-site afterschool programs—to recruit and hire more males into their programs. In addition, if it is true that the "feminine" environment of the elementary school restricts boys from running, throwing, shouting, wrestling, and climbing, then we need to incorporate those very necessary physical activities into the curriculum of school-age programs. Chapter 11 provides specific examples of how to do that. Having young men playing alongside boys is just as critical as having energetic young women helping girls with their math and science homework. In Perspective 7.2 a YMCA staff member provides insight into the role of a male working in an afterschool program.

Another way that school-age program staff can contribute to the success of both boys and girls is by building trust between them. Projects that are imagined, planned, and executed collaboratively can serve as a microcosm of the adult world. With adult guidance, boys and girls can be encouraged to work together toward a goal, as partners and as friends. Youngsters are more likely to achieve developmental outcomes when they are actively engaged in their own learning and development (Walker, Wahl, & Rivas, 2005), and working in mixed-gender groups also helps to prepare them for their future workplace. Think in terms of learning opportunities that permit children and youth to remain engaged for several weeks or months and that are grounded in activities that have meaning and value for the young people themselves. Examples of these include planting a garden, preparing for a major theatrical event, or working on a community service project, such as creating a tutoring program for children of homeless families, painting a public mural, or harvesting and packaging fresh vegetables from a community garden. In projects such as these, individual strengths can be built upon, and children can develop their areas of weakness through the process of growing and sharing. Gender stereotypes disappear in such environments.

Today, either boys or girls may face inequities in formal schooling. A tremendous opportunity to even that balance exists in your afterschool program. Creative programs will use the strengths of the afterschool environment—mixed-age groupings, flexible schedule, activity-based curriculum, and a wide variety of opportunities for interpersonal connections and modeling—to offer youngsters a supportive learning environment.

PERSPECTIVE 7.2

A Male Perspective

Salvador Cortez
Mt. Madonna YMCA, Morgan Hill, California

My Name is Salvador Cortez. I am a 24-year-old Mexican American, and I work with school-age children every day. When I first began working at the Y, I worked as a recreation leader. My role was to incorporate sports and physical activity into the 21st Century Learning Center curriculum our agency runs for the school district. I originally took this job because it fit in to my school schedule, not knowing that the children would change my life and my perspective on the importance of youth work. When I started working for the Y, more males worked as rec leaders than females, because it was more outdoor and sports related, and the kids really seemed to like to have guys to play with. My job became increasingly important to me, because, after working the first year, I began to get attached to the kids.

Glen View Elementary is a predominantly Hispanic school, so I fit right in. I began to develop relationships with the parents, and they began to appreciate the importance of the ASP (afterschool program). Unfortunately, most of the families were single-parent families, and the parents were always working, and older brothers and sisters of the children in the ASP were gang members, in and out of jail, substance abusers, and teenage parents. The children did not have any positive role models in their lives, but when the parents began to see all the positive influences of the ASP, they began to tell me how much they appreciated me being there for their kids. Now, after 6 years of working with the YMCA, I am the assistant director of the ASP at Barrett Elementary School.

The experience of making the difference in a child's life is its own reward. For example, this past year I was part of a very special project. Collaborating with the elementary school staff, the YMCA staff adopted a family within the ASP and gave them a Christmas basket. The basket was full of clothes for the family, toys for the children, and, most important, a Safeway gift card for their Christmas dinner. This was something that I had never done before. To see the look on the family's faces was incredible. To learn that some families do not have the financial resources to celebrate a Christmas holiday and to give them such a gift was a wonderful experience.

Being a male has helped me be a positive influence in the lives of children. The amount of respect and affection I receive from both the students and the parents is enormous. If it weren't for that, I probably wouldn't be in this field. My goal now is to continue with my education and become a high school teacher. I am going to end by thanking the Mt. Madonna YMCA for giving me the opportunity of working and growing with their organization. "We Build Strong Kids, Strong Families, and Strong Communities."

Source: Used with permission from Salvador Cortez.

The Disappearance of Play

Until the 1950s, the hours after school were traditionally the time when children played with other children in their neighborhoods, stretching their bodies as they climbed trees and explored the outdoors, learning about friendship as they formed and reformed alliances, built club houses and forts, scavenging materials from parents and unused pieces of property. In 1955, *The Mickey Mouse Club,* an hour-long children's variety show, made its debut on national television, airing in the late afternoons, five days a week. It was quickly joined by *The Howdy Doody Show; Kukla, Fran and Ollie; Roy Rogers; Sky King; Zorro;* and more. Instead of waiting for the dinner call, children now began coming indoors at 4:00 or 5:00 p.m. to watch television (Chudacoff, 2007). "TV dinners"—precooked meals in aluminum trays that could be heated in the oven and eaten on "TV trays" in front of this new attraction—were invented.

In 1958, the Russians launched *Sputnik,* and the hue and cry that followed this event pointed a finger at American schools for putting too much emphasis on social studies and not enough on math or science. Now homework became the afternoon responsibility of children, frequently bribed by promises of "television when you finish your homework." Other social and economic changes followed, including the two-paycheck family and increased numbers of single-parent families, a reduction of parents' confidence in their children's safety, and increased pressure on educational institutions to improve test scores. By the time modern children entered kindergarten, the unstructured and unsupervised child-created free-play environment that their parents had enjoyed as children had become ancient history. Television, video games, iPods, and cell phones now take up whatever free time children have left over from child care, homework, adult-organized sports leagues, swimming lessons, music lessons, and car pools.

However, play can—and should be—an integral part of afterschool programming. Creativity and imagination are valuable attributes, in childhood and in adulthood, and unstructured child-created play is a natural way to develop them. One youth-serving organization, the Boys and Girls Clubs of America, has partnered with media conglomerate Nickelodeon to create "Let's Just Play," an initiative with a marketing plan and even a pledge.

The YMCA also has a play initiative, called "Activate America." Initially developed to address the growing trend of obesity in American children, Activate America reflects the YMCA's original mission, which defined individual health as the union of spirit, mind, and body. As part of the Activate America initiative, YMCA staff actively challenge the communities in which they reside to provide better opportunities for people of all ages in their pursuit of health and fitness. Boys and Girls Clubs and the YMCA have historically provided a wide range of sports and recreational activities for school-age children, and their play initiatives can provide inspiration for other school-age programs. Regular physical activity for children and adults is linked with improved mood, ability to focus, and higher energy levels, which may lead to children paying better attention to homework and other cognitive tasks. Afterschool programs have many opportunities to integrate playful activity into the curriculum, regardless of their specific program goals. Due to the greater flexibility in the types of activity choices they can offer, afterschool programs can cater to children's interests and diversity in ways that schools often cannot. From tai chi to dancing, the focus can be on enjoyable activity and movement in many forms and can include the creation of outdoor **playscapes** and other environments for unstructured play. In particular, these programs have the ability to offer options beyond competitive sports, which do not appeal to all children. Given the loss of opportunities for free play in children's lives, afterschool programs can help meet parental concerns about leaving children on their own or about safety on neighborhood streets and provide opportunities for play as well.

Children's Use of Tobacco, Alcohol, and Drugs

So far we've been discussing fears and concerns of children about things that are happening around them or to them. It is also important to consider some of the issues of school-age children that result from things they do themselves. Children may be exposed to alcohol, tobacco, and drugs as early as elementary school, and polls show that both parents and teachers underestimate the use of these substances among the young people they know. About 59% of teens report having friends who use marijuana, yet just one in five parents (21%) believes their teen has friends who use the drug.

Having friends who use drugs is a strong warning sign that a youth is also likely to use drugs (Van den Bree & Pickworth, 2005). Drinking, smoking, using drugs—any one of these behaviors can signal problems in children's lives, and the behaviors themselves can lead children into dangerous circumstances.

Drug and alcohol prevention programs are effective ways to discourage use of these substances, and other safety issues can be addressed in afterschool programs as well. Just attending an afterschool program lowers a youth's likelihood of engaging in risky activities: Children who spend no time in extracurricular activities, such as those offered in afterschool programs, are 49% more likely to have used drugs and 37% more likely to become teen parents than are those students who spend 1–4 hours per week in extracurricular activities (National Youth Violence Prevention Resource Center, 2007). Tobacco education programs introduced into the early elementary grades have been effective at reducing the number of new adolescent smokers. If the school districts in your community do not offer these programs, consider incorporating them into your afterschool program. Participating with the children can provide you with valuable information and strategies for helping youngsters, and your very presence increases their likelihood of taking the message seriously.

SUMMARY

School-age youngsters face many different and frightening situations as they grow and develop. While there have always been fears in childhood, today's children live with media scenes of war and violence, which makes their fears more graphic, and they frequently also live with violence in their own homes and neighborhoods. Afterschool staff can help by listening to children, setting up activities and environments that are conducive for reflection and reassurance, and by allowing children to voice their worries and act out their fears or anger in appropriate ways. Consistent boundaries within the school-age program and a regular routine can help children who have chaotic home lives. Many resources are available to help families and professionals assist children in dealing with their fears. Tobacco, alcohol, and drug abuse are also factors that intrude into children's lives. Their families may struggle with addiction, and the children themselves may be pressured to try these substances. You can model ways of making decisions and resisting pressure. Drug-abuse prevention programs that teach strategies and build children's self-assurance can help you develop your own awareness of these societal issues and ways to help today's children cope with them.

TERMS TO LEARN

depression
developmental issues

esteem needs
generational fears

generational issues

learned helplessness

macrocultural

magical thinking

Maslow's Hierarchy of Needs

microcultural

physiological needs

playscapes

safety and security needs

separation anxiety

social anxiety

social needs

social revolution

societal concerns

survival needs

REVIEW QUESTIONS

1. How have gender role changes resulted in parents feeling unsupported in their roles?

2. Distinguish between developmental needs and generational needs. Give some examples.

3. What issues trouble parents and children?

4. List two items from each level of Maslow's Hierarchy of Needs.

5. List two recent events reported in the media that may have elicited fear in children in your community. Would less TV viewing help reduce childhood fear?

6. Distinguish between social anxiety and societal concerns.

7. List five normal fears of childhood.

8. Discuss the appropriate balance of play and structural activities in an afterschool program.

CHALLENGE EXERCISES

1. Interview two parents of school-age children. Ask them what has frightened or worried their child(ren) in the last year. How did the parents handle the situation? What did they say? Did it help?

2. Try to remember something frightening from your childhood. How did you handle it? Did you talk about your fear or keep it to yourself? What frightens you now? How do you deal with your fears?

3. Do you believe program staff should take a stand against smoking, drinking, and drug use when they serve children who may be using these substances? What approach should they take?

4. Interview someone who works in an afterschool program. How does this person feel about helping children to deal with family violence? With drug abuse issues?

INTERNET RESOURCES

C. S. Mott Children's Hospital:
   http://www.med.umich.edu/mott/research/chearhealthconcernpoll.html

National Youth Violence Prevention Resource Center:
   http://www.safeyouth.org/scripts/facts/afterschool.asp

Parents Concern About Children's Safety at School:
   http://www.gallup.com/poll/25021/parent-concern-about-childrens-safety-school-rise.aspx

Rainbows for All Children:
   http://www.rainbows.org

REFERENCES

Brett, D. (1988). *Annie stories: A special kind of storytelling*. New York: Workman.

Bureau of the Census. (2004). *Income, poverty, and health insurance coverage in the United States: 2004* (Series P-70, No. 9). Washington, DC: U.S. Department of Commerce.

C. S. Mott Children's Hospital. (2007, May 3). *National poll on children's health*. A publication of the University of Michigan Department of Pediatrics and Communicable Diseases and the University of Michigan Child Health Evaluation and Research (CHEAR),*1*(2).

C. S. Mott Children's Hospital. (2009, July 14). *National poll on children's health*. A publication of the University of Michigan Department of Pediatrics and Communicable Diseases and the University of Michigan Child Health Evaluation and Research (CHEAR), *4*(2).

Child Trends (2009). *Children in poverty: trends, consequences and policy option*. Washington, DC: Author.

Children's Defense Fund. (2003). *Number of Black children in extreme poverty hits record high: Tabulations of data from the current population survey, March 1991–2002*. Washington, DC: Author.

Chudacoff, H. P. (2007). *Children at play: An American history*. New York: New York University Press.

Dong, Q., Yang, B., & Ollendick, T. (1994). Fears in Chinese children and adolescents and their relations to anxiety and depression. *Journal of Child Psychology and Psychiatry, 35*(2), 351–363.

Edelman, M.W. (2009) Unfair children's health disparities: More reason for reform. *Child Watch*. July 31, 2009.

Erikson, E. H. (1993). *Childhood and society* (Reissue ed.). New York: Norton. (Original work published in 1950)

Evans, J. T. (1999). *Educrisis! What to do when public schools fail?* Houston, TX: West Eagle.

Feiner, J. (1988). *Taming monsters, slaying dragons: The revolutionary family approach to overcoming childhood fears and anxieties*. New York: Arbor House.

Gallagher, T. (2001, November 30). Equal Opportunities Commission conference on boys and girls in the 21st century: Gender differences in learning.

Garatti, M., & Rudnitski, R. A. (2007). Adolescents' views on war and peace in the early phases of the Iraq conflict. *Adolescence, 42*(167) 501–507.

Gardner, H. (1999). *Intelligence reframed: Multiple intelligences for the 21st century*. New York: Basic Books.

Goldin, C., Katz, L. F., & Kuziemko, I. (2006). The homecoming of American college women: The reversal of the college gender gap. *Journal of Economic Perspectives, 20*(4), 133–156.

Greenman, J. (2002). *What happened to the world? Helping children cope in turbulent times*. Watertown, MA: Bright Horizons Family Solutions.

Havighurst, R. J. (1953). *Human development and education*. New York: Longmans, Green.

Jones, J. (2006). *Parent concern about children's safety at school on the rise*. Washington, DC: Gallup.

Katch, J. (2001). *Under Deadman's Skin: Discovering the meaning of children's violent play*. Boston: Beacon.

Katch, J. (2008, August 4). What's the problem with school? *PBS Parents*. Retrieved April 10, 2010, from http://www.pbs.org/parents/raisingboys/school02.html

Kindlon, D. (2006). *Alpha girls*. Emmaus, PA: Rodale.

Kindlon, D., & Thompson, M. (1999). *Raising Cain: Protecting the emotional life of boys*. New York: Ballantine.

King, N. J., Muris, P., & Ollendick, T. (2005). Childhood fears & phobias: Assessment & treatment. *Child & Adolescent Mental Health, 10*, 50–56.

Love, R. (1993). Gender bias: Inequities in the classroom. *Intercultural Development Research Association Journal, 20*(2), 11–12.

Marta, S. Y. (2003). *How to guide children and teens through times of divorce, death, and crisis with the Rainbows approach*. Emmaus, PA: Rodale.

Maslow, A. (1970). *Motivation and personality* (2nd ed.). New York: Harper & Row.

Milne, C. (1994). *Enchanted places*. London: Mandarin Paperbacks. (Original work published in 1974)

Myers-Walls, J. (2005, September). Children as victims of Hurricane Katrina. *Purdue University Extension Knowledge to Go Report, 1*–5.

National Center on Addiction and Substance Abuse at Columbia University. (2005). *Family matters: Substance abuse and the American family: A CASA white paper*. New York: Author.

National Center on Family Homelessness. (2008). *Homeless children: America's new outcasts*. Newton Center, MA: Author.

National Youth Violence Prevention Resource Center. (2007). *Afterschool programs fact sheet*. Retrieved August 4, 2008, from http://www.safeyouth.org/scripts/facts/afterschool.asp

Noonan, J. H., & Vavra, M. C. (2007). *Crime in schools and colleges: A study of offenders and arrestees reported via national incident-based reporting system data*. Washington, DC: Federal Bureau of Investigation.

Ollendick, T., King, N. J., & Muris, P. (2003). Fears & phobias in children: Phenomenology, epidemiology, aetiology. *Child & Adolescent Mental Health, 7*, 98–106.

Ornstein, P. (1994). *School girls: Young women, self-esteem, and the confidence gap*. New York: Doubleday.

Panksepp, J., Burgdorf, J., Turner, C., & Gordon, N. (2003). Modeling ADHD-type arousal with unilateral frontal cortex damage in rats and beneficial effects of play therapy. *Brain and Cognition, 52*(1), 97–105.

Paul, J. (1995, January/February). Violence and young children. *Children's Advocate, 1*.

Rosen, M., & Oxenbury, H. (1997). *We're going on a bear hunt*. New York: Little Simon.

Rosenberg, D., Gegax, T. T., Wingert, P., Briscoe, D., & Shenfeld, H. (2005, March 13). Children of the fallen. *Newsweek*, 32.

Rossman, B. B. (2001). Longer term effects of children's exposure to domestic violence. In S. A. Graham-Bermann and J. L. Edleson (Eds.), *Domestic violence in the lives of children: The future of research, intervention, and social policy* (pp. xi, 237–267). Washington, DC: American Psychological Association.

Sadker, M. P., & Sadker, D. M. (1982). *Sex equity handbook for schools* (2nd ed.). New York: Longman.

Sadker, M. P., & Sadker, D. M. (1994). *How America's schools cheat girls*. New York: Scribner.

Schachter, R., & McCauley, C. S. (1988). *When your child is afraid: Understanding the normal fears of childhood from birth through adolescence and helping overcome them*. New York: Simon & Schuster.

Schaefer, C. E., & DiGeronimo, T. F. (1994). *How to talk to your kids about really important things: Specific questions and answers and useful things to say*. San Francisco: Jossey-Bass.

Scofield, R. (1995). Helping children cope with tragedy. *School-Age Notes, 15*(9), 2–6.

Smith, S., & Reynolds, C. (2002). Innocent lost: The impact of 9-11 on the development of children. *Annals of the American Psychotherapy Association, 5*.

Snyder, A. R., McLaughlin, D. K., & Findeis, J. (2006). Household composition and poverty among female-headed households with children. *Rural Sociology, 71*(4), 597–624.

Snyder, T., Hoffman, C. M., & Geddes, C. M. (1996). Digest of Educational Statistics. *National Center for Education Statistics*. Published by U.S. Department of Education, Office of Educational Research and Improvement, Washington, DC.

Survey and Policy Research Institute. (2007). *What issues concern Bay Area parents?* San Jose, CA: San Jose State University.

Tobin, J. (2000). *Good guys don't wear hats: Children's talk about the media*. New York: Teachers College Press.

Van den Bree, M. B. M., & Pickworth, W. B. (2005, March). Risk factors predicting changes in marijuana involvement in teenagers. *Archives of General Psychiatry, 62*, 311–319.

Walker, J., Marczak, M., Blyth, D., & Borden, L. (2005). Designing youth development programs: Toward a theory of developmental intentionality. In J. L. Mahoney, R. W. Larson, & J. S. Eccles (Eds.), *Organized activities as contexts of development: Extracurricular activities, after-school and community programs*. Mahwah, NJ: Lawrence Erlbaum Associates.

Chapter

8

Understanding and Guiding Children's Behavior

Another responsibility of school-age staff is to understand and moderate the behavior of the children in their care. Several factors contribute to the way children behave in small and large groups. For example, the children in your program may come from widely different family settings, reflecting a variety of cultures, values, and communication styles. Youngsters also vary in their understanding of shared space and time. They differ in conflict-resolution skills. They are in different stages of friendship relationships. Younger children may be only just beginning to use logical thought, and are still egocentric in their worldview, while older members of the group are moving firmly into concrete operational thinking.

CONDITIONS AFFECTING CHILDREN'S BEHAVIOR

To work effectively with school-age children, you must understand and consider these variables. Within a framework of mutual understanding, children and adults can work together to create a safe environment, a mutually agreeable set of expectations, and a system of strategies that will make it possible for everyone to coexist (most of the time) in harmony.

The Guidance System

The process of influencing children's behavior has been called many things. Parents usually call it **discipline**. Educators and psychologists refer to **classroom management** or **behavior modification**. More frequently in recent years this process has been called **guidance**. This last term is helpful, because it reminds us that the process of helping children learn to behave in socially (and situationally) appropriate ways is ongoing. The goal of guidance is not to control children's behavior but to help children learn how to control their *own* behavior.

The guidance system consists of the children, the adults, and the environment.

Dr. Marian Marion, professor and popular speaker and writer on the subject of children's behavior, has described a **guidance system**, which consists of the *children,* the *adults,* and the *environment* (Marion, 2006). She believes that effective interaction with and between children develops when adults understand the workings of this system, accept the responsibility for behaving as leaders and mentors rather than as dictators, and create a self-help environment. Marion's ideas are highly adaptable to before- or afterschool settings as well as recreation programs and drop-in centers. The next sections describe the three aspects of this guidance system, and some of Marion's strategies are described later in the chapter.

The Children Chapter 5 introduced the physical, cognitive, social–emotional, and moral development of children. As you develop your guidance system for a school-age program, it is important to refer to the material in that chapter and consider the behavioral characteristics of children as they occur at different ages and stages. For example, children who are developing physically more slowly than others their age may be left out of some outdoor games or rough-and-tumble play, which will influence their feelings and mood and may in turn influence their behavior inside the classroom.

The cognitive development of younger children may limit their ability to understand what is expected of them or how to practice the give-and-take necessary to get along with other children. Problem solving is governed by brain development and the use of logical thought, even when the "problem" is a social one. You may need to review the steps to solving problems or techniques of conversational turn-taking with children periodically to help them negotiate their relationships with others.

Most older children are feeling increasingly able to take care of themselves physically and are eager for opportunities to try out their new independence and social skills. They are widening their social horizons, making new friends, and trying on new roles at school and in their community. However, they may still need guidance as they take emotional risks, especially when they face rejection or, worse, hostility from others. Insecurities lie just under the surface in most youngsters, even when they appear to be confident. Here are some specific developmental characteristics to be aware of:

5- TO 7-YEAR-OLDS By first grade, some children can begin to think about problems in a logical fashion, but they may still have difficulty controlling their behavior in groups. There is a shift during this period from the kindergartner's dependence on adults to the second or third grader's tight-knit and reciprocal friendships with one another. This means more "tattletales" as children turn to you to solve conflicts. Most of the younger children in school-age programs will be operating at Level 1 moral reasoning (Kohlberg, 1984), which means they follow the rules mostly because they want to avoid punishment, or because they think there might be a reward (extrinsic or intrinsic) for good behavior. You can see this demonstrated in intense but often short-lived friendships, which usually have a personal gain involved for one or the other child ("I'll be your friend if you let me play with your video game").

8- TO 10-YEAR-OLDS By the time children are 8, 9, and 10, they are growing stronger, have more endurance, and are often ready for more physical challenges. Moving into Level 2 of moral reasoning, they develop their own games with complicated sets of rules and hold one another to compliance, although competition is often complicated by close friendships. Children who are 9 or older are beginning to be able to see one another's point of view and can empathize with children whose feelings have been hurt or who are different in some way. Ten-year-olds need things to be "fair," and arbitrary rules or enforcement of them will often set off tears of frustration and anger.

Between 8 and 10, children are still frequently troubled by fears of snakes, spiders, heights, large bodies of water, etc., and may stubbornly refuse to hold the visiting boa constrictor or dive into the pool. Workers in child and youth settings who understand the resulting conflicts (between being good and following the rules, juxtaposed with an occasional gripping sense of fear) can better help children work through the difficulties. If adults scoff at their inability to "get with the program," troubled youngsters, already feeling helpless and frozen in place, may now feel worthless as well.

Most children in the 8- to 10-year-old range are now able to work on projects or homework without much adult supervision or direction and are learning to accept responsibility for their own actions. Their friendships move from being dependent on a one-way benefit to more reciprocal, if possessive, relationships.

11- AND 12-YEAR-OLDS Children over 10 can seriously challenge inexperienced afterschool staff. Secure in their self-perceptions, these older children may test program rules and the authority of anyone around. Some 12-year-olds think it's "cool" to swear or use rude words and may talk back to teachers, coaches, parents, and program staff just to see how it feels. At the same time, older school-agers have learned the two-way street of friendship and are more willing to adjust to one another's individual likes and dislikes. Sometimes this characteristic of older children can be used to mediate difficulties in group interaction.

Around 12 years of age, children's reasoning changes, and they begin to take intentions into account when determining how badly someone has behaved

(Kohlberg, 1984; Piaget, 1932/1965). They find it possible, and even enjoyable, to consider the reasons behind an action and decide that sometimes "the ends justify the means." Loyalty to a friend may cause a child to behave in ways she or he knows are not acceptable; the likely punishment may seem less important than a breach in the friendship. Although they can now think realistically about the consequences of their actions, children sometimes find their judgment being tested by peers and may need the uncritical ear of a caring adult to help them sort it all out.

❀   *Consider This:*   ❀

Did you ever do anything you shouldn't have because a friend asked you to do so? What elements of the situation did you think about before making your decision?

13- TO 16-YEAR-OLDS Young teens are often happier in school than in previous years, although not necessarily because they've suddenly begun to love learning. Social interactions have become the most important part of their life. School and afterschool activities are where most of these encounters take place. If their moral development is continuing on track, they may be in Stage 4 or even 5 of Kohlberg's Level 3 reasoning. Characteristics of these stages are a willingness, even a desire, to meet one's agreed-upon obligations, to keep the social order going, and to uphold the "social contract" of the institutions in which they exist. Unfortunately, those "institutions" can include cliques and gangs as well as classrooms, schools, athletic teams, or other community activities.

Younger teens become extremely busy with friends, outside activities, and school sports or clubs; if college is a goal, older teens begin to settle in to heavy study patterns. Cell phones are a necessity for most youngsters in this age group, who use them to stay continuously connected to their friends. Occasionally they may even be used to talk about homework assignments. Fourteen-year-old girls are more interested in boys than boys are in them, but by age 16 their interest is being reciprocated. Peer pressure can be great. Teens have lots of complaints about the way the school (or the government, or their home, or their soccer team) is being run. Most young people in this age group do not believe they need before- or afterschool supervision. The reality, of course, is that they do, and if you are working in a teen center, you know how much they appreciate having you listen to them and help guide them as they sort out their thoughts and feelings about important events, decisions, and concerns.

The Importance of Friendships Most research into children's friendships shows that those children who form friendships when they begin school are happier and learn better than those who do not. Children who are friendless may even experience emotional and mental problems later in life (Ferrer & Fugate, 2006). This discovery clearly has implications for children's behavior in group settings. The give-and-take required for the formation of mature friendships also has a long-term impact on social and academic success (Grose, 2005; Slee & Shute, 2003) and is therefore a dynamic that you should understand and nurture within your program. Entering into and maintaining friendships requires certain skills (Rubin, 1980):

- Understanding how to gain entry into a group
- Being a supportive, caring and approving playmate
- Knowing how to manage conflict successfully
- Being able to express one's own rights and feelings
- Remaining sensitive to the rights and feelings of others

Children can be taught these friendship skills. The strategies for doing so include modeling and teaching a range of prosocial behaviors such as talking with others while working or playing, showing an interest in others' lives, sharing materials and supplies, and gaining access to an ongoing game or conversation (Ferrer & Fugate, 2006). You can set the stage for children to make friends by building positive, supporting relationships with them and working with the children to develop a limited number of rules for behavior that will help ensure that everyone remains emotionally safe. Help the children learn to phrase the rules in positive words, and discuss what it means to them—e.g., "Respect one another" and "Keep your hands to yourself." As they begin to feel more comfortable in their environment, even shy children will begin to develop the basic trust and self-confidence necessary to reach outside their comfort zone and approach someone in friendship.

You also help children make friends by being a good role model. Youngsters watch when you interact with coworkers, parents, and other adults. Always speak kindly and respectfully; never put another person down (that may be the child's worst fear), and model the mutual respect that you want to see in children's interactions. Another way you can model friendship skills is to initiate friendly conversations with children when they are working together on art or craft activities, and include the quiet children in the exchange. Be fun to be around.

Shy children need help developing several skills that are needed for making and keeping friends. One is knowing how to enter into a conversation and hold up your own end. You can begin this process by greeting each child warmly and by name and letting them know that you are glad to see them. Teach children about conversational turn-taking by asking them about their day or what is going on in their lives, and when they respond, comment on the answer and ask another question. This give-and-take may seem obvious, but some children need help figuring out how it works.

Robert Selman developed a way of categorizing children's friendships, basing his model on the constructivist theory of Jean Piaget. Selman believed that social awareness and friendship skills develop gradually, and each stage of development requires the mental reorganization of social schemas (Selman & Selman, 1979). These stages are shown in Table 8.1. It is helpful to see children's friendship behavior in the context of development, but it is important to remember that the stages overlap, and children may exhibit behaviors from more than one stage at a time. For example, a child who is mostly in the "momentary playmateship" stage might be able to work out a compromise over the choice of a game or activity, which is typically a characteristic of the more mature "fair-weather cooperation" stage.

TABLE 8.1 Developmental Stages of Friendship.

Stage	Approximate Age	Stage	Characteristics
0	3–7	Momentary playmateship	Can't yet consider the viewpoint of another person; can only think about what he or she wants from the friendship. Defines friends by how close they live or by their material possessions ("He's my friend because he lives next door" or "She's my friend because she has a doll house and a swing set").
1	4–9	One-way assistance	Can now tell the difference between his or her own perspective and that of another. Friendship is based on whether someone does what the child wants ("He's not my friend anymore; he doesn't want to play cars"). A close friend is someone you know better than other people.
2	6–12	Two-way fair-weather cooperation	There is a new awareness of interpersonal relationships. Friendship becomes reciprocal but still focuses on the present situation rather than on an enduring relationship. Self-interest is still present, so the friendship may collapse when the children argue.
3	9–15	Intimate, mutually shared relationships	Friendship is now viewed as an entity in itself—an ongoing, committed relationship that is treasured for its own sake and may involve possessiveness and jealousy. ("How can Paula go to the movies with Jemma? She's my best friend!") Older children in this stage may defend one another against outsiders.
4	12 to adult	Autonomous interdependent friendships	Youngsters can now respect their friends' needs for both dependency and autonomy. They also recognize that friends will sometimes need their help in some way; they are no longer so possessive of their time or affection.

Sources: Based on *Children's Friendships,* by Z. Rubin, 1980, Cambridge, MA: Harvard University Press; "Children's Ideas About Friendship: A New Theory," by R. L. Selman and A. P. Selman, 1979, *Psychology Today, 12*(4), pp. 71–80; and *Thinking About Theories,* by P. T. Slee and R. Shute, 2003, London: A Hodder Arnold.

As children begin to venture tentatively into the world of new friendships, keep a reasonable distance, but pay attention to their initial interactions. If you have created a safe, nurturing environment in your program, children are likely to behave kindly to one another. But the road to intimate, mutually shared relationships is a long one, and along the way there may be some conflicts. You can help children learn to settle conflicts in small steps, as needed, without developing a full-blown conflict-resolution curriculum (although some programs have also found that to be effective). Listen to children when they tell you how they feel or what they understand to have just gone wrong between themselves and another child. Restate what they say to you and ask, "Is that what happened?" or "Is that how you feel?" Encourage the unhappy child to replay your exchange with the other child, and offer to sit with them while he does so. Listening to their concerns, help them to identify the problem and encourage them to brainstorm some solutions. By gently coaching children to solve their own conflict this time, you empower them to tackle the next conflict without you.

There are several other steps you can take to promote friendships among the children in your program. Drawing from the research that analyzes the components of children's friendships, the following steps can contribute to children in your program learning social skills and increasing their prosocial behavior (Ferrer & Fugate, 2006). But completely separate from their relationship to nurturing friendships, taking these steps can result in a much more peaceful program!

Step 1. Help children develop empathy. The ability to understand other people's feelings and points of view requires concrete operational thinking, but it develops more readily in children who see other people expressing empathetic feelings. When reading books to children, you can ask how they think the characters feel about various events and interactions in the story. When children tell you about something that happened in school or at home, ask how they felt about it and how they think others felt. By doing this regularly, as a normal part of conversation (don't make it sound like the third degree), children become more accustomed to asking the same questions of themselves: "I wonder how he felt when I said that?"

Step 2. Provide opportunities for children to practice conflict resolution, problem solving, and cooperation. In the course of a normal day, many opportunities abound for children to work together, to create something, or solve a problem or plan a future activity. If you participate some of the time, you can gently encourage discussions about feelings, possible approaches to take to resolve issues, and ways to approach problem solving and planning.

Step 3. Encourage children to show support and appreciation for others. Once again, this is most easily done by modeling, or demonstrating, the behavior. When you see someone doing something positive, say something nice. For example, "I really appreciate the way you put all those game pieces away after you and Anjal finished playing." Or "I have really seen an improvement in your math homework lately. You are making a good effort to keep the numbers lined up and the erasures clean."

Step 4. Help children develop skills that are valued by other children in the program. It doesn't really matter if children excel in sports, or music, or theater, or whatever it is that the culture of your community values. What matters to other children is that their friends respect their interests and don't scorn their achievements. Children without friends sometimes try to protect themselves by denying that they are interested in an activity, when actually they have not been able to figure out how to participate in it. It's easier to join into a game if they know the rules and have mastered some basic skills. And being a good sport about entering into the game even if you know you are not going to excel is a gift that friends can give to another. Teaching ball skills or how to read music or helping children learn lines for the class play—all these are activities that you can easily initiate in your program that will benefit the children on the outside of the friendship groups. If you can gently help them learn just enough to participate, you are contributing to their social competence and happiness in future years.

The Environment   There is a very close relationship between the environment and children's behavior. Elements that influence the environment of your program include the physical, emotional, and temporal dimensions of the program itself but also the outside world in which children reside.

The world has always been a dangerous and, at times, a violent place. One difference today, however, is that in addition to whatever real circumstances exist in the community, danger and violence are also broadcast into our homes via the media. The effects of violent news reporting and entertainment on children's behavior are still unclear, but undoubtedly they are significant. Children who frequently watch scenes in which people kill or hurt one another, and who play video games with violent content, as well as those who are present while their parents argue or fight, inevitably learn different attitudes about conflict resolution than do children whose home environment is calm and whose television and video viewing is restricted and guided. Also, children who watch television see violence that is across the country or across the world and do not understand that it is far away and unlikely to hurt them.

To be responsible members of a group, in which participants act in caring, compassionate, and helpful ways toward one another, children need many opportunities to learn how to be responsible for their actions (Levin, 2003; Ollhoff & Ollhoff, 2007). We cannot control the home environment, but we *can* control the setting in afterschool programs. The goal of the guidance system is not to influence behavior through fear of punishment but to support the development of self-control and problem-solving skills. When you are setting up your program, provide an environment that encourages children's cognitive and social development:

- ❀ Arrange materials and furniture to encourage appropriate behavior.
- ❀ Involve children in making rules.
- ❀ Provide a wide variety of activities from which to select.
- ❀ Plan games and activities that encourage cooperation.
- ❀ Incorporate the home cultures and languages of children.
- ❀ Build strong relationships with families.

When children play strategic games, such as most mancala games, checkers, chess, Othello, Connect Four, or Stratego (especially if program staff members play along with them), they develop the same thinking skills that are needed to work through interpersonal problems. Teaching children to knit, sew, weave, make paper, construct projects out of wood or plastic, or cook helps strengthen their cognitive skills and develops patience. When you encourage children to participate in cooperative activities, such as soccer, basketball, cat's cradle, construction, or making a mural, you are helping them build friendships and learn how to work collaboratively. It is the same with brainstorming about the furniture arrangement, the daily schedule, or how the computer equipment will be shared.

None of the above activities alone will solve children's interpersonal problems or teach conflict-resolution and problem-solving strategies. However, if you encourage such pursuits, while minimizing the availability of violence-oriented action figures and violent video games, films, and television, as well as practicing other guidance techniques described in this chapter, you will encourage children to behave in less aggressive, more cooperative ways. Ideally, the environment of a school-age program allows children to participate in a variety of different activities without getting in one another's way and encourages the development of self-help skills. Other considerations will be covered in Chapter 9, such as arranging the environment to accommodate the changing needs and interests of children. A well-thought-out environment will positively influence children's behavior.

The Adults   An important goal of guiding children's behavior is to encourage **prosocial behavior** and discourage **aggressive behavior**. Children who have good relationships with adults are more likely to make sound decisions and less likely to bully or be bullied (Lawhon, 1997; Levin, 2003). Encourage children to talk about their feelings. If they have been misbehaving, reassure them that you accept the way they feel, but their actions are not acceptable. Provide creative outlets for expressing aggression, and teach children conflict-resolution techniques.

Prosocial behavior is a voluntary action intended to make others feel good or that benefits others (Grusec, Davidov, & Lundell, 2002). Sharing, helping, cooperating, and showing kindness and compassion are examples of prosocial behavior. **Antisocial behavior** is the opposite extreme. Examples of antisocial behaviors seen in children include violations of social rules, defiance of parental or other adult authority and of the rights of others, lying, and stealing. Aggressive behavior is the use of words or actions to injure someone else. For example, here are three scenarios in which children demonstrate aggressive behavior:

1. Jorge and Marco want the same game piece and Jorge wrenches it from Marco's hand, hurting him.
2. Veronica knocks over Ben's carefully constructed 3-D puzzle after he taunts her about how quickly he put it together.
3. Sabrina reaches over and tears a page of Lance's math homework when he refuses to let her see it. Lance is furious and shoves Sabrina off her chair.

Adult intervention is sometimes needed to keep children safe. However, effective adult intervention includes helping children solve their own problems and encourages them to learn from their experiences. Sometimes redirecting children to more acceptable activities is all that is required. At other times, children may need direct help to control their behavior. Use simple, positive reminders to state and restate rules, and help children understand the consequences of their actions. Read on to learn how you might handle those three scenarios.

Aggression among older children may take the form of physical confrontations, putdowns, hostile postures, or freezing opponents out of the activity of the moment. When allowed to go uncorrected, aggressive behaviors can lead to bullying. Understanding why children use aggression toward others is not simple, and labeling a child a bully is not particularly helpful. Dr. Lyn Brown, professor of education at Colby College, decries the labeling of aggressive children as bullies, and discourages the use of bully prevention practices:

> Bully prevention programs typically put kids into three categories: bullies, victims, and bystanders. Labeling children in these ways denies what we know to be true: We are all complex beings with the capacity to do harm and to do good, sometimes within the same hour. It also makes the child the problem, which downplays the important role of parents, teachers, the school system, a provocative and powerful media culture, and societal injustices children experience every day. (2008, p. 30)

Dr. Brown provides alternative suggestions for addressing behavioral issues in school situations, including talking accurately about types of behavior and learning to understand why children use aggression toward others. She also suggests that we adopt methods that reflect the unique environment of our classroom or afterschool setting, create realistic expectations for students, and listen to students. I would add that we should also listen to parents, to teachers, and to one another. In this book, we have discussed all of these ideas; creating a safe and nurturing environment in which all children and staff practice mutual respect in their communication and interactions with one another is a very large step in the right direction to discouraging bullying behavior in your program.

However, children may experience bullying on the school playground, on the bus, while walking to school and home from child care, and in their own neighborhoods, so we cannot and should not ignore it as a social phenomenon. While most overt and dangerous bullying behavior is seen in boys, recent research has identified a parallel behavior in school-age girls. **Relational aggression** is the term used to describe behaviors such as making derogatory comments, spreading rumors, or gossiping in ways intended to tarnish another child's reputation (Crick & Rose, 2002; Simmons, 2002).

The recent appearance of the phenomenon known as **cyber-bullying** is also a form of relational aggression. According to the National Crime Prevention Council, cyber-bullying is when a child is tormented, threatened, harassed, humiliated, embarrassed, or otherwise targeted by another child using some form of technology, such as the Internet or cellular telephones (Patchin & Hinduja, 2009). Ybarra, Mitchell, Wolak, and Finkelhor (2006) interviewed 1,500 students that used the Internet regularly and found that victims of cyber-bullying needed support and intervention just as much as youngsters who have been the target of any other kind of aggressive behavior.

Psychologists recognize the impact of relational aggression and bullying on children's learning and cognitive development as well as on their emotions. When children are faced with a threat, their emotions take over and their brain is unable to effectively process cognitive tasks. When this occurrence happens frequently, long-term effects can result (Fogarty, 2009; Pete & Fogarty, 2007).

When allowed to go uncorrected, aggressive behaviors can lead to bullying.

GUIDING CHILDREN'S BEHAVIOR

Knowing how to intervene and redirect children's aggression will be easier if you understand why it occurs. Some developmental psychologists believe that children are born with an aggressive drive, and many parents justify fighting between siblings or playmates by drawing on that idea. Others believe that aggression is a learned behavior that is influenced by the environment in which the children live. Most theorists acknowledge the role of adults in modeling, teaching, and responding to children's behavior, and some have developed methods for teaching children more acceptable ways to resolve conflict.

The Theories Behind Child Guidance Techniques

Remember the theorists in Chapter 5? Let's review some of them in the context of behavior. B. F. Skinner used his concept of operant conditioning to explain aggression in children. In Skinner's model, children's behavior is shaped by positive or negative reinforcement following random actions, such as damaging another child's painting or engaging in bullying. By definition, a **reinforcer** is anything that causes a behavior to be repeated, so if a child receives attention for his action, that would be considered a reinforcer. Behaviors that are not reinforced tend to reoccur less and less frequently until they disappear (**extinction**).

Theorists Piaget, Vygotsky, Kohlberg, Damon, and Gilligan approach moral decision making, which underlies much of children's behavior, as a combination of cognitive and social development, influenced by the environment in which a child lives and modified by experiences that the child has had. This supports the concept that appropriate behavior can be taught and modeled by adults, as well as mediated.

Rudolf Dreikurs (1964) attributed hostile and aggressive behaviors to **mistaken goals** pursued by some children. He identified four mistaken goals that children sometimes pursue in their quest for a feeling of belonging: **undue attention, struggle for power, retaliation and revenge**, and **complete inadequacy**. Dreikurs and Solz's update (1991) of Dreikurs's classic text, *Children: The Challenge,* is a useful source of theory and guidance techniques for parents, child and youth workers, and teachers. In it the authors suggest ways children can be encouraged to pursue more appropriate goals in their social interactions. Dreikurs encouraged the use of natural and logical consequences to shape children's behavior. This technique will be explained in more detail below.

Albert Bandura (1977) conducted research to support his idea that children learn from their early environment *when* it is appropriate to act aggressively, *what forms* of aggression are acceptable, and *to whom* they can get away with acting aggressively. His findings support Skinner's belief that aggression is a behavior learned through reinforcement and imitation and that therefore can also be *unlearned.*

In terms of day-to-day living, no matter whether aggression is learned from the environment or is instinctive, one of the desired outcomes of socialization is learning to keep it under control. And one of your most important roles as an adult in a school-age program is to help children learn how to do just that.

Effective Child Guidance Techniques   Dealing with misbehavior, including direct and relational aggression, is an important responsibility of afterschool leaders and staff. Knowing how to approach children who are struggling over their place in the **dominance hierarchy**, or simply disagreeing with a friend over a game piece, is the sign of an effective child and youth worker. Children who are regularly afraid and anxious are unable to engage in social interaction or learning and may develop behavior problems themselves if the aggressors are not brought into line and the climate of the school-age program returned to harmony.

Children, like adults, learn in many different ways. Some children learn best by watching others, and some learn best by discussing situations and working out a solution with others. Some children are relatively compliant about following reasonable rules, and others may want to challenge the status quo and negotiate for a different way of doing things. It is important to think about different learning styles and personalities when developing a guidance plan for your program. Sharing power with children helps them to learn from daily experience how to take responsibility for themselves and the operation of their afterschool environment. Creating an environment of trust, mutual respect, and high expectations will go a long way toward ensuring appropriate behavior most of the time (Fink, 1995; Levin, 2003).

STATING EXPECTATIONS OF DESIRED BEHAVIORS   Thoughtful adult leaders do not surprise children. Instead, they prepare them for what is to come that day, the next day, and during the following weeks. Adults who work with school-age children show respect for them by involving them in planning activities and posting activities ahead of time. It is also important to develop and clearly explain behavioral guidelines. Whenever possible, develop them collaboratively with the children and staff, and then present expectations as *positive*, rather than *negative*. For example, say, "In this program we are considerate of one another," rather than "Don't hit." Or "While we are inside, let's keep our voices quieter," rather than "Stop yelling." Keep rules to a minimum, and consider the guidelines shown in Figure 8.1 for developing appropriate limits on children's behavior.

If there are designated times set aside for certain activities, make sure they are prominently posted; if materials or equipment need adult supervision, keep them

FIGURE 8.1   Outcomes of a "Good Limit".

A good limit will do the following:
- Help children achieve self-control.
- Help children develop positive interpersonal skills.
- Protect a child's health and safety.
- Never degrade a child.
- Have real meaning.
- Be developmentally valid.

Source: Based on *Guidance of Young Children* (7th ed., p. 18), by M. Marion, 2007, Columbus, OH: Merrill.

in locked cabinets, clearly labeled. If some children seem to regularly test or ignore the program guidelines, speak to them privately to be sure they understand the expectations and consequences of repeated infractions, then be consistent in your application of those consequences.

Be sure that the rules of the classroom are reviewed by staff members before they are posted and go into effect. You don't want to stipulate that children may not sit on tables only to discover a group leader sitting on a worktable while talking to a cluster of children sitting on the carpet. If it is not safe for children to sit on tables, or if it might damage them in some way, isn't that also true for adults? At least have a good reason why you make a rule, and apply it consistently.

If you and the children develop posters of classroom rules, remind them to be concise as well as positive, and post them prominently so that staff and children can refer to them easily. Send home a copy so that parents can help to clarify them for younger children and support what you are trying to achieve. If inappropriate behavior is a major issue in your program, include a list of important rules in a **behavior contract** such as the one in Figure 8.2. Send two copies of the contract home and ask parents to read it over and discuss it with the child. Ask the parents and the children to sign one copy of the contract and return it to you, signifying that they have discussed the rules and that the child has agreed to comply with them. If the child goes home to more than one house, be sure to provide a copy for each parent or guardian.

Talk about behavior management during staff meetings, and include guidance strategies as you consider future activities. Since most of the activity planning in school-age programs should be done collaboratively, that means these same behavior guidelines should be discussed with the children when you plan the specific activities.

Don't count on one discussion of rules at the beginning of the year to prevent behavior problems all year long. Individual conversations with children that let them know they are on the right track, or need to curb their behavior in one way or another, are far more effective than a single large group review of a list of rules on the wall. Clarify your expectations each time you plan a new activity, and review the rules just before the activity begins. This is especially important if the children are going into a new environment, such as the public library, the cafeteria, or the gym or if they are about to participate in something that could be dangerous, such as a cooking activity with knives or a hot plate. Make sure that children understand what you expect of them. Ask questions. Develop some "What if?" situations to let them role-play their new instructions. Stay close to children who have trouble following directions, and guide them into the appropriate behaviors before they have a chance to do something harmful or distracting. In the long run, preventing behavior problems is far less trouble than solving them (Fink, 1995).

MODELING AND INSTRUCTING Most psychological theories discussing aggression emphasize the role of adults in shaping children's behavior (Bandura, 1977; Erikson, 1993; Skinner, 1953; Vygotsky, 1978). Social learning theory especially would suggest that adults who demonstrate positive behaviors such as respect, generosity, cooperation, thoughtfulness, and helpfulness in their dealings with children, their parents, and other adults in the program will encourage children

FIGURE 8.2 Afterschool Program Behavior Contract.

Expectations of behavior:

1. _____

2. _____

3. _____

4. _____

Privileges granted for meeting the conditions of the contract:

1. _____

2. _____

Consequences/restrictions of failing to meet the conditions of the contract:

1. _____

2. _____

I understand that I must meet all behavior expectations listed above to earn both listed privileges each day. Failure to meet the behavior expectations listed above will result in my earning of both consequences/restrictions listed above.

Privileges and consequences/restrictions will be earned on the same/following day (choose one).

Child's signature	Parent's signature

Staff member's acknowledgment: _____

Date: _____

to do the same. This approach to child guidance is known as **modeling**. It is especially important to model acceptance of individual differences such as cultural practices, conflicting values, and unusual appearance or style of dress.

Learning to work collaboratively with a diverse group of people is one of the developmental tasks of a future teacher or group leader. Group projects in college classrooms are designed to help you learn this skill, so next time your instructor asks you to participate in one, think how fortunate you are to have hands-on experience that has direct application to your career development.

We can also **instruct**, or teach, how to use problem-solving and conflict-resolution techniques, how to control aggressive feelings, how to confront other people appropriately, how to make friends by being a friend, and other social skills. It often seems quicker and easier to intervene in children's difficulties, telling them to "take turns," or "use your words," but those short-term solutions do not usually help children learn to resolve future conflicts; some teaching is necessary because it engages children's brains.

When children misbehave, it is also important to avoid making them feel ashamed. Help children understand that you like them and that that feeling is not conditional on their behavior. Rather than "Get off the couch! Didn't your mother ever tell you not to stand on the furniture?" calmly state, "I can't have you standing on the couch to look out the window; it's dangerous and it's not good for the couch." Being corrected for inappropriate behavior can be humiliating, or it can be educative. Strive to make it educative (Ollhoff & Ollhoff, 2007). It is also helpful to comment positively when children *do* choose appropriate behaviors.

TEACHING PROBLEM SOLVING   Several **problem-solving strategies** have been developed that can be taught to school-age children. A fairly simple one can be outlined on poster board and followed by the children whenever a conflict occurs. The first step is to determine "Who owns the problem?" For example, if Jorge is trying to finish his book report and Susan wants to play on the electronic keyboard, it could be Jorge's problem if he is working on his homework during free activity time. On the other hand, it might be Susan's problem if she wants to play during the study hour. If it is Jorge's problem, he should be encouraged to work through the steps shown in Figure 8.3. If it is Susan's problem, it becomes *her* responsibility to work through the process. This strategy would also work for the conflict between Jorge and Marco over a game piece. Guiding children through problem-solving strategies takes longer than imposing your own solution, but it has longer lasting results (Gordon, 2003).

CONFLICT-RESOLUTION STRATEGIES   Problem-solving strategies work for straightforward problems. However, if the problem appears to have led to a serious emotional conflict, a more appropriate technique to use is **conflict resolution**. This is a process that helps children to view a situation objectively, to consider another child's viewpoint, and, ultimately, to resolve the conflicts without overt aggression or violence (Fink, 1995).

A familiar way of solving conflict between two or more children is for the nearest adult to intervene, ask what happened, and try to make a fair judgment. This approach may lead some children to believe that only adults can solve conflicts and that they are incapable of resolving conflicts without adult help. It may also leave the children involved in the conflict feeling frustrated and unfairly treated or, worse, humiliated. This approach may keep the school-age

FIGURE 8.3   Steps to Problem Solving.

1. Decide who "owns" the problem.

2. Define the problem ("I can't concentrate when Susan plays the keyboard").

3. Generate possible solutions ("Susan uses the earphones; I find another place to work; I wear earplugs").

4. Evaluate and test the various solutions.

5. Decide on a mutually acceptable solution (this depends on both Susan's willingness to compromise and Jorge's persuasive skills).

6. Implement the solution.

environment superficially harmonious. However, several small differences that are resolved unsatisfactorily may go onto a virtual scoreboard in children's heads, waiting to fuel future conflicts. In addition, the adult-intervention model does not prepare youngsters for resolving conflicts *outside* the after-school program when there is no adult to help. Conflicts on the school playground, in a video parlor, at the mall, or elsewhere are usually resolved using the "might makes right" rule. Here those youngsters with more perceived power simply impose their will on those with less. The world would be a better place if children everywhere learned the skills necessary to negotiate and resolve differences peacefully.

Before trying to teach conflict-resolution skills, you need to learn them. There are many institutes, workshops, classes, and books available. These programs are often brought to school districts by anti-gang task groups, who believe that by changing the social climate in the schools and community they can help to produce a long-term effect on children's behavior. If your afterschool program provides an environment in which children practice peace-building and conflict-resolution skills, it may become a model for local schools or other afterschool programs that experience problems with conflicts. Alternately, if you are working on a school site that has already adopted a particular model of conflict resolution, use the same one in your afterschool program. This will support and reinforce the skills children are learning in their regular classrooms.

The basic structure of conflict resolution is similar to the problem-solving technique presented above, except that students are trained to help their peers solve conflicts. Since serious conflicts may lead to heightened emotions, it is desirable to send student facilitators to a formal training program to prepare them for the intensity of feelings that they may face as they try to help. Once trained, these students can often guide their peers through the steps to resolve the conflict and help to keep those with the disagreement on track. Student facilitators, for example, could help Lance and Sabrina from our earlier example resolve their ongoing conflict about sharing math homework solutions. The use of student facilitators sends a message that children can learn to resolve even quite serious problems with a minimum of adult intervention. Adults should remain available to advise the facilitators if they ask for help, or to step in as mediators if necessary, but ideally they remain in the background.

REINFORCING, REWARDING, AND PUNISHING   Adults **reinforce**, or **reward**, children's behavior both knowingly and unknowingly. By definition, a reinforcer is anything that causes a behavior to be repeated (Skinner, 1953), such as a smile, a cookie, or making it to the head of the lunch line. It is important to realize that what we may think of as **punishment**, however (such as placing a child in a time-out corner or delivering a stern lecture on the importance of not eating or drinking at the computer), may feel like a reward to a child who is seeking attention, and consequently it may actually encourage the behavior. However, when one child helps another find a game piece, a quiet "Brian, I really appreciated the way you helped Gillian" can be a very effective reinforcer. **Ignoring** a child's inappropriate behavior, which can be done if it doesn't threaten to injure anyone or anything, is essentially the withholding of a reinforcer. This strategy weakens the behavior, or decreases the likelihood of its repetition.

❀   *Consider This:*   ❀

Which of these behaviors would you ignore, and which would you try to change?

❀ During quiet time, Brenda bounces her pencil rhythmically against the tabletop as she concentrates on her homework.
❀ During free choice time, Josiah calls out, "Can someone help me put some paper in the printer?"
❀ Kirstin pushes to the front of the line forming for snack; Danielle elbows her gently back out of line and tells her to go to the end.
❀ Jessica puts her backpack on the floor instead of in her cubby when she comes into the room.

As adults struggle with children's behavior, they may inadvertently reward and punish behaviors without really understanding what it is that they are reinforcing. Through observation, study, and practice, you can learn to identify the reasons behind many confrontations or situations that occur in group settings. By reinforcing and rewarding only the behaviors that contribute to the harmony of the environment, you can begin to help children reduce the instances of challenging behavior. Even when you do not truly understand *why* unsuitable behaviors occur, you can still use reinforcement theory to decrease their frequency and increase the frequency of desirable ones.

USING COGNITIVE MODIFICATION STRATEGIES   If you find that, in spite of all this planning, you still need to help certain children manage their behavior, consider these three steps: (1) arouse their empathy, (2) help them alter their self-perceptions, and (3) focus on their own values and actions. These are examples of **cognitive modification strategies**, which involve teaching youngsters how to think about a situation, consider several related factors, and change their behavior based on that thinking process (Marion, 2006).

A basketball coach successfully used this technique when the 12-year-old players began to arrive late for practices or miss them altogether. Taking the players aside one by one, the coach pointed out how important it was to the others that each player show commitment to the team (arousing *empathy*). As she discussed the problem with each child, they gave various reasons for the lateness or absence: conflicts with music lessons or schoolwork, problems with rides, illness, tiredness, they "forgot."

Modeling problem-solving strategies, the coach encouraged each player to think of ways to get to practice more regularly. She suggested several ideas, such as planning ahead better, rescheduling music lessons, carpooling, and getting to bed on time (altering *self-perception*). Finally, she pointed out that the players wore their team shirts to school, invited friends to their games, and said that they wanted very much to win games. Didn't these factors seem to conflict with the disinterest they had been showing at practice? Talking to players privately was important, because that allowed them to save face and change their behavior seemingly of their own accord. Helping each player to see the discrepancy between his or her behavior, personal values, and the team goals was all that was necessary to cause a change in most players' behavior.

A Lesson Well Learned

Michael Morrow,
Coordinator of Child Care Services Portland Community College

It was the early 1970s, and I was a rookie teacher in my mid-20s, working with a group of energetic second and third graders. I'll never forget Benji, who was my first year's "that kid," challenging my inexperience at every opportunity—basically setting the bar for me to determine whether I had what it takes to become a teacher. Today he would probably be diagnosed as ADHD, possibly oppositional defiant, but back then he was just "a handful." And as the school's first-year teacher, he was mine.

One day in January, after a full morning of Benji testing my patience, we were preparing for a "science walk" to the park after lunch. For the 15th time that day, Benji was doing what he wasn't supposed to, and I was at my wit's end. I found myself stomping across the room toward him, veins in my neck bulging, and my arms raised, hands poised and aiming for his skinny throat.

Somehow I caught myself. If I'd actually grabbed him, that would have been the end of my teaching career—if not making me a felon. I pointed at him and in a controlled shout yelled, "DON'T MOVE!" and I walked out of the room. I worked in one of those '70s schools constructed with low walls around a library, so I could peek over the wall and ask the teacher next to me to keep an eye on my kids. For a couple of minutes I walked up and down the hall, repeating "You can do this, you can do this, you can do this," while slowing my breathing. After getting a drink at the fountain, I went back to work.

The science walk to the park went okay, and later that afternoon, as the kids were getting ready to head out the door, I motioned Benji over and had him sit next to me. I looked at him and said, "Remember after lunch, when I yelled at you?" He looked at me with that "duh" expression, and nodded yes. "Well," I explained, "I was really angry, and to make sure I didn't do the wrong thing I had to give myself a timeout."

More than 30 years later I still can't forget his expression, and his response. His eyes got big, and after a pause he asked, "Grownups can do that?" It was a wonderful learning experience for him, as a kid who had serious impulse-control issues (and may still have!). But more, it was a valuable learning experience for me, forming the basis for one corner of my "Big Three" triangle for working with kids: *Model what you want them to do.*

And *Model*, along with *Catch Them Being Good* (reward positive behavior) and *Do What You Say You're Going to Do* (consistently, absolutely follow through with stated consequences), form the basis for the philosophy I've developed over almost four decades of working with kids—and it has served me well. Sometimes *almost* doing the wrong thing can lead you to, serendipitously, doing the right thing.

Source: Used with permission from Michael Morrow.

There is a delicate balance between urging compliance with program expectations and encouraging healthy autonomy. Remember, however, that you are responsible for protecting children's health, safety, and feelings. It's not always about being late for basketball practice. Sometimes program leaders have to use stronger measures to urge compliance, such as suspension or expulsion to deal with out-of-bounds or unsafe behavior. Most of the time, however, creative solutions can be found, sometimes by accident, as Mike Morrow demonstrates in Perspective 8.1.

Setting and Enforcing Limits Even though school-age programs should encourage children's participation in decision making as much as possible, plan the physical and emotional environment to support personal freedom, and practice cognitive modification strategies to improve individual behavior, the final responsibility for setting and enforcing limits on children's actions falls on the adults in charge.

What happens when a child absolutely refuses to follow the rules? How do you go about enforcing compliance to the limits once they are set? Before moving to some of the more dramatic measures, it's important to try several other strategies first. The overuse of punishment and rewards may emphasize the dominance of adults over children and destroy youngsters' intrinsic motivation to behave in acceptable ways. Many school-age programs have been successful using **natural and logical consequences** to address inappropriate behavior (Dreikurs, 1990).

NATURAL CONSEQUENCES   Natural consequences can be applied in the following two examples: (1) forgetting a lunchbox and (2) failing to wear a jacket while playing outside on a chilly day.

In the first scenario, Kenta leaves his school-age program in the morning and forgets to take his lunch with him. This has been an ongoing challenge, because Kenta's lunch contains items that need to be kept in the refrigerator. However, following the guidance principles above, the morning staff at Kenta's school-age center have worked with him to place a reminder note in his cubby, and he knows that writing the note and remembering to take the lunch out of the refrigerator is his responsibility.

What are the natural consequences of Kenta's action? He probably will be hungrier than usual when he arrives back at the center after school. He also will probably remember to take his lunch the next day. If his program leader, on the other hand, either (a) delivered the lunch to school or (b) dwelled on the situation after he returned from school, she would be skewing the effectiveness of the natural consequences of Kenta's behavior. In the first situation, she negates their contract that he is responsible for remembering his own lunch, and in the second, she effectively "punishes" him for his forgetfulness, making him feel ineffective and less confident that he'll be able to remember the lunch the next day.

In a second scenario, ignoring the advice of the recreation director, Detra leaves her warm jacket inside when she goes out after school to play baseball on a chilly spring day. An hour in the outfield and she returns quite cold, commenting that *someone* should have brought her coat out to her when she got stuck out there for so long. However, the adult in charge answers, quite calmly, "No, Detra, it was your responsibility to take your coat outside or to ask someone to come in and get it for you. I will give advice about the weather, but I will not take from you your right to face the consequences of your own decisions." Once again, bailing her out would have taught her that someone else—not her—was responsible for her comfort (and also convincing her that, in fact, she isn't capable of taking care of herself). Adding some kind of statement about "I told you that you'd need your coat" sends the same message. Natural consequences do not contain editorial comments, and all by themselves they can be very effective teachers.

LOGICAL CONSEQUENCES   In some cases, natural consequences can be dangerous. No one would encourage a youth worker to send children into the ice, snow, or rain without a coat, and forgetting one's medication or one's inhaler can have disastrous effects. In these situations, adults need to help children to remember the necessary items by brainstorming memory aids. Logical consequences are the alternative. These also must not be enforced via punishment and should also not be accompanied by sermons or threats. Rather, they involve a structuring of events so that consequences logically flow from the misdeed or poor decision.

If, for example, Priya has not finished putting away the game she's been dawdling over for 20 minutes by the time the recreation supervisor leaves for the outdoor playground, she will logically need to stay inside with the staff members preparing snack and finish the task. This is not "punishment" (unless it is presented as such), just the logical consequence of failing to act in a timely manner.

In the same manner, if 8-year-old Marcus spills paint on the table beside the easel, it is only logical that he needs to help clean it up. And if he splashes paint on the children sitting on the table, or pours paint in their hair, it is also only logical that he should assist in the cleanup of *that* mess, as well as in the explanation that will need to be given to the parents. (It is probably also logical that Marcus be refused access to the paints for a period of time if the paint was intentionally applied to his friends' hair.) Logical consequences must be related to the behavior to be effective—requiring Priya to help make the snack because she missed the outdoor play period is not logical, nor is asking Marcus to clean all the tables in the room following the paint incident. It is important to be sure that expectations and responses are appropriate to the child's developmental level and to adjust them if they are not. Ask the youngsters—if it's not a fair consequence, they'll tell you!

Other strategies may be needed if a child's behavior continues to be a problem or if the behavior presents a threat to the safety or well-being of the other children. Limiting free time immediately following an infraction is often effective, especially if it is accompanied by the requirement that the child remain inside (or at least away from the other children) and in the company of a staff member during that period. This is a good time to review the cognitive modification strategies described above. Discuss the broken rules with the child, and work together to figure out possible options for handling the situation if it occurs again. Removing privileges is the next step, trying to relate the privileges revoked to the infraction committed. If the child continues to break program rules, and it doesn't look hopeful that a major improvement is taking place, it is time to involve the parents.

Involving Parents

When the techniques described above are not effective in improving a child's behavior, the child's parents should be asked to a meeting. Depending on your relationship with the family, the situation at home, and a number of other things, this request may produce a reaction from total cooperation to outright unwillingness to help. Since in some cases children receive punishment when they return home after such a meeting, the interpersonal skills the caregiver brings to the meeting may positively influence the outcome of this session.

Since positive reinforcement is more effective than harsh punishment for misbehavior (Ames, Ilg, & Baker, 1989; Damon, 1990), setting up a daily behavior record based on changed behavior in the program is a good approach. In addition to providing a visual reminder of the behavior goals for children, share with parents the concept of shared responsibility for behavior management. They can be encouraged to set up positive behavior charts at home with appropriate rewards for even small improvements.

Because logical consequences can be positive as well as negative, it can be helpful to brainstorm with both parents and children how to match the rewards for improved behavior to the rules or guidelines in question. For example, if the problem being discussed is David's repeated use of offensive language while playing chess with William, a younger child, the original consequence might well have been "no chess with William." This only works as a negative consequence, of course, if the older child *likes* playing chess with William, but let us assume for the moment that he does. If the foul language continues during chess games with others, the consequence becomes "no chess." If it spills over into other games or activities, the consequence becomes "no games with other people." Solitaire, whether with cards or on a computer screen, holds only so much fascination, so a logical reward for a day with no outbursts could be an hour of playing a game with another person. This can be gradually increased in time and in numbers of children, depending on the success of the previous play session. If parents remark that they are having the same problem with David at home, they can be encouraged to set the same guidelines for David playing video games with his younger brothers.

Certain kinds of behaviors—such as repeated hitting, destruction of equipment, use of tobacco or alcohol or other drugs, stealing—risk damaging the physical or emotional environment for other children and should be met with strong measures, such as suspension or exclusion from the program. It is often the case that children, especially older ones, do not want to participate in after-school programs and have little motivation for following group rules. Here is another reason to create an attractive and interesting place for youngsters to be. The threat of exclusion is effective at changing behavior only if it is viewed as a punishment, not a reward.

When behavior problems cannot be solved using effective guidance techniques, then it is time to enlist the help of the parents.

It is also important to build relationships with parents and families *before* it is necessary to address behavior problems. Unfortunately, some parents may view school-age programs as a service, like pay-per-view, dry cleaning, or valet parking that they purchase and forget about (Damon, 1990). In government-subsidized programs such as 21st Century Learning Centers, parents pay a reduced rate or none at all, and in some drop-in programs the children walk in and out of their own accord. In these cases, the motivation for parents to be partners with program leaders may be small. Partnerships with parents must be *developed*. Skillful interpersonal relations and the creation of program policies that address parent values and needs will go a long way toward encouraging parent support and involvement. Developing policies will be discussed in a later chapter.

Assuming that rapport has already been developed with the parents of the child in question, and a positive behavior record/positive consequences contract has failed to improve the child's behavior, it is now time to create a written set of behavioral criteria that the youngster must follow to stay in the program. Ideally, a team that includes a parent or other trusted adult, the child, and a member of the program staff who is close to the child will develop this contract. Behavior needs to change immediately, and consequences must be specified clearly. A time frame for exclusion should also be part of this written contract (e.g., on the next occurrence of the behavior, the child will be excluded for a day, then a week, then a month.) If temporary exclusion does not work, parents should be informed that they must find new arrangements within a certain time frame and helped to find a program that is more suitable for their child.

As a child and youth worker, you have a profound effect on every child with whom you come in contact. Your efforts to help children grow and develop in their ability to respect and get along with other people, to resolve conflicts, and to solve problems will have long-lasting effects on their self-concept and effectiveness as social beings. It is essential that you continue to work on your own personal development, building knowledge, skills, and sensitivity so that your efforts to guide behavior are appropriate for the children in your care to produce an environment of caring, harmony, and mutual respect.

SUMMARY

To effectively guide the behavior of school-age children, it is necessary to understand the factors that contribute to the way they behave. Developmental characteristics play a part, as do individual family experiences and individual differences. The guidance system, consisting of children, adults, and the environment, plays an important role in influencing behavior. The ideas of many theorists contribute to the development of an environment and a way of interacting with children that promotes prosocial behavior and self-help skills. Effective workers in school-age settings understand that children sometimes pursue mistaken goals in their quest for a feeling of belonging and develop their guidance skills to work effectively with the children in their care and their parents to set limits and encourage appropriate behavior. School-age children benefit from learning problem-solving and conflict-resolution skills, and afterschool programs are ideal places to practice these skills.

TERMS TO LEARN

aggressive behavior
antisocial behavior
behavior contract
behavior modification
classroom management
cognitive modification strategies
complete inadequacy
conflict resolution
cyber-bullying
discipline
dominance hierarchy
extinction
guidance
guidance system

ignoring
instruct
mistaken goals
model/modeling
natural/logical consequences
problem-solving strategies
prosocial behavior
punishment
reinforce/reinforcer
relational aggression
retaliation and revenge
reward
struggle for power
undue attention

REVIEW QUESTIONS

1. Identify three factors that contribute to the way children behave in group situations.

2. What are the three components of an effective guidance system?

3. Compare some developmental characteristics of 5- to 7-year-olds with those of 11- to 12-year-olds that might make guidance of mixed age groups a challenge.

4. Give two examples of prosocial behavior and two of antisocial behavior.

5. Distinguish between modeling and instructing.

6. Develop three rules that meet Marion's criteria for "good limits."

CHALLENGE EXERCISES

1. What would be a logical consequence for a child who repeatedly fails to put away game pieces before leaving with her parents?

2. Write an outline for a parent education presentation designed to reduce the number of hours children watch videos and television programs with violent content.

3. Interview a child or youth worker about behavioral contracts. Does this person use them in his or her program? How do staff members involve parents? Are the contracts effective?

4. Call three school-age programs or your local school district and inquire about the use of conflict-resolution training in their schools. Interview a child about the process. Summarize and share with your class.

INTERNET RESOURCES

Mancala Games (history and instructions):
    http://mancala.wikia.com/wiki/Mancala

National Center for Cultural Competence:
    http://www11.georgetown.edu/research/gucchd/nccc/

Rudolf Dreikurs:
    http://www.newworldencyclopedia.org/entry/Rudolf_Dreikurs

REFERENCES

Ames, L. B., Ilg, F. L., & Baker, S. M. (1989). *Your ten- to fourteen-year-old*. New York: Dell.

Bandura, A. (1977). *Social learning theory*. New York: General Learning Press.

Brown, L. M. (2008). 10 ways to move beyond bully prevention (and why we should). *Education Week, 27*(26), 29–39.

Crick, N. R., & Rose, A. J. (2002). Toward a gender-balanced approach to the study of social–emotional development: A look at relational aggression. In P. H. Miller & E. K. Scholnick (Eds.), *Toward a feminist developmental psychology* (pp. 153–168). New York: Taylor & Francis/Routledge.

Damon, W. (1990). *The moral child*. New York: The Free Press.

Dreikurs, R. S. V. (1964). *Children: The challenge*. New York: Dutton Adult.

Dreikurs, R. S. V., & Solz, V. (1991). *Children: The challenge: The classic work on improving parent-child relations—intelligent, humane and eminently practical*. New York: Plume.

Erikson, E. H. (1993). *Childhood and society* (Reissue ed.). New York: Norton. (Original work published in 1950)

Ferrer, M., & Fugate, A. M. (2003). *The importance of friendship for school-age children*. Gainesville: University of Florida IFAS Extension.

Fink, D. (1995). *Discipline in school-age care: Control the climate, not the children.*. Nashville, TN: School-Age NOTES.

Fogarty, R. J. (2009). *Brain compatible classrooms*. Thousand Oaks, CA: Corwin Press.

Gordon, T. (2003). *Teacher effectiveness training*. New York: Three Rivers Press.

Grose, M. (2005, June). *Let's not hurry children through childhood*. Retrieved April 22, 2010, from http://ezinearticles.com/?expert_bio = Michael_Grose

Grusec, J. E., Davidov, M., & Lundell, L. (2002). Prosocial and helping behavior. In P. Smith & C. Hart (Eds.), *Blackwell handbook of childhood social development* (pp. 457–474). Malden, MA: Blackwell.

Kohlberg, L. (1984). *The psychology of moral development*. San Francisco: Harper & Row.

Lawhon, T. (1997). Encouraging friendships among children. *Childhood Education, 73*(4), 228+.

Levin, D. E. (2003). *Teaching young children in violent times: Building a peaceable classroom* (2nd ed.). Cambridge, MA: Educators for Social Responsibility.

Marion, M. (2006). *Guidance of young children* (7th ed.). Columbus, OH: Merrill.

Ollhoff, J., & Ollhoff, L. (2007). *Getting along: Teaching social skills to children and youth*. Farmington, MN: Sparrow Media Group.

Patchin, J., & Hinduja, S. (2009). *Bullying beyond the schoolyard: Preventing and responding to cyberbullying*. Thousand Oaks, CA: Sage.

Pete, B. M., & Fogarty, R. (2007). *Twelve brain principles that make the difference*. Thousand Oaks, CA: Corwin Press.

Piaget, J. (1965). *The moral judgment of the child* (M. Gabain, Trans.). New York: The Free Press. (Original work published in 1932)

Rubin, Z. (1980). *Children's friendships*. Cambridge, MA: Harvard University Press.

Selman, R. L., & Selman, A. P. (1979). Children's ideas about friendship: A new theory. *Psychology Today, 12*(4), 71–80.

Simmons, R. (2002). *Odd girl out: The hidden culture of aggression in girls*. New York: Harcourt.

Skinner, B. F. (1953). *Science and human behavior*. New York: Macmillan.

Slee, P. T., & Shute, R. (2003). *Thinking about theories*. London: Hodder Arnold.

Vygotsky, L. S. (1978). *Mind in society: The development of higher psychological processes* (14th ed.). Cambridge, MA: Harvard University Press.

Ybarra, M. L., Mitchell, K. J., Wolak, J., & Finkelhor, D. (2006, October). Examining characteristics and associated distress related to Internet harassment: Findings from the Second Youth Internet Safety Survey. *Pediatrics, 4*, 118.

Chapter

9

Environments for School-Age Children

There is no one best out-of-school arrangement for all families. A wide variety of options will probably always be necessary in each community in order to meet diverse and changing needs. Some children spend only part of an afternoon or a few afternoons a week in care; others need supervision before and after school each day and for 8 or more hours during school holidays and vacations. The facilities that house these children are also varied. Some children will go to private homes after school; others to multipurpose rooms, classrooms, or portable buildings on their school playground; still others to unused gymnasiums, storefront facilities, or warehouses. But all these facilities will have one thing in common: Once they have been transfigured with imagination and love, they can become great places for children.

PHYSICAL SETTINGS USED FOR SCHOOL-AGE PROGRAMS

This chapter is about environments for children. As with facilities and the program schedules, environments for school-age children should reflect the variety of cultures present in your community and the diversity of their interests and experiences. Many of the ideas presented in this chapter will be useful to Scout leaders, church-school teachers, camp recreation directors, and other youth workers, but the main focus is on designing environments for children in afterschool programs. These programs also come in a variety of forms, and they may be housed in many different kinds of facilities. Figure 9.1 shows the distribution of children in various kinds of facilities. The statistics used to develop this chart were reported by the National Center for Educational Statistics and show that in 2001 over half of children enrolled in school-age programs were housed on public school sites. About a third of the remaining children attended programs evenly divided between child

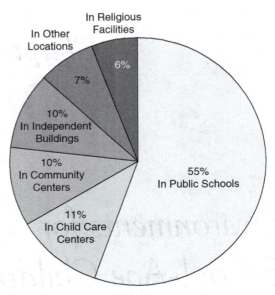

FIGURE 9.1 Where Children Attend School-Age Programs.

Source: Kleiner, B., & Chapman, M. (2004). *Before- and after-school care, programs, and activities of children in kindergarten through eighth grade: 2001.* Washington, D.C.: National Center for Education Statistics, In Neugebaeur, R. (2007). School-Age Child Care Trend Report: Views from the field. *Exchange* (September/October 2007), 4. Used with permission from Exchange Press.

care centers, community organizations, and independent buildings (Neugebaeur, 2007). Some of the most common settings are described below.

Private Homes

School-age programs operated in homes by licensed or registered family child care professionals have a special advantage, because the physical dimension is already homelike. Most providers utilize some portions of the house that are also used by family members but may also dedicate one or more rooms for children's use during the daytime hours. In the first case, one or two rooms may contain books, games, art supplies, and other materials intended primarily for children's use, but members of the family may also use that room in the evening for television, studying, etc.

In other situations, a completely separate portion of the family home, usually a converted family room, basement, or garage, is set aside for the exclusive use of the children, and family members rarely, if ever, enter. In that case, entrances and exits may need to be constructed so that children and their parents never enter the main house.

Unless there is a separate kitchen facility and bathrooms in the dedicated area, the children will need access to the family kitchen, bathroom facilities, and an outside play area in addition to whatever other rooms have been made available to them for naps and play. The caregiver may set certain "inside" and "outside" times or allow the children to move freely from one place to another throughout the time they are there.

Programs housed on school sites should have access to the playground, restrooms, library, and gym or multipurpose room.

School-Site Centers

Before- and afterschool care programs located on school grounds also come in several forms. Some programs are allocated a classroom for their exclusive use, although in heavily populated school districts this is less likely. More commonly, program leaders are offered the use of one or more regular classrooms before and after school and on holidays, if cooperation can be obtained from the teachers assigned to those classrooms in the daytime. This arrangement requires teachers to share their "territory" and sometimes give up precious preparation time, so good communication is necessary for it to work.

Some schools establish before- and afterschool programs in the school library or in a multipurpose room or gymnasium. Well-funded programs may even be able to obtain a portable classroom. This seems to be the option most often used by school-site programs administered by agencies other than the school itself. The most suitable relocatable buildings contain two wheelchair-accessible bathrooms and a kitchen area. All programs housed in classroom space, whatever its form, should also have access to the school playground, restrooms, library, and gym or multipurpose room.

Places of Worship

Programs housed in buildings primarily used for religious education or worship, such as churches, mosques, or synagogues, may find that sharing space with the owners is the only option. This may not be a major problem, however, since such facilities often sit unused during weekdays. Some wonderful spaces can be found this way, affording both cozier rooms and larger halls for program use than can be obtained in private homes or public buildings. However, just as in school classrooms, sharing space requires good communication. As a staff member, you will need to know what rules have been agreed upon for sharing space, such as whether you may hang children's work on the walls, where and how to store equipment, care of the classroom computer, and so forth. More will be said about that later.

Other Community Facilities

School-age programs are often housed in community facilities that would otherwise sit unused much of the time. Exemplary programs can be found in a wing of a senior center, the social room of a country club, a county fair exhibition hall, and even in a meeting room on the grounds of a small airport. Community and cultural centers or large public libraries will sometimes rent one or more large rooms to a program during daytime hours during the week, reserving the right to hold meetings there at other times. Each of these arrangements has unique possibilities and challenges and may provide an affordable option for a program looking for a home.

Permanent or Relocatable Buildings

Some programs have the luxury of occupying a building that can be used at any time of day or night, including weekends. Such is the freedom gained when a corporation or agency obtains or constructs a building for its exclusive use. This allows program staff and children to construct a permanent environment that is just right for them. Much more imagination can be exercised in such a setting than in a shared facility, although careful planning is still necessary to carry your ideas to fruition.

In Gilroy, California, the front windows of a former auto dealership were transformed into an art gallery and the extensive space partitioned with low walls into a charming multi-age-group program. The school-age part of the program operated on the mezzanine level, once occupied by sales personnel and office workers. Another organization secured the federal post office building when it moved to a larger building. Watch for large facilities whose purpose has changed. Among other advantages, both of these programs inherited very large parking lots.

Some large purpose-built centers are designed by architects who take into consideration school-age children's varying heights and weights, the need for varied lighting solutions for different activities, multiple uses of the same areas, and adequate storage. However, it is important that both children and the professionals who work with them be included in the design phase to optimize the construction of an environment that fits the ways in which children and adults will work and play together. If program staff are designing their own environment, they will want to visit lots of other facilities to discuss pros and cons with the children and adults who spend time in those environments.

THE THREE DIMENSIONS OF ENVIRONMENTS FOR CHILDREN

Visit several afterschool programs and you will see many different settings, and you will quickly understand that the environment of a program is far more than the building in which it is housed. The physical arrangement of furnishings in a room and the care with which it is decorated can influence children's emotions, their confidence, and even their self-esteem.

Compare the crisp orderliness of a government office, say the Department of Motor Vehicles or the United States Postal Service, with the cluttered coziness of a tiny quilt shop tucked away in the corner of a downtown street. One environment invites you to touch, breathe deeply, and dawdle, while the other demands an efficient exchange of information: "Take a number; have forms completed before approaching the window." As you design your environment for children, be sure that they feel welcome, nurtured, and encouraged to stay there.

❁   *Consider This:*   ❁

How do you feel after spending an hour sitting in a hard plastic chair in a shabbily furnished airport staging area, staring at pale green walls and bored people, your sensibilities shocked awake periodically by announcements from a loudspeaker right over your head? Contrast that with leaning against pillows and lace on your grandmother's couch, gazing at woven wall hangings and shelves of colorful books and objects d'art, while you listen to her tell story after story about her childhood. Which experience would you prefer? Which one sends the message "You are important. You really matter to me?"

Both indoor and outdoor settings for children should accommodate a variety of play equipment as well as provide sheltered areas for quiet play. Ideally, outdoor areas should include adequate space for sports, group games, gardening, carpentry, and individual activities such as riding bikes, jumping rope, and skateboarding. It should also allow for interaction with nature, including animals, water, soil, plants, trees, and the breezes that rustle their leaves. Obviously, fencing is needed to keep out strangers, but it can be attractively lined on the inside with flowers, shrubs, or large easels to paint and draw on. Children gain many skills while playing outdoors, and they gain an appreciation for nature (Bullard, 2010).

Indoor environments should allow for both individual and group activities, including doing homework or reading for pleasure (at a table, on the rug, or lounging on a couch with feet on a pillow), listening to music, playing board games, making crafts, knitting, and cooking. Separate activities from one another with permanent structures and indoor lofts or with movable dividers and cardboard boxes.

To ensure that environments for children send welcoming messages and encourage many different kinds of desirable behaviors, designers need to understand the three dimensions present in all environments: the physical, temporal, and interpersonal dimensions (Gordon & Brown, 2008).

The Physical Dimension

The **physical dimension** of the environment consists of the site and the structure—the furnishings and equipment as well as the light, color, and sound present in those spaces. You may find yourself working in a less-than-perfect building or space, but wonderful places are the result of creative and imaginative design, not of simply four walls, a ceiling, and a floor.

Plan both indoor and outdoor environments for school-age children so that they meet the unique physical needs of this age group and to encourage independent play and creativity. Indoor space should be large enough that children can work and play without crowding one another or interfering with one another's activities, and they should be decorated in ways that tell children they matter. Comfortable furniture encourages children to "stay awhile," while wall decorations (posters, paintings, or children's artwork) can reflect their interests and role models in sports, film, or music. Adequate storage space allows children and staff to easily access supplies that they use often while including room for equipment and materials that are needed less frequently.

The Temporal Dimension

The **temporal dimension** refers to the way in which time is managed in your program. The word *temporal* means "relating to, or limited by time." The temporal dimension is that aspect of a school-age program that has to do with scheduling the opening and closing times, the daily schedule, and the amount of time allowed for each activity. If the temporal dimension is managed well, staff and children will be generally calm and feel able to participate fully in the program without rushing from one thing to another. Over-scheduling a program can raise the stress level for everyone. A little downtime between activities allows for emotional recharging and also permits children who have not finished to either complete what they started or safely stack their homework, project, or game away for another time.

Review how time is managed in your program. Are the hours that children are present strictly scheduled, with little slivers of the day allocated to particular activities, such as recording attendance, standing in line to go outside, "game time," "music time," "homework time," and so on? Or does the amount of time allotted to various program elements flex and adjust to meet children's needs, with some administrative tasks like attendance completed in conjunction with activities such as snack or free play? Do you find yourself often rushing children or staff to complete activities on an arbitrary deadline, or may they safely store partially completed projects until they have the desire or opportunity to finish them? A well-managed program schedules enough time for children to accomplish some tasks and activities on the same day they started them and also to participate in larger projects that may take several days or weeks to complete.

The Interpersonal Dimension

The **interpersonal dimension** of the environment has to do with the nature of relationships between and among children, staff, and parents, as well as between members of the community, such as classroom teachers, nearby businesspeople, or clergy. Are these relationships formal or informal, inclusive or exclusive, strict or permissive, hierarchical or egalitarian? This dimension is also affected by the ages and numbers of children and staff and the styles of social interaction between and among them. An important criterion is that children have choices and are encouraged to take initiative and explore their interests. A good guideline to follow is to provide twice as many play spaces as there are children (Pratt, 1995).

Ensure that all children will find opportunities to engage in enjoyable activities that reflect their learning style, or "intelligence."

Another criterion to consider in the interpersonal dimension is ensuring that all children will find opportunities to engage in enjoyable activities that reflect their learning style, or "intelligence." For example, a child with strong Linguistic intelligence (Gardner, 1999) will be delighted to find writing materials and a rich selection of books, including those that "play" with language, such as ones containing jokes, riddles, crosswords, or puns. A youngster with Musical intelligence will make good use of a piano and a selection of musical instruments, as well as a CD player, radio, or MP3 player and headphones (for the benefit of the Intrapersonal school-agers playing solitaire or writing in their journal). Don't try to provide a separate environment or activity for each intelligence; children are creative and will find many different ways to interact with materials and environment. Just provide a variety of opportunities (Whitaker, 2002). See Table 5.6 for more examples of how to integrate multiple-intelligence theory into afterschool environments.

Because children grow significantly between the ages of 5 and 12, programs serving those ages should invest in furniture and permanent play equipment that accommodate a variety of sizes and offers progressive challenges (National AfterSchool Association, 1998). Be sure that furniture arrangements encourage children to sit in groups as they engage in reading or listening to music, for example, but that there are also several places to sit comfortably if children wish to be alone.

When all three dimensions in the afterschool environment are carefully considered and optimized so that the environment appeals to children and meets their physical and emotional needs, you will want to ensure that your curriculum supports children in a program that is *nurturing, attractive, interesting,* and *safe.*

A Nurturing Environment   Some children, when asked, will tell you they'd rather go home after school, even to an empty house, than stay in an afterschool program (Vandell, Reisner, & Pierce, 2007). One of the ways in which you can change this opinion is by providing physical arrangements and materials that make children feel welcome and that support their developmental needs. Within a cozy and comfortable environment, adults can more easily interact with children in honest, open ways and show interest in their lives and relationships. A **nurturing** environment such as this is **supportive** of children and their priorities. Adults in such nurturing environments communicate with body language as well as words: "We enjoy having you here; you are a valuable part of our afterschool community; you have interesting things to say; we care about each of you personally."

A nurturing, supportive environment contains logical groupings of interesting areas with rich resources. There are physical boundaries separating noisy and quiet areas, and children can select from a variety of developmentally valid activities or just "hang out." In contrast, in a **nonsupportive** environment, arbitrary rules are imposed, children's movements are rigidly controlled, and materials are locked away or, worse, disorganized and often in short supply. Guidance experts tell us that in supportive settings, children interact on a personal level with involved adults, have opportunities to influence the nature and arrangement of their surroundings, and are allowed to move around freely, play on the floor if they like, and change activities as they wish. These environments not only invite children to stay and play, but they also foster positive adaptive behavior and promote the development of self-control and mastery (Marion, 2006).

When little thought is given to enhancing the comfort and attractiveness of a space, it frequently appears inhospitable, boring, and shabby. Adults who do not understand or encourage children's need to influence their surroundings and interact with one another may appear to be overly stern or hostile when they are actually just fearful of losing control. The effect on the children, unfortunately, is the same. (Remember the parent helper at the amusement park in Chapter 4?)

Children in supportive physical environments are actually *encouraged* to move around and interact with the objects and people they find there. Arrange furniture and materials to encourage the formation of work groups, allow quiet and noisy activities to occur at the same time, and make provisions for privacy for those who wish it. In the outdoors, trees or climbing equipment should allow children to climb, swing, and jump from safe heights. A developmentally appropriate school-age environment can accommodate children of different ages who wish to work individually, in small groups, or in large groups and with varying degrees of independence and self-direction. It might have a separate area for older children and a comfy sofa where they can curl up with a friend to exchange confidences or seek solace. Because some children may arrive at different times of the day than others, separate entry and play areas can minimize interruptions and distractions to children already engaged in activities.

Nurturing children also includes nurturing their interests. This requires having enough supplies for a variety of different activities to take place simultaneously and to allow for changing interests. Let the children guide this process, and encourage them to help collect the needed material or help guide your purchase. One child may want to collect rocks and minerals; another may build a complex maze/house for the resident rodent or reptile. Baseball cards, sodoku puzzles, persona dolls, friendship bracelets, and marbles all have a place in a supportive environment for children. Follow the fad of the moment, and help the children collect the materials they need to build/collect/trade/play with their friends.

Nurturing environments are primarily **child centered** or **child responsive**, not **adult centered**. To work successfully with children in any setting, you must communicate that you respect their opinions and will listen to their ideas. Mostly, you should follow their lead when planning activities, arranging furniture, purchasing supplies, even setting limits for behavior. Child-responsive programs are all about meeting children's physical, social, and emotional needs, giving wings to their ideas and interests, not about satisfying adult needs to control behavior, lead games, or solve disagreements. Be willing to set aside your own agenda and allow children to explain what matters to them. Sometimes this may be how they want to spend their time; at other times it could be about an adjustment to the physical, temporal, or emotional dimensions.

Instead of requiring them to participate in a specific adult-determined activity at a specific time, encourage youngsters to select activities and experiences from a variety of "clubs" or other choices that you have developed after considering their ideas and preferences. In this way, you can address the mission and goals of the program in a way that appeals to the children and is more likely to engage them fully.

Do not underestimate the importance of a nurturing and attractive environment. If they do not feel welcome and respected in your program, school-age children will "vote with their feet" and may persuade their families that they are perfectly safe in self-care. Children do not measure the quality of a program by its ability to prevent juvenile crime, improve test scores, or reduce vandalism in the community. Especially older children are more likely to attend programs that feel welcoming, offer a variety of engaging and challenging activities and experiences in a welcoming and attractive environment, and serve healthy, but tasty, food (Grossman, Campbell, & Raley, 2006; Grossman, Walker, & Raley, 2001). When you create attractive and supportive environments and nurture children's interests, you will attract new families to your programs in the very best way possible: Children and parents will tell their friends.

Family involvement also helps to keep youngsters interested in the program and ensures that the needs of each child and family are met (Fight Crime: Invest in Kids, 2007). By collaborating with families and the school site, you can learn what you need to develop a child-responsive curriculum. As an added benefit, you can use these ideas when you are updating your recruitment and marketing plan. This process will be discussed in Chapter 15. Yet *child responsive* does not mean *child run*. Program leaders must still be the ones who determine the philosophy, goals, and objectives of the program and set the boundaries for behavior. You certainly should listen to families' ideas and opinions when planning activities, but children need you to provide models of behavior, provide opportunities for learning, suggest problem-solving strategies and provide assistance in working with others towards a stated goal.

Homework and the Nurturing Environment The issue of child-responsive vs. adult-centered programming leads rather naturally into a discussion of homework. Afterschool programs are important in the complex process of socialization. Adult leaders work as partners with parents and other adults to provide the role modeling, guiding, and teaching necessary to prepare children for full participation in society. When both parents work outside the home, or when a single working parent is managing a household of children, it can be very difficult to support children's learning. In such circumstances, it is understandable if parents ask afterschool programs to provide time, space, and encouragement for their children to complete their homework and long-term school projects. Research has shown that afterschool tutoring programs can increase the amount of homework turned in and also improve children's self-esteem, sense of accomplishment, responsibility, and attitude toward school (George, 2001).

DEVELOPING A HOMEWORK POLICY   But how does a child-responsive group leader ensure that children actually *do* their homework? Is it your job to be the homework police? Should you use persuasive, even coercive techniques to ensure that the homework is finished before other activities are pursued? This is an issue hotly debated at workshops and professional meetings, in staff rooms, and during parent conferences, mostly without a single satisfactory conclusion.

Many professionals in school-age settings maintain that supervising homework is not their responsibility. In some programs, that is a valid and effective posture. In some school districts, children are expected to complete all school tasks within the school day, taking home only the work they did not finish in the time allowed. In other communities, however, children are given a fairly sizeable number of out-of-school assignments, and youngsters really do need time, an appropriate place to work, and the necessary equipment to complete their tasks.

Parents differ in their availability to supervise homework and in their desire for afterschool staff to take responsibility for this role. In some families, parents place homework squarely in the middle of the "quality time" they spend with children each evening, while others would rather spend that time on the sidelines of soccer practice or supervising children's television watching by sitting down with them and enjoying the shows along with them. Many children and adults are simply too tired after their long days away from home to do an effective job of completing—or supervising—homework.

The best way for each program to solve this dilemma is to examine its mission and goals and then meet with a representative group of parents and children to develop a policy. Homework time may need to be adjusted to be shorter or longer at different times of the year as homework loads change. In most programs, it is best to leave providing motivation for completion of tasks to classroom teachers, parents, and the children themselves. Concentrate instead on providing support for homework time by providing a physical and interpersonal dimension that nurtures their desire to learn and a temporal environment that allows them sufficient time to complete their tasks each day. Some programs ask parents and children to sign a homework contract. Other programs recruit community volunteers to assist with and check homework. Figure 9.2 provides the homework policy of one afterschool program. It may be helpful as you develop your own.

A child-responsive approach to developing a homework center will include adequate lighting, roomy tables, maps and a world globe, online reference materials, dictionaries, rulers, pencils, scissors, and math manipulatives. It may also include soft pillows and a couch or two for reading, a dedicated home-

FIGURE 9.2 Greater Lowell Family YMCA Homework Policy.

Enrollment Packet

Homework Help Agreement

Homework help is structured time set aside in our afternoon for those children who have homework assignments to complete. YMCA staff will help children who require assistance with their homework. YMCA staff will also verify the completion of homework assignments upon the request of parents. Homework help time may also consist of reviewing vocabulary words and math flash cards with a child and providing appropriate reading materials for those children who need to improve their reading skills.

YMCA Staff agree to:

- Provide 50 minutes of structured homework time.
- Provide YMCA staff to assist children who need help.
- Act in a caring, honest, respectful, and responsible manner.
- Verify the completion of homework assignments *upon the request of parents.*
- Allow children to borrow writing utensils.
- Provide homework resources, such as dictionaries, reading books, etc.

Parent agrees to:

- Inform YMCA staff if you do not want your child to do homework at the program site.
- Inform staff that you want YMCA to check your child's homework for completion.
- Understand that getting involved in your child's homework assignments is an excellent way to know what is going on in school.
- Acknowledge that the completion of homework assignments is NOT the goal of the homework help time, but more of a support system for parents.

Child agrees to:

- Realize that completion of homework assignments is their responsibility.
- Be honest when asked if they have homework and during homework help time be caring, respectful and responsible of others.
- Have the necessary supplies with them to complete their homework assignments.
- Ask questions to the YMCA staff when they need assistance.

_____
Signature of Parent/Guardian

_____
Child's Signature

Please verify that my child has completed his or her homework _____ Parent Initials

I do NOT want my child to do homework at the Program Site _____ Parent Initials

Source: Used with permission from Greater Lowell Family YMCA.

work computer, and adults who support the children's efforts by maintaining supplies and equipment, answering questions, and suggesting new strategies for problem solving. Whenever possible, accommodate children's learning styles by encouraging them to do their homework in the way that suits them best.

If they prefer, allow children to do their homework away from others in a soft chair or couch or even on the floor while listening to music (headphones take care of the needs of others for a quiet atmosphere). Some children benefit from the opportunity to talk over strategies and ideas with their friends or even to take breaks from studying or working to chat about their day. All styles of learners need resources to complete the tasks they have been assigned. Adults who trust children to find their own way will be most likely to see exactly those results (see Table 5.6 for additional ideas about materials to provide for homework activities). Adult-centered programs tend toward large bare tables, chairs, and no talking. You can see how it would be difficult to convince some children to spend very much time in that kind of an environment.

Try to have enough staff members present during homework time to allow children free movement between the activity/homework centers and a gym or outdoor recreation area. No child whose body is crying for physical activity should be forced to remain inside for an arbitrary period of time before being allowed to go outside and play. But the reverse is also true; too many children are required to spend long hours sitting on the edge of a playground that holds no interest for them when they would prefer to be inside playing games, working on crafts, or even reading or doing their homework. Although staffing regulations vary, a ratio of one adult to eight children is a good goal, with no fewer than two adults inside or outside at a time; this distribution will allow children to move between intense and relaxed activities in a natural way.

Sometimes children with special needs have personal attendants or **inclusion aides** to assist regular staff in meeting their unique needs. Include these assistants in planning along with the regular staff. It is important for inclusion aides to interact directly with all children in the program so that the children for whom they are responsible are regularly included as part of the larger group during most

Children should have free movement during homework time.

activities. Children with disabilities are children first. Be sure to encourage them to participate fully in play as well as in homework activities.

Long-range homework projects are often assigned to children age 9 and older. Sometimes working in groups is permitted or even encouraged by the classroom teacher, and the afterschool environment is an ideal setting for this to take place. You can facilitate children's developing ability to brainstorm, plan, compromise, and complete complex tasks by listening to their ideas, making suggestions, and helping them obtain the necessary materials or tools for their projects. You can also encourage integration of the school day with the afterschool program by encouraging children to participate in long-term projects they initiate and plan that are suggested by, but not necessarily required by, their classroom curriculum. There will be more said about this in Chapter 10.

Try to schedule a staff member to make a weekly visit with a small group of children to the public library, a tug on working parents' time that may be difficult for them to schedule. Most children respond well to your recognition that their school responsibilities are important. In these and other ways, when children's homework needs are considered during the planning and implementation of before- and afterschool environments, the "police" aspect of homework supervision may disappear completely.

The Nurturing Environment and Cultural Contexts   Ten million children in the United States between the ages of 5 and 17 speak a language other than English at home. These children make up nearly one in five in this age group. Most of them (7.1 million) speak Spanish at home, but many other languages and cultures are represented (U.S. Bureau of the Census, 2009). Noticing language differences can help us become aware of cultural differences that exist in our programs. And cultural differences sometimes create inconsistencies and even conflicts for children as they struggle to behave appropriately in two different environments.

Differences in acting appropriately at home and school are faced by children everywhere, but it is even more of a challenge for children whose family and community social rules are different from those found in American public schools and related programs. An example of the dilemmas children may face is whether to look directly at you when speaking or being spoken to or to respectfully lower their eyes. In the same way, some children have been taught to listen carefully to academic instruction and quietly absorb the knowledge; others (typically middle-class American children) have been encouraged to actively compete with one another and show off their ability (Rogoff, 2003). Your awareness of such dilemmas can help you to be sensitive to a child's discomfort and to act quickly to reassure or guide a child into a way of responding that respects that child's sensibilities but also teaches appropriate ways of behaving at different times in your particular program.

During homework time, there is frequently a marked contrast between children who work best in a quiet environment with those who prefer a collaborative, conversational interchange as they solve math problems or write answers to questions about, say, a social studies lesson. Add in the cultural component that collaboration may be seen as cheating by some people, and chatting during homework time as disrespectful, and you can understand the difficulty. It is important to remember, also, that children who are bicultural do not always speak a different language at home, and they may not have names that give clues to ethnicity or culture. It is up to you to help *all* children distinguish appropriate ways to act during homework time—and any other time—and to provide enough flexibility in terms of work areas, group size, and rules that children's preferences and cultural contexts can also be honored.

The Challenge of Shared Space　Children and staff in school-aged programs deserve to have a place of their own to go before and after school as well as during the holidays and summer vacations. However, space is in short supply in many communities, and afterschool programs may find themselves housed in shared space such as a multipurpose room, gymnasium, cafeteria, recreation center, or even a classroom. School-agers (and their leaders) who have shared facilities in schools or community buildings often report feeling like second-class citizens: Long-term projects are moved or destroyed, personal possessions left in cubbies disappear, artwork is torn from walls. To be fair, some school staff members who have shared their classrooms with afterschool programs have also reported feeling frustrated:

> There is nothing more frustrating for a teacher than to arrive at school, do yard duty, then go to the classroom thinking she is ready to begin the day's lesson and find chairs rearranged, chalk or dry erase markers gone, printer paper gone, teacher desk supplies missing, sewing machine needles missing, marks on the student work displayed in the wall, posters ripped, etc. (Kim, 2004)

Sharing space and resources is a daily reality in most publicly funded programs, and there are fair ways to make it work. Hayin Kim, of the Children's Aid Society, prepared a guide for the federally funded 21st-Century Community Learning Centers, which, due to their large clientele, typically operate in shared space on school sites (Kim, 2004). The following are four useful lessons learned by "veteran space sharers" in the 21st-Century program.

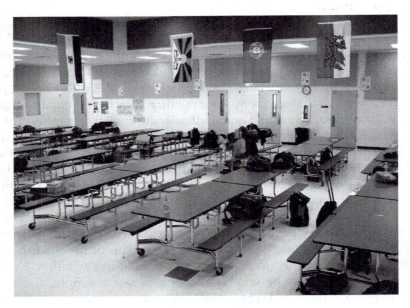

A multipurpose room presents real challenges to environmental planners.

❀ Open communication is critical. Send a letter to a classroom teacher introducing yourself and your role in the extended day program; specify times and days you will be using the classroom; assure the teacher that you will listen to any concerns and suggestions; invite the teacher to meet if it is convenient.

❀ Make sure the room is returned to its original condition. Number one rule of shared classroom use: Do not touch any of the teachers' or students' belongings. Work with the teacher to agree on how chairs and tables should be left at the end of the session; whether to sweep or mop or if a custodian will do that before morning; how to handle accidental breakage or loss of equipment or supplies.

❀ Offer to share resources. Bringing in your own supplies means that teacher supplies will not be used. Perhaps your program has some materials or equipment (such as a paper cutter or laminator) that could be shared with the teacher.

❀ Say thank you. Find a way to do favors for your hosts. Write a nice note periodically, using cheerful note paper or directly on the board so that children can see it also.

Bringing together several services for children and families in one public facility is cost effective, and we will be seeing more of it. Generally at the outset it is advisable to negotiate a shared-use agreement with the other agency or groups using the facility. A roundtable discussion and brainstorming session with representatives from each group can prevent uncertainties, resentments, or unfair situations from developing. If possible, arrange to have at least one child from your program present for this discussion, and request that a representative child from the school be invited also. Children often think of possibilities adults forget. For example, "Will the bathrooms be unlocked?" "May we use the computer?" Be sure you know exactly how many hours a day you will have exclusive use of the spaces and when you may also enter for preparation or periodic meetings or special events. Decide together who will be responsible for cleaning, opening and closing the building, purchasing bathroom supplies, securing building maintenance, and providing security. How much space will you have for storage? This is important if you will be creating and dismantling the environment every day or even every week. Does the landlord have the right to "bump" your program for special events or meetings? If so, where will you go?

You can use equipment owned by your program as bargaining tools, and your generosity might result in permission to use equipment or resources belonging to one of the other groups using the facility or the landlord agency itself. For instance, photocopiers, computers, telephones, fax machines, or laminating machines could be shared by several groups, even purchased jointly if the trust level is high enough. If funds are short, community service clubs such as Rotary, Elks, or Lions can be approached for help obtaining such equipment (offer to share the new acquisition with other nonprofits). Creative problem solving can go a long way in developing ways to share the cost of supplies or utilities equitably. Once the terms are settled, get them in writing. Memories can be unpredictable, and staff can change. If possible, arrange to have periodic meetings with all users of the facility in order to work out any difficulties that may arise later.

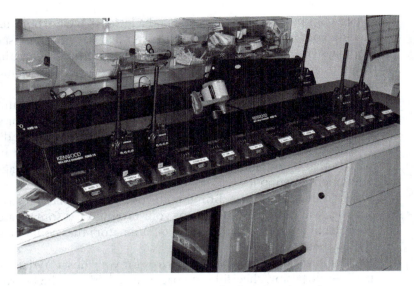

Sharing space with another agency may lead to shared purchases.

The ideas presented in this chapter for making the program feel friendly, especially those encouraging mutual respect and tolerance, should be kept in mind when working in shared space. Get to know your neighbors, especially if others who use the facility are lukewarm or even hostile to your use of the space. Go out of your way to meet the administrators, teachers, administrative assistants, custodians, parents, and parishioners. Share information; invite stakeholders to program-sponsored special events. Win them over with your commitment to the community and to high-quality out-of-school care.

Once the negotiations are complete, and you know where and when you will be housed, how much storage space you will have, how much freedom you have to use wall space or move furniture, you must design your environment for flexibility and portability. Interest areas can be created as kits (prop boxes) that can be set up quickly and stored easily—large plastic storage boxes are helpful here. Ideas for curriculum and contents of prop boxes will be detailed in Chapter 12. Clearly marked labels on the ends of each box can help staff and children select the interest areas they wish to use each day. Administrators should allocate staff time for you to retrieve materials from closets and set up furniture, unrolling rugs, laying out supplies, and hanging up banners, artwork, or posters and then storing them all at the end of the day or the week. Do not give in to the temptation to cut corners and leave everything in boxes or on carts; no matter how portable it is, the environment should make children feel that it was designed especially for them if they are going to feel comfortable there.

Talk with the children about what can be done with the space at hand to make it cozy and comfortable. Brainstorm freely at first, with no discussions or arguments; just list all the ideas on a large piece of paper or board for later discussion. Programs in shared space may need to transform a gymnasium, cafeteria, classroom, or auditorium into a nurturing play space every single day. However, many programs do this quite successfully, with moveable panels made from corrugated cardboard appliance boxes, thin sheets of Styrofoam or other lightweight material, giant hanging banners, furniture on wheels, and carts filled to bursting with supplies, books, games, and equipment. The more challenging the setting, the more fun everyone can have transforming it into a welcoming place. Think of it as designing a set for a play. Children can draw sketches, help hang draperies and wall coverings, and paint furniture. Posters of "heroes"—able bodied and otherwise—help to set a tone for acceptance, high goals, and familiarity.

AN ATTRACTIVE ENVIRONMENT

Most children spend their school days in fairly structured classroom settings, with assigned seating, scheduled activities, and a series of assignments to complete. Effective programs for school-agers offer a change from this experience, allowing children a chance to relax, socialize, and choose the way they wish to spend their time. An attractive, homelike environment will reflect the personalities and cultures of the children within it and change over time with their interests and needs.

One way to learn what environments youngsters consider attractive is to ask them to describe their bedrooms at home. Younger children tend to make nests on the floor or their bed using pillows or stuffed animals; some create thematic play areas with action figures. Older children make statements on the walls with posters, T-shirts, CD cases, or bumper stickers. Siblings sharing rooms often create boundaries with bookcases or lines of possessions or cooperate in the creation of larger floor spaces by moving desks or beds to one side of the room.

Four components of the environment that influence its attractiveness are *furnishings, light, color,* and *sound.* Another important consideration is a *provision for privacy.*

Furnishings (Including Equipment and Materials)

Furnishings should reflect the variety of activities that take place in the program, as well as the differing ages of the children. Be sure there are adequate tables and different-sized matching chairs so that each child can find room to play a board game, study or do homework, read a book, or draw. But also provide softer furnishings—cushions, bean bag chairs, overstuffed chairs or sofas, throw rugs, and gymnastic mats. Fabric wall coverings, banners, posters, and paintings add texture and interest and can help to dampen the sound in an acoustically bright room. They should be topical and colorful and reflect the interests of the children in the program. Be prepared to adapt the environment creatively and individually to enhance access for children with disabilities or physical limitations.

Basic equipment should include outdoor sports equipment such as several different kinds and sizes of balls, bats, skipping ropes, Hula hoops, tug-of-war ropes, pogo sticks, portable goal nets, and yo-yos. Have supplies for indoor activities such as ping-pong, foosball, board games, science experiments, carpentry, fiber arts, arts and crafts, and cooking. This would include microscopes, magnets, mixing bowls, measuring cups or scales, sewing machine, buttons, cloth scraps, thread, yarn, sponges and brushes, paints, colored chalks, interlocking plastic blocks, and the like.

Table 9.1 lists a set of goals for children in out-of-school programs and links them with materials and activities that support those goals. By developing such a chart for your own program, you can identify equipment and materials that you "must have" or "would like to obtain" and work toward acquiring them. This

TABLE 9.1 Selecting Activities and Materials to Meet Program Goals Using Seven Key Areas.

Key Learning Area	Examples of Goals	Possible Activities	Suggested Materials
Literacy	Enrich language development.	Talking, asking questions, listening, recalling experiences, discussions about home and everyday life	Tape recorders, microphones, puppet theatres, dollhouses
	Create habits of listening and concentrating.	Singing, learning rhymes, listening to stories, taking part in conversations	Songs, rhymes, stories, music, games, telephone, sound games
Science	Offer the chance to explore and enjoy natural materials.	Walking and working out of doors, collecting, sorting, planting, weeding, harvesting, painting with natural materials, making collages	Water, clay, wet and dry sand, wood, soil, leaves, fabric, corks, shells, stones, gardening tools
	Extend children's understanding of science and the world around them.	Problem solving, reading, cooking, investigations and experiments, talking to guest speakers	Water, magnets, lenses, mirrors, wood, living and growing things, visitors
Math	Form the basis of mathematical understanding.	Describing, comparing, explaining, classifying, matching, sorting, combining, dividing, pairing	Sand, water, building blocks, wood, collections of objects, construction materials, puzzles, number games
Arts	Stimulate children's imagination and creativity.	Reading, storytelling, acting, painting, dressing up, building, domestic and adventure play, cutting and sticking, modeling	Paint, wet sand, building blocks, music, pencils and crayons, cars, trains, animals, dolls, construction materials
	Encourage the development of manipulative skills.	Cutting, sticking, sorting, piecing together puzzles, building with manipulatives, blocks or wood, cooking, printing, painting	Dough, clay, wood, pencils, crayons, puzzles, paints and water, construction and cooking materials, rubber stamps
	Respond to children's continued need to explore through their senses.	Modeling, playing with different materials, making collages, listening to music, matching scents and sounds	Fingerpaint, dough, water, dry and wet sand, sounds, scents, wood, music
Social Competence	Help children to respect and enjoy companionship of other children and adults.	Conversation, imaginative and adventure play, sharing jokes, long-term building projects	Things to share (climbing frame, road layout, dramatic play area), joint activities (such as singing, outings, stories) construction materials
	Enable children to come to terms with aspects of their own lives and to express their feelings.	Domestic dramatic play, writing or telling stories, conversation, listening to others, reading	Dramatic play materials, paper and writing materials, paint, multicultural books and dolls, pictures, puppets

TABLE 9.1 (*Continued*)

Key Learning Area	Examples of Goals	Possible Activities	Suggested Materials
Fitness and Nutrition	Develop muscular strength and coordination.	Building, climbing and balancing, running, skipping, pushing, pulling, jumping, and playing with balls, woodworking, rolling, hopping, throwing, crawling, and swimming	Climbing and gymnastics equipment, balls, bats, tumbling mats, access to swimming pool, lake, river, or seaside, woodworking tools
Technology	Understanding core concepts of technology	Making things move	Legos and motors
	Characteristics and scope of technology	Writing an assignment using a computer	Computer; Word or other word processing software
	Role of society in development and use of technology	Using digital photography to record a community activity	Digital camera or camcorder

Source: From *Links to Learning: A Curriculum Planning Guide for After-School Programs*, by National Institute on Out-of-School Time, 2005, Nashville, TN: School-Age Notes. Used with permission.

wish list of desired materials and equipment should be developed with the children and purchased as the budget allows. If you wish, you can also stipulate which part of the indoor or outdoor spaces may be used for each activity.

Light and Color

Light and color can set moods that contribute to the emotional well-being of the children and adults in a space (Greenman, 2005). Be sure there is adequate light wherever children play and work. The type of lighting fixtures used is particularly important in an indoor afterschool environment. Most children will be arriving from school, where they will in all probability have been working for several hours under uniform (and probably flickering) fluorescent lights or high-pressure sodium vapor lighting, both of which cause eye fatigue and stress (Hales, 1994; Olds, 1988).

Color and light also have a significant influence on how students learn and retain information (Carter, 2000; Rittner-Heir, 2002). Natural light is the best choice for room illumination, if there are adequate windows to provide it. If not, incandescent or tungsten lamps, alone or in conjunction with fluorescent fixtures, can offer a refreshing change from classroom lighting, and the color of the light they produce is more pleasing to the eyes. Individual desk and table lamps placed strategically can add color and interest to the room. If you must live with tube fittings, try replacing the fluorescents with full-spectrum or color-corrected lamps, which radiate a warm light. Several studies replacing old fluorescent lights with full-spectrum lighting have shown significant benefits to health and academic performance (Heschong Mahone Group, 1999). It is also important to change fluorescent tubes as soon as they begin to flicker, an early sign of deterioration. More recent studies have found positive relationships between skylighting and behavior, physical comfort conditions in classrooms and student learning, and the impact of daylight on human performance (Heschong Mahone Group, 2003).

Some programs are now using low-energy light bulbs, also known as compact florescent lights (CFLs), although there is disagreement about their safety (Lewis, 2008). Rooms with large banks of windows should have curtains, draperies, or blinds to reduce glare from early morning or late afternoon sun.

Color influences mood. Color consultants can create an air of calm reassurance in a hospital or a cheerful, stimulating atmosphere around a factory assembly line simply by their selection of color for wall coverings and furniture. The successful use of color in a school-age setting requires that you not only balance colors but also distribute them well. If you have the option, use a light hue for walls and floor coverings, then allow children to help you plan accents with more intense hues in the furnishings, throw pillows, wall hangings, or accessories. These things can be changed as desired, without major redecorating (Chan & Petrie, 2000; Teachernet, 2007).

Sound

Some settings, such as cafeterias and gymnasiums, have such a characteristically high noise level that viewing a photograph of children playing in these environments will cause people to clap their hands to their ears in sympathy. Yet many before- and afterschool programs must operate daily under such conditions.

Other sound disturbances can be created by vocal dramatizations such as those stimulated by action figures, fashion dolls, road building and block play, computer sound effects, and music played on portable "boom boxes." To help with sound overlap and intrusion, line with cloth the walls of rooms that have bright acoustics, and hang fabric banners from the ceiling. You can also lower the perceived sound level by creating private spaces for children with appliance boxes and large pillows. Programs trying to offer quiet activities in noisy locations (e.g., plagued with traffic or gymnasium noise) might want to build acoustic dividers by covering sheets of Styrofoam with mattress padding or foam. Playing soft music during quiet time can help here, also. Good planning of the physical dimension includes separating loud and quiet activities with bookcases or other dividers, directing speakers away from other people, and asking children to use headphones for private listening. Be conscious of the effect sound can have when it spills over into someone else's area, and involve the affected children in the problem-solving process.

Provision for Privacy

One of the most frequently voiced complaints from youngsters interviewed about their child care settings is that they are never able to get away from the other children and "just be alone." In a home setting, most children can slip away from the action occasionally, even if it is only to a bedroom or a secluded corner of the yard. Privacy and alone time is especially important for children who exhibit intrapersonal intelligence—a strong sense of the self and a desire to understand it better (Gardner, 1993, 1999). Forcing introspective children to join groups and interact after they have just spent 6 hours in a classroom is inconsiderate and unwise.

Children need to be alone sometimes, and it is important to have more than one place for that to happen. A common solution is to have a designated "quiet area," usually stocked with books and magazines, soft seating, and a plush rug. This is fine, unless two children want to read together and plan to do so out loud. Another option is to have one or two comfortable chairs situated away from other activity areas, possibly with a reading lamp on a side table. A third approach, used in home settings for generations, is to drape a sheet or blanket over a table to make a tent. Folding foam pads or Japanese-style futons can be arranged on their sides to create interesting walls for children to climb inside. These hideaway spots can provide restful places for reading and homework or for playing quiet board games with a friend. At the same time, however, all areas must be within someone's earshot or line of sight. There is a fine line between privacy and a dangerous lack of supervision.

Finally, simply having a place to be alone and quiet will not ensure that children who need to be alone will necessarily manage to do so. School-aged youths are often so intensely involved in social development that if large group activities are always happening, they will always choose to engage in them. Program planning that includes periods of downtime with no planned activities ensures that this developmental need to think, unwind, and mull things over can be met (Bellm, 1990).

AN INTERESTING ENVIRONMENT

Interesting. That is a value-laden word. What is interesting to one child may be boring to another; in fact, it undoubtedly will be. So an *interesting* environment must offer a wide variety of activities for youngsters, ranging from quiet solitary pursuits to noisy large-group games.

Most child development professionals agree that the goals of school-aged care programs should be clearly differentiated from those of the educational institutions in which the children spend the bulk of their days. Many parents and educators believe that after school is the time to spend developing the "other three R's"—resourcefulness, responsibility, and reliability (Bergstrom, 1984). School-agers, described by Erikson (1993) as balancing "industry versus inferiority" (see Chapter 5), are especially interested in feeling productive and useful, doing real work, using adult tools, and learning adult skills.

Planning activities that offer children these opportunities is one way of ensuring that the program is interesting. Construction projects, inside and outside the children's own center, can do this. Service projects such as gardening, window washing, making aprons or beanbags for a nearby preschool, or similar pursuits allow children to develop and practice a variety of new skills while simultaneously connecting them with community needs. Remember, however, that although goal-oriented and community service activities are valuable experiences, a steady diet of them can lead to burnout. Children need time to pursue their own interests, make new friends, and enjoy one another's company—in other words, time simply to be children. Perspective 9.1 describes a high quality environment through the eyes of a visitor.

Variety of Materials

Make sure there are a sufficient quantity and a variety of play materials. Provide lots of **open materials**, which have no single "correct" outcome. These include

PERSPECTIVE 9.1

*A Walk Through a School-Age Program:
An Administrator's View*

Dr. Barbara A. Malaspina,
Retired School District Administrator

Walking into an excellent school-age program, the first thing I notice is the busy and productive activities taking place. In one area, the science club is designing a robot to be a greeter in the parent sign-in area. Lots of ideas are flowing, and children laugh as they try different ways to get the robot to move. A group at the writing center is writing thank-you notes to the nurse who came last week to tell them about her role at the hospital.

Construction has been an important and lasting project. The children have marked off a work area with yellow "caution tape" so that they can continue building each day until the elaborate structure is finished.

In the library area, students are debating the merits of the latest Harry Potter movie as compared to the books. As I stroll from one area to another, I scan the walls, which are bright and colorful. Illustrated signs are posted in several areas of the room with rules that have evidently been written by various groups of children. The names of the authors are signed in the corner. Rules include "Listen . . . share . . . be kind," and "Each person gets to say their story; look for solutions that work for everyone!"

Child-made signs like these and the use of caution tape mark specific activities and areas. Quiet areas are grouped together; messy areas

are near water and over the tile flooring. The tables are arranged so that two-children tables are near the game areas. Open spaces are near the music and dramatic play areas and can be used for large meetings. Larger tables are situated near the art supplies and the cooking area. There are clearly designated areas for homework, arts and crafts, puzzles and games, computers, construction, cooking and eating, books and music, as well as current thematic activities. Children are busy and adults are there for conversations, as resources and for help in problem solving.

In wonderful programs such as ones like this, as much attention goes into the outdoor activities and facilities as the indoor spaces. Sports and motor activities like climbing, ball skill building, running, and jump-rope all take place in designated areas. Some activities, such as reading and painting, spill into the outdoors on nice days from the classroom, and others are taken indoors for quieter play—for example, small motor activities with construction materials. Others are usually experienced outside, although once in a while they may be taken indoors for respite from the cold: container gardening, sand and water table play, and science and nature activities. Children keep track of changes in the garden or with nature projects by measuring and recording in journals.

Walking through an afterschool program like this one makes me wish I could return to childhood again so that I could come to a special place like this each day and have so many wonderful opportunities for play and adventure and learning.

Source: Used with permission of Dr. Barbara A. Malaspina.

blocks, clay, paints, and what facility designer Jim Greenman called **loose parts**—materials that are easily moved and transported that can be used by children while playing and constructing things. Children seem to prefer loose parts to fixed equipment, and they serve both as an incentive to play and as a means to manipulate the environment in creative ways. Loose parts can be used separately, combined, collected, sorted, separated again, put together or pulled apart, lined up, and dumped on the ground (Greenman, 2005). Examples of loose parts include "found" materials such as rocks, sticks, leaves, paper, cardboard, and bottle caps. They may also be materials that are provided by the adult staff, like boxes, poker chips, nuts, bolts, screws, washers, or parachutes. Send home a note asking for miscellaneous materials, provide milk crates and shoeboxes to keep it all in, and stand back.

Room Arrangement and Interest Areas

Flexibility is important, but there is also merit in arranging the environment with relatively permanent boundaries and traffic patterns. If certain areas are designated for quiet study and reflection, for instance, it is easier for children to know where to go for solitude and where *not* to sit while excitedly planning a project or outing. A well-arranged physical space with clear limits suggests interesting things to do, but it also helps children match their behavior to the setting. Children wishing to engage in noisy activities should be able to do so without disturbing the rest of the group; painting or cooking activities should be located near a source of water. The reading and writing area needs adequate light, and computers, tape players, or CD players need a power outlet.

Usually, a more effective use of space is to turn bookcases and dividers edgeways from walls as area boundaries rather than leaving them parallel to the walls with large open areas in the middle of the room. Turn sofas and chairs at angles around a rug with their backs to other interest areas, facing one another to encourage conversation. There should be plenty of tables, floor mats, chairs, and shelves.

As you plan your room layout, also consider the active ways in which school-age children move from one place to another. Provide clear, spacious pathways to the outside area, to the bathrooms, and to all doors and especially to fire exits. Allowing 12 to 18 inches around all furniture and other permanent objects in the room will reduce unnecessary bumps and accidents. Figure 9.3 shows two ways this can be done. A good way to plan room arrangement is to draw the space available on graph paper. Each piece of furniture, divider, and so forth can then be drawn to scale and cut out so it can be moved around on the paper until a satisfactory arrangement is found. This method can save lots of sore backs and sharp words.

A SAFE ENVIRONMENT

When parents are asked what they look for in a before- or afterschool setting for their children, a safe environment is usually first on the list. It can be a challenge for caregivers designing environments for children to create an appealing program, with appropriate challenges for rapidly growing school-agers, that provides the level of security and safety parents need and want.

But what do parents mean by "safe"? To understand this and begin to develop a safety plan, consider safety from several perspectives. One view of the subject might be that keeping children safe means to protect them from disease and injuries. Objectively, few caregivers would argue with this as an appropriate goal; however, interpreting that view too narrowly could lead to a severely restricted environment that permitted no climbing or running, no stovetop cooking, no woodworking, certainly no rock climbing, bike riding, or rollerblading, not even visits to the restrooms without an accompanying adult. I have visited many programs where the rules rattle on and on: "Only one child on a swing at a time, no walking up the slide, no water in the sandbox, no sand on the concrete. Don't

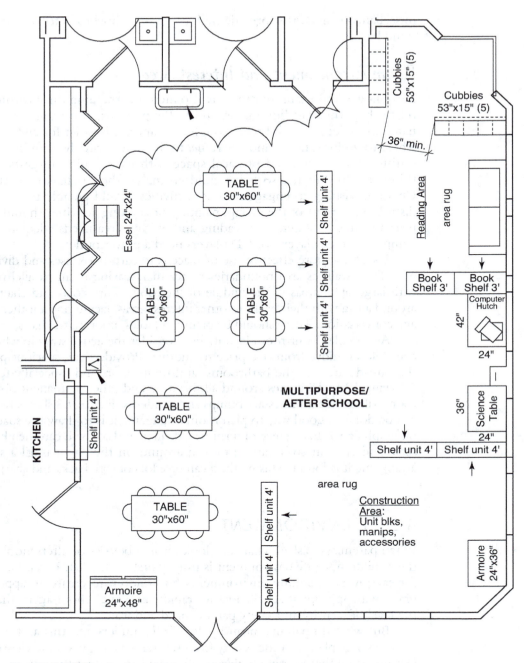

FIGURE 9.3a Multipurpose Room Arrangement Developed by Louis Torelli for the Children's Center at the University of South Carolina, Columbia, South Carolina.

Source: Floor plan developed by Louis Torelli for the Children's Center at the University of South Carolina, Columbia, South Carolina. © University of South Carolina. From Decker/Decker/Freeman/Knopf, *Planning and Administering Early Childhood Programs,* Figure 6.10, p. 151, © 2009 Pearson Inc. Used by permission of the University of South Carolina.

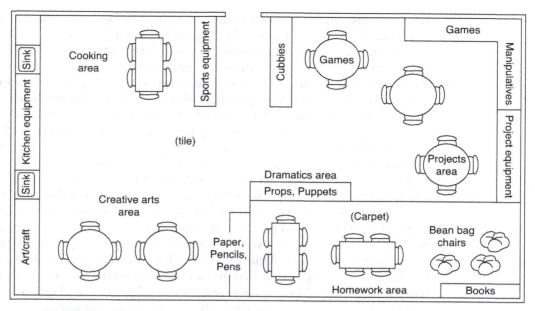

FIGURE 9.3b Careful Planning of Furniture Arrangement Will Encourage Interaction and Creativity.

Source: From *Interactive Curriculum for Development and Learning* by Ralph & Eddowes. Sample Floor Plan, p. 74. Copyright © 2002. Reproduced by permission of Pearson Education, Inc.

climb the tree, don't run, don't stack those blocks higher than your shoulder, no water in the playhouse." Children who are kept *this* safe might as well be wrapped in a cocoon of cotton batting; they certainly are not going to learn how to live in the real world, and they are also not going to enjoy themselves or want to come back again and again. If the afterschool environment presents opportunities for adventure and challenge, both positive aspects, it may also contain some risk of injury to children. To ensure that children are adequately prepared to recognize and avoid dangerous activities (such as running in front of a swing or jumping off a high climber), a risk-management evaluation must be thoroughly undertaken by program staff before embarking on any new activity with children. Rather than avoiding any activity that carries a risk of injury, children and staff should discuss policies and procedures to teach children how to minimize the likelihood of injury and remain vigilant at all times for unnecessary risk taking.

A second view of safety might concentrate on protecting children from dangers present in the outside community, such as being hit by a car on the way home from school; tormented or injured by bullies or gang members; influenced by peers who might encourage the use of drugs, tobacco, alcohol, or other addictive agents; or abducted by someone with ill intent. To avoid such danger is the primary reason many parents place their children in afterschool programs, sometimes at considerable financial hardship—to protect their children from the real or perceived dangers of traveling home from school alone, arriving to an empty house, and spending several hours unsupervised until their parents return from work. This is an area of safety where well-managed school-age environments, even drop-in programs, can be very successful. In fact, programs that teach refusal skills and conflict-resolution techniques and offer drug, alcohol, and tobacco education can actually *reduce* risks to children when they leave the program to spend time in their own neighborhoods, not just while they are in the program itself.

A third view of safety addresses the importance of protecting children from emotional injury. This approach focuses on the interpersonal relationships within the center itself. In an emotionally safe program, adults speak to children using honest, reflective, and nonjudgmental language, and children are taught that put-downs, racist or sexist remarks, and other belittling language will not be tolerated. Some children may have the option of spending before- and afterschool time with friends, neighbors, or family members, but parents who recognize that this emotional safety aspect is not present in those environments may enroll them in afterschool programs instead. The sad reality is that without careful planning and management, these children may face the very same psychologically damaging interactions in afterschool programs that their parents are trying to avoid. This is especially likely when staff members are inexperienced, lack confidence, or are faced with supervising too many children in too small a space with inadequate resources. Some adults feel most safe when they are in control, and attempting to maintain control can cause people to use disrespectful or intimidating words when talking to children. This is an element of safety not always addressed by program leaders and one that deserves a great deal of thought.

All three of these areas of safety can and should be addressed by out-of-school program planners and staff. The steps that need to be taken include (a) setting the standards for supervision and practices, (b) training children to use new or specialized equipment, (c) reducing hazards in the play environment, and (d) responding to accidents and injuries. The following sections discuss these steps in more detail.

Setting the Standards for Supervision and Practice

To administer and implement a safe program for school-agers, program directors must provide training, guidance, and support to staff members and volunteers. This includes developing procedures for handling potentially hazardous activities, such as walking to restrooms or playgrounds, crossing streets, using electrical equipment or sharp tools, and playing outdoors in extremely hot or cold weather. Such standards may include developing a buddy system, requiring children to wear colored T-shirts or name tags, and washing hands before and after eating, after toileting, or playing outside. It may also include posting safety checklists, or supplying all-weather first-aid kits. As a staff member it is your responsibility to follow the procedures your program director has established.

Involve children in making or reviewing safety rules at the beginning of any potentially dangerous activity, such as remembering to wear helmets during skating and cycling. All staff members should be trained in basic first aid and child-abuse reporting procedures, and the adult–child ratio should be such that no adult is ever left alone with the children or unable to supervise their activities adequately. The center should have written procedures for managing children during earthquakes, hurricanes, tornadoes, and fires; all staff members should receive training in those procedures, and the procedures should be posted prominently on the wall. You can ensure that this happens by putting it in your professional development plan and coordinating with administration to schedule trainings for everyone who works with children.

All of the adults in a program must also understand the importance of interpersonal relationships. You may need practice talking with children in ways that communicate respect and caring, even while setting limits or responding to unacceptable behavior. Watch and listen to more experienced staff members, and follow the cues set by someone you notice has good rapport with the children.

To learn how to become responsible members of society, children need to see many models of positive social behaviors, attitudes, and skills. Their life outside your program may not provide these models. They may even be subject to violent and other antisocial behavior at home that leave them with damaging emotional scars. Group-control techniques commonly used by some adults such as timeouts and "use your words" may restore order quickly, but they do not help children feel safe and nurtured, nor do they teach them the behaviors necessary to coexist in a peaceful and empowering afterschool environment (Levin, 2003). Teaching safety is one of the ways you can do this.

Teaching Children to Use Specialized Equipment

School-age children are growing rapidly in their ability to do real work with real tools. As they become interested in doing so, allow them to use staplers, hole punches, paper cutters, blenders, microwave ovens, hotplates, sewing machines, wood-burning kits, soldering irons, hammers, saws, power tools, and even sharp knives. However, before allowing children to use any of these pieces of equipment, be sure to provide adequate training, and always supervise them. Because children's use of such equipment differs from one household to another, no assumptions can be made about previous experience.

Each child should be carefully checked out individually with each tool before being allowed to use it for the first time. Some programs send questionnaires home to parents, inquiring about children's knowledge of cooking or construction activities, and they use that information to develop guidelines for ages at which children may begin to use certain tools. Adaptive versions of some household tools and appliances are available for children with physical limitations. Be sure to ask parents of children with disabilities how they would like these activities to be handled with their children.

Even after learning how to use potentially dangerous equipment, no child should be left unsupervised while doing so. It is probably not necessary to stand directly over children once they demonstrate competency, but be sure that an adult is nearby and watchful in case of questions or problems.

❋　　　*Consider This:*　　　❋

How do you feel about teaching children to use woodworking equipment? Wood-burning tools? Paper cutters? Sharp knives? Were you allowed to use these kinds of tools when you were in elementary school? Can you remember how you learned to use sharp things and electrical equipment safely? You may find this reflective activity helpful if it refreshes your memories and provides some helpful insights for how adults helped you to develop confidence and competence in potentially hazardous situations.

Reducing Hazards in the Afterschool Environment

In addition to developing guidelines and teaching children about safe practices, you must be vigilant in your awareness of potentially dangerous situations in the environment. Don't leave this job to the director. Athletic coaches fill in gopher holes on playing fields and determine that children are wearing the right kinds of shoes; Scout leaders watch for poison ivy and snakes; professionals in school-age settings should be looking for frayed electrical cords, broken chairs or tables or windows, sharp objects sticking out of walls or furniture, backpacks obstructing the doorway, potholes in playground surfaces, and loose swing ropes or rusty chains. Use a safety checklist and teach children to watch for hazards, too. Develop and keep an active "fix-it" list to communicate needs to the program leader.

Selecting Hazard-Free Art Materials When providing art materials for school-age children, it is important to balance their need to explore more complex art forms and media against the potential for health hazards. In general, art safety organizations discourage the use of pastels, chalk, charcoal sticks, powdered clay, powdered tempera paint, plaster of Paris, or instant papier-mâché, all of which create dust that can easily be inhaled and can cause respiratory problems. Sanding dry clay pieces carries the same risk. Replace these items whenever possible with their dustless equivalent, such as oil pastels, dustless chalk, crayons, talc-free premixed clay, liquid paints, and papier-mâché made from black-and-white newspaper mixed with library paste. Instead of sanding clay projects, wipe them with a damp cloth. Products used with children in Grade 6 or under, or in environments with physically or mentally challenged individuals who may not be able to read or understand safety labeling, should be labeled as AP Certified nontoxic by the Art & Creative Materials Institute (Fanning, Gustafson, & Munroe, 2009).

Aerosol sprays also carry respiratory dangers and must be used outdoors or in well-ventilated areas. (Due to a high risk of theft, aerosols should also be kept in locked cabinets.) Other art supplies that programs are often encouraged to avoid include anything containing solvents, such as epoxy, airplane glue, permanent felt-tip markers, shellac, rubber cement, oil-based paints, and mentholated shaving cream. As much as possible, purchase nontoxic paste and glue, water-based inks and paints, vegetable and plant dyes, and water-based markers (American National Red Cross, 1992; Center for Safety in the Arts, 1990). The reason for these guidelines is that regular exposure to toxic materials can cause serious damage to a child's health and cognitive abilities. New research from the U.S. Environmental Protection Agency (EPA) has indicated that chemicals in the environment are implicated in asthma, acute bronchitis and upper respiratory infections, cancer, mental retardation, and attention deficit/hyperactivity disorder.

Scientists' ideas about what might be a "safe" threshold of exposure have been continuously revised downward. What 10 years ago was considered a "safe" level of mercury for human consumption is now known to be a harmful level. Lead and asbestos, for example, were once commonly used and promoted as safe but now have proven to be harmful at any level of exposure (Arkin, Herberg, & Jordan-Cascade, 2003).

As with any potentially harmful activities, however, completely avoiding potentially toxic materials may result in a watered-down (literally!) art program, and children may miss the valuable opportunities to explore their creative talents. Certain arts-and-craft activities declared in one publication to be "not suitable for the child care setting" include airbrushing, ceramic glazing, silk screening, stained glass, metal casting, acid etching, enameling, photo developing, soldering, and wood burning (American National Red Cross, 1992). All of these sound like great fun and under the right circumstances would be entirely appropriate in an afterschool program. So use good judgment. Be aware of the risks. Be sure that if you use any of the dust-producing materials or solvent-based products you do so in a well-ventilated area, preferably outside. Mix powdered tempera, plaster, or papier-mâché away from the children, and wear a dust mask. Teach older children appropriate safety precautions, and ask them to help you watch younger children so they can be protected from hazards created by older children's activities. Always supervise children when they are using any potentially harmful materials or equipment, and always be aware of those children who may be especially vulnerable to environmental hazards, such as children with asthma.

Developing a Safety Checklist Develop a safety checklist customized to your specific environment. Two good resources to use while developing your checklist are the NAA Standards for Quality School-Age Care (National AfterSchool Association, 1998) and the School-Age Care Environment Rating Scale (Harms, Jacobs, & White, 1996). The components of a safety checklist include the facility, equipment and materials, wall hangings toys, games, etc., as well as staff practices, such as latching gates and cupboard doors, monitoring water temperature, and supervising children using equipment.

Inspect your afterschool setting thoroughly at the start of each term and regularly thereafter. If you observe a risky behavior or hazard, note it on a log sheet. Let this become a "fix-it" list. Share your findings with other staff members, administrators, landlords, and children as appropriate. Good safety practices become a habit, and the more eyes and ears that are on the job, the safer your environment will become.

Responding to Accidents and Injuries

Develop policies and procedures for responding to accidents and injuries. Does the closest adult respond to an injury and carry through to contacting parents, or is there a designated person who will take over? Even minor occurrences should be treated and recorded to trace later symptoms and prevent future injury. A simple way to handle minor injuries is with an "ouch report," a simple half-page form completed in duplicate. One copy is given to the parents at the end of the day, and the other is placed in the child's file. A sample of this form, in this case called a "Boo-Boo Gram," is shown in Figure 9.4. More serious injuries should be recorded on a full-page accident or injury report. In addition, all accidents and injuries should be recorded in a log, one line per occurrence. Sample forms can be obtained through your state licensing agency.

A Children's Garden
Child Care and Learning Center **"BOO-BOO" Gram**

Child's Name: _Deborah Eltgroth_ Date: _May 2_

Location of "BOOBOO": _right forearm_ Time: _3.30 pm_

How "BOOBOO" occurred: _Deborah fell on the grass while playing soccer_

_____

Action Taken: _Washed scraped arm and covered it with a bandaid_

_____

Comments: _Deborah said "It's nothing new to me"_

Teacher(s) present: _Miss Jamie and Mr. Tony_

Parent signature: _Marlene G. Eltgroth_

Administrator signature: _____

A Children's Garden
Child Care and Learning Center **"BOO-BOO" Gram**

Child's Name: _____ Date: _____

Location of "BOOBOO": _____ Time: _____

How "BOOBOO" occurred: _____

_____

Action Taken: _____

_____

Comments: _____

Teacher(s) present: _____

Parent signature: _____

Administrator signature: _____

FIGURE 9.4 A Sample Minor Injury or "Ouch" Report.

Source: Used by Permission from A Children's Garden.

In addition, some children may have additional health and safety concerns. Be sure to have, in writing from a parent or doctor, any such information and appropriate responses. Examples are diabetic insulin reaction (when to give orange juice or sugar), bee sting allergy, asthma attack (when to use inhaler), how (or whether) to do cardiopulmonary resuscitation (CPR) on a child confined to a wheelchair.

ENSURING THAT YOUR ENVIRONMENT IS ACCESSIBLE TO ALL CHILDREN

The Americans With Disabilities Act (ADA) sets certain standards and recommendations for physical environments to be accessible and appropriate for children with special needs. You should become familiar with those guidelines and follow them as closely as the facility and finances allow. Sometimes administrators find this process overwhelming, but it doesn't have to be. In general, if the basic ideas presented in this chapter are carried out, and the individual needs of *every child in the program* are considered in developing interpersonal relationships and in organizing spaces, schedules, and activities, the needs of most children with disabilities—and the intent of the ADA—will be met. The ADA Web site listed at the end of this chapter is very useful.

One of the most helpful things you can do to make your class accessible to all is to create an emotionally welcoming environment for all children and their families. That includes helping children in the program understand a new child's disability and helping them to adjust to this new dynamic in their program. Sandall and Schwartz (2002) developed a set of steps for including children with special needs that teachers can use as a guide. Although the original model was developed for use with preschoolers, the steps have been adapted in the list on the following pages for use with older children.

The foundation for inclusive practice is the same high-quality, developmentally appropriate program described so far. All children benefit from an environment that is predictable, nurturing, responsive, and safe. Such an environment includes "engaging interactions, a responsive and predictable environment, many opportunities for learning, teaching that is matched to the child and activity, developmentally appropriate materials, activities, and interactions, safe and hygienic practices, and appropriate levels of child guidance" (Sandall & Schwartz, 2002, p. 11).

In any program, it may be necessary to modify one or more dimensions of the environment because they have become barriers to successful inclusion of one or more children. Many children with special needs can be successfully served in afterschool programs with no individual accommodations. However, if a child is not successful within your specific program, you should work with other staff members to follow the below steps, one at a time. In most cases it is a good idea to allow a week or two, sometimes longer, between each step. Each has features that will work for some children. A few children will need you to work all the way through to the end of the list.

1. *Provide a developmentally appropriate program.* This means that furniture, equipment, materials, activities, and schedule match the developmental needs and abilities of each child. If you have designed a program that serves most children well between 5 and 10 years of age, you are probably on the mark. If a child is not successful within the classroom even with this environment in place, the teacher begins to move through the next steps.
2. *Allow plenty of space in which to move around the classroom.* That way a child with perceptive–motor limitations can move without bumping into things, and children in wheelchairs or using other adaptive devices will find a clear pathway in which to travel.

3. *Modify the environment and the curriculum.* This can be done by changing the physical, interpersonal, or temporal dimension by simplifying activities, allowing more or less time in the schedule for certain activities or changing their order, and providing special equipment or equipment to match the specific needs of the child or children who are having difficulties. For example, children with hearing impairments will benefit from anything you do to muffle the noise in big open areas, and children with visual impairments appreciate having furnishings and dividers stay in the same place from day to day so that they can use the cues of predictable shapes and pathways to help guide them (Greenman, 2005). Evaluate the flexibility of the space to add new activities as interest emerges. For example, if children begin to show an interest in performance arts such as singing, dancing, and reciting poetry, can a portable stage be added somewhere? Real stages are expensive; consider tipping over an unused bookshelf and then hanging some fabric from the ceiling to make a curtain.

4. *Embed opportunities to meet the child's learning goals within the ongoing activities of the group.* This is helpful for any child in your program who seems to be struggling. It is like developing an individualized education program, except the activities are offered to all children in the group without identifying the child with the designated learning goal.

5. *Provide someone to work individually with the child, using specific, child-focused strategies.* This could be a parent, teacher, aide, volunteer, or specially trained inclusion aide. Work with the parents as you implement this step, as they may have developed strategies or be able to recommend an individual to work with the child.

EVALUATING YOUR ENVIRONMENT

Whenever we walk into a room or outdoor space we evaluate it in some way. Is there too much furniture or equipment, or too little? Is it well arranged? Pleasing to the eye? Functional? And so on. We are making judgments, based on how we expect to use that space or behave within it. So it is with the children, parents, and staff who enter environments for children. It is helpful, therefore, to evaluate the environments in your school-age program and see how they measure up to the guidelines provided in this chapter.

Two evaluation tools mentioned earlier provide standards that you can use for this task. The NAA Standards for Quality School-Age Care (National AfterSchool Association, 1998) contain 36 "keys" to quality in six major sections. Standards to evaluate the physical dimension can be found in the Indoor and Outdoor, Safety, Health, and Nutrition sections, and the interpersonal dimension is covered in Human Relationships. The temporal dimension of your program can be evaluated by using selected items from the Activities and Administration sections.

The School-Age Care Environmental Rating Scale (SACERS) is composed of 49 items, including 6 supplementary items for programs enrolling children with disabilities, grouped under seven subscales. The goal of this tool is primarily to measure the developmental appropriateness of group-care programs for children of school age, 5 to 12 (Harms, 1996). However, the Space and Furnishings section can be used to evaluate the indoor and outdoor physical dimensions, while characteristics of the interpersonal dimension are reflected in the Interactions section, and several items for evaluating the temporal dimension can be found in the Program Structure and Special Needs sections.

SUMMARY

Out-of-school child care takes place in a variety of settings, including private homes, school sites, houses of worship, and purpose-built facilities. All environments have three dimensions—the *physical*, the *temporal*, and the *interpersonal*. To meet the physical, social–emotional and cognitive development needs of the children they serve, school-age programs should be *nurturing*, *attractive*, *interesting*, and *safe*. Nurturing environments are supportive and child responsive. Homework and other controversial issues, when addressed within a nurturing environment, can be settled so that they reflect the needs of the local community. Sharing space, while always a challenge, is simplified when the same principles are applied. Light, color, sound, and provisions for privacy all contribute to the attractiveness of the environment. Interesting environments offer a variety of activities, allowing children opportunities for increasingly challenging experiences. Safety should be considered from a variety of perspectives, all of which require thoughtful planning, staff training, and administrative support. All staff members should be familiar with needs of children with disabilities, including the provisions of the Americans With Disabilities Act, and work to ensure that the facility meets them. If after developing a high-quality developmentally appropriate environment, some children are still not having a good experience, a series of steps can be taken to assist in their successful inclusion into the program.

TERMS TO LEARN

adult centered	nurturing
child centered/child responsive	open materials
inclusion aides	physical dimension
interpersonal dimension	supportive
loose parts	temporal dimension
nonsupportive	

REVIEW QUESTIONS

1. Describe four settings where before- and after- school care can be found.

2. What are the three dimensions present in all environments?

3. Explain the difference between a child-responsive and an adult-centered environment. Give an example of each type of response to a group of children who ask if they may build a "fort" in the corner of the child care room.

4. Do you think school-age programs should have a special "homework time"? Why or why not?

5. Give two examples of open-ended materials.

6. Explain how room arrangement can influence children's behavior.

7. Explain how color and sound can influence children's behavior.

CHALLENGE EXERCISES

1. Visit two school-age programs and sketch their floor plans. Evaluate the plans using the guidelines presented in the chapter. Summarize your findings.
2. Interview two professionals in school-age settings and two parents on the subject of homework in school-age programs. Compare their views.
3. After first securing permission to do so, evaluate an afterschool facility using the health & safety components of SACERS or the NAA Standards for School-Age Care. Review your findings with a member of the staff. Summarize.
4. Evaluate your program environments using either the NAA Standards for Quality or the School-Age Care Environmental Rating Scale (obtain from Web sites listed in the Internet Resources section).

INTERNET RESOURCES

Americans With Disabilities Act home page:
http://www.ada.gov/

Color and mood:
http://www.how-to-faux-finish.com/mood-color.html

"Daylighting in Schools": A report prepared for Pacific Gas & Electric Company:
http://www.eco-smart.org/resources/Report-Daylighting_in_Schools.pdf

Healthy Child Care: Ideas for design that consider children's health and safety:
http://www.globalhealthychildcare.org/default.aspx?page=f&content_id=76& language=content

NAA Standards for Quality School-Age Care (click on the Store link):
http://naaweb.site-ym.com

NAA Standards at a Glance:
http://naaweb.yourmembership.com/?page=StandardsAtAGlance

School-Age Care Environment Rating Scale (SACERS):
http://www.fpg.unc.edu/~ECERS/

Development of the SACERS:
http://www.fpg.unc.edu/~ecers/sacersdevelopment_frame.html

Sharing Classroom Space in Afterschool Programs:
http://www.communityschools.org/taas.html

What is your mood? The connection between color and your mood:
http://www.colorquiz.com

REFERENCES

American National Red Cross. (1992). *Child care course: Health and safety units.* Washington, DC: Author.

Arkin, L., Herberg, J., & Jordan-Cascade, J. (2003). *Looking at arts & crafts for unsafe chemicals.* Eugene, OR: Oregon Toxics Alliance.

Bellm, D. (1990). *New ideas for childcare veterans.* San Francisco: California School Age Consortium.

Bergstrom, J. M. (1984). *School's out—Now what? Creative choices for your child's time.* Berkeley, CA: Ten Speed Press.

Bullard, J. (2010). *Creating environments for learning.* Columbus, OH: Pearson.

Carter, R. (2000). *Giving school a radical makeover.* Retrieved July 5, 2009, from http://www.fruition-design.co.uk

Center for Safety in the Arts. (1990). *Art materials: Recommendations for children under 12.* New York: Author.

Chan, T. C., & Petrie, G. (2000). A well-designed school environment facilitates brain learning. *Educational Facility Planner, 35*(3), 12–15.

Erikson, E. H. (1993). *Childhood and society* (Reissue ed.). New York: Norton. (Original work published in 1950)

Fanning, D. M., Gustafson, D. S., & Munroe, D. J. (2009). *Safety: What you need to know.* Hanson, MA: The Art & Creative Materials Institute.

Fight Crime: Invest in Kids. (2007). *After-school programs prevent crime.* Oakland, CA: Author.

Gardner, H. (1993). *Multiple intelligences: The theory in practice.* New York: Basic Books.

Gardner, H. (1999). *Intelligence reframed: Multiple intelligences for the 21st century.* New York: Basic Books.

George, J. (2001). *Homework club provides a model for after-school program.* Red Bluff, CA: University of California Cooperative Extension.

Gordon, A., & Brown, K. (2008). *Beginnings and beyond* (7th ed.). Albany, NY: Thompson Delmar Learning.

Greenman, J. (2005). *Caring spaces, learning places: Children's environments that work* (2nd ed.). Redmond, WA: Exchange Press.

Grossman, J., Campbell, M., & Raley, B. (2006). *Quality time after school: What instructors can do to enhance learning.* Philadelphia: Beacon Centers.

Grossman, J., Walker, K., & Raley, B. (2001). *Challenges and opportunities in after-school programs: Lessons for policy-makers and funders.* Philadelphia: Beacon Centers.

Hales, D. (1994). Kids! 6–10: School lighting, afterschool topics, and other topics. *Working Mother, 17*(4), 68.

Harms, T., Jacobs, E.V., & White, D.R. (1996). *School-age care environment rating scale.* New York: Teachers College Press.

Heschong Mahone Group. (1999, August). *Daylighting in schools: An investigation into the relationship between daylighting and human performance. Pacific Gas & Electric Company report, on behalf of the California Board for Energy Efficiency Third Party Program* (pp. 24–29). Gold River, CA: Pacific Gas and Electric Company.

Heschong Mahone Group. (2003, October). *Windows and classrooms: A study of student performance and the indoor environment.* Gold River, CA: California Energy Commission.

Kim, H. (2004). *Sharing classroom space in afterschool programs.* Washington, DC: Coalition for Community Schools.

Koralek, D., Newman, R. & Colker, L. (1995). *Caring for school-age children.* Washington, DC: Teaching Strategies.

Levin, D. E. (2003). *Teaching young children in violent times: Building a peaceable classroom* (2nd ed.). Cambridge, MA: Educators for Social Responsibility.

Lewis, R. (2008, June 30). Mercury-absorbent container linings for broken CFLs created by Brown Researchers. *Medical News Today.* Retrieved April 10, 2010, from http://www.medicalnewstoday.com/articles/113258.php

Marion, M. (2006). *Guidance of young children* (7th ed.). Columbus, Ohio: Merrill.

National AfterSchool Association. (1998). *NAA standards for quality school-age care.* Boston: Author.

National Institute on Out-of-School Time. (2005). *Links to learning: A curriculum planning guide for after-school programs.* Nashville, TN: School-Age Notes.

Neugebaeur, R. (2007, September/October). School-age child care trend report: Views from the field. *Exchange,* 4.

Olds, A. (1988). Places of beauty. In D. Bergan (Ed.), *Play as a medium for learning and development* (pp. 181–185). Portsmouth, NH: Heinemann.

Pratt, D. (1995). Enriching your outdoor environment. *CSAC Review, 8*(3), 1–5.

Ralph, K. S., & Eddowes, E. A. (2001). *Interactions for development and learning* (2nd ed.). Columbus, OH: Merrill.

Rittner-Heir, R. M. (2002). Color and light in learning. *School Planning and Management, 4*(2), 57–58.

Rogoff, B. (2003). *The cultural nature of human development.* New York: Oxford University Press.

Sandall, S. R., & Schwartz, I. S. (2002). *Building blocks for teaching children with special needs.* Baltimore: Paul H. Brookes.

Teachernet. (2007). *Giving the schools a radical makeover.* London: Department for Children, Schools and Families.

U.S. Bureau of the Census. (2009). *American FactFinder.* Washington, DC: Author.

Vandell, D. L., Reisner, E. R., & Pierce, K. M. (2007). *Outcomes linked to high-quality afterschool programs: Longitudinal finding from the study of promising afterschool programs.* Irvine, CA, and Madison, WI: University of California, Irvine; University of Wisconsin–Madison; Policy Studies Associates.

Whitaker, D. L. (2002). *Multiple intelligences & after-school environments: Keeping all children in mind.* Nashville, TN: School-Age Notes.

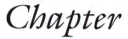

Chapter

10

Cooperative Program Planning

Planning is very important if you are going to achieve the goals that have been set for your program. There are many factors to juggle in running a high-quality school-age program, and planning helps teaching staff to manage many of those factors as they develop a curriculum.

THE "CURRICULUM" OF SCHOOL-AGE PROGRAMS

When planning is discussed in texts intended for classroom teachers or child care providers, the word **curriculum** is inevitably used. Sometimes it is defined; more often it is not. The term *curriculum* is also used in college classes when we discuss what we plan for children in early childhood centers or afterschool programs.

There are many definitions of *curriculum,* many of them specific to elementary or secondary school instruction. Most definitions address only one aspect of teaching and learning, such as the use of textbooks, reciprocal teaching, or state and district standards; or they refer to a complete **course of study**, such as a math curriculum or a social studies curriculum.

The definition provided by the Pennsylvania Office of Child Development and Early Learning (2008), in its document, *Using Curriculum and Assessment to Strengthen Classroom Practice,* is more helpful:

> *A description of the content or information that is going to be taught and the methods that are going to be used to teach that content. This content information is based on scientifically-researched information and reflects age, culture, and linguistically appropriate skills and developmental stages of the children in your program. (p. 1)*

The word *curriculum* itself comes from the Latin word *currere,* which means "to run a course" or "make one's way around a known route" (Wien, 2008, p. 5).

Another definition that shows this intentionality of the concept and applies well to school-age programs is "the totality of learning experiences provided to students so that they can attain general skills and knowledge" (Marsh & Willis, 2007, p. 32).

For the purposes of this book and for the school-age environments in which you will work, the last definition is the one we will use. Effective afterschool programs *provide learning experiences*—they do not, and should not, replicate or merely extend the hours of the classroom day. Most learning opportunities provided in a well-designed program will contribute to children's acquisition of social, emotional, cognitive, and physical skills. However, although what takes place in school-age programs often includes "teaching and learning," it is not, nor should it be, the same thing as the formal "course of study" occurring in conventional classrooms (National AfterSchool Association, 1998; National Institute on Out-of-School Time, 2005). Even when academic enrichment is the primary mission of the program, highly qualified afterschool professionals structure learning experiences differently than would most classroom teachers.

When program leaders talk about curriculum in school-age programs, they are usually referring to the experiences and activities in which children and adults engage, the context from which they emerge, and the social–emotional climate in which they take place. This includes spontaneous activities as well as planned ones. Ideally, school-age curriculum *emerges* from the needs and interests of the children and adults within a program, and each activity is allowed to continue for as long as desired to satisfy that interest or complete the tasks the participants set for themselves.

An Emergent Curriculum

The idea of an **emergent curriculum** is not new, but it has not always been known by that term. Teachers in the 1940s and 1950s used **thematic units** such as Ancient Greece, Explorers, Hurricanes, or Dinosaurs to integrate broad areas of knowledge, such as social studies, mathematics, or science with the teaching of the four major language skills: reading, writing, listening, and speaking. Perceptive teachers soon learned, once they had introduced a theme, to listen to the children's questions and ideas and encourage their inquiries. I was in such a sixth-grade teacher's classroom during that period, and I still remember the exciting journey my classmates and I took with explorers Lewis and Clark as we developed a script and sound effects for a radio program modeled after Walter Cronkite's contemporary radio history program *You Are There*. For 3 months we grappled with maps, geography, and natural history books; read about the geography, flora, and fauna and economic value of the future Louisiana Purchase; and read aloud contemporary accounts of Lewis and Clark's interactions with the Shoshone, Nez Perce, Blackfeet, and other native tribes. I'm sure that Mr. Chambers had a plan for what he hoped we would learn while studying about this period in American history, but that 30 minute radio show, painstakingly recorded on reel-to-reel tape, was the result of a rich and fruitful inquiry process by 25 youngsters, fed and directed by our own enthusiasm and desire to create the most authentic and exciting radio performance our school had ever heard. Sadly, few of today's children have many such opportunities for self-directed learning.

In the 1960s, **open classrooms** emerged, inspired by idea that children want to learn and will do so naturally if left to their own initiative. Open classrooms were marked by learning areas, often without walls. Students were free to move from area to area, learn at their own pace, and enjoy unstructured periods of study. Developed originally in Great Britain, this school model thrived in alternative communities and university towns, but by the mid-1970s open classrooms were criticized by parents and educators advocating a return to a more traditional emphasis on reading and writing fundamentals and more structured classrooms. The open classroom concept had a fatal flaw—children were usually encouraged to study whatever they wished, and the teachers often failed to make sure that curriculum content for the grade was being covered. When standardized test scores dipped dramatically in the 1970s, open classrooms were thought to be the cause, and they soon disappeared from most public schools.

In the early 1990s, a town in Italy named Reggio Emilia won the hearts and kindled the spirit of teachers around the world by demonstrating a wondrous way of fostering young children's development through projects of active exploration and symbolic representation. Delegations of educators flocked to Italy to see the schools for themselves, and soon the "Reggio Emilia approach" became a popular subject for conference workshops and journal articles in the United States. Out of this period also came two new terms: **emergent curriculum** and the **project approach**.

Emergent curriculum came to be known as the approach to planning used in Reggio Emilia that builds upon the interests of the children but is actually watched over and guided by the teachers. Team planning is an important part of emergent curriculum. Teachers meet frequently to discuss several directions a project could take, the materials needed, and possible parent and/or community support and involvement (Malaguzzi, 1987).

Projects, on the other hand are more in-depth studies of concepts, ideas, and interests that arise from within the group and warrant further exploration and study. Often considered by the children to be personal adventures, projects may last a few days or could continue throughout the school term, making them ideal for afterschool programs. During a project, adult volunteers or staff serve as facilitators, helping children make decisions about the goals of the study, the way in which the group will study the topic, the representational medium that will be used to document and showcase the topic, and the selection and acquisition of materials needed to complete and represent the work (Malaguzzi, 1987).

❀   *Consider This:*   ❀

Think about a time in your life when you became interested in a subject so much that you began to study it on your own. Perhaps it was finding out what other songs a favorite musical artist had sung, a topic or historical event presented in a film you saw, or even a hobby such as knitting or skiing. What made this inquiry interesting? Did you find the resources you needed to learn what you wanted about the subject? Did you approach anyone else to help you in your inquiry?

Finding a Balance Between Academic Enrichment and Recreation

Today, since many American schools still struggle with low test scores, state- and federally funded afterschool programs are often charged with raising districtwide academic achievement. If you work in one of these programs, you may be asked to provide homework support and design activities aimed at increasing children's knowledge base and improving school-related skills. Programs funded by private, sometimes nonprofit organizations and city recreation programs, not held to the restrictions of public funding, are more likely to use an emergent curriculum approach that emphasizes emotional and social development over academic skills. However, some parents and staff members feel that *neither* of these approaches is ideal and would be more satisfied with a curriculum that balances academics with children's interests. Funders may expect you to give priority to academic standards and raising test scores, but your ultimate responsibility is to developmentally appropriate practice with children, so you must find a balance that works or the children will stop attending the program—and then you can't help them at all.

As was demonstrated in Chapter 1, children, parents, and communities have a wide variety of nonacademic expectations for afterschool programs, including safety and supervision, reduction in juvenile delinquency and crime, and the development of positive social relationships and life skills. Most parents do value school success and request individual tutoring and homework help, but they sometimes raise doubts (and current research would support those doubts) that narrowly academically focused afterschool programs in and of themselves improve children's success in school.

Most research findings support integrating into afterschool programs an array of interesting enrichment and recreational activities, academic supports, and opportunities for interpersonal and social development, character education, and fun. According to the Harvard Family Research Project, which compared and analyzed the findings of 11 in-depth evaluative research studies, three primary and interrelated factors that are critical for achieving positive youth outcomes are (1) access to and sustained participation in programs, (2) high-quality programming, and (3) strong partnerships (Little, Wimer, & Weiss, 2008). The most successful programs had weekly program schedules that included homework help, individual tutorials, long-term project-based activities, arts and crafts, performing arts, and recreation (Birmingham, Pechman, Russell, & Mielke, 2005). This chapter will provide ideas for using a variety of planning tools and procedures as you develop a curriculum that reflects this research and meets the goals and objectives of your program, while maintaining the flexibility desirable when encouraging children to participate and direct much of their own learning.

Afterschool workers are a widely diverse group of people. They include classroom teachers, paraprofessionals, college students, artists, and community members, and they come with a variety of educational backgrounds and skills. Good planning allows program leaders to take advantage of these skills and to engage all children in interesting, challenge, and ongoing activities each day that help them to grow and develop both as scholars and as well-rounded human beings.

DEVELOPING CURRICULUM PLANS

Why, one might ask, should we plan at all? If curriculum is "emergent," why not just let it emerge? Carol Anne Wien, author of *Emergent Curriculum in the Primary Classroom: Interpreting the Reggio Emilia Approach in Schools* (2008), explains why:

> Emergent curriculum is a term that brought into relation the notion of an intentional course to follow, a plan with logic, and its apparent opposite, an emergent or unplanned process. The term *emergent curriculum* thus captures a seeming paradox: an intentional course is implied by the use of the word *curriculum*. But paradoxically, the course of this curriculum is not known at the outset. It is emergent—that is, its trajectory develops as a consequence of the logic of the problem, the particular connections that develop as participants bring their own genuine responses to the topic and collaboratively create the course to follow out of these multiple connections. (pp. 5–6)

Planning Activity Areas

Figure 10.1 lists three steps you can follow to combine the intentionality of curriculum planning with the flexibility of an emergent curriculum. First, create an environment that encourages and supports a wide variety of activities. Within that environment, develop interest areas that are supplied and "ready to go" and can be used without advance arrangements. Such interest/activity centers provide the core of many afterschool programs, and children find security in the consistent availability of certain interest areas where they can engage in activities of their own choosing. These areas traditionally include spaces for art, reading and relaxing, block building, puppets or drama, kinesthetic endeavors (water play, clay modeling, listening to music, fine and gross motor activities), science, music, crafts projects, and computers. Modify the spaces occasionally or build new ones to meet the current interests of individual children or to renew interest in a particular area. Finally, suggest inquiry or activity possibilities through the arrangement of materials and by stocking the areas with related books and props.

To be effective, these interest areas should offer children different ways of approaching concepts and ideas. See Figure 10.2 for some examples of how traditional interest areas can be augmented and expanded to encourage the development of an emergent curriculum that supports a variety of learning styles. Table 5.6 in Chapter 5 also lists materials and activities that engage the children with diverse learning modalities. All interest areas should be kept well supplied and maintained, with obsolete and damaged material and equipment removed or repaired frequently.

FIGURE 10.1   Three Steps to Developing an Emergent Curriculum.

1. Create an environment that encourages and supports a wide variety of activities.
2. Within that environment, develop interest areas that are supplied and "ready to go," and add new ones as children's interests emerge or change.
3. Suggest inquiry or activity possibilities through the arrangement of materials and by supplying the areas with related books and props.

FIGURE 10.2   Examples of Expanded Activity Areas That Encourage Emergent Curriculum.

Artistic Endeavors

INSIDE: easels; large and small sheets of art paper; brushes, paint, pastels, charcoal, felt pens; clay, Sculpy, Play-Doh, and sculpting tools; books and DVDs of artists' lives and techniques.

OUTSIDE: freestanding easels or fastened to fences; same supplies as inside augmented by large painting projects such as finished wood, Styrofoam or cardboard constructions, murals, banners.

Block Building and Construction

INSIDE: lots of large and small blocks on low shelves; vehicles and people to play with inside the block constructions; Legos, Lincoln logs, erector sets; architecture books, maps, GPS computer programs.

OUTSIDE: even larger blocks; woodworking tools and bench; materials and plans for constructing things (wood, Styrofoam, large cardboard boxes, etc).

Literacy Skills

Notepads, paper, pens, pencils; computer with browsers and lists (can be compiled by children) of useful Web sites for various school projects, homework topics, and individual interests; maps, globes; current newspapers and news or topical magazines; library books on topics of current interest with book request forms to be completed for next library visit.

Math and Science/Inquiry and Research

Scales, rulers and yardsticks, magnets, weather stations, calculators, unit blocks, abacuses, magnifying glasses, microscopes and slides, telescope, binoculars; books of science experiments, math puzzles, and games; biographies of famous scientists and mathematicians; cooking equipment, including measuring spoons, cups, etc.

Regional/Cultural Activities

INSIDE (or OUTSIDE on a nice day): bead stringing, bead looms, books about Mardi Gras and/or other cultures that make beaded necklaces and objects; spinning, weaving, knitting, quilting, constructing fishing lures, books about those or other similar activities; earphones and MP3 players or tapes, CDs or vinyl records and stereo equipment, instruments, sheet music, books about musicians and their lives and work; examples of regional music; introductory instruction books for selected instruments; regional toys and games.

In some programs, staff and children develop individual centers together and arrange them within the space available to create the kind of atmosphere they want for their specific program; then they stock the centers with supplies and use as desired. Chapter 9, on environments, gave several specific examples of activity areas, and more will be described in later chapters.

Augment traditional activity areas with a constant supply of raw materials, or "loose parts": familiar objects such as balls, hoops, blocks, costumes, and items less commonly found in afterschool programs, such as string, tape, rubber bands, glue, clothes pins, sand, leaves, seeds, and miscellaneous donated materials from teacher supply depots. Children experiment with their creative and physical abilities as they manipulate loose parts (Greenman, 2005), and these loose parts can also be used to engage in the kind of explorations, investigations, and constructions that form the heart of emergent curriculum. Collect books and posters on a variety of topics, and augment your collection with visits to the library to gather more as interests change. Once you begin to see an interest "emerging," you can meet with one or more children and other staff members to brainstorm ways to study the topic in depth. More will be said later in this chapter about developing long-term projects.

Clubs

Clubs can be considered a variation on the project approach. A club is an ongoing group organized around topics of interest to several children, but many different activities (including projects) can take place in a club over the weeks and months that it meets. Examples of topics that lend themselves to clubs are dinosaurs, the Middle Ages, magic, jewelry, rocks and minerals, photography, or fiber arts. Children may want to read or watch a film about their topic, invite a guest speaker, learn how to play games, use tools, make objects, or embark on long-term projects with outcomes such as a book or a play (Middle Ages), a large construction (dinosaurs), a show (magic, jewelry, and rocks and minerals), or a sale (photography and fiber arts). Clubs can meet once or twice a week, or less often, depending on interest. Some topics appeal more to younger children and others to intermediate ages. Many activities can be designed to engage children of different ages and skill levels, but sometimes it works best to have two different levels of a club to plan activities or projects that are suitable for younger and older (or beginning and advanced) children. For example, Photography I might cover learning to use a digital camera to take photographs in different lighting, learning about composition, and uploading photos to a computer, while Photography II could be about learning to use Photoshop or other program to size, enhance, or use photographs in reports, craft projects, or displays.

There are several advantages to clubs. Since children are asked to sign up for a specific number of sessions—say 6 weeks or 3 months—it helps them learn to make a commitment and stick to it. While it may not be a major catastrophe if some children do not stay with the club until the end, there are some drawbacks to the group if the participants are not consistent, and their peers will probably let them know what they are. Clubs are, however, only a short-term commitment, and children can join several different clubs throughout the year, exploring new topics and getting to work with children of different ages.

Club leaders can be staff members or older children. However, every club should also have an adult adviser to assist with needed equipment, supplies, and technical details such as space reservation, field trips, and speaker clearances. Advisers could be staff members or a community volunteer, such as a parent or other interested adult. Middle and high school students make good leaders, also. They may be required to complete a **service learning** project for school or to meet requirements for a Scout badge or leadership award. Review your goals for the clubs and the basic guidelines for activities, behavior, and assessment, and decide together an appropriate size for the group, and invite children to sign up.

Brainstorming Curriculum Ideas

Afterschool program leaders often use a brainstorming tool called a **web** to record children's ideas because webs are flexible and can be modified quickly. A web doesn't show everything that will be learned but instead identifies many things that *could* be learned. A web is great for visualizing possibilities, but a web is not a "plan." Before developing a plan, you need to identify areas of current interest and

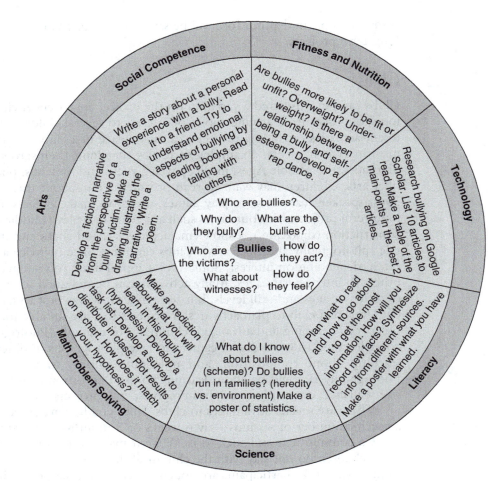

FIGURE 10.3   Webbing a Curriculum Brainstorming Session.

brainstorm ways that children could pursue them, various kinds of investigative and hands-on activities that could take place within the constraints of your program. As Elizabeth Jones (Jones, Evans, & Stritzel, 2001) described it, "Putting all the activities on a web gives you a road map full of possible journeys" (p. 194). Once you have completed a web, you can begin to develop a plan. An example of webbing such a brainstorming session is shown in Figure 10.3. Webbing is best done on a large blank surface, such as a chalkboard, white board, or butcher paper. After the first brainstorming session, it can be useful to recopy your web onto a smaller sheet of paper to refer to it during future planning sessions. Several companies have developed downloadable software that you can use to modify and document webs. Some are listed in the Internet Resources section at the end of this chapter.

THE BENEFITS OF ADVANCE PLANNING

Even though child-initiated and **spontaneous** activities are important, there are valid arguments for staff and children working collaboratively to plan some parts of their curriculum ahead of time. Planned activities do not need to consume most of the program day; the routines of before- and afterschool programs should be peppered with interesting short- and long-term projects and activities to keep children engaged and to teach organization and planning skills, as well as persistence. But planning is important for a variety of reasons, and including children in the process helps them to learn a wide variety of important skills. For example, if you work in a summer program that meets all day every day for several months, you will need to reserve buses, purchase tickets for field trip destinations, and schedule the use of equipment and supplies for projects. Children and families need advance notice of certain activities, outings, clubs, and projects to ensure that they have the appropriate clothing, permission slips, etc. Including children in the planning process helps them see that major activities take major effort and require a longer timeline than other activities. Even youth sports and community service organizations whose schedules, activities, and fund-raising projects are most commonly adult initiated and planned benefit from the engagement and creative ideas that result when adults and youngsters collaborate in the planning process.

Thinking about activities and experiences in advance allows for scheduling of key areas; acquisition of materials, equipment, and supplies; and allocation of adult staff. It allows staff to thoughtfully consider how to include and adapt activities for children with special needs. In addition, advance planning helps children to learn important skills, enjoy the anticipation of events or activities, and contribute their ideas about when, where, and how they will take place. Finally, advance planning permits program staff to include components in the planning process and during the activities themselves that promote the stated goals of the school-age program.

Whether your program has as its goal supervision and care of school-age children, athletic training and competition, academic enrichment, or leadership and community service, adult staff who pay attention to the seeds planted during activity planning can reap a plentiful harvest. This means it is important that children are not just included in the process but are listened to and their ideas considered seriously. The process of planning, in itself, provides a model of involvement that is likely to continue throughout the activity. Engagement, focus, and communication are also important outcomes of this process.

If involving youngsters in the planning process is a new concept for your staff, it may take some time to develop an environment of mutual trust in which ideas and opinions can be freely offered and exchanged. As well, some children (and some adults) have not been accustomed to listening or being listened to, to respecting or being respected, or to working collaboratively with adults. Helping children (and staff) develop needed skills and attitudes will take time, but it is time well spent.

Scheduling Key Areas

Many activities require specific features of a program environment, such as a sink, computer, table, whiteboard, basketball court, or stage. With advance planning, you can ensure that these **key areas** are available on the date needed and reserve them. A procedure should be developed so that children and staff *not* participating in the activity have advance warning and can negotiate different dates and times if they desire. This helps teach children the habit of considering the needs of others.

FIGURE 10.4   Activity Area/Equipment Reservation Request.

Activity Area/Equipment Reservation Request

Date needed: _____/Time: _____

Staff leader: _____

Youth leader: _____

Activity area(s) needed: _____

_____

_____

Equipment needed: _____

_____

_____

Description of proposed activity: _____

_____

_____

_____

_____/_____

Signature of requesting person/date

The same kind of reservation process is also advisable for the use of special-purpose supplies and equipment that may be needed during the planning or preparation of the activity, such as felt pens and a dry-erase board, a photocopy machine, or a basketball. A simple form, such as the one shown in Figure 10.4, serves both functions very nicely.

Obtaining Materials, Equipment, and Supplies

Perhaps the activity being planned requires the use of equipment that the program does not own or supplies and materials that will cost money. Advance planning allows staff and children to participate in a **scrounging mission**, which in itself requires planning and the development of certain problem-solving and communication skills. Sometimes you may be able to borrow specialized equipment from another program or agency and obtain supplies or materials through donations and trades. If that is not possible, the planning process will need to include fund-raising, a necessary component of every active program.

Scheduling Staff

For activities to be successful and safe, pay attention to **allocation of staff**. Sometimes program staff members initiate activity ideas or are present when someone else suggests an activity they'd like to do. In other cases, the idea may come directly from the children, who plan it pretty much on their own. In either case, be sure that an adult will be available for backup or supervision when the activity is actually happening. Staff–child ratios and group sizes must always be appropriate so that the safety of children will be ensured. These ratios vary according to the ages and abilities of the children but should be within 1:10 to 1:15 for children age 6 and older and 1:8 to 1:10 for children under 6. Keep group sizes small when children are learning a new skill or doing something that requires careful supervision, and never allow groups to be larger than 20 children.

Occasionally, parents or community members can be invited to lead outings or special projects; sometimes the nature of the activity is such that the youngsters can manage on their own. It is still a good idea to be sure that the project is entered on the staff planning calendar, just to make sure that a member of staff will be available to participate.

Encouraging Children to Contribute Their Ideas

One of the strongest arguments for planning activities in advance is to make sure that the children who want to take part have a chance to participate. Perhaps a staff member suggests a skate day—nothing wrong with that, in and of itself—but scheduling a skate day without first polling the children and their families might result in a conflict with an afterschool softball tournament or fall on a day when several students are studying for a social studies quiz and wouldn't be able to participate. Some children have music lessons or outside activities that cause them to leave the afterschool program earlier on certain days. They would certainly like to have some influence on the dates and times when interesting things are going to take place. Finally, youngsters can often identify resources in the community that can be utilized in a particular project, such as a travel agency with a van; a church with a basketball court; the location of empty boxes, folding chairs, puppet theaters; or someone who has lots of fabric scraps.

There is another reason that children should be active participants in the planning process, especially children over 7 or 8 years of age. During this period of development, children benefit from opportunities to build interpersonal skills and learn how to accomplish more complex tasks (Erikson, 1993). These tasks can include the activities being planned or even the planning process itself. Also, children are often the most creative source of ideas about how to adapt an activity to include a friend with disabilities or someone who attends the program only 2 or 3 days a week. Whether their ideas are accepted by the group or not, all children benefit when they regularly participate in collaborative experiences. Planning that takes place without regard for their opinions, especially if it is perceived as a message that they "don't count" or "can't do it," undermines their sense of worth and can result in discouragement and negativity. Spirits may plummet, and behavior problems sometimes follow. The activity may even be a failure due to lack of participation. It's far more helpful to include children from the earliest stages of planning than to risk problems later.

Learning Important Skills

Planning for any future activity demands certain steps. If you plan a road trip with your friends, you need to figure the mileage between cities, estimate driving time, and reserve motels or campsites at appropriate spots along the route. You will also need to calculate how many meals you will eat on the road (how much food to pack) and in restaurants (how much money to bring). The number of pairs of socks, the correct warmth of outer clothing, and how many CDs to bring in the car all must be calculated if the trip is to be a success.

Planning a bake sale, a puppet show, a trip to a local museum, a tournament season, or a construction project requires the same kind of thinking into the future—speculating on elapsed times, calculating costs, considering the needs of all participants, allocating resources, raising funds. The more often children are encouraged to participate in activity planning, the better they will become at these skills. Projects of any size demand a certain amount of thought and organization. If these elements are missing, complications or disappointments may occur. Unfortunate results may serve as natural consequences, resulting in children planning more successful projects later, especially if thoughtful evaluation follows the debacle. However, in most cases, unpleasant results can be prevented with careful planning.

In addition to teaching planning skills, group process of any kind offers rich opportunities for youngsters to work on the developmental tasks of childhood. Robert Havighurst (1972) identified the following tasks for children between the ages of 5 and 12:

- ❀ freeing oneself from primary identification with adults
- ❀ beginning to establish independence from adults
- ❀ forming friendships with peers
- ❀ accepting oneself as a worthwhile person
- ❀ clarifying the adult world and the child's world
- ❀ learning rules
- ❀ beginning to identify with same-sex social contemporaries
- ❀ learning more realistic ways of studying and controlling the physical world

Repeated activity planning, especially if done in groups, contributes to the development of these skills. For example, forgetting to pack a frying pan for an overnight campout might mean that breakfast becomes cold cereal rather than the pancakes everyone had hoped for. Failing to take enough stakes along could result in tents or tarps flying around in the evening wind. These events tend to be memorable; the next time these same children plan a similar activity, they will remember both the pan and the stakes.

Enjoying the Anticipation of the Event or Activity

One of the greatest pleasures in life is looking forward to something enjoyable. Even though I have enjoyed many spur-of-the moment trips to the movies or amusement parks, I can still remember the deliciousness of savoring the *idea* of going to a movie theater alone with my father when I was about 8. We planned it one evening, peering together at the movie reviews and ads in the newspaper. When we had decided on the film, we looked at my father's appointment diary. Thinking very hard, we found a day and time some 2 weeks in the future that did not conflict with his lodge night or bowling or with my music lesson. Then we talked about where we would eat—a picnic in the park or soup in a cafe? And what would we buy at the snack bar? Could I please have a chocolate bar? And maybe an orange drink?

More than 40 years have passed since that event, and I have long since forgotten what film was playing the night we went to the theater. However, the planning, the negotiating, and the delightful anticipation as night after night we talked about our "night out" are with me still. All children deserve to look forward to something. Too often youth workers surprise children with projects or activities and expect them to change gears from whatever they were doing and "get involved." Or they put a field trip or other off-site activity on the monthly calendar that goes home to parents without mentioning it to the children.

Sometimes it is the anticipation of a desirable activity that will bring a child back to an afterschool program often enough to make friends, begin to fit in, and perhaps even to start enjoying himself. At the very least, children deserve to know what to expect when they arrive at their afterschool program site. Sometimes the expectation of events to come can serve to reassure children that there is some consistency in their otherwise chaotic world. Posting a schedule for children of activities and outings that they have helped to plan in advance is one way of providing that consistency and anticipation.

Achieving the Stated Goals of the Program

By planning program activities in advance, you can make certain that over the course of a school year you address and achieve the goals that have been developed for the children in your program.

Dr. Joan Bergstrom (1990), educator and author, has suggested that the hours outside the school day are best spent developing what she calls the "other three R's": resourcefulness, responsibility, and reliability. Other program goals, as mentioned elsewhere, include raising test scores, developing workplace skills, fostering character development, or improving social skills. Goal setting is discussed in more detail in Chapter 14. Whatever the goals may be for children in a program, thoughtful activity planning can ensure that they experience a variety of interesting experiences that lead to their attainment.

PLANNING THE YEAR

Long-term program planning takes many forms. Some of it may be scratched out on a paper napkin in a fast-food restaurant, quick jottings about activities that occur to you when you least expect it. Some of it is simply carried over from previous years if the activities being planned were successful. Some planning cannot take place until the children are present, but it is a good idea to do some advance thinking about what you are trying to accomplish, and you should have some tentative planning completed before they arrive.

A necessary precursor to planning activities is laying out the calendar year. Usually this is done by the program staff and is then revisited and revised later with the help of the children, although some programs may include one or two older children in even the initial discussions. The most effective method I have seen for year-long calendar creation is to fasten a very long sheet of butcher paper—about 10 or 12 feet in length—horizontally on a wall at eye level. Using broad felt-tip markers, the starting and ending dates of the year are indicated at the beginning and end of the paper, and it is divided into calendar months with vertical lines. Months can then be divided into 5-day weeks (unless your program is also open weekends, in which case those days should also be reflected) and the hours of operation indicated. Holidays, vacation days, and special commemorations are then indicated (staff or children's birthdays, Ground Hog Day, Valentine's Day, and so on; some of these will be determined by the cultural and ethnic makeup of the community, and others that you don't think of will be remembered by the children).

In addition to dates that are celebrated, it is important to indicate dates that trigger a change in programming, such as beginning and end of school terms, intramural sports, holidays and minimum days, teacher-training days, and others. On those days, you will have more children for longer hours. That will affect both staffing and activity planning. If your program serves children from more than one school, some of these days may differ for different children. Post school district calendars, individual school calendars, and hours of operation on the wall near your planning sheet. In some communities, public libraries and other useful resources operate on limited days and restricted hours. It is helpful to post the days and hours such resources are open. Every member of the planning team

Using a Gantt Chart for Long-Term Planning.

should have a list of the goals and objectives of your program to be sure that they keep these goals in mind as they propose projects, activities, and trips. As dates for long-term and short-term projects are determined, enter them on the planning calendar as a horizontal line, starting and ending on the appropriate dates. This kind of planning format is called a **Gantt chart**. If you wish, you can transfer your finished chart to a computer-formatted spreadsheet or text file. An example of how that might look can be seen in Figure 13.2, which shows how a Gantt chart is used to plan a month-long-reading and gardening activity.

Identifying Goals, Objectives, and Leadership Strategies

A separate planning process, one that should have taken place long before you began planning the year, is undertaken to develop the program goals, which should reflect the overall philosophy and mission of the school-age program. Missions and goals differ from one program to another, and this visioning process usually takes place at a retreat with program administrators, parents, and staff who focus on the reasons the program is in existence and the desired outcomes.

Afterschool programs occur in diverse settings, use various approaches, and have many different goals. For example, school-age child care funded by the federal Child Care and Development Fund (CCDF) seeks to keep children safe and secure and provide enriching activities while their parents work. Other publicly funded programs, such as the federal 21st Century Community Learning Centers (21CCLC) program, aim primarily to raise students' academic achievement. State accountability for student achievement under No Child Left Behind, along with relevant changes to 21CCLC and related programs, have heightened the importance of linkages between the school-day curriculum and afterschool programs (more on that in Chapters 14 and 15), and if the mission and goals state that, it will guide your planning.

Here are three examples of how understanding the mission and goals of a program might guide your planning process: (1) An afterschool center located on-site at a highly academic elementary school may offer arts and crafts, music and movement, and other creative activities to relieve stress and provide outlets for individual expression. (2) A drop-in youth program at an inner-city recreation center may encourage youngsters to participate in team sports and emphasize responsibility, regular attendance, and skill building, and it may also provide tutoring and a study skills workshop to help develop academic skills. (3) An afterschool program in a school district that has reduced weekly minutes devoted to physical education in order to spend more time teaching literacy skills might initiate 30 minutes of yoga and contemporary dance sessions before beginning homework time.

You can identify the mission and goals of the program in which you work by examining parent handbooks, staff training manuals, and marketing brochures. For example, one guide for the staff of 4-H–sponsored afterschool programs emphasizes the development of self-concept and independence, cognitive skills, physical development, life skills, and community involvement (Albrecht & Plantz, 1993). A Girl Scout training manual for troop leaders identifies its goals as teaching values, decision making, leadership skills, and respect for others (Girl Scouts of Northern California, 2008). The mission statement of one YMCA afterschool program shows that it has similar objectives:

We believe that focusing on character development as a central theme encourages children to grow and foster positive values. We believe it is essential to demonstrate the values of caring, honesty, respect, and responsibility at all times and to challenge children to demonstrate these values as well. (Mounday, 2008, p. 1)

Contrast those goals with these, from the Boys and Girls Club of Citrus County, Florida:

The JCPenney Afterschool Fund has provided us with the resources we need to create a comprehensive and effective curriculum that encourages kids to excel. We know from research and firsthand experience that kids need support in order to excel. Otherwise, they accept lower standards of academic achievement which can result in lower aspirations for higher education. This program provides members with a variety of one-on-one, small-group and large group activities to support academic goal setting, learning and success in school. (Pope, 2005, para 5)

Children's Choice Child Care Services in Albuquerque, New Mexico, lists their mission statement on their Web page; it is the first thing parents see:

Children's Choice Child Care Services, Inc., is dedicated to facilitating the positive development of children by developing and maintaining school-age care programs that are a model of quality care—programs where children play, learn, grow, and make friends—programs where children are nurtured and develop life skills. We will use these programs as a source of training and technical assistance for the larger community of school-age care practitioners.

A parent looking for information about this program would then be likely to click on Parents and Programs, and this is what they see:

Children's Choice school-age care program to give each child an opportunity to . . .

1. *Develop physical, intellectual, and social skills.*
2. *Develop a sense and understanding of positive values.*
3. *Develop self-confidence, self-respect and self-reliance.*
4. *Develop good decision-making, leadership and social competency skills.*
5. *Develop positive family and peer relationships.*
6. *Develop interpersonal and cultural competencies.*
7. *Develop interest, respect and understanding of our natural world.*
8. *Develop sportsmanship, teamwork and a sense of fair play.*
9. *Develop a commitment to learning.*
10. *HAVE A WHOLE LOTTA FUN!*

(Used by permission of Mike Ashcraft, Founder and CEO of Children's Choice Child Care Services, Inc.)

Whatever the mission, goals, and objectives of your program, you cannot begin to plan until you know what they are. Ask program administrators to provide mission and goal statements to everyone who will be planning day-to-day activities. Refer to those often when planning and evaluating your program year to be sure that your curriculum matches the program intention.

Ensuring a Balanced, Integrated Curriculum

All quality assessments of school-age programs examine the **breadth** of activities available to children. It is important to offer a wide variety of activities from which

FIGURE 10.5 Elements Found in a Balanced, Integrated Curriculum.

- Active physical play
- Creative arts and drama
- Quiet activities and social interaction
- Academic enrichment and higher level thinking
- Indoor and outdoor play
- Small and large motor activities
- Teacher-led and child-initiated activities
- Quiet and loud activities
- Lots of choices every day

youngsters may choose and to create a curriculum that is both **balanced** and **integrated**. A balanced curriculum means that there are daily opportunities for a number of different kinds of activities, such as active physical play, creative arts and dramatic play, quiet activities, and socializing as well as enrichment activities that support the development of basic academic skills and higher-level thinking (California School-Age Consortium, 2008; National Institute on Out-of-School Time, 2007). There should be a balance between indoor and outdoor activities, small and large motor activities, teacher-directed and child-initiated activities, and quiet and loud activities. Figure 10.5 summarizes these elements. Such differentiated programming offers many opportunities to enhance the growth of each child in all domains of development (National Childcare Accreditation Council, 2008). It also encourages children of different ages and abilities to play together and to grow and develop at whatever stage is appropriate for them.

An integrated curriculum draws on several different subjects or developmental areas at the same time. For example, writing a letter to a pen pal requires a child to reflect on his or her personal experiences as well as the reader's interests. This integrates social–emotional development (self-knowledge and empathy) with language development (writing) and possibly, depending on how far away the pen pal lives, cognitive development (geography). Group cooking projects typically incorporate math and science with interpersonal relations; if they are offered as part of a nutrition and fitness awareness focus, physical education, health, and self-esteem are integrated as well.

It is important for goals to reflect the microsociety of the afterschool program and also of the wider community. Historically, different geographical regions have varied somewhat in values and expectations for the childhood years; additional variations within a region may derive from cultural and ethnic diversity in the community. Be sensitive to families' needs and desires for their children, and be sure to include those as you develop the goals for your program.

Not all programs for school-agers are designed with a mission and goal at the forefront of their identity. Some may look more like a social club or have grown primarily out of parents' desire for their children to be safe after school or participate in art or music lessons (Musson, 1999). However, in practice, all programs have an *intent*, and that intent can be translated into a philosophy and a set of goals. Once the overall goals are determined, focus groups of parents, children, staff, and community members can be held to identify specific objectives that contribute to the attainment of these goals. Finally, activities and leadership strategies that will help children achieve the identified objectives should be recorded and kept in the forefront of the entire planning process.

PLANNING THE SEASON

Seasonal planning may seem unnecessary at first. After all, the seasons are obvious, aren't they? Not necessarily, and not to everyone. Even long-term residents of the Midwest may forget to take the possibility of snow into consideration if they are planning a January outing in August, and inexperienced activity planners may need a reminder that large containers of cold drinking water would be a good idea during outdoor summer activities almost anywhere. September planning for outside events occasionally overlooks daylight saving time ending at the beginning of November. And rain is common in certain places during October; in other regions, it may be summer storms that you need to plan around. To help in weather-related planning, use color-coded strips of paper or thickly drawn lines to indicate the likely weather patterns during certain months. Some commercial calendars indicate weather-related activities in their featured photographs, and these can be pasted above or below the calendar strip as reminders or activity suggestions.

PLANNING THE MONTH

Two kinds of monthly calendars should come out of your program planning process:

- ❁ One calendar on which the staff records detailed activity plans
- ❁ Another for parents to take home and post for year-round use

Monthly Staff Planning Calendar

Once the basic structure of the program year has been plotted on the planning calendar, it is time to involve the children and parents in brainstorming activities, projects, and outings that they would like to suggest for the year. The best way to accomplish this is with a combination of questionnaires sent home with children and small discussion groups, during which staff members or an older child keeps track of all suggestions. This will form the basis for your year's curriculum, but it should be flexible enough to allow for changes to occur and for new activities to be added as they emerge from the children's interests. If too many activities are suggested, you may need to vote for the most popular, cluster similar activities together into one, or offer some activities specifically for smaller groups. (Certainly it should *never* be a requirement that every child participate in every activity.) If you have children in your program who have an **individualized education program** (IEP) designed to address a specific learning or behavioral goal, be sure to incorporate some of those elements into your overall program planning.

Part of the brainstorming process should include deciding on a good time of year for these activities to occur. Some, such as kite flying or planting vegetables, are more obviously suited for certain times of the year. Kites can be constructed when it is raining, but the windy days of early spring are usually best suited for flying. Many indoor projects, such as sewing, construction, or making masks, can be used as relief from winter doldrums, and supplies can be pulled out or put away as desired during the long, wet days of fall or winter. They may also be enjoyed when the temperatures rise and hot playgrounds send children indoors for shelter. You might want to schedule certain outings, such as attending a play or sporting event, before or after other related events (such as putting on a puppet show or forming a softball team).

It is important that this planning process does not leave children or staff with the impression that all projects, outings, or activities *must* be entered on the calendar in order to happen—nor that planned activities can never be scratched or rescheduled. This would result in an inflexible program that would soon lose its appeal and would not allow for emergent ideas.

Activity planning is an ongoing process, and although many activities are made far more successful by advance planning, some do not need to be planned ahead at all. It might be a good idea to schedule additional planning meetings once a month with all interested children and staff. In these meetings you will evaluate activities once they are over, add new activities or events to the schedule, and reconsider or reschedule previously planned events. To keep these sessions interesting and lively, consider having children take turns leading **evaluation sessions**.

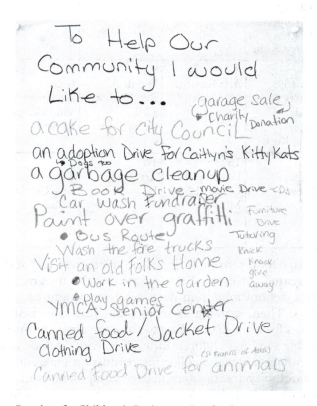

Results of a Children's Brainstorming Session.

FIGURE 10.6 Example of Staff Planning Calendar.

Summer Planning Calendar

	Monday	Tuesday	Wednesday	Thursday	Friday	Notes
Pre-program (June 8–12)	8 Staff Planning All day	9 Last day of School parent orientation	10 Classroom setup	11 Planning groups	12 Summer Training and Kickoff	
Week 1 (June 15–19)	15 T-shirt Decorations Sasha Pool 3: 15–4 Mowra	16 Art: Friendship Bracelets George	17 Fieldtrip: Pump It Up 2:30–4pm Sasha George	18 Fieldtrip: Rec Center 12:15 Sasha Kurt	19 Fieldtrip: Roller gardens 9–12pm Kurt	*"Welcome Week"*
Week 2 (June 22–26)	22 Art: Collection Boxes Mowra Café: Trail Mix Sasha	23 Hike/ Scavenger hunt George	24 Fieldtrip: Rec Center 12:15 Sasha George	25 Library Kurt Flea Market 1–3pm Sasha George	26 Fieldtrip: Zoo 11:30–3:30 All	*"A Hike in the Woods"*
Week 3 (June 29– July 3)	29 Art: Patriotic Kits Mowra	30 Fieldtrip: Rec Center 12:15 George Sasha	1	2		*"4TH of July"*
Week 4 (July 6–10)	6 Library Mowra Pool 1:45–2:30 George	7 Fieldtrip: Chutes & Ladders 1–3pm Sasha Kurt	8 Art: Favorite MN Fish George	9 Fieldtrip: Rec Center 12:15 Sasha Kurt	10 Café: Ice Cream Sandwiches Mowra	*"Local Lakes and Fish"*
Week 5 (July 13–17)	13 Fieldtrip: Science Museum 1-3pm Kurt George	14 Library Mowra	15 Fieldtrip: Rec Center 12:15 Mowra	16 Art: Bug Houses Kurt	17 Café: Bug Crackers Sasha	*"Bugs"*

Once the initial long-term planning is complete, monthly staff planning calendars can be created for each of the months of the program year. Begin by entering holidays, school minimum days, teacher-training days, birthdays, and other special days. Then, working as far into the year as is feasible, transfer the suggested activities from the Gantt chart to the appropriate monthly calendar and identify responsible staff and children for each activity. Include dates for making arrangements, sending home and collecting permission slips, and reminding children to bring skates, bicycles, or other needed equipment from home. If **special accommodations** are needed for an outing (like a van with a lift or large print materials), be sure to request them well ahead of time. Monthly calendars can be placed in a loose-leaf notebook and updated as new ideas emerge. This is illustrated in Figure 10.6. Once a month, information resulting from the planning process should be transferred from the staff planning calendar to a family calendar and sent home.

Monthly Family Calendar

You can use an ordinary commercial calendar and neat handwriting for the monthly calendar or use computer software that allows you to insert text and graphics into each day's square. A sample family calendar is shown in Figure 10.7. Transfer important dates from the yearly calendar to the monthly one: birthdays, holidays, minimum days, and others. Identify dates such as special outings, deadlines for signups, and fundraisers; also highlight some of the month's activities and projects. If parents or other volunteers work in your program, identifying the days on which they are scheduled to work will help them to remember their commitment. If snacks or meals are served, it may be better to create a separate menu calendar than to include that information along with the programmatic details. The menu calendar can be printed on the reverse side of the activity calendar.

Planning a Week

So far, the planning process has focused primarily on activities and events that require a fair amount of lead time in order to arrange for equipment, materials, special purpose areas, or advance reservations. The yearly planning process looks at the entire program and attempts to ensure that the program is balanced, integrated, and organized. The monthly plan takes note of important dates and staffing. However, it is the day-to-day flow of the school-age program that directs weekly planning and requires that it be kept current.

Weekly planning, when done regularly, can encourage creative thinking among staff and children. A simple theme, built around an individual's interest or discovery (for example, the birth of puppies or a local athletic or artistic event), can lead to research, gathering of materials, cleaning/rearranging projects, or other endeavors that were not considered during the year-long or even monthly planning process.

Some afterschool programs do their weekly planning on Fridays, when children are often freed from homework responsibilities. Friday planning allows children and staff the weekend to locate material they need for a project and furnishes something for children to look forward to on Monday. Planning for the week can also be done when children arrive at the beginning of the week, especially if the activities being planned do not require extensive preparation.

Begin by reviewing the monthly calendar with the children. After activities have been confirmed or canceled and any adjustments to interest areas have been decided upon, record the activities on a weekly planning sheet, which can then be posted for everyone to see.

Although yearly and monthly planning takes into account major events and dates, which should be recorded also on the weekly planning sheet, weekly plans include regular activities and changes to the usual routine, special visitors, new materials, or projects that will be available in interest areas or projects that are continuing from previous weeks. An example of a weekly planning sheet is shown in Figure 10.8.

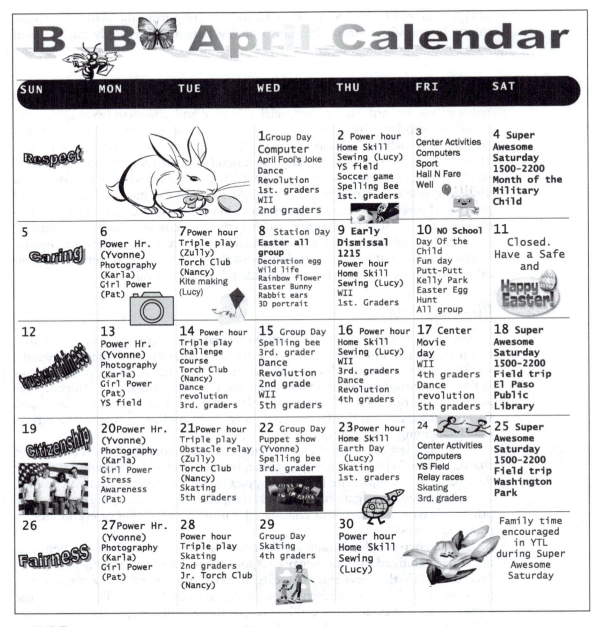

B B April Calendar

SUN	MON	TUE	WED	THU	FRI	SAT
Respect			**1** Group Day Computer April Fool's Joke Dance Revolution 1st. graders WII 2nd graders	**2** Power hour Home Skill Sewing (Lucy) YS field Soccer game Spelling Bee 1st. graders	**3** Center Activities Computers Sport Hail N Fare Well	**4 Super Awesome Saturday 1500-2200 Month of the Military Child**
5 Caring	**6** Power Hr. (Yvonne) Photography (Karla) Girl Power (Pat)	**7** Power hour Triple play (Zully) Torch Club (Nancy) Kite making (Lucy)	**8** Station Day **Easter all group** Decoration egg Wild life Rainbow flower Easter Bunny Rabbit ears 3D portrait	**9 Early Dismissal 1215** Power hour Home Skill Sewing (Lucy) WII 1st. Graders	**10** NO School Day Of the Child Fun day Putt-Putt Kelly Park Easter Egg Hunt All group	**11** Closed. Have a Safe and Happy Easter!
12 trustworthiness	**13** Power Hr. (Yvonne) Photography (Karla) Girl Power (Pat) YS field	**14** Power hour Triple play Challenge course Torch Club (Nancy) Dance revolution 3rd. graders	**15** Group Day Spelling bee 3rd. grader Dance Revolution 2nd grade WII 5th graders	**16** Power hour Home Skill Sewing (Lucy) WII 3rd. graders Dance Revolution 4th graders	**17** Center Movie day WII 4th graders Dance revolution 5th graders	**18 Super Awesome Saturday 1500-2200 Field trip El Paso Public Library**
19 Citizenship	**20** Power Hr. (Yvonne) Photography (Karla) Girl Power Stress Awareness (Pat)	**21** Power hour Triple play Obstacle relay (Zully) Torch Club (Nancy) Skating 5th graders	**22** Group Day Puppet show (Yvonne) Spelling bee 3rd. grader	**23** Power hour Home Skill Earth Day (Lucy) Skating 1st. graders	**24** Center Activities Computers YS Field Relay races Skating 3rd. graders	**25 Super Awesome Saturday 1500-2200 Field trip Washington Park**
26 Fairness	**27** Power Hr. (Yvonne) Photography (Karla) Girl Power (Pat)	**28** Power hour Triple play Skating 2nd graders Jr. Torch Club (Nancy)	**29** Group Day Skating 4th graders	**30** Power hour Home Skill Sewing (Lucy)		Family time encouraged in YTL during Super Awesome Saturday

FIGURE 10.7 A Monthly Calendar Keeps Families Informed.

Source: From Army School-Age Program Calendar. Used by permission of the School-Age Coordinator, Fort Bliss, TX.

PLANNING A DAY

Programming needs are different when the length of the program day varies. For example, an athletic coach may plan a particular schedule of activities for a weekly 2-hour practice session (warm-ups, laps, drills, and scrimmage). However, when he or she plans a week-long summer camp, the wise coach will vary the activities and the length of time spent on each and may also offset focused skills training with team-building activities and other enjoyable pursuits to keep the team motivated.

FIGURE 10.8 Weekly Planning Sheet.

MONDAY 4.	TUESDAY 5.	WEDNESDAY 6.	THURSDAY 7.	FRIDAY 8.
2:30 p.m. Nancy-sign in Kammi-snack	ELECTION DAY 2:30 p.m. Nancy-snack Kammi-sign in	1:30 p.m. MINIMUM DAY Nancy-sign in Kammi-snack	1:30 p.m. MINIMUM DAY Nancy-snack Kammi-sign in	1:30 p.m. MINIMUM DAY Nancy-sign in Kammi-snack
3:00 p.m. Nancy-group 1 Christmas magnets Kammi-group 2 Christmas magnets	3:00 p.m. Nancy-group 2 Fieldtrip Kammi-group 1 Fieldtrip	2:00 p.m. Nancy/Kammi HOLIDAY SAFETY VISIT FROM FIREMEN	2:00 p.m. Nancy-group 2 make fire extinguisher out of can Kammi-group 1 make fire extinguisher out of can	2:00 p.m. Nancy-group 1 paper mâche Christmas bulb Kammi-group 2 paper mâche Christmas bulb
4:00 p.m. Nancy-group 1 homework Kammi-group 2 homework	5:00 p.m. Nancy-group 2 small snack Kammi-group 1 small snack	4:00 p.m. Nancy-group 1 small snack Kammi-group 2 small snack	3:30 p.m. Nancy-group 2 outdoor freeplay Kammi-group 1 outdoor freeplay	3:30 p.m. Nancy-group 1 Twister Kammi-group 2 Twister
4:30 p.m. Nancy-continue homework Kammi-freeplay	5:30 p.m. Nancy-group 2 homework Kammi-group 1 homework	4:30 p.m. Nancy-group 1 homework Kammi-group 2 homework	4:00 p.m. Nancy-group 2 homework Kammi-group 1 homework	4:00 p.m. Nancy-group 1 freeplay Kammi-group 2 freeplay
5:00 p.m. Nancy-paperwork Kammi-small snack	6:00 p.m. Nancy/Kammi Close	5:00 p.m. Nancy-continue homework Kammi-freeplay	4:30 p.m. Nancy-freeplay Kammi-continue homework	4:30 p.m. Nancy-freeplay group 1 vs. group 2 Kammi-Wheel of Fortune
5:30 p.m. Nancy-continue paper Kammi-story time		5:30 p.m. Nancy-paperwork Kammi-group 1 & 2 story time	5:00 p.m. Nancy-group 2 small snack Kammi-group 1 small snack	5:30 p.m. Nancy-paperwork Kammi-small snack
6:00 p.m. Nancy/Kammi Close		6:00 p.m. Nancy/Kammi Close	5:30 p.m. Nancy-group 1 & 2 story time Kammi-paperwork	6:00 p.m. Nancy/Kammi Close
			6:00 p.m. Close	

In much the same way, experienced program planners take note of the times of day and the length of time children will be in their program and make appropriate accommodations for those different circumstances. Many such programs operate on split-day sessions, operating for an hour or two before school then closing until one or three o'clock in the afternoon when they open again until six or seven o'clock that evening. Other programs remain open all day, serving a mixed age group before and after the regular school day and kindergarten children during the half day that they are not in class. A third scenario combines children who are on and off track in year-round schools; these schools might have 6- or

9-week sessions followed by 2- or 3-week breaks. And nearly all programs face periodic teacher-training days or school holidays that require children to stay at the school-age center for 8 hours or longer. Still others offer evening activities, or even overnight "campouts." Each of these scenarios should be planned separately and recorded clearly on the monthly and weekly calendars.

Remember to consider the varying developmental and individual needs of all the children as you plan their program day. (It may help to review earlier sections in this book on developmental stages, special needs, guidance, and issues facing today's children.) Quality programs are paced to meet differing children's needs. Balance time for quiet activities with more active pursuits, and be sure that your arrangements permit several different kinds of activities to take place simultaneously. Allow for changes in plans; be flexible enough to reschedule an event that couldn't happen due to illness or an unexpected conflict and to cheerfully cancel

FIGURE 10.9   Example of a Daily Plan Sheet.

Plan I: Before School

7:00   Snack and juice available for self-service

Homework Table Staff:	Interest Area 1: Storytelling Staff:
Interest Area 2: Arts and crafts Staff:	Interest Area 3: Puzzles, card games, board games, Legos Staff:

Conversation Pit: Friend to friend

7:45   Clean-up activities and knapsacks

7:55   Closing activity: Yoga, deep breathing, meditation, singing Staff leader:

8:00   Line up for class

Plan II: Afterschool Program

3:00   Arrival, sign-in, and announcements

3:15   Snack and free choice activities (naps, snacks, raps, and laps)

3:45   Group meeting and planning time; sign up for Friday clubs; staff set up activities

4:00   Homework, planned activities, free choice

Inside homework Staff:	Outside homework Staff:
Math/science lab Staff:	Patio constructions Staff:
Couch/pillow area Max 4 children	Outside free play Staff:

Craft table/easels/jewelry bench – ask for help if you need it

6:00   Activity cleanup; individualized activities (6:00 box), free play outdoors; clean out cubby and prepare to go home

6:30   Center closes

an activity that loses its appeal between the time it was planned and the time it is to take place. Plan backup projects that can be set up quickly. Figure 10.9 shows one example of such a daily plan for a before- and afterschool program with staffing assignments.

PLANNING AN ACTIVITY

When you are considering a specific activity, a helpful strategy is to develop a plan sheet that includes all the program features necessary for success. In addition to providing an organized record of the planning process, written plans allow program staff to record evaluative thoughts and comments following the event. If kept in a binder where they can be located later, these reports can be invaluable the next time a similar activity is undertaken. Did you have sufficient equipment? Supplies? Was the area large enough? Written plans also permit future program leaders and participants to benefit from the planning and experience of others, even of staff members and children who may no longer be present. An activity plan form designed for use in school-aged programs is shown in Figure 10.10.

Another element of activity planning, especially useful for keeping abreast of the several emergent curriculum projects that may be taking place at any time, by using the simplified Emergent Curriculum Planning Form shown in Figure 10.11. The first section of the form allows you to record the date of the beginning of the project, the topic, and the children's interests that initiated the project. Below are columns for you to record developmental skills or knowledge being addressed, activities or outcomes being planned, materials and supplies needed and potential sources for that material, and a final column for evaluation data. There is enough room on the form to record four sets of each of these items, which is useful as the project develops and may change its course. Finally there is a place for the signatures of the curriculum designers. These are usually the children planning the activities, although they may include one or more adults who are collaborating with the children in planning the curriculum. Transfer the relevant elements, such as supplies or equipment needed, scheduling of specific areas, and need for adult supervision, to the monthly teacher planning calendar so that these items do not get overlooked.

PLANNING LONG-TERM ACTIVITIES

My adult children, each of whom spent 3 to 6 years in school-age child care, still remember with affection the activities and inquiries they took part in that lasted several weeks or even months after school. Sometimes these projects were related to the school curriculum (nearly all California children construct a replica of one of the 21 historical missions during fourth grade, and two of the four my children made were constructed primarily at their afterschool center). Other activities were suggested by the interests of one of the other children in the program. These activities tended to spill over into our daily lives (such as digging into the attic trunk for bean-bag fabric for the carnival or hauling tools to school for the vegetable garden) and provided opportunities for growth and learning that are still apparent today.

Regular staff planning sessions are essential to an effective program.

Many writers on the subject of childhood have observed the limited opportunities modern children have for developing problem-solving strategies, for developing a sequence of steps leading to a goal, and for seeing a project all the way through from planning to completion (Gardner, 1999; Goleman, 1995; Katz, 2007; Secretary's Commission on Achieving Necessary Skills, 2006). Long-term

FIGURE 10.10 Sample Activity Plan.

ACTIVITY PLAN

Title of activity: Date:

Where it will take place:

Group size: Time of day:

Staff contact/role:

Goal(s):

Objectives:

1.

2.

3.

Material/equipment needed:

Special accommodations needed:

Procedures, if applicable:

Costs:

Evaluation:

FIGURE 10.11 Emergent Curriculum Planning Form.

Date of beginning curriculum: _____

Topic: _____

Children's current interests guiding curriculum: _____

_____

Developmental Skills or Knowledge Being Addressed (Target Child?)	Activities and/ or Outcomes	Materials & Supplies Needed	Who Can Provide the Material & Supplies?	How Did It Work Out? What Went Well? What Could Be Changed?

Names of curriculum designers: _____

_____

_____

_____

Source: Developed by Matt Kaplan, Ph.D., Pennsylvania State University. Used with permission.

projects provide practice in each of these skills and also create an interesting reason to go to the afterschool program each afternoon.

Many long-term projects grow naturally from someone's personal interests, part of the emergent curriculum discussed earlier. When my son was in sixth grade, the director of his afterschool center designated a corner of the room "Australia," in which children could sequester themselves when they didn't feel like being sociable. Several children, interested in enhancing the decoration and environment of the area, dived into a lengthy study of Australian flora and fauna, writing to the Australian tourist board for posters and spending hours designing and crafting stuffed wallabies, kangaroos, wombats, kookaburras, and gum trees. The result was a maze made from large appliances boxes, decorated inside and out, and a handful of children who could talk your ear off about the geography, geology, and biology of Australia.

Other long-term projects may be initiated by a program leader, either to meet a goal of the program or to engage certain children in an endeavor that will help them develop new skills or support academic targets. Such a project was Larvae, Ladies and Learning, developed by two teachers in Canada who led first graders in an exploration of Painted Lady butterflies and linked their activities with the Ontario Science Technology Curriculum (Whitham & Killoran, 2003).

Long-term projects engage students in a variety of observation, play, hand-on tasks, and real-world challenges. Project-based learning complements classroom learning because it makes use of the skills the children are developing and makes abstract knowledge concrete and relevant. In this case, the project was designed specifically to complement the provincial curriculum (insects and science concepts are both part of the Grade 1 learning goals), while the Australia project, which in fact also complemented classroom learning in areas of biology, geography, and geology, emerged directly from the interests of the children.

Dr. Lilian G. Katz, Professor Emerita of early childhood education at the University of Illinois, has long been a proponent and a teacher of the project approach. Recently, Dr. Katz suggested that project work may contribute to children's development of intellectual dispositions. In other words, the process of pursuing a research goal through project work strengthens children's motivation to acquire academic skills (Katz, 2009). Just watching the intense engagement of children planning or carrying out a project of their own invention, supported by adults as an endeavor of importance, and listening to the children as they brainstorm how to learn what they need to know to complete their research, you would surely agree.

Dr. Sylvia C. Chard (2009), Professor Emeritus of early childhood education at the University of Alberta, Canada, wrote:

> The Project Approach builds on natural curiosity, enabling children to interact, question, connect, problem-solve, communicate, reflect, and more. This kind of authentic learning extends beyond the classroom to each student's home, community, nation, and the world. It essentially makes learning the stuff of real life and children active participants in and shapers of their worlds. (para 1)

And what a great way to use afterschool time! Some activities require field trips. Others beg for outside speakers, film viewing, or library research. Wherever the project leads, embrace it. It's probably going somewhere useful. (For more suggestions for long-term project ideas, see Chapters 11, 12, and 13). Long-term projects can require several hours of planning, so it's best to schedule three or four planning sessions before you expect to begin. Figure 10.12 illustrates this planning process, and Perspective 10.1 provides an example of a long-term project that took place in a third-grade classroom in Alberta, Canada.

THINKING BROADLY ABOUT YOUR PROGRAM

Figure 10.13 illustrates a checklist that can help you think broadly about your program, looking at weekly and monthly activities to ensure that the curriculum is balanced over time. Enter material on this form as you complete the plan sheets described above, and make sure that each element appears in the curriculum as often as you want it to. Your form may contain different components, and you may plan certain curriculum activities more or less often than shown here; customize the form to meet your program needs.

FIGURE 10.12   Long-Term Project Planning Guide.

Three (Actually Four) Phases of Project Development
Phase 0: Preliminary Planning
Projects, like good stories, have a beginning, a middle, and an end. This temporal structure helps adults to organize the progression of activities according to the development of the children's interests and personal involvement with the topic of study.
During the preliminary planning stage, the group leader tentatively selects the topic of study (based on the children's interests, program and curriculum goals, the availability of local resources, etc.). The leader also brainstorms from her own experience, knowledge, and ideas and represents them in a topic web. This web will be added to throughout the project and used for aligning the project activities with curriculum goals and for recording the progress of the project.
Phase 1: Beginning the Project
The group leader proposes the topic with the children to find out the experiences they have had and what they already know about it. The children represent their experiences and show their understanding of the concepts involved in explaining them. The adult helps the children to develop questions that could guide an investigation. Collaboratively, they agree to embark on the project. Sometimes a note about the study is sent home to parents, and the leader encourages parents to talk with their youngsters about the topic and to share any relevant special expertise.
Phase 2: Developing the Project
Opportunities for the children to do fieldwork and speak to experts are arranged. The group leader provides resources to help the children with their investigations; real objects, books, and other research materials are gathered by the children. The leader and children brainstorm ways to carry out a variety of investigations. Each child is involved in representing what he or she is learning, and each child works at his or her own level in terms of basic skills, constructions, drawing, music, dramatic play, etc. The leader and any other adults who may be involved in the project enable the children to be aware of all the different work being done through small or large group discussion and display. The topic web designed earlier provides a shorthand means of documenting the progress of the project; new bubbles are added as needed.
Phase 3: Concluding the Project
The group leader and children plan a culminating event through which the children share with others what they have learned. The children can be helped to tell the story of their project to others by featuring its highlights for the rest of the afterschool program, the principal, and the parents. One of the responsibilities of the leader is to help the children select material to share and, in so doing, involve them purposefully in reviewing and evaluating the whole project. The leader also offers the children imaginative ways of personalizing their new knowledge through art, stories, and drama. Finally, the leader uses children's ideas and interests to make a meaningful transition between the project being concluded and the other topics to come.

Source: Adapted with permission from *Engaging Children's Minds: The Project Approach,* by L.G. Katz and S.C. Chard, (2000). New Jersey: Greenwood. Retrieved April 12, 2010, from www.projectapproach.org. Used with permission.

EVALUATING CURRICULUM

Monthly planning meetings should include an evaluation of activities and projects that have taken place during the previous few weeks. It is important to collect feedback in a timely manner, before memories fade, especially if the activity is a new one to your program. Some of this can be done informally, by simply recording

The Building Project

A Project by Third-Grade Students at an Elementary School in Edmonton, Alberta, Canada

Length of project: 12 weeks
Teachers: Darlene Williams, Carmelle Workun

PHASE 1—BEGINNING THE PROJECT

The topic of "building" integrated a number of curriculum goals. It was also a topic that the children had prior knowledge of and were interested in studying, and there were resources and local experts to be called on. The teachers began the project by telling the children simple stories about recent home renovations they had both done to their houses. Children then shared stories about their homes and their experiences with building. After sharing stories, the class brainstormed a list of possible activities from which to choose to give them another opportunity to share and represent their experiences with building. The children drew and labeled houses, surveyed classmates about the types of houses they live in, and constructed models of buildings. Throughout this phase, children's questions about building were collected on a chart that was displayed in the room. These questions were used to focus the research of our project: How does electricity get into the house? How do you build a basement? Why are some roofs flat and some sloped? How do you know if a building is safe once it is built? What materials do they use to build a skyscraper? How did they build the pyramids in Egypt? Do all houses look the same around the world?

PHASE 2—DEVELOPING THE PROJECT

There were several guests who visited the classroom to help the children with their research. Among them were a roofer, a carpenter, a tool safety expert, an old-fashioned-tool worker, a surveyor, and a bridge builder. The class also made weekly visits to a house construction site. They visited a pioneer village and went on a tour of the neighborhood. The children engaged in a variety of investigation and representation activities. Some wrote research reports on famous buildings. One group wrote a play based on a talk-show format, explaining the various steps involved in building a house. Some presented their information in a multimedia format. One group made a booklet on tools and tool safety. Children also made observational drawings of buildings and building materials, a poster on old-fashioned tools, a comic strip about pioneers building a homestead, a book report on different houses around the world, and a Venn diagram comparing old and new tools. Many discussions and sharing sessions took place where the children had opportunities to appreciate and comment on one another's work and to contribute new understanding and knowledge to the group. Children's work was displayed throughout the classroom, on school bulletin boards, and in the display case at the entrance to the school. Questions generated in Phase 1 were reviewed regularly, and children able to respond to a particular question shared their newfound knowledge and insights with the class.

PHASE 3—CONCLUDING THE PROJECT

The children decided to have a photo slide show for their parents to highlight key features of the project. Each child chose two slides and wrote up his or her narrative, focusing on describing what was happening in the slide and what learning took place from the experience. Each child also selected work from his or her project folder for parents to see. The class then spent a wonderful afternoon with parents presenting the story of our project in a slide show, sharing their project portfolios with their parents, and taking their parents around to the various bulletin boards and display cases showing them their work and the work of their classmates. As a final culminating activity, a group of fathers organized a birdhouse-building activity. Each child had the opportunity to design and build his or her own bird house. To remember our project, the class put together a memory album consisting of photos taken during the project and anecdotal stories written by the children.

COMMENTS

This project on "building" was the focus of a master's thesis study focusing on assessment and evaluation in project work. Believing that traditional assessment and evaluation methods are inadequate to capture the amount and diversity of learning taking place during project work, we wanted to experiment with a wider variety of assessment and evaluation tools and techniques to best document children's learning. Some of the assessment and evaluation tools used during the project included learning logs, field notes, quality work charts, project work planning sheets, self-assessment and evaluation criteria for Phase 2 activities, peer evaluation strategies, a project study sheet, portfolio and project self-evaluation sheets, and anecdotal notes. The most significant insights gained from this study of assessment and evaluation in project work concerned the necessity to involve children in the assessment and evaluation process from the very beginning of the project. Children were helped by knowing up front the expectations concerning their work and behavior, and they needed to be a part of the process that determined these expectations.

Source: *Engaging Children's Minds: The Project Approach,* by L.G. Katz and S.C. Chard, (2000). New Jersey: Greenwood.

Venn Diagram On Old and New Tools

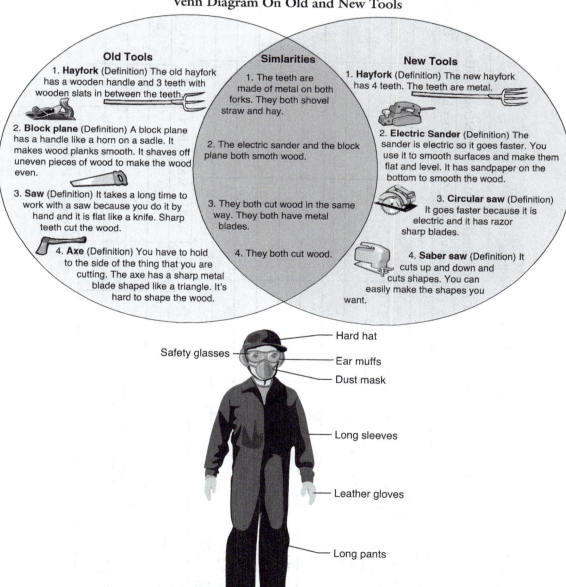

FIGURE 10.13 Components of an Afterschool Program: A Planning Guide and Checklist.

COMPONENTS OF AN AFTERSCHOOL PROGRAM: A PLANNING GUIDE AND CHECKLIST

Daily	Monday	Tuesday	Wednesday	Thursday	Friday
Recreation/Play					
Homework Support					
Fitness and Health					
Three or more times per week					
Arts					
Literacy					
Social-Competence					
Math Problem-Solving					
One or more times per week					
Science					
Technology					

Once a month	JAN	FEB	MAR	APR	MAY	JUN	JUL	AUG	SEP	OCT	NOV	DEC
Planning w/children and youth												
Community Service												
Three times per year (minimum)												
Family Event												

Source: From *Links to Learning: A Curriculum Planning guide for After-School Programs*. Used with permission of the National Institute on Out-of-School Time.

FIGURE 10.14   Simple Activity Evaluation Form.

Name of activity:	
Group leader:	Date of activity:
This is how I felt about the activity:	
What I enjoyed most:	
What I think we should do differently:	
Other comments:	
Name: _____	

comments made by the children during or immediately following the event. If you ask the children how they liked the field trip, they'll tell you! You can use a simple evaluation feedback form such as the one shown in Figure 10.14 to collect this information.

A more formal evaluation session can be scheduled for a day or two later, perhaps during a snack or another time when most of the participants and staff are sitting together anyway. Begin the process with another informal discussion about the activity. This allows the children to remember specific details of the event and provides an opportunity for you to solicit positive suggestions for improvement as you or one of the children records comments on a chart. This process sends an important message—that program participants play an important role, not just in developing and implementing program activities but also in the process of evaluation and making changes for the future.

The final evaluation of each activity takes place when staff members meet to review the children's comments and add their own ideas for improvement. Individual activity evaluation is part of the continuous program improvement process discussed in Chapter 3.

SUMMARY

The curriculum of school-age programs must reflect the mission and goals of the program, but the development of activity ideas differs from that carried out by teachers in regular classrooms. To maintain the interest of children in the programs, curriculum should be balanced and integrated and driven primarily by children's needs and interests. A good way to ensure this is to include children and families in the planning and evaluation process.

Program leaders should involve staff, children, and parents in their initial planning and also keep them involved throughout the year. Although curriculum should emerge from the interests and needs of the children, and be flexible to those changing needs, advance planning allows for scheduling of key areas; acquisition of materials, equipment, and supplies; allocation of adult staff; and helps children to learn important skills, enjoy the anticipation of events or activities, and contribute their ideas about when, where, and how they will take place, permitting program staff to promote the stated goals of the school-age program. Plan the year first, taking into consideration goals, objectives, leadership strategies, and local holidays. Then plan the month, the week, the day, and the activity. Use a checklist to ensure that all program areas are included in activities and that emergent curriculum is recorded for later evaluation. Long-term activities can offer children valuable experience in problem solving and follow-through. The curriculum planning process concludes with an evaluation.

TERMS TO LEARN

allocation of staff	key areas
balanced	open classrooms
breadth	project approach
course of study	projects
curriculum	scrounging mission
emergent curriculum	service learning
evaluation sessions	special accommodations
Gantt chart	spontaneous
individualized education program	thematic units
integrated	web

REVIEW QUESTIONS

1. Why is it important to plan an activity?

2. Why is it important to evaluate?

3. Describe and define *balanced* and *integrated curriculum*. What opportunities do these curriculum styles offer to children?

4. How does the chapter suggest that school-age programs define curriculum?

5. When is the best time to evaluate an activity? Why? Please give an example.

6. What developmental task of childhood does Robert Havighurst identify that justifies teaching basic planning skills to children between the ages of 5 and 12?

7. How can you get children involved in planning and evaluating the curriculum?

CHALLENGE EXERCISES

1. Plan a week's curriculum that reflects a balanced and integrated curriculum that also reflects the cultural and ethnic diversity in the community.
2. Write a 1-month lesson plan for one of the following:
    a.   Drop-in center (open M–F)
    b.   Drop-in center (one night)
    c.   Child care setting program
3. Choose a school-age center to observe. Drop in and observe for a half hour each day for 2 or 3 days. Can you tell what their curriculum is based on?
4. Visit two school-age programs and observe the centers' planning calendar for the month, week, and day. Summarize your findings.

5. Ask an afterschool program staff member for a summary of the best and worst activities they can remember planning. Ask what could have made it better or what made it work.
6. Plan and participate in an activity with a small group of school-age children. Discuss and evaluate the activity with the participants and write a summary.

INTERNET RESOURCES

ReadWriteThink webbing tool (free download):
http://interactives.mped.org/view_interactive.aspx?id=127&title

Service learning with children:
http://www.childrenforchildren.org/index.php?q=node/57

Using a Gantt chart for planning:
http://www.conferencebasics.com/2009/04/planning-your-conference-using-a-gantt-chart/

Webbing: An Intergenerational Approach (includes webbing tool):
http://intergenerational.cas.psu.edu/webbing.htm

Integrating children's academic and career goals into afterschool curriculum:
http://www.citrusbgc.com/news1.htm

Activities for children and youth in your program:
http://www.afterschool.gov/

About Gantt charts:
http://www.ganttchart.com/

Some thoughts on emergent curriculum:
http://chiron.valdosta.edu/whuitt/CGIE/yule.pdf

Citrus County Boys and Girls Club:
http://www.citrusbgc.com/news1.htm

Resource Center and Lending Library:
http://www.californiaafterschool.org

REFERENCES

Albrecht, K., & Plantz, M. (1993). *Developmentally appropriate practice in school-age child care programs* (2nd ed.). Dubuque, IA: American Home Economics Association.

Ashcraft, M. (2009). *Children's choice child care service.* Retrieved April 24, 2010, from www.childrens-choice.org

Bergstrom, J. M. (1990). *School's out—Now what? Creative choices for your child's time* (2nd ed.). Berkeley, CA: Ten Speed Press.

Birmingham, J., Pechman, E. M., Russell, C. A., & Mielke, M. (2005). *Shared features of high-performing after-school programs.* Washington, DC: Policies Studies Associates.

California School-Age Consortium. (2008). *After school: Policy brief.* San Francisco: After School Corps: CalSAC's After School Workforce Development Project.

Chard, S. (2009). *The project approach: Engaging children's minds.* Retrieved April 12, 2010, from www.projectapproach.org

Erikson, E. H. (1993). *Childhood and society* (Reissue ed.). New York: Norton. (Original work published in 1950)

Gardner, H. (1999). *Intelligence reframed: Multiple intelligences for the 21st century.* New York: Basic Books.

Girl Scouts of Northern California. (2008). *Leadership essentials.* San Jose: Author.

Goleman, D. (1995). *Emotional intelligence.* New York: Bantam.

Greenman, J. (2005). *Caring spaces, learning places: Children's environments that work* (2nd ed.). Redmond, WA: Exchange Press.

Havighurst, R. J. (1972). *Developmental tasks and education* (3rd ed.). New York: McKay.

Jones, E., Evans, K., & Stritzel, K. (2001). *The lively kindergarten: Emergent curriculum in action*. Washington DC: National Association for the Education of Young Children.

Katz, L. (2007). Viewpoint: Standards of experience. *Young Children, 62*(3), 94–95.

Katz, L. (2009). *The contribution of the project approach to the intellectual development of young children*. Paper presented at the Chicagoland Project Approach Summer Institute Chicago, Illinois, July, 2009.

Little, P. M. D., Wimer, C., & Weiss, H. B. (2008). *After school programs in the 21st century: Their potential and what it takes to achieve it*. Cambridge, MA: Harvard Graduate School of Education.

Malaguzzi, L. (1987). *The hundred languages of children*. Reggio Emilia, Italy: Department of Education.

Marsh, C. J., & Willis, G. (2007). *Curriculum: Alternative approaches, ongoing issues* (4th ed.). Upper Saddle River, NJ: Pearson.

Mounday, C. (2008). *Child care parent manual 08/09*. Santa Anita, CA: Santa Anita Family YMCA.

Musson, S. (1999). *School-age care: Theory and practice* (2nd ed.). Don Mills, Ontario: Addison-Wesley.

National AfterSchool Association. (1998). *NAA standards for quality school-age care*. Boston: Author.

National Childcare Accreditation Council. (2008). *Quality child care for school age children: A NCAC factsheet for families*. Surry Hills, New South Wales: Australian Government.

National Institute on Out-of-School Time. (2005). *Links to learning: A curriculum planning guide for after-school programs*. Nashville, TN: School-Age Notes.

National Institute on Out-of-School Time. (2007). The afterschool program assessment system (APAS). Wellesley Center for Women, Boston: Wellesley College.

Pennsylvania Office of Child Development and Early Learning. (2008). *Pennsylvania early learning keys to quality: Using curriculum and assessment to strengthen classroom practice*. Harrisburg: Author.

Pope, A. (2005). Children in after-school programs can achieve! *Boys and Girls Club of Citrus County News*. Retrieved November 10, 2008, from http://www.citrusbgc.com/news1.htm

Secretary's Commission on Achieving Necessary Skills. (2009, December 15). *What work requires of schools*. Retrieved April 24, 2010, from http://wdr.doleta.gov/SCANS/whatwork/

Whitham, L., & Killoran, I. (2003). Larvae, ladies and learning: The project approach. *Canadian Children, 28*(1), 29–34.

Wien, C. A. (Ed.). (2008). *Emergent curriculum in the primary classroom: Interpreting the Reggio Emilia approach in schools*. New York: Teachers College Press.

Chapter
11

A Health and Fitness Curriculum: Fighting Back Against Childhood Obesity

Being healthy and fit is a basic right of childhood. As adults we speak of "wellness," and many of us strive toward that goal, spending hours at the gym or trying to eat more healthfully. Children who have regular physical exercise and eat nutritional meals are more energetic and resilient, still showing energy and high spirits even at the end of the school day. Unfortunately, between budget limitations and the recent focus on standardized test scores, many elementary and middle schools have reduced physical education and nutrition/health classes to focus on core academic subjects. In some cases the length and even number of recesses have also been reduced, even though studies show that periodic physical activity breaks lead to higher academic performance (Trost, 2007).

Research tells us that increased physical activity and improved nutrition lead to better health and to clearer thinking and reasoning, so decisions like this shortchange children in multiple ways. Regular physical activities and games that encourage movement contribute to the development of healthy muscle tissue and physical coordination, which can lead to improved perception and self-assurance (Shephard, 1997; Sibley & Etnier, 2003). Today's children are typically more sedentary than children in previous generations, and the reduction of physical activity in schools seriously exacerbates the problem.

Afterschool programs are well suited to provide children with engaging, enjoyable, and challenging physical activity each day. If you also work nutrition education into your curriculum and offer healthy snacks, you will build children's awareness of the need for them to learn how to make good food choices. There are some compelling reasons for you to do this.

AN EPIDEMIC OF OBESITY

Human beings experience a highly extended period of physical growth compared to other animal species, and children's body proportions and composition normally vary as they grow. For instance, rapid gains that take place in height and weight during infancy slow down once a child begins to walk. Growth continues at a slower rate, with periodic "spurts" in height or weight well into middle childhood. Then, during early **puberty**, growth becomes rapid once again (Cole, Cole, & Lightfoot, 2009). Do you remember returning to school after summer vacation when you were 12? Typically, the girls had shot up in the intervening months, now standing nearly a head taller than most of the boys their own age.

The same trend occurs with body fat composition. A normally developing infant has a significant amount of baby fat during the first 9 months of life but sheds it gradually through early and middle childhood. Historically, during the later years of elementary school, girls gain slightly more body fat than boys and carry it through early puberty and then regain their slim adult proportions by adolescence.

But a shocking thing has happened in recent years. The number of school-age children who are overweight and obese—across socioeconomic status and other demographic categories such as culture and geography—has become a serious national concern. Statistics from the National Health and Nutrition Examination Survey (NHANES) show that in the United States between 1988 and 2004 the prevalence of obesity increased from 11% to 19% among 6- to 11-year-olds and from 11% to 17% among adolescents aged 12 to 19 (Centers for Disease Control and Prevention [CDC], 2008). **Body mass index (BMI)**, expressed as weight divided by height and then squared ($BMI = kg/m^2$), is used by medical practitioners to identify children who are overweight or at risk of becoming overweight. BMI ranges for children and teens are calculated to account for normal differences in body fat between boys and girls and differences in body fat at various ages. Cutoff criteria used in most research reports are based on the 2000 CDC BMI-for-age-growth charts for the United States. **Overweight** children fall in the 85th to 95th percentile. Children with BMI values at or above the 95th percentile of the sex-specific BMI growth charts are categorized as **obese**. Technically, **obesity** means having *too much body fat*. However, as a guiding principle, youngsters are assumed to be obese if their weight is more than 20% higher than the ideal weight for a boy or girl of their age and height.

According to the NHANES surveys, obesity in children and adolescents was relatively stable at about 4% from the 1960s to 1980 (CDC, 2008). However, the next published survey, covering the years 1976 to 1994, showed that obesity had nearly doubled among children and adolescents, and the trend continued upward through 2004 (see Table 11.1). Researchers now estimate that 15% of all children in the United States are overweight, and nearly 25% of black and Hispanic children weigh too much. However, this trend is definitely not limited to people of color. It affects a wide age range, most ethnic groups, and families of every socioeconomic status (Ebbeling, Pawlak, & Ludwig, 2002).

TABLE 11.1 Prevalence of Obesity Among Children and Adolescents Ages 6–19 Years, for Selected Years 1963–65 Through 1999–2004 (Percents).

Age (Years)	NHANES 1963–65	NHANES 1966–70[1]	NHANES 1971–74	NHANES 1976–80	NHANES 1988–94	NHANES 1999–2000	NHANES 2001–02	NHANES 2003–04
6–11	4.2	4	6.5	11.3	15.1	16.3	18.8	
12–19	4.6	6.1	5	10.5	14.8	16.7	17.4	

[1]Data for 1963–65 are for children 6–11 years of age; data for 1966–70 are for adolescents 12–17 years of age, not 12–19 years.

Source: CDC, 2006

The Dangers of Obesity in Children

As you can imagine, once these figures were first released in 2000, the topic of childhood obesity became a common subject in the media. By this time, physicians were seeing many more cases of weight-related childhood **diabetes** than they had in the past, and other health problems such as heart disease, high blood pressure, and elevated fasting blood glucose levels were beginning to surface (Rosener, 1998; Steies, 2003). Public health departments and universities spearheaded task forces, workshops, and conferences to explore and address the situation.

The American Academy of Child and Adolescent Psychiatry encouraged parents to reduce children's television watching (American Academy of Pediatrics Committee on Public Television, 2001). The *Early Childhood News* called childhood obesity "a new epidemic," and listed a variety of causes, including family income, television, food choices, lack of physical activity, and parenting beliefs and practices (Steies, 2003). The same year, *Parents* magazine published "The Big Issue of Obesity," which contained the frightening prediction from a Yale University obesity expert that "today's American children may be the first generation in modern history to live shorter lives than their parents did" (Brownell, cited in Laliberte, 2003, p. 1).

Unfortunately, all the attention from professionals and the media didn't at first halt the trend of weight gain in children. The statistics for 2003–2004 showed an increase in overweight and obesity from 2001 to 2002. In 2004, the National Association for the Education of Young Children published "The O Generation: Our Youngest Children Are at Risk for Obesity." In it, authors called the situation "the most preventable and avoidable cause of illness and death in the United States" (Huettig, Sanborn, DiMarco, Popejoy, & Rich, 2004, p. 52). Emphasizing the findings that obese children were apparently at risk for the same health problems as obese adults, and at a much earlier age, they appealed to child development professionals, teachers, and families to address the issue in child care settings, schools, and at home.

Perhaps we are finally beginning to notice. A 2008 NHANES survey finally found that obesity prevalence among children and adolescents had shown no significant increase between 2003–2004 and 2005–2006. According to that study, in the combined years 2003–2006, 16.3% of children and adolescents aged 2–19 years were obese, at or above the 95th percentile of the 2000 BMI-for-age growth charts (Ogden, Carroll, & Flegal, 2008). Now that we have been alerted, it is important for all of us who work with children to help them to develop healthful lifestyles and habits.

Understanding the Causes of Childhood Obesity

It is clear that such a widespread demographic shift over five decades cannot be explained as the result of only one or two variables. Experts still do not agree on the exact combination of causes that have resulted in the situation. Life was simpler in the 19th century, when Louis-René Villermé, a public health worker, determined that the average height of a population was positively correlated with the productivity of the soil. Since in a self-contained single-industry economy wealth and wellness were directly related to the food being cultivated locally, Villermé observed that the taller the people and the faster their growth, the healthier their children and the wealthier their village (Komlos & Kriwy, 2002). The puzzle becomes even more complex when we consider figures showing that the number of Americans living in households lacking consistent access to adequate food soared in 2008, to 49 million, the highest number since the government began tracking what it calls "food insecurity" (Nord, Andrews, & Carlson, 2009).

Food and Fitness In an attempt to get an easy-to-explain handle on the current problem and its causes, the U.S. National Institute of Environmental Health Sciences (2006) sponsored a conference on obesity and the environment in Washington, DC. The conference sponsors reviewed findings from researchers at institutions of higher learning, public health, and medicine. Their conclusion was that the recent increase in childhood obesity is the result of several different factors interacting with certain environmental contexts that influence eating and physical activity. At the conference, researchers reported that the most significant characteristics of our social and cultural environments influencing children's food and fitness habits are these:

- ❀ Urban and suburban designs that discourage physical activity
- ❀ Economic and time pressures on families that result in frequent consumption of convenience foods
- ❀ Reduced access to and affordability of nutritious foods in many communities
- ❀ Decreased opportunities for walking or biking to, at, or after school
- ❀ Parental fears encouraging children to stay indoors while parents are at work
- ❀ Increased amounts of time spent viewing television and engaging with technology (para. 4)

Government Policies Following the conference, the Robert Wood Johnson Foundation (RWJF) offered to fund proposals that implemented certain approaches to address childhood obesity. The recommendations included engaging children in at least 15 minutes of age-appropriate physical activity several times a day, totaling from 1 to several hours a day most days of the week. They also stipulated that children participate daily in several different types of activity designed to achieve optimal health, wellness, fitness, and performance benefits, and that

FIGURE 11.1 Robert J. Wood Foundation's Approach to Ending the Increase in Childhood Obesity.

The goal of RJWF's work on childhood obesity is to help halt the rise in rates of the condition by promoting healthy eating and physical activity in schools and communities throughout the nation. RJWF places special emphasis on reaching children at greatest risk: African-American, Hispanic, Native American and Asian/Pacific Islander children living in low-income communities.

RJWF has a four-pronged approach to halting the increase in childhood obesity:

- Building the evidence regarding what works to promote healthy eating and increase physical activity among children.

- Testing innovative approaches in order to spread promising models.

- Educating leaders and investing in advocacy strategies.

- Working on ways to help health care providers screen and counsel to prevent and manage childhood obesity.

Source: National Institute of Environmental Health Sciences (2005), Obesity and the Environment (pamphlet) July 1, 2005; Robert Wood Johnson Foundations (2006) Childhood Obesity (position paper), February, 2006. Used with permission.

periods of 2 or more hours of inactivity be avoided in the planning of their day (U.S. National Institute of Environmental Health Sciences, 2006). Figure 11.1 lists these recommendations in more detail.

In 2009, the RWJF released a position paper to highlight the types of legislative changes that could significantly address the quality of food being consumed by children participating in subsidized school meals and other government assistance programs (Child Nutrition Working Group, 2009). Representatives from the RWJF Center to Prevent Childhood Obesity urged legislators to improve and enhance federally funded child nutrition programs such as the National School Lunch Program (NSLP), School Breakfast Program (SBP), and the Special Supplemental Nutrition Program for Women, Infants, and Children (WIC).

As a school-age professional, you are ideally situated to address several of these issues. School-age programs provide many valuable opportunities to promote healthy eating and physical activities. The remainder of this chapter will help you learn how you can do that.

❀ *Consider This:* ❀

Where did you grow up? How did you get to school? Did you walk or take a bus? Did you have a bicycle? Talk to other students in your class about how they traveled to school or around their neighborhood during their childhood. How do the children who come to your program arrive?

Parents and teachers have been informed. The increased rate of childhood overweight and obesity is serious and must be curbed. Your first step as a school-age professional is to understand the concerns and the causes. Next, provide excellent role models for children, and help them and their families to find ways to improve their health and fitness. The final step is to incorporate healthy eating and fitness into your regular curriculum.

Trends in Activity Levels and Eating Habits of School-Age Children

One of the most significant physical changes to occur during the years of middle childhood is the development of **gross motor skills**. During the school years, children improve their balance, strength, agility, and flexibility. They get better at catching, throwing, running, jumping, hopping, and ball handling. Not long ago, it was quite common to find 8-year-old children bursting into sprints at recess as they raced across the school playground, engaging in intricate patterns of hopscotch, kicking or dribbling soccer balls, or swinging bats at balls pitched by their classmates. Depending on their interests and body composition, boys and girls began to develop differing capabilities in these motor skills over the course of middle childhood.

I recently watched a group of third- and fourth-grade children during a school recess. Rather than jumping up and down trying to catch a ball or get a turn at some other playground game, most children sat in groups on benches or directly on the blacktop, chatting to one another, talking on cell phones, texting and reading messages, or listening to MP3 players. After sitting for 2 hours in a classroom, rather than enjoying the free play time that was being provided for them, these children preferred to sit some more, and talk. A survey of 15,000 school districts found that 40% were either eliminating recess or cutting back on it or considering one or the other (Clements, 2004, p. 70). Yet even when time is provided for outside recreation, children may need to be coaxed into using the time for active play.

Another important growth pattern of middle childhood takes place in the brain. New and different connections form—the **myelin sheath**, the fatty substance covering the **neural pathways** that improves cognitive processes, continues to develop, and numerous cognitive activities begin to take place in different parts of the brain. These expanded functions ultimately result in a more mature thinking process for the school-age child. The connection here is that regular participation in activities involving large muscles, using a full range of motion at the joints, and raising their heart and breathing rates contribute to children's overall fitness and health, including the health of the neural pathways in the brain. If the children I saw sitting with their cell phones and iPods had truly understood this relationship, perhaps their newly mature thinking processes would have encouraged them to choose active play over more sedentary pursuits.

The report by the U.S. National Institute of Environmental Health Sciences (2006) also reported that American families are eating more convenience foods than in the past. This was attributed to economic and time pressures on families and possibly also a reduced access to and affordability of nutritious foods in many communities. Convenience foods tend to be high in salt, sugar, and fat and can contribute to obesity, diabetes, and heart disease (Ludwig, 2007). The following sections will explore these two issues more thoroughly and provide some ideas for helping children and families develop new and healthy lifestyles.

DEVELOPING HABITS OF LIFELONG HEALTH AND FITNESS

The topic of health-related fitness in children has become one of great interest in recent years, especially since the trends in childhood obesity have become so noticeable. At the same time, Western society's emphasis on physical appearance, combined with many youngsters' belief that they must follow in the footsteps of talk-show guests and fashion dolls and hurry into adulthood, seems to have made eating disorders such as anorexia and bulimia permanent fixtures of the middle years (Elkind, 1998, 2006; Mendoza, Zimmerman, & Christakis, 2007).

Meanwhile, of course, researchers have discovered that many other children have low aerobic endurance and high levels of body fat. These are all serious issues because underweight, unfit, and overweight children are *all* more liable to show early signs of coronary heart disease, high cholesterol levels, and high blood pressure (Rosenbaum & Leibel, 1989; Rosener, 1998; Steies, 2003).

It's not too difficult to understand two of the reasons for this unhealthy situation: (1) Children spend too much time in sedentary activities, and (2) they eat too many of the wrong foods. A third explanation, that eating disorders are related to self-esteem, is also significant. The American Academy of Pediatrics (AAP) Committee on Public Television (2001) has recommended that school-age children limit their viewing of TV and videos to 1 to 2 hours per day, but many of them watch much more than that. The AAP also recommends that the shows children watch be nonviolent and educational. Above all, TV should not be a substitute for activities like playing, exercising, reading, or social engagement with their friends and family.

Most American children between the ages of 2 and 12 watch between 21 and 28 hours of television per week (American Academy of Child & Adolescent Psychiatry, 2002). In addition, they spend a very small portion of each day participating in high-intensity physical activity. While most elementary schools have a physical education program, many children spend as little as 1 hour in planned physical activity per week (Endres, 2003). Also, sports played during physical education periods are typically those that promote agility and specialized skills, such as baseball, basketball, soccer, or volleyball. Activities that develop cardio-vascular fitness and can continue to be enjoyed throughout adulthood, such as cycling, swimming, running, dancing, yoga, and tennis, are more useful to children's overall fitness and self-concept but less often seen in formal PE programs.

The National Content Standards for Physical Education established in 2004 recommend 150 minutes per week for elementary school students and 225 for middle and high school. For reasons mentioned earlier, most schools have been unable to meet these guidelines (National Association for Sport and Physical Education [NASPE], 2004).

Your Role in Modeling Health and Fitness

So how do you fit into this picture? Here is another place where the adults in a child's life—possibly even you—model behaviors, attitudes, and values that are then internalized and eventually become part of the child's own personality. Parents who commute long hours and work all day may have difficulty modeling physical fitness to their children. Even if physical activity is a regular part of their lives, it may take place away from home, out of the child's view (an aerobics class on the way home from work, for example, or a racquetball game at noon).

In addition, parents who work away from home may be less in control of what their children eat than those who in generations past had the time to cook nourishing breakfasts and be waiting with freshly made snacks after school. Children's eating habits, not to mention TV- and video-watching habits, are now more heavily influenced by their friends, teachers, coaches, and after-school program staff than they are by their parents.

Adults who spend lots of time with children will want to model good eating patterns and healthy levels of physical activity. Be sure to share your experiences with children if you regularly participate in physically challenging games and activities directly with youngsters—your own enjoyment of these activities may spark an interest in one of them.

❀   *Consider This:*   ❀

What do you like to eat for breakfast? What kind of snacks do you eat after you get home from school or work? Do they comfort you? Make you more or less energetic?

What criteria do you use when you choose your meals or snacks? Cost? Convenience? Health? Do you consider yourself a good model of nutritional habits for school-age children?

A highly respected leader in afterschool program development, Rich Scofield (1987), liked to say that children "play" in response to their natural developmental needs. For example, children 7 years old and older want to do "real work with the real tools" (p. 2) of the adult world, using woodworking equipment, an electric

Provide opportunities for a variety of physical activities.

drill, a stove and vacuum cleaner, and paintbrushes. They also "strive to become competent at a particular skill" (p. 2). This could include throwing a football, playing hopscotch, jumping rope, in-line skating, and learning tricks with a yo-yo as well as bending wire, cutting cloth, drawing a floor plan, and hanging a picture. These activities become "not only skills to learn but also social statements as they strive for peer acceptance" (p. 2).

Adults working with school-age children can and should capitalize on children's natural physical development. It is very important to provide materials, equipment, and opportunities for lots of different kinds of physical activities—not just outdoor sports but also dancing, dramatic performances, building projects, and rearranging the furniture. Provide activities in which children with a wide range of physical capabilities can be successful.

Increasing Physical Activity

The NASPE has developed guidelines for integrating physical activity into the complete school day (see Figure 11.2), but with the recent emphasis on increasing test scores in elementary, middle, and high schools, many schools and school districts have been unable to implement these guidelines. Afterschool programs, however, are ideally suited to integrate physical activity into their curriculum.

FIGURE 11.2   Physical Activity Guidelines for Children Ages 5–12.

Purpose of the Guidelines

NASPE seeks to provide meaningful physical activity guidelines for parents, physical education teachers, classroom teachers, youth physical activity leaders, administrators, physicians, health professionals, and all others dedicated to promoting physically active lifestyles among children. The guidelines provide information concerning how much physical activity is appropriate for preadolescent children (ages 6 to 12). Physical activity, broadly defined, includes exercise, sport, dance, as well as other movement forms.

The Guidelines

The full document contains detailed interpretations of the following brief guideline statements. Other sections include a rationale for the guidelines, importance of sound nutrition, important concepts about physical activity for children, appropriate activity models for children, using the physical activity pyramid to help children make activity choices, and recommendations for promoting physical activity in schools and physical education.

Guideline 1. Children should accumulate at least 60 minutes, and up to several hours, of age-appropriate physical activity on all, or most days of the week. This daily accumulation should include moderate and vigorous physical activity with the majority of the time being spent in activity that is intermittent in nature.

Guideline 2. Children should participate in several bouts of physical activity lasting 15 minutes or more each day.

Guideline 3. Children should participate each day in a variety of age-appropriate physical activities designed to achieve optimal health, wellness, fitness, and performance benefits.

Guideline 4. Extended periods (periods of two hours or more) of inactivity are discouraged for children, especially during the daytime hours.

Source: From *Physical Activity for Children: A Statement of Guidelines for Children Ages 5–12* (2004), with permission from the National Association for Sport and Physical Education (NASPE), 1900 Association Drive, Reston, VA 20191, USA. www.naspeinfo.org.

Factors Affecting Physical Growth

Many factors influence physical growth. Some researchers believe that heredity is the primary contributor to *patterns* of physical growth, while environmental influences affect *actual* physical growth and development. How tall a child will become or what her body composition will be at the end of adolescence is influenced by attributes inherited through the genetic process from her parents and other relatives. Other contributions to physical growth are made by socializing agents in the child's environment, which can include the afterschool setting. These contributions include nutrition, emotional well-being, and culture.

Good Nutrition　Good nutrition is an example of an environmental factor that supports healthy growth and development. Ingesting adequate proteins, fats, and carbohydrates is essential for growth and maintenance of body tissues as well as for providing the body fuel to function. Without adequate nutritious food, children are not able to grow according to the plan embedded in their genes. The child's usual breakfast, for example, may consist of whole grains, fruit, dairy, and eggs, which contribute complex carbohydrates for energy, fruit for fiber and vitamins, dairy for calcium and other minerals, and protein for growth. Or it could contain sweet pastries, a sweetened and colored fruit juice substitute, and a greasy sausage patty, which fail to supply the child's body with the resources it needs to build muscle and bones and with the energy needed to run and jump and play (and learn) in the waking hours ahead. A lifetime spent eating nourishing food on a regular basis—or of not doing so—can be seen in the growth and development patterns of children during middle childhood.

Emotional Well-Being　A second environmental factor affecting growth is emotional well-being. Lack of affection and attention has been shown to result in growth disorders. Growth depends not only on genetics, but it is also dependent on messages that come from the interpersonal environment. Even if adequate nutrition is provided, a child will not grow normally without nurturing (Cole et al., 2009). Developing children's awareness of their body through yoga or dance and teaching them lifelong habits of fitness by organizing regular cycling or hiking events can contribute to increased feelings of competence and self-worth.

Culture　A third environmental aspect that contributes to physical differences is culture. How a culture teaches people to "obtain and preserve food, how to make shelters, and how to heal the sick and injured" are all examples of how cultural practices can affect growth patterns (Cole et al., 2009, p. 77). In other words, it is the responsibility of a society to provide clean, nutritious food, housing, and health care for its children, as well as to implement immunization and disease control so that children's bodies will have the ability to absorb foods and avoid infections. This means having clean air and water and a health-care system that is accessible to all populations. We all need to do everything we can to make these things high priorities in our society. Starting locally and on a small scale, by proposing a classroom recycling program or publishing a monthly "Green Afterschool" newsletter, for example, can bring issues of the environment into children's awareness. The shortage of affordable housing or the prevalence of families without medical insurance can be studied and discussed in a group that collaboratively writes a report for the newsletter to raise the awareness of other students and their families.

Teaching and Modeling Healthy Food Choices

Nutrition is a term that relates to the quality, frequency, and amount of food eaten each day (National Institute on Out-of-School Time, 2005). Being active and also eating nutritious food contributes to a child's overall wellness, including his readiness for learning. If leaders model healthy eating and provide only nutritious food choices, they can gradually teach and encourage children to develop good nutritional habits that will last their whole lives.

Eat only healthful foods yourself when you are around the children in your programs. Lean toward fresh fruit and vegetables, whole grain breads, and low-fat or nonfat milk or water, rather than soda or fruit juice. Become more physically active around the children—for example, shooting baskets or leading cycling trips around town. Talk to children about some of your physical activities outside the program, such as playing tennis, swimming, or sailing or hiking.

If you or someone close to you has had a weight problem, it's okay to share the ongoing challenge of changing eating habits with youngsters. Solicit suggestions from them about how you can reduce your consumption of empty calories that you personally enjoy, such as potato chips, soda, french fries, or chocolate. It is helpful for children to know that adults need to work to stay healthy, too, and that their trusted adults think it is worthwhile to do so.

A Nutritious Snack Curriculum

Providing healthy snacks after school is an effective way to promote a healthy nutritional environment and help children begin to practice healthy eating habits. Purchasing, preparing, and serving snacks should be an integral part of your curriculum. All children will have opinions about favorite foods, but if you take a leadership role in helping them to plan, you can make a real difference in their understanding of the balance of nutrition and health with enjoyable eating.

In some afterschool programs, snack is a boring routine, and one that does not engage the children in either the selection or preparation of foods. Mike Ashcraft, director of the Children's Choice Child Care Services in Albuquerque, New Mexico, once commented that much of the food he was serving ended up in the trash "because kids weren't hungry yet or didn't like what we were having" (Ashcraft, personal communication). The traditional pattern in many programs is for children "to stand in line to sign in as they arrive from school, wait in a group for announcements, and continue to wait passively for snack portions to be served" (Ashcraft, personal communication). He found that switching to family-style snacks rather than individual portions and encouraging children to serve themselves resulted in less waste, happier children, and healthier eating habits. After that discovery, the afterschool staff at Children's Choice began to make snacks available for several hours after the children arrived and completely changed how snacks were prepared and served in order to give the children more options. Mike concluded by saying that, after the snack menu changed, the word out on the schoolyard was that Children's Choice was the place to go after

Chicken Quesadillas

Find your group of at least 3-4 friends

1. Wash your hands first!!!

2. 2 friends grate the cheese. Be careful not to cut your self. That means we are going to have a calm body and not be too silly.

3. 2 friends cut the chicken into small –medium pieces.

4. Now that your prep is done, place chicken, and cheese on your tortilla and bring to Ms. Cindy or Ms. Amanda and we will cook it on fryer.

5. Now you can put your sour crème and /or salsa and enjoy your cooking project!

Good job friends

Reusable laminated recipe cards show recommended serving sizes or directions for building snacks.

school. Several new enrollments came as a result of their child-friendly snack policy, and no more snacks went into the trash.

Ashcraft suggests that actual menus and portions should be adjusted to meet the needs of your children and your own understanding of nutrition. Taking a cue from this program's success, here are some guidelines for engaging children in selecting and preparing their own food:

- ❀ Provide large bowls or plates filled with several choices of fruit, vegetables, crackers, and cheese.
- ❀ Purchase small and medium-sized containers with spouts to fill with juice and water that children can pour themselves.
- ❀ Provide serving implements, napkins, and paper cups so that children can serve themselves when they are ready and can select the type and amount of food that they want.
- ❀ Increase children's participation in the snack curriculum by encouraging them to help develop the menus and even prepare some of the food. Make reusable laminated recipe cards to indicate recommended serving sizes or directions for building such multipart snacks as tacos, fruit parfaits, or stuffed bell peppers.

USDA Food and Nutrition Service Guidelines for Afterschool Program Snacks   Figure 11.3 shows the U.S. Department of Agriculture's Food and Nutrition Service guidelines for afterschool program snacks, which are often used by programs to guide serving portions and content. Government nutritionists have developed two 4-week-cycle menus to help afterschool programs get started serving healthy snacks. These cycles, summer menus, and other information can be obtained from the Food and Nutrition Service Web site at the end of this chapter.

FIGURE 11.3   USDA Food and Nutrition Service Afterschool Snacks Program.

The FNS Afterschool Snacks meal pattern is based on the nutritional needs of children ages 6 to 12 years and is as follows:

The National School Lunch Program offers cash reimbursement to help schools serve snacks to children in afterschool activities aimed at promoting the health and well-being of children and youth in our communities. A school must provide children with regularly scheduled activities in an organized, structured, and supervised environment and include educational or enrichment activities (e.g., mentoring or tutoring programs). Competitive interscholastic sports teams are not eligible afterschool programs. The programs must meet state/local licensing requirements, if available, or state/local health and safety standards. All programs that meet the eligibility requirements can participate in the National School Lunch Program and receive USDA reimbursement for afterschool snacks.

Two different components from the four listed must be served:

Milk, fluid	**1 cup (8 ounces)**
Meat or meat alternate	**1 ounce**
Fruit or vegetable or full-strength juice	**3/4 cup**
Grains/breads	**1 serving**

Because afterschool snacks are available for children through the age of 18 years, additional foods may be needed to meet the calorie and nutrient needs of children ages 13–18 years. To assist snack providers, each cycle menu has been divided into two age categories: ages 6–12 years and ages 13–18 years. For each menu, the required two components in the appropriate amounts are included.

In addition, one optional food component is added for the 13–18 years age group. This optional component is included to assist providers in offering a satisfying snack and in meeting the nutritional needs of the older age group. The optional items are marked on the menus with an "O." Many afterschool care programs (like the Department of Education's 21st Century Schools Program) provide some funding for snacks and may supplement what you receive from USDA should you find that participants require a larger snack than USDA reimbursement rates will provide.

Source: From U.S. Department of Agriculture Food and Nutrition Service, 2009.

The recommended snack menus and recipes Web site is a good place to start, because it provides recommended nutritional guidelines. Information from the government Web site can also help you offset the cost of the food, which may increase once you switch from traditional snack portions to self-regulated family-style eating—and once you begin to offer fresh, tasty food. Directors of programs who have begun offering more nutritious and more attractive snacks have reported a surge in snack expenses at first, but once children knew that they could go back for seconds and thirds if they wanted—but are encouraged to take only what they will actually eat—they begin to regulate their portion sizes over time.

Recognizing that eating healthier food is frequently more expensive than traditional snacks, the Department of Agriculture's National School Lunch and Child and Adult Care Food Programs were expanded through the Child Nutrition Reauthorization Act of 1998 to offer cash reimbursement for snacks provided to children through age 18 years in certain afterschool programs. You may also be able to obtain nutritional grants through your own state public health department or agricultural extension program.

These yogurt/raspberry parfait cups incorporate fruit into a delicious sugarless dessert.

Here are some suggestions to get you started:

- Offer raw vegetables, such as carrot, celery, and jicama for meals and snacks, rotating low-fat dips such as plain yoghurt, hummus, and blended soybeans (edamame) mixed with a small amount of horseradish or other spices.
- Limit fruit juices to 6 ounces a day and offer fresh, cold water both indoors and outdoors all day long. Avoid artificially flavored and sweetened imitation fruit drinks.
- Use both familiar and new vegetables to make soups and stews. With supervision, even small children can help select, wash, and prepare vegetables for cooking.
- Find ways to incorporate a variety of fresh fruits into sugarless desserts, such as smoothies, parfait layers, ices, and sauces.
- Talk about seasonal foods and the advantages of purchasing foods from local farmers and ranchers. Older children may enjoy learning about the "slow food" movement and discussing its political and economic implications.

Preparing Snacks With Children   Preparing the snacks with children is a good way to introduce ideas about healthy eating into the curriculum and encourage children to prepare their own snacks at home. If you have limited kitchen facilities, secure some basic equipment and staple supplies before embarking on a full-blown cooking curriculum. Begin with a few utensils, such as cutting boards, knives, spoons, and can openers and access to refrigeration, and gradually build up your "kitchen" through donations, fundraisers, and yard sale scrounging. If

Some afterschool programs may be able to use kitchen facilities.

you are fortunate enough to have traditional kitchen/institutional facilities, such as a refrigerator and freezer, conventional and/or convection oven, microwave, and blender, there should be no limit to the variety of snacks and meals you and the children can prepare.

The purchase price of individual food items should be recorded and included in the planning and purchasing process, and older children should be regularly included in those sessions, working together with staff members to calculate average portion sizes based not only on nutritional value of the food but also on the cost of the ingredients. See Chapter 12 for guidance in integrating academic enrichment activities into an expanded snack preparation and cooking curriculum.

INCORPORATING AEROBIC ACTIVITY INTO YOUR PROGRAM

Afterschool programs can become effective weapons in the fight against obesity by creating environments that are conducive to healthful eating and physical activity. Health and school success are interrelated (Story, Kaphingst, & French, 2006). Children do better in school when they are healthy and fit. In the same way, you will enjoy your work—and be a more effective group leader—if you are physically active for part of each day. Your enthusiasm will be contagious, and your children will want to be active like you. The subsequent sections will explore a few suggestions for promoting physical activity in your program.

Encourage Children to Walk or Bike to School

In the early years of the 20th century, most children walked or rode a bicycle to school. Ask any grandparent. The story in our family is that my father walked

3 miles. Uphill. Both ways. In the snow. Perhaps he did. I only walked a mile and a quarter (and only one way was uphill!), because beyond that radius a big, yellow school bus picked up children and deposited them at their school. However, I have many happy memories of the years I spent walking to and from my neighborhood school, talking and joking with my friends, stopping in the Devonshire Market for snacks, collecting rocks or flowers or bottle caps along the way. We had a tremendous sense of freedom during our walk. We solved minor problems like leaking lunchboxes or muddy shoes and made our way into the world each day with a confidence that I suspect helped to shape us in ways that we will never understand. Our parents expected us to get safely to school and safely home, and most of the time we did so without incident. In 1950, 7 million children were transported in 115,000 school buses. Fifty years later, 448,307 school buses transported nearly 23 million children to and from public schools (Editors of *School Bus Fleet* Magazine, 2001). Today 25 million children, about 54% of all K–12 students in the country, travel in school buses to and from schools and school-related activities (American School Bus Council, 2008), and many others are driven by parents.

When escalating transportation costs caused many school districts around the country to eliminate or reduce the use of free busing, instead of children returning to walking or riding their bicycles, parents formed car pools and drove their children to school, creating traffic jams at schools everywhere. Even in school districts that still run buses, most children living too close to school to use them are driven to school each day. In some school districts, nearly all children are transported to school by a parent, a car pool driver, or in a district-owned vehicle. Just 15% of American children today walk or ride their bicycles to school, compared with 42% in 1969 (CDC, 2007).

There are many contributing causes for this trend. Many neighborhood schools had been abandoned in favor of larger buildings on the outskirts of town. Magnet schools that emphasized science and math or dramatic arts had become attractive to many parents, who would drive their children across town to attend them. More mothers were at work, leaving many neighborhoods empty during the week. Gone were the friendly neighbors who had watched out for us from their front porches or kitchen windows. Fears of accidents, predators, and other unforeseen threats have caused parents to worry about the safety of children in their communities. Television has heightened fears by broadcasting any incident, no matter how far away. With the increasing need for afterschool supervision, more families enrolled their youngsters in recreational, sports, music, and academic enrichment programs. Family schedules became busier.

Increasing the safety and practicality of walking or bicycling to school is one way you can make a difference in the health and fitness of the children you serve. The idea is growing in practicality. Since 1997, communities around the United States have been celebrating Walk to School Day. In 2008, participation reached a record high with more than 2,800 events from all 50 states and the District of Columbia registered on the U.S. Walk to School Web site (www.walktoschool.org). The primary goal of Walk to School Day is to motivate parents to leave their cars at home and walk with their children to school. By encouraging children and parents to spend time together and practice safe pedestrian behavior, the activity increases children's awareness of individual responsibility and reassures parents

FIGURE 11.4   Goals of the International Walk-to-School Movement.

International Walk to School is about more than just getting together with children and going for a walk to school as a special event. This is certainly important, but the event's greater aim is to bring forth permanent change in communities across the globe. Below are some of the initiative's goals:

- **Encourage physical activity** by teaching children the skills to walk safely, how to identify safe routes to school, and the benefits of walking.

- **Raise awareness of how walkable a community is** and where improvements can be made.

- **Raise concern for the environment.**

- **Reduce crime and take back neighborhoods** for people on foot.

- **Reduce traffic congestion, pollution, and speed** near schools.

- **Share valuable time with local community leaders, parents, and children.**

Source: http://www.iwalktoschool.org, *National Center for Safe Routes to School* of the University of North Carolina Highway Safety Research Center.

of their safety. By publicizing the event, parents and school leaders promote a healthier lifestyle for children and families and encourage the entire community to make it safer for children to walk, bike, and play outside (Kong et al., 2009).

A primary school in Dorset, England, launched a walk-to-school promotion in 2000 that grew to involve more than 400 children. It resulted in car pool usage being reduced by 18% and walking and cycling increased by 16%. The movement now has its own international Web site, www.iwalktoschool.org, with links all over the world. Figure 11.4 lists the six stated goals of the International Walk to School (IWS) program, which you can use as a guide to help develop a program in your own community.

In 2002, 70% of the student body of Topa Topa Elementary School in Ojai, California, walked or rode their bikes to school on the monthly Walk to School Day compared to approximately 25% on a typical day. After participating in the international event for 3 years, the sixth-grade teachers and children had expanded the annual project into a monthly one by means of a service learning project. Guided by suggestions on the Safe Routes to School (SRTS) Web site (www.saferouteinfo.org), the children analyzed surveys and other feedback from the three previous annual events, made safety recommendations to the district, and publicized what they had done in order to increase participation. On average, 30% more children walked or biked to school on the monthly Walking Wednesdays than on other days, with a significant decrease in traffic. After a successful year with the monthly event, parent volunteers partnered with the city police department youth education to move Walking Wednesdays from a monthly event to a weekly one (Learn and Serve America National Service Learning Clearinghouse, 2003).

In Massachusetts, organizers in several communities encouraged travel by foot through weekly or daily walking groups. To encourage children to participate, sponsors offered free pencils or colorful wrist bands and sometimes arranged for the appearance of a special guest star—usually the school principal or teacher or local celebrity—along their walking route. Some parents were fearful of letting their children leave home on their own, and so some school districts have made sure that their initial walking groups are led by an adult.

The actual risk of harm to students walking to and from school is low, as long as they are taught to avoid strangers, walk with a friend or in a group, and exercise basic safety precautions such as looking both ways before crossing streets. Although many parents have come to believe that walking to school is not as safe as it used to be, the statistics don't actually show an increase in accidents on school routes or children being approached or snatched (Mason, 2007; Vaznis, 2008). As with many things in today's media-saturated world, one frightening event in an individual community far away may be talked about all over the country the next day, increasing our sense of vulnerability and fear.

You and the children in your afterschool program can combat this trend by organizing your own Walk to School activity or creating a Safe Routes to School program. Encourage a group of interested children to follow the links listed at the end of this chapter to see what other communities have accomplished. Discuss the goals of the International Walk to School Movement listed in Figure 11.4 and the steps for establishing a Safe Routes to School (SRTS) program in Figure 11.5. If there is continued interest, engage parents, school officials, and community leaders in the project. If you and the children project enthusiasm for the idea, develop relationships with families and businesses along the walking routes, and review basic rules of safety and good sense, you can make walking to school a common occurrence once again in your community.

FIGURE 11.5 Steps to Creating a Safe Routes to School Program.

Starting a Safe Routes to School (SRTS) program is an opportunity to make walking and bicycling to school safer for children and to increase the number of children who choose to walk and bicycle. On a broader level, SRTS programs can enhance children's health and well-being, ease traffic congestion near the school, and improve air quality and community members' overall quality of life. The steps outlined below are meant to provide guidance by providing a framework for establishing a SRTS program based on what has worked in other communities. Detailed suggestions for implementing each of the steps is provided in *The SRTS Guide*, available as a PDF document at http://www.saferoutesinfo.org/guide/pdfs.cfm.

Some communities may find that a different approach or a reordering of these steps works better for them.

1. Bring together the right people.

2. Hold a kick-off meeting.

3. Gather information and identify issues.

4. Identify solutions.

5. Make a plan.

6. Act on the plan.

7. Evaluate, make improvements, and keep moving.

An SRTS program has the potential to improve walking and bicycling conditions near a school and spread interest into other parts of the community. Coalitions that persist in their efforts and make measurable improvements based on their evaluation will be rewarded with safer places for children to walk and bicycle and more children choosing safe routes to school.

Dance, Yoga, and Music

A growing body of research shows that yoga, stress reduction, and creative arts programs can also positively affect physical and mental health (Watson, Poczwardowski, & Eisenman, 2000). There are many benefits of including creative arts, yoga, music, dance/movement activities, and other nonverbal forms of expression into your afterschool program. When offered to children and teens on a regular basis, such activities can increase self-esteem, reduce stress, improve personal responsibility, and improve school success (Coe, Pivarnik, Womack, Reeves, & Malina, 2006; McKenzie et al., 2006; Webber et al., 2008). These types of activities may be more attractive to children who avoid team sports or other more active endeavors.

Body image issues and poor eating habits plague many young people today. Left to their own devices, youngsters begin to spend less time in physical activity as they reach the later years of elementary school and more time in social networking, listening to music, or watching videos. The moderate to vigorous movement easily achieved in structured programs that range from hip-hop dancing to full musical productions can increase the overall amount of physical activity for young preteen and teenage youngsters to the point that it could prevent excess weight gain of up to 2 pounds a year (Webber et al., 2008) and improve overall body image. Participating in enjoyable activities such as dance or yoga has also been shown to reduce eating disorders (Daubenmier, 2005; Sands, Tricker, Sherman, Armatas, & Maschette, 1997). Enjoying music in the classroom can be a subtle first step toward participating in a more active musical experience, such as dance or yoga.

Dance   Finding a dance instructor is not usually too difficult. Many adults who took dance lessons as children are able to teach a few basic moves to interested youngsters. Older children who are themselves taking dance lessons can also

School-age children usually enjoy learning new dance steps.

serve as leaders, and the children can be encouraged to ask their friends and parents to help them locate other resources. Sometimes paying someone a small fee to come once a week to teach new steps and moves will be enough to kick off a dance curriculum that can lead to performances for parents and community members and a ready supply of enthusiastic dancers ready to teach the "next generation" of children as they join the group.

Yoga   It may be more difficult to find a yoga instructor. If no one on your staff has been trained to teach yoga to children, ask parents and teachers at local colleges or high schools if they know someone who will volunteer to start a program at your site. If program leaders and other staff members take the class along with interested youngsters, that would have the double benefit of motivating more youngsters to participate and building a supply of future teachers. If no teacher can be found, you could purchase or rent a yoga or Pilates video. In that case, it would be wise for one or more staff members to familiarize themselves with the yoga positions to be covered in advance so that they can help children with them.

Children who practice yoga are often better able to regulate their emotions, manage stress, and calm themselves. Instructors and parents also report that children who regularly participate in yoga classes choose better foods to eat and engage in more physical activity than children who do not (Binzen, 2007). In 2007, the International Yoga Association sponsored a Symposium on Yoga Therapy and Research in Los Angeles, and several groups presented the results of studies on the benefits of yoga for children. One study examined the benefits of yoga for adolescents with eating disorders. Mostly suffering from low self-esteem, these teens attended yoga classes as part of a psychiatric day treatment program, and nearly 75% reported an increase in well-being. They used the terms *relaxed, calm, energized* and *more awake* to describe how they felt after class. Other studies looked at anxiety, depression, trauma, mood regulation, sense of well-being, self-esteem, and "increased wellness," and all reported positive results (Binzen, 2007).

Physically active and fit children tend to be more self-assured and do better in school. Dance and yoga can help to improve children's health and fitness and can also help them to find a comfort level with their bodies that will encourage healthier eating and lifestyle habits. Besides—it's fun!

Music   Music has long been considered to be a potentially healing and stress-relieving art form. In 1697, Congreve, an early poet, wrote:

> *Musick has Charms to sooth a savage Breast,*
> *To soften Rocks, or bend a knotted Oak.*
> *I've read, that things inanimate have mov'd,*
> *And, as with living Souls, have been inform'd,*
> *By Magick Numbers and persuasive Sound*

Although in recent times we usually see the above misquoted to say that music can charm a savage *beast,* when the poem was written the author was referring to a human breast, or possibly soul. Certain kinds of music are known to induce relaxation and relieve anxiety, which is why we hear it in hospital waiting rooms, cancer treatment centers, dentist offices, and hotel lobbies. Some teachers and parents believe that music can help to accelerate learning, focus attention, and even enhance health. One popular book, *The Mozart Effect: Tapping the Power of Music to Heal the Body, Strengthen the Mind and Unlock the Creative Spirit* (Campbell, 1997), has encouraged many parents and teachers to explore the use of music as a therapeutic and cognitive enhancement tool.

LISTENING TO MUSIC   Clinical investigations into the study of the effect of music and sound on the human nervous system (called *psychoacoustics*) have shown that certain musical compositions can actually improve ear and brain function while providing a pleasant listening experience. A number of published works support the idea that listening to Mozart's work, for example, may temporarily increase cognitive skills (Campbell, 1997; Mahler, Lawrence, & Arcangelos Chamber Ensemble, 2000; Plante, Marcotte, Manuel, & Willemsen, 1996). However, everyone doesn't like classical music, and a temporary cognitive improvement isn't going to help much when chapter tests or final exams come around.

Fortunately, Finnish researchers discovered that verbal memory and focused attention improved significantly more in stroke patients who listened to their favorite music for several hours a day than in those who listened to audio books or nothing at all (Sarkarmo et al., 2008). And two other studies showed that listening to music can also enhance attention, learning, communication, and memory in healthy subjects (Schellenberg, Nakata, Hunter, & Tamoto, 2007; Thompson, Moulin, Hayre, & Jones, 2005).

Music has a well-documented effect on alleviating anxiety, depression, and pain in patients (Siedliecki & Good, 2006). One particularly interesting study examined the influence of aerobic exercise activity, soothing music-and-nature scenes, and suggestion on coping with test-taking anxiety. The conclusion of the researchers was that any or all of these activities can play a role in reducing anxiety (Sacks, 2006). So whether or not children get smarter if they listen to Mozart, there are many other good reasons for introducing music into their lives (Schwartz, 2008).

Try playing soft, melodic music or nature sounds (such as water passing over stones) during homework time or at other times during the day when children are engaging in quiet activities such as reading, writing, or creating art. Many children find such background sounds pleasant and relaxing, and you might observe that certain children are actually soothed and refreshed by the experience. Introduce music as a physical activity by encouraging children to stretch to music before sitting down to do homework or on a rainy afternoon when they've been cooped up indoors for hours. Stretches can become dance steps; dance steps can become aerobic activity. Music may be the key to getting some children off the couch and moving.

MUSICAL INTELLIGENCE   Certain children, identified by Howard Gardner as having **musical intelligence**, have a particular sensitivity to pitch and tone that allows them to detect and produce musical structure. They tend to notice non-verbal sounds in the environment and sometimes even use rhythm or melody to help themselves learn school material, such as lines in a poem or play, math facts, or sequences of events in a story or historical event. Some children study more effectively with music in the background or played through headphones, so make that a choice if you have the means to do so.

Some children may enjoy listening to music in a more focused manner—for example, with high-quality earphones during free-choice time when they can actually concentrate on the music. Children with musical intelligence not only enjoy listening to music but also may want to learn how to make music as well. In that case, music serves the dual function of helping to balance a child's emotional life and providing an opportunity for enjoying a physical activity.

LEARNING TO MAKE MUSIC   Learning to sing, read music, or play a musical instrument can be life changing for a child. Unfortunately, opportunities to do so within a public school setting have been reduced drastically by changing priorities and limited education funding. Fewer children today have the opportunity to feel the vibrations of well-crafted music flow through their bodies as they draw a bow, pass their breath over a reed, or excite a drum head.

The main focus of an afterschool music program should not be so much on performance as on the impact that making music can have on the children themselves. Seek out a retired music educator who may enjoy the opportunity to bring quality music education to your children. As with any other program that you initiate, it is important to develop and to maintain good communication between school-day and afterschool personnel, especially if there is already some kind of music education in place in the school. Engage the participation of families whenever possible, both in supporting the idea of an afterschool music education program and in the actual procurement of instruments, teachers, and places to practice. Other valuable resources are community-based music organizations, such as symphonies or special-interest music groups, which in turn can engage their own networks, volunteers, and suppliers to publicize or support your program. Engage as many students as you can in your program, not just children who seem to be, or whose families think they are, "talented." All children benefit from some formal music instruction, and if they show any interest at all they should not be excluded through an audition process. Read Perspective 11.1 to see how this can play out in a well-planned regular offering of music education to children.

The National Association for Music Education (MENC) supports afterschool music learning opportunities that capitalize on children's natural interests and provide materials, equipment, and opportunities for expressive musical involvement. They are concerned that afterschool programs may substitute for or supplant music education programs in the regular day program of the school. However, afterschool music programs can add variety to existing programs and may ignite interest in developing music education in the school district day programs through the excitement and energy they elicit from children and families.

Tailor instrumental and vocal music activities to the age and needs of the children, and strive to ensure that children *want* to participate rather than are compelled to by parents or staff (Wagener, 2008).

Other Creative Ways to Get Children Moving

The goal of this section is to help you find enjoyable ways to get children up off the furniture and moving. There are many ways to do this, and the sections that follow are merely intended to give you some ideas of what can work. Some of the examples provided below were pilot projects, funded with one-time money and operating for only a year or two. However, using certain elements of one or more

Afterschool Music Program Hopes to Keep Kids in Tune

Cathryn Creno, January 24, 2009, Arizona Republic

At the beginning of the school year, 7-year-old Conrad Varela was happy just to know how to strum a few chords on his father's old guitar. But by December, the student at Shaw Elementary School near downtown Phoenix had his own instrument and was playing songs. "I like rock and roll, you know, the hard stuff," the second grader said. "My parents are really surprised I am learning so fast."

Conrad can thank five Tempe and Ahwatukee teenagers who teach music once a week to about 60 participants in Shaw's afterschool program. They have named their volunteer group Sounds of the Community. "We weren't sure what the outcome would be," said Mountain Pointe High School senior Christian Appleby, who teaches guitar. "Some of the kids who had never played an instrument before asked for guitars for Christmas. For me, that has been the coolest part."

Sounds of the Community has been so successful that Janel White-Taylor, an Arizona State University assistant professor of educational technology, assisted the teens in getting a $1,000 grant to purchase additional instruments and to pay gas costs for the group to commute to the central Phoenix school. White-Taylor, who directs a program called Project eXcellence, also is urging the teens to recruit and train replacement volunteers to keep the music going next year.

Sounds of the Community is the brainchild of Appleby and Corona del Sol High School senior Molly Yang, who teaches piano to Shaw students. The two volunteered as art instructors in the Dominican Republic last summer through a program called Sister Island Project. When they returned home, they decided to continue their efforts at a school in a low-income part of the Valley. Appleby and Yang rounded up three friends from Mountain Pointe—Nicole Ortiz to teach art, Ben Backhaus to teach guitar,

and Rodney Mitchell to teach drums—and approached Shaw officials with the idea. Lisa Norwood, Shaw's learning intervention specialist and afterschool program coordinator, said her school had never received a volunteer offer from teens—let alone teens that are a 30-minute drive away.

"When I got the call I was like, 'Really?'" Norwood said. "And then when I found out where they were from, it was an even bigger surprise. But it was clear these were smart kids who had done their homework and knew what they were doing." Norwood said Sounds of the Community was an immediate hit with more than half of the 100 children who attend the afterschool program. "You can just see the excitement when Friday comes because it is music day," she said. "They line up to take turns playing the instruments."

Briana Durant, 10, had never picked up any instrument before joining Sounds of the Community's guitar class. Now the fourth grader can play a few chords and enjoys writing lyrics, too. Yang, who has studied piano for 12 years, said she wants to foster the children's appreciation for music and art. "Ultimately, this is about helping them find a passion for whatever type of art appeals to them," Yang said.

Sandra Stauffer, a music education professor at Arizona State University's Herberger College of the Arts, was not surprised that the Shaw students have progressed quickly. She suspects the volunteer work also is helping the teens become better musicians. "We know that peer tutoring is good for both the tutor and the student," she said. "Both get something out of it."

Yang said she thinks her piano playing has improved. "I thought I could just go in and say, 'Put your hands like this and play like this,'" she said. "It didn't work that way. Instead, I have had to stretch my own boundaries to think of ways to teach them." White-Taylor, whose Project eXcellence is an effort to boost afterschool learning at low-income schools like Shaw, sees so much benefit from Sounds of the Community that she is urging the current volunteers to find replacements for when they leave to go to college next year. "This group is kind of amazing," she said. "With most high-school students, you have to give them direction."

Last fall, White-Taylor suggested the volunteers apply for a grant from Ashoka's Youth Venture. The organization, which helps youths start businesses and volunteer programs for social change, awarded Sounds of the Community the $1,000 grant. "In many parts of the Valley, kids can afford their own instruments and private music lessons after school," White-Taylor said. "But that doesn't happen in low-income districts. This program can close the gap."

Source: Creno, C. (2009, January 24), *The Arizona Republic.* Used with permission of *The Arizona Republic.*

of the models provided, you can create a physical activity program that matches the children's interests and can be supported with the resources existing in your community. Read on for ideas.

All Children Exercise Simultaneously   Now a signature program of the Youth Fitness Coalition, All Children Exercise Simultaneously (ACES) was created as a way to motivate children to exercise. ACES takes place on the first Wednesday in May as part of National Physical Fitness and Sports Month and National Physical Education Week. At 10 a.m. local time, children in schools all over the United States and in many countries around the world hop, skip, jump, run, walk, and play together, in a "symbolic gesture of fitness and unity."

This fitness event was started in 1989 by physical education teacher Len Saunders of New Jersey. The program has been growing each year. The first year, 240,000 children participated worldwide. In 2009, Michigan alone had over 500,000 participants. Project ACES is now organized by the nonprofit Youth Fitness Coalition but is still managed by its founder. Participating in ACES could be a kickoff activity for your new health and fitness curriculum, a way to publicize your commitment to offer a variety of opportunities for children to experience enjoyable physical activity. Individual school districts and programs have total flexibility in organizing their events. You may play music, invite celebrity guests or speakers from the community, or even invite local media to participate in the activity as well as cover your ACES workout. The ACES Web site (see the Internet Resources section at the end of this chapter) provides ideas, contact names, and suggestions for ways to motivate children and include the community, including a downloadable certificate that you can print and award to participants.

Virtual Trail Walking   A creative spinoff from the ACES idea was developed by a teacher whose third-grade class had participated in the annual exercise activity in the past. This time she helped her students measure their steps, chart them on a map, and "walk" the 2,175 miles of the Appalachian Trail (they actually walked on the school track), which was studied as part of the social studies curriculum. Drawing material from the Appalachian Trail Conservancy (http://www.appalachiantrail.org), she posted an enlarged map of the Appalachian Trail on a bulletin board, printed out related historical material for children to read, and encouraged them to research the trail conditions, flora and fauna, and weather as they virtually inched their way along the entire trail.

You could easily adapt this idea to your own program. For example, an excellent documentary DVD is available, titled *Walking With Freedom: A Hike Along the Appalachian Trail.* It was made by long-distance hiker and filmmaker Michael Daniel, who took his video camera along as he hiked the entire trail. The videography is excellent, showcasing for the children both the Appalachian Trail itself and many of the animals and people one can find while traveling along it.

You could show it to children in segments as a reward for completing designated portions of their own virtual trail or hold a public screening at the beginning of a planned walking event. Because it shows the natural settings along the actual trail, the DVD can enhance the experience and make the children's participation even more interesting and educational. You could also engage a local amateur videographer to walk along with you and the children and document the actual trail they are walking and incorporate short interviews with the children and "nature talks." The final product can be shown to parents and used the following year as a motivational tool to encourage a new group of children to hike.

WALK ACROSS AMERICA   Find a copy of Peter Jenkins's watershed book *Walk Across America* (2001) and read it, one chapter at a time, to a group of older children. Suggest that they plot the route taken by Jenkins on a U.S. map, and begin a virtual walk that they can mark in a different color along the same route. Most virtual trail walks use a proportionate number of miles walked by the children to count for the actual miles of the trail. For example, 5 miles walked in your neighborhood, or on the school track, could be recorded as equal to 50 miles of the walk across America. Or you could count steps, equating 6,000 steps (or 600 steps, for younger children) to 60 miles of the total distance. A way to be sure that children of different physical capabilities are equally able to participate would be to count walking minutes instead of steps or miles and equate those to miles. If you do that, for example, 60 minutes walking could be charted on the map as 60 miles.

VIRTUAL TRAILMAPS AND GUIDES   The idea of photographing major hiking trails has become quite popular, and many "virtual navigation experiences" are now available on the Internet. One source is called Trailmonkey: Your Virtual Guide to Adventure in the Great Outdoors. Many national parks and trails are available on this site, including Crater Lake, Glacier, Yellowstone, and Banff (in Canada). Each trail listing leads you to a detailed park and trail description and a photo index. The trail maps are great and can be printed for a variety of classroom uses. If you access the maps on a computer, you can take advantage of links to photos of scenes along the route marked with camera icons. Click on a camera and the appropriate photo pops up on your screen, illustrating that part of the trail. Enlarge the map of the trail the children select and post it on a bulletin board; then the children can print out the appropriate photos and link them with a length of string to the matching locations along the trail.

Other Web sites provide photo essays and virtual trail walks for the Inca Trail in Peru, the route taken by Lewis and Clark in the future Louisiana Territory, and a 2,500-mile virtual "Walk to Yellowstone National Park" undertaken by elementary school children and teachers in Georgia. Use a search engine (or encourage your children to do so) to find others. Motivate one another to walk each day by posting the trail in a public place, such as the cafeteria, tallying the total miles walked each week and marking the group's progress on the map.

Fit for Learning, Fit for Life   The original Fit for Life concept was developed by health and fitness consultant Ron Jones, through a collaboration between the Boys and Girls Clubs and Kaiser Permanente Health Care. The initial program targeted three elementary schools and the local Boys and Girls Club in Bakersfield, California. Participation was approved by parents or guardians. All children were invited to participate regardless of their fitness levels or weight. The goal was to model health a through a combination of educational lessons and enjoyable games. The Fit for Life program emphasized physical activities that children could participate in anywhere, such as strength conditioning, balance and agility training, flexibility, aerobic activities incorporating walking, running, and playing with Frisbees. The trainers taught children how to think differently about play and playground environments and to learn habits of wellness and nutrition that would extend beyond the length of the program. Although the original Fit for Life program was a pilot and lasted only a year, schools and after-school programs all over the country have since used the model to create similar programs.

One successful program is in Santa Clara County, California. Santa Clara County's initiative is called Fit for Learning, and it resulted from a partnership between the school district, the YMCA of Santa Clara Valley, Kaiser Permanente, and several private nonprofit foundations. The program unobtrusively appears in classrooms in the form of resource guides for activity leaders. The guide provides ways to weave fruits, vegetables, and the importance of exercising into existing lesson plans that also conform to California's teaching standards. In its most successful form, Fit for Learning has been integrated into the regular language arts, geography, and social science classroom curriculum and the afterschool programs run by the YMCA. By fostering exercise and physical activities led by classroom teachers and afterschool group leaders, the program involves adults and children in learning new habits and has been successful in raising awareness of healthful eating and changing activity habits. The Fit for Life Web page (at the end of the chapter) contains guidelines for setting up a similar program, activity leader handouts, and nutrition mini-lessons.

Electronic Interactive Exergames   It's ironic that overuse of video games has been identified as one of the contributors to children's lack of fitness, and now the video game industry is marketing games advertised as offering a partial solution to the same problem. Ask around to see if anyone's family has a Wii console that you could use as another way to incorporate physical activity into the afterschool curriculum. Several companies now make programs that work with the Wii (pronounced *we*), and many children find them appealing enough to engage in strenuous physical exercise while playing alone or competing with their friends. The Wii Fit collection of games, in which the player does mini-exercises from pushups to running, includes a fitness log that can be completed after each workout; by graphing the number of minutes on a classroom chart you can set up a motivating competition, and everyone wins.

Not enough time has passed to see if individual children will persist in playing interactive games long enough to make a significant difference in their fitness, but in an afterschool environment they can be included as just one option in a broad fitness program, especially useful when it's raining or snowing outside. The program makes it easy for children to work toward personal fitness goals by responding to cues on the screen to block virtual soccer balls, swivel hips to power virtual Hula hoops, and leap off virtual ski jumps. It calculates their Wii Fit

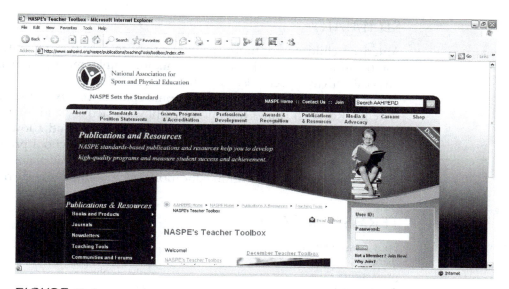

FIGURE 11.6 National Association for Sport and Physical Education Teacher Toolbox Web Page.

Source: Reprinted with permission from the National Association for Sport and Physical Education (NASPE), 1900 Association Drive, Reston, VA 20191. www.naspeinfo.org.

age from their BMI reading and tests of their center of gravity and balance. Children can check their daily progress, set goals, check their current Wii Fit age, and even enter exercise time they've spent in addition to Wii Fit activities. By making the Wii console, balance beam, or mat controllers available regularly, and providing external motivation such as a fitness challenge linked to successful achievement of game milestones, interest can be created in other forms of the physical activities encouraged by these electronic partners, such as yoga, dancing, soccer, tennis, and running. NASPE's Teacher Toolbox website, shown in Figure 11.6, suggests other activities to introduce.

Fit Kid Activities The North Carolina Wellness Trust Fund has developed a Web page (see end of chapter for URL) that contains links to resources for teachers and afterschool activity leaders. These resources provide enjoyable and meaningful physical activities that children can engage in during relatively short periods of time. My favorites are the Brain Breaks, which integrate activity and academic enrichment into enjoyable games that engage both the body and the brain. Presidential Race, for example, combines speed walking, hopping, and jumping jacks with a card game in which electoral votes for each state are counted out using physical activity by teams who vie for the presidential post. Another activity combines middle school social studies with Tinikling, the national dance of the Philippines. Participants learn to identify examples of cultural borrowing, such as language, traditions, and technology, and evaluate their importance in a variety of societies. As part of the activity, children learn to do the Tinikling and maintain a rhythmic beat with bamboo instruments. The instructions for each activity are clear and easy to understand, and many have accompanying videos that demonstrate the games.

SUMMARY

American children are more sedentary than in previous generations, due to a combination of factors that include changing employment patterns, reduction of physical activity in schools, easy and inexpensive access to convenience and fast foods, and an attractive array of electronic entertainments and social networking systems. Research shows that increased physical activity and improved nutrition lead to better health, clearer thinking and reasoning, and a lower incidence of diabetes, high blood pressure, and heart disease. Afterschool programs are well suited to provide children with engaging, enjoyable, and challenging physical activity and can easily include nutrition education and cooking in the curriculum.

TERMS TO LEARN

body mass index/BMI
diabetes
gross motor skills
musical intelligence
myelin sheath

neural pathways
nutrition
obese/obesity
overweight
puberty

REVIEW QUESTIONS

1. What changes have occurred in society to cause obesity rates to rise in children of all ages?
2. Explain three dangers of obesity in young children.
3. What three environmental factors contribute to children's physical growth?
4. List three activities that children can participate in during out-of-school time that will help them to develop habits of health and fitness.

CHALLENGE EXERCISES

1. What can leaders in afterschool programs do to counter the rise of obesity in young children and adolescents?
2. Take a survey of school-age children (see if you can do this activity at a nearby afterschool program) until you find 10 who live less than a mile from school. To do this you may need to plot their houses on a map that shows the school with a mile-radius circle drawn on it. Record how those children get to school each day. What percentage of them walk or ride a bicycle?
3. Locate someone who has a Wii Fit program and ask him/her to demonstrate it in class.

INTERNET RESOURCES

BMI charts for children and adolescents:
    http://www.cdc.gov/nccdphp/dnpa/healthyweight/assessing/bmi/childrens_BMI/ about_childrens_BMI.htm

International Walk to School:
    http://www.iwalktoschool.org

Kids Walk to School: A guide to promote walking to school:
http://www.cdc.gov/nccdphp/dnpa/kidswalk/pdf/kidswalk.pdf

Food and Nutrition Service snack cycle and funding information. (Many links provided with specific information about afterschool and summer snack menus and reimbursement policies):
http://www.fns.usda.gov/cnd/menu/cyclemenu.htm

Mileage clubs and other incentives to encourage walking and bicycling to school:
http://www.saferoutesinfo.org/guide/encouragement/mileage_clubs_and_contests .cfm

National Association for Sport and Physical Education (NASPE) Teacher Toolbox: Integrating physical activity into the complete school day:
http://www.aahperd.org/naspe/publications/teachingTools/toolbox/index.cfm

Fit kids activities (physical activities that integrate academics):
http://www.fitkidsnc.com/SeeLearnDo.aspx

All Children Exercise Simultaneously (ACES):
http://www.lensaunders.com/aces/aces.html

Trailmonkey: Your Virtual Guide to Adventure in the Great Outdoors:
http://www.trailmonkey.com/virtual.htm

Fit for Life:
http://www.ronjones.org/Health&Fitness/FitforLife/index.html

U.S. Department of Agriculture Food and Nutrition Service Child and Adult Food Care Program afterschool snacks: Fact Sheet and Q&A:
http://www.fns.usda.gov/cnd/afterschool/

U.S. Department of Agriculture Food and Nutrition Service Child and Adult Food Care Program afterschool snack cycle menus:
http://www.fns.usda.gov/cnd/menu/cyclemenu.htm

Source of music and videos for aerobic dance, yoga and Pilates, and guided meditation:
http://www.workoutmusicvideo.com/aerobics.html

Virtual Trail Walking:
http://walking.about.com/cs/measure/a/webwalkingusa.htm

The Inca Trail:
http://www.raingod.com/angus/Gallery/Photos/SouthAmerica/Peru/IncaTrail

Mr. Hathaway's Virtual Trail:
http://www.pcs.k12.va.us/http://www.appalachiantrail.orgvtrail

Web Walking USA:
http://walking.about.com/cs/measure/a/webwalkingusa.htm

REFERENCES

American Academy of Child & Adolescent Psychiatry. (2002). Children and watching TV. *Facts for Families, 54,* 1–2.

American Academy of Pediatrics Committee on Public Television. (2001). Children, adolescents, and television. *Pediatrics, 107*(2), 423–426.

American School Bus Council. (2008). *Background/history about the American School Bus Council.* Retrieved July 29, 2009, from http://www.americanschoolbuscouncil.org/index.php?page = faq

Binzen, M. (2007). *Experience of yoga meets experimentation of the West at SYTAR.* Paper presented at the Symposium on Yoga Therapy and Research Los Angeles, March 6–7, 2007.

Campbell, D. (1997). *The Mozart effect: Tapping the power of music to heal the body, strengthen the mind and unlock the creative spirit.* New York: Avon.

Centers for Disease Control and Prevention. (2006). Prevalence of Overweight Among Children and Adolescents: United States, 2003–2004. Retrieved April 10, 2010 from http://www.cdc.gov/nchs/pressroom/06facts/obesity03_04.htm

Centers for Disease Control and Prevention. (2007). National prevalence and correlates of walking and bicycling to school. *American Journal of Preventive Medicine, 33*(2), 98–105.

Centers for Disease Control and Prevention. (2008). *National health and nutrition examination survey.* Atlanta, GA: Author.

Child Nutrition Working Group. (2009). *Child nutrition programs: Federal options and opportunities.* Little Rock, AK: Robert Wood Johnson Foundation Center to Prevent Childhood Obesity.

Clements, R. (2004). An investigation of the status of outdoor play. *Contemporary Issues in Early Childhood, 4*(1), 68–80.

Coe, D. P., Pivarnik, J. M., Womack, C. J., Reeves, M. J., & Malina, R. M. (2006). Effect of physical education and activity levels on academic achievement in children. *Medicine & Science in Sports & Exercise, 38,* 1515–1519.

Cole, M. C. S., Cole, S., & Lightfoot, C. (2009). *The development of children* (6th ed.). New York: Worth.

Daubenmier, J. J. (2005). The relationship of yoga, body awareness, and body responsiveness to self-objectification and disordered eating. *Psychology of Women Quarterly, 29*(2), 207–219.

Ebbeling, C. B., Pawlak, D. B., & Ludwig, D. S. (2002). Childhood obesity: Public health crisis, commonsense cure. *Lancet, 360*(9331), 473–483.

Editors of *School Bus Fleet* Magazine. (2001). *School bus fleet 2001 fact book.* Torrance, CA: Bobit. Retrieved April 10, 2010, from http://education.stateuniversity.com/pages/2512/Transportation-School-Busing.html

Elkind, D. (1998). *All grown up & no place to go: Teenagers in crisis.* Cambridge, MA: DeCapo Press.

Elkind, D. (2006). *The hurried child: Growing up too fast too soon* (25th anniversary ed.). Cambridge, MA: DeCapo Press.

Endres, J. B., and Rockwell, R. E. (2003). Exercise and physical fitness. In *Food, Nutrition, and the Young Child* (5th ed.). New York: Prentice Hall.

Huettig, C. I., Sanborn, C. F., DiMarco, N., Popejoy, A., & Rich, S. (2004, March). The O Generation: Our youngest children are at risk for obesity. *Young Children,* 50–55.

Jenkins, P. (2001). *Walk across America.* New York: Harper.

Komlos, J., & Kriwy, P. (2002). Social status and adult heights in the two Germanies. *Annals of Human Biology, 29*(6), 641–648.

Kong, A. S., Sussman, A. L., Negrete, S., Patterson, N., Mittleman, R., & Hough, R. (2009). Implementation of a walking school bus: Lessons learned. *Journal of School Health, 79*(7), 319–325.

Laliberte, R. (2003, September). The big issue of obesity. *Parents.*

Learn and Serve America National Service Learning Clearinghouse. (2003). *Walk to school campaign.* Retrieved July 29, 2009, from http://www.servicelearning.org/slice/index.php?ep_action=view&ep_id=216

Ludwig, D. S. (2007). Childhood obesity—The shape of things to come. *New England Journal of Medicine, 357*(23), 2325–2327.

Mahler, G., Lawrence, R., & Arcangelos Chamber Ensemble. (2000). *Music to de-stress.* Unpublished Musical Recording Label Notes. Advanced Brain Technology.

Mason, N. (2007). Walk this way. *American School & University, 79*(10), 44–47.

McKenzie T. L., Catellier D. J., Conway T., Lytle L. A., Grieser M., Elder J. P. (2006). Girls' activity levels and lesson contexts in middle school PE: TAAG baseline. *Medicine & Science in Sports & Exercise, 38*(7), 1229–1235.

Mendoza, J. A., Zimmerman, F. J., & Christakis, D. A. (2007). Television viewing, computer use, obesity, and adiposity in the U.S. preschool children. *International Journal of Behavioral Nutrition and Physical Activity* (4:44doi:10.1186/1479-5868-4-44)

National Association for Sport and Physical Education. (2004). *Physical activity for children: A statement of guidelines for children ages 5–12* (2nd ed.). Reston, VA: Author.

National Institute on Out-of-School Time. (2005). *Links to learning: A curriculum planning guide for after-school programs.* Nashville, TN: School-Age Notes.

Nord, M., Andrews, M., & Carlson, S. (2009). *Household food security in the United States, 2008.* Washington, DC: U.S. Department of Agriculture.

Ogden, C. L., Carroll, M. D., & Flegal, K. M. (2008). High body mass index for age among US children and adolescents, 2003–2006. *Journal of the American Medical Association, 299*(20), 2401–2405.

Plante, T. G., Marcotte, D., Manuel, G., & Willemsen, E. (1996). The influence of brief episodes of aerobic exercise activity, soothing music–nature scenes condition, and suggestion on coping with test-taking anxiety. *International Journal of Stress Management, 3*(3), 1555–1166.

Rosenbaum, M., & Leibel, R. L. (1989). Obesity in childhood. *Pediatrics in Review, 11*(2), 43–57.

Rosener, S. (1998). Childhood obesity and adulthood consequences. *Acta Paediatrica, 87*(1), 1–5.

Sacks, O. (2006). The power of music. *Brain 2006, 129*(10), 2528–2532.

Sands, R., Tricker, J., Sherman, C., Armatas, C., & Maschette, W. (1997). Disordered eating patterns, body image, self-esteem, and physical activity in preadolescent school children. *International Journal of Eating Disorders, 13*(4), 369–384.

Särkämö T., Tervaniemi M., Laitinen S., Forsblom A., Soinila S., Mikkonen, M., et al. (2008). Music listening enhances cognitive recovery and mood after middle cerebral artery stroke. *Brain and Cognition, 131*(2), 1–11.

Schellenberg, E. G., Nakata, T., Hunter, P. G., & Tamoto, S. (2007). Exposure to music and cognitive performance: Tests of children and adults. *Psychology of Music, 35*, 5–19.

Schwartz, E. (2008). *Music therapy and early childhood.* Gilsum, NH: Barcelona.

Scofield, R. (1987). *School-age notes.*

Shephard, R. J. (1997). Curricular physical activity and academic performance. *Pediatric Exercise Science, 9*, 113–126.

Sibley, B. A., & Etnier, J. L. (2003). The relationship between physical activity and cognition in children: A meta-analysis. *Pediatric Exercise Science, 15*, 348–359.

Siedliecki, S. L., & Good, M. (2006). Effect of music on power, pain, depression and disability. *Journal of Advanced Nursing, 54*, 553–562.

Steies, A. (2003, March/April). Childhood obesity: A new epidemic. *Early Childhood News*, 15–23.

Story, M., Kaphingst, K., & French, S. (2006). The role of schools in obesity prevention. *Future of Children, 16*(1), 109+.

Thompson, R. G., Moulin, C. J., Hayre, S., & Jones, R. (2005). Music enhances category fluency in healthy older adults and Alzheimer's disease patients. *Exp Aging Res, 31*, 91–99.

Trost, S. G. (2007). *Active education: Physical education, physical activity and academic performance.* San Diego: San Diego State University.

University of North Carolina Highway Safety Research Center. (7/8/2010). National Resource Center for Safe Routes to School. Retrieved 7/14/2010, from http://www.iwalktoschool.org/about.htm

U.S. Department of Agriculture Food and Nutrition Service. (2009). Afterschool Snacks Cycle Menus. Washington, DC: U.S. Department of Agriculture Food and Nutrition Service.

U.S. Department of Agriculture Food and Nutrition Service. (2009, 04/09/2010). *Afterschool snacks cycle menus.* Retrieved April 25, 2009, from http://www.fns.usda.gov/cnd/menu/cyclemenu.htm

U.S. National Institute of Environmental Health Sciences. (2006). *Media briefing highlights: Findings of 2005 national conference on childhood obesity.* Princeton, NJ: Author.

Vaznis, J. (2008, September 19). Walk-to-school movement afoot across Massachusetts. *Boston Globe.* Retrieved December 7, 2008, from http://www.boston.com/news/local/articles/2008/09/19/walk_to_school_movement_afoot_across_mass/?page = 1

Watson, D. L., Poczwardowski, A., & Eisenman, P. (2000). After-school physical activity programs for adolescent girls. *Journal of Physical Education, Recreation & Dance, 71*(8), 17.

Webber, L.S., Catellier, D.J., Lytle, L.A., Murray, D.M., Pratt, C.A., Young, D. R., et al. (2008). Promoting physical activity in middle school girls. *Journal of Preventive Medicine, 34*(3), 173–184.

Chapter

12

Engaging Children in Indoor Activities

Whenever possible, the majority of children's physical activities should take place out of doors, and a short outdoor activity time after school can help children transition into their afternoon pursuits. However, when it rains or blusters—or worse, snows—children come into your program after already being cooped up for hours and subjected to one planned activity after another, and unless you are lucky enough to have a multipurpose room, gymnasium, or pool, it can be a real challenge to provide them with the physical activity their bodies crave. A "structured unstructured time" after arrival may be the answer.

THE IMPORTANCE OF CHOICE AND PLAY: NAPS, SNACKS, RAPS, AND LAPS

What I generally feel like doing after a long day is to collapse into a comfy chair with the newspaper or a good book and "veg out" for a while with a cup of tea before facing more people or activities. Many youngsters say they feel the same way (although their choice of snack may be different!). Some children enjoy having time to talk with their friends or program leaders about their day, and still others want to go immediately into the gym or outside to shoot hoops or run around.

❀   *Consider This:*   ❀

What do you like to do when you finish the school day, or when you get home from work? Do you have the freedom most days to indulge in that activity, or do you rush from one activity to another without a break? How do you feel on days when you get that "me" time? How do you feel when you do not?

One afterschool leader calls these kinds of activities "naps, snacks, raps, and laps" and allows 45 minutes after they arrive from school for youngsters to choose some variation on one of those stress busters before embarking on organized activities. She moves enough furniture to allow children to dance or do yoga on the carpet in one area of the room, sets out a self-service snack, assigns one or more group leaders to accompany the children who want to go outside, and then withdraws to a quiet corner, where she picks up a book and lets the youngsters have this time to themselves (P. Brasher, personal communication).

Structured vs. Unstructured Play

Sadly, some school-age program managers believe that **structure** is more important than ever at this time of day, to keep school-agers' pent-up high spirits under control. Staff members with this perspective may plan a full afternoon of "interesting group activities," starting the moment the children arrive, and then become frustrated or discouraged when children do not want to participate. It is important for children to have time and freedom both for a transitional "de-stress" period and for additional long periods of **unstructured play**.

The Importance of Play

The importance of play cannot be understated. Play offers children a unique and often magical way of relating with the world and with others. It leads them to learn new cognitive and physical skills and practice others. Play provides children with many opportunities to work with others, develop acceptable ways of behaving and speaking, and build confidence and competence. Play is also important to healthy brain growth. Play is so important to children's optimal development that it has been included by the Office of the United Nations High Commission for Human Rights (1989) as a right of every child.

A 2007 report from the American Academy of Pediatrics (AAP) emphasized that free and unstructured play is healthy and, in fact, essential for helping children reach important social, emotional, and cognitive developmental milestones as well as helping them manage stress and become **resilient**, or able to bounce back from change or misfortune. Engaging in fantasy play is one of the ways children practice newly developed social skills (Henig, 2008). Through role-playing, they learn to share, take turns, negotiate, feel empathy, and effectively express how they feel.

❀   *Consider This:*   ❀

The United Nations General Assembly adopted the **Convention on the Rights of the Child** and opened it for signature on November 20, 1989 (the 30th anniversary of its Declaration of the Rights of the Child). It came into force on September 2, 1990, after it was ratified by the required number of nations. As of December 2008, 193 countries had ratified it, including every member of the United Nations except the United States and Somalia (UNICEF, 1989). What do you think this says about the place of childhood and play in American culture?

Play allows children to create and explore a make-believe world.

Play allows children to use their creativity while developing their imagination, dexterity, and physical, cognitive, and emotional strength (American Academy of Pediatrics, 2007). Play allows children to create and explore a world they can master, conquering their fears while practicing adult roles, sometimes in conjunction with other children or adults (Ginsburg, Committee on Communications, & Committee on Psychosocial Aspects of Child and Family Health, 2007).

Strategies for Involving Children in Activities

It is important, therefore, to offer children a wide variety of things to do, and places to do them, while remaining watchful for signs that a youngster may need help to get started, needs more physical activity, or just wants a change of pace. If faced with no structure at all, some children will have difficulty focusing on a self-directed pursuit, soon acting bored, disruptive, or destructive. While you should never coerce children into participating in a specific game or activity if they express unwillingness to do so, it is fine to stimulate their interest through positive and creative approaches. Sometimes this takes the form of **modeling** interest yourself. Demonstrate how to arrange the beads into a pattern, how to chop the snack vegetables, or how to shape a pinch pot. One technique that helps get the ball rolling is to interest one or two class leaders in a group game. Usually other children will join in if the leaders appear to be having fun. But always allow children to merely observe if that is their wish. Perspective 12.1 addresses the importance of encouraging children to play together.

BALANCING ACADEMIC ENRICHMENT AND APPLIED KNOWLEDGE

Industry leaders have been concerned for many years that youngsters are graduating from high school and college without the necessary skills and knowledge to succeed in the world of work. In 1990, the Secretary of Labor appointed a com-

PERSPECTIVE 12.1

The Interplay Experiment

Bernie DeKoven, aka Major Fun

It was 1971—can you believe it?—that I made public the startling discovery that kids who play together work together better.

All right, not startling. But at least I got to prove it. (Probably. Actually, 40 years is a long time ago, and I can't find the research paper, and don't exactly remember if my memory is that reliable, anyway.)

We put groups of 20 or so kids in this almost empty room. Empty except for four piles of scrap Masonite and recycled computer paper, and a big mirror (two-way, hee, hee, hee).

We asked them to build a city for us. That's what we asked. "Could you build a city out of this stuff?" we asked, and then we added, "We'll come back in a while to see what you made."

Some of the groups of kids had spent a couple of hours a week over the last couple of months participating in a program I called Interplay. Basically, this program involved kids in playing games with each other: physical/social games like hide-and-seek; tug-of-war; and Duck, Duck, Goose; for a couple hours a week. The rest of the groups were kids who were from the same class but had not participated in the Interplay sessions.

We gave them 15 minutes. This is what we discovered: *The kids who had played together worked better together.* The kids who hadn't, spent most of their time stealing supplies from each other. Even though the materials were purposefully selected to be of the no-apparent-appeal-to-anyone junk variety, the kids spent more time fighting over the materials than in building with them. They had divided themselves up in groups around each pile. And in each group, most of the kids had made different cities of their own.

The kids who played together, can you believe it, built a single city, sometimes by connecting individual cities, but still generally all connected into one. The kids who played together better worked together better. Proof conclusive.

So, 40 years ago, the School District of Philadelphia published my curriculum. A six-volume set of kids games. They published two editions before the money ran out.

Kids who play together work better together. We knew this 40 years ago. So how come this is still such big news? How come we continue to be surprised by the connections between laughter and learning, games and leadership, fun and health, play and growth? Why are recesses still so short? Why are our playgrounds still so isolated, still so separate from our learning grounds? Why do we still allow physical education to become physical intimidation? To degenerate into an endless series of no-win tests and competitions? Why do we still have spelling bees when the only kids who win are the ones who don't need to learn spelling? Why do we still make our kids—day by day, grade by grade—divide themselves and each other into winners and losers, achievers and failures, when what we really want is for them to join together into a community of learners?

Why are we still so surprised that our kids spend so much of their time fighting over junk when together they could be rebuilding the world?

Source: From Major Fun, http://www.deepfun.com/intrplay.htm. Used with permission of Bernie DeKoven.

mission to determine the skills young adults need to succeed in the workplace and to contribute to successful business enterprises in the nation. Figure 12.1 lists those skills and competencies.

The necessary skills and competencies include such items as management of time, money, and human and physical resources; acquiring, interpreting, evaluating, and communicating information; participating in collaborative projects; and working within cultural contexts (SCANS, 1991, 2006). The commission published a series of documents to help educators incorporate the SCANS competencies

FIGURE 12.1 SCANS Skills: Foundation and Competencies.

The 1991 report *What Work Requires of Schools: A SCANS Report for America 2000* of the Secretary's Commission on Achieving Necessary Skills (SCANS) identified a three-part foundation and five basic competencies that have since come to serve as guiding principles for career-foundational curricula:

A: A Three-Part Foundation

Basic Skills: Reads, writes, performs arithmetic and mathematical operations, listens, and speaks

- *Reading* - locates, understands, and interprets written information in prose and in documents such as manuals, graphs, and schedules
- *Writing* - communicates thoughts, ideas, information, and messages in writing; and creates documents such as letters, directions, manuals, reports, graphs, and flow charts
- *Arithmetic/mathematics* - performs basic computations and approaches practical problems by choosing appropriately from a variety of mathematical techniques
- *Listening* - receives, attends to, interprets, and responds to verbal messages and other cues
- *Speaking* - organizes ideas and communicates orally

Thinking Skills: Thinks creatively, makes decisions, solves problems, visualizes, knows how to learn, and reasons

- *Creative thinking* - generates new ideas
- *Decision making* - specifies goals and constraints, generates alternatives, considers risks, and evaluates and chooses best alternatives
- *Problem solving* - recognizes problems and devises and implements plan of action
- *Visualizing* - organizes and processes symbols
- *Knowing how to learn* - uses efficient learning techniques to acquire and apply new knowledge and skills
- *Reasoning* - discovers a rule or principle underlying the relationship between two or more objects and applies it when solving a problem

Personal Qualities: Responsibility, self-esteem, sociability, self-management, integrity, and honesty

- *Responsibility* - exerts a high level of effort and perseveres toward goal attainment
- *Self-esteem* - believes in own self-worth and maintains a positive view of self
- *Sociability* - demonstrates understanding, friendliness, adaptability, empathy, and politeness in group settings
- *Self-management* - assesses self accurately, sets personal goals, monitors progress, and exhibits self-control
- *Integrity/honesty* - chooses ethical courses of action

B. Five Competencies

Resources: Identifies, organizes, plans, and allocates resources

- *Time* - selects goal-relevant activities, ranks them, allocates time, and prepares and follows schedules
- *Money* - uses or prepares budgets, makes forecasts, keeps records, and makes adjustments to meet objectives
- *Material and facilities* - acquires, stores, allocates, and uses materials or space efficiently

FIGURE 12.1 (*Continued*)

- *Human resources* - assesses skills and distributes work accordingly, evaluates performance and provides feedback

Interpersonal: Works with others

- *Participates as member of a team* - contributes to group effort
- *Teaches others new skills*
- *Services clients/customers* - works to satisfy customers' expectations
- *Exercises leadership* - communicates ideas to justify position, persuades and convinces others, responsibly challenges existing procedures and policies
- *Negotiates* - works toward agreements involving exchange of resources, resolves divergent interests
- *Works with diversity* - works well with men and women from diverse backgrounds

Information: Acquires and evaluates information

- *Acquires and evaluates information*
- *Organizes and maintains information*
- *Interprets and communicates information*
- *Uses computers to process information*

Systems: Understands complex interrelationships

- *Understands systems* - knows how social, organizational, and technological systems work and operates effectively with them
- *Monitors and corrects performance* - distinguishes trends, predicts impacts on system operations, diagnoses deviations in systems performance, and corrects malfunctions
- *Improves or designs systems* - suggests modifications to existing systems and develops new or alternative systems to improve performance

Technology: Works with a variety of technologies

- *Selects technology* - chooses procedures, tools, or equipment including computers and related technologies
- *Applies technology to task* - understands intent and proper procedures for setup and operation of equipment
- *Maintains and troubleshoots equipment* - prevents, identifies, or solves problems with equipment, including computers and other technologies

Source: Figure excerpted from *What Work Requires of Schools: A SCANS Report for America 2000*, by Secretary's Commission on Achieving Necessary Skills, 1991, Washington, DC: U.S. Department of Labor, pp. xvii–xviii.

into school curriculum, but the recent emphasis on teaching and evaluating specific academic skills pretty much sidelined those efforts. Here is another place where afterschool programs can offer children opportunities to learn useful life skills that they may not learn otherwise.

Using the Project Approach to Teach Life Skills

Lilian Katz (2007), a leader in the field of childhood education and a strong proponent of the project approach to curriculum development, has written widely expressing dismay that academic standards have become so heavily emphasized in elementary schools. Dr. Katz believes that individual children should be encouraged to engage in long-term projects consisting of real experiences that support them in their quest for meaning and understanding. By working closely with individual children and small groups, teachers are able to evaluate what children are learning as they are learning it. You can discover a great deal by observing how children communicate to others what they have done, what they think about it, and what they have figured out. This is exactly what the SCANS report writers meant when they wrote the "information competency": "acquires and evaluates information, organizes and maintains information, [and] interprets and communicates information."

Katz points out that we can measure educational experiences not merely by the facts learned but also by the level of engagement and absorption exhibited by the children. In addition, we can see the value of the experiences by the intellectual challenge resulting from sustained investigations and by the confidence children have in the importance and relevance of their questions (Katz, 2007; Katz & Chard, 2000). The project approach, pioneered at Reggio Emilia, Italy, and introduced in Chapter 10 as part of a discussion on emergent curriculum, provides a natural way for these "sustained investigations" to take place. By engaging in an extended study of a topic, self-selected and pretty much self-directed, children can discover a depth and breadth of understanding that is difficult to achieve in daily assignments. Several examples of long-term projects will be provided in this chapter and the next.

Children who feel that they belong to a group of their peers, and who learn to engage with others about the various inquiries each is carrying out, are likely to be successful in school and in life, no matter whether they have yet mastered a particular math, science, or language standard (Davies, 2008; Grotberg, 1995). Thus, wherever possible, provide opportunities for children to participate in sustained exploration, short- and long-term projects, and some kind of outcome that can be shared with and evaluated by the children themselves as well as by the adults responsible for measuring children's progress.

Afterschool Programs and Academic Standards

However much some of us would like to ignore academic standards, it is a fact of life that many afterschool programs are under contract to support children's acquisition of the standards upon which they, and their schools, will be measured. In addition, many parents ask program staff to help their children complete their homework and better understand the lessons of the classroom. It is important, therefore, that afterschool staff familiarize themselves about the state and local benchmarks and standards for each subject, and at each grade. This information is readily available at school district offices and may also be posted on the state and county department of education Web pages. Standards exist for nearly every subject taught in elementary and high school and can be woven into many of your activities in such a way that children are hearing the concepts, applying the concepts, and connecting the concepts all while participating in enjoyable activities. Figure 12.2 illustrates how this can be done. Several resources that demon-

FIGURE 12.2 Linking Activities to Standards.

Aesop and Ananse: Animal Fables and Trickster Tales

Introduction to activity: Fables and trickster tales are "narratives, found in many cultures, that use animal characters to convey folk wisdom and to help us understand human nature and human behavior" (Bernstein, 2002). In this activity, fables and trickster tales will be read to mixed-age groups of children. These tales typically have a high interest value, and through listening to the stories and talking about them, children will learn to see how both types of traditional literature employ various animals in different ways to portray characteristics of certain stereotypical human types.

After reading a story, lead the group in an informal discussion of the narrative and thematic patterns that occur in the tale. On succeeding days, ask 2nd-grade and older children to take turns selecting and reading stories from a collection of age-graded fables and trickster tales. Keep a dictionary handy for them to use to look up unfamiliar words. After several days of participating in this activity, children will (depending upon their age and stage of development) be able to:

- Identify the definition and understand specific elements of fables and trickster stories
- Recognize Aesop's fables and Ananse spider stories
- Compare and contrast themes of tales from different cultures
- Differentiate between the cautionary lessons and morals of fables and the celebration of the wiles and wit of the underdog in trickster stories

More specifically, they will have learned or practiced the following skills included in the Grade Three Reading Standards for the state of California:

1.3 Read aloud narrative and expository text fluently and accurately and with appropriate pacing, intonation, and expression

1.6 Use sentence and word context to find the meaning of unknown words

1.7 Use a dictionary to learn the meaning and other features of unknown words

2.1 Ask questions and support answers by connecting prior knowledge with literal information found in, and inferred from, the text

2.4 Recall major points in the text and make and modify predictions about forthcoming information

3.1 Distinguish common forms of literature

3.2 Comprehend basic plots of classic fairly tales, myths, folktales, legends, and fables from around the world

3.3 Determine what characters are like by what they say or do and by how the author or illustrator portrays them (Hill, 2007)

Guiding Questions:

What is a fable? How are fables different from other types of stories? What is a trickster tale? How is it different from other types of stories and from fables? What are the elements ("parts") that are common to fables and trickster tales? Where do these stories come from? How have they been passed down from one generation to another? What kind of wisdom about human nature and human behavior can we learn from fables? How can we use that wisdom in our daily lives?

Note: This activity demonstrates how afterschool curriculum can be linked to state academic standards. By telling or reading the stories in small mixed-age groupings, and allowing the children to select the stories and read them aloud in the order in which they wish, you are keeping the setting informal and enjoyable. As you begin to lead an informal discussion of the story you create a learning opportunity

(continued)

FIGURE 12.2   Linking Activities to Standards. (*Continued*)

that is markedly different from the scripted large-group lessons children are likely to have experienced during the classroom day.

The content of the activity was suggested by a lesson planning resource developed by the National Endowment for the Humanities, and more information about the fables and trickster stories used in it can be found on that web site, which is cited below.

Sources: Concept and story selection adapted from Lesson #240, Aesop and Ananse, Animal Fables and Trickster Tales. Used by permission of EDSITEMENT, National Endowment for the Humanities. The California State Reading Standards were accessed via a Web site entitled Developing Educational Standards, maintained by the Wappingers (New York) Central School District (http://edstandards.org/Standards.html#State). Used with permission.

strate how to develop activities and projects that link to state standards are listed at the end of the chapter.

The Use of Seven Key Learning Areas to Balance Curriculum

According to Richard Murnane, a professor at the Harvard Graduate School of Education, and Frank Levy, professor of urban economics at MIT, the skills needed for youngsters to succeed can be grouped into what they call the "new basic skills" (Murnane & Levy, 1996). These are classified both as "hard" skills such as math and reading and "soft" skills, which include the ability to work in groups and make presentations. They also emphasize the need for all youngsters to become skilled at using technology. The activities in this chapter and the next are organized by seven key learning areas that incorporate these skills as well as the SCANS competencies. These seven areas are identified by David Alexander, the primary author of *Links to Learning,* as "central to comprehensive, high-quality after-school programs" (National Institute on Out-of-School Time, 2005, p. 9).

- ❀ Literacy
- ❀ Science
- ❀ Math problem solving
- ❀ Arts
- ❀ Social competence
- ❀ Fitness and nutrition
- ❀ Technology (integrated into other sections)

The most effective afterschool programs offer a balance of academic support, enjoyable ways to apply or expand academic skills (enrichment), recreation, and cultural activities. When school-day subject matter, workplace skills, and recreational activities are presented as an integrated package, children gradually come to understand that education and learning are continuous processes, occurring outside the classroom as well as inside, and with practical uses at many different levels and in diverse contexts. Children who spend extended time in a program with these attributes will be well on their way to becoming independent lifelong learners. Table 12.1 maps the curriculum activities described in this chapter into one or more of the seven key learning areas; select activities from each area in order to balance children's experiences.

TABLE 12.1 Use of Seven Key Learning Areas to Balance Indoor Curriculum.

Key Learning Areas	The Project Approach	Curriculum Webs	Writing Personal Letters	Online Pen Pals	Cooking in the Classroom	Math Problem Solving	Using a Sewing Machine	Making Puppets	Making Jewelry	Tie-Dyeing	Fantasy Play	Dramatic Performance	Prop Boxes	Puppet Play	Indoor Active Games	Large Constructions	Photography
1. Literacy	X	X	X	X	X	X	X				X	X	X	X			
2. Science	X	X			X						X		X				
3. Math problem solving	X	X			X	X	X		X		X	X	X	X		X	
4. Arts	X	X					X	X	X	X	X	X	X	X			
5. Social competence	X	X	X	X							X	X	X	X	X	X	
6. Fitness and nutrition	X	X			X						X	X	X	X			
7. Technology	X	X	X	X	X	X	X	X	X	X	X	X	X	X		X	X

Source: From *Links to Learning: A Curriculum Planning Guide for After-School Programs.* Used with permission of the National Institute on Out-of-School Time.

ACTIVITIES THAT SUPPORT LITERACY LEARNING

As children begin to read, they begin to make connections between what they are reading and other parts of their lives, and they may enjoy sharing their favorite stories with other children. Soon they discover that they can write stories themselves, as well as plays and puppet shows, and they may enjoy dramatizing stories they are reading in school. Classroom teachers use literature webs to build an integrated curriculum, and school-age program staff can use the same process to help children apply concepts learned from books and other print media in a variety of interesting ways.

Creating and Using Curriculum Webs

Think of a web as a selection of related concepts. The core concept or idea (it can also be the title of a book) is written in the center of a piece of paper, and lines are drawn forming a set of spokes going away from it. The second level of ideas, or **web strands**, represents different categories of information related to the core concept. If relationships exist between various web strands, they can be connected with strand ties. Sometimes an additional level of ideas, or **strand supports**, is added to represent information or facts that add meaning or relevance to the web strands (Freedman & Reynolds, 1980). In *Webbing with Literature: Creating Story Maps with Children's Books,* author Karen Bromley (1991) explained that diagramming literature themes enhances understanding and appreciation of literature and helps children identify important issues in children's books.

Figure 12.3 shows a web of activities relating to Konigsburg's *From the Mixed-up Files of Mrs. Basil E. Frankweiler* (1973). The learning concepts illustrated in the web were identified by a parent who led the activities during a

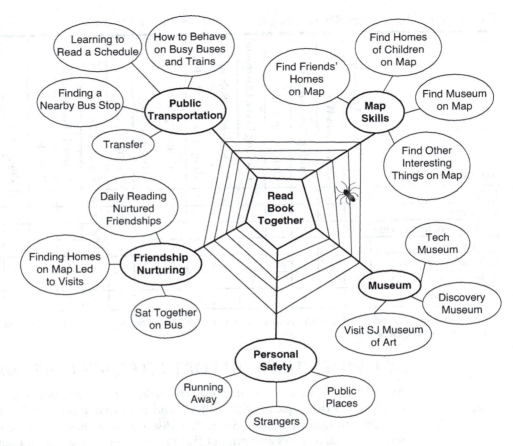

FIGURE 12.3 Sample Literature Web.

summer program for school-aged children (a detailed description of the activities is presented in Chapter 6). Activity webs such as these can be developed by children or by children and staff together as ways to extend the enjoyment of a book. In these situations, the learning concepts tend to be discovered as the children's interests lead them forward rather than being determined by an activity leader in advance of the project.

Benefits of Creating and Using Curriculum Webs

- ❀ Providing a variety of experiences that develop and support literacy skills
- ❀ Demonstrating connections between ideas
- ❀ Supporting literacy development at various levels

Connecting Geography to a Pen-Pal Activity

Making friends in other countries can be a horizon-broadening experience. Not only do children learn about distant places, but during an exchange of letters with someone their own age they will also learn details about living in those countries that they may not learn during classroom geography lessons. Discuss the idea of developing a Global Friendships project with other staff members and interested children, and then expand your inquiries to parents, friends, and professional colleagues. You probably know someone who has traveled internationally and who may be able to connect you with a teacher whose students would be interested in exchanging letters with the children in your program. Other good contacts are ministers, community college instructors, and international student advisers.

Learning to Write a Personal Letter

Once you have found a place to send the letters, locate it on a world map and help the children research and learn correct letter-writing style. E-mail is great, but nothing beats receiving a real letter with a foreign stamp. Also, learning to write an effective personal letter is a good beginning for youngsters who may one day need to know how to write a correctly formatted business letter (Powell & Davidson, 2005). Resources for format and style can be found at the end of this chapter, and Figure 12.4 shows a sample of a personal letter with a heading, salutation, and complimentary close.

Be sure everyone puts a readable return address on the letter itself, in case the envelope becomes damaged. Discuss with parents whether they would like their child to receive answers to the letters at their home address, or if you should have them use the address of your program facility.

Letters should begin with the return address and the date in the upper right-hand corner. That is called the **heading**. Start the message portion of the letter **salutation** (or greeting) with "Dear New Friend" or the like, or the name of a child if it is known, and end the letter with a **complimentary close** ("Yours truly," or "Sincerely") and the writer's name. When new at letter writing, children usually need help coming up with something to write about—the body of

FIGURE 12.4 Sample of a Friendly Letter.

123 Main Street
Anytown, US 54321
November 4, 2009

Dear Aunt Docia,

Hi, Aunt Docia! I am writing to invite you to a play that my friends from our afterschool program will be performing in two weeks. We are putting on a modern version of Hansel and Gretel, and we made all the sets and costumes ourselves in our Building and Sewing Clubs. I am playing Gretel (actually, in our play she is called Griselda), and I am very excited. Please say you will come!

How is Lucky? He is still my very favorite dog, mostly because Mom and Dad still don't think we should have a dog since we are all away from the house so much. I am looking forward to coming to visit you at Thanksgiving so that I can play with him.

Thank you for ordering greeting cards and wrapping paper. They should be here by the day of the play and I will give them to you then.

Love,
Nathan

P.S. The details of the play and how to get to the Little Theater are on the school Web site, and you can go online anytime to get them.

the letter. A group brainstorming session can be helpful to get everyone started. Encourage youngsters to suggest suitable topics and list them on a whiteboard or flip chart for others to use. A good place to start is a brief introduction to themselves and their families, the things they like to do, and what they are learning in school.

Ask each student to write a rough draft of his or her letter, and then ask another child to read it for clarity, spelling, grammar, and punctuation. Be available to review letters upon request, and be ready to help with nuances of grammar, such as plurals, possessives, and capitalization. After they have made any necessary changes to the draft, the children are ready to write a final version in blue or black ink or type it on a computer.

Now it is time to address the letters. This is often a brand-new experience and can be a bit tricky, especially if the letters are going to a country in which English is not the standard language. Sometimes house numbers appear in a different relationship to the street name than they do in the United States. Help everyone review their addresses to make certain that the house numbers, street names, cities, countries, and postal codes are all in the correct places on the envelope and copied accurately from the addresses you have received. In addition to the recipient's address, make sure there is a return address on each envelope. Provide each child with a checklist similar to the one in Figure 12.5, which shows each component in a complete letter.

A trip to the post office to weigh each letter and purchase the correct postage is the next step. In addition to individual letters, some programs like to put together a package to send to the overseas class, containing an issue of a local newspaper, information about your program and the community, and a state or national map showing the location of your community.

FIGURE 12.5   Letter-Writing Checklist.

Be sure to include all of these parts in your letter:

☐ Return address
☐ Date
☐ Salutation (greeting)
☐ Body
☐ Closing
☐ Postscript (p.s.)
☐ Signature

Have a friend or an adult review your letter and proofread it carefully to check for each of these:

☐ Correct spelling
☐ Correct capitalization
☐ Correct punctuation
☐ Correct grammar

PERSPECTIVE 12.2

Mystery Pen Pals

Sue Edwards,
Waugh Kids Care, Petaluma, CA

Our small school district afterschool program in California exchanged letters with a similar program on the East Coast. We "hooked" kids up based on their ages, and we would send letters back and forth in large envelopes—one letter for each child. Imagine the excitement when the big envelope would arrive and we'd have to wait for the afternoon program to open it up and distribute letters! We tried to send replies twice a month, and this lasted for the school year. The most exciting time was the winter holiday when they sent us a video of themselves playing on the snow-covered playground and each child introduced themselves.

We did the letter, note, or postcard writings at the end of homework time—it's an incentive to complete the homework for many children!

Used with permission.

While they are waiting for the replies to their letters, children might enjoy learning about the country where their letters are going. Provide them with a world map or globe and encourage research and discussion about the location of the country, its neighbors, and what kinds of things they might be liable to do there. In addition to online research, bring in magazine articles and geography books or make a trip to the public library to borrow books about the country. Develop a bulletin board to collect the material children locate, and encourage them to engage in mini-research projects as they encounter new topics and questions.

You can also nurture the children's interest in the project by bringing in literature, music, or news articles about the region. Letters take about a week to get to Europe from most of the United States and a week to come back, longer to the Middle East or Africa. It may be a month or more before the first answer arrives.

A map showing the location of pen pals' homes teaches geography while enhancing the pleasure of receiving letters.

However, programs that have initiated international pen pals in years past report that some of the children end up with lifelong friends, and the long initial wait is worth it. Sometimes "old-fashioned" paper letters and envelopes will start a friendship that can later continue communication through Facebook or e-mail, but in other cases the child at the other end does not have access to modern technological communication systems, and traditional letters will be the permanent means of contact.

In addition to writing to children in other countries, it can be rewarding to exchange letters with children in another program in the United States or Canada. As staff members travel to conferences and workshops in different states, encourage them to make connections with leaders from other parts of the country and offer to trade letters with their children for a year. Follow the same steps as described for the Global Friendships project, and post a U.S. and state map on which you can plot the location of the state and the community where the other afterschool program or classroom is located. By exchanging letters with programs in a different state each year, you can encourage children to learn about different parts of the nation, both by exchanging letters and by embarking on inquiry projects that are inspired by the contents of some of the letters.

Technology Tie-in: Teaching Children to Use E-mail

Making friends online can also be fun. It may be more of a challenge to encourage children to use formal writing skills in the less structured e-mail environment, but interest level is usually high when e-mail begins arriving from children who live far away. However, be very cautious about how you obtain e-mail addresses for children, and don't assume that because you find a Web site that advertises "pen pal service" that it is necessarily legitimate, although some are. One site, http://www.epals.com/, offers an online "global community" with a wide variety of activities for children to participate in and a secure e-mail system that includes translation and safety procedures. There is a cost involved to the school district or school-age program, but it receives high commendations from users. Unless you are confident of a source of e-mail addresses, it is usually best to obtain them directly from colleagues or friends. Encourage children to share their e-mails with you and with other children, and monitor both incoming and outgoing messages to ensure appropriate content and good manners (Platt, 1993).

Some Benefits of Writing Letters and Pen Pals

- ❀ Developing letter-writing skills
- ❀ Applying literacy skills to a practical activity
- ❀ Learning about children in other countries

SIMPLE SCIENCE PROJECTS

Children learn about the world by playing within it. (Here is that word *play* again!) Many simple science experiments and projects lend themselves to afterschool settings and often provide a link to concepts being taught in academic classrooms. Take children to the public library to locate books about topics of interest, many of which will suggest ways in which the ideas presented can be demonstrated. Children may suggest their own experiments by asking questions:

"I wonder if this floats?" "How can you tell a worm from a caterpillar?" "Which is harder, a diamond or a piece of glass?"

The important thing to remember is that it is the *children* who are supposed to be doing the science, not the adults. If children aren't challenged to think, they may never know how well they *can* think. If children never get a chance to be curious and track down the answers to their own questions, they may not think of themselves as independent learners and will instead depend on adults to set the agenda, pose the questions, and produce the answers (Helm & Beneke, 2003).

Staff in school-age settings can support the process of inquiry by creating an environment that nurtures exploration and by helping children locate resources, tools, and materials and by supervising and assisting wherever there is a possibility of accidents. However, the youngsters should lead the inquiry forward and wherever possible set up the experiments themselves. Otherwise it's just like being in school. Science inquiry is also a wonderful place to begin developing "projects" with children, although the project approach can be used in any area of interest (Helm & Beneke, 2003).

Here are some science experiments to get you started:

THE EGG-EATING BOTTLE

MATERIALS

An egg
A bottle with a mouth/neck slightly smaller than the egg
A piece of paper
A match (and an adult to help with the lighting)

STEPS

1. Place the egg in cold water in a pan, bring to a boil, and cook egg for about 10 minutes, until hardboiled.
2. Cool egg, then remove shell and skin.
3. Make sure that the egg will rest on the top of the bottle without falling through (a quart-sized milk bottle or wine carafe will usually work).
4. Wrinkle up the piece of paper and put it into the bottle.
5. Light the match and drop it into the bottle so that it lights the paper on fire.
6. Quickly fit the egg onto the mouth of the bottle. The egg will be sucked into the bottle!

Questions children may ask: Why does the egg get sucked in? Why did the fire go out so quickly? How do I get the egg back out of the bottle?

EXPLANATION

As the paper burns, it uses the oxygen in the air. Placed in the mouth of the bottle, the egg seals the opening so that no more air can get in to replace the oxygen. The air pressure inside the jar drops, and the egg is sucked in.

THE ERUPTING VOLCANO

Children aged 6 to 8 seem to enjoy this activity best. Older children may not find it as exciting, since similar activities sometimes show up in intermediate science curriculums. If that is the case, the fourth-, fifth-, or sixth-grade children could plan the construction of the volcano and combine the ingredients the first time, and then the younger children can play with the effects.

MATERIALS

A volcano shape made out of wire-covered **papier-mâché**, or a pile of gravel or sand
A hidden center made out of a plastic water bottle with a fairly wide top, or a narrow-topped bottle and a funnel
One-cup measuring cup
Baking soda
Vinegar
Large pan or tray to contain volcano and the mess it will make.

STEPS

1. Build the volcano with the plastic bottle in the center. (This can be as simple or as complicated a process as the children wish. In one center, the volcano construction and painting took nearly a week, resulting in a realistic model that was later incorporated into a model train board.)
2. Place volcano on the tray (or build it on a large flat surface that will contain spills).
3. Place about 1/4 cup of baking soda into the bottle, using the funnel if necessary.
4. Using the measuring cup, pour about half a cup of vinegar into the bottle, and stand back. (This process can be made more realistic by adding red food coloring to the vinegar.)

EXPLANATION

Placing baking soda and vinegar together causes a chemical reaction that results in carbon dioxide gas, or foaming bubbles. This is similar to the process that happens in real volcanic eruptions, which are caused by extremely hot gases exploding through weak spots in the earth's crust.

MAKING A MAGNETIC COMPASS

MATERIALS

Bar magnet
Steel sewing needle
About 8 to 10 inches of fine thread
Pencil or pen
Drinking glass or jelly jar
A piece of paper about 1×2 inches

STEPS

1. Thread the needle and tie a knot in one end of the thread. Leave the other end free so it can be pulled through the paper. Fold the paper in the middle to make a 1-inch square. Now spread the paper a little and push the needle through the center fold from the inside. Gently pull thread through the paper so the knot is not pulled through. Take the needle off the thread.
2. Magnetize the needle by stroking it 20 to 30 times *in the same direction* across one end of the magnet.
3. Tie the free end of the thread around the middle of the pencil and lay the pencil across the top of the glass. The length of thread should suspend the paper about an inch above the bottom of the glass.

4. Make the paper into an upside-down V and insert the needle horizontally through the center of both parts of the paper. Lower the paper inside the glass again so that it and the needle are suspended by the thread and held up by the pencil. If the needle is free to turn, it will align itself north and south.

EXPLANATION

Earth is a huge magnet. One magnetic pole is near the North Pole, and the other is near the South Pole. A magnetic field is made up of lines of force that travel in a circular pattern from one pole to the other. In the experiment, the needle turns a few times and then aligns itself north and south with the lines of force in Earth's magnetic field.

Benefits of Simple Science Projects

❀ Nurturing the process of inquiry
❀ Developing independent learning strategies
❀ Encouraging problem solving

MATH PROBLEM SOLVING

Problem solving is a valuable skill, and the application of math concepts and skills to real-world activities helps children understand their usefulness. Most school district math standards have been developed from the National Council of Teachers of Mathematics' Thirteen Curriculum Standards, listed in Figure 12.6.

Cooking is an excellent way to use math standards in the classroom and apply them in enjoyable ways. The examples of problem-solving exercises shown in Figure 12.7 emerged at the 2008 National AfterSchool Association meeting in Ft. Lauderdale during the preparation of recipes by participants in a workshop and are reproduced here to demonstrate how linking children's class-room and homework problems to real activities can take place in your program. Cooking can also be used to help support science and communication curriculum standards.

Cooking in the Classroom

One of the most motivating statements a staff member in a school-age setting can make is "Let's cook." Not only is there an obvious reward at the end of the task, but most children enjoy the social interaction inherent in the process and the opportunity to pour, measure, stir, and shape ingredients. It is not a stretch to say that cooking incorporates elements of literacy, science, math problem solving, social competence, and nutrition. If you have access to a sink and counter space, food preparation can be a daily event. Pizza, popcorn, cheese balls, soups, pies, pasta, brownies, pretzels, peanut brittle—there is no end to the cooking projects in which children can participate.

In fact, with a little instruction at the beginning of the program year, older children can plan, organize, and supervise food projects that allow younger children to participate and learn future leadership roles. Children can videotape one

FIGURE 12.6 Thirteen Curriculum Standards for Elementary Mathematics Education.

1. **Problem Solving.** Children will use problem-solving techniques to investigate situations, formulate problems based on observation, generalize solutions, and acquire confidence by using math meaningfully.

2. **Math as Communication.** Children can model situations, reflect on the mathematics, and then discuss ideas meaningfully.

3. **Math as Reasoning.** Younger children can apply deductive and inductive reasoning to a problem. Older children can make and evaluate math conjectures and arguments.

4. **Math Connections.** Children will explore problems and describe results in graphical models.

5. **Estimation.** Children can make educated guesses about quantity.

6. **Number and Number Relationships.** Children can represent numerical relationships in two-dimensional graphs.

7. **Number Systems and Number Theory.** Children can use fractions of whole numbers and decimal representations of fractions. Older children can order decimals.

8. **Computation.** Younger children can use arithmetic functions. Older children can use algebraic and geometric functions and solve proportion problems.

9. **Patterns and Functions.** Children can describe, extend, analyze, and create a wide variety of patterns, tables, graphs, and rules.

10. **Algebra.** Middle school children can turn correlation graphs into algebraic functions. Younger children can categorize objects by color, shape, and function and write simple algebraic equations to describe how many of each they have.

11. **Statistics and Probability.** Older children can systematically collect, organize, and describe data and use them to construct charts and graphs and then make comparisons. Younger children can tally the occurrences of an event and make a simple bar graph.

12. **Geometry and Spatial Sense.** Children can comprehend shapes and relationships in space.

13. **Measurement.** Children can use different systems of measurement in practical applications.

Source: Adapted with permission from *Curriculum and Evaluation Standards for School Mathematics,* by National Council of Teachers of Mathematics, 1989, Reston, VA: Author. All rights reserved.

another preparing dishes and then edit the tape and dub in music, printed recipes, and interviews to create a "cooking show" that can then be shown to other children or parents.

Entire meals, such as a harvest or Passover feast, a formal evening dinner for parents, "stone soup," or just plain lunch, can be made by school-agers, especially during the long days of winter and spring breaks or summer vacation when there is plenty of time to spend in preparation and cooking. Food beyond regular snacks can be purchased with money earned through fund-raising projects, included as curriculum supplies in the program budget, or donated in turn by parents.

Chapter 11 describes the benefits of developing a healthy snack program as part of a health and fitness curriculum. Refer to that chapter for a list of needed equipment and materials. The ideas in this chapter primarily relate to extending the cooking curriculum to practice arithmetic skills and math problem solving.

FIGURE 12.7   Examples of Cooking-Related Problem-Solving Exercises.

Print or type these questions on 4 × 6 cards. Decorate them with illustrations and laminate for use in games.

How would you alter this recipe if you need 9 dozen cookies? How about 2 dozen? What kinds of mathematical challenges does that offer? (*Hint:* Proportions are important.)

What calculations would you need to make if you only had metric measuring cups and spoons to work with?

This recipe should be baked at 375°F for 11–13 minutes. What temperature would you set the oven to if you are baking it in London while on vacation—and the oven is marked in Celsius?

There is a very specific proportion of baking powder, baking soda, and acid that is used to raise quick breads, cakes, and cookies. How would we figure out what that proportion is?

How much flour and how much oil do you combine to make a roux (base for cream sauce)? How much roux will it take to thicken a cup of liquid? Where would we find this information? How could we test it?

How much cornstarch will it take to thicken a cup of gravy?

Your recipe, taken from the Internet, tells you to bake your casserole at 220°F. Your oven is calibrated in Fahrenheit with 50° increments. Where should you set it?

You're visiting your aunt in Canada and plan to make her some cookies as a surprise. Your recipe calls for 1/2 cup of butter, but the measuring equipment in her cupboard is labeled in mL (milliliters). How will you know which measurement to use?

If it takes turkey 24 hours per 5 pounds to thaw in the refrigerator, how long should your mother allow for an 8-pound turkey to thaw?

If we decide to cook a turkey this year for our harvest festival, and the butcher tells us to cook the turkey for 20 minutes per pound, how long should we cook a 12-pound turkey?

The brownie recipe calls for a 9 × 10 square pan, but we only have an 8" × 10" and a 10" × 12" pan. Which one of those two should we use?

Teaching Food-Preparation Skills

Learning to do simple tasks in the kitchen, such as separating an egg, grating cheese, or popping popcorn, can be the focus of a whole cooking activity. Likewise, children can conduct experiments with different types of foods, such as toasting whole wheat, white, and rye bread to see which takes the longest (Di'Amico & Drummond, 1996). Making predictions and recording what happens is a simple way to engage children's problem-solving skills. Make foods from scratch that are usually purchased ready-made, and ask children why certain foods are added in a particular order, or help them relate physical changes to temperature or combinations of ingredients. Shake whipping cream in jars until it becomes butter, and spread the butter on hot slices of bread made from flour that the children have ground themselves (Bumgarner, 1997). Mix cereal squares together with pretzels, nuts, and Worcestershire sauce and then toast to create a crispy snack mix.

Take things one at a time. At the beginning of the year, develop cooking activities that teach just one skill, such as hand washing, cutting, measuring, or safety rules such as "stay behind the yellow tape on the floor when a staff member is using the fryer." Keep a record of which children have participated in each activity and who has been checked out with each safety rule and skill. As older children become proficient at washing vegetables, using sharp knives, or measuring dry and wet ingredients, ask them to supervise a younger child who has been trained but is not yet ready to use the skill when alone.

Here are recipes that have received thumbs-up from school-agers:

HAWAIIAN PIZZA

DOUGH:

> 1 tablespoon (package) dry yeast
> 1 cup warm water
> 2 tablespoons vegetable oil
> 1/4 to 1/2 teaspoon salt
> 3 to 4 cups flour

TOPPING:

> 8 ounce jar pizza sauce
> Sliced mushrooms
> Ham slices, finely chopped (or use vegetarian ham)
> Pineapple chunks
> 1 or 2 cups grated cheese
> Grated Parmesan cheese

Wash hands and have all ingredients ready. In a medium-sized bowl, dissolve yeast in warm water. Allow to stand for 10 minutes to start bubbling, and then stir well. (To speed up the fermenting process, you can add up to 1 tablespoon sugar or honey to the warm water.) Stir in remaining ingredients, adding just enough flour to form a stiff dough, one that requires your hands to get it mixed and pressed into a ball. Knead dough on a floured surface for about 5 minutes until warm and elastic. Rinse the bowl in hot water if necessary to remove flour residue, dry with a paper towel, and then spray with vegetable oil. Turn ball of dough around in the bowl to coat, then cover with a towel and let it rise in a warm place about 1½ hours, or until it has doubled in size. Punch ball down and divide into two pieces. Roll out each piece and place on a greased 12–14-inch pizza pan or cookie sheet and push to the edges, forming a rim around the outside. Brush dough with vegetable oil. (All or half of the dough can also be frozen for use another day.)

To make pizza, spread with prepared pizza sauce (you can buy that in the supermarket or make it from scratch from a recipe book) and either the topping listed above or something different (other favorites are browned and drained ground beef or sausage, vegetables, sliced mushrooms or olives, and pepperoni). Top with 1 or 2 cups grated mozzarella cheese. Bake at 425°F for 15 to 20 minutes, until crust is golden brown. Cool slightly and cut into wedges. Enjoy!

Note: To incorporate math problem-solving skills into this cooking activity, ask the children to double or triple the recipe. How much flour will they need? How much cheese and tomato sauce? What if they only have a 10-inch pan? Can they figure out how to make just enough pizza dough for that sized pan without wasting any ingredients? Ask similar questions for each of the following recipes.

BERRY PARFAITS (see photo on p. 284)

For each parfait:

> One 6-ounce plastic tumbler. Layer into the tumbler, starting with yogurt and ending with fruit:

Lay out taco ingredients, so everyone can participate in food preparation.

Vanilla low-fat yoghurt
Low-fat granola
Fresh or frozen berries (raspberries, strawberries, boysenberries, blueberries)
Hand out spoons. Enjoy!

TACOS

For each taco:

1 taco shell; spoon into prepackaged shell each of the following:
2 tablespoon lean ground beef, fried and drained (by the teacher for younger children), or black beans
2 tablespoon chopped tomatoes
2 tablespoon lettuce torn into small pieces
2 tablespoon grated cheese
Several kinds of hot sauce and salsa to sample

QUESADILLAS

For each quesadilla:

2 whole wheat tortillas
2 tablespoons grated cheese
2 tablespoons finely chopped chicken (cooked in advance by teacher, or precooked in packages)
2 tablespoons finely chopped tomatoes
1 tablespoon thinly sliced or chopped lettuce

Sprinkle cheese, chicken, tomatoes, and lettuce on one tortilla. Top with the second tortilla. Grill and cut into wedges. (Early in the year, or for younger children, a staff member should grill the meat and the quesadillas.) These can be cooked in the microwave, using only one tortilla and folding it over; they are not crisp.

HOT DOG BEAN SOUP

1 cup navy beans, soaked overnight in 8 cups of water
1 large onion, finely chopped
2 or 3 carrots, diced
2 stalks celery, diced
1 teaspoon salt
2 tablespoons molasses
1 teaspoon mustard
1 tablespoon flour
1 cup hot water
3 to 6 nitrate-free chicken or turkey sausages, sliced

Drain beans and cover with fresh boiling water. Add onion, carrots, celery, and seasonings and cook over low heat until beans are tender, at least 2 hours. (This can be safely done in a slow cooker; add more water as necessary to keep from sticking.) Remove 1/2 cup beans from pan and squash them into a creamy texture with a spoon. Stir in flour and 1 cup hot water until smooth. Return flour/bean mixture to pan, add molasses and mustard, and stir until blended. Continue cooking until soup thickens, about 5 to 10 minutes. Add sausages, heat through, and serve on a cold wintry day. (Serve soup to vegetarian staff and children before adding sausages.)

Cooking can be a very informal activity in the afterschool program, in which sharing, inclusion, and cultural exchanges are facilitated by eating the resulting meal in a family-style setting with casual conversation. It can also be a precursor to snack time, or a full-blown "club" or selected activity. As has been shown, cooking activities can also be used to demonstrate mathematical or scientific concepts, but that takes a reasonable amount of thought and preparation on the part of the adult guiding the activity. If one of your program goals is raising academic standards, spend some time each week reviewing the math or science standards being taught to each grade represented by your children, and during staff meetings develop a plan of cooking activities that can be used to support those standards.

Other Activities That Strengthen Math Problem-Solving Skills

In addition to cooking, there are many enjoyable games and activities that can develop mathematical problem-solving and spatial concepts. Here are just a few:

PUZZLES. Browse the Internet or old puzzle books for classic math puzzles to solve and post them periodically for group challenges. Example: Five people are lined up in order from tallest to shortest. Jorge is ahead of Cam. Myra is behind Kim. Ben is the tallest. Cam is not ahead of Myra. What is the correct order? Help the children think through the facts that are known, and use manipulatives—blocks or stuffed animals—to represent each child. (Answer: Ben, Kim, Myra, Jorge, Cam)

CONSTRUCTIONS. Make boxes and other shapes from cardboard. Collect several small gift boxes, and then carefully take them apart with scissors. Using paper marked into squares, duplicate the shapes of the boxes in different sizes and fold them into box shapes, holding them together with tape. Rulers can help as the sizes get larger, and calculators can help children figure out the relationships between differently sized edges as they get bigger. Once the children get good at cubes and three-dimensional rectangles, suggest that they make "rocket ships" by affixing a cone to the end of a paper towel roll. Figuring out what shape the paper needs to be to curve into a cone helps children understand geometric concepts.

INTERACTIVE ONLINE PROBLEM SOLVING. Several Web sites offer math problem-solving challenges to children that include suggested strategies and hints. For example, on Scholastic's Math Maven's Mysteries Web site, children are presented with a lunchtime scenario in which children are discussing their food selections, good and bad. The task is to use logic to match each student with his or her favorite food based on comments that they make. AfterSchool KidzMath utilizes stories, games, and activities to reinforce number relationships, measurement, and geometry. While the primary program depends on a set of 10 or 20 storybooks that would need to be purchased by your program, interactive games are also available on the Web site, such as Funny Bug, in which children are invited to roll a die, add up the numbers, and draw different parts of the bug based on the total which is then located on a chart. Exploratorium's Math Explorer presents a variety of scenarios and math activities for older children. One great example is Breaking the Mayan Code, in which children are challenged to decipher a page from an ancient Mayan book by combining mathematical skill with logic and trial-and-error investigation. In addition to figuring out what the Mayan document means, children learn how the Mayan system of counting is similar to or different from our own and how closely Mayan beliefs were tied to their understanding of mathematics. All of these online resources are listed at the end of the chapter.

Benefits of Math Problem Solving

❀ Gaining experience solving math problems using number relationships, estimation, computation, and measurement
❀ Learning to work with others to solve problems
❀ Learning to see mathematical skills and concepts in contexts that include cooking, constructing objects, human relationships, reading, writing, speaking, and listening

CREATIVE ARTS

Learning experiences in the creative arts can be provided in a variety of ways. Just about any opportunity that you can provide for children to explore artistic media such as paint, clay, pens, pencils, textiles, metal, music, dance, photography, or theater will offer new experiences and different ways of seeing the world, expressing their feelings and ideas, and appreciating the expressions of others. Exactly which art forms you choose to teach will depend somewhat on the interests and preferences of your staff members and volunteers, although children's interests should also guide you in seeking out leaders in areas in which local expertise is lacking.

Learning to Use a Sewing Machine

Here is a "real" activity that many children enjoy and very few learn at home. Simple straight-sew and zigzag sewing machines may be found in garages, basements, and attics. Ask parents and staff if you can borrow some for your program. (Many people will freely give them to you.) If no one in the program knows how to use a sewing machine, ask someone from a local fabric store to show you, or invite a member of the retired community to come and give sewing lessons. You can usually find people affiliated with a local quilting guild, craft bazaar, or 4-H club who would enjoy the opportunity to introduce children to their hobby. Following simple safety instructions, children (and staff) can quickly learn how to thread the machine and practice sewing straight seams. In just a few hours, most children are ready to make something "real."

Easy first projects include bean bags, shopping/book bags, simple curtains, furniture slipcovers, covers for tables to turn them into puppet theaters or forts, and tablecloths or sets of napkins for special occasions. These require only the simplest of construction techniques and are satisfying to make because they each have a function. Many children enjoy exploring the "art" of sewing, creating quilts, machine embroidery, or combining several techniques to make wall hangings or pictures to frame.

After completing several projects with straight seams, children who want more challenging projects might enjoy visiting a fabric store and selecting simple craft patterns. Most stores include directions for making decorator pillows, simple stuffed toys, Christmas stockings, or other whimsical items. Collect fabric scraps, thread, buttons, scissors, etc. by sending notes home with children, or ask their classroom teachers to request donations. (Teachers may have suggestions of their own; children in one school-age program sewed simple skirts, capes, and hats for a school play.) After the initial learning phase, make sewing projects a free-choice option.

Benefits of Learning to Use a Sewing Machine

- ❀ Learning to following instructions or patterns
- ❀ Developing orderly steps and sequences
- ❀ Using the medium to express creative ideas

Making Puppets

Making puppets is a very popular activity, because children know that once the puppets are finished, there are many different ways to play with them. There are many different kinds of puppets, and children of all ages can make some kind of puppet to enjoy. Learning to make and use puppets is sometimes part of college children's literature class curricula, but if you are not familiar with different types of puppet construction, locate a book at the public library or search the Web, collect the needed materials, and follow the directions. Several books and Web sites are listed in the resources sections at the end of this chapter.

With a group of children, practice making stick puppets, paper bag puppets, or sock puppets. For older children, introduce papier-mâché techniques and suggest that they make the heads of characters from a favorite story. Ask your sewing machine experts to make simple bodies for hand puppets. Facial features and clothing can be cut out of fabric scraps and glued on. See the Dramatic Play section in this chapter for puppet play activities.

Benefits of Making Puppets

- ✿ Working creatively with open-ended materials
- ✿ Learning to work with others to share materials and ideas
- ✿ Designing one or more puppets to match a specific story or book
- ✿ Becoming familiar with several different types of puppets

Making Jewelry

With every passing school year there seems to be a new friendship bracelet, necklace, or pin in style. Establishing a jewelry-making center to allow children to construct the fashion of the year can lead to the creation of more complex jewelry projects. Some youngsters will enjoy spending several afternoons threading beads, tying knots, or twisting plastic strands to decorate their ankles, wrists, necks, and clothing or those of their friends. Younger children may be content to dye macaroni with food coloring, threading it on string, but older children will be more interested in colored wooden or plastic beads, shrinkable colored plastic, or tying repetitive macramé-like knots to form their adornments. Provide plenty of beading supplies, including fasteners, wire, pliers, and boxes with several compartments for storing materials. Make earrings, necklaces, and friendship bracelets. Be to sure have one adult at the table to provide a helping hand, demonstrate the safe use of scissors and wire cutters, etc. Consider asking a local craftsperson or jewelry instructor to come in and give a demonstration. Teen magazines are good sources of craft ideas, or you can also invite junior high or high school students to lead jewelry-making workshops. Collect supplies at yard sales and flea markets, and ask children's parents for their discards. Previously worn jewelry with broken catches or broken chains with working clasps can be taken apart and restrung. Some younger children will even find the process of organizing the found materials into egg cartons or muffin tins an enjoyable occupation. Some programs have sold repaired and re-crafted jewelry as a fund-raising project.

Benefits of Making Jewelry

- ✿ Developing and using imagination and creativity
- ✿ Learning to use tools and a variety of materials
- ✿ Possibly developing an interest in learning more complex jewelry-making skills
- ✿ Learning skills to make gifts for others

Tie-Dyeing

Youngsters will come to an activity table to tie-dye just about anything—shirts, jeans, socks, sheets, pillow cases, scarves, capes, or hats. Tie-dyeing is fun, creative, and very easy. Children can create unique designs and colors by tying fabric with rubber bands or string and immersing in one, two, three, or more dye colors. Just make sure that the fabric contains at least 60% cotton or other dyeable fiber. Materials that are 100% polyester will not hold the dye and will bleed out during washing.

Manufacturers of fabric dye provide detailed directions on their product packages or Web sites, but here are the basics:

The point of tie dyeing is to prevent the dye from reaching the fabric in certain parts of the garment. Anywhere that the dye can't reach will remain the color of the original fabric. Once children understand how it works, they can create beautiful gradations of color from bright to light. They do this by folding the fabric, tying it with string, wrapping rubber bands around it, etc. and then soaking it repeatedly in a dye bath, sometimes allowing it to dry out, refolding and retying the fabric a second or even third time, and dying it again in a different color. The folding and tying can be done a day or two before the actual dyeing process takes place, although tie-dyeing one garment ahead of time to demonstrate the process helps children understand what it is they are trying to accomplish.

Prepare powdered or liquid dye according to package directions. Most dyes today are mixed with cold tap water and do not require long simmering over a heat source like they did in our grandmothers' days. However, you still need to wear protective gloves to keep your hands from being discolored and sore. Some dye manufacturers recommend that the garments be prewashed and then soaked in a sodium carbonate solution to make the dye adhere better to the fabric (Burch, 2008). Prepared dye concentrates can be stored in glass jars for several days. Have a few large sinks and containers available before beginning the actual dyeing, as you will need one for each color of dye and one for rinsing.

Once the garments are ready, place them in containers of dye one or two at a time for at least 15–20 minutes. The longer the garments are in the dye mixture, the darker and richer the colors will be. Remove from the dye bath and rinse according to package directions, usually in cold running water. Wring out the garment until the water runs clear.

If someone wants to dye a garment one solid color rather than tie it, be sure that the garment easily fits into the dye bath with room to stir it around; tied garments take up less space.

Benefits of Tie Dyeing

- ❀ Developing an awareness of color and design
- ❀ Working collaboratively with others
- ❀ Completing a multipart task

DRAMATIC ACTIVITIES: FANTASY PLAY, STAGED PLAYS, PROP BOXES, AND PUPPETS

Louisa May Alcott and the Brontë sisters wrote their first stories during long winter evenings. Long winter days at the school-age child care center can also be productive, if staff and children work together to create dramatic productions. (So can long summer days, actually.)

Fantasy Play

One way to pique children's interest in drama is to create dramatic play areas suited to the school-age child. Diverging from household settings usually seen in preschools, this area may have different furnishings at different times throughout the year, and boxes of theatrical props can be developed that suggest certain themes. An ice cream shop can be created with ice cream scoops, a box of cones, containers of toppings such as nuts and cherries, aprons, hats, and materials to make menus. Children can serve imaginary ice cream made out of balls of pink, white, or brown yarn or prepare real ice cream snacks for their friends. A restaurant **prop box** could contain tablecloths and napkins, cutlery, flowers, salt and pepper shakers, etc. Food packages and posters help identify the type of food served—e.g., ethnic, health food, fast food, pizza. Children can develop a service station with a box of work clothes and hats, oilcans and rags, paper towels, plastic spray bottles, miscellaneous tools, and posters from local garages or tire stores. Children exploring these materials may be able to track down one or two real tires to work on with a lug wrench. Office prop boxes can be made from plastic or cardboard file boxes purchased from office supplies or stationery stores. They may contain file folders, envelopes and pads of paper, pens, pencils and holders, clear plastic tape and dispensers, a telephone, staplers, stamps, hole punches, etc. Larger objects, such as telephones and a computer, could be permanently situated in a corner of the classroom, where they can be used by children throughout the program day.

This realistic dramatic play offers valuable opportunities for children to interact with others, exercise their imaginations, share and take turns, and try out new roles (Humphrey, 2001). They can also integrate their imaginary play with other activities taking place in the program. For example, the "office workers" might enjoy typing thank-you letters to volunteers or designing fund-raising posters. "Restaurant workers" could provide a special meal for Valentine's Day or other celebration. "Service station mechanics" might offer to check the brakes or lubricate their friends' bicycles before a ride around the neighborhood. Ideally, these ideas would flow naturally out of the play and be initiated by other children rather than by the adult staff.

Benefits of Fantasy Play

- ❀ Interacting with others
- ❀ Exercising their imaginations
- ❀ Sharing and taking turns
- ❀ Trying out new roles

Staging a Play

Children's use of the dramatic play area may go no further than enjoyable hours spent in fantasy play, but it may also lead to someone suggesting, "Let's put on a play." Plays can be staged with memorized parts or with some children reading the script and other children acting it out or operating puppets. Some effective plays are taken directly from stories children already know, while others are made up by the children. Some children are content to use only the costumes and props provided by the program, but others get quite elaborate and bring in lots of materials to set the scene.

Dramatic ventures may be spur of the moment, and they need only amuse the children who wish to participate in them or observe—they don't need to be very complicated at all. Sometimes, however, they may turn into big productions, and that, for the most part, is okay, too. Some program staff members, staying up all night sewing costumes or painting the night before a play, might think things got out of hand (and they probably *did* if the adults are doing the costumes instead of the youngsters!), but once it is all over they are usually ready to start again.

Benefits of Staging a Play

❀ Learning to construct scenery, costumes, scripts, and roles
❀ Understanding the purpose of written dialogue (scripts)
❀ Working with others on a variety of tasks
❀ Learning to give and receive positive critiques

Prop Boxes

Some school-age programs have taken prop boxes beyond the realm of merely suggesting dramatic play activities and have developed interesting collections of materials that are portable (for taking to the park, for example) and easy to store in cupboards or on shelves (Barbour, 2002). For example, the Butte, Montana, Coordinated Child Care Council lists 11 afterschool prop boxes that may be checked out from their agency:

Large Prop Boxes

Each prop box has a different theme and comes complete with games, activities, props, books and everything you will need to have fun with that theme! You may check out a prop box anytime you would like and keep it for up to a month. They're great life-savers when you are running low on ideas or are just looking for something different for the kids! And, there is no charge—so please take advantage of these resources anytime!

After School 1—Fun for outside games and play. Box contains parachute and sack race bags.
After School 2—Rainy day weather? Play with these games inside. Leap Pad, Marble Madness, and much more.
After School 3—Prop box full of manipulative games. There are magnets, marbles, games, and experiments.
After School Bugs/Insects—Explore bugs and insects with this box full of interactive fun bug stuff. Everything from bug counters and puzzles to magnifying glasses and bug catchers.
After School Games 1—Great for an inside day. Games for all ages. Traditional favorites and new ones, too.
After School Games2—This box contains games for all ages. Includes Bingo, marble races, and Battleship.
After School Play-Doh—Everything you can imagine for Play-Doh fun! You just provide the Play-Doh.
After School Science Exploration—Ever wonder how things work? Come and check out this box to get the children involved in solving those questions.
After School Outside 1—This box is a must have for sunny days spent outside. Parachute play with rings, ropes, and scooters.
After School Parachute—Large 20 foot parachute, race sacks, plenty of scarves to twirl around; this is an all around fun outdoor box for summer.
After School Puppets—Multicultural people puppets, zoo and farm animal puppets along with a portable puppet stand make up this fun box.

Source: *Used with permission of Butte 4-C's Community Coordinated Child Care. www.butte4-cs.org.*

The use of prop boxes enhances curriculum both indoors and out and offers individualized choices of activities for the children. They are especially valuable for programs that must re-create their environment every day—such as school-age sites in cafeterias, in gymnasiums, at parks, or in other shared space—and can reduce behavior problems caused by a lack of interesting things to do.

The director of one school-age program I visited uses prop boxes to as a way to extend a portable classroom into the outdoors. Children are invited to select a prop box and take it outside with them. There they can set up a "mini-classroom" using supplies and equipment contained in the box. Interesting props for outside boxes include magnifying glasses (for looking at insects, leaves, or toes); small gardening shovels and rakes; bats, balls, and mitts; beanbags and folding targets; bubble solution and straws; and modeling clay.

Select containers and supplies that are durable and require little or no maintenance, and keep them lightweight and easily accessible. Great prop boxes can be made from cardboard file carriers with finger holes at each end or from clear plastic housewares boxes with tight-fitting lids. Brainstorm ideas with children and staff, and remember to keep the contents simple to make them cost effective. Good sources for prop material include flea markets, service club stores, parent donations, and a variety of community resources, such as hospitals, fire departments, post offices, and police departments.

A special kind of prop box I have seen is known to the children as the "five o'clock box." About that time of the day, explains program director Maureen O'Hanlin, some children's parents start arriving to take them home, and the need arises to clean up the projects that have occupied children's attention that day. Before the five o'clock box system was invented, program staff had to choose between asking the children who stayed the latest to put away material left out by children who left earlier or make them wait for their parents in a neat, but boring, room (personal communication, 2008).

Their creative solution to this dilemma was to engage everyone in cleaning up before the majority of parents arrived, usually between 4:30 and 5:00 p.m. Then, when the room was returned to order for the next day, they would bring out the five o'clock boxes. These are plastic boxes of small games and objects that are interesting to play with but do not make a big mess. Two or three children can take out a box together, and the individual games can be quickly returned to the box as each youngster leaves. Examples of good materials for five o'clock boxes are string and diagrams for playing cat's cradle, plastic handheld puzzles, miniature Etch A Sketch, travel games in Ziploc bags, decks of cards and card game books (also books with word search, crossword, or sudoku puzzles). Colored pencils and small coloring books, magnifying glasses and tiny objects to magnify, and magnets and metal objects all can be packaged into interesting pastimes for those last few minutes of the day. Putting colored inventory dots on each game or object that corresponds with the box from which it came simplifies clean-up when parents arrive. Figure 12.8 provides some other prop box curriculum ideas.

Benefits of Prop Boxes

- ❀ Exploring a variety of different activities
- ❀ Developing new skills and learning new ways to use existing skills
- ❀ Making good use of short blocks of time
- ❀ Adapting to different circumstances

FIGURE 12.8 Ideas for Prop Boxes.

QUIET BOX	MUSIC BOX
Books to read	Multicultural instruments
Blanket	Tape recorder and cassette tapes
Walkman	Ribbons for dancing
Cassette story tapes	Earphones
Word searches	Material for making instruments
Crossword puzzles	Rhythm instruments

GAMES BOX	WRITING/DRAWING BOX
Small jigsaw puzzles	Writing paper and pens
Handheld computer games	Rulers, French curve, templates
String and cat's cradle instructions	Colored pencils
Jacks and ball	Crayons
Bag of marbles	Felt pens

BLOCK BOX	HOMEWORK BOX
Cars	Dictionary
Animals	Atlas
Carpet	Pencil sharpener
Foam blocks	Ruler
Colored unit blocks	Erasers

ART BOX	BEAUTY BOX
Beads and string	Curling iron
Art supplies	Rollers
Table top easel	Blow dryer
Laptop easel	Mirrors
Donated plastic containers with tops	Clips
Watercolors	Hot rollers
Origami paper and idea book	Hair products

Source: Based on O'Hanlin, 1997.

❀ Creating themes and collecting material
❀ Cleaning up takes little time

Puppet Play

This activity has elements of literacy and social competence, but it is a natural outcome of puppet construction, which logically belongs in the creative arts. Vida Zuljevic (2005), a teacher of Russian bilingual kindergarten and a proponent of puppet theater for children, wrote, "For centuries, people of diverse cultures have created and used puppets, finding an almost magical power in their capacity for creating open, honest, and trustworthy communication between the puppeteer and the audience" (p. 37).

In her work with children in Bosnia, Croatia, Germany, and the United States, Ms. Juljevic has found has found that "no matter what culture children belong to or what language they speak, they play with puppets freely, using their hands, thoughts, language, and feelings, and they develop lasting friendships that are beneficial for their further development" (Zuljevic, 2005, p. 37). Sometimes the children who like to make puppets are not the same children who want to put on puppet shows, so there may need to be some group decision making about who "owns" a puppet once it is made. Some of the puppet builders might agree to make a selection of characters that will remain in the center for others to use in their productions. Puppets are great for fantasy play, so don't restrict their use to formal presentations. Some children talk to the puppets and develop complex dialogs with puppet characters. For them, an audience would only get in the way. A box of puppets and a small puppet theater that sits on a table can be the source of a great many hours of entertainment.

Benefits of Puppet Play

- ❀ Developing an appreciation of literature
- ❀ Enhancing creative thinking and expressions of feelings
- ❀ Improving self-confidence
- ❀ Drawing connections between different subject areas

FITNESS AND NUTRITION: ORGANIZED ACTIVE GAMES

Chapter 11 discusses concerns about the health and fitness of American children and identifies a variety of ways in which fitness and nutrition activities can be woven into the afterschool curriculum. In addition to those activities, organized indoor games are excellent vehicles to get children moving, even on days when weather does not permit outdoor play (and, as Bernie DeKoven—also known as Major Fun—points out in Perspective 12.1, they have lots of other benefits as well). Be sure to keep ideas fresh, and ask the children to request games that they especially like to play. This is a good opportunity for older staff members to teach children games that they once enjoyed at birthday parties or family gatherings. With the gradual disappearance of daily physical education sessions in elementary schools, many modern children have never played any of these games before. Written instructions for many indoor games can be found in public libraries or on the Internet under "party games" or "children's games." Other sources are listed in the resources at the end of this chapter.

Indoor Hide-and-Seek

Since hiding places large enough for children are hard to come by in most classroom settings, the child who is It hides his or her eyes while each child hides an object instead. The objects must be things that will be recognized by It when found, such as stuffed animals, trucks, blocks, etc. and must be in plain sight when It gets close to them. The children will need to set ground rules about where they stand while their object is being located so that there is an element of reason in the dash to "base." Certain areas may need to be placed off-limits before play begins, and the children may want to set a limit on how many objects can be hidden in each round of play.

The leader of the game (not necessarily an adult) begins each round by asking each child to show the person whose turn it is to be It the object that he or she will be hiding. All other parts of the game, including counting to 100 (or some other agreed-upon number) and running for base, are the same as in the traditional outdoor version of hide-and-seek.

Follow-up Activities

Variation 1: It hides designated objects around the room. Then the rest of the players have to retrieve the hidden objects, announce their find, and race It to base.

Variation 2: Instead of one person seeking the hidden objects, designate just one person to hide one object, and everyone looks for it and then races the person who finds it to base.

Variation 3: Set a kitchen timer that ticks for a specific amount of time, such as 5 or 10 minutes. Everyone tries to find the timer before it rings.

Variation 4: This is called "four corners." All the children crowd into the corners of the room (depending on the arrangement of your center, there may be more than four corners). The person who is It hides his or her eyes during this process and then calls out a name and races the called person to base.

Leapfrog

Players line up, one behind another. The first player squats down, knees bent, hands on knees, head down. The second player now places his hands on the first player's shoulders, spreads his or her knees wide, and jumps over the first player. The third player jumps over the first two, one at a time. The fourth player jumps over the first three, and so on. When all players are squatting in a row, the last player leaps over all of them, and the first one begins again. This can continue all over the room, for as long as the players wish.

Duck, Duck, Goose

This is a very old game, but it seems to be just as enjoyable to primary-aged children today as it was in our grandparents' time. Older children have a tendency to tap one another's heads a bit too hard, and the running around the circle sometimes becomes a chase across the play yard. Allow older children to participate at your own discretion and with clear guidelines. It is a good idea to set a timer for a designated length of time before beginning this game and the two variations, because they have no natural end point.

1. Ask 10 or more children to sit in a circle facing one other. These are the "ducks."
2. You begin by being the "fox."
3. Slowly walk around the outside of the circle, gently touching the top of each child's head while saying "duck" each time you do so. After you have gone around the circle once or twice, select a "goose." This is done by touching one of the ducks' heads and saying "goose!"
4. The goose quickly jumps up and chases the fox (you) around the circle, trying to tag you before you can get to the spot where the goose was just sitting. If the fox succeeds in taking the goose's place he or she is now safe

and the goose becomes the fox. If the fox is tagged while running from the goose, he or she must start the game again.

Follow-up Activities

Duck, Duck, Goose reinvented: This variation on Duck, Duck, Goose is played in pairs, which means each participant will move around a lot more than in the traditional game.

What you need:

❀ Masking tape
❀ Chalk

What you do:

1. Using the masking tape and chalk, mark two parallel lines about 10 to 15 feet apart. The space outside those lines is designated as the "safety zone."
2. Each child stands facing a partner in the center of the space marked by the lines.
3. They take turns tapping each other on the shoulder, saying either "duck" or "goose."
4. Nothing happens with "duck." But when one child says "goose," that player has to turn around and run toward the safety zone before being tagged by his partner.
5. If the second player tags the first before the safety zone is reached, you both return to the center and the tagger starts the next round.
6. If the chasing player is unable to tag the player who said "goose" before reaching the safety zone, the chasing player starts the next round.

Source: Activity written by Rae Pica, children's activity specialist. Used with permission.

Drop the Handkerchief:

1. Form a circle with the children holding hands. One child stays outside the circle.
2. The child on the outside of the circle skips around the circle, touching each one of the children gently with the handkerchief while singing this song: "A tisket, a tasket, A green and yellow basket, I wrote a letter to my love, But on the way, I dropped it."
3. As the child reaches the last line in the song, he or she drops the handkerchief behind one of the players, who in turns picks it up and tries to catch the first child before that child can run around the ring and jump into the vacant place.
4. As soon as this happens, the first player joins the ring.
5. It is now the turn of the second child to "drop the handkerchief."

Freeze Dance (Statues)

Twelve-year-old Deborah described this game to me: "Someone (It) turns on some music and everyone dances around. Then the person who's It turns off the music and everyone freezes. Anyone who moves is out. The last person to be out is It. No one wants to be out because they like to dance, so everyone works really hard to stay still, even though they're usually laughing so hard they can't."

Here is another way to explain how the game works: Select a student or staff member to be the music monitor. You can use any source of music that can be started and stopped repeatedly: a piano or guitar; radio; or CD, tape, or MP3 player with external speakers. Select the music and begin playing, stopping the music every minute or so. Children dance any way they wish (safely) until the music stops, at which time they must "freeze," or stop moving. The music monitor looks around to see if anyone was still moving when the music stopped. These children are out and can help the monitor watch the remaining children. The last one still "in" is the winner.

Benefits of Active Indoor Games

- ❀ Promoting healthy, active movement
- ❀ Helping develop listening skills
- ❀ Developing social skills
- ❀ Encouraging enjoyment of group activities

TECHNOLOGY

Technology is such a basic part of modern life that we would be remiss if we did not offer youngsters opportunities to use tools of all kinds. It is generally agreed that being knowledgeable about and comfortable with industrial and computer technology are critical skills for employment, and these skills are best achieved when we use technology as a tool for learning rather than teaching it as a separate subject (Harvard Family Research Project, 2004; Murnane & Levy, 1996; National Institute on Out-of-School Time, 2005). By incorporating elements of technology into academic enrichment activities you can not only harness the valuable contribution of the specific tool—be it an electric drill, digital microscope, computer, digital camera, or scanner—but you can also increase the interest level of most children, who find technological equipment to be interesting and motivating.

Integrating Technology Into Afterschool Programs

When we hear the term *technology* today, most of us immediately think of computer technology. However, industrial technology also provides youngsters with opportunities to develop competencies and skills that will help them in the workplace and in their lives.

Industrial Technology As school budgets shrink, many districts eliminate industrial technology classes such as wood shop, metal shop (including welding), auto mechanics, and auto body. It is probably not feasible to offer youngsters the opportunity to weld or work on cars, but you can certainly teach simple carpentry and basic tool skills. You can also buy small rocket ships in kit form. Children can work in pairs to assemble the rockets, decorate them, and then see whose flies the highest. Making kites from newspaper or butcher paper is another fairly easy technology project (see Chapter 13 for instructions).

Middle school and high school engineering classes have been constructing milk carton boats, balsa wood racing cars, and "better mousetraps" for years. Such activities teach cause and effect as well as a variety of basic physics and engineering concepts. Educator Walter McKenzie developed a Build a Better Mousetrap

Web site and invited classrooms from all over the world to participate in the development of inventions that met certain criteria, which changed from project to project. Many of the inventions have been archived on the Internet (see Internet Resources at the end of the chapter) and could be a source of great ideas for integrating industrial technology in your program.

Other ways an afterschool program can integrate industrial technology include the following:

❀ Accumulating a collection of tools, both hand powered and electric, that can be used with wood, cardboard, and Styrofoam. Visit flea markets and yard sales for good buys on tools. Obtain construction materials from recycling centers or teacher donation stations.

❀ Providing access to tools on a regular basis, not just during special club time. If none of the staff members feels able to supervise this endeavor at first, recruit a retired teacher or craftsman to teach interested children how to use the tools and care for them. Making tools and equipment available regularly will help students develop their skills in handling them and using them safely.

❀ Providing the time and sustained training and development for afterschool staff to understand the importance of encouraging children to become comfortable tool users; brainstorm projects that staff members can construct themselves, such as building shelves for staff supplies, installing a birdhouse away from squirrels, or making a puppet theater.

Computer Technology   Computers and access to the Internet provide many opportunities for afterschool learning to reinforce reading, math, and writing skills as well as to complete homework and school assignments that require research, gathering information, and writing reports. More complex math, science, and art projects often necessitate simulations and problem solving that can also be enhanced by using computers. In addition, technology can enable schools to reach families at home and access other community resources such as museums, libraries, and local projects via the Internet.

Examples of how an afterschool program can integrate computer technology include the following:

❀ Providing access to current model computers, educational software, and high-speed Internet to all afterschool participants, allowing them practice using the technology and developing information research and management skills

❀ Making technology resources available after school, on weekends, and during school holidays to help students enrich their learning and assist parents and grandparents to learn to use computers

❀ Providing the time and sustained training and development for afterschool staff to learn to use technology to improve their teaching, upgrade their skills, and integrate online learning opportunities into enrichment activities

Large Constructions

Many children like to build things. If the materials are lightweight, such as cardboard, Styrofoam sheets, or fabric, the constructions can be quite large and impressive. One of my students recalled spending several weeks during sixth grade building and decorating a set of interconnected tunnels using appliance cartons and a roll of duct tape. The oldest boy at the afterschool center, he retreated inside his "house" whenever he felt overwhelmed by the younger children, but every once in a while he actually allowed his young friends to play inside it. Other uses for large boxes include dollhouses, mailboxes, ships, fantasy-corner furniture, and reading centers. Computer-aided-design software is now available for children, and by using it they can design structures with electronic building blocks that click into place. One very cool program, for example, is Google SketchUp, which can be downloaded free from http://sketchup.google.com and then used to "create, modify and share 3D models." Encourage children to design a structure on the screen and then build it with real materials (Knowledge Adventure, 2004).

To construct large objects, it will usually be necessary to use tools and materials such as saws, hammers and nails, screwdrivers and screws, pliers, and measuring tape. As children become more proficient in building, they may wish to graduate from cardboard, foam boards, and fabric to wood. Now it becomes appropriate to use those battery-operated and electric tools you have. Using drills, assisted screwdrivers, and powered sanders or jigsaws should take place out of doors and will be discussed under Working With Wood in Chapter 13.

If puppets are popular at your center, a puppet theater may be the object of a construction project. Refrigerator boxes are good for this. The result doesn't have to be terribly sturdy or long lasting. It's the construction process that is the main point, and if it eventually gets bent and squashed . . . well, there are more boxes at the appliance store.

Programs that operate in large spaces, such as multipurpose rooms, can use children's building projects to provide privacy or permit different activities to take place at the same time. In fact, children often suggest this kind of project themselves. Dividers can be made from Styrofoam sheets or from light wood frames covered with cloth or burlap. Even large banners hanging from suspended horizontal poles can be construction projects—large pieces of felt can be cut into shapes and glued onto sheets of burlap or other cloth. Large constructions can include papier-mâché dinosaurs, California missions, space ships, and sets for dramatic productions. Younger children usually need suggestions to get started with a large construction, but older children may prefer to make and carry out their own plans without much assistance (or interference) from adults. If they know it's okay to come up with ideas for projects, they probably will, and if they need you, they'll tell you. A nurturing environment allows this kind of creativity to happen.

Benefits of Large Constructions

- ❀ Developing an understanding of spatial relationships and measurement
- ❀ Learning how to use tools
- ❀ Planning and completing a major project
- ❀ Learning to work with others

Photography

Taking photos, uploading them to a computer, learning to use image-processing software such as Photoshop, printing, making photo collages, albums, scrapbooks, posters—these are all projects that children can initiate and enjoy. If you can make a digital camera available to the children in your program, there are many benefits, both to the children themselves and also to the program. For example:

1. Children can document one another's long-term projects, such as the production of a play or the planting of a vegetable garden, then make a bulletin display for others to enjoy.
2. A budding photojournalist might decide to edit a program newsletter; other children can work together to design the layout, write articles, plan, and take photos for inclusion in the final production.
3. Photo montages of ongoing activities or special guests or projects can be created by the children and used to decorate parts of the room.
4. Photos can be uploaded for use in a homework project.
5. A "rogue's gallery" of photos can be created, with one or more interested children photographing everyone in the program and posting their photos with their names on an introductory bulletin board.

Benefits of Photography

- ❀ Learning to use a camera and take increasingly improving photos
- ❀ Enjoying the use of a new technology in a variety of settings
- ❀ Experiencing new ways of seeing the world through the composition of photographs.

SUMMARY

Children who have been in school all day need opportunities to de-stress in their afterschool program. For some children, unstructured play is the best choice, and these children benefit from being allowed to read, listen to music, chat with their friends, or just "vege out." Others, after a brief interlude, are ready to participate in group activities or games. On days when weather doesn't allow outdoor play, school-agers may appreciate some adult leadership to organize things to do. Children raised in the TV generation may not be familiar with traditional indoor games or pursuits. Adult staff can serve in valuable roles both as resource agents and participants as new games and activities are introduced.

TERMS TO LEARN

complimentary close/closing	resilient
Convention on the Rights of the Child	salutation
heading	strand supports
modeling	structure
papier-mâché	unstructured
prop boxes	web strands

REVIEW QUESTIONS

1. Explain why structured programming may not be appropriate in school-age programs on bad weather days.

2. Describe two ways of encouraging children to participate in activities other than requiring them to do so.

3. Name three things you can do in the kitchen without a recipe.

4. What is a prop box, and what can you do with one?

CHALLENGE EXERCISES

1. Locate someone in the community who has a skill that school-age children might like to learn. Coordinate with the director of a school-age program to invite this person to teach the children the skill. Observe and write a summary of the session.
2. Think about how you liked to spend your time on rainy days after school. Which of the activities you enjoyed could also be enjoyed in a school-age center?
3. Develop a literature web for a school-age children's book. Plan three activities and demonstrate them in class.

Curriculum Resources

Crowley, R. (2008). The consequences of poor nutrition and obesity in children. *Connections, Journal of the California Association for the Education of Young Children, 37*(1), 18–20.

Links to Learning: A Curriculum Planning Guide for After-School Programs, by the National Institute for Out-of-School Time. School-Age Notes, 2005.

Schreiber, D., & Bloom, A. (2008, Fall). Recipe for success: Serving nutrition education through cooking programs. *Afterschool Review, Journal of the National AfterSchool Association*, 31–35.

Children's Books

Some of these are out of print but can be found in public libraries.

175 Science Experiments to Amuse and Amaze Your Friends, by Brenda Walpole
Alice in Pastaland: A Math Adventure, by Alexandra Wright
Cooking With Kids: Exploring Chinese Food, Culture, and Language, by Ni Hao Productions
How? More Experiments for the Young Scientist, by Dave Prochnow & Kathy Prochnow
Kids Cooking: A Very Slightly Messy Manual, by the authors at Klutz Press
Kids in the Kitchen: 100 Delicious, Fun & Healthy Recipes to Cook & Bake, by Sarah Bracken and Micah Pulleyn
Math in the Kitchen, by William Amato
Pigs in the Pantry: Fun With Math and Cooking, by Amy Axelrod
Puppet Mania! by John Kennedy
Puppet Planet: The Most Amazing Puppet-Making Book in the Universe, by John Kennedy
Science Projects and Activities, by Helen J. Challand
The Math Chef, by Joan D'Amico & Karen Erich Drummond
The Science Chef, by Joan D'Amico and Karen Erich Drummond
What? Experiments for the Young Scientist, by Robert W. Wood

INTERNET RESOURCES

AfterSchool KidzMath program (Grades K–2 and 3–6):
http://www.devstu.org/afterschool/askm/videos/index.shtml

Build a Better Mousetrap:
http://surfaquarium.com/mousetrap/rubric.htm

Cooperative game ideas 1:
http://www.lessonplanspage.com/PEHungrySnakeCooperativeLearningGameIdea24.htm#

Cooperative game ideas 2:
http://www.irvingisd.net/pe/PEWEB/cooperative_games.htm

Easy-to-use flour mill:
http://www.lehmans.com/shopping/product/detailmain.jsp?itemID=449&itemType=PRODUCT

Friendly or personal letters:
http://englishplus.com/grammar/00000143.htm

Grinding wheat for baking:
http://www.preschooleducation.com/art17.shtml

Just for fun: Emily Post's 1922 guidelines:
http://www.bartleby.com/95/27.html

Letter Generator (online template for children's letters):
http://readwritethink.org/materials/letter_generator/

Letter-writing etiquette:
http://www.advancedetiquette.com/newsletter/apr04_issue.htm

Math Explorer:
http://www.exploratorium.edu/math_explorer/search.php

Math Maven's Mysteries:
http://teacher.scholastic.com/maven/

National Center for Quality Afterschool:
www.sedl.org/afterschool/toolkits

NCTM's Thirteen Standards for Mathematics Curriculum:
http://www.nctm.org/standards/default.aspx?id=58

NNCC developmental guidelines:
http://www.nncc.org/Curriculum/fc46_cook.kids.html

Principles and Standards for Elementary Mathematics:
http://www.usi.edu/science/math/sallyk/Standards/document/index.htm

San Francisco's Exploratorium:.
http://www.exploratorium.edu/afterschool/activities/index.php

Standards for each state:
http://statestandards.org.standards.html

REFERENCES

American Academy of Pediatrics. (2007). The importance of play in promoting healthy child development and maintaining strong parent-child bonds. *Pediatrics, 119*(1), 182–191.

Barbour, A. (2002). *Prop box play: 50 themes to inspire dramatic play.* Beltsville, MD: Gryphon House.

Bernstein, L. (2002). *Aesop and Ananse: Animal fables and trickster tales* (EDSITEment Lesson Plan). Retrieved August 15, 2009, from http://edsitement.neh.gov/view_lesson_plan.asp?id=240

Bromley, K. (1991). *Webbing with literature: Creating story maps with children's books.* Boston: Allyn and Bacon.

Bumgarner, M. A. (1997). *The new book of whole grains.* New York: St. Martin's Press.

Burch, P. (2008, July). *All about hand dyeing.* Retrieved August 22, 2009, from http://www.pburch.net/dyeing/howtotiedye.shtml

Davies, L. (2008). Ten ways to foster resilience in children. Retrieved April 26, 2010, from http://teachers.net/gazette/

DeKoven, B. (1971). *The interplay experiment.* Retrieved April 26, 2010, from http://www.deepfun.com/intrplay.htm

Di'Amico, J., & Drummond, K. E. (1996). *The math chef: Over 60 math activities and recipes for kids.* New York: Wiley.

Freedman, G., & Reynolds, E. (1980). Enriching basal reading lessons with semantic webbing. *Reading Teacher, 33*(6), 677–684.

Ginsburg, K. R., Committee on Communications, & Committee on Psychosocial Aspects of Child and Family Health. (2007). The importance of play in promoting healthy child development and maintaining strong parent–child bonds. *Pediatrics, 119*(1), 182–191.

Grotberg, E. H. (1995). *A guide to promoting resilience in children: Strengthening the human spirit.* The Hague, Netherlands: Bernard Van Leer Foundation.

Harvard Family Research Project. (2004). YouthLearn: Using technology to create meaningful learning experiences for youth. *Evaluation Exchange, 10*(3), 1.

Helm, J. H., & Beneke, S. (2003). *The power of projects.* New York: Teachers College Press.

Henig, R. M. (2008, February 17). Taking play seriously. *New York Times.* Retrieved January 2, 2009, from http://www.nytimes.com/2008/02/17/magazine/17play.html

Hill, C. (2007, April 17). Developing educational standards. Retrieved July, 2009, from http://edstandards.org/Standards.html#State

Humphrey, J. H. (2001). *Learning the 3 Rs through active play.* Hauppauge, NY: Nova Science Publishers.

Katz, L. (2007). Viewpoint: Standards of experience. *Young Children, 62*(3), 94–95.

Katz, L., & Chard, S. (2000). *Engaging children's minds: The project approach.* Norwood, NJ: Ablex.

Knowledge Adventure. (2004). *Kid CAD: The amazing 3D building kit* [Computer software] (Version XP; Windows 98). Westborough, MA: Author.

Konigsburg, E. L. (1973). *From the mixed-up files of Mrs. Basil E. Frankweiler.* New York: Simon & Schuster. (Original work published by Dell in 1967).

Murnane, R., & Levy, F. (1996). *Teaching the new basic skills: Principles for educating children to thrive in a changing economy.* New York: The Free Press.

National Institute on Out-of-School Time. (2005). *Links to learning: A curriculum planning guide for after-school programs.* Nashville, TN: School-Age Notes.

Office of the United Nations High Commissioner for Human Rights. (1989). *Convention on the rights of the child.* Retrieved January 2, 2009, from www.unhchr.ch/html/menu3/b/k2crc.htm

O'Hanlin, M. (1997, Fall). Lecture on prop boxes at Gavilan College.

Platt, C. W. (1993). Mystery pen pals. *Learning, 22*(2), 74.

Powell, R., & Davidson, N. (2005). The donut house: Real world literacy in an urban kindergarten classroom. *Language Arts, 82*(5), 248–256.

Secretary's Commission on Achieving Necessary Skills. (1991). *What work requires of schools: A SCANS report for America 2000.* Washington, DC: U.S. Department of Labor.

Secretary's Commission on Achieving Necessary Skills. (2006, March 9). *What work requires of schools.* Retrieved July 28, 2008, from http://wdr.doleta.gov/SCANS/

UNICEF. (1989). *UNICEF: Convention on the rights of the child.* Retrieved July, 2009, from http://www2.ohchr.org/english/law/crc.htm

Zuljevic, V. (2005). Puppets—A great addition to everyday teaching. *Thinking Classroom: A Journal of Reading, Writing, and Critical Reflection, 6*(1), 37.

Chapter

13

Engaging Children in Outdoor Activities

Children grow healthier, wiser, and more content when they are more fully connected throughout their childhood to the natural environment in as many educational and recreational settings as possible. These benefits are long term and significant and contribute to their future well-being and the contributions they will make to the world as adults.

(NEBRASKA DEPARTMENT OF EDUCATION, 2008)

The quotation above is from a Call to Action initiated by the Nebraska Department of Education in partnership with several other agencies and presented at the International Working Forum on Nature Education in July 2008. The collaborators cited dozens of authorities—scientists, physicians, educators, naturalists, landscape architects, city planners, artists, and historians—who support the need for providing children with more opportunities to experience the natural world. They also provided many ideas for doing so. This chapter incorporates some of those ideas.

CREATING AN OUTDOOR ENVIRONMENT FOR CHILDREN

It is just as important to examine and reevaluate the outside play area available to the children in your program as it is to plan your indoor classroom design. First, the area should be large enough and designed in such a way that children can run around without bumping into one another or into obstacles, where they can be themselves, and where they can make a lot of noise and a lot of mess. The play space must be safe, but it also needs to offer challenges appropriate to the ages of the children. For many generations, youngsters have crossed streams on slippery stones, hung from long rope swings, and ridden their bicycles on gravelly and

TABLE 13.1 Use of Seven Key Learning Areas to Balance Outdoor Curriculum.

Key Learning Areas	Unstructured Play	A Field Trip to the Woods	Planting a Garden	Greening the Planet	Parachute Games	Hiking, Cycling , Skating	Team Sports	Outdoor Games & Sports	Working with Wood	Raising Animals
1. Literacy	x	x	x						x	x
2. Science	x	x	x	x						x
3. Math problems	x		x						x	x
4. Arts	x		x							
5. Social competence	x	x	x	x	x	x	x	x		x
6. Fitness and nutrition	x	x	x	x	x	x	x	x	x	x
7. Technology	x	x	x						x	

Source: From *Links to Learning: A Curriculum Planning Guide for After-School Programs.* Used with permission of the National Institute on Out-of-School Time.

rutted dirt roads. They have fished from logs, jumped rope, and played hop-scotch, catch, and hide-and-seek. Try to think of how your children might want to use this outdoor space, and then make sure there are places for those activities to happen. Include a variety of different textures and materials, plants, trees, flowers, streams, loose parts, places to be alone, and objects to climb and swing on (Greenman, 2005; Keeler, 2008). Fasten easels to fences or walls, construct hard-surfaced pathways for wheeled toys, sandboxes with covers, grassy areas, large rocks, a gravel base under a faucet. Leave some areas of dirt untouched, for digging in and soaking with a hose to make lovely mud. It doesn't have to be done all at once, and if you are working with an existing playground on a school or church site, for example, you might need to add an additional play area to the one that is already there in order to provide some of these features.

The main purpose of this chapter is to convince you that it is a valuable use of your time to create wonderful outdoor environments for children and to provide you with some ideas to facilitate children's outdoor play. Table 13.1 shows how each of the activities in the chapter aligns with the seven key learning areas introduced in Chapter 12. As you develop year-long, monthly, and weekly outdoor curriculum plans, select activities that provide a healthy and intellectually stimulating balance of learning experiences.

Benefits of Outdoor Play and Activities

As you read in Chapter 12, free and unstructured play is healthy and, in fact, essential for helping children reach important social, emotional, and cognitive developmental milestones as well as helping them manage stress and be able to bounce back when life presents sudden changes or misfortune. While this general statement is absolutely true, regular and extended opportunities for structured and unstructured *outdoor* play are now known to be even more essential to children's development and well-being (Louv, 2008; Wells, 2003). Outside play also increases metabolic rates, so that children digest their food better and have better appetites (Pellegrini, Horvat, & Huberty, 1998). Sunlight is considered by many people to be the best source of vitamin D for children (Kelland, 2010), but many children are not getting enough of this important vitamin. Vitamin D deficiency is implicated in heart disease, stroke, hypertension, autoimmune diseases, diabetes, and other health conditions, so it is important to include fish or fish oil, dairy products, and/or vitamin supplements in children's diets. In addition, several hours a day of outdoor play will lead to a significantly increased intake of vitamin D, even when children's skin has been protected from harmful rays by sunblock and hats (Morgen, 2010).

❀   *Consider This:*   ❀

Where did you like to play out of doors when you were a child? Did you get to play outside regularly, or only on special occasions, such as when you visited friends or relatives or went on vacation? What do you remember about the most enjoyable time you ever spent out of doors during your childhood?

Natural outdoor settings are filled with continually changing sounds, colors, textures, and new places to explore. Researchers tell us that unstructured outdoor play "has the potential to improve all aspects of children's well-being: physical, emotional, social and cognitive" (Burdette & Whitaker, 2005, p. 1). This is especially the case if they have the freedom to move around a fairly large area, select their own materials and pursuits, and engage in activity for long periods of time (Johnson, Christie, & Wardle, 2004). While playing out of doors, children are presented with repeated opportunities to solve problems, engage socially and emotionally with others, learn new physical skills and refine others, and become more aware of their own feelings (Nelson, 2008).

One of the known outcomes of playing outdoors, of course, is that children are active and move around a lot. Left to their own devices, they run, climb, jump, spontaneously do somersaults, and slide down slippery hills. Teachers know that children who engage in active play at recess are more easily able to focus on reading and math when they return to the classroom. Regular active outdoor play helps children to manage stress, frustration, and anxiety. But there are even more valuable outcomes. Eric Nelson, director of the Outdoor Classroom Project at the Child Educational Center in La Canada, California, credits their outdoor curriculum with children's attainment of at least seven learning and developmental objectives:

1. Meets health challenges by establishing a pattern of ongoing, vigorous, and extended physical activity
2. Fosters learning through self-initiation, control, and personal responsibility
3. Achieves social–emotional mastery and builds communication skills through projects and group activity
4. Builds a healthy, balanced internal psychology through time spent alone
5. Develops an interest in science and math through connecting with nature

6. Creates a successful learning environment for the active learner
7. Manifests classroom harmony (Nelson, 2008; Orfalea Foundations, 2010)

Dr. Stuart Brown (2008), a physician, psychiatrist, clinical researcher, and the founder of the National Institute for Play, has made a career of studying the effects of play on people and animals. He wrote that "Nothing lights up the brain like play. Three dimensional play fires up the cerebellum, puts a lot of impulses into the frontal lobe—the executive portion—helps contextual memory be developed, and . . . and . . . and . . ." (n.p.). It would seem to me that this brain activity would be even more noticeable if the play were taking place out of doors.

Most American Children Live Indoors

Children today spend less time outside, interacting with nature, than their parents did. Even a generation ago, children spent more time out of doors because it was the normal thing to do. If their mothers didn't work outside of the home, and most did not, very young children typically spent most of their playtime in the family yard, and older children roamed about the neighborhood, on foot, bicycles, skates, or skateboards.

In more urban settings, children gravitated to overgrown vacant lots and city parks, which were likely to have more trees and grass than the professionally designed playgrounds of today. Until the mid-1980s, city parks had an interesting balance of things to do that put children directly into contact with the real world. Swings, teeter-totters, and child-powered roundabouts provided youngsters with opportunities to pump their legs, jump and land, run and climb, as well as feel the air rushing through their hair and over their faces. Public park sandboxes were huge, and even 8- and 10-year-old children found them fun to dig in. I remember burying my bare feet into the cold, moist sand at the bottom of a large hole and collaborating with my friends to build complex castles and cities that required shovels, forms, and lots of water. Today an adult watching such a scene would undoubtedly be concerned about the health hazards of an uncovered public sandbox, and rightly so. Still, "digging holes to China" in a public sandbox was a game enjoyed by thousands of children who came to no harm.

Before developers of tract houses were required to build neighborhood parks, children could often find undeveloped land nearby that contained rivers and streams in which to wade, swim, or fish; trees to climb and play under; and hills to hike up and slide down. Children whose mothers were working were probably "watched" by a relative or the mother or grandmother of one of their friends. And "watching" generally consisted of being instructed to change out of school clothes, offered a nutritious snack, and reminded to return home by suppertime.

Between 1981 and 1997, children's unscheduled play time dropped by 25%, and much of the time remaining was being spent in sedentary and passive activities such as watching TV, using a computer, and playing videogames (Burdette & Whitaker, 2005; Gies, 2008). With the recent increase in children's use of "smart" phones, MP3 players, and laptop computers, that statistic has increased even more. We need to get our children outdoors again and engaged in active play.

Modifying Outdoor Environments and Maintaining Safety

I am not suggesting that we should reconstruct the wooden swings, see-saws, roundabouts, and sandboxes on which our parents and grandparents played. Nor that we should ignore contemporary playground design principles and safety standards that have been developed through credible research and the observation of children and their injuries. Children in our programs deserve to have places to play outdoors that are safe, engaging, and fun.

We *can,* however, build outdoor environments for children that integrate safety and freedom or modify and simplify existing playgrounds so that they more nearly replicate a natural outdoor environment and offer more opportunities for creative play (Frost, 2006).

An excellent source of inspiration for modifying an outdoor environment, or for creating an imagination-friendly outdoor environment, is *Natural Playscapes,* by Rusty Keeler (2008). The author, an artist–designer with a strong belief in the importance of play in the development of emotional health, calls this "creating outdoor play environments for the soul" (p. 15). Here is *his* "call to action":

> You can do it. You can create extraordinary outdoor places for young children without highly complex play contraptions surrounded by a sea of wood chips or gravel . . . . Places for children that tickle the imagination and surprise the senses . . . . Places for young ones of all abilities to discover themselves and the world around them. [There is] a new movement in children's outdoor play areas, natural playscapes—Where the entire space is filled with art, hills, pathways, trees, herbs, open areas, sand, water, music, and more . . . . Where children find places to run, climb, dig, pretend, and hide, with opportunities to bellow or be silent. (p. 15)

It is not necessary to embark on a full-fledged construction project to create wonderful outdoor spaces for children. Begin with a simple area that you can redesign with your staff, parents, and children, and see how much they enjoy it. Some suggestions for developing **playscapes** are included in this chapter, and many others can be found in the resources listed at the end of the chapter. Figure 13.1 lists safety guidelines for public and school playgrounds. Use this list to evaluate the existing play facilities at your site and guide you as you begin to explore ways to reconnect children with nature.

FACILITATING UNSTRUCTURED OUTDOOR PLAY

Creating open space that fulfills childhood needs to jump, run, climb, swing, shout, roll, hide, and create wonderful messes is the first step to increasing the time they spend in outdoor play. Well-designed outdoor environments fulfill children's basic desire to experience freedom, adventure, experimentation, and taking risks (Greenman, 2005). But they shouldn't stop there. Children also need opportunities to quietly observe the unknown, the unpredictable, and the challenging. They thrive with long stretches of unscheduled time to marvel at nature. Introduce children to the sound of birds in the trees, the patience of ants and snails and worms making their way through newly turned soil in the garden, and to the wondrous vision of a moth or butterfly emerging from its chrysalis and gracefully fluttering away in the summer breeze (Johnson et al., 2004).

FIGURE 13.1 Public Playground Safety Checklist.

Consumer Product Safety Commission
Public Playground Safety Checklist
CPSC Document #327

Is your public playground a safe place to play?

Each year, more than 200,000 children go to U.S. hospital emergency rooms with injuries associated with playground equipment. Most injuries occur when a child falls from the equipment onto the ground.

Use this simple checklist to help make sure your local community or school playground is a safe place to play.

Public Playground Safety Checklist

1. Make sure surfaces around playground equipment have at least 12 inches of wood chips, mulch, sand, or pea gravel, or are mats made of safety-tested rubber or rubber-like materials.

2. Check that protective surfacing extends at least 6 feet in all directions from play equipment. For swings, be sure surfacing extends, in back and front, twice the height of the suspending bar.

3. Make sure play structures more than 30 inches high are spaced at least 9 feet apart.

4. Check for dangerous hardware, like open "S" hooks or protruding bolt ends.

5. Make sure spaces that could trap children, such as openings in guardrails or between ladder rungs, measure less than 3.5 inches or more than 9 inches.

6. Check for sharp points or edges in equipment.

7. Look out for tripping hazards, like exposed concrete footings, tree stumps, and rocks.

8. Make sure elevated surfaces, like platforms and ramps, have guardrails to prevent falls.

9. Check playgrounds regularly to see that equipment and surfacing are in good condition.

10. Carefully supervise children on playgrounds to make sure they're safe.

This document is in the public domain. It may be reproduced without change in part or whole by an individual or organization without permission. If it is reproduced, however, the Commission would appreciate knowing how it is used. Write the U.S. Consumer Product Safety Commission, Office of Information and Public Affairs, 4330 East West Highway, Bethesda, MD 20814.

Increasing Opportunities for Engagement

To become engaged in learning that they have initiated and that adults actively support and encourage, children need to be able to stick with one activity long enough to learn how to do something new or discover something they don't know. Typically this can take as long as 45 minutes or an hour—a length of time well beyond typical unstructured play periods scheduled by classroom teachers or afterschool leaders, and sometimes also beyond the attention span of children raised indoors. But if provided with such an expanse of time on a regular basis, guided by adults with gentle suggestions for things to do and explore, and with the materials and tools needed to do so, most children begin to develop both a love of learning and confidence in their ability to learn out of doors (Nelson, 2008). They can experiment, satisfy their curiosity, manipulate materials in new ways or create things of their own, and make messes. This is very new territory for many children of the electronic age, and it might require gradual steps toward the final goal, but it can be very rewarding. Be patient.

Encouraging Different Types of Play

The authors of *Play, Development and Early Education* encourage teachers of young children to facilitate a wide variety of play out of doors (Johnson, Christie, & Wardle, 2005). School-age children need the same wonderful environments and often just as much "facilitation." As you examine your outdoor environment, be sure that each of the following types of play are encouraged by your arrangement of spaces, choice of equipment and materials, and scheduling of outdoor time:

❀ *Physical play*—Climbing equipment, swings, bike paths; large areas of grass and hills punctuated by partially buried barrels, large boulders, and patches of shade.

❀ *Constructive play*—Sand and water, easels and paint, a bench and tools for woodworking, big table and natural clay for shaping, lots of paper and pens, loose objects such as baskets of pine cones, leaves, dried flowers. "Access to water is critical," wrote Jim Greenman (2005, p. 32), a leader in the field of child care environmental design: "A dirt pile for digging, a rock pile for building, sticks and cloth for making a home or shop, magnifying glasses for observing nature—with a few simple materials and a shift in outlook, we can transform outdoor spaces into environments that encourage exploration" (p. 32).

❀ *Social play*—Select equipment that encourages the engagement of more than one child (pushing one another on the swing, pulling a wagon carrying another child, playing together in the sand, and so on). Projects such as gardening, sitting together for a picnic lunch, observing the weather, or looking at leaves through magnifying glasses can all be social activities.

❀ *Sociodramatic play*—Create forts, playhouses, greenhouses, and other structures that children can change, adapt, restructure, and make into anything they can imagine. Such structures, if simple and basic in design, can serve as palettes on which children can paint details, information, and meaning; they can also reflect on the cultures of the children who use them, and they can be a classroom one day, a falafel restaurant the next.

❀ *Games with rules*—Many of the games described in the previous chapter can also be played outside, as well as other traditional games such as Red Light/Green Light, Simon Says, and Follow the Leader. Running is safer and falling down much more pleasant on grass than on hard classroom floors (Johnson et al., 2004).

Adapting your outdoor spaces to encourage different types of play can be a challenging task. You not only need to consider the developmental needs of school-age children but also ensure that there is appropriate supervision, safety, and access by children with physical challenges. However, the importance of this undertaking cannot be overstated. As you improve your outdoor environment to make it more interesting, more flexible, and more developmentally appropriate, you will see that the spaces also become better utilized than they have been in the past, and children will, without coercion, want to spend more time enjoying outdoor pursuits.

Thinking Creatively About Outdoor Activities

Many opportunities are already directly in your hands to increase children's participation in outdoor play. Take a group of children out of doors and simply play with them in the natural surroundings. In full-day programs during spring and summer breaks, plan day-long hikes away from the center and schedule field trips or overnight campouts to interesting outdoor locations (Cox, 2007). Plant a garden. Work with wood. Fly a kite. The rest of this chapter contains ideas to help you get started and resources to help you develop and expand your outdoor curriculum.

Benefits of Unstructured Outdoor Play

- ❀ Improving emotional well-being
- ❀ Learning social interaction
- ❀ Practicing problem solving
- ❀ Increasing metabolism and vitamins A and D
- ❀ Discovering the world of nature

NATURE AND ECOLOGICAL ACTIVITIES

It seems to me that adults who played outdoors regularly as children have healthier attitudes toward their physical environments. Many hikers and rock climbers, for example, work to preserve open space and maintain trails; sports fishermen and hunters often advocate actively for thoughtful forestry management and the prevention and recovery of polluted rivers and streams; some cyclists publicize the relationship between combustion engines and climate change. Spending time in outdoor environments can help children understand their relationship to nature and the need to conserve and preserve the environment.

Field Trips to Outdoor Places

In his provocative book *Last Child in the Woods* (2008), chairman of the Children and Nature Networks, Richard Louv, wrote about an English teacher in Santa Cruz, California, who had been taking her students on field trips to the Sierra Nevada or the equally distant Central Valley to connect the literature read in class with the environments in which some of the action had taken place. After a conversation with her students about the much closer coastal mountains and state forests, she learned that most of them had never been to either one. So she dropped the road trips, Louv reported, and began teaching closer to home. For example, while the students were reading John Steinbeck's novel *Cannery Row,* she took the students to tide pools in nearby Monterey Bay, where Steinbeck had often visited.

In the same way, you can initiate visits to natural environments in your own community that are suggested by a book one of the children is reading or with a subject that some of the children are studying in class. Select stories or nonfiction books from the library reading corner and then propose a field trip that relates to one of them. Find a stream, a hill, a wood, or a tide pool, and imagine with the children that you are exploring the stream beside Laura Ingalls Wilder's home in *The Little House in the Big Woods* (2005), the woods where the lamp post glimmered in the *The Lion, The Witch, and the Wardrobe* (Lewis, 2004), or the coastal puddle where the hermit crabs and turban snails live in *One Small Place by the Sea* (Brenner, 2004). Even an old churchyard, a flea market, or an abandoned drive-in theater, all of which are likely to be overgrown with weeds, can be fun to explore. Take the children out of doors often. Wander around together. Play. Talk about what you did.

Follow-up Activities

❀ *Sketchbooks*—Children can record what they see on outings. Provide them with some examples of naturalists' illustrated notebooks so they know that this is a "real" endeavor and has value.

❀ *Journals*—Children may enjoy writing about things other than just what they see and hear, such as also how they feel, what they are thinking, topics that the outdoor environment reminds them about. Sitting in a peaceful, quiet place and writing is an activity that dates back hundreds of years.

❀ *Photograph/scrapbook*—Purchase some scrapbook supplies and put together a basic blank book. Encourage children to use a digital camera to record outdoor activities and explorations. Pictures can be uploaded to a computer and printed, along with mementos of the activities and outings, such as leaves, conifer needles, dried flowers, and found materials.

Benefits of a Field Trip to the Woods

❀ Linking literature and the environment
❀ Expanding children's knowledge of nature
❀ Increasing interest in and concern for the environment

Planting a Garden

Some children may be fortunate enough to have worked in a family garden, but for many more, nurturing plants is an unexplored and wonderful adventure that they can experience at their afterschool program. A good way to begin the project is to take walks around various neighborhoods and parks with small groups of children, introducing the idea of growing living things, and see who shows an interest. Some youngsters may prefer to grow flowers, and others vegetables. Either is fine, and both are even better. Don't expect everyone to be enthusiastic. It is far better to have a small group of dedicated gardeners than a larger group who have to be talked into going outside to pull weeds on a hot day.

If no garden area has previously been allocated to your program, tour the grounds with some of the children, selecting several areas that seem suitable. It is a good idea to do this at different times of the day and in different types of weather, to ensure sufficient sunshine, access to water, adequate drainage, and safe routes for walking. If your program is located on a school site, ask the principal of the school for the correct procedure to request the use of one of the areas. Sometimes it will be necessary to prepare a presentation to a school site council or the board of trustees, which can be a useful exercise in itself for the children to participate in, but sometimes the onsite administrator can approve your project directly.

❀   *Consider This:*   ❀

Did you ever plant flowers or vegetables when you were a child? Recall if you did so with your family or if the activity took place in school or at a special event of some kind. Do you know any gardeners? What have you noticed about how they act when they are in their gardens or talking about them? Does this kind of activity appeal to you?

Organize a group of children to write letters to plant nurseries, hardware stores, or parents requesting the donation of child-sized tools, soil amendments, and seeds. (See the letter-writing activity in Chapter 12 for some hints to help the children get started.) Sometimes local gardening club members will join you for a session and teach children about composting; preparing soil for planting, mulching, cultivating; or other techniques that will ensure success. Service clubs such as Rotary, Lions, or the Elks may also be willing to help, and retired community members often enjoy assisting children with such enterprises. Formulating and writing letters and tracking down addresses can fill many hours of the rainy season and build motivation for the project when the planting season finally arrives. During this time it might also be fun to bring in seed catalogs and gardening books and to visit a garden center or commercial garden and talk with the owner about suitable plants for your area.

Small gardens can be contained in enclosures made from discarded chunks of concrete or several long pieces of wood. Avoid using vehicle tires or railroad ties for vegetable plantings, as both contain harmful chemicals. Many plants benefit from being started inside before it is warm enough for outdoor gardening, and in some regions it might even be necessary to build a **cold frame** or **greenhouse**. Cut-down milk cartons, clear plastic liter-sized bottles, and concentrated juice cans make good containers for seed nurseries. During the weeks while the seeds are germinating, tools are being located, and the plot secured, children can draw pictures of their fantasy garden and eventually develop a realistic plan. If you live in a rural or semirural area, rodent screens under the planting boxes are a good idea, as are fences to keep out deer, rabbits, passing dogs, etc. Pathways between rows will help to protect the plants from enthusiastic feet and allow accessibility for children, staff, or visitors who use wheelchairs. Gardens grown in the middle of the city are attractions for passersby, and benches set on the edges of the garden will sometimes fill with teachers or community workers eating lunch or taking a break from work.

As part of a long-term curriculum planning project, one of my college students developed a summer "reading room" in conjunction with an existing, but neglected, garden. Reflecting on the need for children to have productive activities during the long summer months as well as a cool place to spend the hot afternoons, she designed a long-term curriculum plan that included children's activities in the garden during the cooler hours of the morning and in the reading room after lunch where the temperature could be somewhat controlled with ventilation and fans. Targeted for about 20 children in an all-day summer program, Monica's plan is laid out in the Gantt chart shown in Figure 13.2.

FIGURE 13.2 Gantt Chart of Long-Term Curriculum Project: Garden Reading Room.

Schedule of Proposed Long-Term Curriculum Project				
Week of June 15–19				
	Monday	Tuesday	Wednesday	Thursday	Friday
10:00	First day introductions	Morning hellos	→		
11:00	↓	Exercise time	→	Introduce garden project	Introduce reading room project
12:00	Lunch	→			
1:00	Craft time	Reading time	Craft time	Reading time	
					Field trip: Walk to library
2:00	Games	Water fun	Games	Water fun	↓
Week of June 22–26				
	Monday	Tuesday	Wednesday	Thursday	Friday
10:00	Morning hellos	→			
11:00	Discussion: What do we want in our garden?	Talk about garden design: Which plants to use?	Activity: Let's make a garden map	Flower planting	Flower planting
12:00	Lunch	→			
1:00	Field trip: Walk through creek	Discussion: What do we want in our reading room?	Field trip to nursery	Talk about reading room design	Activity: Let's make a library map
2:00	↓	Water fun	↓	Water fun	Water fun
Week of June 29–July 3				
	Monday	Tuesday	Wednesday	Thursday	Friday
10:00	Morning hellos	→			
11:00	Activity: Create rules for garden	Discussion: What are good bugs?	Activity: Leaf rubbings	Activity: Make me a scarecrow	Reading time: Garden & reading room
12:00	Lunch	→			
1:00	Organizing of bookshelves and reading room	Activity: Create rules for reading room	Paint posters for party in English and Spanish	Activity: Make me a scarecrow	Preparations for party and BBQ
2:00	↓	Water fun	↓	Water fun	↓
					Family Fun Night & BBQ 6:00 to 8:00 pm

Source: Used with permission of Monica D. Martinez-Guaracha.

PERSPECTIVE 13.1

A Garden Room

Monica Martinez-Guaracha

This plan combines outdoor play with quiet activities. Some children prefer one or the other, but other children participate in both. The close proximity of our neglected school garden to the portable classroom allows the children to move in and out of the garden and into the reading room easily. Because this project is planned for the summer months, the afternoon heat may make working in the garden unbearable, so most of the work will be done in the mornings. Having the children engaged in a variety of activities inside the reading room in the afternoons will be a nice alternative from the boring summer days they have historically spent in one classroom.

Three times a week I will take library carts of books into our garden so that children can read there during lunchtime. Because we don't have any tall trees in the garden, I'll need at least three portable canopies to give the children shade when they work in the beds and read. I've broken down the two big parts of my projects into a number of smaller activities in the Gantt chart. Materials needed will be listed in each individual activity plan.

Source: Used with permission from Monica Martinez-Guaracha.

During the school year, several classes plant, maintain, and harvest the garden, which is then left unattended during the summer months. This plan encourages the summer children to rake leaves and harvest late vegetables and plant seeds that would grow in the summer months, such as corn and squash, spinach, mustard greens, and chard. While the Gantt chart shows only 3 weeks of activities, in reality the children could continue enjoying the reading room and the garden for the rest of the summer, and a variety of additional activities could be developed. Perspective 13.1 describes the project.

Consider integrating a pleasant outdoor environment into *your* curriculum in a way that builds on children's interests and increases engagement. It doesn't have to be a vegetable or flower garden; it could simply be a pleasant outdoor

Many children today have not had an opportunity to grow plants or flowers.

FIGURE 13.3   Making a Windowsill Garden.

After the gardening season is over, show a group of children how they can plant a "windowsill garden" of herbs that will continue to grow through the late fall and winter. An easy way to do that is to use egg cartons made of recycled paper. They will need a sunny window and cool temperatures (60°F) for best growth. Here are the steps:

1. Cut the lid off the egg carton and poke small holes in each section with a sharp pencil.
2. Place potting mix in each section, about 2/3 full.
3. Sprinkle 3 to 6 herb seeds into each section (avoid planting coriander, dill, anise, or fennel, as they grow best when planted directly into the garden).
4. Cover seeds with about ¼ inch more potting mix.
5. Place the carton in a window where it will receive light but not direct sun.
6. Water carefully and regularly.
7. To avoid overflow, place a plastic tray under each carton.

Good choices of herbs for this project include parsley, sage, rosemary, and thyme, as well as basil, cilantro, and chervil.

space, perhaps, as Monica suggests, with a pavilion or canopy to provide shade in the hot summer, where children enjoy reading or talking and participate in imaginative play or active games. Integrating the outside into the inside makes the natural setting seem more *normal* somehow, one that doesn't require a "special event" in order to enjoy.

During the growing season, children can share their project with friends and family; if the garden is close to a school or preschool, participants can host field trips to the garden. Harvest time can be celebrated with a feast made from vegetables grown by the children, served on tables decorated with their own flowers. The looks on the youngest children's faces will be worth all the muddy footprints left on the center floor. Once the growing season has ended, some gardening activities can take place inside, as shown in Figure 13.3.

Follow-up Activities   Some programs have discovered many enjoyable activities that can result from having a garden in their program. For example:

- ❀ Older children can lead younger ones in matching games made from the pictures in seed catalogs, and they can teach one another the names of the different plants.
- ❀ Make picture frames and stationery from flowers that children dry and press.
- ❀ Dry extra flowers to be sold in bunches.
- ❀ Donate excess vegetables to a food bank, and help children deliver their bounty in person.
- ❀ Make snacks and meals from the harvest of the garden.
- ❀ Plant herbs and flowers in large containers by the front door, and package fresh cuttings for parents as they arrive in the evening.

Benefits of Planting a Garden
- ❀ Developing an understanding of the cycle of living things
- ❀ Recognizing the relationship between food and the seasons

❀ Starting and completing a long-term project
❀ Opportunities for social interaction and personal growth

A long-term project such as a garden produces many rewards besides flowers and vegetables. Walking in a garden at the end of a long day can have a mellowing effect on parents, children, and staff, and the lessons learned from patiently removing pesky weeds, watering thirsty vines, and harvesting delicious vegetables or sweet-smelling flowers will last forever. In addition, organizational skills developed while planning and maintaining a garden can be used later in school or community projects. Figure 13.3 demonstrates how you can introduce children to the idea of growing things with a **windowsill garden** even before outdoor planting season arrives.

Greening the Planet

A high school teacher in San Jose, California, teamed his 10th grade students with 6th graders in a nearby elementary school in a water-quality research project being conducted by a local agency. Each week, a staff member from the nearby Children's Discovery Museum taught the biology students how to collect, test, and document a different kind of soil or water sample. At the creek behind the elementary school, high school students taught their younger research partners the techniques they had learned and supervised the collection of samples. Together they tested the samples and recorded the results, including mapping and sketching the environment from which the samples had been taken. What had begun as a mildly interesting service learning project eventually developed into a working partnership between teens and 11-year-olds, resulting in a presentation at a statewide conference, long-term friendships, and a broader appreciation of the need to protect natural resources (M. Stark, Pioneer High School, personal communication).

Partly as a result of this productive collaboration, the City of San José Environmental Services Department set aside up to $50,000 for watershed projects throughout the county. The Request for Proposals form identified an applicant eligible to receive a Youth Watershed Education Grant as an

educator or youth leader affiliated with a school or a charitable, nonprofit, [or] nonsectarian [organization and who has] experience in at least one of the following areas:

1. conducting hands-on environmental education activities for youth;
2. implementing curricula or developing new curricular activities for youth between the ages of 5 and 18; or
3. training educators or peers in curricular activities. (Freitas, 2008, para 12)

If that sounds like you, or someone you work with, then inquire about similar programs in your community for which your program may be eligible. More and more cities and counties are turning to service agencies and educators to help them meet "green" goals. What better way to encourage children to spend time in nature than to engage them in real work that helps to protect their local natural environment?

Benefits of Greening the Planet
❀ Understanding the importance of ecological environments
❀ Engaging in community service
❀ Interacting with other children and adults
❀ Developing an awareness of local environmental issues

OUTDOOR GAMES AND SPORTS

Games that have traditionally been played outdoors are softball, football, soccer, badminton, tennis, and other such activities that require a designated space and room to run around. Others active pursuits, usually engaged in during vacations or at least away from the city, include swimming, hiking, long-distance cycling, and mountain climbing. Some of these activities may be difficult to arrange in some afterschool settings. But even traditional children's activities such as running and jumping, playing hide-and-seek, walking long distances, and riding bicycles have all but disappeared from today's playgrounds, and with a little thought you can begin to reverse that trend.

Parachute Games

Children (and many adults) love being inside parachutes on a hot day and under them as they billow in the breeze. They enjoy running in circles watching the silk fronds swell and enjoy collapsing in laughing heaps among the folds when they finally deflate and fall. School supply houses sell colorful parachutes designed specifically for children's play, but many school-age centers prefer the larger surplus-store parachutes that were once carried in military airplanes. Either type is a good investment.

Most parachute games begin by placing 6 to 20 children around the outside of a parachute, where they each take firm hold of the edge and either walk around in circles or lift the parachute up by rhythmically raising their hands up and down. While most games can be played in a gym or cafeteria, children may be safely allowed to be more boisterous if the parachute is enjoyed in a soft grassy area.

Here are some enjoyable things to do with parachutes:

Bounce the Beach Ball Throw a beach ball on top of a taut parachute. By moving the edge of the chute up and down in a wave, children can move the ball around the edge of the parachute, or they can attempt to move it to the center of the chute. Sometimes there is a hole that can be the target, and you can also play

Parachutes teach physical and social skills and are a favorite with all ages.

this game with a smaller ball. This can be a two-team challenge—one group tries to get the ball in the middle, while the other group tries to keep the ball toward the edge. Also try using a smaller, lightweight ball.

Slithering Snakes   Everybody takes off their shoes and sits on the grass in a circle, with the parachute covering their legs but pulled fairly tight. One person is declared "It" and remains under the chute, in the "lake." Slithering under the "water," the person who is It touches someone on the foot and pulls that person under the water. Now both of them slither around looking for a new victim. The last person to be selected becomes the new It.

Parachute Cave   This is a favorite game on a hot day. Everyone stands around the parachute and pulls it taut. Using a rhythmic up and down movement, the parachute is gradually filled with air and raised up higher and higher until it billows full. Then, on the count of three, the children bring the chute down to the ground, duck under it, and sit down, with the chute wrapped around their backs and tucked under them. By rocking back and forth just right, the children can eventually learn to keep the parachute afloat around them for 10 or 15 minutes, and it's nice and cool in there. Other ideas can be found in books and videos sold by the supply houses that sell parachutes.

Benefits of Parachute Games
- ❀ Developing listening skills
- ❀ Increasing social interaction
- ❀ Using physical strength
- ❀ An opportunity for simply having fun

Hiking, Cycling, and Skating

Children who spend several years in child care are dependent on high-quality programming to offer them a wide variety of experiences. Whenever possible, find ways to allow the children in your program to enjoy the same kinds of activities and pursuits that they would be able to participate in if their parents were available to provide supervision and transportation and help them to develop lifelong habits of healthy play. This can and should include opportunities to swim, ride bikes or scooters, skate, skateboard, Rollerblade, jump on Pogo sticks, or spin Hula hoops or other outdoor activities that are popular at the moment.

If it is safe to do so, schedule frequent jaunts around and out of the neighborhood. Some children may walk, but others may prefer to skate or ride their bicycles. These trips can be designed in a variety of ways—searches for **collage** supplies, garbage pickup, scavenger hunts, or simply explorations and adventures. For everyone to enjoy these outdoor activities, keep the group size small, and allow the leaders to plan them on fairly short notice. One way to avoid inconveniencing parents who may not always arrive for pickup at the same time is to set aside 1 or 2 days a week for these kinds of "away" activities. Involve both parents and children in deciding which days they should be and what time the group should return. Then, the day before a hike or outing, have interested children sign up for the event and take home a reminder notice. Be sure also to plan an interesting activity for those who cannot participate and must remain at the center.

Benefits of Hiking, Cycling, and Skating
- ❀ Learning the enjoyment of active physical play
- ❀ Enjoying the company of others
- ❀ Learning to care for equipment
- ❀ Understanding the importance of safety guidelines

Team Sports

Sometimes the scheduling limitations caused by parents working away from the community in which they live, or working long hours, prevents children in after-school programs from participating in recreation leagues organized for softball, soccer, football, swimming, hockey, or other team sports. School-age center staff can make the difference for these children by coordinating between parents, coaches, and teachers to assist with transportation to and from practices or by organizing a team that practices at the program facility. Inquire into the existing recreation activities in your community, and see what sports are offered, where, and when. If you have enough children within an age group, fielding your own team and participating in the community league may be the best approach, although it may not be practical for a staff member to coach the team. See if a parent or community volunteer can take that role. You will need to work closely with parents on every step of this process, as they may be required to pay league fees, provide uniforms, and transport children on weekends. Perhaps there is a way the school-age program can raise money to help with some of these needs, and it may be possible for staff members to participate in the weekend games.

Whether or not participation in organized athletic leagues is feasible, or even desirable, helping children to organize team games after school can be a very enjoyable endeavor. If your program does not have money for equipment, allow children to bring their own or request donations from community agencies. Locate a rulebook for the "sport of the month" and encourage the children to refer to it. If they request help with skills, and a staff member knows how to develop skill-building activities, go for it. Generations of youngsters enjoyed pickup basketball and softball games in vacant lots and city gyms long before parents began organizing leagues; the afterschool program is a perfect environment to allow these pastimes to develop naturally if the interest is there.

Cooperative games focus on participation, fun, and interaction rather than competition and winning. Introducing cooperative games into the afterschool environment can increase children's sense of safety and belongingness, while encouraging active play out of doors. Some goals of cooperative team games include:

- ❀ Working together as a group for individual and collective success
- ❀ Helping one another pursue a goal using constructive feedback
- ❀ Overcoming challenges or fears that arise during the game
- ❀ Having fun together

One example of a cooperative team game is All on One Side. In this game, only one team plays at a time, and it starts on one side of a volleyball net with no one on the other side. The object is to get your team to the other side of the net and back as many times as possible in the time allowed. Using a balloon for a ball, each player volleys the balloon to another player and then scoots under the net to the other side. The last player to touch the balloon taps it over the net and scoots under. The receiving players try to keep the balloon in play and repeat the process. Other cooperative games may be found in the Organized Outdoor Games section of this chapter.

Benefits of Team Sports
- ❀ Learning a variety of skills
- ❀ Understanding the concept of sportsmanship
- ❀ Social interaction
- ❀ Increasing physical strength and skills

ORGANIZED OUTDOOR GAMES

One of the cornerstones of afterschool programs is recreational games, both indoors and out. After 6 or 7 hours sitting in school, children need to move, and this is a good way to begin an afternoon session. Because you may end up organizing and leading outdoor games almost every day during good weather, it is important to develop a repertoire of different games that can be played with large groups. Even the most enthusiastic participants of the newly reintroduced traditional games, whether it is Duck, Duck, Goose or Steal the Bacon, eventually tire of them when they are played day after day. Many books are available with instructions for outdoor games. Two excellent ones are *School-Age Ideas and Activities for After School Programs*, by Karen Haas-Foletta, et al., and *The Complete School-Age Child Care Resource Kit*, by Abby Barry Bergman and William Green. Good sources of cooperative games include *Cooperative Games and Sports*, by Terry Orlick, and *Everyone Wins! Cooperative Games and Activities*, by Josette and Sambhava Luvmour.

Working with children during their out-of-school time requires a unique set of skills and abilities (Haas-Foletta, Cogley, & Ottolini-Geno, 2005). When you work with school-age children, it is important to participate in the games as well as to organize them. Don't worry that you're not in great physical shape . . . that will change! More important than your skill is your good humor and your enthusiasm. Many school-age children are unaccustomed to regular exercise and may even be overweight. Enjoyable games that require vigorous movement can go a long way toward offsetting this trend and may even kindle an interest in sports. Another thing to remember is that school-age children need to participate in deciding what games are played, for how long, and how often. They can actually do much of the organizing, too, if you model the process and encourage them to take a larger and larger role.

Most games can be easily adapted to include children with special needs, even though Annie's walker slows her down or Jamal doesn't really grasp the rules. Encourage all children to help each other play together. Doing this not only promotes inclusion of the children with disabilities, but it also makes participation more fun for all the other children who aren't athletic "stars."

Outdoor games can include circle games (Duck, Duck, Goose, Telephone, A Tisket a Tasket), team sports, individual "silly stuff" (like Follow the Leader, Water Balloon Pop, or the Bunny Hop), or you can provide equipment for children to toss beanbags, jump rope, or play sets of giant dominoes. Some programs might want to schedule certain days when children can bring their Rollerblades, skateboards, or bicycles and adapt favorite games to be played on wheels. In addition to the ideas to follow, descriptions of group games can be found in manuals for adult leaders of Campfire, Scouts, YMCA Indian Guides and Princesses, and other youth organizations. Other helpful sources are books written for elementary physical education instructors. Two such texts are *Children Moving,* by George M. Graham, Melissa A. Parker, and Shirley Ann Holt/Hale (2001) and its accompanying manual of lesson plans, *On the Move,* by Shirley Ann Holt/Hale (2006). Search libraries and the Internet for other sources of games, especially those that encourage children to work together toward a goal. The following were adapted from *Cooperative Games for Indoors and Out,* by Jim Deacove (1990). Other sources of cooperative games can be found in the Internet Resources section at the end of the chapter.

Volley-Up

Two groups on either side of volleyball net try to keep the volleyball aloft for as many hits as possible. A good goal is to get to 100. One player starts by serving from the end of the court, and the ball has to go over the net from one side to the other, as usual. Three successive hits by one side are permitted. The last player to touch the ball on a dropped ball or unsuccessful hit is the one to serve it into play again (you might want to limit this to three successive tries). One person serves as a scorekeeper to **tally** the hits.

Stop and Go

This is a variation on softball that develops skills and involves all the players. Use a bat and ball and set up bases as usual. All remotely feasible positions are assigned, including just one batter. Everyone is a team when the scoring is tallied. The batter stays up and hits. The hit is chased and stopped or caught. When caught or stopped, the person fielding it shouts, "Got it!" The batter running around the bases stops wherever he or she is, even if on the base path between bases. The person fielding the ball now becomes the third baseman and everyone moves up a position, including the fielders, left, center, right, first right, second right, etc., depending on the number of players. If a player in the infield catches it, then everyone moves up one place. The catcher becomes the batter. If the ball is caught rather than fielded, then the one catching it becomes the next batter, and the first batter stays on the base path as far as he or she ran before the ball was caught.

The individual can therefore work for himself both when at bat and in the field, but he also works to add more enjoyment for everyone by trying his best to field or catch the ball. Scoring is done this way: Everyone on the base path tries, in order, to get around to home. Each runner who makes it in counts as one run. The runner in goes out into the field and enters the batting order. He can bat twice if he fields the ball or catches it and moves up again.

The whole team scores the number of runs achieved in one inning. An inning is over when you get the same number of hits as you have players playing—i.e., if you have 10 people playing, then 10 hits make up an inning.

Three innings allow you a chance to see what kind of a score you can get. The number of players can vary as for any baseball game. You need at least a batter, a catcher, a pitcher, and a few fielders. You can play without a catcher if you have a good backstop. There are no strikeouts or walks. Each batter stays up until she is given a pitch she can hit, and of course she can also wait for a pitch she likes best. There is no reward or competitive inducement to this game, and when you play it you will notice that even children who don't usually care to play softball tend to play better and have more fun.

Scramble

This game is a variation on musical chairs except that the object is to make sure than no one is left out. Jim Deacove (1990), author of the classic *Cooperative Games for Indoors and Out,* wrote, "Our **cultural conditioning** gets us worrying about getting ahead in the musical chairs of society and all the time our hearts are worrying about those who don't get a chair. It would be nice if we could build a society that made sure anyone got a chair" (p. 2).

The game works nicely with 10 to 15 players, but more or fewer can play, depending on what you use as the chair. You can literally use a chair, but you can also use a tree stump, a sturdy wooden box, a tree, a small circle drawn on the ground, or whatever you wish. Assign four corners of the playing area, naming them North, South, East, and West. Everyone but the caller is scattered around the four areas, and the caller describes an activity the players must engage in while the caller waits for the right moment—hopping, walking, running, crawling on all fours, etc.

Now the caller runs around the playing area and suddenly calls out one of the areas. He or she may shout, "North!" At once, the players in the North area scramble to the chair, stump, tree, or whatever and try to get a place on it. Everyone must somehow manage to get on the object, or at least touch it, and hang on. Everyone has to help the scramble work. A time limit of 30 seconds can be made if you wish. The caller calls the time, and if everyone is still on the object, the game is won, and the first on board becomes the caller. If everyone cannot get aboard, the caller resumes running around the playing area, and the children resume their activity. This can be made even more interesting by calling two areas or even three. Be sure to use a large and sturdy object as the base.

Tag and Freeze Tag

Don't forget old standby games like tag. Freeze tag is just like regular tag except when you get tagged you're frozen, and you stay frozen until someone who's not frozen tags you. If you get tagged three times you're It. If everyone gets frozen, then whoever's been tagged the most is It.

Benefits of Outdoor Games
- ❀ Promoting healthy active movement
- ❀ Helping development listening skills
- ❀ Developing social skills
- ❀ Encouraging enjoyment of group activities

Source: Descriptions of Volley Up, Stop & Go, Scramble, and Tag and Freeze Tag used by permission of Family Pastimes Ltd.

OTHER OUTDOOR PURSUITS

Other outdoor activities, most of which can be set up within the school-age center grounds, include Ping-Pong (table tennis), shuffleboard, croquet, miniature golf, and ten-pin bowling. Try to obtain "real" game sets, not the "kiddie" versions. They can often be found at flea markets or yard sales. It can be fun to keep score and develop tournaments. Perhaps you might want to invite local "experts" to teach game-specific skills, but don't let competition overcome enjoyment. As in all areas of curriculum, enthusiastic youth leaders are the key to finding enjoyable things to do out of doors and engaging the interest of the children in participating.

Water Fun

Running through sprinklers on a sunny day . . . sitting in 2 inches of cool water and reading a book . . . making a dam or stepping stones across a creek . . . sailing milk-carton boats down the gutter. Children have enjoyed these and other delightful pursuits in and around water for generations, and children who spend their days in afterschool programs should have opportunities to experience them, too.

Many of the children in school-age programs are unaccustomed to "playing"—with water or with anything else. However, Stuart Brown, president of the National Institute for Play, says that in terms of building memories and producing learning and well-being, "play is as fundamental as any other aspect of life, including sleep and dreams" (cited in Henig, 2008, para 1). It may take creative leadership to bring out the little boys and girls trapped inside the sophisticated young people in your program, but rest assured, once you find them, they'll be there to stay, and that's a good thing. Make sure everyone has a change of clothes or obtain a washer and dryer, so children won't be worrying about ruining their clothes. Be sure the day is reasonably warm. Here are some more things school-age children have been known to enjoy doing with water:

- ❀ Make large hoops out of coat hangers and craft pipe cleaners. Dip them in a soap solution and make giant bubbles (see Figure 13.4 for bubble recipe). You can also use plastic straws (teach the children to blow, not suck!), plastic strawberry baskets, serving spoons with holes.
- ❀ Dig a ditch and fill it with water (this can take all day). Paddle barefoot in it.
- ❀ Dam up a stream created by a rainstorm. Build a bridge over a natural stream.
- ❀ Fill a water table with water and do "big kid" kinds of things with it.
- ❀ Take some water out to a dirt patch and make mud. Play in it.
- ❀ Make water balloons. Throw them on the ground and watch them burst. Throw them at each other (set some ground rules first, like how far back

FIGURE 13.4 Making Liquid Soap for Bubbles.

Soap solution: *2/3 cup liquid dish soap to 1 gallon of water. For stronger bubbles, add 1 tablespoon glycerin (available in cake-decorating sections of grocery or craft stores).*

you need to stand so you don't hurt anyone). Turn the hose on and wash everyone's feet.

❀ Water the garden. Water the plants. Fill a birdbath.
❀ Dump a pile of sand on the ground. Sprinkle it with water and make a sandcastle.

Benefits of Water Fun
❀ Enjoying sensory play
❀ Discovering scientific properties of water and objects placed within it
❀ An outlet for playful aggression
❀ Opportunities for cooperative play

Working with Wood

Many schools have put away their woodworking tools, and fewer parents amuse themselves in garage workshops than in years past. Budget cuts have even restricted the offering of woodshop in many middle and high schools. But working with wood is a very satisfying activity, and many patterns for simple projects such as birdhouses, planters, and letter racks still exist in public libraries, although you may need to request a book from the main branch. If no one on staff feels confident enough to teach a woodworking workshop, try asking parents or contacting a branch of the 4-H, Scouts, or Camp Fire Inc. to see if they have a suggestion. You can also check local middle and high schools for teachers who may have taught woodshop in the past or who still pursue the craft. Staff members and children can learn together. A great resource for non-woodworkers is *Woodshop for Kids,* by Jack McGee. My father was a cabinet maker, so I was taught to use real tools at a very young age, and under his tutelage I learned to use them correctly and without injury to myself or others. McGee believes that it is possible for all children to do so. He suggests beginning with wood sanding and wood oiling, progressing to matching games and building small projects from precut kits (McGee, 2005).

I usually start children working with wood the same way my father started me, creating art sculptures by gluing or nailing miscellaneous pieces of wood together in interesting ways rather than diving immediately into a structured project that requires the use of tools. Starting simply allows children to become comfortable with the texture and feel of wood, progressing to the use of sandpaper, hammers and nails, and the safety precautions necessary to use those and other woodworking tools. Children 5 to 7 years old are often perfectly happy to cut, hammer, and glue wood together without being too concerned about the outcome. Older youngsters may want assistance to build specific projects, such as birdhouses or cutting boards.

Lumberyards that cut wood to order can sometimes provide free wood scraps. If children have several different kinds, sizes, and shapes of wood as well as different sized nails, there will be more interest. Handsaws, drills, screwdrivers, vises, and chisels can be introduced one at a time, and projects can be designed to provide practice with these additional tools. Supply the younger children with chunks of balsa and other soft woods that can be cut with a small **coping saw** and glued together. Harder wood, hammer, nails, and **crosscut saws** can come later. Balsa wood can usually be purchased in hobby shops or online (see Internet Resources for sources).

Youngsters who want to try making specific projects can make an online search or leaf through magazines, books, and pamphlets that you have collected for them. Learning how to enlarge patterns and transfer them to the wood is a logical next step, then follows measuring, cutting, fastening the pieces together, smoothing with sandpaper, and applying a finish. Encourage good workmanship rather than speedy production. One of the advantages of woodworking in an afterschool program is that children can take advantage of long stretches of time and do a really careful job.

After they become proficient with small projects, some children might want to tackle larger ones. Several youngsters could collaborate to build a playhouse, a tree house, or a puppet theater. One of my college students remembered his satisfaction at age 10 when he used strips of plywood to build a complex exercise area for the center's pet hamster. Modeled after a mouse maze, it contained nooks and crannies in which their furry friend could sleep, as well as interesting areas to explore. Open at the top, and accessible from the hamster's cage, it provided hours of enjoyment for both rodent and children.

Somewhere in your community you might have a retired builder or furniture refinisher who can teach the fine points of wood construction or finishing. With patient and gentle guidance from their teacher, three 10-year-olds at one center I visited covered a kitchen work area with ceramic tiles. Their sense of competence soared, and they proudly showed off their work to visitors. Be sure to make sure there is adequate ventilation whenever paint, varnish, or other solvent-based products are used, and, if possible, schedule these activities out of doors. Other good resources for woodworking activities are listed at the end of this chapter.

Benefits of Working with Wood
❀ Learning the properties of wood and glue
❀ Learning how to use tools
❀ Enjoying the experience of building something
❀ Discovering a lifelong hobby

Building and Flying Kites

With the popularity of Khaled Hosseini's recent book *The Kite Runner,* and the film made from that book, an increased interest in kites of all kinds has emerged. A simple diamond-shaped kite is very easy to make, and once several children have constructed and decorated their kites, the activity can move outside on a breezy day. Several Web sites are devoted to the construction of several different styles of kites, as well as detailed instructions and strategies for flying them successfully. Try making a simple kite yourself. Once you understand the process, bring in enough material for a group of children to make their own kites, encourage them to decorate them so they can be told apart in the sky, and then schedule a kite-flying activity out of doors.

Benefits of Making and Flying Kites
❀ Engaging creatively in the construction process
❀ Experiencing the pleasure of beginning and completing a project
❀ Enjoying the serenity of holding a flying kite for an extended period
❀ The Chinese believe that flying kites on a regular basis prolongs life

Raising Animals

In some before- and afterschool environments, it is feasible to include animals in the curriculum. Whether the animals are small and caged, such as guinea pigs, hamsters, snakes, or iguanas, or much larger animals, such as sheep, pot-bellied pigs, ponies, or ostriches, children will never forget their animal friends and will learn many valuable lessons from helping to care for them.

Invite veterinarians, local small farmers and ranchers, dog or cat breeders, 4-H members, or representatives of the National FFA Organization to visit your program. Their presentations may lead to an interest in animal care among your group. Sometimes speakers from a pet-rescue organization or wild-animal rehabilitation group will bring in injured animals and talk about the care necessary to return their patients to the wild.

Pets arrive in afterschool settings from a variety of sources. Sometimes one of the staff members or parents has a pet that he or she can no longer care for at home. School-age children like to earn money, and the acquisition of a center pet could become the focus of a fundraising effort. It is important that before any animals are brought into the center, however, local health regulations are reviewed, the cost of required immunizations and possible neutering are considered, and the source of funds for the animal's feed is defined. Obviously, if you share your facility with other people, they will also need to be consulted. Bringing an animal into your program is not only an enjoyable experience but is also a long-term commitment and one that deserves a great deal of thought and planning (Carroll, 2001). You will also need to develop a plan for the animal's care, possibly outside the program facility, during weekends and holidays. A rotating schedule that sends small animals home to children's families in turn works well for some programs, but a large animal such as a goat or pony will require that staff members travel to the facility where the animal is kept to manage the feeding, exercising, etc.

Once the kind of pet has been determined, make a visit to the public library with a few children to borrow books about caring for the animal. Together, plan where the pet will live, and discuss how the cleaning, feeding, and exercising will be scheduled and supervised. Work with the children to figure out how you will need to rearrange the program space to accommodate the cage and supplies, or make arrangements to build fencing and a shelter. After all these considerations are dealt with, enjoy the new addition to your program!

Animals that have been cared for in school-age programs include the following:

birds	hamsters	cats	dogs	gerbils
horses	mice	rabbits	snakes	ducks
fish	iguanas	frogs/toads/turtles	heifers	ostriches
guinea pigs	pot-bellied pigs	sheep	chickens	

Two useful books to add to your classroom library if you decide to embark on animal care are *The ASPCA Complete Guide to Pet Care*, by David L. Carroll, and *Taking Care of Pets*, by Susan Ring (English/Spanish). Others are listed at the end of this chapter.

Benefits of Raising Animals
- ❀ Connecting with living things
- ❀ Understanding the physical needs of pets and how to care for them
- ❀ Social interaction with others
- ❀ Developing responsibility

SUMMARY

Children who participate in programs after school need lots of physical activity to develop normally and develop lifelong habits of healthy living. Developing an outdoor environment that encourages children to play actively and engage in a variety of activities is an important part of planning an outdoor curriculum. Organizing outdoor games and activities takes planning and preparation. It also takes an enthusiastic attitude and a willingness to participate along with the children. Outdoor activities such as gardening, woodworking, and animal husbandry provide opportunities for children to engage in long-term commitments and see the results of their efforts. Athletic activities such as team sports and recreational swimming, hiking, cycling, skating, and skateboarding may take special arrangements, but they can add a great deal to the value of a school-age program.

TERMS TO LEARN

cold frame

collage

cooperative games

coping saw

crosscut saw

cultural conditioning

greenhouse

playscapes

tally

windowsill garden

REVIEW QUESTIONS

1. Why are recreational games an important part of the school-age program?

2. What does Jim Deacove mean when he compares musical chairs to our society?

3. List four possible sources of free gardening equipment or supplies.

4. Describe three things you can do with a parachute.

5. How can children in afterschool programs participate in team sports?

CHALLENGE EXERCISES

1. Lead a group of 10 school-age children in a game that most of them do not know. How did it go? Describe in a few paragraphs what steps you went through to explain the rules, demonstrate the play, and clarify confusion.
2. Call your local chamber of commerce and ask for a list of service clubs in your community. Which clubs could be the source of supplies or equipment for outdoor activities?
3. Draw a sketch of a school-age site with which you are familiar. Where might you put a small garden? Explain why it is important to select several sites before approaching the school or agency administration for permission to plant a garden.

4. What challenges might you face when you decide to plan a bike day at your center? How could you handle each of the problems you think of?

Children's Books

The ASPCA Complete Guide to Pet Care, D. L. Carroll

Barnyard in Your Backyard: A Beginner's Guide to Raising Chickens, Ducks, Geese, Rabbits, Goats, Sheep, and Cows, by Gail Damerow

4-H Guide to Raising Chickens, by Tara Kindschi

Taking Care of Pets, Susan Ring

How to Build Animal Housing: 60 Plans for Coops, Hutches, Barns, Sheds, Pens, Nestboxes, Feeders, Stanchions, and Much More, by Carol Ekarius

INTERNET RESOURCES

Balsa wood for carpentry and crafts:
   http://www.nationalbalsa.com/

Cooperative games:
   http://www.irvingisd.net/pe/PEWEB/cooperative_games.htm

Cooperative team games:
   http://www.ultimatecampresource.com/site/camp-activities/cooperative-games. page-1.html

Guide to cooperative games for social change:
   http://freechild.org/gamesguide.htm

How to Make and Fly Kites (an excellent online resource for kite construction and flight instructions):
   http://www.howtomakeandflykites.com/

Making and Flying Kites: Learn about kites—how to make, how to fly:
   http://www.making-and-flying-kites.com/

You Tube: How to Make a Traditional Kite out of a plastic bag:
   http://www.youtube.com/watch?v=Z2QLdTiOU3c

Make Your Own Kite—instructions for making a very simple diamond-shaped kite.
   http://www.skratch-pad.com/kites/make.html

REFERENCES

Brenner, B. (2004). *One small place by the sea*: New York: HarperCollins.

Brown, S. (2008, May 7). *Why do we play?* Paper presented at the Art Center Design Conference, Pasadena, CA. Retrieved April 26, 2010, from http://www.ted.com/talks/ stuart_brown_says_play_is_more_than_fun_it_s_vital.html

Burdette, H. L., & Whitaker, R. C. (2005, January). Resurrecting free play in young children. *Archives of Pediatric Adolescent Medicine, 159,* 5.

Carroll, D. L. (2001). *The ASPCA complete guide to pet care.* New York: Penguin/Plume.

Cox, P. (2007). *Summer adventures: Terrific themes for a carefree summer program.* Nashville, TN: School-Age Notes.

Deacove, J. (1990). *Cooperative games for indoors and out.* Perth, Ontario, Canada: Family Pastimes.

Freitas, S. (2008). *Youth watershed education.* San Jose: City of San Jose Environmental Services Department, retrieved April 27, 2010 from http://www.sanjoseca.gov/esd/ schools/youth-watershed-education-grants.asp

Frost, J. L. (2006). *The dissolution of children's outdoor play: Causes and consequences.* Paper presented at The Value of Play: A Forum on Risk, Recreation and Children's Health, May 31. Retrieved November 10, 2008, from http://cgood.org/assets/attachments/ Frost_Common_Good_FINAL.pdf

Gies, E. (2008, Fall/Winter). Playing it smart! *Land & People,* 8.

Greenman, J. (2005). *Caring spaces, learning places: Children's environments that work* (2nd ed.). Redmond, WA: Exchange Press.

Haas-Foletta, K., Cogley, M., & Ottolini-Geno, L. (2005). *School-age ideas and activities for after school programs.* Nashville, TN: School-Age Notes.

Henig, R. M. (2008, February 17). Taking play seriously. *New York Times Magazine.* Retrieved January 2, 2009, from http://query.nytimes.com/gst/fullpage.html?res= 9404E7DA1339F934A25751C0A96E9C8B63

Johnson, J., Christie, J., & Wardle, F. (2005). *Play, development and early education.* Boston: Pearson/Allyn & Bacon.

Keeler, R. (2008). *Natural playscapes.* Redmond, WA: Exchange Press.

Kelland, K. (2010, March 10). Scientists find why "sunshine" vitamin D is crucial. *Reuters.* Retrieved April 26, 2010, from ttp://www.reuters.com/article/idUSTRE6261IX20100308

Lewis, C. S. (2004). *The Lion, the Witch, and the Wardrobe.* New York: HarperCollins.

Louv, R. (2008). *Last child in the woods: Saving our children from nature-deficit disorder.* Chapel Hill, NC: Algonquin.

McGee, J. (2005). *Woodshop for kids.* Bellingham, WA: Hands on Books.

Morgen, C. (2010). The sunshine vitamin: Are children getting enough? Retrieved from http://www.seattleschild.com/article/20100104/SCM04/100109939

Nebraska Department of Education. (2008). *Call to action: Re-connecting the world's children to nature.* Paper presented at the Working Forum on Nature Education: New tools for connecting the world's children with nature, July 21–23, 2008, Nebraska City, Nebraska.

Nelson, E. (2008, September/October). The outdoor classroom: No Child Left Behind, beginnings workshop [Handout]. *Exchange,* 39–43.

Orfalea Foundations. (2010). *About the outdoor classroom.* Retrieved April 27, 2010, from http://orfaleafoundations.org/go/our-initiatives/outdoor-classroom/about-the-outdoor- classroom/

Pellegrini, A. D., Horvat, M., & Huberty, P. (1998). The relative cost of children's physical play. *Animal Behavior, 55*(4), 7.

Wells, N. M. (2003). At home with nature: Effects of "greenness" on children's cognitive functioning. *Environment and Behavior, 32*(6), 20.

Wilder, L. I. (2005). *Little house in the big woods.* New York: HarperFestival.

Chapter
14

Working With Older School-Age Children and Teens

One of the most significant challenges for out-of-school programs, especially those offering traditional before- and afterschool care, is designing environments and planning activities that appeal to children beyond fourth grade, generally ages 9 and older. Many of these youngsters have been in group care since early childhood and would prefer to go home, even to an empty house, after school. They know all the board games, they are tired of the routines, and they want a more individualized and interesting way to spend their time. Even more challenging to engage in afterschool activities are middle school and high school youths, who by virtue of having left elementary school behind and entered the world of 50-minute classes, lockers, and school dances usually appear rather grown up and capable.

OLDER SCHOOL-AGERS AND TEENS: INTERMEDIATE GRADES, MIDDLE SCHOOL, JUNIOR HIGH, AND HIGH SCHOOL

Definition of Terms

This chapter is about older children—those from ages 9 to 11 in elementary schools and from ages 12 to 18 in secondary schools. Depending on the school district, these youngsters are generally found in the intermediate grades of elementary schools (usually Grades 4–5 or 6), in middle schools (generally Grades 5 or 6–8), junior highs (Grades 7 and 8 or 7–9) and high schools (Grades 9–12 or 10–12) (Manning & Bucher, 2009). Most of the material in this chapter applies to all age groups, but some of it is specific to one age group or another. Generally children from age 9 to 11 will be referred to as "older children," although that term can also refer to fifth, sixth, or even seventh graders in middle schools.

Middle school youngsters are also sometimes called "preteens" or "young adolescents." "Teens," since it specifically refers to youngsters 13 to 19, usually refers to children in junior high and high school or youngsters who have left school but are in programs intended for that age group.

The arguments against self-care presented in the early chapters of this book are primarily targeted at older children and young adolescents. Few parents believe that 7- or 8-year-olds are ready to leave at home unsupervised, and even if they allow their children some modicum of self-care, they usually feel uneasy about it. But a 12-year-old? A 16-year-old? In a society where 50 years ago children that age were earning wages—and some still are—it seems a bit of a stretch to tell these youngsters and their parents that they are not old enough to take care of themselves after school.

Yet, the truth is that we live in a different world from the one our grandparents lived in, and today's preadolescent children and young teens are far more vulnerable to violent crimes, drug and alcohol habits spawned by boredom, and stress-related illnesses than were their forebears. Most of the crimes perpetuated by and against teenagers in the United States take place between 3:00 and 8:00 p.m. (Fight Crime: Invest in Kids, 2007; Gottfredson, Gottfredson, & Weisman, 2001), and the afterschool habits of unsupervised 10-year-olds may predispose them to be included in those statistics.

Safety of Older School-Age Children

The parents of more than 28 million school-age children work outside the home. As many as 14 million children, including over 35% of 12-year olds, go to empty houses on any given afternoon. A 2006 survey of over six hundred 12- to 17-year-olds found that youngsters who were left unsupervised 3 or more days per week were twice as likely as supervised youths to associate with gang members, three times as likely to be engaged in criminal behavior, and more than three times as likely to use illegal drugs (Fight Crime: Invest in Kids, 2007). In nearly every survey recorded by agencies compiling out-of-school statistics, working parents report that their number-one concern is the safety of their children during the afterschool hours (Duffett & Johnson, 2004; National Youth Violence Prevention Resource Center, 2007). A 2008 survey showed that 97% of parents believed afterschool programs kept their children safe. Unfortunately, during this period of economic challenge, only 79% of the respondents believed that afterschool programs were affordable for their families (Prime Time Palm Beach County, 2008).

In most communities there seem to be fewer wholesome and safe activities for older children to participate in with their friends than there were 20 or 30 years ago, and fewer parents and grandparents are available to "keep an eye" on them near home as they try out their maturing skills. Without a meaningful attachment to a group, some youngsters are drawn to gangs. Adolescents crave excitement and group activity. If they cannot find it in programs organized by responsible adults, they may find it in less desirable places.

Communities that have developed programs for older school children have seen a decrease in vandalism and school failure (Goldsmidt, Huang, & Chinen, 2007; Shernoff & Vandell, 2007; Yohalem, Wilson-Ahlstrom, Ferber, & Gaines, 2006). Many parents in those communities who have previously spent most afternoons worrying about and communicating with their school-age children are now able to concentrate on their jobs. This increase in parental **productivity** is another outcome of school-age programming that has encouraged increasing numbers of communities and businesses to provide financial support for out-of-school options. Parent productivity goes down when parents are worried about their children. This angst is so widespread that researchers have even given it a name: Parental Concern About After-School Time (PCAST) (Nierenberg, 2006).

According to a 56-page report about the high cost to business of unsupervised children, working parents are more likely to experience this parental concern when their children begin to spend more time unsupervised, when they are the parent responsible for securing child care, and when they work more than half-time (Nierenberg, 2006). Parents of older children (Grades 6–12) are at the highest risk of PCAST, because their youngsters are the least likely to be supervised after school. Even when programs targeted for these ages exist, many parents struggle to convince their youngsters to attend. For this reason it is essential for you to understand the developmental characteristics of older children as well as what is necessary to create programs that meet the needs of this older population and entice them to participate.

DEVELOPMENTAL CHARACTERISTICS OF OLDER CHILDREN AND TEENS

Erikson describes children aged 6 to 12 as being in the stage of industry vs. inferiority. Although they are forming friendships with peers during this stage, children also carefully observe teachers, older siblings, and sometimes relatives or friends of their parents to learn how the adult world works (Erikson, 1993; Havighurst, 1972). It is important to children in this stage to learn how to do real, grown-up tasks, and they develop a sense of competence from doing so. Refer to Chapter 5 for more details about Erikson's views about this stage of development.

Fourth-, fifth-, and sixth-grade children are moving into Level 2 of moral reasoning (Kohlberg, 1984) and like to develop their own games or change the rules of games they played as younger children. They are better at understanding other people's points of view and can work together collaboratively to paint a mural, build a structure, plan events, or decorate a room. Offer them active games to play, interesting things to think and talk about, problems to solve, and a variety of ways to work with one another. See Table 14.1 for more details about the development of these "mid-aged" children.

Middle school youth want even more challenge. Early adolescence is a time of rapid physical, psychological, social, and cognitive change (Cole, Cole, & Lightfoot, 2009). Between the ages of 10 and 16, most youngsters move from the familiar one-classroom elementary model to a school day that may include as many as five different classrooms, teachers, and unique groupings of students. Within a 6-hour period they may be undressing and suiting up with their peers for physical education classes, struggling to produce a pleasant sound with their voice or a musical instrument, or grappling with the nuances of a foreign language, mathematical formula, or ethical dilemma.

TABLE 14.1 MILESTONES in School-Age Development.

Age	Physical	Cognitive	Language	Social-Emotional
6 yrs.	Has 90% of adult-size brain Reaches about two-thirds of adult height Begins to lose baby teeth Moves a writing or drawing tool with the fingers while the side of the hand rests on the table top Can skip Can tie a bow	Begins to demonstrate concrete operational thinking Demonstrates conservation of number on Piaget's conservation tasks Can create series operationally rather than by trial and error	Might use a letter-name spelling strategy, thus creating many invented spellings Appreciates jokes and riddles based on phonological ambiguity	Feels one way only about a situation Has some difficulty detecting intentions accurately in situations where damage occurs Demonstrates Kohlberg's preconventional moral thinking
7 yrs.	Is able to make small, controlled marks with pencils or pens due to more refined finger dexterity Has longer face Continues to lose baby teeth	Begins to use some rehearsal strategies as an aid to memory Becomes much better able to play strategy games May demonstrate conservation of mass and length	Appreciates jokes and riddles based on lexical ambiguity Begins to read using a print-governed approach	May express two emotions about one situation, but these will be same valence Demonstrates Kohlberg's conventional thinking Understands gender constancy
8 yrs.	Plays jacks and other games requiring considerable fine motor skill and good reaction time Jumps rope skillfully Throws and bats a ball more skillfully	Still has great difficulty judging if a passage is relevant to specific theme May demonstrate conservation of areas	Sorts out some of the more difficult syntactic difficulties, such as "ask" and "tell" More conventional speller More fluent reader	Expresses two same-valence emotions about different targets Understands that people may interpret situations differently but thinks it's due to different information
9 yrs.	Enjoys hobbies requiring high levels of fine motor skill (sewing, weaving, model building)	May demonstrate conservation of weight		Can think about own thinking or another person's thinking but not both at the same time
10 yrs.	Girls may begin to menstruate	Begins to make better judgments about relevance of a text Begins to delete unimportant information when summarizing		Can take own view and view of another as if a disinterested third party
11 yrs.	May begin preadolescent growth spurt if female	May demonstrate conservation of volume	Begins to appreciate jokes and riddles based on syntactic ambiguity	Still has trouble detecting deception Spends more time with friends
12 yrs.	Has reached about 80 percent of adult height if male, 90 percent if female Has all permanent teeth except for two sets of molars Plays ball more skillfully due to improved reaction time Begin to menstruate	Shows much greater skill in summarizing and outlining May begin to demonstrate formal operational thinking		May begin to demonstrate Kohlberg's postconventional moral thinking

Source: Schickedanz, Understanding Children and Adolescents, © 1998 Reproduced by permission of Pearson Education, Inc.

The developmental tasks of preteens and teenagers include finding an identity, gaining gradually more independence from others, and acquiring knowledge and skills necessary for advanced academic pursuits and the world of work (Havighurst, 1972). Older teens may already be working some days after school or on weekends and be challenged by interpersonal relationships or the development of new skills that are needed on the job. Since development is both continuous and noncontinuous, rates and degree of maturation vary considerably from one individual to another, confusing matters even more. See Table 14.2 for more details of adolescent development.

Fortunately, researchers have studied the characteristics of effective programs for older youths. The remainder of this chapter will identify those characteristics and will provide some examples of exemplary models that you can follow and look to for ideas.

SOME DIFFERENCES IN PROGRAMS FOR OLDER CHILDREN AND TEENS

Programs that are effective in serving the needs of older school-age children may look quite different from other programs. Sometimes the facility looks like a family room; other models include a soda shop, a sports bar, and a computer lab with comfy chairs. One Pennsylvania community first experimented with care for older children when the school district moved fifth and sixth graders from local elementary schools into a newly constructed middle school. In a description of their program, director Tracy Yanouzas admits that she and her staff had begun with no clear idea how they would proceed but quickly came to realize that programming for the intermediate grades was quite different from what they had been doing before (Yanouzas, 1993).

Create Separate Programs for Older School-Agers, Middle School Youngsters, and Teens

The expansion of afterschool programs for older youngsters has taken place at a rapid rate. Today there are thousands of afterschool programs on intermediate and middle school campuses and many others in community facilities. These afterschool programs help young adolescents develop academic and other skills in a safe and caring environment and increases their engagement in learning. It has been shown repeatedly that middle school students who are engaged in learning behave better in school and have more effective work habits, improved attitudes toward school, a greater sense of belonging to the community, and better relationships with their parents (Fairfax County Office of Public Affairs, 2006). A majority of middle school youth are **latchkey children** who without afterschool programming would return to empty houses at the end of the school day (Killian, 2000).

Public funding often requires that programs for middle school students offer both an academic and an enrichment component every day. The academic component may include activities like tutoring, homework help, and assistance in specific academic content areas. Enrichment includes general recreation as well as art, dance, music, theater, cooking, gardening, and violence-prevention activities.

TABLE 14.2   MILESTONES in Adolescent Development.

Age	Physical	Cognitive	Language	Social-Emotional
13 yrs.	Has reached and passed peak of growth spurt if female Has probably reached puberty (begun menstruation) if female Has begun growth spurt if male Experiences heightened concern about appearance	May demonstrate formal operational thinking Begins to imagine several possibilities for solving problems May become a self-regulated learner	Speaks in longer sentences, uses principles of subordination Understands metaphors, multiple levels of meaning Increases vocabulary	Still has weak sense of individual identity, is easily influenced by peer group Spends more time with friends, usually same sex Might begin sexual relationships, especially with early maturation
14 yrs.	Is reaching peak of growth spurt if male Is gaining muscle cells if male, fat cells if female May develop anorexia or bulimia, especially if female Is getting deeper voice if male Has probably reached the conclusion of the growth spurt if female	Continues to gain metacognitive abilities and improve study skills Begins to generate hypotheses to explain possible outcomes May have more advantages if in a small high school	Improves reading comprehension abilities and study skills Writes longer, more complex sentences Likely to be very involved in electronic communication	Seeks increasing emotional autonomy from parents Fewer parent-adolescent conflicts with authoritative or democratic parenting Involvement in volunteer activities leads to higher levels of prosocial reasoning
15 yrs.	Has probably reached puberty (begun sperm production) if male May reach fastest reaction time	Can think in terms of abstract principles If creative, can think about problems in novel ways and generate unique approaches to solve problems	Improves analogical reasoning of self-referencing strategies Language is more efficient and coherent in expression	Seeks intimate friendships and relationships May have had sexual intercourse but may not use contraception
16 yrs.	Has probably reached the conclusion of the growth spurt if male May reach peak performance level in some sports Body image concerns lead some to eating disorders and steroid use	Can argue either side in a debate Shows growing interest in social and philosophical problems Better able to organize studies and establish self-set study behavior	May fail to develop writing ability if not instructed Continues interest in electronic communications	Is actively involved in search for personal identity Is likely to be sexually active May use alcohol, cigarettes, and marijuana Romantic relationships are influenced by dating scripts
17 yrs.	Is still gaining muscle strength if male Is likely to have had an automobile accident Is likely to have had a sexual relationship	Shows hypothetico-deductive reasoning Can think in terms of abstract concepts about broad principles May take SAT or ACT test as part of college admissions process	With instruction and practice, metalinguistic abilities and study skills continue to improve May have learned a second language	Likely to be involved in continuing process of identity formation May have part-time job May make decisions that bear on later occupational choices May be preparing to leave home, separate from parents

Source: Schickedanz, Understanding Children and Adolescents, © 1998 Reproduced by permission of Pearson Education, Inc.

Afterschool programs for high school youngsters are significantly different from programs designed for elementary and middle school programs. To be successful, programs for older teens need to incorporate a variety of activities that are relevant and interesting to students of these ages and to provide opportunities for them to have input and leadership roles within the program.

❀ *Guideline 1: Don't call your program "child care."* Tracy Yanouzas's first suggestion for program designers is not to call your program "child care." Instead, think of a catchy name and then develop a **logo**, perhaps incorporating the school logo into it (some programs have a contest to select a logo), and a **mascot** (Yanouzas, 1993). Her program, run by a nonprofit organization called Lebanon, was called Lebanon Kids. Many use the word *club* in their name, as in Kids Club or Clubhouse Kids. Some programs select a name that reflects the kinds of environment and activities youngsters can expect to find there, such as the Learning Center, the Afterschool Safe Place, or the Youth Activity Center. Others, such as the After School Center in Philadelphia, have selected a name that leaves them completely free to change the nature of their program over time. And still others have catchy names like Kaleidoscope and Tapestry or acronyms such as RAMS (Ralston After Middle School), SAP (School Age Program), and ASK (After School Kids). Figure 14.1 shows how the logo and mascot help to create an appealing online home page for Cipriani After School Care, which operates Ralston RAMS After School Program in Belmont, California and Perspective 14.1 introduces the Ralston RAMS site director.

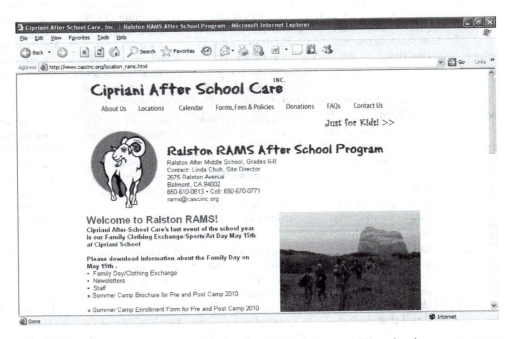

FIGURE 14.1 Creating a logo and mascot can make a middle school program more appealing to youngsters and their families.
Source: Used by permission of Cipriani After-School Care.

PERSPECTIVE 14.1

Working in a Middle School Program

Linda Chuh,
Site Director, Ralston After Middle School (RAMS),
Belmont, California

What I like about working at RAMS is the youth and their natural curiosities. They are not inhibited and they are very empathetic to the needs of their peers and the world. It's a pleasure to be part of their continuous metamorphose. My goals for RAMS are to offer an engaging environment and to provide a safe enriching supervised setting and a nurturing program. We are also working on reducing at-risk behaviors and on developing positive relationships with peers and adults. I enjoy helping youth build skills to succeed in life.

Used with permission.

❧ *Guideline 2: Make the environment appealing, comfortable, and "cool."* Naming your program something unique isn't enough, however. Successful programs for older youngsters don't *feel* like child care, either; they often look and sound more like cafes, coffee houses, or recreation programs than afterschool programs. The goal is to make the environment appealing, comfortable, and even "cool." Some ideas for how to make this happen are included later in this chapter.

❧ *Guideline 3: Provide new games, new challenges, and new rules.* Another lesson Yanouzas's staff learned was that the games, activities, and art projects they had used in the elementary program did not appeal to their new clientele. The older children wanted new games, new challenges, and new rules. Jane Winters, director of school-age programs at Beacon Cove Intermediate School in Jupiter, Florida, emphasizes that this difference, which her school-age staff also discovered quickly, was not a bad thing. Rather, she thinks it put "new energy" into staff planning and engagement. Mandi Vargas, a teacher who formerly worked in preschool and elementary afterschool programs, explained it this way: "Having just older children in our program meant that we could pretty much forget about having to create three separate versions of every activity or read the instructions and game cards to younger children. These older children understand the concepts, the rules, the goals, and objectives much more quickly" (personal communication, January 9, 2009). In many cases, the youngsters are highly involved in planning the activity, so they know exactly what to do.

Used with permission.

Dimensions of Programs for Older School-Age Children   Afterschool activities for intermediate grades and middle school youngsters not only look different from programs designed for children in grades K–3; they usually also have different desired outcomes. In the earliest years of school-age care, a middle school program design team at Work-Family Directions, a nonprofit agency that provides work–life solutions and services to the corporate sector, proposed a three-dimensional way of thinking about programs for older children, and their model still stands as a useful tool (Work-Family Directions Middle School Design Team, 1995).

ACTIVITIES   The first dimension of this model is the *activities* dimension of the program. In this component, staff and youngsters develop a schedule of things that the youngsters think they would enjoy doing, that staff feel competent to lead, and that members of the community could teach. Examples of the activities dimension could include a recreational basketball league, an arts module that allows participants to work with authentic art media (such as acrylic paint rather than tempera and true clay instead of Play-Doh), and a landscaping/architecture component taught by the city planner.

SOCIAL VALUES AND CHARACTER BUILDING   The second dimension is the **social values** and **character-building** component of the program. As discussed in Chapter 6, adults in afterschool programs are agents of socialization, and program activities always contain a values component. Without preaching or lecturing, adults model and reinforce positive values such as mutual respect, teamwork, and cooperation. In some cases, if you're not paying attention, youngsters could be learning far less desirable characteristics from one another, such as disrespect, self-ishness, and cheating. To make certain that the values component is considered, it should become an element of planning and discussed during the curriculum de-velopment phase of each program year.

CARE STRUCTURE   The third dimension of the Work-Family Directions model rep-resents the **care structure**. This refers to the policies, procedures, and routines that help staff members to care effectively for children and youth and the contractual obligations, written and implied, between the provider/agency and the families of the children served. Chapter 16 will cover this dimension in detail, but for the mo-ment it might be helpful to think about the days and times that your program is open to older youngsters. Does the program close for school holidays? Is it available before school for children whose parents leave home several hours before the school day be-gins? Does the program stay open late enough to accommodate families who com-mute and may need to pick up other children from various child care arrangements? Scheduling decisions, which are often made by school district or agency administra-tors, may affect your ability to effectively serve the families in your community.

Implications for School-Age Staff   So what does this model tell us about the role of afterschool staff? To implement the *activities* dimension of the program, staff members will need to develop weekly schedules and lesson plans in collabora-tion with students to ensure that the program meets all requirements defined for the afterschool program. They will also need to provide leadership for part-time site staff, students, and volunteers and provide the necessary coaching, training, and performance assessment to ensure that quality programming is delivered to the participants. This may involve collaborating with school administrators, school staff, and parents regarding program activities and student needs and optimizing the quality of homework assistance and student enrichment by recruiting and integrating volunteers and community-based partners into to the program.

Implementing the *social values* and *character-building* dimensions involves supporting students in making positive behavior choices and taking disciplinary measures when appropriate, as well as fostering an engaging environment that students, program staff, and volunteers want to be part of each day. It can also take additional forms, such as building student leadership skills, perhaps encouraging them to host visitors and explain the program to them, to represent the program at community events, or participate in service learning projects.

Implementing the *care structure* involves recruiting well-educated staff members and supporting them in their leadership roles. It also includes developing and managing the budget effectively so students and staff have appropriate program supplies, materials, and opportunities to attend trainings and special events. Ensure student safety at all times by regulating the ratio of adults to children and personally assisting in setup, breakdown, and ongoing maintenance of equipment and facilities and keeping the school or community site clean and orderly. Schedule staff development and training on a regular basis, and ensure that it meets the individual needs of staff members.

Make the Program Look Different

A popular approach taken in program planning for older children in programs that also include younger children is to distinguish some activities, especially **clubs**, as appropriate for specific ages. Clubs are interest groups led by adults or teens who have a particular skill or interest in the same subject, and they can be targeted specifically for younger or older participants. Programs for older elementary school children and those in middle schools often make a heavier use of clubs in program planning than those designed for younger children. Popular clubs include dance, computers, drama, painting, karate, cooking, basketry, math, music lessons, rocket building, or competitive sports. Some programs allow children to select the club they wish to attend each time they meet, but most encourage youngsters to stay with the same club for at least 6 weeks. Some clubs meet for an entire school term.

Many clubs operate much like a seminar or class, with the leader teaching certain skills that take several weeks to develop and culminate in some kind of a product that is produced by the participants. For example, one program's cooking club put on a "'50s diner evening" for their parents. A logical ending to a drama club session would be a play or a puppet show. A sewing club might stage a fashion show or make stuffed animals for a children's center or hospital. In this model, the sports club might include studying sports statistics, related history, or creative writing as well as learning to play one or more sport.

Clubs at Jupiter Middle School of Technology in Florida include podcasting, during which students learn how to create storyboards, write scripts, and synthesize 2-minute digital videos that will be entered into a local film festival. Other Jupiter clubs include Students Working Against Tobacco, Tree Huggers, and WJMS, the school radio station. In addition to on-campus clubs that meet before and after school, the out-of-school section of the local parks and recreation department contracts with individual "recreation consultants" to create modules for intermediate and middle school youth (Prime Time Palm Beach County, 2008). Modules meet 1 or 2 days a week for up to 10 weeks and include the Sushi Experience (find out where sushi started and why it was developed), What's for Dinner (during which participants prepare a complete meal consisting of a main dish, salad, and a beverage), Bonsai Basics, and Marine Archaeology Exploration. Other popular clubs Include Stamp and Coin Collectors, Model Building, Fiber Arts (sewing, knitting, crocheting, tapestry, and quilting), Wood Carving, Dancing, Karate, and Yoga. Figure 14.2 illustrates the approval process used for screening such consultants.

❀ *Consider This:* ❀

Have you ever collected rocks, stamps, coins, model dinosaurs, sports cards, or other objects? Do you know anyone (possibly an older adult) who did? Why do you suppose children like to collect things? Some adults say that they enjoy learning about the objects they have collected and being recognized by their friends as an "expert" on the category of objects they like to collect. Do you think this is the case for children, too?

FIGURE 14.2 Class Module Instructor Background-Check Approval Process.

Palm Beach County Parks & Recreation Department/Out of School Programs

Middle School After-School Program, School District of Palm Beach County

Recreation Consultant Background Check Approval Process

Prior to becoming an approved Recreation Consultant, a Nationwide Background Check must be conducted and approved by the School District of Palm Beach County Police. To initiate this background check process, prospective Recreation Consultants must complete the following:

- ❀ Complete and submit the Recreation Consultant Application (includes the Code of Conduct Form).
- ❀ Meet with Parks and Recreation Department for interview and program overview.
- ❀ Submit and receive approval for each Recreation Module being offered.
- ❀ Have scheduled modules and a pending contract to work in the Middle School After-School Program.

Once your contract is ready to be processed you will be contacted by the Middle School After-School Office. All prospective Recreation Consultants must have a Nationwide Background Check conducted and approved by the School District of Palm Beach County Police (this includes substitutes and volunteers). Upon approval, the Recreation Consultant will be issued a School District photo ID badge with an expiration date on the badge. Prior to the expiration date on the photo ID badge, School District Police requires all Recreation Consultants to renew their Nationwide Background Check (every five (5) years) and annually, School District Police will conduct the Florida Department of Law Enforcement (FDLE) Background Check and photo ID badge renewal. All fees for Background Checks are to be paid by the prospective consultant. Please contact the Middle School After-School Office at (561) 982-0925 for the cost of all background checks.

Please contact School District Police to make arrangements to pick up your photo ID. Once you have received your photo ID you are cleared to work in Palm Beach Schools. The Photo ID is required at all times when working in the schools. Consultants will not be allowed on campus without it.

If the results are unfavorable:

- ❀ Written notification will be sent to the individual (details of disqualifying offense(s) are provided), OR
- ❀ Written notification will be sent to the business (if any) that employs the individual. Details of disqualifying offense(s) are **NOT** provided.
- ❀ The individual will have the opportunity to appeal the disqualifying offense.

Although the Parks and Recreation Department will be notified of the prospective Recreation Consultant clearance status by the Middle School After-School office, they will not be given details of the disqualifying offense(s). Be advised that all information is confidential and the School District is not at liberty to discuss any disqualifying offenses with any business that employs Recreation Consultants.

Source: Used by permission of Palm Beach County Parks & Recreation Department.

If your staff will be leading club activities, or at least serving as the primary source of ideas and curriculum, it is a good idea to add "interest areas" to your employment application. The interest areas are not intended to be a determining factor in hiring, but they help to develop a selection of enthusiastic leaders for clubs as well as ideas for club topics. Many programs use the 1- or 2-day-a-week model, and some even ask parents not to pick up their children early on those days, so they can finish whatever they start. To ensure consistency between offerings, ask instructors to develop a resource binder for each club or module, containing goals and objectives, necessary equipment and supplies, a description of activities, and a list of reference material they have found to be helpful. Request a summary of each topic to be included in a list of club or class offerings, to be given to parents when their children are enrolled in the program and to be posted periodically through the year with a schedule of new start dates. Keep the binders in a central location for future references.

If you plan to use outside instructors, paid or volunteer, it is important to obtain references, require the same fingerprinting and background screening required of regular staff, and view a sample lesson before agreeing to include them in your offerings. The Palm Beach County Out-of-School Programs coordinator at the Parks and Recreation Department developed a background check and curriculum-approval process for outside instructors. Figure 14.3 shows the class module summary form and sample lesson plan forms that prospective instructors are required to complete.

Even if clubs are the core of a program for older children, it is also important to offer alternatives to club activities on the days when they meet. Not all children want to participate in the activities scheduled or perhaps in any group activity at all. They should be able to read, play games, do homework, listen to music, or participate in an individual project of some kind. If youngsters lose interest in a club and no longer want to participate, it's generally best to let them drop out until the next set of clubs begins and then make a different selection. For them to miss several meetings, then start again, especially if they do it frequently, can be disruptive. Most clubs last from 60 to 90 minutes on the days that they meet. That's plenty of time for children to become engaged in an activity and complete a task. Program directors report that if they go too long the enthusiasm and enjoyment start to diminish. Special activities, such as field trips and final presentations at the end of each session, can of course take longer if necessary.

Change the Role of the Staff

Staff members moving into programs for older children find they have a different interpersonal role to play than they had played with younger children. It is still important to research and plan new and interesting activities to engage the program participants. However, you may also be asked to teach athletic skills and new dance steps, take groups to the library, help children practice speeches and parts for the school play, and even plan "the perfect outfit" for the promotion dance. To help youths feel ownership of their program, you'll want to encourage them to increase their participation in planning activities and to take on some leadership roles in carrying them out. For example, if the drama club plans to stage a play, encourage two or three individuals to review one-act plays beforehand and pitch

FIGURE 14.3 Sample Class Module Summary Form and Lesson Plan Forms.

PALM BEACH COUNTY

Parks and Recreation Department
Out of School Programs
Recreation Module Summary
To be completed per each Recreation Module offered.

Name of Module: _____	**Days of Week Available:** _____
Recreation Consultant: _____	**# of Sessions per Module** *(Example: 2, 4, 6, 8)*: _____
Grade Level Preference: ☐ K-12 ☐ K-5 ☐ 6-8 ☐ 9-12	**Recreation Module Fee** *(Please Circle One)* **Hourly Rate/Flat Rate/Rate per Participant:** *(Please complete Recreation Module Fee Worksheet below)*
Minimum and Maximum Number of Participants: *Ex. :(Minimum 10/ Maximum 25)* _____	**Is Recreation Module Fee Inclusive of Supply Cost?** ☐Yes ☐No If no, please list supply costs:
Length of Module Session *(45mintues to 1 hour)*:	

Summary of Module to be published in the Out of School Programs Resource Guide

_____
_____
_____
_____
_____

Please complete the attached Lesson Plan and include in detail the following information.

Goals and Objectives: *State what participants will learn by the end of each session. What will the participants be able to do or talk about when they have completed each session. These goals should be measurable based upon the outcomes of planned activities.*

Equipment and Supplies: *List in detail the equipment and supplies needed to effectively facilitate each session. Be sure to include what the Recreation Consultant will provide and what the After School Program will provide.*

Session Format: *List the activities the participants will actually engage in to accomplish your goals and objectives for each session.*

Recreation Module Fee Worksheet
Please estimate your total fixed and consumable costs for each Recreation Module offered.

Types of Expenditure	Estimated Cost
Fixed Cost: *i.e. insurance; transportation (vehicle to transport specialty equipment); staff wages; reusable equipment and supplies; athletic and game equipment; art supplies; etc.*	
Consumable Cost: *i.e. perishable items; paint; glue; clay; prizes and awards; paper; etc.*	
Total Estimation of Cost	

*Please note that when establishing your Recreation Module Fee, School Board Policy does not allow for mileage to be included in program fees. Mileage maybe included during Contract Development with the School District.

FIGURE 14.3   Sample Class Module Summary Form and Lesson Plan Forms. (*Continued*)

Out of School Programs
Recreation Module Lesson Plan

SESSION

GOALS AND OBJECTIVES:

_____

_____

_____

_____

EQUIPMENT & SUPPLIES PROVIDED BY RECREATION CONSULTANT:

_____

_____

_____

EQUIPMENT/SUPPLIES/FACILITY NEEDS PROVIDED BY AFTER SCHOOL PROGRAM:

_____

_____

SESSION FORMAT:

_____

_____

_____

_____

_____

Source: Used by permission of Palm Beach County Parks & Recreation Department.

their favorites to the group. A "producer" can be in charge of sending letters home requesting help with props and costumes, and a "director" can lead actors through stage blocking and learning their speeches. Other leaders can guide the production of scenery, the acquisition of snacks for sale at intermission, and the production of the program.

Youngsters who plan and organize events and activities, make decisions, and complete specific tasks usually feel proud of their achievements and are more likely to stay involved. This means that you must be sensitive to the ebb and flow of responsibility in the program, gradually shifting control to the participants but being prepared to pick up the slack where they are unable to follow through. (Discovering on production night that no one remembered to arrange the chairs may mean that you end up moving some furniture, but making everyone wait until the responsible person arrives may not be feasible.)

By providing structure and guidance that is not intrusive, you can help young adolescents to develop skills that lead to maturity and confidence (California Department of Education, 2002).

Give Older Children a Room of Their Own

Some programs differentiate care for older children in their regularly established school-age programs by allowing children of different ages to group together at various times during the day or week. Having their own space can be extremely morale boosting, for older children especially. Children's advocate and writer Don Bellm described a program housed in a large multipurpose room with a sign in one corner that read, "Third graders, teachers and parents only. All other children KEEP OUT!" (Bellm, 1990, p. 7). One family child care provider allowed fifth and sixth graders to clean out an unused workshop in her back garden and turn it into a clubhouse. It soon became the site of special "older kid" meetings and planning sessions, a homework retreat on fair afternoons, and a quiet place to read for one or two children at a time. Because the workshop was designed with large windows, line-of-site supervision wasn't a concern. And even though their caregiver could keep an eye on them, the children valued the opportunity to have a space that was all theirs.

One California program housed in three portable buildings designates four-thirty as the time each afternoon when children above fourth grade retreat into one of the portables for club time. During that period, the older children may choose to work on long-term projects, read, do homework, or talk quietly in a conversation area. Their group leader is an avid photographer, and several years ago he set up a film enlarger in a closet for a 6-week Introduction to Photography workshop. It's still there. During long, gloomy winter afternoons, the older children can be seen peering at negatives and contact sheets and designing collages or cropping images for enlargements, the results of which decorate two of the building's walls. A do-it-yourself snack center in the kitchen area of the portable provides a break area or a focus of cooking activity for some children, and a well-equipped art corner appeals to others. Other activities this creative leader has introduced include African fabric dyeing, which produced large, brightly colored banners that now welcome visitors to the afterschool program, and a kitchen renovation project led by a local builder, who showed children how to remove cupboard doors to the outdoors for repainting and helped them fasten ceramic tiles to a stained and worn sink surround.

This program recognizes the value of mixed-age groupings for certain activities, especially sports and games, yet also communicates to the older children that they have the right to develop and enjoy unique interests, tastes, likes, and dislikes. Once again, flexibility is the key. It is important that the older children have their space, but it's counterproductive to the program if they are cliquish or snobbish about it or unwilling to allow "their space" to be occasionally used for other activities. Sometimes (subject to approval from their peers) older youngsters in the California program invite a younger friend to visit during club time, or they may accompany a younger sibling or buddy into one of the two remaining buildings after four-thirty to assist with a project, help with homework, or just hang out. This interaction is encouraged by adult staff members. It doesn't take away from the older children's privileged privacy, and it helps to maintain relationships between the different age groups.

CHARACTERISTICS OF SUCCESSFUL PROGRAMS

In addition to having dedicated space and time with their peer group, older children have other developmental needs. Experienced out-of-school program designers agree that successful programs for older children:

- ❀ Offer extended day programs during breaks or off-track periods
- ❀ Involve youngsters in planning and leading activities
- ❀ Ensure flexibility for individual needs
- ❀ Provide a wide variety of activities
- ❀ Challenge their skills, help develop new abilities, and supervise safe risks
- ❀ Create and nurture links with community agencies

(Gootman, 2000; Killian, 2000; Yanouzas, 1993)

Offer Extended Day Programs

Longer days during winter, spring, and summer breaks or when year-round schools are off track provide opportunities for you to plan and undertake projects that take several days or weeks to complete. Snow days or other kinds of winter emergency closings offer this opportunity also, but they have the added stress of requiring everything to be done inside. Some programs are open for 10 or more hours a day during long breaks, so it's important to have a rich collection of ideas and projects ready for these days before they arrive.

For example, collect miscellaneous inexpensive items throughout the year in a "prize box." Good things to put in the box include pens and pencils, souvenir cups, hats, and novelty items of all kinds. When children are cooped up for long hours, play Jeopardy!, Wheel of Fortune, or Bingo. The oldest youngsters can take turns organizing the games and keeping score, letting children select their own prizes as they win individual rounds of play. Perhaps this could even be operated like a carnival, with children turning in two or three collected small prizes for one of greater value. Obviously, you can't overuse this activity, or you'll run out of prizes and it will cease to be fun, but it's a good activity once in a while.

Long, inclement days provide good opportunities to get out the Monopoly board, the chess and checker sets, the wood-burning kit, and the bead looms. Some of these old hobby/activities from years gone by are ideal for days with long time frames. Supply a bookcase with especially engaging books to read, either out loud in small groups or individually, and collect popular magazines for days when homework is simply not an issue. Keep a running list of things to do "when there's time." Recruit a group of bored youngsters to help you put magazine clippings in file folders, sort the parts to all the games, or send for all the free things you've collected offers for. Figure 14.4 lists guidelines for planning projects for older school-age children.

Long-range projects that lend themselves well to long summer (or winter) days and incorporate some of these goals can include (a) writing and putting on a play, musical performance, talent show, etc., (b) publishing a newsletter for parents, community, or school pals, (c) redecorating the whole environment, (d) setting up a penny carnival for neighborhood children, (e) forming a basketball (volleyball, soccer, softball) team and learning to play *really well,* and (f) making puppets, building a puppet theater, and presenting shows for community children.

FIGURE 14.4   Guidelines for Planning Projects for Older School-Age Children.

Effective projects for older school-age children allow them to do one or more of the following:

- ❀ Develop a new skill
- ❀ Advance to the next skill level
- ❀ Gain a feeling of personal satisfaction and accomplishment
- ❀ Give something to the community
- ❀ Help people in need

Source: Based on *Summer Program Tips, Strategies, and Activities for School-Agers 5–14 Years Old,* by R. Scofield, 2001, New Albany, OH: School-Age Notes.

Summer activities can take the form of specialty **camps** (e.g., drama, cheerleading, computers), sports clinics, open recreation periods, classes, and trips to local points of interest. With additional staff and training, some programs offer horseback riding, rock climbing, and water sports. Any of these ideas could be incorporated into school-age programs for older children.

Full-day school-age programs can play an important role in the growth and development of mid-aged children. But to do so, you need to develop attractive programming options that appeal to these age groups. Careful planning and appropriate activities will keep older children interested and engaged, provide opportunities to develop new skills and extend others, and prepare youngsters for the transition into responsible self-care when their families agree it is time to do so.

Involve Youngsters in Planning and Leading Activities

Encourage active participation from children in the planning process. As young people grow and develop in their ability to solve problems of time, space, and personal interaction, the tasks of planning future activities should gradually be handled more by them and less by the program staff. For example, when planning a bicycle outing for a group of second and third graders, you might sketch the streets to be traveled; remind children to bring such important necessities as helmet, sturdy shoes, water bottle, and light jackets; and write the permission slips.

A bicycle outing for seventh and eighth graders will be far more successful if the participants actually plan the route, develop a menu for the picnic lunch, and brainstorm lists of things that could go wrong or need to be brought along. The role of the adult becomes that of a facilitator, occasionally asking a question or suggesting an alternative plan. The activity is pretty much in the hands of the cyclists themselves.

Ensure Flexibility for Individual Needs

Even when youngsters plan their own activities, they may change their minds about participating or decide to postpone the activity until another day. Preteens' and teenagers' moods are highly changeable and influenced by circumstances of the school day, affairs of the heart, media coverage of local and national events, the weather, and even their hormones. It's a good idea to have backup plans for everything and to keep a good sense of humor.

Flexibility includes being willing to change the location of an activity if someone else needs the room or figuring out how to manage when certain supplies or equipment is missing, broken, or being used by someone else. Modeling flexibility is an important role for child and youth workers; the problem solving that goes along with it encourages creativity and spontaneous thought.

Rules should contribute to positive youth development and not be arbitrary or inflexible. The purpose of rules in a program for older children is to be sure everyone is safe, physically and emotionally, not to arbitrarily exclude someone from an activity because a permission slip didn't make it into the director's hand by a specific day or time.

Provide a Wide Variety of Activities

Older youngsters are constantly seeking new challenges. Playground games that engaged them when they were 6 and 7 years old have become too predictable and boring. The daily routine, important for providing a sense of security in their earlier years, now seems dull. As an adult in an afterschool program, you have an opportunity to provide children with activities that may be unavailable to them in financially beleaguered school districts or in the limited amount of time they spend with their families. The following ideas are just a few examples to get you started.

Request Donations of Musical Instruments When you have received enough instruments, you can advertise for a retired musician and then form a band or an orchestra. The Teen Center in Santa Cruz, California, offers free rehearsal space for local bands, which has become a draw for area youth, who come into the center with their friends, purchase a soda and a snack, and listen to music without having to buy a ticket.

A participant in an online newsgroup for afterschool providers wrote that she listened to classical music with the young teens in her program. With some explanations and repetitions, the youngsters learned to love the music as much as she did, "Not just the sounds, like at raves," she wrote, "but the music itself." (M. Teterin, personal communication, 2009). Her program in the Ukraine provided a music studio where teens could record their own songs, and once or twice a year they prepared performances for the community. Even without a proper studio, however, with a computer and a synthesizer you can provide a group of budding musicians with many hours of enjoyable experimentation.

Invite a Local Scientist or Mathematician This professional can run a science club one afternoon a week or coach youngsters in their design of science fair projects.

Many science and mathematics professional organizations have entered into partnerships with schools and afterschool programs. One of the goals in doing this is to expand opportunities in math and science for women and people from diverse cultural backgrounds, which fits perfectly with the mission of school-age programming (Froschl, Sprung, Archer, & Fancsali, 2003; Walker, Wahl, & Rivas, 2005). Contact local aerospace or computer firms to see if they have an education component, and invite them to help you set up and supply a math or science lab and/or provide a volunteer to lead the youngsters in explorations and activities. Parents or college students can also be asked to volunteer occasionally to come by for the last hour of the day to help students with math homework.

Older students in your program could staff a homework lab for younger children in the program.

Invite the Local Community Theater   The theater group can put on their next play at your center, and the children can offer to build the sets and sew the costumes.

Many communities have amateur theater groups that are scrounging for places to rehearse and stage their plays. A dance studio in my community once hosted the production of a musical review based on a 1930s radio show. Their part of the bargain was to build a temporary stage, provide rehearsal space, make costumes, and staff the box office. In exchange, all students of the dance studio were offered parts in the performance or invited to work on the stage crew or intermission staff. All rehearsals were held at the dance studio, as were the five performances at the end of several months. Many lasting friendships grew out of this partnership, and the studio gained new paying customers who hadn't even known the studio existed until they attended a performance of the play. This kind of partnership could work equally well in an after-school program or youth center.

Design an Environment That Invites Older Youngsters   Most older school-agers, especially teens, enjoy settings that are decorated in a theme, such as a pool hall, a coffee house, or a '50s malt shop. The way a program feels when you walk through the door is almost as important as what happens once you get there. Older children also want to have a personal impact on their environment. If they decorate the space they've been provided, they are far more likely to enjoy being in it. If you can obtain permission to paint walls, build temporary dividers, or add floor coverings, there is no limit to what you and they can do. But very creative environments have also been designed without hammering a nail. For example:

- ✦ Inflate a rubber raft and fill it with pillows. Create a "river" of blue carpet or butcher paper, and surround it with river rushes and overhanging trees made from cardboard tubes and construction paper.
- ✦ Set up a dome tent. Equip it with folding camp chairs, pillows, books, and homework supplies and hang an electric light from the ceiling. Place it on a tarpaulin, and add a picnic bench, ficus tree, or hammock.
- ✦ Use a combination of cardboard appliance cartons and Styrofoam boards to create a separate room within a room. Paint it or decorate with artwork, construction paper creations, or cover with cloth. Furnish it with sofa, comfortable chair, coffee table, and board games.
- ✦ Ask youngsters to bring in unused activity items from home. Especially search for a pool table, a piano, a dartboard, an air hockey game . . .

Make Homework an Integral Part of the Program   Unlike younger children, who can probably finish their homework once they return home in the evening, most older students cannot. After fifth or sixth grade, several hours of studying and completing out-of-class assignments are generally expected of all American schoolchildren. By setting up an area that is conducive to study and quiet work, you show that you think this endeavor is an important one. And by being available to resolve questions and confusion, you can assist parents with this important task. Consult with parents and decide if a certain amount of time should be dedicated strictly to homework and when, or whether it is your role simply to facilitate the process. It's also important to provide the tools that these older students will need to do their homework, which becomes more academically challenging and specific than it was in the early grades. Have more than one computer available for use, and develop reference libraries that include copies of textbooks.

Challenge Their Skills, Encourage New Abilities, and Supervise Safe Risks

Providing a wide variety of activities may offer opportunities for youngsters to grow and learn, but only if you exercise creativity as you help the children plan those activities. Simply buying new and different board games or teaching new sports is not enough. Competition is a natural characteristic of many older school-agers, and while it can get out of hand if not mediated by skillful staff, a certain amount of competition can spur youngsters to new growth (Scofield, 2001).

Older children need opportunities to take risks within a safe environment. Growing and stretching is one of their major developmental tasks, and if they don't have chances to do so with supportive adults to help them, they'll do it without that guidance. Depending on the community in which you live, tasks such as chopping and stacking wood, lighting campfires or fireplace fires, carving soap or wood, learning to shoot a bow and arrow, and using power tools all might fall under this heading. Native American people have historically taught 10- to 16-year-old children the tasks and responsibilities of adulthood. In fact, throughout most societies of the world this has always been an important time for young people. Instead of simply "hanging out," they can be spending time developing important skills that they will need in the coming years. Plan activities for long summer days, such as hikes, rock climbs, or horseback riding, and bring in speakers or other community resources to teach map-reading skills, outdoor safety, and care of specialized equipment.

Developing **prosocial behaviors** is another goal that can be achieved during out-of-school time (Durlak & Weissberg, 2007). One program set up a system (devised by the youngsters themselves) to award variable numbers of points for a selection of useful activities around the program—sweeping the floor, vacuuming the carpet, tutoring a younger child, sorting out the game closet, alphabetizing the last month's supply receipts, etc. Points were recorded and collected to purchase prizes or buy privileges such as sitting at the program director's desk to do homework, 10 minutes of telephone usage, a banana split, or other small rewards.

Cooking, woodworking, sewing, generating computer graphics, learning a foreign language—there is an endless number of interesting things that older children can be exposed to and encouraged to learn. Program staff can share their own interests and also bring in experts from the community. Hobbies provide many adults with countless hours of pleasurable activity, and most of these spare-time pursuits were begun in middle or late childhood. Research confirms that to be effective, skill-development activities should be sequential, active, focused, and explicit (Durlak & Weissberg, 2007). This is easy to do. When planning activities, be sure that an adult begins each session prepared to teach children the skills needed for the activity, in the order in which they will be needed, and allow plenty of time for youngsters to practice their new skills in a relaxed, safe, and friendly setting.

Create and Nurture Links With Community Agencies

Some programs for older children connect with community service clubs or recreation departments to develop competitive athletic or other activities during out-of-school time (Coatsworth & Conroy, 2007). If the program can't field an entire team, perhaps the children can join together with youngsters from another afterschool program to do so. Some children may enjoy participating in or leading a Scout troop, 4-H project, or Campfire club, and inquiries to local youth-serving organization staff members may reveal ways in which they can do so. These associations have been working with middle and high school youth for decades and have a lot to offer afterschool programs. Another approach is to work with some of these groups to fill a community need. For example, you could adopt a street or a park and then plant trees, bushes, and flowers. Organize a monthly street or park patrol to clean up litter and keep an eye on things. Work with schools or the arts community to paint murals on areas that are vulnerable to graffiti.

Many opportunities exist for alliances between out-of-school programs and community civic organizations. For example, for a number of years members of the Teen Scene Club in Charles County, Maryland, joined with children in an afterschool activity program at the local public library to participate in reader's theater presentations, to plan and host afternoon teas for library trustees, and to publish a library newsletter (Dowd, 1991). The Seattle Library has created teen centers in the main library and each of the branches for middle and high school youth and has partnered with several afterschool programs in Seattle as well as with Starbucks, which funds much of the marketing material. Replete with an excellent collection of books, videos, and CDs, the teen centers invite young people to linger in comfortable seating with books and homework. Developed initially for latchkey teens, outreach coordinators have invited afterschool programs to transport youngsters to the teen centers for special programs or for help with research projects and homework. Afternoon and evening activities include book, meme, and cartooning groups; homework help; SAT preparation; and teen readings, and the Seattle Library Teens Web site contains a monthly calendar of events, a blog, a podcast, and an online chat feature for youngsters who want to seek help from a librarian.

Many other examples exist of collaboration. For example, eight afterschool programs in Boston offered a science component as the result of a partnership between the Museum of Science and the Boston MOST Initiative (Harvey & Shortt, 2001; Shortt, 1997). The Miami Science Museum collaborates with the National Science Foundation to provide hands-on investigative science activities at 87 afterschool sites run by local community-based organizations (Brown, 2007). In San Jose, California, the Metropolitan YMCA of Santa Clara County teamed up with Kaiser Permanente Health Foundation and other local organizations to develop and administer a health and fitness curriculum in afterschool programs at 228 elementary schools (Santa Clara County Office of Education, 2009).

The National Building Museum in Washington, DC, works with several nonprofit agencies, professional photographers, designers, museum staff, and local middle and high schools to offer a summer outreach program called Investigating Where We Live. During each 4-week session, participants learn to use digital photography and creative writing as a means of understanding and documenting

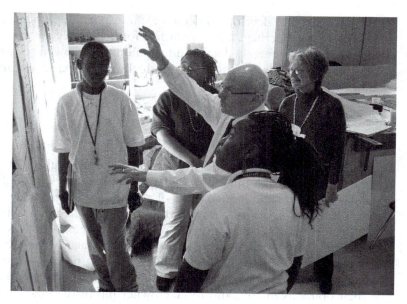

An *Investigating Where We Live* participant prepares one of the walls for the exhibition of student work.

local neighborhoods. In a series of site visits, each team of 10 gathers information about the community's history and identity. Following the information-gathering phase, the teens spend the rest of the summer assembling the information to create an exhibition of their own design, which is then displayed at the National Building Museum. Students showcase their photographs, poems, and narratives and offer their interpretations of the city's communities (Andrew Costanza, personal communication). In 2009, students examined the neighborhoods of Columbia Heights, Shaw, and U Street. Their photographs, writings, and artwork were then featured in an exhibition at the National Building Museum. A related program, CityVision, uses design as a framework to teach District of Columbia public school students how to become active participants in shaping their communities. Through extensive fieldwork and careful mentoring at the National Building Museum throughout the regular school year, students identify needs and propose solutions designed to help local neighborhoods. This award-winning collaboration, now in its 16th year, has helped many youngsters develop technical skills and connections that have led to scholarships and jobs.

Other possibilities for partnerships include collaborative training, workshops and conferences, and shared curriculum. Invite members of the business community to offer workforce-preparation workshops building on the competencies (see Chapter 12) and foundation skills identified by the secretary of labor's Commission on Achieving Necessary Skills (Killian, 2000; Secretary's Commission on Achieving Necessary Skills, 2006). Tap into the energy and idealism of young people. Involve them in service learning projects that confront community issues, such as homelessness, vandalism prevention, and safety. Challenge them to explore individual community service opportunities such as volunteering as library pages, hospital candy stripers, or preschool aides.

You will need to develop guidelines for transporting participants to and from these activities and perhaps adjust your fees for hours they are away from the program. But these are merely details and shouldn't be allowed to get in the way of helping young people learn to take gradually more expansive and responsible roles in their community.

PROGRAMS FOR TEENS

The high-school-age population is particularly challenging. Many interesting activities compete for young adolescents' attention after school. They have busy schedules that may include work, care of a sibling, or other family responsibilities. They are less likely to want to stay on the school campus and much less likely than younger children to attend a program 5 days a week (Hall, Israel, & Shortt, 2004). For non-drivers to get to a program, the facility must be accessible by public transportation or by walking. The decorating and room arrangement should be supervised, if not carried out, by the teens themselves. For teens to feel that their opinions matter, and to take ownership of the program, they must be participants in every step of the developmental process.

There are several reasons why older youth are underserved in out-of-school time programming. Funding sources tend to support programs for younger school-age and middle school-age youngsters in the belief that investment has more impact when made at the earliest possible intervention level. Also, afterschool programs have been primarily seen as a support to working parents, rather than as programs that can aid high school students in preparing for the workforce or higher education and to avoid **at-risk** behaviors (Hall et al., 2004). Many mixed-age programs change their goals and activities somewhat during long breaks from school, and opportunities during full-day programs for long-term projects and traveling away from the program site do make them more attractive to older youths.

Almost everything that has been said so far in terms of naming programs, providing age-appropriate environments, and collaborative planning also applies to the teen population. However, programs for teens cannot be approached the same way as programs for younger children with regard to the goals and objectives of the programs. To be attractive and effective, programs for teens must be developed specifically with the needs of older youths clearly at the forefront.

In 1990, the Carnegie Council on Adolescent Development convened its 26-member Task Force on Youth Development and Community Programs to examine community-based youth development organizations. They were trying to determine how, or even if, existing community organizations met the needs of children and adolescents during the non-school hours. This investigation was driven by a growing body of research indicating that young teens were increasingly at risk for crime, violence, and substance abuse. The first major report, released in 1992, stated that by the age of 15 many American youths would already be at risk of reaching adulthood unable to obtain or hold a job, meet the commitments of relationships, or function as a responsible member of our democratic society (Carnegie Corporation of New York, 1992). The funding for teen programs during the decade following that report was primarily earmarked for programs hoping to improve that situation.

Unfortunately, according to the National Crime Victimization Survey (NCVS) (Bureau of Justice Statistics, 1999), one in five students and nearly one in three males among inner-city high school students had been shot at, stabbed, or otherwise injured with a weapon at or in transit to or from school. Although adolescents represent approximately 14% of the general population, in 2000 they represented about 25% of people suffering a violent victimization (Bureau of Justice Statistics, 2001). Those figures may be low, however, because the NCVS is a random-digit dial telephone survey and the information is collected from whoever answers the telephone. According to data from the Adolescent Health Survey, which used questionnaires and face-to-face interviews of high school students, approximately 20% of the adolescents reported having a knife or gun pulled on them or being shot, stabbed, or jumped in the past year. These data indicated that adolescents would probably suffer about three times the number of violent victimizations reported in the NCVS.

The use of guns is a serious risk to teenagers; an increase in homicides of juveniles in the 1990s showed a clear connection to the use of firearms (Bureau of Justice Statistics, 2002). Young people are victims of homicide at alarming rates, and although actual numbers of homicides have begun to recede since their peak in 1993, firearm usage in homicides of young people has been increasing since the mid-1980s. The situation has not improved much in recent years. More than a thousand children between the ages of 12 and 17 were killed in 2006, and 90% of the reported deaths were caused by a firearm (Puzzanchera & Kang, 2008). Although adolescents continued to represent approximately 14% of the general population, they now constituted about 31% of the victims of violence and were twice as likely as any other age group to be victims of violent crime (Office of National Drug Control Policy, 2007). Numerous studies validate the fact that teens who use drugs are more likely to engage in violent behavior, steal, abuse other drugs, and join gangs. And teens who participate in gangs are more likely to be involved in violent acts and drug use (Fight Crime: Invest in Kids, 2007; Howell & Decker, 1999).

The major recommendations of the Carnegie report were influential in focusing many federal and nonprofit agency grant-making efforts over the next decade. To address the vulnerability of teens, communities were encouraged to build networks of affordable, accessible, safe, and challenging programs that would appeal and respond to the diverse interests of older children and youths. With this in mind, community programs should:

- ❀ Tailor program content and processes to the needs and interests of adolescents
- ❀ Recognize, value, and respond to the diverse backgrounds and experience of participants
- ❀ Extend the reach of programs to underserved populations
- ❀ Actively compete for the time attention of youngsters after school
- ❀ Strengthen the quality and diversity of adult leadership in the program
- ❀ Reach out to families, schools, and a wide range of community partners
- ❀ Enhance the role of young people as resources in their community
- ❀ Serve as vigorous advocates for and with children and youth
- ❀ Specify and evaluate program outcomes
- ❀ Establish strong organizational structures, including energetic and committed board leadership

Source: From *A Matter of Time: Risk and Opportunity in the Nonschool Hours.* Carnegie Council on Adolescent Development. Task Force on Youth Development and Community Programs. Copyright © 1992 by Carnegie Corporation of New York. Used with permission.

In the years following publication of the Carnegie report, many communities responded to the challenge. In 1996, the American Business Collaboration for Quality Dependent Care, a national coalition led by 21 major corporations, provided funding for research and development of resources that could help increase the supply of quality programs. In addition, the coalition invested funds to develop a national model middle school program that could be replicated nationwide. This vote of confidence and commitment by the business community was an important factor in helping to expand the number and quality of out-of-school programs that rapidly began appearing in communities all over the United States. Since 2000, afterschool programs for older children and teens have undergone an exciting period of expansion. Federal funding for 21st Century Learning Centers increased from a million to a billion dollars between 1992 and 2002, accompanied by a much stronger focus on academic outcomes, accountability, and helping middle school children perform better on assessments (Afterschool Alliance, 2006).

A Model Program: LEAP   One early program that developed as a model was LEAP—Leadership, Education, and Athletics in Partnership. This program demonstrated a comprehensive, community-based model that served children from eight economically disadvantaged neighborhoods in Connecticut when it opened in 1992 and is still in operation today. Delivered through community-based afterschool sessions and summer programs, LEAP works closely with school curricula to reinforce literacy and academic achievement goals. This is an important factor in programs for adolescents, since research consistently shows a relationship between school failure and vandalism, drug/alcohol usage, and violence (Carnegie Corporation of New York, 1992; Gottfredson et al., 2001; Zaf, Calkins, Bridges, & Margie, 2003).

One of the most innovative and probably most important characteristics of the LEAP program is that from the beginning it has worked toward preventing problems facing poor young children at the same time it addresses the out-of-school needs of older children and adolescents. College and high school students are trained to work as counselors for younger children. In the original model, one college student was paired with a high school student to work with a group of eight gender- and age-matched children from a targeted neighborhood. While the LEAP program is primarily literacy based, program designers recognized the need for children to develop socially outside the classroom environment as well, so arts workshops, athletic leagues, wilderness camping trips, and visits to other cities were incorporated into the year-round program. In the LEAP program, both group leaders and group participants benefit—while younger children develop skills and interests that will buffer them from many at-risk situations and behaviors, older participants receive valuable training in leadership, curriculum development, conflict resolution, and interpersonal relations. More information about LEAP can be found on their Web site, listed in Internet Resources section at the end of this chapter.

Nighttime Programming Challenges and Solutions   Adolescents also need safe and interesting places to go at night. An unfortunate kneejerk response to the frightening statistics in the Carnegie report was for many cities to institute curfew laws. Justifying the wholesale sweep of underage youngsters from the streets as "**for their own good**," city after city began to round up teens having no immediate destination after 9:00 or 10:00 p.m. In some cases, communities could demonstrate a slight drop in juvenile crime and crimes perpetuated against juveniles, but a second result was more quickly evident—a loud and collective wail from teenagers and their parents that "there's nothing to do" and especially "there's nothing to do that doesn't cost money." In other words, young people on their way to or from sporting events, films, restaurants, pool halls, bowling alleys, or coffee houses were exempt from the curfews, while those without the financial means to attend those events or places were picked up by the sweep.

Create Safe and Friendly Havens for Adolescents

In a well-meant effort and supported by research, to reduce the number of adolescents in public places at night, curfew and anti-loitering laws curtail what for many teens is a primary source of entertainment—"hanging out." Cities who are truly listening to their young people provide ways for them to do this safely.

When they listen, what do they hear? What do teens want in a youth center? The responses are fairly consistent:

"It has to have music."
"Dancing is cool, especially with strobe lights, and so is gymnastics."
"Be sure there's a hangout room, lots of food, restrooms, telephones, and a video arcade."
"I like to play pool—can it have some pool tables and a Coke machine?"
"We would do our homework there if we could do it in a cool place—not a boring, quiet room like in the library." (The Seattle Public Library, however, seems to have overcome this objection with their Teen Center.)

Having a safe environment at night and on weekends can be critical for some teens.

"Sometimes could we have speakers and help finding jobs?"

"I'd like some help filling out applications for jobs and college."

Not too surprisingly, what youths say they want in teen center programs closely parallels the findings of the Carnegie Corporation and other research groups. Over a decade later, research funded by the Time Warner Foundation found that to be successful in reaching high-school-age youth and sustaining their interest, community organizations need to do the following:

- ❀ Listen to youth voices and incorporate their ideas in decision making.
- ❀ Offer employable skills, such as office work skills.
- ❀ Provide opportunities for young people to interact with community and business leaders.
- ❀ Promote partnerships with schools and principals.
- ❀ Introduce participants to the world outside their local neighborhood.
- ❀ Provide assistance in navigating the post–high school experience. (Hall et al., 2004)

The Role of the Adult in Programs for Teens

And what about adult leaders? Even after careful planning, teen centers can fail if the staff is not selected carefully. To be effective, adults in teen programs should serve the youngsters as mentors, teachers, and friends. The Search Institute (2003) calls these people **assets**. Researchers conducted surveys in thousands of communities around the country and concluded that most successful young people have *many* assets in their lives—parental support, community involvement, internal motivation, and high self-esteem among them (Benson & Glickman, 1997; Benson, Roehlkepartain, & Sesma, 2004). However, having adults in your program who serve as assets to adolescents is critical. Such adults love and support teens, are approachable and available when kids have something to talk about, and will take the time to talk seriously on just about any topic. Over 3 million young people have been surveyed by the Search Institute in thousands of communities. Consistently the data show that the most successful young adolescents have three or more adults in their lives to whom they can regularly turn for advice and support (Search Institute, 2003). So you want to find these people, and hire them for your program.

It's clear that communities need to work closely with young people and school-age professionals to develop successful networks of affordable, accessible, safe, and challenging programs that appeal to the diverse interests of teens from all sectors of society. Work with the business community to provide a computer lab, with the parks and recreation department to find a suitable facility and matching funds, and with teens and local artists to paint murals on the walls. Watch **craigslist** for a serviceable pool table or air-hockey game. Survey teens to learn what activities are most popular and what should be included in a snack bar menu. Balance activities that promote academic success and workplace skills with those that are just plain fun. As more teen programs emerge in communities around the country, out-of-school professionals like you will be there to ensure that each one is successful.

SUMMARY

Developing out-of-school programs for older school-agers and teens is challenging because the interests of these age groups are different from those of younger children. There is also a widespread perception that they do not need care in the hours before and after school. Successful programs help youngsters develop a new skill or advance to the next skill level, give a feeling of personal satisfaction and accomplishment, and link program participants to their community in some way. Even more challenging are programs that operate all day during school vacations and holidays and programs designed for children over 13. These programs must incorporate youth participants in environmental design, program planning, and evaluation of activities and may need to seek funding from the business community to survive. Research supports the need for community-linked programs for older youngsters, which can reduce teen involvement in drugs, alcohol, and violent crime.

TERMS TO LEARN

assets	for their own good
at-risk	latchkey children
camps	logo
care structure	mascot
character building	productivity
clubs	prosocial behaviors
craigslist	social values

REVIEW QUESTIONS

1. What is meant by "older children" in this chapter?

2. Identify three characteristics of programs for older children that differentiate them from those of younger school-agers.

3. What was an unfortunate "kneejerk" reaction in some communities to the publication of the Carnegie report?

4. List four positive ways to structure time for older school-agers during extended day programs.

5. How should the goals of a teen program differ from those of a program for younger children?

CHALLENGE EXERCISES

1. Interview a small-business owner about older school-age children in the community. Has this group been identified by the community as a "problem"? If so, why? Determine if there are programs for older youngsters in the community. Do you think there is a relationship?

2. Locate a teen center in your community. Visit it when it is open. Describe the environment, the activities, the interaction between staff and teens. Does it appear to be a place youngsters enjoy being?

3. Read the local news section of five consecutive issues of your community newspaper (you can find them in the public library). Highlight every time the word *teen* is used. Make a table identifying the topics discussed and their incidence. Summarize your findings.

INTERNET RESOURCES

CityVision (National Building Museum; District of Columbia):
http://www.nbm.org/families-kids/teens-young-adults/cityvision.html

craigslist (online local classifieds and forums, community moderated and largely free):
http://www.craigslist.org

Curriculum packets from the National Aviation and Space Administration:
http://education.nasa.gov/divisions/informal/overview/R_NASA_and_Afterschool_Programs.html

Federal resources for afterschool programs:
http://www.afterschool.gov/

LEAP (Leadership, Education, and Athletics in Partnership):
http://www.leapforkids.org/

Research and resources for afterschool programs:
http://www.middleweb.com/afterschool.html

Search Institute research page:
http://www.search-institute.org/research/assets

Seattle Public Library teen programs:
http://www.spl.org/default.asp?pageID=info_attend_teen

REFERENCES

Afterschool Alliance. (2006). *21st Century Community Learning Centers: A foundation for progress.* Washington, DC: Author.

Bellm, D. (1990). *Challenges of shared space.* San Francisco: California School Age Consortium.

Benson, P. L., Roehlkepartain, E. C., & Sesma, A. J. (2004). Tapping the power of community: The potential of asset building to strengthen substance abuse prevention efforts. *Search Institute Insights & Evidence, 2*(1), 1–14.

Brown, J. A. (2007). *Hands-on curriculum for afterschool programs.* Miami: Center for Interactive Learning, Miami Science Museum.

Bureau of Justice Statistics. (1999). *National crime victimization survey.* Washington, DC: U.S. Department of Justice.

Bureau of Justice Statistics. (2001). *National crime victimization survey.* Washington, DC: U.S. Department of Justice.

Bureau of Justice Statistics. (2002). *National crime victimization survey.* Washington, DC: U.S. Department of Justice.

California Department of Education. (2002). *New school age curriculum framework, draft,* Sacramento: Child Development Division, California Department of Education.

Carnegie Corporation of New York. (1992). *A matter of time: Risk and opportunity in the nonschool hours.* Waldorf, MD: Carnegie Council on Adolescent Development.

Coatsworth, J. D., & Conroy, D. E. (2007, Fall). Youth sport as a component of organized afterschool programs. *New Directions for Youth Development, 115,* 56–74.

Cole, M. C. S., Cole, S., & Lightfoot, C. (2009). *The development of children* (6th ed.). New York: Worth.

Dowd, F. S. (1991). *Latchkey children in the library and community: Issues, strategies, and programs.* Phoenix, AZ: Oryx.

Duffett, A., & Johnson, J. (2004). *All work and no play? Listening to what kids and parents really want from out-of-school time.* New York: Public Agenda.

Durlak, J. A., & Weissberg, R. P. (2007). *The impact of after-school programs that promote personal and social skills.* Chicago: Collaborative for Academic, Social, and Emotional Learning.

Erikson, E. H. (1993). *Childhood and society* (Reissue ed.). New York: Norton. (Original work published in 1950)

Fairfax County Office of Public Affairs. (2006, April 14). *Fairfax County board of supervisors and Fairfax County school board to kick off middle school after-school program expansion.* Retrieved September 4, 2009, from http://www.fairfaxcounty.gov/news/2006/102.htm

Fight Crime: Invest in Kids. (2007). *After-school programs prevent crime.* Oakland, CA: Author.

Froschl, M., Sprung, B., Archer, E., & Fancsali, C. (2003). *Science, gender, and afterschool.* New York: Educational Equity Concepts, Inc., and Academy for Educational Development.

Goldsmidt, P., Huang, D., & Chinen, M. (2007). *The long-term effects of after-school programming on educational adjustment and juvenile crime: A study of the LA's BEST after-school program.* Washington, DC: U.S. Department of Justice.

Gootman, J. (2000). *Afterschool programs to promote child and adolescent development.* Washington, DC: National Academy of Science.

Gottfredson, D. C., Gottfredson, G. D., & Weisman, S. A. (2001). The timing of delinquency and its implications for after-school programs. *Crime and Public Policy, 1*(1), 61–80.

Hall, G., Israel, L., & Shortt, J. (2004). *It's about time! A look at out-of-school time for urban teens.* Boston: Wellesley College.

Harvey, B., & Shortt, J. (2001). *Working together for children and families: A community guide to making the most of out-of-school time.* Boston: National Institute on Out-of-School Time.

Havighurst, R. J. (1972). *Developmental tasks and education* (3rd ed.). New York: McKay.

Howell, J. C., & Decker, S. H. (1999, January). The youth gangs, drugs and violence connection. *Juvenile Justice Bulletin.* Retrieved April 10, 2010, from http://www.safeyouth.org/scripts/facts/docs/gangs.pdf

Killian, E. (2000). *Designing workforce preparation programs: A guide for reaching elementary and middle school youth after school.* Chevy Chase, MD: 4-H Afterschool.

Kohlberg, L. (1984). *The psychology of moral development.* San Francisco: Harper & Row.

Manning, M. L., & Bucher, K. T. (2009). *Teaching in the middle school* (3rd ed.). San Francisco: Allyn and Bacon/Pearson.

Miller, B. M. (2003). *Critical hours.* Boston: Nellie Mae Foundation.

National Youth Violence Prevention Resource Center. (2007). *Afterschool programs fact sheet.* Retrieved August 4, 2008, from http://www.safeyouth.org/scripts/facts/afterschool.asp

Nierenberg, S. (2006). *Afterschool worries: Tough on parents, bad for business.* Retrieved January 7, 2009, from http://www.catalyst.org/publication/146/after-school-worries-tough-on-parents-bad-for-business

Office of National Drug Control Policy. (2007). *Teens, drugs & violence.* Washington, DC: Executive Office of the President of the United States.

Prime Time Palm Beach County. (2008). *The state of afterschool in Palm Beach County 2008.* Boynton Beach, FL: Author.

Puzzanchera, C., & Kang, W. (2008). *Easy access to the FBI's supplementary homicide reports: 1980–2006.* Washington, DC: Office of Juvenile Justice and Delinquency Prevention.

Santa Clara County Office of Education. (2009). *Fit for learning.* Santa Clara, CA: Author.

Scofield, R. (2001). *Summer program tips, strategies, and activities for school-agers 5–14 years old.* New Albany, OH: School-Age Notes.

Search Institute. (2003). *Coming into their own: How developmental assets promote positive growth in middle childhood.* Washington, DC: Author.

Secretary's Commission on Achieving Necessary Skills. (2006, March 9). *What work requires of schools.* Retrieved July 28, 2008, from http://wdr.doleta.gov/SCANS/whatwork/

Shernoff, D. J., & Vandell, D. L. (2007). Engagement in after-school program activities: Quality of experience from the perspective of participants. *Journal of Youth Adolescence, 36,* 891–903.

Shortt, J. (1997). *Creative solutions: The MOST initiative.* Boston: National Institute on Out-of-School Time.

Walker, G., Wahl, E., & Rivas, L. (2005). *NASA and afterschool programs: Connecting to the future*. New York: American Museum of Natural History.

Work-Family Directions Middle School Design Team. (1995). A new way of thinking about the middle school "program." *School-Age Notes, 16*(4), 1.

Yanouzas, T. (1993, June). Middle school-age care. In S. Krampitz (Ed.), *Kids* (p. 3). Storrs, CT: University of Connecticut Cooperative Extension.

Yohalem, N., Wilson-Ahlstrom, A., Ferber, T., & Gaines, E. (2006). Supporting older youth: What's policy got to do with it? *New Directions for Youth Development, 111*, 117–129.

Zaf, J., Calkins, J., Bridges, L., & Margie, N. (2003). *Promoting positive mental and emotional health in teens: some lessons from research*. Washington, DC: Child Trends.

Chapter

15

Developing Partnerships with Families, Schools, and the Community

Family involvement in schools and school-age programs increases student achievement. The benefits of parent and family involvement include higher test scores and grades, better attendance, more completion of homework, more positive attitudes and behavior, higher graduation rates, and greater enrollment in higher education (Decker, 2000; Fletcher, 2005). Although parents usually participate in their children's education and afterschool activities more when the children are young, continued involvement through the middle grades and at the secondary school level is important in encouraging and guiding children's development and achievement. That said, it is not unusual for parents to feel that afterschool programs pretty much run themselves and that they are not needed. In addition, staff views about parents, which can vary widely, can have important effects on a program's ability to engage parents (Newman, 2008).

Therefore, it is important for staff to examine their current attitudes toward parents and consider how they may help or hinder their ability to build positive relationships with parents as well as to learn what strategies are most effective in engaging them in afterschool programs.

❀   *Consider This:*   ❀

When you think about the parents of children in afterschool programs, do any of the following statements match your feelings? (a) Most parents today don't care enough to spend time with their children. (b) Afterschool staff need to work together with parents to provide quality experiences for the children. (c) Most parents don't actually care whether the afterschool program is high quality or not, as long as it is affordable. (d) Today's parents don't know how to discipline their children—that's why they behave so badly. (e) Most parents really want to spend more time with their children but can't because they have too many other responsibilities.

When afterschool program staff regard their relationship with families as a partnership in which they both share responsibility for children's learning, and communicate that to the parents, the result is usually higher family involvement. When the vision of partnership is extended to include the larger community, the benefits are even greater. Perhaps most important is that when responsibility for children's learning is shared by the school, home, and community, children have more opportunities for meaningful, engaged learning and begin to see the connection between the school curriculum and the skills required of the real world (C. S. Mott Foundation, 2007; Stedron, 2007).

Out-of-school programs hold a unique place in the field of child and youth work. By their very nature, programs that are designed for children during the hours when their parents are not available to care for them operate at times when parents are not usually available to participate. That seems obvious, but it is easy to forget.

Before- and afterschool programs are indispensable for millions of families who juggle work, family, and school responsibilities with childrearing. However valuable they may recognize your role to be, though, most parents who depend on these programs have very little opportunity for regular contact with the program director or staff.

Some children arrive at your center by bus, van, or taxi before and after school and may be retrieved by a rushed relative or neighbor at the end of the day. Others ride in carpools with rotating drivers who also race to their evening responsibilities. Even if parents are able to physically come inside the center to fetch their children, they may be distracted (as they should be) by their children's reports of the day's activities. Staff members may be involved with children or other parents and unable to carry on an extended conversation.

In non-school-based programs—such as athletic, enrichment, or club activities—coaches, dance or piano instructors, and adult leaders may be setting up or putting away the day's equipment or interacting with children or other staff when parents are present. Without advance planning, it is difficult to have a meaningful conversation under these circumstances. However, in spite of the obstacles, regular, open communication between families and staff is essential. Without it, no one in the parenting–socializing team has the whole picture—of the child, of the family, or of the program. When you facilitate two-way communication, you open the door to full family engagement and participation and improve outcomes for the children.

BUILDING RELATIONSHIPS WITH FAMILIES

Chapter 6 discussed the role of adults in the socialization of children. We know that children learn academic content, attitudes, dispositions, and values from many of their interactions with adults. Research also tells us that if children in out-of-school programs are to receive a consistent, positive set of messages about themselves and learn how to function effectively in society, program leaders must work closely with their families to make that happen. Researcher Dan Bellm (1990) described the situation this way:

> Caregivers may know more about child development and group care, and about how the child spends the school day, but parents know much more about the child's history, personality, home life, and culture. A good partnership is based on cooperation, the sharing of knowledge, and mutual respect. (p. 4)

In 2005, the Harvard Family Research Project (HFRP) introduced the **complementary learning framework**, the concept that an integrated approach to learning that combines school and non-school supports increases the ability of children to learn the skills they need to succeed (Bouffard, Goss, & Weiss, 2008). School-age programs can develop complementary learning frameworks by building links between school and children's families. You can help parents support their children's learning in a variety of ways. By nurturing relationships with families, you can improve communication between parents and classroom teachers, provide opportunities for parents to participate in their children's learning experiences, and address parents' concerns about their children's progress.

On the most basic level, families and programs enter into partnership when the children are first enrolled (Baker & Manfredi-Petit, 2004; Seligson & Allenson, 1993). This is a **contractual partnership**, in which parents agree to give money, vouchers, or at least permission to attend in exchange for peace of mind about their children's safety and development, and the program agrees to provide some kind of child care or enrichment. If nothing is done to foster the relationship between the adults who contract for services and the program providing those services, this is as far as the partnership will go. Roberta Newman (2008), director of a large, multisite school-age program and well-known developer of training and curriculum materials for out-of-school programs, developed a manual for working with teachers and staff to learn how to build relationships with parents and families. In that manual, she wrote

> The one unifying theme among today's parents may be that many of them are stressed by the challenges of earning a living and fulfilling their obligations in the workplace while trying to build and maintain healthy relationships with the significant people in their personal lives. . . . Some parents have more capacities and skills for handling this balancing act successfully than others. The extent to which parents feel that their lives are manageable and under some degree of control has a strong influence on the extent to which they are able and willing to be resourceful partners with their children's out-of-school programs. (p. 7)

The Role of Adults in the Family–School Partnership

It is important before we go any further to think about whom those adults might be who enter into these contractual partnerships. Contemporary families are very diverse. The adults who care for a child may include people outside the **nuclear family** unit, which traditionally has consisted of father, mother, and child. Grandparents, aunts and uncles, stepparents, foster parents, adoptive parents, noncustodial parents—even family friends—all may be involved in the raising of a child (Chase, Arnold, & Schauben, 2006; Susman-Stillman & Banghart, 2008). It is important for you to recognize the roles that these people take in a child's life, to respect their knowledge and experience, and to make them feel included. For convenience and clarity, in this chapter the terms *parents* and *families* mean "all of the significant others in a child's life" who share or assume parent and family roles and responsibilities. It is important to build positive relationships with these important people.

If nurtured, the contractual relationship between a family and an out-of-school program can grow into a **committed partnership**. Ideally, each party recognizes the richness of the contribution of the other in the growth and development of a young human being and works to build on it (Jeppson et al., 1997). Parents typically are deeply concerned about their children's health, safety, and school success. They are, as the author of one government report phrased it, "consumers with an avid personal interest in the outcome of the partnership needs" (Zimmerman, 2000, p. 3). The process of developing a relationship with each family begins with the first contact and continues throughout the year with every interaction between staff and family members.

Setting the Tone at the First Contact

Parents inquire about school-age programs at various times during the year. They may be preparing for a job change or relocation of residence, changing work hours or commuting arrangements, or planning ahead for a child who will be attending elementary school in the coming year. First contacts may come at inconvenient times, sometimes taking the form of telephone calls in the middle of group activities or drop-in visits while staff is in the middle of a meeting. A helpful strategy is to develop a brief script and a packet of informational material that can be quickly pulled from a file and handed to a visitor or mailed to a caller. The next step is to arrange for an appointment and site visit at a more convenient time.

When you first meet with a parent or other family member, remember that this person will not know your program philosophy. Explain that first, before getting into details about admission agreements, rules, and scheduled hours. Recognize that the parents may have a story to tell, that they may feel some stress around the cost or effectiveness of afterschool care, or even suspect that their child may be opposed to the idea. Before you get too caught up in telling the parents about your program, provide opportunities for them to tell you about their child and their family situation. Listen carefully and communicate in a positive manner. As you explain the philosophy of your program, provide the visitors with a copy of your mission statement, a description of the program goals and objectives, and a summary of services and fees. If parents decide that your program is right for their child, a more detailed discussion of specific details can follow.

Reassure parents that you are accessible and that communication between your program and their family is important to you. Encourage them to study the material you have provided and to ask any questions that occur to them before enrolling. This is a good time to ask about the child you will be serving and about the rest of the family. Ask parents to tell you something about their family traditions or culture. Learn if a language other than English is spoken at home. Showing that you honor the child's culture during this initial meeting will help you to develop connections between home and school later and go far in ensuring that children and their families feel valued and welcome (Gonzalez-Mena, 2005; Novick, 1996). Identify any special needs to be accommodated and explain

Provide visiting parents with a copy of your mission statement, goals and objectives, and fee schedule.

relationships that you have developed with local schools and the community. Let them know that you value family participation, and describe a few ways in which they can become involved. Be as accepting and supportive as you know how to be. This will help parents to feel welcome and valued.

Keep a file of community resources and share some of those materials with new parents. Families who have recently moved into the community will appreciate information on bus routes, enrichment and athletic programs, and other services. Even long-time residents may be unaware of the existence of certain children's activities or resources.

❀   *Consider This:*   ❀

Think about a family you know who is facing personal or economic challenges. What kinds of day-to-day issues are they dealing with? What services in your community would be useful for this family to know about? How do you think these family issues affect the child or children in your program? What can you do to help?

Admission and Enrollment Policies

Parents have many assets to contribute to your program, and they can provide valuable insights into family and community. However, for parents to behave as partners, they must understand the terms of the partnership. For this reason, it is important that admission and enrollment policies be clearly written and reflect program philosophy, including waiting list priorities, educational and developmental goals, discipline guidelines, and expectations of parents. It is also important that the policies themselves meet real parent needs. For example, is your program open on school holidays that are not usually included in the business holiday calendar? Are your hours of operation long enough to work for parents who commute some distance to work? How do you handle homework? Which religious and cultural celebrations do you recognize and honor?

Enrollment Packets   Enrollment packets should be prepared and made up well in advance of parent need. Keep a supply handy for parents who may drop in without an appointment, and make sure that they include all the necessary information required for parents to register their child. Typical contents include a personal information form that includes medical information and releases, emergency contacts, and an agreement to comply with the terms of the parent handbook. A complete and current fee schedule and a copy of the actual contract should also be included in the packet, as should a checklist for parents to complete that identifies some of the skills, services, or talents they would be willing to share with the program (see Figure 15.1 for a sample parent talent list). Wherever possible, provide parent handbooks and enrollment packets in the languages spoken by the families of children in your program.

The responsibility for writing and maintaining policies and procedures, creating enrollment packets, and writing parent handbooks is generally that of the director in conjunction with the owner or a board of directors. However, program staff will be called on to locate information or explain it, and so you should be familiar with the documents and the location of topics within them. It's also important to discuss any areas of confusion or conflict at staff meetings to facilitate clarification and modifications of either the policy or the written material if appropriate. Also periodically discuss a selection in the NAA Code of Ethics (Appendix).

Parent Handbooks   Parent handbooks, being lengthier and more expensive to produce than enrollment packets, are not usually provided to parents until after they enroll their children, although many programs are now making these documents available as PDFs on the program Web site. Certainly a printed copy should be made available for parents to review at the initial meeting and any time in the future. Handbooks should be written in clear language and contain all of the information parents will need throughout the year. Typical contents include a current program calendar and schedule, sign-in and sign-out procedures, instructions for late pickup of children and payment of additional fees, procedures for emergencies and illness, discipline guidelines, procedures for meals and snacks, and any materials parents are expected to supply. Parent handbooks should include expectations for parent involvement and clear guidelines for families who wish to take their children on extended vacations. Parents should know how they can maintain their child's place without depriving the program of needed funds and what the procedures are for termination of services by either party. Figure 15.2 shows an example of a parent involvement policy and a description of parent responsibilities.

Program policies should comply with all state and federal guidelines, and handbooks must always be kept up-to-date. Chapter 16 will discuss the legal and budget aspects of admission and enrollment policies in more detail.

Schedule Open Houses, Back-to-School Nights, and Parent Conferences

A review of research by the Southwest Regional Educational Developmental Laboratory found a positive and convincing relationship between family involvement and benefits for students, including academic achievement (Henderson &

FIGURE 15.1   Sample Parent Talent List.

Parent Talent Self-Assessment Tool

Check each of the following talents you have. Rate your talents between 1 and 5, with 5 being very talented and 1 being a little talented.

I am able to organize

_____ plan

_____ think logically

_____ clarify

_____ be efficient

_____ synthesize ideas

_____ analyze

I can see opportunities

_____ imagine/envision

_____ design things

I can lead

_____ motivate

_____ inspire

_____ persuade

_____ initiate

_____ execute

_____ persist

I can instruct

_____ advise

_____ tell stories with lessons

_____ experiment

I can manage

_____ juggle many responsibilities

_____ be self disciplined

I can put people at ease

_____ mediate

_____ negotiate

_____ harmonize

_____ balance

_____ tolerant

_____ generous

_____ cooperative

I am able to

_____ make things work (mechanical)

_____ build things

_____ be artistic

_____ make beautiful things

_____ perform

_____ express ideas with words

_____ express ideas through art

_____ express ideas through music

_____ interpret

Other talents I have are:

Source: From *A Guide to Engaging Parents in Public-Private Partnerships* by Elaine Zimmerman, developed as part of the Child Care Partnership Project. Used by permission of The Finance Project, Washington DC.

Mapp, 2002). Engaging parents and families through special programs is an enjoyable way to build regular family involvement in your program. Make it a priority at staff meetings to talk about the best ways to talk to families, request time to plan and organize parent activities, and encourage a mind-set among the program leaders that recognizes and appreciates the advantages of program leaders and parents working together. It may take some time. Develop a culture that embraces the notion of having regular personal contact with parents and not

FIGURE 15.2   Parent Involvement Expectations and Parent Responsibilities Should Be Clearly Written.

Parent Involvement

Parent involvement is an integral part of the After School Center community and families who enroll agree to participate in the work that we do. Families are expected to participate in evening or weekend activities for at least ten hours each year, although we welcome more time if you can spare it. (Any member of the family over 16 years of age may earn participation credit.)

Parent/Guardian Responsibilities

Before school, parents and guardians must accompany children to the Early Birds classroom and sign the child in, noting the time on the attendance sheet form and using a full legal signature. Please greet the supervisor on duty so that the supervisor knows that your child has arrived. The Early Birds program cannot be held responsible for children not signed in by a parent or guardian.

After school, parents and guardians should sign the child out from the Afterschool Club, once again noting the time. Please make eye contact with the supervisor and let him/her know that the child is leaving.

Waiver forms are available for children 10 years old and older. Using a waiver form, parents and guardians may give permission for children to sign themselves in or out of the program. A written list of dates must be provided when these waivers will be in force.

Parents are responsible for notifying staff in advance of their children's schedule changes and absences, and for calling the Early Birds classroom on sick days.

Thank you for helping us to keep your children safe!

Source: Adapted from *Parent/Guardian Responsibilities,* by Ann Arbor Public Schools Child Care Program, Ann Arbor, MI: Author. Used with permission.

waiting to have problems before contacting them. If parents are treated as the assets they are to the children, they will be much more likely to participate in social activities and other events.

Open Houses   Holding an open house toward the end of each school year and another in late summer can be an excellent way to showcase your program and market it to area families. Make it an informal opportunity for parents to talk with group leaders and the site director and to learn about your mission, goals, and program. Consider having a special activity, such as a scene from the spring musical or a harvest feast of the children's garden bounty, to be an icebreaker. Ask some of the children and their families to help staff host the evening so that parents and children can talk to one another about the program. This can be the all important "first contact" with a parent who may volunteer to help with costumes for next year's play.

Back-to-School Night   After the initial enrollment and contract signing, parents can become lost in the blur of day-to-day program operation. One way to avoid this is to encourage them to attend a back-to-school night for new and returning families during the first or second week of school in the fall and spring. This event should be primarily social in nature or have a very short program that highlights some of the special events of the coming year. Newly enrolled families can visit the site and meet with program staff as well as other parents and children. Match returning families with newcomers in some kind of game or activity, and post carpool maps and sign-up sheets for workdays, potluck suppers, snacks, or fundraising activities. To accommodate working parents, schedule this event after normal program hours or on a weekend, and provide refreshments. Following a welcoming evening such as this, new children and families are more likely to get involved and will have familiar faces to greet them as they arrive each day.

Parent Conferences   Consider holding parent conferences once or twice a year to talk in greater depth about the child or your program. While this may be a good time to discuss challenges or issues that have arisen, don't schedule conferences only when there is a discipline or other problem; use them to build trust and communication with families and to facilitate two-way communication. Programs at school sites may want to coordinate these meetings with parent–teacher conferences, allowing parents to sign up for a conference on the same day they meet with their children's classroom teachers. In some cases, a leader from the afterschool program may accompany parents to the teacher conference if circumstances suggest it and all parties agree. Children do not always function in formal classroom environments the same as they do in less structured afterschool settings. Sometimes the entire parenting–care-giving team talking together can identify areas of need that elude the notice of any one individual. School-age program staff can serve as advocates and facilitators for children and families, and the conference process can help to identify areas where this advocacy might be welcome.

❀   *Consider This:*   ❀

Think about when you were a child and your parents were scheduled to meet with your teacher. How did you feel about this happening without you being there? Did your parents share the content of the meeting with you? Did you dread parent conferences or look forward to them? How can you make conferences a positive experience for parents and children?

Family Fun Nights and Parent Information Meetings

Parent involvement in the day-to-day operation of the program, although always difficult to achieve, increases when families get to know individual members of the program staff. They soon also become acquainted with other parents and families in the program and begin to feel more comfortable at the center. You can facilitate this process with enjoyable social events such as pizza parties, video viewings, hayrides, or family fun nights, when you bring out the board games, play Bingo, or enjoy other recreational experiences together. Some programs meet off-site, sometimes at a local bowling alley, miniature golf course, or pizza restaurant that will donate a small amount of their revenue to your program. Other groups who meet on site order food ahead of time and ask each family for a contribution toward the cost. In other communities, preparation of the meal is a shared activity.

Friendships between families can develop at family fun nights.

These evenings work best if they are scheduled when there is minimum calendar conflict. Find out when practice occurs for the sport of the season; what night the school is holding award ceremonies or school site council meetings or whatever other regular event might conflict. Announce the date in the monthly parent calendar, and send home reminders a few days before each event. Inquire whether individual families need help with transportation, care of younger children, or translation, and develop "buddy pairs" among the families who can assist with one or more of those needs. Occasionally invite one or more teachers from the regular school program or the principal or a counselor. Use your judgment; ask people who are supportive of your program and who are genuinely interested in the children and families you serve.

Some of the program's social events should be just that—social. Think of them as opportunities for building friendships, and eventually partnerships. At other times the children might like to present plays, puppet shows, or musical productions for their families. Still other evenings might include a short business meeting, where you can present ideas for future activities that would benefit from family input to the planning process. Other family activities that afterschool programs have enjoyed include picnics, family trips to the county fair, ice cream socials, and tailgate parties before local high school football games.

Parenting Education and Support

It can be helpful to also schedule one or two evening sessions a year devoted to parent education or support, inviting speakers to discuss issues such as homework, competitive sports, conflict resolution, or other topics suggested by the parents. Other ways in which your program can assist parents in resolving parenting or child development issues include acquiring and organizing a lending library of books on topics of interest to parents, maintaining a section of the parent-communication bulletin board devoted to parenting topics, and listening to parents who need someone to talk to when they run into difficult times with their children. Sometimes all a parent needs to hear is that other parents are facing the same challenges.

Some family members will choose not to confide their frustration. In fact, many people find it difficult, even intimidating, to speak with other adults about their children, especially when things are not going well. Fortunately, very few parents can ever hear too much about their children, especially if the information is positive and helpful. A good way to achieve an exchange of information is to speak informally with family members about the positive experiences you have with their children, what you notice about their achievements, and how much you enjoy being with them. This helps to build positive relationships, contributes to children's self-confidence and self-esteem, and shows family members that you care about them (Fletcher, 2005). Soon parents may feel comfortable enough to broach difficult subjects.

Including Fathers and Other Males in Family Activities

When planning events that include parents and families, be sure to include the men in children's lives. Chapter 1 discussed changing family structures and the increasing number of children who live in single-parent households, reconstituted or blended families, foster-parent homes, extended families with relatives, and other family configurations. Another important change in family dynamics is the increased role of fathers and other male family members in the active parenting of children (McBride, 1996; Roggman, 2005).

Traditionally, school parent–teacher conferences took place between the teacher and one parent, usually the mother, because they were most often scheduled during the workday. Increasingly, schools and afterschool programs have recognized the need to schedule these events in the evenings. The shift may have been primarily a response to women joining the workforce, but the result has been that many more fathers, grandfathers, and older brothers now participate in this important interchange.

Sometimes, however, there is a perception that noncustodial fathers, especially those of low-income and "high-risk" backgrounds, do not participate in childrearing and therefore should not be included in activities such as parent conferences, back-to-school nights, or open houses. According to many studies, this perception is wrong (McBride, 1996; Roggman, 2005; Roy, 2008).

Research findings show that regular and consistent interaction between children and their fathers is alive and well in most families and thrives even more when schools and other programs welcome their participation. However, male involvement is not limited to fathers. Increasingly, especially in single-parent families, the male role is augmented by grandfathers, uncles, older brothers, mothers' boyfriends, stepfathers, foster fathers, and friends of the family. Focusing program interactions exclusively on parents may exclude these important people and communicate to them that their role is unimportant.

Listen carefully when you are in conversation with children and parents; they may mention a cousin who comes to family events, an uncle who lives in the apartment over the garage, or the grandpa who drives everyone to church or temple. Pay attention at events throughout the year and note mention of older brothers, stepfathers, and live-in boyfriends. When you know who the significant males are, encourage them to participate in program activities. Trust takes time to develop, so be patient, but repeat your invitations each time an event is scheduled until all members of the child's "family" feel included. (The same approach is increasingly important regarding children's older female siblings, aunts, mothers, and cousins.)

Day-to-Day Communication

Communication is the key to building committed partnerships. Keeping families informed is important, and it can be accomplished in a variety of ways. It is also important to provide multiple ways for family members to inform *you* about changes in their family, concerns about their child, and other issues. Individual conferences, parent handbooks, informal gatherings, and family evenings have already been mentioned. Here are some other ideas.

A parent bulletin board can help to build parent involvement.

FIGURE 15.3 A Well-Designed Web Site Can Enhance Communication with Parents.
Source: Used by permission of Mike Ashcraft, Founder and CEO of Children's Choice Child Care Services, Inc.

Your Public Front Door   Some programs develop voice-mail systems or Web sites that provide information about their location, hours, goals, procedures, and coming events. Children's Choice Childcare Services has gone even further, by including links to Facebook, Twitter, and YouTube, where director Mike Ashcraft posts informational bulletins about parenting, school success, and coming events (see Figure 15.3 for a screen shot of the Children's Choice home page). Some Web sites are informational only, but others are interactive and allow parents to send e-mail messages to group leaders, the site director, and even their children. To be helpful, these sites must be kept current, and staff must read their email often. In the same way, the outgoing message on the voice-mail system should be current and include information in all languages represented in the program. Periodically refine the information provided by surveying parents and asking them what kind of information they find most (and least) useful (Caplan & Calfee, 1999). Be sure that if you include photographs of children, staff, or families on your Web page, that you have signed release forms giving you permission to do so.

Bulletin Board   Maintain a bulletin board in a location convenient for parents to read. Post the daily schedule and information about staff members, parent meetings, special speakers, field trips, and other significant events. This is a good place to post sign-up sheets for shared meals, field trips, phone trees, and carpools. Recruit parents to "adopt" the bulletin board for a month or a term. Children can also take some responsibility for keeping the bulletin board items current.

Newsletters Weekly or monthly newsletters are excellent vehicles to inform parents and families of coming events, past successes, and a variety of newsworthy items. However, parents receive newsletters and flyers from many sources, so if you want yours to be read and remembered, it should be brief, informative, and interesting. Have children take turns doing the artwork, or include an article on individual children each time, to keep parents reading. Include important dates, procedural or schedule changes, and upcoming events. Some programs include a parenting tip in each issue. See Figure 15.4 for an example of a parent newsletter.

Arrange the information in a clear, easy-to-read format, and if the document is posted on your Web site, print out additional copies to be kept in the classroom, and place a copy of each issue in a permanent binder kept in a location that is available to both parents and staff. (Some parents may not have Internet access at home and may be left out of the loop if that is the only way to obtain the newsletter.) Be sensitive to the differences in educational levels and English language proficiencies among families of the students in your program, and provide articles in more than one language if possible. Never communicate important program information exclusively in writing. Find alternative ways to make sure that everyone is included in the communication loop (Caplan & Calfee, 1999; Fletcher, 2005).

Personal Conversation Sometimes it's good just to chat. Surprise a parent by occasionally asking her how the workday went. Ask a father returning from an absence how his mother is recovering from surgery. Compliment parents when you observe them taking extra time to respond to a child's request to inspect their latest art project or emerging plant in the garden. Share with them something positive their child told you about a family event. Parents need affirmations as much as do children and staff. Direct personal contact is almost always the best way to communicate important information and feelings (Katz, Aidman, Reese, & Clark, 1996).

Telephone Contact Periodically, take a few minutes during the workday to call parents and ask them if they have any questions or concerns they have forgotten to share with you. Don't do this too often or it will be an intrusion, but once or twice in a school year sends the message that you care about their child and the whole family. Encourage them to call you during the day if they want to discuss something that doesn't lend itself to end-of-the day conversation. If something important is going on at home, parents may be anxious about their child during the day. A brief phone call after an emotional morning leave-taking to say that the child has settled into an activity or gone cheerfully to class can be reassuring and allow the parent to focus on work responsibilities for the rest of the day. It can be helpful both to parents and to staff if 1 hour a day can be identified when you can be most easily interrupted by a telephone call.

Notes A short note in a child's backpack saying something nice about that child can give parents a wonderful lift. Of course, it's also necessary to send a note home if there is a serious discipline issue—or an injury, no matter how small. But you can also use this vehicle to share a positive interaction you noticed between their child and other children or a special accomplishment. Extend the "eyes" of parents who miss seeing something special that happened during their child's day.

A Children's Garden
Child Care and Learning Center

Monarch Newsletter
May

Sunscreen

Please see our list on the door of kids who currently have sunscreen. If your name is missing, **please bring in a small bottle this week.** Thanks!

Family Conferences

We are offering family conferences this month. This is a wonderful opportunity to gain insight on your child's experience while in the Monarch room! Each conference will run **20 minutes** with either Miss Shay or Miss Sandra. We encourage you to see one of us to **schedule a meeting time** as soon as you can. "Primary Conference Groups" are

Huddle Topics

We have had several class discussions about __conflict resolution__, while using respectful words with one another and finding a common ground to compromise.

The children have also practiced **endurance in the physical, mental, and emotional capacities.**

We are working toward the understanding of __differences__ between people, and **including everyone** around us! :)

Summer Adventure Camp

Registration forms for are **due ASAP** Check out our display near the front desk for more exciting news!

Healthy Snacks

We have always enjoyed munching on the birthday goodies that our kids have brought in to celebrate their special day! However, it is time that we modify our treats in order to lessen the sugar highs and lows that the children experience. Below, are a few ideas to accommodate this change, and as always, these items must be store bought. Thank you for your consideration!

- **100% Juice** (ex: not Sunny D or Tampico)
- **Cereal bars**
- **Muffins**
- **Popsicles** (no sugar added)
- **Fresh fruit**
- **Popcorn**
- **Fruit snacks** (100% fruit juice)
- **Parfaits** (provide yogurt, berries, & granola—the kids will make them here!)
- **Smoothies** (we can blend the ingredients here!)
- **Whole wheat pita pockets** (the kids can stuff them with a variety of fun ingredients!)
- **Mini bagel pizzas** (the kids can put them together and bake them here!)
- **Invent your own healthy birthday treat!!!**

Thank you for considering one of these alternative treats to share!

Special Projects

We have had fun making flubber (glue & liquid starch), sugar cube creations, spa, crazy hair, English muffin pizzas, sand painting, musical chairs, karaoke, and endurance runs, among countless other activities! Everyday is a new project!

Karate Classes!

Evan Sweeney (Miss Brandi's brother) will be instructing the Karate Enrichment classes on **Wednesdays, beginning June 10th from 11:30—12:15** (tentatively). We are waiting until the summer time to offer these classes to the School-Age kids in order to not interfere with our homework time. Please sign the **"Release of Liability Agreement"** and **pay the $10 per class session.** Don't miss out on the fun experience!!!

FIGURE 15.4 Newsletters Keep Families Informed.
Source: Used by permission of A Children's Garden.

PERSPECTIVE 15.1

Encouraging Positive Connections Between Families and Afterschool Programs

Julie Hancock,
LINKS for Learning, Livingston, Montana

Encouraging positive connections between families and the school is an important goal of the LINKS program. LINKS staff work to create family-friendly environments at the end of the day. We encourage parents to spend time in the program before taking their children home. Over the past 2 years we have increasingly more parents who take time to observe the program, play a game with their child, or visit with staff. This is important time for creating a positive connection with the LINKS program and with the school.

A popular family activity offered by the LINKS program is "soup night." These are free soup (or pancake) suppers followed by literacy or math activities. Attendance at soup nights is very high—over 80% of participating children attend with parents, grandparents, and siblings. Students help prepare and serve the meals. These are very relaxed evenings, with parents, staff, and children enjoying time to visit and learn new games. These soup nights have been instrumental in developing a strong sense of community among LINKS families and staff.

Used with permission.

Photos   Invest in a digital camera and teach some of the older children to use it (chances are, they already know!). Once every few weeks, post photos of children's activities on the class bulletin board or Web site, and send pictures home with each family throughout the year. When photos are taken down from the bulletin board, have children arrange them in a scrapbook with artwork and descriptions of the activities that are pictured. Bring the books to family fun nights and keep them in the room where children can share them with their families. In Perspective 15.1, the director of a large afterschool program describes ways to engage parents' interest.

Results of Effective Parent Partnerships   Parents and staff who work together to develop partnerships can create out-of-school programs that foster children's development in all areas. Research has shown that parent and family involvement in after-school programs increases achievement and school success (Perkins, Christner, Hoy, Webster, & Mock, 2004). Children benefit in many ways when their parents are involved in their activities. They tend to exhibit more positive attitudes and behaviors when their parents are present, and youth risk behaviors, such as alcohol use, violence, and antisocial behaviors, decrease as parent involvement increases. The keys to engaging parents in your program are respect, understanding, and communication. The end result is parents who feel valued, children who recognize the value of afterschool activities, and staff who understand the importance of working collaboratively with schools and families.

Resolving Parent–Staff Differences

In spite of your best efforts to develop a climate of open communication and committed partnerships, parents and staff will occasionally disagree about such things as program policies, peer relationships, or discipline strategies. Dealing with direct disagreements requires **respect** and **discretion** (Katz et al., 1996).

Respect parents' rights to their views, and avoid direct conflict with cultural beliefs or practices. Before discussing disagreements in detail, be sure that you know your program's policy for resolving conflicts with families. Are program leaders free to work out the solution directly with parents, or should the director be included? Should the child participate in some or all of the process, or should the adults discuss the situation in private?

Always use discretion about where and when children and their families are discussed and where you discuss conflicts with parents. Never talk about children or their families in public or social settings, and don't discuss one child with another or with another parent. Confidentiality is extremely important if you are to maintain the trust between families and program staff. Handled respectfully and discreetly, the resolution of differences between a program and a family can be a positive experience, and it can serve as a model of constructive behavior for the children at the center of the conflict.

DEVELOPING PARTNERSHIPS WITH SCHOOLS

High-quality afterschool programs create connections with the curriculum and instruction offered by local schools. While you should not attempt to duplicate or repeat the school experience, developing authentic partnerships with teachers, schools, and districts helps you to plan afterschool activities that support and reinforce what is learned during the traditional school day (Caplan & Calfee, 1999; Diedrich, McElvain, & Kaufman, 2007).

Advantages

One of the advantages of the afterschool environment is that it is natural to depart from formal teaching methods and offer creative, hands-on ways for children to apply the concepts and skills they are taught in the classroom (Fletcher, 2005). Models can be found in nearly every state, and good ideas implemented by large, funded projects can be replicated on a smaller scale in your program. For example, in Central Falls, Rhode Island, the extended school-day program provides activities specifically designed to boost academic achievement. The leaders of the program collaborated with the YMCA, Boy Scouts, several Hispanic social service agencies, and the city of Central Falls to offer the program in three schools. Afterschool officials reported that students who participated missed less school and earned higher grades than those who did not, and the De Witt Wallace Reader's Digest Fund provided sufficient additional money to expand the district to seven schools (Pardini, 2001).

An afterschool program on a single school site could accomplish the same goals for the children it serves by working with the principal and teachers to align program activities with academic goals and individual children's needs. Programs that serve more than one school can bring together administrators and teaching staff from each one at the beginning of each year to agree on the goals and scope of the **collaboration**. After that, afterschool staff would need to regularly communicate with teachers at each school to keep activities aligned with school curriculum.

Afterschool programs that successfully build relationships with school personnel can support student learning while maintaining their goal of providing a safe, healthy, enjoyable, and developmentally appropriate environment for children and youth. However, while supporting academic achievement is a worthy goal, it shouldn't be the only one. Providing afterschool activities that are interesting and challenging strengthens cognitive skills in all areas and can create a general enthusiasm for learning (Fletcher, 2005). A wise youth worker of my acquaintance said that children come for the activities but stay for the relationships. This might also be said about the school and community representatives who partner with afterschool administration and staff.

Children who work together on long-term projects such as dramatic or musical presentations, large constructions, gardens, and newsletters develop skills in problem solving, making decisions, and thinking critically. Point that out to teachers and principals whenever you have the opportunity to do so. Coordinated alliances between afterschool programs and schools can improve school outcomes and school climate, but they can also connect families to support services and engage, guide, and motivate students to succeed—all goals that school administrators understand and appreciate (National Institute on Out-of-School Time, 2007).

Concerns

There are certain factors that need to be taken into consideration when working with teachers and administrators, and this is a role for the director or board members of your program. Principals worry that if the children in their schools do not succeed on standardized tests that the school district will lose federal and state funds, and teachers in their schools are under pressure to place more emphasis on academic achievement than in past decades. They sometimes feel that the afterschool program is taking up valuable space in their classrooms, cafeteria, gym, or playground and may be increasing their liability in some way. However, principals and teachers are also concerned about opportunities that children and young people miss because of the recent emphasis on core subject areas. You can strengthen your relationship with schools by showing principals, board members, and teachers how your program supplements the school day by offering opportunities for children to apply what they learn in school in interesting ways. One way to do that is to invite teachers to parent conferences and principals to special events such as plays, talent shows and service projects, or to regular meetings of the Science Club, Young Authors, or Math Challengers. Another is to include teachers and school administrators on an accreditation self-study team.

On some school campuses the afterschool program, or "day care" as it is sometimes called, is seen as an add-on, a babysitting service, or, even worse, a nuisance that takes up space. However, time spent talking about the importance of children having a safe, positive place to be after school, and the kinds of activities that can help schools achieve their goals, is time well spent. Trust takes many months to develop, and an understanding of what exactly you do in your program can take even longer. Whenever possible, demonstrate the kinds of enrichment experiences you offer, and point out the differences between high-quality programs and mere "homework help."

DEVELOPING COMMUNITY PARTNERSHIPS

Nurturing relationships with the families of children served by your program is important, but so is working within the wider community. Community service is one way to make what is learned during the school day relevant to the lives of children. Drawing on resources that exist within the community can also yield many positive outcomes for children and their families. Individual members of every community, such as business owners, members of the clergy, librarians, city council members, and teachers, all have a stake in developing high-quality out-of-school programs for children, and once they understand the role they can play, they are usually happy to collaborate.

Forming Partnerships with Businesses, Community-Based Organizations, and Public Agencies

There are many ways to collaborate with members of your community. One of the simplest is to request donations from a business in exchange for advertising in a school newsletter or performance program. For example, the program coordinator might request gardening supplies and seeds from a plant nursery; scrap lumber, nails, and a few hammers from a building supply center; and vegetables for a cooking project from a supermarket. A small notice in that month's newsletter could thank the nursery and the building supply center for their donation, listing the name and address of the business and suggesting that parents support the business owners. When the next month's snack schedule is published, the cooking project can be included in it, along with the name and address of the supermarket that donated vegetables, with a thank-you to the manager who made the donation. Increasingly, as afterschool programs are supported by a combination of public and private monies, they are discovering that the terms and conditions of that funding require that parents, staff, representatives of public and private agencies, and school personnel work together to address shared goals or objectives and to share decision-making and management responsibilities (Child Care Partnership Project, 1999). This is a **public–private partnership**: when the government, or the **public sector** (federal, state, local, and/or tribal officials or agencies), joins with ordinary people, or the **private sector** (families, employers, philanthropies, media, civic groups, and/or service providers) to attain a shared goal (Zimmerman, 2000).

With a little effort and creativity, programs can collaborate with nonprofit community agencies, health-care workers, and other professionals to provide services for children and families such as vision screenings, dental examinations, glasses, immunizations, and assistance with utility or food costs. Recruit literacy aids from the Lions or Rotary clubs, and invite business owners to lead clubs or provide single-session presentations on their fields of expertise. Health-care agencies may sponsor hikes, nutritional cooking projects, or exercise classes. Representatives from the Small Business Administration, often retired businesspeople, can talk about starting a small business and help interested youngsters develop a business plan for a newspaper or a window-washing service, for example. Julie Hancock, Director of an afterschool program in Livingston, Montana, provide some examples of successful community partnership in perspective 15.2.

Working with Community Partners

Julie Hancock,
LINKS for Learning, Livingston, Montana

LINKS enjoys strong working relationships with community partners. Coordinating with mental health providers allows us to more effectively serve children and families with specific needs. Local businesses offer field trip opportunities and on-site programs and have donated books, games, and materials.

Big Brothers and Sisters of Park County coordinate our America Reads program. We have 27 reading mentors, 20 of whom are high school students. These volunteers spend 45 minutes each week with a LINKS student. Half of the time is spent reading, and half of the time is devoted to developing the mentoring relationship. Board games, playing outside, or participating in LINKS activities together allow mentors and "littles" time to get to know each other. Evaluations of reading fluency have shown this program to be very effective. National studies indicate that such mentoring programs are also effective in reducing substance abuse in both the "little" and the mentor. It is extremely popular with children and parents and provides high school students with an opportunity for community service.

Used with permission.

Partnerships That Strengthen Students' Academic Performance

Many afterschool programs partner with museums, art galleries, and colleges or universities to provide enrichment activities that support and strengthen children's interest in science and math.

In Chapter 13, the Santa Clara County Children's Discovery Museum BioSITE project was described as a way to encourage youngsters to spend more time out of doors. High school students mentor third- through fifth-grade students in water quality testing and monitoring the health of the Guadalupe River in San Jose. The Santa Clara County Watershed Watch campaign is another aspect of this partnership, in which many organizations and agencies work together to protect the quality of the San Francisco Bay and coastal waters affected by runoff from this watershed. Many science applications have come from these relationships. Children who participate in the BioSite or Watershed Watch work closely with geologists, biologists, ecologists, and museum curators in the course of their work. This interaction serves as a natural career education seminar, frequently igniting an interest in science in children who had not previously shown such an interest. If no such programs exist in your community, contact science or technology museums, high school or college science teachers, or your city or county water district to discuss starting such a partnership.

Another way that children's academic interest and success can be increased is by partnering with higher education institutions. There are many mutual benefits for colleges and universities to partner with schools and programs serving school-age youth. For example, elementary and middle schools provide institutions of higher education with their future students. In addition, since colleges and universities prepare and train most future teachers, professors are always looking for opportunities for their teacher interns to spend time working with children. A study conducted in Illinois found that even non-education majors who volunteer to work with youth are more likely to follow a career in education (American Youth Policy Forum, 2006).

In Corvallis, Oregon, students from Oregon State University helped more than 700 disadvantaged youngsters develop the skills needed to graduate from high school, go on to college, and pursue a career in math or science. They accomplished this by working in after-school clubs, outdoor science camps, field trips, and activities that took place on the university campus (Afterschool Alliance, 2007).

In Boston, students from Harvard University tutor youth at the Mission Hill After-School Program four afternoons a week. University students help one or two children with homework, take them on field trips, and participate in projects designed to enhance academic learning. Students at California State University at Long Beach collaborate with students from Long Beach City College and the University of California system to teach afterschool students about computer literacy and Web site design (Afterschool Alliance, 2007).

Workforce Development Through Community Partnerships

Community partnerships also make it possible to help older children and youth develop job skills. **Workplace skills** that are needed for successful employment include not only skills directly related to the production, marketing, or maintenance of a product but also include interpersonal skills, critical thinking, and an awareness of diverse learning and communication styles (Secretary's Commission on Achieving Necessary Skills, 2006). Workforce development or investment boards throughout the nation develop Requests for Proposals (RFPs) from qualified organizations to develop programs that connect workplace skills training to other youth education and development programs serving youngsters from 12 to 18 years of age.

The federal Workforce Investment Act (WIA), originally passed in 1998, offers a comprehensive range of workforce development activities through statewide and local organizations. The purpose of these activities is to promote an increase in the employment, job retention, earnings, and occupational skills improvement by participants. This, in turn, improves the quality of the American workforce, reduces welfare dependency, and improves the productivity and competitiveness of the nation. Title I of the WIA authorizes services for youth, adults, and laid-off workers. Eligible youth must be 14 to 21 years of age, low income, and meet at least one of six specific barriers to employment. This program, which emphasizes services for out-of-school youth, emphasizes attainment of basic skills competencies, enhances opportunities for academic and occupational training, and provides exposure to the job market and employment. Activities may include instruction leading to the completion of secondary school, tutoring, internships, job shadowing, work experience, adult mentoring, and comprehensive guidance and counseling.

By working closely with employers and workforce developers in your community, you can learn about programs funded by the WIA and partner with them to offer job-related skills training to the children in your program. In addition, by offering interesting and challenging activities such as woodworking, outdoor construction, gardening, or cooking you can help older children develop skills and dispositions—such as punctuality, safety, and persistence—that will increase their job readiness and eligibility for workforce development programs when they become old enough to participate in them.

Building the Capacity and Sustainability of Out-of-School Programs

In the early 1990s, the phrase "after-school programs" was rarely heard in policy discussions about meeting the developmental needs of children from low- or moderate-income homes. Yet there was a serious shortage of such programs, especially in neighborhoods needing them most. Even where they existed, barriers such as cost or lack of transportation placed them out of reach for many families. In 1994, DeWitt Wallace–Reader's Digest launched a program to develop community-based coalitions in five cities. The models developed and administered over the next 5 years as a result of the MOST (Making the Most of Out-of-School Time) initiative illustrated creative ways in which public and private funding can be combined to increase programs for school-age children. These models are described in Figure 15.5.

With an initial grant in 1993, Wellesley College's National Institute on Out-of-School Time managed the MOST initiative and provided training and technical assistance to MOST sites. In June 1999, the Wallace Foundation held a public briefing in Washington to raise awareness of the need for quality after-school programs. Finally, the Wallace Foundation commissioned a two-phase evaluation study of MOST to capture lessons on how to increase the supply and quality of after-school programs.

They learned that more than 6,000 children now had access to affordable programs in target cities. Providers had received training to improve their quality. The MOST initiative produced concrete evidence about the importance of concerted efforts by families, community organizations, the school system, businesses, and political and cultural institutions to work together to provide more and better programs and sustain them over time.

The MOST model has now been replicated many times. The afterschool movement is strong and appears to be well received by most families and communities. The federal and state governments have consistently supported afterschool

FIGURE 15.5   Creative Partnerships Illustrated by the MOST Models.

Creative Solutions: The MOST Initiative

- Seattle MOST leveraged funds for new programs. By bringing together the Children's Museum, Seattle Housing Authority, and the YMCA, MOST initiated a partnership that received federal funds to create a new YMCA school-age program in a public housing community.

- Together, Chicago MOST and the Chicago Park District transformed over 40 drop-in recreational programs in diverse neighborhoods into high-quality after-school programs.

- Chicago MOST fostered "Friendship Circles": connections among school-age programs in different neighborhoods that exposed children and staff to diversity. Through Friendship Circles, over 500 children and staff came together to share activities.

- A partnership between Boston MOST and Boston's Museum of Science added a science component to eight established after-school programs.

- MOST involved the federal AmeriCorps organization to improve school-age care programs in Boston. Among seven program sites, typical AmeriCorps efforts included managing volunteers at a large school-based program and informing parents about school-age programs within a housing development.

programs, and the passage of the No Child Left Behind Act makes public support of additional learning opportunities all the more important (Gayl, 2004). However, ensuring **sustainability**, or continued funding, is necessary to develop a permanent and secure system of afterschool programs for children. Depending on one stream of funds to augment parent fees, such as school district, state, or federal grants, is unwise. Program administrators need to develop policy, guidelines, and political action agendas in order to secure a broad platform of support. Non-interrupted access to funding, staffing, space, and supportive policies all must be secured to experience true sustainability. Sometimes it takes years to build the networks necessary to develop the kinds of collaborations described in this chapter. However, while separately each program can touch dozens of children's lives each year, when you collaborate with parents and communities, you can together affect the lives of many more.

SUMMARY

Developing partnerships with parents requires open and frequent communication. Beginning with the first contact, out-of-school programs need to develop ways to help parents get to know the program staff and other families served by the program and keep them informed of changes and upcoming events. It is also important to develop partnerships with communities. This is time-consuming, but the effort put into working collaboratively with community agencies and organizations can pay off in a high-quality program with strong connections to the neighborhoods it serves. Developing partnerships with parents or with communities takes time, patience, and excellent interpersonal skills

TERMS TO LEARN

collaboration
committed partnership
complementary learning framework
contractual partnership
discretion
nuclear family

private sector
public sector
public–private partnerships
respect
sustainability
workplace skills

REVIEW QUESTIONS

1. Why is it more challenging to get parents involved in out-of-school programs than in other types of child care or classrooms?

2. List three ways in which program staff can facilitate communication with parents.

3. What is meant by *contractual* vs. *committed* partnerships?

4. List three successful community partnerships described in the chapter.

CHALLENGE EXERCISES

1. Develop a script for a conversation with a parent calling for information about your program.

2. Develop a list of items you would put into an initial mailing to an inquiring parent.

3. Interview a program director and learn what strategies are used in his or her program to develop partnerships with parents.
4. Research examples of successful community partnerships in your community. Write a summary and present to the class.
5. Search the Internet for a Web site designed by or for a school-age program. Bring a printout of it to class.

REFERENCES

Afterschool Alliance. (2007, September). Afterschool partnerships with higher education. *Afterschool Alert: Issue Brief #2.*

American Youth Policy Forum. (2006). *Helping youth succeed through out-of-time-programs, a policy brief.* Washington, DC: Author.

Ann Arbor Public Schools Community Education & Recreation. (2010). *School-age child care parent/guardian responsibilities.* Retrieved April 27, 2010, from http://www.aaps.k12.mi.us/reced.childcare/parent_responsibilities

Baker, A. C., & Manfredi-Petit, L. A. (2004). *Relationships, the heart of quality care.* Washington, DC: National Association for the Education of Young Children.

Bouffard, S., Goss, C. B., & Weiss, H. (2008). *Complementary learning: Emerging strategies, evolving ideas* (No. ED502276). Boston: Harvard Family Research Project.

C. S. Mott Foundation. (2007). *A new day for learning.* Flint, MI: Time, Learning and After-School Task Force.

Caplan, J., & Calfee, C. S. (1999). *Strengthening connections between schools and after-school programs.* Oak Brook, IL: North Central Regional Educational Laboratory.

Chase, R., Arnold, J., & Schauben, L. (2006). *Family, friend, and neighbor caregivers—Results of the 2004 Minnesota statewide household child care survey.* St. Paul, MN: Wilder Research Center.

Child Care Partnership Project. (1999). *A guide to successful public-private partnership for child care.* Washington, DC: The Finance Project.

Decker, L. E. (2000). *Engaging families & communities, pathways to educational success.* Boca Raton, FL: National Community Educational Association, Florida Atlantic University.

Diedrich, K. C., McElvain, C. K., & Kaufman, S. (2007). *Beyond the bell: Principal's guide to effective afterschool programs.* Naperville, IL: Learning Point Associates.

Fletcher, A. J. (2005). *A guide to developing exemplary practices in afterschool programs.* Sacramento, CA: Center for Collaborative Solutions, the Community Network for Youth Development, and the Foundation Consortium for California's Children and Youth.

Gayl, C. L. (2004). *After-school programs: Expanding access and ensuring quality.* Washington, DC: Progressive Policy Institute.

Gonzalez-Mena, J. (2005). *Diversity in early care and education: Honoring differences.* Boston: McGraw-Hill.

Henderson, A. T., & Mapp, K. L. (2002). *A new wave of evidence: The impact of school, family, and community connections on student achievement.* Austin, TX: National Center for Family & Community Connections With Schools: Southwest Educational Development Laboratory.

Jeppson, E., Thomas, J., Markward, A., Kelly, J., Koser, G., & Diehl, D. (1997). *Making room at the table.* Chicago: Family Resource Coalition of America.

Katz, L. G., Aidman, A., Reese, D. A., & Clark, A. M. (1996). *Preventing and resolving parent–teacher differences.* (ERIC Document Reproduction Service No. ED401048)

McBride, B. A. (1996). *Father/male involvement in early childhood programs.* (ERIC Document Reproduction Service No. ED400123)

Newman, R. L. (2008). *Building relationships with parents and families in school-age programs* (2nd ed.). New Albany, OH: School-Age Notes.

Novick, R. (1996). *Developmentally appropriate and culturally responsive education: Theory in practice.* Portland, OR: Northwest Regional Educational Laboratory.

Pardini, P. (2001). School–community partnering. *School Administrator, 58*(7) 6–11.

Perkins, D. G., Christner, B. J., Hoy, P. E., Webster, P., & Mock, L. (2004). *After-school programs parent involvement plan.* University Park: Department of Agricultural and Extension Education, Pennsylvania State University.

Roggman, L.A. (2005) Father involvement in early head start programs. *Fathering: A Journal of Theory, Research, and Practice About Men as Fathers, 3*(1), 29–58.

Roy, K. (2008, Spring). *A life course perspective on fatherhood and family policies in the United States and South Africa. Men's Studies Press, 6*(2), 92–112

Secretary's Commission on Achieving Necessary Skills. (2006, March 9). *What work requires of schools.* Retrieved July 28, 2008, from http://wdr.doleta.gov/SCANS/

Seligson, M., & Allenson, M. (1993). *School-age child care: An action manual for the 90s and beyond.* Westport, CT: Auburn House.

Stedron, J. (2007, March). A new day for learning. *State Legislatures: The National Magazine of Policies and Politics.* Retrieved April 27, 2010, from http://www.ncsl.org/default. aspx?tabid=12815

Susman-Stillman, A., & Banghart, P. (2008). *Demographics of family, friend, and neighbor child care in the United States.* New York: National Center for Children in Poverty.

Zimmerman, E. (2000). *A guide to engaging parents in public-private child care partnerships.* Washington, DC: U.S. Department of Health and Human Services Administration for Children and Families.

Chapter
16

Administrative Issues: Licensing, Policies, and Personnel

Administering a school-age program requires a broad range of skills and knowledge. In addition to understanding the developmental and academic needs of elementary, middle, or high school youngsters, it is important to know how to manage the overall and day-to-day operation of the program, and it is vital for program administrators to have a clear understanding of the licensing and other legal requirements that govern your program, as seen in Figure 16.1.

You may not see yourself as a site director just yet, but everyone working in an afterschool program needs to understand the breadth of the task to carry out the mission and goals of the program and assist administrators and site supervisors in keeping the program in legal compliance. This chapter will not tell you how to do the job of an administrator; it merely outlines the tasks that the administrators, sometimes assisted by senior staff members, need to be aware of to manage the program effectively.

LICENSING ISSUES

An important indicator of quality in school-age programs is compliance with state licensing regulations and accepted quality standards. A challenge faced by many states is that child care regulations have typically evolved to protect infants, toddlers, and preschoolers in response to the demands of families, research on the benefits of high-quality programs, and persistent legislators. These regulations may not perfectly match the needs of children in school-age programs, and afterschool programs situated on public school sites may be exempt from licensing regulations.

The goals of most state child care licensing requirements are to ensure the basic health and safety of children in supervised care and to promote children's healthy development. School-age programs, which have a variety of goals and

FIGURE 16.1 Typical Job Description for a School-Age Site Director.

The School-Age Site Director is responsible for planning, administering, coordinating, and managing a recreational and enrichment afterschool program that meets the physical, intellectual, and emotional needs of school-age children. The School-Age Site Director ensures that child care regulations are met; policies and procedures are followed; oversees the collection of child care fees; and recruits, hires, trains, evaluates, and supervises site staff.

Source: Adapted from an actual position announcement posted on craigslist.com, August 24, 2009.

exist in many different kinds of settings, may find it challenging to be constrained by licensing requirements originally developed for use with children from 0 to 5 years of age.

Licensing and Regulations

Licensing is the process by which an individual, organization, or corporation procures from the appropriate state agency a permit to operate a school-age program. The purpose of having licensing requirements is to assure **minimum standards** for all licensed programs. Many out-of-school programs, such as service organizations, athletic teams, homework clubs, or drop-in centers, have historically been exempt from licensing because they operate infrequently or for specific, noneducational purposes. These programs may be covered under an umbrella of regulations through their association with a parent agency.

The Challenge of Varied Licensing Regulations Many programs for school-agers are covered by previously existing **early childhood legislation**, which stipulates required square footage, ratios of children to adults, number of bathrooms, diaper-changing procedures, and so on. As unique school-age programs develop to fill unmet needs, state legislators are gradually writing special regulations to govern them. In addition, various funding streams have resulted in disparate rules for what may appear to be similar programs. For example, California requires most child care centers and family child care homes to be licensed by the California Department of Social Services under Title 22 of the California Code of Regulations. However, some categories of programs are exempt from licensure, including parent-run cooperatives and programs operated during limited hours by park and recreation departments. In addition, programs funded by the California Child Development Division of the Department of Education are regulated by Title 5 of the California Education Code and must meet those standards in addition to Title 22 Regulations. Federally funded Head Start programs (including school-age programs such as Even Start) must meet federal standards as well as Title 22 licensing requirements but are not required to meet the state Title 5 standards (Bolen, 2008).

Other states exempt some afterschool programs from licensing requirements, and some have different regulations for different types of programs, such as those that are strictly tutorial, operate for less than 4 hours a day, are located on public or private school grounds, or are operated by certain nonprofit agencies. For example, in Florida, **license-exempt programs** include those that are strictly instructional or tutorial in nature or are strictly recreational (e.g., ballet, karate, gymnastics, sports,

Administrators identify which regulations apply to their programs and communicate that to parents and staff.

etc.) (Department of Children and Family Services, 1999–2007). In most states, programs that are administered under the auspices of public or certain nonprofit agencies are exempt from Social Services or Health and Welfare oversight because the state regulatory agencies assume that a system other than the child care system will monitor quality (National Association for Regulatory Administration, 2004). To effectively function within this confusing array of rules and regulations, administrators and leaders of school-age programs must understand the purposes of regulations and identify which ones in their state apply to their specific program.

Understanding the Licensing Provisions That Apply to Your Program
Determining who governs your program and locating a copy of the regulations may be a lengthy task. For example, a program operated on school grounds by a private agency may be governed by the Department of Social Services, Human Services, or Child and Family Services, depending on the state in which the program is operated. The same agency, whichever it is, may operate other programs under contract with the state Department of Education, which would then be the governing agency for those programs. But if the local school district administers the program, whether or not it is located on the school grounds, the agency governing the school district would be the one specifying the regulations for the afterschool program.

Some states address this challenge by developing licensing standards with a specific focus on the unique needs of school-age programs. They may do this by developing supplemental sections in their licensing documents; other states embed requirements for school-age programs into each section of their child care regulations. In 2005, less than half of the states had separate school-age standards in their licensing regulations, but many others were in the process of developing such legislation (Finance Project, 2006; Urzedewski, 2006).

To support state efforts to provide quality afterschool opportunities, the federal Child Care Bureau awarded a contract to the Finance Project, a nonprofit research, consulting, technical assistance, and training firm for public- and private-sector leaders. This contract resulted in the Afterschool Investments project, which provides technical assistance to certain federal grantees and to many state and local leaders supporting afterschool efforts. The Afterschool Investments project has also developed **afterschool profiles** for every state.

These profiles provide key data and descriptions of afterschool programs throughout the nation, including a range of out-of-school-time programming that take place before and after school, on weekends, and during summer months. The profiles are designed to serve as a resource for policymakers and administrators, but they can also be extremely helpful for afterschool leaders and providers trying to understand their own state's combination of funding, regulations, and guidelines. An easy-to read (PDF) document can be downloaded and printed for each state that will generally include the following information:

- Demographics
- Child care and development fund awards
- Provider reimbursement rates
- Temporary Assistance for Needy Families (TANF) and child care
- Program licensing policies
- Systems/quality supports (credentials, rating systems, afterschool network)
- 21st Century Community Learning Centers funding
- State initiatives
- Statewide organizations
- Additional resources

The Web site for these state-by-state afterschool profiles is listed in the Internet Resources section at the end of this chapter.

Licensing regulations address generally the same areas in each state: organization and administration, staffing, physical environment and equipment, health and safety, program, discipline, and parent rights. Educational agencies and professional organizations take over where licensing leaves off, usually recommending lower child–adult ratios and enhanced environment and programming and stipulating guidelines for parent and community participation. It is important for staff of these programs to be current with local licensing laws, contract funding terms and conditions, and the recommendations of professional organizations to ensure legal compliance and a high-quality out-of-school program.

Liability: Who Is Responsible?

A reasonable area of concern to private agencies and individuals operating any kind of business is **liability**, or the potential for lawsuits. Three principles usually apply in legal actions involving programs for children:

1. *Employee liability:* Employees are hired to perform certain types of duties and are expected to be adequately prepared to perform those duties as well as to understand the expectations of the employer. When employees act within the scope of the employer's expectations, they are not liable for the

results of their actions. However, when they act beyond them or fail to act up to them, they are considered **negligent**, and they *are* liable.

2. *Employer liability:* Except for cases of employee negligence, employers are liable for all actions of their employees carried out while they are at work.
3. *Board liability:* Boards of directors are responsible for the actions of all employees hired by the board, as the board essentially becomes the "employer." (Decker & Decker, 2004)

Liability varies depending on many factors. The form of ownership of the agency, its tax status, and how the program is funded will determine exactly what provisions of law apply, as will the expectations of all individuals involved in the program. Everyone who works in a program should be aware of these legal principles and understand their own responsibilities regarding the safety and well-being of the children and families being served. In addition, basic principles of **risk management** should be understood by everyone employed by the program. Program administrators need to be very clear about their role in the protection of children and work diligently to prevent incidents and accidents, protect children, and reduce liability. Coalition for Children, a not-for-profit (501c3) organization, has developed a risk-reduction education program, which includes material on the screening and training of employees, child abuse reporting, effective supervision, prevention programs, and perimeter issues, including children walking to the program and to the bus, equipment, pickup and release of children, and field trips. Coalition for Children has developed an informational Web site that can be found in the Internet Resources section at the end of this chapter.

❀   *Consider This:*   ❀

Remember somewhere you especially enjoyed playing when you were a child. Did you feel safe and secure there? Looking back now, do you still think it was safe? Who do you suppose was legally responsible for maintaining that environment? What about that play space stands out in your mind? How do you think your perception of safety influenced your play experience?

Types of Ownership and Liability   In terms of ownership, school-age centers can function as proprietorships, partnerships, or corporations. **Proprietorships** are businesses owned by one person, who assumes full responsibility for debts, taxes, and legal issues. **Partnerships** involve more people and their stability depends on the continued interest, either financial or emotional, of all members of the partnership. Each partner is held responsible for his or her own taxes, but liability and decision making is shared with other partners. **Corporations** are sometimes formed to limit the liability of individuals wishing to operate a school-age program or center. Corporations may be for-profit or nonprofit and are governed by a board of directors. Corporations identified as **for-profit** run essentially like proprietorships; their main purpose is to make a profit. Stockholders in the corporation pay taxes on this profit, as does the corporation itself. Private **nonprofit** corporations are permitted to make a profit, but that is not their main goal, and they must put any profit back into the program. Generally, out-of-school programs organized as nonprofit corporations serve a specific population or geographic area that could not support a program on tuition and fees alone.

The owner of the building in which the program is housed, the driver who runs the van service between schools and the school-age center, even the independent contractor who provides piano lessons or coaches a soccer team—each of these individuals has varying degrees of **legal exposure**. It is important to learn what is expected of your program and the people working in it and to understand clearly your potential liability. For example, make sure you don't inadvertently violate the Americans With Disabilities Act or other civil rights laws by having policies or admission requirements that are discriminatory. A good idea is to ask a local attorney or legal aid volunteer to present a workshop to staff and parents to be sure everyone understands his and her rights and obligations. All administrators and site supervisors in school-age programs should complete at minimum one college-level course in child care administration.

POLICY ISSUES

When an afterschool program is designed and planned, most organizers will meet with community stakeholders, such as parents, school administrators and faculty, and community leaders, to identify community needs and develop a vision and goals. The vision is usually translated into a **mission statement**, and the goals guide administrators and staff as they develop their program design, student learning objectives, and curriculum. All of these things need to be done before program administrators can write policy and develop procedures for the smooth operation of the program.

Contracts with Parents

Once the director and staff have determined which regulations and guidelines govern their program and have designed a program to meet them, they must explain those requirements to parents along with any other stipulations necessary for the smooth running of the program. Some of the ways in which those explanations can be made are through (a) a mission statements, (b) admission agreements, and (c) parent handbooks.

Mission Statements   A mission statement identifies your purpose for being and becomes the framework for goals and objectives, policies and procedures, curriculum, daily schedule, budget, staffing requirements, and just about everything else about the program. An effective mission statement is concise and identifies the underlying assumptions that guide decision making. It should also outline the broad goals the program is hoping to achieve, describe the community the program is designed to serve, and state the values and general principles that define its standards.

Mission statements are usually written by administrators and approved by boards of directors or funding agencies. Line staff rarely have input into a mission statement of the program for which they work, although some administrators hire staff early and encourage them to participate in the process. Whether or not you

FIGURE 16.2   Three Sample Mission Statements.

To enhance the economic stability of County families by offering affordable, high quality, developmentally appropriate before and after school and vacation care at County elementary schools.
Prince William County, Virginia, School Age Care Program

To provide each child an environment where he/she is able to develop a positive self-image and to offer peace of mind to our families through loving care and communication.
Children's Creative Learning Centers, Sunnyvale, California

To support the needs of children through strong partnerships with families, schools, and communities, together providing social, academic, and cultural learning opportunities that build upon individual strengths and interests necessary for lifelong success.
For Kids Only Afterschool, Salem, Massachusetts

had anything to do with the development of the actual documents, the community served by your program, and the funding agents if you are a public or nonprofit entity, may expect your mission statement to be a promise to deliver some specified social value (Leonard, 2006). It is therefore important that you understand what it means and be prepared to live up to its provisions. (See Figure 16.2 for three actual examples of mission statements.)

Developing Admission Agreements   Most states require licensed child care programs to enter into contracts with the parents or legal guardians of each child registered in the facility. The most common form of contract between parents and programs is called an **admission agreement**. This written contractual form must be completed and maintained in the center's files, signed by both parties. While most regulatory agencies do not stipulate the exact wording or contents of these agreements, most require at least the following provisions:

- ❀ basic and optional services
- ❀ payment rates and provisions for payment
- ❀ rules for modifying any part of the agreement
- ❀ conditions permitting refunds
- ❀ right of licensing agencies to inspect the facility, audit records and require physical examinations of the children
- ❀ right of parents to visit the program without advance notification
- ❀ conditions for termination (Child Care Law Project, 1998, p. 1–2)

It is also wise to include a statement in the admission agreement that the parents agree to abide by the program's rules and regulations as described in the parent handbook and keep a log for parents to sign verifying that they have received a copy of the handbook and will comply with its contents. Contract law stipulates that once you have told a parent that there is space available for the child to begin on a certain date for a set fee, you have made an "offer" of services. If the parent accepts your offer, the law will recognize that a contract has been made. To be very clear about the terms of that contract, and to prevent any future dispute from escalating because the two parties to the agreement have different memories of the specifics, most regulatory bodies require a written contract as well. If each of you has a copy of the contract, the chances for misunderstanding are smaller.

As well, the process of reviewing and signing the written document signals to the parent that your program is legally compliant and that you take your role seriously (Ashcraft, 2005).

Parent Handbooks   Unlike admissions agreements, which are heavy with legal terminology, **parent handbooks** should clearly explain specific details of the program and outline the responsibilities of both the administering agency and the parents. They should be well organized and clearly written and include the program mission, goals, objectives, policies, procedures, opportunities for family involvement, and information about fees and hours of operation (Ashcraft, 2005; Fletcher, 2005). Provide each family with a copy of the handbook, in their home language if possible.

As you prepare your mission statement, admission agreement, and parent handbook, remember that a **family-centered program** is most helpful to the children you will serve. It is important to review program details and guidelines with parents and children to ensure that their needs will be met, and be prepared to revisit policies and procedures if you discover that they will not. Programs that ignore parents' working hours, commute time, and need for care during school holidays and teacher in-service days, for example, add stress to already stressed families. Your program will be far more effective (and successful) if it is seen as an advocate rather than as an adversary of parents. Once you have reviewed the handbook with parents, possibly agreed to make some allowances for their individual needs, and given adequate time for questions and clarification, it is time to ask parents to sign the admission agreement.

Staff Policies and Procedures Manual

The art of writing a handbook of policies and procedures lies in combining clear directions to the staff with as many possibilities for potential problems as everyone in the organization can think of. Generally, the owner or governing board will set policy, and the director, in collaboration with his or her staff, will develop the procedures for implementing the policy (Sciarra, 1998) and write the manual. For example, the board may establish a policy to admit all children between the ages of 6 and 12 who can benefit from the program, given that space is available. The director then meets with staff and possibly parents to develop the procedures necessary to achieve the children's enrollment, including planning publicity; designing, distributing, and reviewing registration forms; and informing parents that their child has been accepted or placed on a waiting list. Here, again, you must keep up-to-date on the implications of the ADA and other antidiscrimination laws and be sure that your policies comply with appropriate provisions in the NAA Code of Ethics (Appendix).

Procedures need to be clear and unambiguous, but if they are overly detailed they won't be read or followed. Certain components of a policies and procedures manual—such as a mission statement, program goals and objectives, job descriptions, staff orientation, training, and evaluation—should be revisited every year and adjusted as appropriate. For cost reasons, these manuals are not generally distributed to parents, but they should be available for review if requested, and every staff member should have a copy. As with the parent handbook, employees should be asked to sign a log indicating that they have received a copy of the policies and procedures manual and agree to comply with its contents.

Determining an Operating Schedule

Scheduling school-age programs can be a very complex task. Programs for school-age children that include kindergarteners operate over a large portion of the day. Other programs may meet before and after school when school is in session and for extended days only during school holidays, vacations, and teacher in-service days. Some programs serve several different schools that may be on different calendars; others serve only one school or schools from one district that all follow the same schedule. In either case, you will need to make a policy decision about whether your program will provide care and activities when school is not in session and how early and late it will be open. Three sample schedules are shown in Figure 16.3. The Monarch figure demonstrates a school-year schedule for second through six graders, while the Caterpillar figures show a school-year schedule for K–1 children and a summer camp schedule.

FIGURE 16.3   Sample Schedules for School-Age Programs.

Typical 2nd–6th Afterschool Schedule

After-School Daily Routine
2nd~6th Grade Monarchs

A Children's Garden
Child Care and Learning Center

Monday & Wednesday

2:00–3:00	Peer connections (2:30–3:00 Snack)
3:00–3:30	Special Projects (introduction)
3:30–4:00	Study Time (HW & Academic Binders)
4:00–4:30	Homework Club/Independent Club
4:30–5:00	**Outdoor enrichment and playtime**
5:00–5:35	Special projects (conclusion)
5:35–5:45	Close down room, walk to Caterpillars
5:45–6:00	End of the day activities

Tuesday & Thursday

2:00–3:15	Peer connections (2:30–3:00 Snack)
2:45–3:15	**Outdoor & indoor playtime**
3:15–3:30	Huddle at tables
3:30–4:00	Study Time (HW & Academic Binders)
4:00–4:30	Homework Club/Independent Club
4:30–5:00	**Outdoor enrichment and playtime**
5:00–5:35	Special projects
5:35–5:45	Close down room, walk to Caterpillars
5:45–6:00	End of the day activities

Friday

2:00–3:30	Peer connections (2:30–3:00 Snack)
2:45–3:30	**Outdoor enrichment & playtime**
3:30–3:45	Huddle on carpet
3:45–4:30	Cooking activity & Village play
4:30–5:30	Extended special projects
5:30–5:45	Detailed clean up, walk to Caterpillars
5:45–6:00	End of the day activities

FIGURE 16.3   Sample Schedules for School-Age Programs. (*Continued*)

Typical Kindergarten Half Day Schedule

A Children's Garden
Child Care and Learning Center

Caterpillar Daily Schedule

11:45–12:30	Greeting/lunch/opening activities (free choice)
12:45–1:00	Clean-up and get mats ready
1:00–2:00	Rest/nap time
2:00–2:45	Wake-up/staggered snack/free choice
2:45–3:00	Caterpillar huddle
3:00–4:00	Outside (free/organized play and magic basket)
4:00–4:30	(or 4:45) homework time
4:30–4:45	Caterpillar huddle
4:45–5:30	Centers/art/sensory
5:30–5:45	Clean-up /prepare closing activities
5:45–6:30	Center combines/close

Summer Day Camp Combined Schedule

A Children's Garden
Child Care and Learning Center

Caterpillar Daily Schedule

8:00–8:30	Opening activities with Monarchs
8:30–9:00	Outside
9:00–10:20	Staggered snack/work time/Special Project
10:20–10:35	Caterpillar Huddle – plans for enrichment
10:35–11:35	Outside enrichment/Gardening
11:35–12:00	Open activities
12:00–1:00	Lunch preparation/lunch/prepare for rest
1:00–2:00	Rest time
2:00–2:45	Calm activities/staggered snack
2:45–3:45	Clean up/outside enrichment/Gardening
4:00–4:35	Group A: Focused Learning Group B: Art/Special Projects (rotate every-other day)
4:40–5:30	Open activities
5:30–5:45	Clean-up/prepare closing activities
5:45–6:30	Caterpillars and Monarchs together again/close

Source: A Children's Garden. Used with permission.

Funding and Finances

Programs for school-agers obtain their start-up and operating funds in a variety of ways. They may be sponsored by youth-serving organizations such as YMCA and Boys and Girls Clubs, or by churches, parks and recreation departments, housing associations, military bases, or government agencies. State-funded programs may be supported fully, or the funding may be partial, with contributions from local sources expected to make up the difference. Privately owned school-age centers receive most of their income from parent-paid tuition and fees. Some programs may receive start-up funding from a public or private agency and then must operate on a combination of private and public funds. Nearly all school-age centers participate in some kind of fund-raising to assure adequate funds for supplies, field trips, and "extras." Sometimes benefactors can be found in the community who will sponsor specific expenditures that match their community service goals. If a local service organization sponsors a grant-writing workshop, be sure to attend. Take advantage of the tips offered to learn how to apprise such benefactors of your needs and watch for workshops at conferences that teach proposal writing and direct you to potential sources of funding for programs such as yours.

Budget development is a specialized skill, and successful **fiscal** management and planning is crucial for the success of any community program. Anyone having responsibility for budget building and the management of funds must learn the process and confer with appropriate financial advisors for the first few years. Community colleges and business schools often advertise courses in business administration, and community colleges usually offer specialized coursework for child care program management.

Understand the goals and objectives of your program so you can prioritize expenditures. When you need to decide whether to use this year's budget to resurface the playground, purchase a new computer, or add services for 12- and 13-year-olds, referring to a mission statement can make the decision much easier. Be sure your program has one.

Transportation and Parking

How will the children arrive at your program? They can come in a variety of ways—by private car, in vans operated by schools or afterschool centers, alone or with their parents on public transportation, on foot, even in taxis and limousines. Consider the various routes and means by which your children will be traveling so you can provide adequate parking, turnaround space, greeters, or traffic control.

An urban program may need to be situated near a public transportation hub or run its own shuttle bus; programs situated on school sites may want to negotiate with the school district for automobile access to the portable building or classroom where the program is located for the convenience of parents dropping off or picking up their children. One child care agency received major start-up funding from a local transportation agency because they were willing to locate at the intersection of a bus route, light rail, and train depot. However, when the ad-

Consider how your children will be arriving at your program, and provide adequate parking, turnaround space, greeters, or traffic control.

ministrators discovered that over 70% of their clients drove their own cars to the center, they had to enlarge the parking lot and turnaround area (Cornell Cooperative Extension, 2004).

Getting Along with Your Neighbors

Being a good neighbor can be considered both a legal and a financial responsibility. For example, when you are designing a new program for school-agers, be sure that fences, driveways, parking lots, and drive-throughs are planned with the needs of local residents in mind. Of course, you will obtain the necessary permits and permissions to construct such items, but you must also pay attention to traffic patterns, footpaths, noise, and visual impact. If your center is situated in a residential area, get to know one or more families before completing the plans. Sometimes a chat over a fence (or over a cup of coffee) can save hours of wrangling at public meetings. Even the color of the building can become an issue; residents have been known to bring suit against child care centers painted in primary colors amidst a group of paler buildings. If your program operates in a business district, consider how the comings and goings of parents and children will affect nearby merchants. It may be helpful to join the chamber of commerce or other local business association. Working with people on community projects provides opportunities for relationships to develop that may make future negotiations easier to accomplish.

Once your afterschool program is open, monitor the times of day when children's spirited voices can be heard in neighbors' homes and yards, and do whatever is necessary to keep arrivals and departures from negatively affecting the neighborhood. Let the community know the positive impact of organized school-age programs through public service announcements and visits to service clubs, churches, and other neighborhood agencies. Involve the children

FIGURE 16.4 A Clear Set of Goals Helps Staff Develop Program Priorities.

This list is posted on New Mexico's Children's Choice school-age care program Web site for the convenience of parents and potential clients.

Goals: It is the goal of the Children's Choice school-age program to give each child an opportunity to develop:

1. Physical, intellectual, and social skills.
2. A sense and understanding of positive values.
3. Self-confidence, self-respect, and self-reliance.
4. Good decision-making, leadership, and social competency skills.
5. Positive family and peer relationships.
6. Interpersonal and cultural competencies
7. Interest, respect, and understanding of our natural world.
8. Sportsmanship, teamwork, and a sense of fair play
9. Commitment to learning
10. HAVE A WHOLE LOTTA FUN!

Source: Used by permission of Mike Ashcraft, Founder and CEO of Children's Choice Child Care Services, Inc.

and staff in community clean-up days and other activities so that if conflicts do arise, neighbors will already associate faces, names, and personalities with the program. It is much easier to resolve problems when the disputants see one another as human beings rather than merely representatives of faceless institutions.

Referring to the goals, objectives, and mission statement of your program will help here. For example, if a goal is to relieve parents from some of the stress of worrying about their children's welfare while they are at work, consider how they will feel if the program does not operate during the summer, winter break, or during teacher in-service days. Even major holidays are workdays for retail workers, parents who are employed in the fields of recreation or transportation, or those in a medical profession. Figure 16.4 provides some examples of goals for an afterschool program. If your board decides the program should remain open for most of the public holidays and all other times when school is closed, the site director will need to hire enough staff members to allow for rotation of holidays and vacations among employees, and the staff must understand why this is important to the program's mission. If the program closes during days when parents must work, you might want to compile a list of licensed care providers who will take school-age children and assist parents to find alternative arrangements.

PERSONNEL ISSUES

The relationship between afterschool staff and the children with whom they work is the single most important factor of a successful afterschool program (Birmingham, Pechman, Russell, & Mielke, 2005; Otterbourg, 2000). The administration and governing board need to focus on an intentional recruiting and hiring process, including a comprehensive job description and an interview that includes practical situational questions.

Staffing Considerations

Hours of operation will determine your staffing pattern. Programs that open more than an hour before school starts and stay open until six or seven in the evening will need to employ several part-time people and possibly also institute split shifts. This can make recruiting and retaining a high-quality staff a real challenge. Remember that early-morning routines may include more **caregiving** than later in the day, which is often a time for homework and active play. Children who arrive early in the morning may need some time and a quiet place to awaken gradually. They may also benefit from a snack or breakfast before starting school. Staff members who work during these early hours should be aware of the nurturing aspect of their role and be willing to read stories or snuggle with youngsters as they prepare for their day. Don't expect these to be the same people who lead in lively games 9 hours later. Perspective 16.1 discusses other criteria for hiring staff.

Blurring of Roles and Shared Decision Making   The unique scheduling and staffing needs of programs before and after school usually lead site directors to work directly with children, at least part of the time. This can make life easier, as managerial decisions are then frequently made by the same people who implement them. Conversely, it can also make life harder, because meeting the immediate needs of children may cause directors to postpone paperwork or other administrative duties.

Unlike programs for younger children, where administrative and teaching duties are usually separated, staff working in school-age programs may find that lines of authority and responsibility are drawn less clearly, and the teaching staff may be more often included in the decision-making process. It is important

Teaching staff should be included in making decisions.

PERSPECTIVE 16.1

Hiring the Right People for the Right Reasons

Dr. Andrea Fletcher,
Center for Collaborative Solutions

When I was hired as the first director at Sacramento START, one of California's pioneering afterschool programs, the most pressing issue was how to hire the best possible people in the shortest possible time—a challenge many of you are facing right now. I had 6 weeks to fill positions at 20 sites with 120 staff members. We met that target, and I learned a lot about what works and what doesn't. I've learned even more over the past several years working as a consultant to hundreds of new and established programs. I'm convinced that two things matter more than anything else: hiring from neighborhoods where your sites are located and hiring for attitude over experience.

The advantage of hiring locally is huge. It ensures that the racial, cultural, and linguistic diversity of your staff reflects the student population, contributing in important ways to creating and maintaining an emotionally safe environment and developing supportive relationships between adults and children and young people. It reconnects neighborhoods with the schools, providing pathways for parent involvement and helping parents become more effective partners in their children's education. It provides jobs for low-income families and for local community college and university students. And it increases your staff's commitment to your program. The impact is powerful—student attendance increases, and so does staff retention and program quality.

With this geographic focus in hiring, the question is how to select the right individuals. There's a real difference in what you should be looking for in site directors and program leaders—those folks who work directly with students. The primary responsibilities of site directors are to develop a high-performing staff, to work effectively with principals and teachers to develop an authentic partnership, to build positive relationships with community members, and to set and achieve meaningful goals that contribute to program quality. The best site directors are inspirational leaders; effective managers, team builders, and coaches; and partnership developers. They're open to learning and committed to excellence. They have a strong sense of personal responsibility. They get along well with people and are passionate about making a difference. And, perhaps most important, they understand that their success depends on the success of those who work for and with them.

The best advice I can give on choosing program leaders is to hire for attitude and train for skills. Regardless of their formal qualifications, previous experience, or credentials, their real work is about engaging and supporting students and helping them build their skills and self-confidence, expand their knowledge, and increase their enthusiasm for learning. People who do this especially well have a very positive outlook on life, a talent for meeting children and young people where they are, and a real commitment to helping students succeed. Look for these qualities in interviews and it will make all the difference in hiring the right people and getting the new year off to a great start!

Used with permission.

---

that, especially given this multiplicity of tasks juggled by director and line staff, there be enough people to go around. Be sure that staff–child ratios and group sizes always permit the staff to meet the needs of children and youths; their safety and well-being must come before balancing the budget, at least during the program day.

The integrated nature of school-age program administration often means that the management function takes place at the centers as much as it does in centralized offices. For this reason, all members of the staff must understand

The management function may take place at the afterschool site as well as in a centralized office.

the program philosophy, goals and objectives, and priorities. These should be reviewed each year with them. A benefit of this knowledge is a greater opportunity for **shared decision making**, in which both staff and management contribute to developing policy and finding solutions to administrative challenges.

Be sure to support families' involvement in your programs by including them in decision making as well. If you offer an orientation session for families at the beginning of each year and for each new family and nurture communication throughout the year, you may discover that they can offer valuable insight and information.

Hiring and Retaining Effective High-Quality Staff Successful afterschool programs recruit staff members that "reflect the cultural and linguistic backgrounds of their students" (McNear & Wambalaba, 2006, p. 22). However, afterschool professionals enter the field by different paths, and that can make training and professional development difficult. Just the same, training and professional development have been shown to be two key elements in developing and retaining effective, high-quality staff, so directors and site supervisors should focus on this area and plan time to release program and group leaders to attend trainings that meet their individual professional growth needs. Providing targeted training allows staff to be better equipped to work with the youth in their program and can have a positive effect on the long-term achievements of the children (Bowie & Bronte-Tinkew, 2006).

The site director clearly needs to have specific knowledge of child care administration. Most colleges and universities offer coursework that will prepare directors to hire and supervise staff, develop and oversee a budget, understand legal and liability issues, and determine a philosophical direction for curriculum development. Figures 16.5 and 16.6 present recommended competencies for various levels of leadership in school-age programs. In no way does this chapter

FIGURE 16.5 Levels of Responsibility.

LEVELS OF RESPONSIBILITY
Program Administrator Overall direction of the program • developing a mission, goals, and policies for the program • program implementation and evaluation • administration, including fiscal management • organizational development, including management of human resources
Site Director Daily operations of the program • supervising staff • communicating with families • building relationships with the host community • overseeing all program activities
Senior Group Leader Supervision and guidance of children in the program • program planning • communicating with families • supervising support staff • relating to the community
Group Leader Supervision and guidance of children in the program under the direction of a Senior Group Leader • same as the Senior Group Leader
Assistant Group Leader Supervision and guidance of children under the direct supervision of a Group Leader

Source: Levels of Responsibility: National Afterschool Association. (1998). *NAA Standards for Quality School-Age Care.* Boston: National Afterschool Association. Used with permission.

provide the needed administrative training. The goal of this chapter is to present an overview of the kinds of administrative issues that exist in school-age settings, in order for staff members and administrators alike to understand what is required.

Titles vary, so the responsibility assumed by that staff member will determine the qualifications required.

FIGURE 16.6 Recommended Minimum Qualifications for Staff in School-Age Programs.

MINIMUM QUALIFICATIONS			
Position	**Experience**	**Education**	**Professional Preparation**
Program Adminstrator	One year	Associate's or Bachelor's Degree in Related Field	Six credit hours: • child and youth development (3) • administration (3)
	Two years	Bachelor's Degree in Unrelated Field	Twelve credit hours: • child and youth development (3) • administration (3) • other areas related to sac programming (6)
	Eighteen months	AA Degree or two years of college in a related field or equivalent certification	Nine credit hours: • child and development (3) • other areas related to sac programming (6)
Senior Group Leader		Bachelor's Degree in related field	
	Three months	Bachelor's Degree in unrelated field	Six credit hours: • child and youth development (3) • other areas related to sac programming (3)
	Six months	AA Degree or two years of college in related field or equivalent	Six credit hours: • child and youth development (3) • other areas related to sac programming (3)
	One year	AA Degree or two years of college in unrelated field	Six credit hours: • child and youth development (3) • other areas related to sac programming (3)
Group Leader	None	Bachelor's Degree in a related field	
	Three months	Bachelor's Degree in unrelated field	Three credit hours: • child and youth development
	Six months	AA Degree in related field	
	Nine months	AA Degree or two years of college equivalent	Three credit hours: • child and youth development
	Eighteen months	HS Diploma or GED	Six credit hours: • child and youth development (3) • other areas related to sac programming (3)
Assistant Group Leader	None	Minimum age 16	See section on orientation and in-service training

Source: From *NAA Standards for Quality School-Age Care*, by National Afterschool Association. (1998). *NAA Standards for Quality School-Age Care*. Boston: National Afterschool Association. Used with permission.

SUMMARY

There is usually more overlap between the responsibilities of management and staff in school-age programs than in programs serving younger children. Shared decision making is more effective if all members of staff understand the program philosophy, goals and objectives, and priorities. Site directors of school-age programs should be knowledgeable about licensing regulations, liability issues, and fiscal matters. Directors may work with a governing board, teachers, and parents in the development of admission agreements and a policies and procedures handbook. Other matters that will need to be understood and overseen by program directors include transportation and parking, community relations, and the development of program calendars and schedules that serve parent needs. Staff retention is improved by effective training and professional development, so program administrators should schedule time for staff members to obtain ongoing in-service education that matches their individual professional growth needs.

TERMS TO LEARN

admission agreements
afterschool profiles
caregiving
corporations
early childhood legislation
family-centered program
fiscal
for-profit
legal exposure
liability

license-exempt programs
minimum standards
mission statement
negligent
nonprofit
parent handbooks
partnerships
proprietorships
risk management
shared decision making

REVIEW QUESTIONS

1. Explain how the role of a school-age program director may differ from that of the director of a program for younger children.

2. Describe what is meant by shared decision making.

3. List three things that a director can do to improve the way a neighborhood feels about having a school-age program in its midst.

4. What is the difference between the role played by state licensing regulations and the terms and conditions of a funding agency?

CHALLENGE EXERCISES

1. Request a copy of a parent handbook from a school-age program. Try to identify within it the philosophy, goals and objectives, and priorities of the program. If they are not listed specifically, see if you can figure out what they are from the text of the handbook. Summarize.

2. Obtain the yearly calendar from two school-age programs serving the same school district. Are they open the same number of days? What are their policies on minimum school days and school holidays or vacations? Interview a parent from each program about the availability of child care during summer vacations in their community.

3. If possible, attend a parent, staff, or board meeting for a program for school-agers. List the agenda items and the kinds of solutions that were reached at the meeting.

INTERNET RESOURCES

Afterschool profiles by state:
http://nccic.org/afterschool/statep.html

Beyond the Bell: A Toolkit for Creating Effective After School Programs (2nd edition):
http://www.ncrel.org/after/bellkit.htm

National Association of Child Care resource and referral agencies:
http://www.naccrra.org

Resource guide for planning and operating afterschool programs:
http://www.sedl.org/pubs/fam95/

Risk-management resources:
http://www.safechild.org/risk.htm

REFERENCES

Ashcraft, M. (2005). *Best practices: Guidelines for school-age care programs.* Farmington, MN: Sparrow Media Group.

Birmingham, J., Pechman, E. M., Russell, C. A., & Mielke, M. (2005). *Shared features of high-performing after-school programs.* Washington, DC: Policies Studies Associates.

Bolen, E. (2008). *Analysis of Title 22 and Title 5 regulations affecting preschool programs.* San Francisco: Child Care Law Center.

Bowie, L., & Bronte-Tinkew, J. (2006). The importance of professional development for youth workers. *Research-to-Results: Practitioner Insights* (2006–17).

California Department of Education. (1996). *School-age care in California.* Sacramento: Child Development Division.

Child Care Law Project. (1998). *Admission agreements for child care centers.* Los Angeles: Author.

Cornell Cooperative Extension. (2004). *Linking economic development and child care.* Ithaca, NY: Cornell University Press.

Decker, C. A., & Decker, J. R. (2004). *Planning and administering early childhood programs* (8th ed.). Upper Saddle River, NJ: Prentice Hall.

Department of Children and Family Services. (1999–2007). Florida administrative code: Child care standards, rule 65C-22.008 (subparagraph 65C-22.008(2)(c)1). Tallahassee: Florida Department of State, Family Safety and Preservation Program.

Finance Project, The. (2006). *Promoting quality in afterschool programs through state child care regulations.* Washington, DC: Child Care Bureau.

Fletcher, A. J. (2005). *A guide to developing exemplary practices in afterschool programs.* Sacramento, CA: Center for Collaborative Solutions, the Community Network for Youth Development, and the Foundation Consortium for California's Children and Youth.

Leonard, H. B. (2006). *Should mission statements be promises?* Cambridge, MA: Harvard University Press.

McNear, G., & Wambalaba, M. (2006). *Literacy in afterschool programs: Focus on English language learners.* Portland, OR: Northwest Regional Educational Laboratory.

National AfterSchool Association. (1998). *NAA standards for quality school-age care.* Boston: Author.

National Association for Regulatory Administration. (2004). *Child care licensing study.* Washington, DC: National Child Care Information Center.

Otterbourg, S. D. (2000). *How the arts can enhance after-school programs.* Washington, DC: U.S. Department of Education, National Endowment for the Arts.

Sciarra, D. J., & Dorsey, A. G., (1998). *Developing and administering a child care center* (4th ed.). San Francisco: Delmar.

Urzedewski, P. (2006). *What's up? Department policy issues.* Lincoln: Nebraska Health & Services System.

Appendix

National Afterschool Association Code of Ethics
January 2009

ACKNOWLEDGMENTS

The National Afterschool Association would like to acknowledge the Ohio Afterschool Association (OAA) in their role in developing the initial draft of the Code of Ethics. The Ohio team members, led by Christine Schmidt were Teresa Gagnon, Lucy Goodkin, Donna Holland, Leslie Mitchell and Linda Loshe Smith. The initial Code of Ethics draft was peer reviewed by more than 100 afterschool professionals across Ohio.

The National Afterschool Association formed a national committee to review and edit the Ohio document. The National Committee co-chaired by Eddie Santiago and Christine Schmidt included Deborah Chase, Selma Goore and Denise Sellers. Once this document was reviewed and approved by the NAA board, it was disseminated to state affiliate leaders and NAA members for review.

When developing this Code of Ethics, both the Ohio and national teams reviewed several Codes of Ethics from child-serving organizations as well as national membership organizations. A special thanks goes to Concordia University, St. Paul, Minnesota, the National Association for the Education of Young Children, the National Staff Development Counsel and the National Recreation and Parks Association for their progressive work that served as a reference and inspiration.

NAA has taken reasonable measures to develop the Code in a fair, open, unbiased and objective manner, based on currently available data. However, further research or developments may change the current state of knowledge. Neither NAA nor its officers, directors, members, employees nor agents will be liable for any loss, damage or claim with respect to any liabilities, including direct, special, indirect or consequential damages incurred in connection with the Code or reliance on the information presented.

CONTACT INFORMATION

The National Afterschool Association

P.O. Box 34447
Washington, DC 20043
1-888-801-3NAA (3622)
www.naaweb.org

INTRODUCTION

The National Afterschool Association (NAA) has provided leadership in fostering the expansion and inclusion of quality afterschool programming across the nation. NAA has stressed the value of afterschool programming for the individual positive growth and development of children ages 5–18. Its members are dedicated to the common cause of assuring that all children and youth ages 5–18, regardless of abilities, have the opportunity to find accessible, quality afterschool programming that meets the positive growth and development needs of the individual child and the family. Members of NAA are encouraged to support the efforts of the Association and profession by supporting state affiliate and national activities and participating in continuing education opportunities, certification and accreditation. The Association has consistently affirmed the importance of well-informed and professionally trained personnel to continually improve the implementation of afterschool programs.

This document outlines personal and professional excellence, and encourages the professional development of those working in the afterschool field. The highest standards of professional competence, fairness, impartiality, efficiency, effectiveness and fiscal responsibility are integrated within the sections while avoiding any activity that is in conflict with the performance of job responsibilities.

The NAA Code of Ethics sets standards of conduct for the afterschool professional. It was designed as a resource to assist the afterschool professional in understanding the ethical responsibilities inherent in providing afterschool programs for children ages 5–18. The following document has two sections that can be used separately or together. The first document, Statements of Ethical Conduct for Afterschool Professionals, is a brief overview expressed in broad statements to guide sound, ethical decision-making. These statements provided a framework for the creation of the second document, the NAA Code of Ethics. The NAA Code of Ethics is divided into four sections that outline the ethical responsibilities the afterschool professional has towards children, families, colleagues and the community. The NAA Code of Ethics is intended to define the principles and practices that guide ethical decision-making strategies of afterschool professionals to ensure safe, nurturing environments and positive relationships for children and youth.

> The purpose of the NAA Code of Ethics is to raise awareness of our personal commitment to ethical conduct as we carry out our professional responsibilities, conforming to accepted professional standards of conduct. Our Code of Ethics adheres to the highest standards of integrity and honesty in all public and personal activities to inspire public confidence and trust in the afterschool profession.

CONCEPTUAL FRAMEWORK

The Afterschool Code of Ethics sets forth a set of professional responsibilities that focus on four sections: (1) Children, (2) Families, (3) Colleagues and (4) Community and Society. Each section outlines the responsibilities the afterschool professional strives for in building the relationships mentioned above. The set of principles outlined in this document are meant to establish a framework that outlines the conduct of the afterschool professional while the set of practices is meant to provide guidance when ethical dilemmas occur. Although this document provides a framework and guidance for addressing ethical dilemmas, it is understood that the afterschool professional at all times needs to combine the material in this document with sound professional judgment. Similarly, the Code of Ethics is not meant to substitute for or replace any established organizational policies and procedures.

Each section outlines the core responsibilities of the afterschool professional and practices for a given relationship. This approach is meant to strengthen and affirm our commitment to the core values of the field of Afterschool. Afterschool professionals who face ethical dilemmas are encouraged to use this Code of Ethics as a guide to resolve conflicts with the best interest of the child in mind while maintaining the core values outlined in this document.

BASIC ASSUMPTIONS

> Assumption I—Ethical dilemmas will occur.
> Assumption II—The manner in which ethical situations are handled has a direct impact on the individuals involved.
> Assumption III—Real life ethical dilemmas are rarely easy. Often the best ethical course of action to take is not obvious. One important value may contradict another. It is our professional responsibility to work with those involved to find the most ethical action to take.

Above all we will bring *NO harm* to any child. We *will* participate in practices that respect and *do not* discriminate against any child by denying benefits, giving special advantages or excluding from program activities on the basis of his or her race, ethnicity, religion, gender, sexual orientation, national origin, language, ability or their status, behavior or family beliefs.

KEY DEFINITIONS

Afterschool is defined as before school, after school, school vacations/holidays and summer.

Afterschool Programming is defined as any organized program provided for children and youth ages 5–18 during a time when they are not in school.

Afterschool Professionals are those individuals who work in any organized program for children and youth ages 5–18 during a time when they are not in school.

Core values are ethical behaviors that are rooted in the history of our field and grounded in research and best practices in afterschool programming.

Ethics is defined as the responsibility to intentionally choose what is right, moral and just in practice and in principle.

Family includes all persons who are responsible for and involved with the child/youth and who the child/youth identifies as having significant impact in their lives.

Practice is systematically putting the principles into action in afterschool programming by the afterschool professional.

Principles are fundamental codes of conduct.

STATEMENT OF ETHICAL CONDUCT FOR AFTERSCHOOL PROFESSIONALS

The Afterschool Professional shall:

- ❀ Demonstrate the highest standard of individual conduct, personal accountability, trustworthiness, integrity, fairness, consideration of the rights of others and the highest principles of good business practices and relationships.
- ❀ Understand that every individual is a unique and valuable asset to the afterschool community.
- ❀ Design environments and activities based on the knowledge of how children grow and learn.
- ❀ Develop programs that strive to build a strong community among children where play is maximized, children and youth are empowered, self-esteem and maturity are guided and self-discipline is taught and encouraged.
- ❀ Provide opportunities that enhance individual uniqueness, positive choice, critical thinking, creativity, curiosity and a love of learning.
- ❀ Appreciate, support, encourage and respect close ties between the child and family.
- ❀ Recognize that understanding that children achieve their full potential when supported in the context of family, culture, community and society.
- ❀ Base all relationships with children and families on trust, respect and acceptance.
- ❀ Communicate openly and clearly with the afterschool community, staff, children and youth, families, hosts, employees and other professionals.
- ❀ Uphold basic principles of trust, honesty, integrity and respect in all professional and business practices.
- ❀ Serve as an advocate for children, their families and their teachers in the local community and society.
- ❀ Recognize how personal values, opinions and biases can affect professional judgment.
- ❀ Be committed to their own learning and professional development.

❀ Respect colleagues in afterschool programming and support them in maintaining the NAA Code of Ethics.

❀ Respect and protect the confidentiality of the child, families, colleagues, program and partner organizations and agencies.

❀ Honor the ideals and principles of the NAA Code of Ethics.

Afterschool professionals provide programming in a variety of settings that offer a wide range of activities and programming for children ages 5–18. Those who provide services to the afterschool child and youth operate on a central core of beliefs that each child needs to be treated as an individual and deserves caring professionals who provide a safe, nurturing environment. These environments are planned with the child in mind and encourage independence, exploration, a feeling of self-worth and provide activities and events that create opportunities for social-emotional growth, recreation and educational learning. The afterschool professional needs to work in the best interest of the child.

SECTION I: ETHICAL RESPONSIBILITIES TO CHILDREN AND YOUTH

The school age years are a period of rapid growth and exploration for all children. Each child grows and develops at his or her own unique, individualized pace. It is the responsibility of afterschool programs to provide a safe, nurturing and enriching environment where all children can develop their cognitive, physical, emotional and social competencies to the fullest extent possible.

We dedicate ourselves to these principles:

P-1.1 Expand our understanding of children and youth ages 5–18 by staying current with the knowledge related to afterschool programming and demonstrate this knowledge within the afterschool program.

P-1.2 Allow children and youth to participate in planning the environment and activities that assist in individual growth in social, emotional, physical and cognitive development.

P-1.3 Appreciate and honor the uniqueness and potential of each child or youth.

P-1.4 Support and respect the child's and their family's race, ethnicity, gender, ability, religion and socioeconomic status.

P-1.5 Ensure that each child has opportunities to build positive relationships based on trust, honesty and respect.

P-1.6 Ensure that each child will have access to the most appropriate programs and resources in the most inclusive environment possible.

P-1.7 Protect the safety, health and nutrition of each child within the program.

P-1.8 Ensure that confidentiality is maintained unless the well-being of a child is in question.

P-1.9 Work as a team with families, staff and schools to set goals for each child, working with outside specialists when necessary.

As Afterschool Professionals, we:

❀ Plan environments that foster the social, emotional, physical and intellectual needs of all children and youth while allowing for independence and creativity by creating a playful, friendly, empowering program space that celebrates the gifts and talents of the children and youth.

❀ Provide a wide variety of age and developmentally appropriate activities and interactions to encourage a love of learning through curiosity.

❀ Provide a structure using guidelines and procedures that clearly communicate boundaries and expectations through the use of positive guidance methods, encouraging and supporting cooperative solutions.

❀ Create a balance within the daily activities that is responsive to the children's abilities, interest, talents, cultures, feelings and temperament.

❀ Maintain confidentiality of information related to the child unless the child's welfare is at risk. However, when there is reason to believe that a child's welfare is at risk, it is permissible to share confidential information with agencies and individuals who may be able to intervene in the child's interest.

❀ Report all instances of any form of suspected child abuse and/or neglect as outlined by the laws of the individual state/municipality.

❀ Advocate for policies, procedures and laws that promote quality afterschool programming.

❀ Establish child-centered practices that will support the development of skills of self-discipline and self-control.

❀ Ensure that the children's ideas, interests and needs guide the curriculum.

❀ Provide appropriate curriculum and qualified staff to support the changing needs of children and youth as they grow and mature.

❀ Provide opportunities for children to become socially and emotionally competent.

❀ Respect and protect the confidentiality of the children, families, colleagues and the organization.

❀ Involve all those with relevant knowledge of the child (families, staff, school and specialist) to create an appropriate environment for children and youth.

SECTION II: ETHICAL RESPONSIBILITIES TO FAMILIES

Families are the primary influence in the lives of children. As afterschool professionals we have a responsibility to work in partnership with family members. Building relationships through these partnerships will support the growth and development of each child or youth. Recognizing that all children grow and develop within the context of their family, the community and their culture will allow opportunities for success for each child by enhancing his or her development.

We dedicate ourselves to these principles:

P-2.1 Develop positive relationships with the families served that are based on mutual trust.

P-2.2 Appreciate, accept and respect each family's uniqueness of culture, language, customs, beliefs and ethnicity.

P-2.3 Recognize the parents' right to make decisions for their children and respect different childrearing value systems.

P-2.4 Report all instances of all forms of suspected child abuse and/or neglect as outlined by the laws of the individual state/municipality.

P-2.5 Share information with families that help them to understand the child's growth and the value of developmentally appropriate afterschool programming.

P-2.6 Provide opportunities for parents to interact with program staff and other families, and provide information about community resources and professional services to improve their understanding of their children and improve their skills as parents.

P-2.7 Ensure that confidentiality is maintained unless the well-being of a family is in question.

P-2.8 Protect the safety and health of each child within the program.

As Afterschool Professionals, we:

- Welcome all families into our afterschool programming.
- Communicate to families the program philosophy, policies, procedures and personnel qualifications.
- Focus on the strengths and assets of each family unit by encouraging family involvement in our programs.
- Involve families in significant decisions affecting their child(ren).
- Provide community resources to benefit families.
- Communicate with families in a timely manner about incidents involving their child(ren), risks such as exposures to contagious diseases that may result in infection and occurrences that might result in emotional stress.
- Communicate with integrity, honesty and respect to build a trusting, positive relationship with families.
- Develop written policies for the protection of confidentiality and the disclosure of children's records.
- Maintain confidentiality of information related to the child unless the family's welfare is at risk. However, when there is reason to believe that a family's welfare is at risk, it is permissible to share confidential information with agencies and individuals who may be able to intervene in the child's interest.
- Help family members in conflict by working openly, sharing our observations of the child and helping all parties involved make informed decisions. Refrain from becoming an advocate for one party while working within any existing legal order.
- Report all instances of any form of suspected child abuse and/or neglect as outlined by the laws of the individual state/municipality.

SECTION III: ETHICAL RESPONSIBILITIES TO COLLEAGUES

Based on our core values of honesty, integrity, trust and respect, our primary responsibility is to create a caring and cooperative workplace. Within this environment professional satisfaction is valued, human diversity is respected and positive relationships are modeled. The same attitudes and behaviors that support a child's growth and development are equally important with co-workers, employers and employees. Although it is understood that throughout a career in the afterschool field professionals may have different roles and responsibilities, the commitment to ethical conduct remains constant. This code is designed to outline the responsibilities of afterschool professionals to their Co-worker, Employee and Employer.

We dedicate ourselves to these principles:

P-3.1 Establish and maintain relationships with other afterschool professionals based on honesty, respect, integrity, trust and cooperation.

P-3.2 Implement high quality services that align the mission of the program and the needs of the children.

P-3.3 Provide ongoing program evaluation, information sharing and identify program improvement.

P-3.4 Support success of all employees through evaluation, mentoring and enhancing knowledge and skills though professional growth opportunities.

P-3.5 Promote and support professional growth opportunities to enhance knowledge and skills.

P-3.6 Resolve issues of disagreement in a professional manner and according to the policies and procedures of the agency/organization.

P-3.7 Maintain a stable workforce for those who work on behalf of children and youth, through mutual support, teamwork and equitable compensation (salary, benefits, working conditions and schedules).

P-3.8 Work collaboratively and cooperatively with co-workers.

P-3.9 Support and encourage co-workers and colleagues in meeting individual needs for professional growth and development.

P-3.10 Promote policies, procedures and working conditions that encourage mutual respect, competence, well-being and positive relationships among staff members.

P-3.11 Recognize the importance of professionalism in the workplace at all times.

P-3.12 Ensure that confidentiality is maintained unless the well-being of a child or staff member is in question.

We will support these principles by implementing these practices:

❀ Provide support for and participate in professional growth opportunities to enhance knowledge and skills.

❀ Establish a fair, respectful and non-threatening evaluation process that is based on relevant employee performance as it relates to the work responsibilities for children and youth as well as program.

❀ Develop and maintain comprehensive written personnel policies and procedures. These policies shall be reviewed by and made available to all staff members.

❀ Provide a workplace that is safe, nurturing and emotionally supportive.

❀ Address the need for programmatic or policy changes through appropriate and established procedures.

❀ Speak and act on behalf of the organization only when authorized.

❀ Take appropriate action in the event of the violation of the operating laws or regulations designed to protect children and youth in the event that a colleague's behavior is harmful to the program's emotional climate.

❀ Base hiring and promotions decisions solely on a person's record of accomplishment and ability to carry out the responsibilities of the position. Participation in discrimination based on race, ethnicity, religion, gender, national origin, culture, disability or sexual preference is strictly forbidden.

❀ Address issues of concern or disagreement with co-workers in a dignified, honest and respectful manner according to the policies and procedures of the agency/organization.

❀ Share information and resources with appropriate parties to support quality afterschool programming.

❀ Maintain confidentiality of information related to staff members unless the staff's welfare is at risk. However, when there is reason to believe that the staff's welfare is at risk, it is permissible to share confidential information with agencies and individuals who may be able to intervene in the staff's interest.

❀ Engage in collaborative and thoughtful planning with colleagues, children and youth to ensure the alignment of the program's mission with the needs of the children, youth and families.

SECTION IV: ETHICAL RESPONSIBILITIES TO COMMUNITY AND SOCIETY

Our responsibility to the families, community agencies and organizations concerned with the welfare of children and youth is to provide high quality programming staffed with educated, qualified and responsive individuals who have an understanding of the abilities and developmental needs of children and youth. Our responsibility to society is to encourage and support the socialization of the children and youth by providing opportunities to develop leadership and communication skills that will enable them to develop in a socially acceptable way. Our responsibilities include engaging in and facilitating collaborations and cooperative agreements that will enhance programming, educating (and informing) others about the need and benefits of afterschool programming and advocating for the welfare and protection of all children and youth.

We dedicate ourselves to these principles:

P-4.1 Provide the community with high quality afterschool programming that meets the needs of the children, youth, their families and the community.

P-4.2 Provide access to afterschool programming that promotes the well-being of every child and youth by facilitating positive development through age and developmentally appropriate practices.

P-4.3 Work cooperatively with child-serving agencies and organizations to share the responsibility for the care and education of children and become a collective voice for the rights and welfare of all children and youth.

P-4.4 Develop positive relationships that work collaboratively to maximize resources and programming available to children and youth.

P-4.5 Educate and inform others as to the vital role of afterschool programming in the lives of children and the community at large.

P-4.6 Support the development of policies and laws that promote the well-being of children, youth and families.

P-4.7 Further the professional development of the field of afterschool programming.

P-4.8 Promote the afterschool field's commitment to realizing its core values as reflected in this Code.

P-4.9 Ensure that organizational confidentiality is maintained.

P-4.10 Work collaboratively with programs, schools and community agencies/organizations to ensure effective transitions for children and youth.

We will support these principles by implementing these practices:

- ❀ Provide professional and accessible afterschool programming that will enhance the community's ability to raise and support healthy children.
- ❀ Establish and/or participate in community organizations that further the development of afterschool programming and professionals.
- ❀ Recommend for employment only those who are competent and qualified.
- ❀ Learn how the legislative process works in order to advocate for children, youth and families.
- ❀ Create a learning environment that encourages, facilitates and supports ongoing professional development.
- ❀ Become familiar with and implement laws and regulations within your state that serve to protect the children and youth in your program.
- ❀ Create interpersonal and public opportunities to support programs that are advancing and developing children and the afterschool field and take responsibility for observing, monitoring and evaluating programs that fall short of this mission.
- ❀ Work collaboratively with community agencies/organizations to ensure the effective transition of children and youth to the afterschool program.
- ❀ Maintain confidentiality of information related to the agency/organization unless the welfare of the children or staff is at risk. However, when there is reason to believe that the children's or staff's welfare is at risk, it is permissible to share confidential information with agencies and individuals who may be able to intervene in the children's or staff's interest.

Source: National AfterSchool Association Code of Ethics © 2009. Used with permission.

REFERENCES AND BIBLIOGRAPHY

American Association of Grant Professionals (2006). Code of Ethics. Retrieved February 2, 2008, from: http://www.grantprofessionals.org/about/images/codeofethics.pdf.

Boys & Girls Clubs (2007). A Matter of Trust: Alliance of Boys & Girls Clubs Code of Ethics.

Charron, L. (2001) "Code of Ethics for School-age Care." SAC Monograph No.1. St. Paul, MN: Concordia University, Concordia School of Human Services.

Harms, T., Jacobs, E. and White, D. (1996). School Age Care Environmental Rating Scale. Columbia University, New York: Teachers College Press.

International Federation of Social Workers (2002). Draft document: Ethics in Social Work Statement of Principles. Retrieved from http://www.ifsw.org/en/p38000252.html

MacDonald, C. (2006). Considerations for Writing A Code of Ethics. Retrieved February 14, 2008, from: www.ethicsweb.ca/codes/writing-a-code-of-ethics.htm.

National AfterSchool Association (1999). The NAA Standards for Quality School-age Care. Boston, MA: National Afterschool Association.

National Association for the Education of Young Children (2005). Code of Ethical Conduct and Statement of Commitment. Washington, DC: National Association of the Education of Young Children.

National Recreation and Park Association. NRPA Professional Code of Ethics. Retrieved May 23, 2008, from: (http://www.nrpa.org/content/ default.aspx?documentId=493.

National Staff Development Council (2000). A Staff Development Code of Ethics. Retrieved February 12, 2008, from: http://www.nsdc.org/publications/getDocument.cfm?articleID=488.

University of Illinois at Chicago. The Collaborative for Academic, Social, and Emotional Learning (CASEL). Retrieved May 19, 2008, from: http://www.casel.org/home/index.php.

YMCA of the USA (2005). Code of Conduct. Washington, DC: YMCA of the USA.

Index

Abuse, 163
Academic achievement
  afterschool care and, 33
  community partnerships to strengthen,
    420–421
  family involvement and, 401, 406
  gender and, 166–168
  poverty and, 140
  program quality and, 57
  support for, 139–141
Academic enrichment
  balance between recreation and, 238
  balancing applied knowledge with, 304–310
Academic programs, for child-care professionals,
    82, 84, 85
Acceptance, 145–146
Accessibility, 229–230
Accidents, 227–228. *See also* Safety
Accommodations, 111, 254
Accountability, 140
Accreditation
  explanation of, 66, 67
  goals of, 67–68
  national system for, 70–71
  personal perspective on, 69
  process of, 68, 70
  standards for, 71–73
Activate America (YMCA), 170
Activities. *See also* Indoor activities; Outdoor
    activities; Play
  to address fears of children, 159–161
  benefits of planned, 242–243
  evaluation of, 263, 265, 267
  linked to standards, 309–310
  long-term, 259–265
  looking forward to, 246–247
  for older children, 377, 387–389
  older children and adolescents leading, 386
  opportunities for diverse, 63
  spontaneous, 242
  strategies to involve children in, 304

that support literacy learning, 311–316
  use of multiple intelligences theory to plan, 114
Activity Area/Equipment Reservation Request
    Form, 244
Activity areas, 221, 239–241
Addams, Jane, 16
Adema, Willem, 47
Admission agreements, 432–433
Admission policies, 405–406
Adolescents. *See also* Children; Older school-age
    children; School-age children
  creating safe and friendly options for, 395–396
  developmental characteristics of, 272, 375
  explanation of, 371
  programming for, 374, 376–387
  safety issues for, 371–372
Adult-centered environment, 207
Adults, role in family-school partnerships,
    403–404
Adult supervision
  with full accountability, 25
  in programs for adolescents, 396
  with some accountability, 25
Aerosol sprays, 226
Africa, school-age care in, 47
African Americans
  health care access for, 152
  obesity among, 272
  poverty among, 153
Afterschool, origin of term, 16
Afterschool Alliance, 40–41
Afterschool care. *See also* School-age care
  academic achievement and, 33
  academic standards and, 308–310
  elements of effective, 50–51
  historical background of, 3–4, 15–19
After School Education and Safety (ASES)
    program (California), 32–33
Afterschool inclusion aides, 78
Afterschool profiles, 429
Afterschool program leaders, 78

Agents of socialization
   adults as, 135–136
   explanation of, 129
Age-specific development, 82
Aggression
   behavior modeling to combat, 187
   explanation of, 183–184
Alcohol consumption. *See* Substance abuse
Alcohol prevention programs, 171
Alexander, David, 310
All Children Exercise Simultaneously (ACES), 294
Allocation of staff, 244–245
All on One Side game, 359–360
American Academy of Child and Adolescent
      Psychiatry, 273
American Academy of Pediatrics (AAP), 277, 303
American Camp Association, 85–86
American Home Economics Association (AHEA), 37
Americans with Disabilities Act (ADA), 7, 229
Andrews, Rosa, 67, 70
Animal fables, 309–310
Animal-related activities, 366–367
Annie Stories: A Special Kind of Storytelling (Brett), 164
Anorexia, 143
Antisocial behavior, 183
Anxiety. *See also* Fears
   music and, 291
   separation, 156
   signs of, 157, 158
   social, 156
Aptekar, Louis, 49
Art & Creative Materials Institute, 226
Art materials, hazard-free, 226–227
Ashcraft, Mike, 281, 282, 412
The ASPCA Complete Guide to Pet Care (Carroll), 366
ASQ: Assessing School-Age Quality, 67, 70
Assessment, 66
Assessment of Afterschool Program Practices Tool
      (APT), 64
Assets, 396
Assimilation, 111
Athletic programs, 41
At-risk behaviors, 392
Attitudes, 130
Australia, school-age care in, 46
Autonomy vs. shame and doubt stage, 102

Baby Boomers, 158
Back-to-school night, 408–409
Balanced curriculum, 250–251
Bandura, Albert, 116, 135, 185
Beacon Cove Intermediate School (Jupiter, Florida), 377
Behavior
   aggressive, 183

antisocial, 183
at-risk, 392
child development and, 176–178
environment and, 181–184
explanation of, 129
friendships and, 178–181
guidance system to influence, 175–184
methods to guide, 185–196
prosocial, 183, 389
role of adults and, 183–184
stating expectations of desired, 186–187
Behavior contracts, 187, 188
Behavior modification, 175
Bellm, Don, 384, 403
Benodjehn Child Care Center (Leelanau County,
      Michigan), 37
Benson, O. H., 17
Bergman, Abby Barry, 360
Berry parfaits, 322–323
Biking, 285–288
BioSITE project (Santa Clara County Children's
      Discovery Museum), 420
Blades, Joan, 38
Blended families, 19
Bobo Doll experiment, 135
Bodily/kinesthetic intelligence, 114
Body mass index (BMI), 272–274
Boeree, George, 106
Boston Children's Mission, 16
Boston MOST Initiative, 390
Bounce the beach ball activity, 357–358
Boys and Girls Clubs of America, 17, 36, 41, 170,
      250, 295
Boy Scouts, 18
Brain Breaks, 297
Brain function, play and, 346
Breadth, 250
Brett, Doris, 164
Bromley, Karen, 311
Bronfenbrenner, Urie, 121–124, 135
Brown, Lyn, 183–184
Brown, Stuart, 346, 363
Bulimia, 143
Bulletin boards, 412, 413
Bullying, 184

C. S. Mott Children's Hospital, 152
California
   afterschool programming in, 32–33
   licensing requirements in, 427
California State University at Long Beach, 421
Camps, 386
Canada, school-age care in, 46, 47
Caregiving, 439

Care structure, 378, 379
Caring and relationship theory, 119–120
Carnegie Council on Adolescent Development, 392
Carroll, David L., 366
Centrate, 110
Certification. *See also* Licensing
    for child-care professionals, 82, 84, 85
    requirements for, 73
    state requirements for, 85
Character building, 377–378
Chard, Sylvia C., 262
Chèches, 49
Check-in programs, school-sponsored, 27–28
Child and Adult Care Food Program (Department of
    Agriculture), 283
Child and youth development, 15
Child and youth workers, 58
Child Care and Development Fund (CCDF), 249
    explanation of, 35
Child Care Bureau, 429
Child Care Exchange, 12
Child-centered environment, 207
Child development
    guidance system and, 176–178
    knowledge of, 82
    milestones in, 96
    overview of, 14–15
Child development theories
    characteristics of, 97
    cognitive development, 108–114
    domains of, 97–98
    ecological systems, 121–124, 135
    learning theories, 115–116
    moral development, 117–120
    overview of, 96–97, 124
    physical growth and development, 98–100
    social-emotional development, 100–103, 105–108
Child neglect, 163
Child Nutrition Reauthorization Act of 1998, 283
Children. *See also* Adolescents; Preschool-age
    children; School-age children
    concerns of, 153–154
    concerns of parents about, 152–153
    developmental changes in, 14–15, 176–178
    developmental issues of, 151–152
    developmental tasks for, 106–108
    effect of divorce on, 162–164
    ethical responsibilities to, 450–451
    gross motor skills in, 276
    homeless, 162, 164
    normal fears of, 156–157
    obesity in, 143, 144, 152, 272–276
    relationship development in, 60–61
    role in planning activities, 245
    safety needs of, 154–155
    scheduling needs of, 5
    substance use among, 170–171
    time spent indoors, 346
Children: The Challenge (Dreikurs & Solz), 185
Children Moving (Graham, Parker Holt/Hale), 361
Children's Choice Child Care Services
    (Albuquerque), 250, 281–282, 412, 413
Children's Defense Fund, 152, 153
Children with special needs
    accessibility issues for, 229–230
    attendants or inclusion aides for, 210–211
    games for, 360
    suitable programs for, 5–7
Chuh, Linda, 378
CityVision, 391
Classroom aides, 79
Classroom management, 175
Clubs
    explanation of, 241
    for older children and adolescents, 376, 379–380
Code of ethics (National Afterschool Association),
    446–448
    basic assumptions, 448
    conceptual framework, 448
    key definitions, 448–449
    responsibilities to children and youth, 450–451
    responsibilities to colleagues, 452–454
    responsibilities to community and society,
        454–455
    responsibilities to families, 451–452
    statement of ethical conduct for afterschool
        professionals, 449–450
Cognitive development, 108–111, 176–178
Cognitive development theories
    multiple intelligences, 112–114
    Piagetian, 108–111
    use of, 113–114
    Vygotsky's sociocultural, 111–112
Cognitive modification strategies, 191–193
Cohort effects, 14
Cohorts, 14
Cold frame, 352
Collaboration, 417
Collage, 358
Colleagues, ethical responsibilities to, 453–454
Color, in school-age care sites, 217–218
Committed partnerships, 404
Committee on Public Television (American Academy
    of Pediatrics), 277
Communication, methods for family-program,
    412–416
Communities
    ethical responsibilities to, 454–455

Communities (*continued*)
  knowledge of, 163
  protecting children from dangers in, 223, 393, 396
Community facilities, 202
Community organizations
  alliances with, 390–391
  development of workplace skills in, 421
  partnerships between programs and, 419–423
  programs for adolescents in, 392–394
  support services in, 164
Community volunteers, 79–80
Compact florescent lights (CFLs), 218
Competence, development of, 140–141, 145
Competencies, for working in school-age child care, 91–93
Complementary close, in personal letters, 313
Complementary learning framework, 403
Complete inadequacy, 185
The Complete School-Age Child Care Resource Kit (Bergman & Green), 360
Computers, 337. *See also* Internet; Technology
Concrete operational stage, 110
Conflict resolution
  as behavior technique, 189–190
  developing skills in, 181
Connectivity, 118
Conservation of liquid task, 110
Construction activities, 324–325, 337–339
Constructive play, 349
Constructivist theory, 108
Continuous, 109
Continuous program improvement, 71–72
Contractual partnership, 403
Conventional moral level, 117
Convention on the Rights of the Child (United Nations), 303
Cooking
  to enhance math problem-solving skills, 319–321
  learning skills for, 321–324
Cooperative games, 359. *See also* Games
Cooperative Games and Sports (Orlick), 260
Cooperative Games for Indoors and Out (Deacove), 362
Coping saw, 364
Cortez, Salvador, 169
Corvallis, Oregon, 421
Council for Early Childhood Professional Recognition, 67
Council on Accreditation (COA), 70–73
Course of study, 82, 235
Craiglist.com, 396
Creative arts, activities related to, 325–328
Crèches, 49, 51
Credentials, 85
Creno, Cathryn, 293–294

Crime, 19–20
Crime Poll (Gallup), 153
Crosscut saws, 364
Crowe, Bonnie, 30
Cultural conditioning, 362
Cultural diversity
  nurturing environment and, 211–212
  socialization and, 136
Cultural schemas, 130
Culture
  physical growth and, 280–281
  socialization and, 130, 133–134
Curriculum
  creating balanced and integrated, 250–251
  emergent, 236–241
  evaluation of, 263, 265, 267
  explanation of, 235–236
  use of learning areas to balance, 310–311
Curry, N.J.C., 146
Cyber-bullying, 184
Cycling, 358

Daily plans, 256–259. *See also* Plans/planning
Damon, William, 120, 185
Dance, 289–290
Daniel, Michael, 294
Darwin, Charles, 96
Deacove, Jim, 362
Decision making, 147, 185
Defense mechanisms, 100
Deferred, 68
De Kalb Public Library, 43
DeKoven, Bernie, 305, 333
Denmark, school-age care in, 45, 46
Department of Agriculture, U. S., 282, 283
Department of Education, U. S., 167
Depression, in children, 152, 153
Developing Cross-Cultural Competence: A Guide for Working With Young Children and Their Families (Lynch & Hanson), 134
Developmental characteristics
  explanation of, 151–152
  of older children and teens, 372–375
  of school-age children, 82, 87–89, 106–108
Developmentally appropriate, 82
Developmental milestones, 96
Developmental tasks
  competence and, 145
  explanation of, 106–108
DeWitt Wallace Reader's Digest Fund, 417, 422
Diabetes, 273
Dimensions of self-esteem, 145–147
Directional, 14–15
Discipline, 90, 175

Discontinuous development, 15
Discretion, 416
Dispositions, 87
Distal supervision, 24
Divorce, 162–164
Dolna Crèche program, 51
Domains of development, 14, 97–98
Dominance hierarchy, 186
Dramatic activities
    fantasy play, 328–329
    prop boxes, 329–332
    puppet play, 332–333
    staging plays, 329–330
    visits by local theaters, 388
Dreikurs, Rudolf, 185
Drop-in programs, 41
Drug abuse. *See* Substance abuse
Drug prevention programs, 171
Duck, Duck, Goose activity, 334–335, 360
Duncan, Arne, 6

Early childhood legislation, 427
Early Childhood Program Accreditation, 70
Eating disorders, yoga and, 290
Ecological systems theory
    explanation of, 121–123
    socialization and, 135
    use of, 123–124
Edelman, Marian Wright, 152, 160
Edwards, Sue, 315
The Egg-Eating Bottle experiment, 317
Ego, 100
Egocentric, 109
Ego integrity vs. dispair stage, 105
Eisenhower, Dwight D., 90
Elkin, Frederick, 129, 134
E-mail activities, 316
Emergent curriculum
    activity areas to encourage, 239–241
    explanation of, 236–237
    funding sources and, 238
*Emergent Curriculum in the Primary Classroom:
    Interpreting the Reggio Emilia Approach in
    Schools* (Wien), 239
Emotions
    explanation of, 129
    physical growth and, 280
    socialization and, 133
Empathy, 181
Endorsers, 68
Energy, to work with children, 89
Engagement
    emphasis on, 63
    increasing opportunities for, 348–349

Enrichment programs
    benefits of, 142
    explanation of, 41–42
Enrollment policies, 405–406
Environments. *See also* School-age care sites
    accessibility of, 229–230
    for adolescents, 377
    attractiveness of, 215–217
    behavior and, 181–183
    dimensions of, 202–203
    evaluation of, 230–231
    indoor, 203
    interesting, 219–223
    interpersonal dimension of, 204–215
    light and color in, 217–218
    nurturing, 205–212
    for older children and adolescents, 388
    outdoor, 203, 343–344, 347
    physical dimension of, 203–204
    privacy in, 218–219
    safe, 221, 223–228
    shared spaces in, 212–215
    sound in, 218
    temporal dimension of, 204
    types of, 62–63, 199–200
Equipment. *See also* Materials
    basic, 215
    for planned activities, 244
    in shared spaces, 213–214
    to support program goals, 216–217
    teaching children to use specialized, 225
Erikson, Erik, 12, 88, 100–103, 105, 106, 134,
    165, 219, 372
The Erupting Volcano experiment, 317–318
Esteem needs, 155
Ethical caring, 119–120
Ethical decision making, 147
Ethics of caring theory, 118
Europe, school-age care in, 45–47
Evaluation sessions, 253
Everyone Wins! Cooperative Games and Activities
    (Luvmour & Luvmour), 260
Existential intelligence, 114
Exosystem
    explanation of, 123
    socialization and, 135–136
Extended day programs, 385–386
Extended families, 19
Extinction, 116, 185

Fables, 309–310
Families. *See also* Parents
    abuse and neglect in, 163
    academic achievement and involvement of, 401, 406

Families (*continued*)
blended, 19
building relationships with, 196, 402–417
changes in structure of, 170
conflicts between staff and, 416–417
conversations with, 414
daily communication with, 412–416
ethical responsibilities to, 452–453
extended, 19
in-home care by, 27, 29
involvement in day-to-day operations, 409
need for school-age care, 19–20
nuclear, 19, 403
partnerships between schools and, 403–404
reconstituted, 19
setting tone with, 404–405, 408
strategies to support, 163–164
substance abuse in, 162
types of, 19, 162, 403
Family calendars, 255
Family-centered programs, 433
Family child care providers, 81
Family fun nights, 410–411
Fantasy play, 328–329
Fathers, inclusion of, 411–412
Fears. *See also* Anxiety
of children, 153–154
generational, 158
methods to address, 159–161, 164
of parents, 152–153
Female-headed households
nontraditional work schedules and, 39
poverty and, 140
statistics of, 151
Females. *See also* Gender
academic achievement and, 166–168
gender roles and, 165–166
Field trips, 350–351
Firearms, 393
Fit for Learning (Santa Clara, California), 296
Fit for Life program, 295–296
Fitness. *See also* Health
dance and, 289–290
focus on, 143, 144
modeling, 277–279
music and, 290–292
obesity and, 274
Walk to School programs and, 286–288
yoga and, 290
Fitness activities
duck, duck, goose, 334–335
freeze dance, 335–336
indoor hide-and-seek, 333–334
leapfrog, 334

Fletcher, Andrea, 440
Flexibility, 89–90
Florida, licensing requirements in, 427–428
Food and Nutrition Service (FNS) (Department of
Agriculture), 282–283
Food-preparation skills
activities to learn, 321–324
to enhance math problem solving, 319–321
Formal child care, categories of, 2–3
Formal operational thinking, 110–111, 157
For their own good, 394
Forum for Youth Investment, 64
Foundations, Inc., 85
4-H programs, 17
Frames of Mind (Gardner), 112
France, school-age care in, 45, 46
Freeze dance activity, 335–336
Freeze tag, 362
Freud, Sigmund, 100, 102
Friendships
developmental stages in, 179–180
importance of, 178
methods to promote, 180–181
skills for, 179
From the Mixed-up Files of Mrs. Basil E. Frankweiler
(Konigsburg), 311–312
Funding
for private programs, 36
for school-age programs, 34–35, 139–140, 238,
374, 436
Furnishings, 215

Games
cooperative, 359
to enhance math problem solving, 324–325
function of, 134
organized outdoor, 360–362
with rules, 349
for students with special needs, 360
types of outdoor, 357–360
Gamines, 49–50
Gardening projects
explanation of, 351–352
personal perspective on, 354
reading room for, 352, 353
strategies for, 354–356
Gardner, Howard, 112–114
Gender. *See also* Females; Males
academic achievement and, 166–168
implications for programs, 168
moral reasoning and, 118
Gender roles
learning, 165–166
same-sex role models and, 167–168

Generational fears, 158
Generational issues, 152
Generation X, 123
Generation Y, 123
Generativity vs. stagnation stage, 105
Geography, pen-pal activities and, 312–313, 315
Gesell, Arnold, 98–100
Gesell Institute of Child Development, 98–100
Gilligan, Carol, 118, 120, 185
Gilroy, California, 202
Girl Guides, 18
Girl Scouts, 18
Global Friendships project, 312–313, 316
Graham, A. B., 17
Graham, George M., 361
Grand Traverse Band, 37
Grant, Jodi, 6
Grassroots programs, 37–38
Greece, school-age care in, 45
Green, William, 360
Greenhouse, 352
Greening the planet project, 356
Greenman, Jim, 220
Gross motor skills, 276
Guidance
    effective and positive styles of, 90
    explanation of, 92, 175
Guidance system
    adults and, 183–184
    children and, 176–181
    environment and, 181–184
    explanation of, 128, 176
Guidance techniques
    conflict-resolution strategies as, 189–190
    elements of effective, 186
    logical consequences as, 193–194
    modeling and instructing as, 187–189
    natural consequences as, 193
    reinforcing, rewarding, and punishing as, 190–192
    setting and enforcing limits as, 192–193
    stating expectations or desired behaviors as, 186–187
    teaching problem solving as, 189
    theories behind, 186
Guided instruction, 112

Haas-Foletta, Karen, 360
Hall, G. Stanley, 96
Hancock, Julie, 416, 420
Harvard Family Research Project (HFRP), 238, 403
Harvard University, 421
Havighurst, Robert, 106, 145, 246
Hawaiian pizza, 322
Heading, in personal letters, 313

Head Start programs, in Native American communities, 37
Health. *See also* Nutrition; Obesity
    in curriculum, 271
    focus on, 62, 143–144
    modeling, 277–279
    obesity and, 273–274 (*See also* Obesity)
    outdoor play and, 345
    parents' concerns related to, 152–153
Heart House (Austin, Texas), 36, 37
Hide-and-seek, 333–334
Hierarchy of needs (Maslow), 63, 154–155
Hiking, 358
Hiring, 441–443
Hispanics
    health care access for, 152
    obesity among, 272
    poverty among, 153
Holt/Hale, Shirley Ann, 361
Homelessness
    distress in children observing, 164–165
    explanation of, 162, 164
Homework
    child-centered policy for, 208–211
    nurturing environments and, 207–208
    older children and adolescents and, 388–389
Homework Help Agreement, 209
Homework Libraries (De Kalb County, Georgia), 43
Homicide rate, 393
Hosseini, Khaled, 265
Hot dog bean soup, 324
Houchen Settlement House (El Paso, Texas), 17
How to Talk to Your Kids About Really Important Things: Specific Questions and Answers and Useful Things to Say (Schachter & McCauley), 161
Human Services Reauthorization Act, 35
Humor, 90
Hurricane Katrina, 158, 161, 165
Hurried child syndrome, 19

I, development of, 134
Id, 100
Identity vs. role confusion stage, 103, 105
Ignoring, 190
Imitation, learning through, 135, 136
Inclusion aides, 210–211
Income Maintenance Administration (Department of Human Services), 39
India
    school-age care in, 49, 51
    shelters for children in, 48–49
Individualized education program (IEP), program planning and, 252

Indoor activities. *See also* Activities
  academic standards and, 308–310
  balancing academic enrichment and applied
    knowledge and, 304–307
  creative arts, 325–328
  dramatic play, 328–333
  fitness, 333–336
  importance of choice and play and, 302–304
  learning areas for, 310, 311
  project approach to teach life skills and, 307–308
  strategies to involve children in, 304
  to support literacy learning, 311–319
  to support math problem solving, 319–325
  technology-related, 336–339
Indoor hide-and-seek, 333–334
Industrial technology, 336–337
Industry vs. inferiority stage, 88, 102–103
Informal child care
  athletic and recreational, 41
  background of, 38–39
  drop-in, 41
  enrichment programs as, 41–42
  explanation of, 3
  library programs as, 42–43
  for nontraditional hours and services, 39–41
In-home care, 27, 29
Initiative vs. guilt stage, 102
Injuries, 227–228. *See also* Safety
Instruction, 188
Integrated curriculum, 250–251
Intentional socialization, 129
Interaction, emphasis on, 63
Interest areas, 221, 239–241
Interest groups, 379. *See also* Clubs
Interesting environments
  characteristics of, 219
  materials in, 219–221
  room arrangements in, 221
Internalize, 129
Internalized conversation, 134
International Nanny Association, 29
International school-age care programs
  in Africa, Asia, India, the Middle East, and Latin
    America, 47–50
  in Europe, Canada, and Australia, 45–47
  overview of, 43, 45
International Walk-to-School Movement, 287
International Yoga Association, 290
Internet
  cyber-bullying and, 184
  fitness programs on, 294–297
  problem-solving activities on, 325, 337
  program communication using, 412
  puzzles on, 324

  safety issues for children using, 152
  time spent indoors and, 346
Interpersonal dimension, of environment, 204–205
Interpersonal intelligence, 114
Intimacy vs. Isolation stage, 105
Intrapersonal intelligence, 114
Ireland, school-age care in, 46, 47

Japan, school-age care in, 48
Jewelry-making activities, 327
Job interviews, 83
Job skills, 137–138
Johnson, Carl, 146
Jones, Ron, 295
Jupiter Middle School of Technology (Florida),
  379
Juvenile crime, 19–20

Kaiser Permanente Health Care, 295, 296, 390
Katch, Jane, 167
Katz, Lilian G., 262, 307–308
KDK-Harman Foundation, 37
Keeler, Rusty, 347
Kenya, school-age care in, 47
Key areas, schedules for, 243–244
KidMover (Dade County, Florida), 40
KidsPark, 39–40
Kim, Hayim, 212
Kindlon, D., 166, 168
The Kite Runner (Hosseini), 265
Kites, 265
Kohl, Herb, 104–105
Kohlberg, Lawrence, 117–118, 147, 185
Korea, school-age care in, 48

Last Child in the Woods (Louv), 350
Latchkey children
  explanation of, 25–27, 374
  support systems for, 27
Latency period, 102
Latin America, child care in, 48
Leapfrog, 334
LEAP program, 394
Learned helplessness, 153
Learning theories
  explanation of, 115
  operant conditioning, 115–116
  social learning, 116
  use of, 116
Lebanon KIDS, 376
Legal exposure, 431
Letter-writing activities, 312–316
Levy, Frank, 310
Liability, 429–431

Liberia, school-age care in, 47
Library programs, 42–43
Licensed family child care homes, 30–32
License-exempt programs, 427
Licensing. *See also* Certification
    goals of, 426–427
    requirements for, 427–429
Life experiences, 14
Life skills
    development of, 137–138
    project approach to teach, 307–308
Life span, moral development through, 120
Light, in school-age care sites, 217–218
Limits, setting and enforcing, 192–193
LINKS program, 416, 420
Links to Learning (Alexander), 310
Literacy
    activities that support, 311–316
    explanation of, 142
Logical consequences
    effects of, 195
    explanation of, 193–194
Logical/mathematical intelligence, 114
Logo, 376
Loose parts, 220–221
Louv, Richard, 350
Low, Juliette, 18
Luvmour, Josette, 360
Luvmour, Sambhava, 360

Macrocultural influences, 165–166
Macroprograms, 49
Macrosystem, 123, 136
Magical thinking, 161
Making a Magnetic Compass, 318–319
Malaspina, Barbara A., 220
Males. *See also* Gender
    academic achievement and, 166–168
    gender roles and, 165–166
    as school-age care professionals, 167–169
Marion, Marian, 128, 176
Martinez-Guaracha, Monica, 354
Mascot, 376
Maslow, Abraham, 63, 154–155
Materials
    in interesting environments, 219–221
    open, 219–220
    for planned activities, 244
    in shared spaces, 213–214
    to support program goals, 216–217
Mathematicians, visits by, 387
Math problem-solving skills
    cooking activities to enhance, 319–325
    games and activities to enhance, 324–325

Maturational theory, 98–100
Maturation theory
    explanation of, 98
    use of, 99–100
Me, development of, 134
Mead, George Herbert, 134
Mental model, 108
Mesosystem, 122
Miami Science Museum, 390
Microcultural influences, 165
Microprograms, 49
Microsystem, 122, 135
Middle East, child care in, 48
Milne, Christopher Robin, 29, 151
Milner, Debbie, 40
Minimum standards, 427
Mission Hill After-School Program, 421
Mission statements, 431–432
Mistaken goals, 185
Mixed-age grouping, 31–32, 384
Modeling
    appropriate behavior, 187–189
    culturally relevant behavior, 136
    function of, 87, 116, 188, 304
    health and fitness, 277–279, 281
    problem-solving strategies, 141, 191
MomsRising.org, 38
Monkey Tail Gang After-School Club (Philadelphia), 36
Monthly plans, 252–256. *See also* Plans/planning
Moral decision making, 185
Moral development theories
    caring and relationship, 119–120
    ethics of caring, 118
    moral reasoning, 117–118
    through life span, 120
    use of, 120
Moral reasoning
    development of, 147, 372
    explanation of, 117–118
Moral virtue, 146–147
Morrow, Michael, 192
MOST initiative, 422
Motivation, 133–134
Mueller, W., 147
Multiple intelligences theory
    activity planning by using, 114
    explanation of, 112–113
Mumbai Mobile Crèches, 49
Murnane, Richard, 310
Music
    healing and stess reduction through, 290–291
    learning to make, 292–294, 387
    listening to, 291

Musical intelligence, 114, 291–292
Myelin sheath, 276

Nannies, 29, 30
National Afterschool Association (NAA)
    accreditation and, 70–71
    code of ethics, 446–455
    establishment of, 16, 57
    function of, 40–41
    problem-solving exercises and, 319
    quality pyramid of, 59–63
National Association for Music Education (MENC),
    292
National Association for the Education of Young
    Children (NAEYC), 70, 273
National Building Museum (Washington, D.C.),
    390–391
National Center for Educational Statistics, 166
National Content Standards for Physical Education, 277
National Council of Teachers of Mathematics, 320
National Crime Prevention Council, 184
National Crime Victimization Survey (NCVS), 393
National FFA Organization, 366
National Health and Nutrition Examination Survey
    (NHANES), 272
National Improvement and Accreditation System, 70
National Institute for Play, 346, 363
National Institute of Environmental Health
    Scientists, U.S., 276
National Institute on Out-of-School Time (NIOST),
    15, 38, 422
National Physical Education Week, 294
National Physical Fitness and Sports Month, 294
National School-Age Care Alliance (NSACA), 57, 67,
    70. See also National Afterschool Association
    (NAA)
National School-Age Child Care Alliance (NSACCA),
    16
National School Lunch Program (NSLP)
    (Department of Agriculture), 275, 283
National Science Foundation, 390
Native Americans, 37–38
Natural caring, 119
Natural consequences, 193
Naturalistic intelligence, 114
Natural Playscapes (Keeler), 347
Nature activities
    field trips to outdoor places, 350–351
    gardening, 351–356
    greening the planet, 356
Nature vs. nurture, 98
Nee, Judy, 47
Needs, Maslow's Hierarchy of, 63, 154–155
Neglect, 163

Negligent, 430
Neighbors, 437–438
Nelson, Eric, 33, 45
Netherlands, school-age care in, 46
Neural pathways, 276
Newman, Roberta, 403
"The Newsletter for School-Age Care Professionals"
    (School-Age Notes), 16
Newsletters, 414, 415
Nighttime programs, 394–395
No Child Left Behind Act (NCLB), 32, 35, 423
Noddings, Neil, 119
Nonprofit organizations, 36–37
Nonsupportive environment, 206
North Carolina Wellness Trust Fund, 297
No supervision, 24
Notes for families, 414
Nuclear families, 19, 403
Nurturing environment
    child-centered, 207
    cultural contexts and, 211–212
    explanation of, 205–207
    homework and, 207–211
Nutrition
    modeling good, 278, 281
    physical growth and, 280
    in school-age children, 276
    in school-age programs, 62
    school lunch program and, 275
    snacks for good, 281–285

Obesity. See also Health
    causes of childhood, 274–276
    dangers of, 273–274
    incidence of, 143, 144, 152, 272, 273
Objectivity, 118
Office of Farmer Cooperative Demonstration Work, 17
Office of the United Nations High Commission for
    Human Rights, 303
O'Hanlin, Maureen, 331
Ohio State University, 17
Older school-age children
    activities for, 387–389
    activities led by, 386
    creating programs for, 374, 376–381
    developing skills and abilities, 389
    developmental characteristics of, 372–375
    explanation of, 370–371
    extended-day programs for, 385–386
    flexibility in programs for, 386–387
    links between community agencies and, 390–392
    nighttime programming for, 394–395
    in planning role, 386
    programs for high school, 392–395

role of adults in programs for, 396

safety of, 371–372, 395–396

setting aside separate space for, 384

staff roles for, 381, 383–384

Ollhoff, Jim, 129

Ollhoff, Laurie, 58, 129

Ontario Science Technology Curriculum, 262

On the Move (Holt/Hale), 361

Open classrooms, 237

Open houses, 408

Open materials, 219–220

Operant conditioning, 115–116

Orderly, 14

Oregon State University, 421

Orlick, Terry, 260

Orr, Jeremy, 79

Others, 139

Outdoor activities. *See also* Activities

with animals, 366–367

benefits of, 344–346

environment for, 203, 343–344, 347

games and sports, 357–362

with kites, 365

nature and ecological, 350–357, 366–367

safety in, 347

trends in, 346

unstructured, 347–350

water-related, 363–364

with wood, 364–365

Outdoor Classroom Project (Child Educational Center, La Canada, California), 345–346

Out-of-home care

grassroots solutions for, 37–38

licensed family child care homes as, 30–32

nonprofit programs operating, 36–37

privately funded, 36

publicly funded school-age programs as, 32–35

types of, 30, 31

Out-of School Programs (Palm Beach County, Florida), 380–382

Out-of-school time, 16

Out-of-School Time Program Evaluation, 64

Overweight, 272. *See also* Obesity

Palm Beach County Parks & Recreation Department, 380–382

Papier-mâché, 318

Parachute cave, 358

Parachute games, 357–358

Parental afterschool stress, 19

Parental concern about after-school time (PCAST), 372

Parent conferences, 409

Parent education sessions, 411

Parent handbooks, 433

Parents. *See also* Families

abuse and neglect of, 163

building relationships with, 196

conflicts between staff and, 416–417

contracts with, 431–433

conversations with, 414

fears and concerns of, 152–153

involvement in improving behavior, 194–195

knowledge of children's likes and dislikes, 12–13

need for school-age care, 19–20

with nontraditional work schedules, 39–40

setting tone with, 404–405

strategies to support, 163–164

substance abuse among, 162

workforce statistics for, 24

Parent Talent Self-Assessment Tool, 407

Parker, Melissa A., 361

Parking, 437

Partnership for After School Education (PASE), 85

Pen-pal activities, 312–313, 315

Persona, 103

Personality

of child-care professionals, 86–91

role of adults in development of, 134–136

Personal letters, 313–316

Photographs, 416

Photography activities, 338–339

Physical activity. *See also* Fitness

academic achievement and, 167

guidelines for, 279

health and, 277–279

incorporated into programs, 285–288

methods to promote, 292, 294–298

Physical dimension, of environment, 203–204

Physical growth, 280–281

Physical growth and development theories

Gesell and, 98

use of, 99–100

Physical play, 349

Physical settings. *See* Environments; School-age care sites

Physiological needs, 154

Piaget, Jean, 108–109, 179, 185

Piagetian cognitive development theory, 108–111

Pitts, Leonard, Jr., 131–133

Places of worship, 201

Plan, Development and Early Education (Johnson, Christie & Wardle), 349

Plans/planning

advance, 242–243

calendar year, 247–252

checklist for, 266

children as participants in, 245

Plans/planning (*continued*)
  daily, 256–259
  goals and objectives as elements of, 249–250
  monthly, 252–256
  seasonal, 252
  skills for, 245–246
  weekly, 255, 257
Plateau effect, 166
Play. *See also* Activities
  benefits of outdoor, 344–346
  disappearance of, 169–170
  function of, 134
  importance of, 303–304
  personal perspective on, 305
  structured, 303
  types of, 349–350
  unstructured, 303, 347–350
Playgrounds
  historical background of, 16
  safety in, 347, 348
Plays, 329–330. *See also* Dramatic activities
Playscapes, 170, 347
Postconventional moral level, 117
Poverty, 140, 153
Powell, Colin L., 77
Powell, Robert Baden, 18
Power, 145
Precausal thinking, 110
Preconventional moral level, 117
Preoperational stage, 109–110
Preschool-age children, 14
Presidential Race, 297
Preteens. *See* Older school-age children
Privacy, in school-age care sites, 218–219
Private homes, 200
Privately funded programs, 36
Problem-solving skills
  activities to enhance math, 319–325
  as behavior technique, 189, 190
  development of, 140–141
  modeling of, 191
Productivity, 372
Professional development programs, 85–86
Program Observation Tool (POT), 64
Program quality
  accreditation and, 67–73
  assessment of, 66
  challenges effecting, 56–57
  effects on children, 57
  quality pyramid and, 59–63
  rapid growth and, 57–59
  tools for evaluating and improving, 64–66
Program Quality Self-Assessment (QSA), 65
Programs. *See* School-age programs

Progressive Education Association, 106
Project approach
  clubs as, 241
  explanation of, 237
  to teach life skills, 307–308
Project Home Safe, 37
Prop boxes
  benefits of, 330–331
  in fantasy play areas, 329
  ideas for, 330, 332
Prosocial behavior
  development of, 389
  explanation of, 61, 183
Psychosocial theory
  explanation of, 100
  life crises and, 100–101
  stages in, 101–103, 105–106
Puberty, 272
Public libraries, programs at, 42–43
Publicly funded school-age programs
  explanation of, 32–33
  funding for, 34–35
  locations of and transportation to, 33–34
Public-private partnerships, 419
Public sector, 419
Punishment
  as behavior technique, 190–191, 194
  operant conditioning theory and, 115
Puppets
  creation of, 326–327
  dramatic play with, 332–333
Puppet theaters, 338
Puzzles, 324

Quality, 57. *See also* Program quality
Quality Assurance System (QAS), 65
Quality pyramid
  activities and, 63
  environment and, 62–63
  explanation of, 59–60
  human relationships and, 60–61
  program organization, procedures and policies and, 60
  role in programming, 63
  safety, health, and nutrition and, 61–62
Quesadillas, 323

Racism, 131–133
Rainbows for All Children, 163
Receptivity, 119
Reciprocal interaction, 120
Reciprocal teaching, 112
Reconstituted families, 19
Recreation programs
  balance between academic enrichment and, 238

benefits of, 142
explanation of, 41
Recruiting, 441–443
Reggio Emilia approach, 237, 308
Registration, 72
Reinforcers
as behavior technique, 190
explanation of, 115, 185
positive, 194
Relatedness, 119
Relational aggression, 184
Relationships, 60–61, 63. *See also* Friendships
Resilient, 303
Respect, 416
Responsiveness, 119
Retaliation and revenge, 185
Rewards, 190–191
Reynolds, Cynthia, 158
Ring, Susan, 366
Ríos, José Luis, 8–9
Risk management, 430
Robert Wood Johnson Foundation (RWJF), 274, 275
Roman, Steve, 43
Room arrangements, 221
Rowe-Finkbeiner, Kristin, 38

Safe Routes to School (SRTS), 287, 288
Safety
accident and injury policies and procedures and, 227–228
checklist for, 227
children's need for, 154–155
hazard-free art materials and, 226–227
of older school-age children, 371–372, 395–396
in outdoor environments, 347, 348
overview of program, 221, 223–224
standards for, 61–62, 224–225
in use of specialized equipment, 225
Salutation, 313
Salvation Army, 36
San Jose, California, 356, 390, 420
Santa Clara County Children's Discovery Museum, 420
Santa Clara County Watershed Watch, 356, 420
Saunders, Len, 294
Save the Children Out-of-School Time Rural Initiative project (Charleston, South Carolina), 41
Saws, 364
Scaffolding, 112
SCANS competencies, 305–308, 310, 391
Schedules
for key areas, 243–244
nontraditional, 39–41
Schema, 111
Schofield, Rich, 16, 278

School-age care
budgeting issues facing, 6
contemporary, 4
elements of effective, 50–52
environment for, 181–183, 199–231 (*See also* Environments)
generations of, 58
historical background of, 3–4, 15–19
meeting interests of children in, 7, 9–11
need for, 19–20, 24–25
origin of term, 15–16
parent expectations for, 12–13
scheduling requirements for, 5
School-age care centers
contracts with parents and, 431–433
funding for, 34–36, 139–140, 238, 374, 436
liability issues for, 429–431
licensing requirements for, 426–429
operating schedules of, 434, 435
ownership of, 430–431
personnel issues for, 438–443
relationships between neighbors and, 437–438
staff polices and procedures manuals for, 433
transportation to, 32, 33, 286, 436–437
School-Age Care Environment Rating Scale (SACERS), 65, 67, 227, 230–231
School-age care options
informal care as, 38–43
in-home care as, 27, 29
in other countries, 43–50
out-of-home care as, 30–38
overview of, 24–25
self-care as, 25–27
School-age care professionals
afterschool inclusion aides as, 78
afterschool program leaders as, 78
behavior guidance and, 183–184
certificates and degrees for, 82, 84–85
classroom aides as, 79
community volunteers as, 79–80
conflicts between families and, 416–417
credentials and state-issued certificates for, 85
family child care providers as, 81
gender distribution of, 168, 169
levels of responsibility of, 442
overview of, 77
personality, temperament and disposition for, 86–91
personnel issues related to, 438–443
polices and procedures manuals for, 433
professional development for, 85–86
qualifications of, 443
scheduled planned activities, 244–245
school-age program site supervisors as, 81

School-age care professionals (*continued*)
service club leaders as, 80–81
skills and knowledge for, 91–93
socialization role of, 129
working with older children, 378–379, 381, 383–384
School-age care sites. *See also* Environments
community facilities as, 202
floor plans for, 222–223
permanent or relocatable buildings as, 202
places of worship as, 201
private homes as, 200
school-site centers as, 200–201
shared spaces in, 212–215
School-age children. *See also* Children
activity levels and eating habits of, 276
assimilation and accommodation in, 111
developmental characteristics of, 82, 87–89, 106–108, 372–375
educational options for people working with, 82, 84–86
interaction with, 86–87
needs of, 76–77, 104–105
older, 370–397 (*See also* Older school-age children)
personality and temperament for working with, 86–91
preschool-age vs., 14
professionals who work with, 77–81
relationship development in, 60–61
role-models for, 87
scheduling needs of, 5
skills and knowledge for working with, 91–93
School-age Community Child Care Act of 1985, 32
School-age Ideas and Activities for After School Programs (Haas-Foletta), 360
School-age programs
activities and, 63
activity areas for, 239–241
addressing children's fears in, 159–161
administrator's personal perspective on, 220
admission and enrollment policies for, 405–406
advance planning for, 242–243
allocation of staff for, 244–245
anticipation of, 246–247
balance between academic enrichment and recreation in, 238
brainstorming curriculum ideas for, 241–242
checklist for, 262, 266
children as participants in planning for, 245
clubs approach in, 241
communication methods between families and, 412–416
daily plans for, 256–259
emergent curriculum and, 236–237

environment and, 62–63
evaluating curriculum for, 263, 265, 267
flexibility in, 386–387
goals for, 247
human relationships and, 60–61
long-term activities in, 259–263
long-term plans for, 247–252
materials and supplies for, 244
monthly plans for, 252–256
for older children and adolescents, 374, 376–387, 392–395
overview of, 235–236
planning skills for, 245–246
program organization, procedures and policies and, 60
safety, health, and nutrition and, 61–62
scheduling areas for, 243–244
seasonal plans for, 252
weekly plans for, 255, 257
School-age program site supervisors, 81
School Breakfast Program (SBP), 275
School lunch program, 275
Schools
building partnerships with, 417–418
publicly funded programs in, 33–34
relationships between families and, 403–404
year-round, 5
School-site centers, 200–201
School-sponsored check-in programs, 27, 28
Schuylkill Center for Environmental Education, 36
Science activities, 316–319
Scientists, visits by, 387
Scramble game, 362
Scripps Howard News Service, 154
Seasonal plans, 252. *See also* Plans/planning
Seattle Public Library
After School Happenings, 43, 44
teen centers in, 390
Second-language learners
personal perspective of, 8–9
program suitability for, 7
statistics for, 211
Second Street Learning Center (Reading, Pennsylvania), 39
Secretary's Commission on Achieving Necessary Skills (SCANS), 306–307
Security needs, 154
Self, development of, 134
Self-care
effects of, 26–27
explanation of, 25
safety concerns of, 371
support systems for, 27
Self-efficacy, 144

Self-esteem
    dimensions of, 145–147
    explanation of, 140
    homelessness and, 162
    role of positive, 144
Self-regulation, 134
Self-respect, 144–145
Self-study, 66
Seligson, Michelle, 15, 51
Selman, Robert, 179
Sensorimotor stage, 109
Separation anxiety, 156
Service club leaders, 80–81
Service learning, 241
Settlement houses, 3, 16–17
Sewing machine activities, 325–326
Shared spaces, 212–215. *See also* Environments;
    School-age care sites
Single-parent households. *See* Female-headed
    households
Skating, 358
Skinner, B. K., 115–116, 185
Slithering snakes activity, 358
Smith, Jamie R., 83
Smith, Shannon, 158
Snacks
    Food and Nutrition Service Guidelines for
      Afterschool Program, 282–283
    importance of healthy, 281–282, 320
      (*See also* Nutrition)
    prepared with children, 284–285
    suggestions for, 284
Social anxiety, 156
Social capital, 80
Social-emotional development theories
    developmental tasks, 106–108
    explanation of, 100
    psychosocial theory, 100–103, 105–106
    use of, 108
Socialization
    agents of, 129, 135–136
    culture and, 130, 133–134
    early exposure to, 128
    out-of-school settings for, 139
    personality development and, 134–136
    types of, 129
Social learning theory, 116
Social needs, 155
Social networking, 152, 412
Social play, 349
Social revolution, 151
Social skills, 138–139
Social values, 377–378
Sociocultural theory of cognition, 111–112

Sociodramatic play, 349
Sound, in school-age care sites, 218
South Africa, school-age care in, 47
Southwest Regional Educational Developmental
    Laboratory, 406
Special needs. *See* Children with special needs
Special Supplemental Nutrition Program for Women,
    Infants, and Children (WIC), 275
Spontaneous activities, 242
Sports, team, 359–360
Sri Lanka, school-age care in, 48
Stable, 15, 97
Staff planning calendars, 254. *See also* Plans/planning
Stakeholders, 66
Standards
    for accreditation, 71–73
    afterschool care and, 308–310
    for mathematics education, 320
    for safety, 61–62, 224–225
Standards for Quality School-age Care (National
    Afterschool Association), 70, 227, 230
Starr, Ellen, 16
Statues, 335–336
Steal the Bacon game, 360
Stop and go game, 361–362
Storytelling, 164
Strand supports, 311
Stress, 152
Structure, 303
Structured play, 303. *See also* Play
Struggle for power, 185
Substance abuse
    among children, 170–171
    among parents, 162
    homelessness and, 164
Superego, 100
Supervision, 24, 25
Supplemental Education Services (SES), 32
Supplies. *See* Equipment; Materials
Supportive environment, 206
Survival needs, 154
Sustainability, 423
Sweden, school-age care in, 45

Tacos, 323
Tag game, 362
Taking Care of Pets (Ring), 366
Taming Monsters, Slaying Dragons (Feiner), 160
Teachers
    adults as, 136–137
    gender role development and same-sex, 167–168
    knowledge of school-age children, 13–15
Team planning, 237
Team sports, 359–360

Technology. *See also* Internet
  computer, 337
  email and, 316
  industrial, 336–337
Teenagers. *See* Older school-age children
Teen Center (Santa Cruz, California), 387
Teen Scene Club (Charles County, Maryland), 390
Telephone contact, 414
Television
  children's programming on, 169–170
  fitness and, 273, 277
Temperaments, 14
Temporal dimension
Temporal dimension of environment, 204
Terrorism, 153–154, 158, 161, 165
Thematic units, 236
Thompson, M., 166, 168
Thought and Language (Vygotsky), 112
Tie-dying, 327–328
Tinikling, 297
Tobacco education programs, 171
Tobacco use, 171
Tobin, Joseph, 167
Todd, Christine, 24
Topa Topa Elementary School (Ojao, California), 287
Traditionalists, 158
Trailmonkey: Your Virtual Guide to Adventure in the Great Outdoors, 295
Transportation
  to child care homes, 32
  cost of, 286
  methods of, 436–437
  to publicly funded programs, 33
Trickster tales, 309–310
Trust vs. mistrust stage, 101
21st Century Community Learning Centers, 33, 35, 139, 196, 212, 249

Underutilization, of school buildings, 33
Undue attention, 185
Unintentional socialization, 129
Union Park Action for Safe Families (Orange County, Florida), 37
United Kingdom, school-age care in, 46, 51
United Neighborhood Houses of New York City, 17
United Way, 36
University of California, 421
Unstructured play, 303, 347–350. *See also* Play
Urban Institute, 29

Validators, 68
Values clarification, 147
Vandalism, of school buildings, 33
Vargas, Mandi, 377
Verbal/linguistic intelligence, 114

Villermé, Louis-René, 274
Violence
  adolescents as victims of, 393
  effects on children, 153
  risk for, 157
Virtual trail walking, 294–295
Visual/spatial intelligence, 114
Volley-up, 361
Vygotsky, Lev, 111–112, 121, 185

Walk Across America (Jenkins), 295
Walking, 285–288
Walking With Freedom: A Hike Along the Appalachian Trail, 294
Walk to School Day, 286, 288
Walk Wednesdays, 287
Water activities, 363–364
Watershed projects, 356
Webbing with Literature: Creating Story Maps with Children's Books (Bromley), 311
Webs
  curriculum, 311–312
  explanation of, 241–242
Web strands, 311
Weekly plans, 255, 257. *See also* Plans/planning
Well-baby clinics, 98
Wellesley College, 15, 38, 422
Wellesley School-Age Child Care Project, 15, 51
Whirlpool Foundation, 37
Wien, Carol Anne, 239
Wii Fit, 296–297
Windowsill garden, 356
Winters, Jane, 377
Wood activities, 364–365, 389
Woodshop for Kids (McGee), 364
Workforce Investment Act (WIA), 421
Workplace skills, 421
Work schedules, parents with nontraditional, 39–40

Yanouzas, Tracy, 376, 377
Year-round schools, 5
Yoga, 290
Young Men's Christian Association (YMCA), 18, 41, 170, 209, 249, 296
Young Women's Christian Association (YWCA), 18, 41
Youth Camp Outcomes Questionnaires, 65
Youth Enhancement Facility (YEF) (Oklahoma), 37–38
Youth Fitness Coalition, 294
Youth Program Quality Assessment (YPQA), 66
Youth work, 15

Zone of proximal development, 112
Zuljevic, Vida, 332–333